DEMOCRACY AND
DEVELOPMENT IN INDIA

'Readers committed to social democracy will welcome Atul Kohli's carefully crafted and persuasively argued analyses on how the shift from "Socialism to Pro-business" has penalized the poor and advantaged the rich.'

—LLOYD I. RUDOLPH AND SUSANNE H. RUDOLPH
University of Chicago

'Atul Kohli is one of the foremost interpreters of India's development experience in [a] comparative perspective ... He combines fieldwork with deep historical knowledge and can knit together sensitivity to regional variation with a focus on the central government ... This is an indispensable volume for anyone [interested in] state–society relations in India.'

—PRATAP BHANU MEHTA
Centre for Policy Research

'Kohli is a towering intellectual force in the study of Indian politics and political economy. These essays, written with characteristic lucidity, bring together his compelling intellectual output of the last two decades.'

—ASHUTOSH VARSHNEY
Brown University

'This is an outstanding collection of essays on the consolidation of democracy in India ... [The] book makes a strong argument for a social democratic model of development and questions the growing power of [the] business and corporate sector, which is ... pertinent at this time of financial crisis. It is the single most important exploration of India's transformation and of great value to scholars of democracy and comparative politics.'

—ZOYA HASAN
Jawaharlal Nehru University and National Commission for Minorities

ATUL KOHLI

DEMOCRACY AND DEVELOPMENT IN INDIA

FROM SOCIALISM TO PRO-BUSINESS

OXFORD
UNIVERSITY PRESS

OXFORD
UNIVERSITY PRESS

22 Workspace, 2nd Floor, 1/22 Asaf Ali Road, New Delhi 110002, India

Oxford University Press is a department of the University of Oxford.
It furthers the University's objective of excellence in research, scholarship,
and education by publishing worldwide in

Oxford New York
Auckland Cape Town Dar es Salaam Hong Kong Karachi
Kuala Lumpur Madrid Melbourne Mexico City
Nairobi New Delhi Shanghai Taipei Toronto

With offices in
Argentina Austria Brazil Chile Czech Republic France Greece
Guatemala Hungary Italy Japan Poland Portugal Singapore
South Korea Switzerland Thailand Turkey Ukraine Vietnam

Oxford is a registered trademark of Oxford University Press
in the UK and in certain other countries

Published in India
by Oxford University Press, New Delhi

First published 2009
Oxford India Paperbacks 2010
Digitally Printed in 2024

ISBN-13: 978-019-806847-1
ISBN-10: 019-806847-6

Typeset in Dante 11/13
by Eleven Arts, Keshav Puram, Delhi 110 035
Printed at Manipal Technologies Limited, Manipal
Published by Oxford University Press
22 Workspace, 2nd Floor, 1/22 Asaf Ali Road, New Delhi 110002, India

Contents

III POLITICS AND DEVELOPMENT IN SELECT STATES

Tables and Figures

FIGURES

Publisher's Acknowledgements

The publisher acknowledges the following for permission to include articles/extracts in this volume:

Cambridge University Press for 'Centralization and Powerlessness: India's Democracy in a Comparative Perspective', in Joel Samuel Migdal, Atul Kohli, and Vivienne Shue (eds), *State Power and Social Forces: Domination and Transformation in the Third World*, New York, 1994, pp. 89–107.

The Journal of Asian Studies for 'Can Democracies Accommodate Ethnic Nationalism? Rise and Decline of Self-Determination Movements in India', 56(2), May 1997, pp. 325–44; published by Cambridge University Press.

Journal of Democracy for 'Enduring Another Election: India Defies the Odds', 9(3), July 1998, pp. 7–20; published by Johns Hopkins University Press.

Asia Society for 'From Majority to Minority Rule: Making Sense of the "New" Indian Politics', in Marshall M. Bouton and Philip Oldenburg (eds), *India Briefing, 1990*, New York, 1990, pp. 1–24.

Cambridge University Press for 'India's Fragmented-Multiclass State and Protected Industrialization', in Atul Kohli, *State-Directed Development: Political Power and Industrialization in the Global Periphery*, New York, 2004, pp. 257–90.

Economic and Political Weekly for 'Politics of Economic Growth in India, 1980–2005, Part I: The 1980s', 1 April 2006, pp. 1251–9.

Economic and Political Weekly for 'Politics of Economic Growth in India, 1980–2005, Part II: The 1990s and Beyond', 8 April 2006, pp. 1361–70.

World Development for 'Politics of Economic Liberalization in India', 17(3), March 1989, pp. 305–28; published by Elsevier.

Pacific Affairs for 'Regime Types and Poverty Reform in India', 56(4), Winter, 1983–4, pp. 649–72.

Cambridge University Press for 'Breakdown in a "Backward" State: Bihar', in Atul Kohli, *Democracy and Discontent: India's Growing Crisis of Governability*, 1991, New York, pp. 205–37.

Cambridge University Press for 'Growing Turmoil in an "Advanced" State: Gujarat', in Atul Kohli, *Democracy and Discontent: India's Growing Crisis of Governability*, 1991, New York, pp. 238–66.

Asian Survey for 'Parliamentary Communism and Agrarian Reform: The Evidence from India's Bengal', 23(7), July 1983, pp. 783–809, published by the University of California Press, © 1983 Regents of the University of California.

Asian Survey for 'The NTR Phenomenon in Andhra Pradesh: Political Change in a South Indian State', 8(10), October 1988, pp. 991–1017, published by the University of California Press, © 1988 Regents of the University of California.

Journal of Commonwealth and Comparative Politics for 'Karnataka's Land Reforms: A Model for India?', XX(3), November 1982, pp. 309–28.

Introduction

Written over nearly three decades, the essays in this volume analyse the interaction of democracy and development in India. When I started thinking and writing about India in the late 1970s, Indira Gandhi dominated India's political scene. A commitment to *garibi hatao* (alleviate poverty) was in the air, India's democratic institutions were under severe strain, and the economy muddled along at the sluggish 'Hindu rate of growth'. The sense of unity and hope of the early Nehru years was already a distant history, replaced by a number of economic crises, on the one hand, and by contentious, populist, and personalistic politics, on the other hand. Over the subsequent three decades India experienced significant political and economic progress. While not quite 'India shining', as India's image makers would have it, democracy in India indeed put down firmer roots and economic growth accelerated. At the same time, however, the quality of governance remained low, a variety of economic and political inequalities widened, and the number of poor, unhealthy, and illiterate people living in India continued to be unacceptably high. The essays in the volume interpret political and economic changes in India over the critical three decades during which a country committed to socialism was transformed into what many now describe as pro-business 'India incorporated'.

In this brief introduction I outline several connected themes that provide a degree of coherence to what may otherwise appear to be disparate essays. First, the essays share a theoretical and normative unity: they are all informed by a state–society frame of reference and argue—implicitly or explicitly—for a social democratic model of development in India. These issues are discussed very briefly in the first section below. A discussion of three substantial themes follows: political change, political economy, and uneven regional development. Among the political changes I focus on are how and why democracy in India put down firm roots, on the one hand, but why, on the other hand, the quality of governance offered by India's democracy continues to be low, especially below the national level. The interrelated political economy themes that I discuss concern acceleration of economic growth, worsening inequalities, persistence of poverty, and growing power of business groups. And finally, a discussion of political and economic changes in select states ought to provide an inkling of why progress across Indian states continues to be uneven. The key development that helps make sense of these interrelated changes over the last three decades is the growing economic and political power of business groups within India.

STATE–SOCIETY FRAMEWORK

Disagreements about how to interpret India's political economy are only in a small part rooted in disagreements about the nature of underlying facts. These disagreements for the most part stem from alternative theoretical and normative commitments. Such 'paradigmatic' differences are not easily resolved. Instead of fighting 'paradigmatic wars', it may be useful to outline in brief the 'first principles' that I embrace and that inform the empirical essays in this volume.

The state–society frame of reference that structures my scholarship harkens back to the classical political sociology of Marx and Weber.[1] Several key assumptions help distinguish this scholarly tradition from other competing ones. First, not only Marx and Weber but also other classical sociologists, including Durkheim, shared the view that social reality is *sui generis*. From this standpoint, the study of society, including that of politics and economics, requires societal level concepts and theories that go well beyond aggregating individual level phenomena. These foundational assumptions of modern political sociology often developed in opposition—especially in the writings of Durkheim—to the economic individualism of other classical thinkers, such as that of Adam Smith. From the very beginning then, the sociological tradition that I embrace took a different fork in the social science road than economics, eschewing methodological individualism, on the one hand, and insisting that markets and states are deeply embedded in societies, on the other hand.

Of course, Marx and Weber differed on profound issues. While Weber found much of use in Marx, he also argued persuasively that politics and culture of a society could not be reduced to the underlying class forces, especially in the short to medium term. At the same time, both Marx and Weber

---

[1]For a fuller statement see Joel Samuel Midgal, Atul Kohli, and Vivienne Shue (eds), *State Power and Social Forces: Domination and Transformation in the Third World*, New York: Cambridge University Press, 1994, especially Atul Kohli and Vivienne Shue, 'State Power and Social Forces', pp. 292–326.

appreciated the importance of economic factors in moulding longer term processes of historical change. These theoretical sensibilities then constitute the second important set of initial principles on which the state–society framework rests. I share the Weberian assumption that state and society, or patterns of authority and association, are empirically interrelated but analytically autonomous.[2] This assumption does not preclude a serious consideration of class and economic forces in the study of politics. On the contrary, for anyone studying complex societies in detail, these initial assumptions provide enormous flexibility, allowing one to focus on the impact of state on society when studying some problems, and reversing the causal focus, say, to class determinants of political structures and processes, when investigating yet other issues. This scholarly posture put me at odds with both Marxist and modernization theories during the Cold War years, and, more recently, with neo-classical economics and its off-shoot, the rational choice approach to the study of politics.

Analytical predispositions often condition normative preferences of scholars. For example, Marxists in the past were often sympathetic to the goal of revolutions and communism; modernization theorists championed democracy against communism; and many neo-classical economists today hold that free markets are capable of solving major societal problems. In a parallel fashion, the state–society frame of reference that I adopt shares an elective affinity with social-democratic preferences. This affinity is rooted in the core assumption that states and societies have their own partially autonomous logics of action that, in turn, mutually influence patterns of political and social change. This assumption allows one to imagine the possibility of democracy in poor societies, to argue for a vigorous role for states in promoting economic growth and welfare provision, and at the same time to logically worry about the growing power of capital in political and social life.

POLITICAL CHANGE

Democracy has put down firm roots in India but the quality of government that India's democracy provides remains low. I have explored these related trends in a number of my scholarly writings, only some of which are included in this collection.[3] Brief schematic comments on both these trends—

---

[2]For such an interpretation of Weber, see Reinhard Bendix, *Max Weber: An Intellectual Portrait*, New York: Anchor Books, 1962. I sought to apply this framework to India in Atul Kohli (ed.), *India's Democracy: An Analysis of Changing State–Society Relations*, Princeton, N.J.: Princeton University Press, 1988, see especially the 'Introduction'.

[3]The issue of consolidation of democracy in India is explored in Atul Kohli (ed.), *The Success of India's Democracy*, Cambridge: Cambridge University Press, 2001, especially in the

democratic consolidation but poor governance—may be helpful at the outset for introducing the subject, as well as for situating specific essays in this volume within the broader study of political change in India.

First, how does one best understand consolidation of democracy in India? It is clear that India's democracy has succeeded against considerable odds: a low-income economy, widespread poverty and illiteracy, and immense ethnic diversity. How did India do it? It is my suggestion here, as elsewhere, that Indian democracy is best understood by focusing not mainly on its socio-economic determinants, but on how power distribution in that society is negotiated and renegotiated.[4] A concern with the process of power negotiation, in turn, leads one to analyse leadership strategies, the design of political institutions, and the political role of diverse social groups, or, in short, the interaction of the state and society.

More specifically, India's democratic record suggests that two related sets of political processes have guided the management of power conflicts in that society. First, a delicate balance has been struck and restruck between forces of centralization and decentralization. And, second, the interests of the powerful in society have been served without fully excluding the weaker groups. The record on both of these fronts is far from perfect; the failures have actually put a great strain on Indian democracy. Nevertheless, accommodation of those who mount powerful challenges by granting them greater autonomy and/or a share of resources has been central to the strengthening of democracy.

As federal democracies go, India is a relatively centralized state. While many critics have made this observation, the fact is that demands for decentralization only make sense within the context of centralized authority; authority and power, like wealth, have to exist before they can be distributed. Over the years, as democracy has spread, numerous mobilized groups in India have demanded further redistribution of power. These demands were often resisted, sometimes wisely, but at other times unwisely and at a great cost. Overall, however, enough concessions were made so that the Indian political system by now possesses significant decentralized traits. Notable features of these are to be found in the practice of federalism, in the changing character of local governments, and in the evolving constitutional design.

No electoral democracy can long survive without protecting the interests of the powerful, whether these are propertied groups, groups with high status, or groups with effective political organization. Long-term exclusion

---

'Introduction'. Problems of governance in India constitute a central theme in Atul Kohli, *Democracy and Discontent: India's Growing Crisis of Governability*, New York: Cambridge University Press, 1991.

[4]Here, I am drawing on my 'Introduction' to Kohli (ed.), *The Success of India's Democracy*.

of weaker groups is also not healthy for a democracy. How has this balance been managed in India? While the rhetoric of the Indian state has often been redistributive—socialism, abolition of traditional privileges, reform of the caste system, and populism—political practice has been considerably more conservative, eschewing any decisive redistribution. The Indian state has thus been criticized both for its excessive socialist commitments and for its failure at substantial redistribution. However, the political impact of these twin tendencies—radical in tone, conservative in practice—may well have strengthened democracy. This is because the powerful in society feel well served by the system, but weaker groups do not feel totally excluded or hopeless, at least not so far.

A brief chronological sketch of several phases of political change in India may now help further clarify how strategies of power management in India have evolved. Institutions and practices of democracy found considerable acceptance during the first phase, which was dominated by Nehru and which lasted from, say, about 1950 to the mid-1960s. Aside from Nehru's own commitment to democracy, India benefited in this phase from the presence of two very important institutions: a well-functioning civil service and a popular ruling party, the Indian National Congress (or Congress).[5] The civil service constituted the heart of the state that India inherited from the colonial period, and India's 'new' civil service was essentially built on this colonial base. This civil service contributed to effective government and imparted political stability.

The Congress, by contrast, had spearheaded a successful national movement and, as a result, enjoyed considerable popularity and legitimacy. These new rulers of India, especially Nehru, utilized the inherited political capital wisely, accommodating rival elites within the larger political umbrella that was Congress. Moreover, while Nehru and others employed the rhetoric of socialism, political practice was considerably more conservative. The Congress, for example, built its political networks on the back of the powerful members of society—often the landowning upper castes— exchanging state patronage for electoral mobilization. This strategy enabled the Congress to succeed for a while, at least long enough for practices of democracy to take root.

[5]I have not studied this period in any detail. Useful scholarly works on this early phase on which I am drawing include Bipan Chandra, Aditya Mukherjee, and Mridula Mukherjee, *India after Independence, 1947–2000*, New Delhi: Penguin,1988; Francine Frankel, *India's Political Economy, 1947–1977: The Gradual Revolution*, Princeton, N.J.: Princeton University Press, 1978; Rajni Kothari, *Politics in India*, Boston: Little, Brown & Co.,1970; W.H. Morris-Jones, *The Government and Politics in India*, London: Hutchinson, 3rd edn, 1971; David C. Potter, *India's Political Administrators: From ICS to IAS*, New Delhi: Oxford University Press, 1996; and Myron Weiner, *Party Building in a New Nation*, Chicago: University of Chicago Press, 1976.

Indian democracy was also helped by the fact that Indian political society in this early phase was not all that mobilized, certainly far less than in the subsequent decades. Political conflict mainly took the form of claims and counterclaims by rival elites, especially regional elites demanding a greater share of power and resources vis-à-vis the central government. These conflicts could have proven difficult but were successfully accommodated by creating a federal system that recognized linguistic communities as legitimate political components. Elite versus mass conflict in India in these decades was, however, minimal. What class conflict existed was limited to a few regions. Given India's political heterogeneity, such conflicts seldom spread from one region to another. Mobilization of lower castes was also in its infancy and limited to a few southern states. Most of India's poor were lower-caste, landless peasants. These groups were generally dependent for their livelihood on those above them, the landowning upper-caste elites. These vertical ties of patronage and dependency, in turn, constrained the political behaviour of poor, illiterate Indians.

Democracy has often had undemocratic roots. India's case has been no different, as least not on this score. An effective civil service and relatively low levels of political mobilization meant that, unlike numerous other post-colonial experiments, Indian democracy was not seriously debilitated at the outset by poor governance and multiple political conflicts. The Congress further provided the key governing institution that not only transformed nationalist legitimacy into a ruling force, but also incorporated rival elites into a loosely knit organization, and promised future incorporation to India's unkempt masses. While the Congress repeatedly won elections during this first phase and dominated India's political landscape, a broader political change was also underway: institutions and practices of democracy took root.

The second major phase during the 1970s and 1980s was dominated by Nehru's daughter, Indira Gandhi. Indian politics during this phase became considerably more turbulent, even temporarily threatening democracy. As the memory of anti-colonial nationalism declined, numerous new elites entered the political arena, challenging Congress's hold on power. A rapidly growing population also produced a new generation of potentially mobilizable citizens. The spread of commerce and democracy started undermining the vertical ties of clientelism that had constrained the political choices of the lower strata in the past. India's economic development was also relatively sluggish and elitist, leaving a majority without any significant improvement in living conditions. The political situation was by now ripe for dramatic changes.[6]

---

[6]I analysed the subsequent political changes in some detail in Kohli, *Democracy and Discontent*. Also, see Lloyd Rudolph and Susanne Rudolph, *In Pursuit of Lakshmi*, University

After Congress's popularity declined in the second half of the 1960s, Indira Gandhi recreated the Congress during the 1970s and the 1980s as a much more populist and personalistic organ. The old Congress, with its modest organizational base, was destroyed in this transformation, creating a significant institutional vacuum in the Indian polity. Indira Gandhi instead promised 'alleviation of poverty' to India's poor masses, generating considerable popular support. She used this popularity to concentrate power in her person, further undermining existing institutional constraints on the use of power. Indira Gandhi appointed loyal minions to significant political offices across the country, squeezed whosoever challenged her, and when the opposition itself became strident—as it did in the mid-1970s—imposed a 'national emergency' for two years (1975–7), limiting democratic practices and bringing India's democracy to the brink.

Indira Gandhi's personalistic and populistic politics definitely weakened some of India's democratic institutions. The old Congress party was transformed into a personal tool that went into a slow but steady organizational (though not necessarily an electoral) decline following her death. The civil service was politicized. Centralization of power also weakened the federal system, evoking strong opposition in some regions that did not readily accept loss of autonomy. As in many other democracies, personalistic power simultaneously created a viable political centre but weakened institutional politics.

The balance sheet of political developments during this phase, however, was not only towards the weakening of Indian democracy. Contrary trends also deserve to be underlined. First, elections were held regularly throughout the period, and political power remained a function of securing popular majority support. Even Indira Gandhi's personal power was a function of her widespread electoral appeal to India's poor masses. It was a need to reconfirm this legitimacy that pressured her to call elections after a brief authoritarian interlude (1975–7). The fact that she was voted out of power following the Emergency only confirmed the efficacy of Indian democracy: those who tamper with the basic system will lose popular support. Second, and related to the first point, following the Emergency, a number of India's political groups—for example, some of India's communists, who had hitherto held an ambivalent attitude towards democracy—realized how much there was to lose without liberal political freedoms, and became recommitted to democracy. And finally, Indira Gandhi sharply politicized the issue of widespread poverty in India. Even while she failed to deliver on her promises to the poor, Indira Gandhi broadened the scope of Indian democracy towards a greater inclusion of the lower strata.

of Chicago Press, 1987; Paul Brass, *The Politics of India since Independence*, Cambridge: Cambridge University Press, 1994; and Chandra, *et al.*, *India after Independence*.

Indira Gandhi's assassination in the mid-1980s, and that of her son Rajiv Gandhi a few years thereafter, brought to an end the era of Congress's dominance via family rule. Even though democracy had by now taken a firm foothold in India—notice that even the assassination of the highest leaders was 'dealt with' by yet another round of elections to select alternative leaders—the quality of government that this democracy was capable of delivering remained rather uncertain. The critical issue was the absence of cohering institutions amidst a rapidly politicizing society. The third and current phase that began around 1990 has thus been characterized by a variety of national-level political experiments to find a substitute for the old Congress rule. I explore this transition from the second to the third phase in Chapters 3 and 4.

The decline of Congress's hegemony has been met by two important political developments: the rise of the Bharatiya Janata Party (BJP), especially in India's Hindi-speaking 'heartland' that comprises states in north-central and western India; and the growing significance of regional parties, especially in southern India, but also in 'peripheral' states as West Bengal, Punjab, and Kashmir. The BJP is a right-leaning, religious-nationalist party that has successfully mobilized support at the national level by simultaneously demonizing India's religious minorities, especially Muslims, and championing causes that appeal to the majority Hindus. Over time, however, the BJP has had to moderate its strident religious nationalism, both to broaden its electoral support and to seek coalition allies.[7] Ironically, the BJP's electoral loss in 2004 underlined some upper limit on the party's performance-based popularity.

Regional nationalism has greater appeal than Hindu nationalism in many of India's 'peripheral' regions. A variety of regional parties have thus become quite significant over the last few decades. Since many of these parties arose in opposition to the Congress, they often built their power base around intermediate castes—the so-called 'backward castes' in India—that the Congress failed to incorporate. Championing the cause of their respective regions, and especially of the middling groups within the region, these parties seldom have strong left or right ideological views. When it comes to participating in national politics, they can thus swing more to the Left, or to the Right, depending on the political opportunities available, and on ambitions and convenience of their respective leaders. The recent rise of a party of the lower castes, the Bahujan Samaj Party (BSP) led by Mayawati, also seems to be following a similar pattern.

The third and most recent phase of Indian politics has thus been characterized by minority national governments and some related governmental

[7]Useful studies of the BJP include Christophe Jaffrelot, *The Hindu Nationalist Movement and Indian Politics, 1925 to the 1990s*, New York: Columbia University Press, 1996.

instability. While India's first eight general elections were spread out more or less evenly over the early four decades (1950–90), India held five general elections in the 1990s alone. By contrast, the most recent minority governments headed by the BJP (1999–2004) and the Congress (2004 to present) have not only managed coalitional support well but also offered a fair amount of policy coherence and stability. How does one best understand the phenomenon of minority governments without debilitating policy instability? The main underlying political trends are in tension: the growing fragmentation of India's political society, on the one hand, and a narrowing of the ruling alliance involving technocratic policy makers and big business, on the other hand.

Ever since the decline of anti-colonial nationalism in the 1950s and the 1960s, growing political fragmentation has been an important, steady trend in India. First, the political elite fragmented. This led to and was accompanied by growing assertiveness of a variety of oppositional elites, including some of India's regional elite. Indira Gandhi and India's regional elite, in turn, reached deeper into the social hierarchy to build political support. Thus, parties belonging to and championing the cause of the backward castes emerged in numerous regions. At the same time, class politics became salient in a few regions. A variety of single issue social movements also occupied new spaces created by a vibrant democracy. And finally, and more recently, even the lowest castes have been mobilized by their own parties, capturing power in one region or another. Given problems of coordinating collective action, these mobilized interests and identities in India by now generate formidable obstacles to creating cohesive majority governments.

If political fragmentation was the only trend, Indian politics by now would be a lot more unstable than it is. A variety of political and social developments also continue to impart cohesiveness to Indian democracy. In the political sphere, for example, while the Congress by now is only a shadow of its former self, it nevertheless remains a powerful national party, fully capable of offering responsible government. The successful mobilization of Hindu nationalism by the BJP has probably been the most important political development in recent decades; irrespective of our judgments about the desirability of this development, the fact is that, like the Congress, the BJP, as one of India's two national parties, remains fully capable of forging a stable national government. Beyond the political sphere, India's civil service continues to provide effective government, especially at the apex. A powerful armed force also remains an effective coercive tool to influence politics in the last instance; while coercion is clearly antithetical to democracy, it is also the case that many developing country democracies disintegrate as the political capacity to create order declines. And finally—and probably most importantly—the power and influence of India's indigenous business groups has grown steadily. While not quite hegemonic in the Marxist sense of that term, it is the case that Indian business groups wield political influence via powerful national organizations. These organizations not only transcend many regional and other political divisions of India but also offer clear policy preferences that narrow the policy range within which political parties operate. The results include policy stability in some key areas as economics. From a social-democratic standpoint, the growing power of business in India is of course a mixed blessing: on the one hand, it limits political uncertainty, a condition that is essential for a capitalist economy to flourish; on the other hand, the more the Indian state works for Indian capital, the more politically marginalized become India's numerous other social groups.

The discussion so far has focused on the evolution of India's democracy. It is also important to comment briefly on the quality of government offered by India's democracy. Since my somewhat bleak 1991 book on the subject,[8] the situation in India has improved along some dimensions, but continued along grooves of earlier origins in many other areas. The quality of governance in India thus remains mixed. Judged by the standards of developing countries, India is a moderately well-run country. It is widely perceived today as a growing democratic power in which ethnic diversity has been accommodated, the economy is growing, foreign and economic policies are sound, and where an educated middle class is growing. This image is valid but incomplete. First, this is a relatively recent image. And second, it is an image that is more likely to appeal to friends of India who do not deal with daily India, but less to a common office worker in Lucknow or to a poor farmer in Andhra Pradesh. Many such Indian citizens by contrast experience the Indian state as relatively ineffective, corrupt, more an obstacle than a source of solutions, even venal, and, more often than not, simply absent when needed.

In order to understand the mixed quality of governance in India it helps to keep in mind that the Indian state is a lot more competent in some areas and places (and not in others), on the one hand, and regularly prioritizes some problems to solve (and not others), on the other hand. It is also important to bear in mind that state authority in India runs relatively shallow; the farther down the political hierarchy one travels, the more the state lacks public purpose, serving instead personal or sectional interests. For example, India's ruling elite at the apex tend to be relatively competent. And yet, this competence did not translate into effective governance during the Indira Gandhi years. The main reason was that she prioritized socialism but failed to create an institutionalized power base that incorporated the popular sectors. The mismatch between the ambitious political goals and shallow authority ensured that she as well as her son Rajiv Gandhi often failed to translate their considerable electoral popularity into substantial policy

---

[8]See Kohli, *Democracy and Discontent.*

achievements. These issues are explored in greater detail in Chapter 1 as well as Chapter 8.

The relative competence of India's highest bureaucratic elites and the concomitant shallowness of public authority are two characteristics of the Indian state that have not altered dramatically over time. What has altered over time instead are the priorities of India's leaders, who are increasingly focused on economic growth and political stability. There is also an effort underway to insulate—as much as possible—decision making at the apex from popular pressures. Narrower priorities have enabled India's competent rulers to achieve some important goals, though not without cost, and only when policy accomplishment did not require downward penetration of state authority. For example, some of the most significant regional movements for greater self-determination, or even secession, have by now declined in intensity. While some of this was a result of accommodation and clever statecraft, a fair amount of brutal state repression was also used, incurring serious human costs. I explore this issue in some detail in Chapter 2. A narrow alliance of a technocratic elite with business groups has similarly succeeded in steering India onto a higher growth path, but at the expense of widening inequalities. These issues are explored in Chapters 6 and 7.

If policies aimed at securing political stability and promoting economic growth exhibit considerable state competence at the national level, the same does not hold for a variety of policy areas that influence distributive and welfare outcomes. The commitment of the state elite to India's poor has generally been rhetorical, and the state authority to accomplish such tasks has also been limited. As a result, redistributive land reforms and a variety of other efforts that may enhance the life chances of the poor have often failed in India.[9] Some related issues are discussed in Chapters 9, 10, 14, and 20. The failure of primary education in India is also well known.[10] In more recent years, buoyant economic growth has filled state coffers; aimed at improving India's image as a global player, the state elite, in turn, has assigned increased resources to such areas as primary education and health. Unfortunately, the capacity of lower level governments to translate these shifting national priorities into real gains for India's poor remains quite meagre.

Most state and local governments in India do not govern effectively. While there are exceptions, even important exceptions, on the whole the generalization holds. I documented related trends and analysed why this should be so in my first two books;[11] I also analyse these issues in a number of essays in

---

[9] I have analysed this issue in some detail in my first book. See Atul Kohli, *The State and Poverty in India: The Politics of Reform*, Cambridge: Cambridge University Press, 1987.

[10] One good study of the subject that points to leadership priorities as the main culprit is Myron Weiner, *The Child and the State in India*, Princeton, N.J.: Princeton University Press, 1991.

[11] See Kohli, *The State and Poverty*; and Kohli, *Democracy and Discontent*.

Section III of this book. Since I wrote the essays, the situation has not altered substantively. The failures are manifest in a variety of outcomes, including the inability to collect taxes in the countryside or on services, distorted priorities for public expenditures, corruption, politicization of the bureaucracy, and ineffective policy in such areas as public education, public health, and the provision and maintenance of infrastructure. The deeper causes include the facts that sub-national and local politics in India often lack public purpose, and that the state and local bureaucracies in India are not very professional.

POLITICAL ECONOMY

The political economy themes that have interested me over the years include politics of economic growth and redistribution, on the one hand, and the growing power of capital in Indian politics, on the other hand. Over the three decades that my work on these themes spans, the Indian state has increasingly prioritized economic growth, and the economic and political importance of indigenous business groups within India has grown. The results include acceleration of economic growth, some reduction in poverty, but widening inequalities. These issues are well covered in this volume (see Section II) and require only a brief introduction; in my comments here I will focus only on issues that are not well developed in the essays.

The neo-liberal accounts of India's economic performance blame the statism of Nehru and Indira Gandhi for India's sluggish growth and attribute post-1991 growth acceleration to liberal economic policies.[12] While not without merit, especially because of their logical consistency, I have often found these accounts unsatisfactory because they fail to situate economic processes within their political and social context, and thus often lead to erroneous conclusions.[13] Focusing instead on political determinants of economic growth, I argue that Nehru used his considerable nationalist legitimacy to prioritize growth of heavy industry and achieved considerable success; by contrast, Indira Gandhi's populism hurt both public and private investments and thus led to a decline in industrial growth (see Chapter 5).

---

[12]See, for example, Jagdish Bhagwati and Padma Desai, *India: Planning for Industrialization*, London: Oxford University Press, 1970; Isher Judge Ahluwalia, *Industrial Growth in India: Stagnation since the Mid-Sixties*, New Delhi: Oxford University Press, 1985; T.N. Srinivasan and S. Tendulkar, *Reintegrating India with the World Economy*, Washington, D.C.: Institute for International Economics, 2003; and Arvind Panagariya, *India: The Emerging Giant*, New York: Oxford University Press, 2008.

[13]A variety of alternative economic accounts that I have found more satisfactory include Gunnar Myrdal, *Asian Drama: An Inquiry into the Poverty of Nations*, New York: Pantheon, 1968; Pranab Bardhan, *The Political Economy of Development in India*, New Delhi: Oxford University Press, 1998; and Bimal Jalan, *India's Economic Crisis*, New Delhi: Oxford University Press, 1991.

In Chapters 6, 7, and 8, I also develop an alternate account of India's growth acceleration since about 1980. Put very briefly, following the Emergency, Indira Gandhi slowly but surely abandoned her commitment to garibi hatao, prioritized economic growth, and embraced Indian business as a ruling ally. A process of state and capital alliance for growth was thus initiated and this process has been unfolding in fits and starts ever since. Rajiv Gandhi's efforts to liberalize India's economy ran into numerous political obstacles, the most significant of which was opposition from Indian business groups, who felt threatened by any sharp opening of the economy to global forces (Chapter 8). By contrast, when liberalization came in 1991, this was in part facilitated by an economic crisis, in part by growing confidence and assertiveness of a section of Indian business groups over the 1980s, and in part by careful political calibration of the liberalization process to suit the needs of indigenous Indian capital. I thus argue that the acceleration of economic growth in India began around 1980, and not in 1991; it was a product, not of liberal policies adopted in 1991, but of a growing state–capital alliance for economic growth that was initiated by Indira Gandhi, and that has by now matured into a central feature of India's political economy (Chapters 7 and 8).

Politics of redistribution and poverty alleviation are the other political economy issues that I have analysed in some of my scholarly writings. In my early writings I focused on the failure of Indira Gandhi to translate her commitment to poverty alleviation into tangible gains for the poor. I attributed this failure in part to state capacity, by which I meant to draw attention to the ideology and organization of the state elite, and in part to the underlying class nature of state power.[14] More importantly, I examined and further developed this argument with reference to a number of Indian states. The study documented that the Communist Party of India (Marxist) in West Bengal implemented some redistributive policies more effectively than the Congress and Janata parties in such states as Karnataka and Uttar Pradesh. The argument was that this relative success of the Communist Party of India (Marxist) or the CPI(M) resulted from its social-democratic ideology and social support, on the one hand, and its effective organization as a party, on the other hand (see Chapters 9, 14, and 20).

I updated these concerns of politics of redistribution in a recent essay that is not included in this volume.[15] Eschewing numerous details that I cover in this essay, a few of the more important developments in India in this area may be worth summarizing. Over the last three decades the Indian

[14]See, Kohli, *State and Poverty in India*.

[15]See Atul Kohli, 'State and Redistributive Development in India', forthcoming (available at http://www.princeton.edu/~Kohli/workingpapers.html).

state has shifted from a reluctant pro-capitalist state with a socialist ideology to an enthusiastic pro-capitalist state with a neo-liberal ideology. This shift has significant and, on the whole, negative implications for pursuing redistributive policies in India.

On the one hand, the state's warm embrace of capital has been accompanied by higher rates of economic growth. Some of this is bound to help India's poor. On the other hand, however, the state–capital alliance for growth is leading to widening inequalities along a variety of dimensions: urban–rural and across classes and region. Not only does rapid economic growth then not benefit as many of the poor as it could if inequalities were stable, but also the balance of class power within India is shifting decisively towards business and other property owning classes. This creates the possibility, nay, makes it likely, that future patterns of development will be even more unequal.

It is quite ironical that the shift away from socialism was initiated by Indira Gandhi herself. As already indicated, seeking higher economic growth, Indira Gandhi in the early 1980s reordered the Indian state's class underpinnings, tilting it towards capital and against labour (see Chapter 6). Both she and her son Rajiv Gandhi thus moved the Indian state away from its socialist ambitions to a growth-promoting state that worked closely with the corporate sector. The distributional impact was negative but not as negative as what was to follow in the 1990s. State elites increasingly downplayed the rhetoric of socialism. A major fatality of this ideological shift was that land redistribution and tenancy reforms lost luster as policy options. While these policies had never succeeded much in India, now even their desirability became questionable. Also, very few new efforts emerged to improve primary education and public health. Mercifully, both Indira and Rajiv Gandhi kept up public investments. As some of these public investments were channelled into the countryside and others into India's poorer states, they put a brake on growing inequalities across the rural–urban and rich–poor state divides.

The state–business alliance for growth has pretty well continued to characterize India's model of development since about 1980, with another important liberalizing shift in 1991, when integration with the global economy also picked up speed (see Chapter 7). Unlike some other parts of the world, India's leaders did not push en masse privatization of the public sector, state shrinkage, or rapid opening to global investment. What they did instead was to slowly but surely reduce tariffs, liberalize foreign investment laws, and cut back on public investments. The more economic growth was led by private investors, the more the benefits accrued to owners of capital and to their agents. A significant urban middle class has also been growing in the shadow of this growth upsurge. All this is not surprising.

What the Indian state has also done is to throw its weight behind the winners of the new economy, without compensating those who are being left behind. It is this activist role of the state that has further contributed to growing inequalities. The Indian state has thus continued to support Indian capital in various ways so as to enable it to compete against global competition. A variety of 'public–private partnerships' are also beginning to absorb public initiative and resources. By contrast, investments into agriculture have not kept pace, and the poorer states of India have been left to their own resources. Since new private capital has not rushed into these areas, inequalities in India continue to grow, and the county's poor do not benefit as much from growth as they might under a modified policy regime.

Contrasting developments across Indian states put redistributive politics in India in sharper relief. Over the years the states in which poverty has come down the most include Kerala, West Bengal, Punjab, Andhra Pradesh, and Tamil Nadu. By contrast, poverty has come down the least in Assam, Jammu and Kashmir, Bihar, Madhya Pradesh, and Rajasthan.[16] While rates of economic growth are a significant predictor of these trends, an interesting fact is that for a unit of economic growth in various Indian states poverty came down much more rapidly in some states than in others. Thus, for example, one unit of growth in Kerala or West Bengal has been four times more 'efficient' in reducing poverty (as indicated by what economists call the growth elasticity of poverty) than, say, in Bihar or Madhya Pradesh.[17] More concretely, this means that it will take four times the growth rate of Kerala and West Bengal to reduce the same amount of poverty in Bihar and Madhya Pradesh. How does one best understand such different capacities across Indian states to reduce poverty?

The two states in which poverty has come down the most—Kerala and West Bengal—are states with long experience of left governments. All the southern states—Kerala, Andhra Pradesh, Tamil Nadu, and Karnataka—are among the top-half of the states in which poverty has come down the most. By contrast, India's BIMARU states—Bihar, Madhya Pradesh, Rajasthan, and Uttar Pradesh—are among the bottom-half of the states in which poverty has come down the least. Leaving proximate determinants of such patterns aside (for example, irrigation infrastructure, growth of farm yields, access to credit), the deeper explanation of such a pattern probably lies in the nature of social and political power in these states, and related to that, different

---

[16]For details, see ibid. The data on which this discussion is based is drawn from Timothy Besley, Robin Burgess, and Berta Esteve-Volant, 'The Policy Origins of Poverty and Growth in India', in Timothy Besley and Louise J. Cord (eds), *Delivering on the Promise of Pro-poor Growth*, Washington, D.C.: Palgrave Macmillan and the World Bank, 2007, pp. 49–78.

[17]See Besley, *et al.*, Table 3.1

policies whose results have accumulated over decades. Put as a hypothesis, it may be suggested that poverty has been reduced the most in states where effective governmental power rests on a broad political base; in such cases, rulers have minimized the hold of upper classes on the state, successfully organized the middle and lower strata into an effective power bloc, and then used this power to channel resources to the poor.

This simple hypothesis can be used to explain varying capacities across Indian states to reduce poverty. First, let us consider the two cases of India's left-leaning states, Kerala and West Bengal. There is more of a consensus around the case of Kerala than West Bengal. Poverty in Kerala has been reduced sharply and its human development indicators are far superior to that of rest of India.[18] And all this was accomplished while economic growth rates in Kerala have been close to the all-India average. Underlying these redistributive achievements are complex historical roots, including the political mobilization of lower castes and classes well before independence.[19] This broadened political base then facilitated the rise of a well-organized communist party to power. A more pro-poor regime interacted with a more efficacious citizenry, creating what Drèze and Sen have rightly called a 'virtuous' cycle. This created both a supply of and demand for a variety of successful pro-poor public policies, including land reforms, higher investments into and better implementation of education and health policies, and greater gender equality. The fact is that, when compared to other Indian states, by now the cultivated land in Kerala is distributed most evenly and wages of landless labourers in this state are highest in India.

While the case of West Bengal is more mixed, the main dynamics of poverty alleviation again seem to be that a well organized regime with a broad political base has been relatively effective at pursuing tenancy reform, helping push up minimum wages—though only somewhat—and implementing centrally sponsored anti-poverty programmes more effectively than in other states. Land inequality in the countryside in West Bengal is also among the lowest in India by now, though wages of agricultural labourers are only marginally above the all-India average. There is also some evidence that tenancy reforms—via enhanced security and bargaining power—have helped agricultural productivity, thus making growth in West Bengal more inclusive.

If India's 'social-democratic' states have effectively leveraged superior party organization and a broad political base to pursue modest redistributive reforms, how does one interpret the fact that all of India's southern states

---

[18]See, for example, Jean Drèze and Amartya Sen, *India: Development and Participation*, Oxford: Oxford University Press, 2002.

[19]See, for example, Patrick Heller's chapter on Kerala in Richard Sandbrook, Marc Edelman, Patrick Heller, and Judith Teichman, *Social Democracy in the Global Periphery: Origins, Challenges, Prospects*, New York: Cambridge University Press, 2007.

are above average in their poverty alleviation capacities? India's southern states share two sets of distinguishing political traits, one well researched and the other much in need of research. The well-established fact is that narrow domination of Brahmins was more effectively challenged in all the southern states relatively early in the twentieth century.[20] Since independence, the political base of power in these states has generally been middle castes and classes, and in some instances even lower classes. This is quite distinct from the Hindi-heartland states, where Brahmanical domination was only challenged relatively recently. The other fact is that the quality of state-level bureaucracy in the south has generally been superior. While this 'fact' needs to be documented by further scholarly research, over years of field work I was repeatedly struck by a sharper sense of professionalism among state-level bureaucrats, especially in Tamil Nadu, more akin to the Indian Administrative Service (IAS) than to prevailing practices in the Hindi-heartland.

How might prolonged rule by governments with broader political base and more effective bureaucracy influence poverty alleviation? Leaving Kerala aside, land redistribution has not been very effective in the southern states. The main policy instruments of poverty alleviation have instead been somewhat different. Over the last several decades the southern states have invested more heavily in education and health than in the Hindi-heartland states.[21] Another study notes that, on the whole, southern states have benefited more from subsidized public distribution of wheat and rice;[22] populist leaders and superior bureaucracy must get the credit. With a more effective bureaucracy, other poverty alleviation programmes (such as a variety of employment generation programmes) have also been implemented better.

The contrast with BIMARU states of northern India is striking. Of course, these states experienced low growth rates. However, the contrasts in the social and political structures are also notable. Well into the late twentieth century, the main mode of politics in these states was Congress rule that rested on a narrow political base of upper castes and classes.[23] With patron–client ties

[20]See, for example, Francine Frankel and M.S.A. Rao, *Dominance and State Power in India*, 2 volumes, New Delhi: Oxford University Press, 1990.

[21]See, Prerna Singh, 'World's Apart: A Comparative Analysis of Social Development in India', doctoral dissertation in preparation, Princeton University, chapter 4.

[22]See John Harniss, 'Do Political Regimes Matter: Poverty Reduction and Regime Difference across India', in Peter Houtzager and Mick Moore (eds), *Changing Paths: International Development and the New Politics of Inclusion*, Ann Arbor: University of Michigan Press, 2003, pp. 204–31.

[23]The fact that the lowest castes also voted for the Congress in these states, say, up until the end of the 1960s, did not make Congress a broad-based party. Members of the lowest castes often depended on members of upper castes and were entangled in a variety of patronage relationships. In spite of an apparent broad social base, Congress's effective political base in these states was thus quite narrow.

as the key defining unit of the political society, factional bickering among the patrons was the core trait of state politics. This personalistic bickering detracted from any type of constructive use of state power, whether in promoting growth or distribution. With long traditions of *zamindari* or *taluqadari* rule (forms of indirect rule), the quality of state-level bureaucracy that these regions inherited was also generally low. Virulent patronage politics politicized the bureaucracy in post-independence years, further diluting the state's developmental capacity. For some three to four decades following independence then, a narrow political base, personalistic factionalism, and a less-than-professional state-level bureaucracy characterized the nature of state power in this region of India.

Land reforms were very poorly implemented in the Hindi-heartland states. With upper-caste landowners wielding considerable power—both in the state and in the society—and with a readily corruptible bureaucracy, this failure was not surprising. A variety of other state interventions that might have helped the poor were also ineffective.

In recent decades, the political base of state power in all of these states has broadened, though social power of upper-caste landowners remains significant. Over time this broadening of state power may lead to some greater benefits to the poor, as has recently been evident in Rajasthan and Madhya Pradesh. Meanwhile, factional bickering and politicized bureaucracy have nearly been institutionalized in the Hindi-heartland areas, leading to policy ineffectiveness. Decades of malign neglect and policy ineffectiveness have thus accumulated in creating the largest concentration of the poor within India.

POLITICS AND DEVELOPMENT IN SELECT STATES

Developmental performance of Indian states continues to diverge along several dimensions, including economic growth, distribution and poverty alleviation, and quality of governance. Why this should be so remains a complex, important, and under-researched area of research. I have already made a few comments on the politics of redistribution across Indian states. The essays in this volume do not provide anything close to a systematic answer to this critical puzzle of diverging developmental performance across Indian states. What they provide instead are insights into the political and developmental dynamics within some of India's important states. A central theme in these essays is that varying politics and authority structures across Indian states are a key determinant of regional developmental dynamics. Here I provide a simple typology of Indian states that may help organize comparative analyses of authority patterns—causes and consequences—across Indian states.

State-level governments in some parts of India simply lack public purpose. Instead of using state authority and resources to pursue the public good, ruling elites in these settings use their power for personal and sectional gains. Bihar and Uttar Pradesh typify these neo-patrimonial states of India. Politics in these and a few other states of India tends to be under-institutionalized and instead characterized by some shared traits: the political arena is dominated by a single leader, surrounded by loyal minions; modal political relationships are vertical, of a patron–client type; bureaucracy is politicized; symbolic appeals are used regularly to build diffuse electoral support; the zero-sum quality of politics makes those excluded from power feel totally excluded; and instead of any systematic public policy, leaders channel public resources for personalistic and narrow gains.

Understanding the causes and consequences of such neo-patrimonial governments in some of India's states is an important research problem for others to pursue. Equally important is to explore ways in which one might get out of the deleterious trap created by mutually reinforcing influences of low levels of economic development and poor governance. In Chapter 11 on Bihar, I investigate how state disintegration and caste conflicts contributed to poor governance. Elsewhere I have analysed the policy ineffectiveness of governments in Uttar Pradesh.[24] While my analyses of Bihar and UP predate the emergence, say, of Laloo Prasad Yadav and Mayawati in these states, respectively, they do provide the political context for understanding these more recent developments.

Indian states in which governmental authority is used more constructively can be conveniently thought of as states that are either more on the Left, or more on the Right. Given democracy, these ideological tendencies can, of course, shift. Nevertheless, it is fair to characterize some such states of India as Kerala and West Bengal in recent periods as India's left-leaning states (or, as noted above, social-democratic states), and states like Gujarat as right-leaning, developmental states of sorts, in which the government has worked closely with business groups to promote economic growth. Politics in India's left-leaning states is typically characterized by mobilized lower classes and castes, on the one hand, and by the presence of a well-organized left-of-centre political party, on the other hand, that systematically incorporates this mobilized support into a social-democratic power bloc. The presence of this power bloc, in turn, has added public purpose to state politics. I analyse in some detail in Chapters 13 and 14 how politics of this type emerged in West Bengal and how state power in turn was used to pursue certain constructive ends as tenancy reforms. I also analyse

---

[24]See Kohli, *The State and Poverty in India*, chapter 5.

in Chapter 15 how similar efforts to create a social-democratic power bloc failed in a state like Karnataka, the main culprit being the absence of a well-organized left party.

Since economic liberalization and related shift of initiative from the centre to states, a few of India's states have sought actively to promote business and industry. Narendra Modi in Gujarat and Chandrababu Naidu in Andhra Pradesh are two recent examples. While I do not analyse these specific cases, I do provide the political context for understanding these developments. Narendra Modi in Gujarat has created an efficient pro-business government with the help of the well-established business class of Gujarat and a relatively well-organized BJP that has mobilized a pro-Hindu majority against Muslims. In Chapter 12 on Gujarat, I analyse the long-standing 'tradition' in the state of fomenting deliberate violence so as to capture state power for narrow elites. An attempt was also made in Andhra Pradesh in recent years to institutionalize a pro-business activist state. This effort, however, was heavily dependent on the political fate of a single leader, Naidu. The social context that gave rise to a leader-dependent polity in Andhra Pradesh is analysed in Chapter 15.

To sum up, the essays in this volume analyse the evolution of democracy and development in India over a period of three decades, three decades during which India's rulers abandoned socialism and embraced pro-business ethos and practices. While the essays were all written separately, they do share some unity. They are framed by a state–society framework and are informed by a normative preference for social-democratic outcomes. The essays shed light on aspects of political change, political economy, and state-level politics within India.

I

Political Change

The essays in this section should be read in conjunction with the Introduction to this volume, especially the summary discussion on 'political change'. Two important patterns of political change that I analyse are in apparent tension. On the one hand, democracy as a formal system of rule has put down firm roots in India. On the other hand, however, the quality of government offered by India's democratic state remains poor, especially below the national level. The two opening chapters in this section help shed light on these themes, while clarifying that the tension between democratic success and poor governance in India is more apparent than real.

Among the political processes that have contributed to the strengthening of democracy in India is the establishment of a successful federal system. This has been essential in creating a degree of political cohesion among diverse ethnic regions. For example, some of the most contentious 'ethnic nationalist' conflicts in India were/are the struggles involving Tamils, Sikhs, and Muslim Kashmiris with New Delhi. How these struggles unfolded and, on balance, were 'accommodated' is analysed in the chapter entitled 'Can Democracies Accommodate Ethnic Nationalism?'. This essay was written in the 1990s. I have not tried to update the information. The core argument, namely, that democracy with a strong central government is in a good position to accommodate ethnic nationalist demands, stands.

In spite of a firm democratic foundation, the Indian state often fails to diagnose and solve pressing problems within India. This conundrum is especially puzzling when leaders won power with handsome majorities, as was the case with Indira Gandhi and Rajiv Gandhi. A variety of policy failures of these popular leaders of the past are analysed in the chapter on 'Centralization and Powerlessness'. The argument is that translating popularity into successful policy outcomes requires cohesive political organizations, such as parties and bureaucracies. Their absence, especially below the national level, has repeatedly made it difficult for India's rulers to offer effective governance.

Changing patterns of politics in India can also be studied usefully in a chronological fashion. In the Introduction to this volume, I suggested that it made some sense to think of political change in independent India in terms of three periods: the Nehru years; the Indira Gandhi years, including the last few years under her son, Rajiv Gandhi; and a third and a more recent phase in which a variety of political forces have competed vigorously to capture and retain power. Two essays focus on the transition to and the evolution of this most recent phase of Indian politics. While originally written for a broad audience in the West, the essays do contain serious scholarly analyses. In the essay, 'From Majority to Minority Rule', I analyse the underlying forces that propelled the end of the Gandhi dynasty rule, ushering in the era of competitive but unstable governments. The rise of the BJP, in turn, is the analytical focus of the second essay, 'Enduring Another Election'. These essays provide the necessary background for understanding the most recent efforts in the twenty-first century by both the Congress and the BJP to craft functioning national governments.

1

Centralization and Powerlessness
India's Democracy in a Comparative Perspective*

During the 1970s and 1980s, a recurring pattern characterized political change in India: control over governmental decisions tended to centralize in leaders who ruled by virtue of personal popularity, but who found it difficult to transform their personal power into a problem-solving political resource. A number of political consequences typically followed. Governmental legitimacy became hard to sustain; there was a high leadership turnover below the highest ranks; the state continued to perform at a low level of efficacy—in terms both of accommodating conflicting interests and of solving developmental problems; and political violence as well as poverty continued to dominate the political landscape. This chapter attempts to explain the roots of the simultaneous tendencies towards centralization and powerlessness in India's low-income democracy.

It is argued that such tendencies towards centralization and powerlessness are generated by the near absence of systematic authority links between the state's apex and the vast social periphery. In years past, especially during the 1950s, India's nationalist party, the Congress, forged patronage links with regional and local influentials, thus creating a chain of authority that stretched from the capital city to villages. Over the last two decades or so, these links in the authority structure eroded, owing to a number of forces: the spread of democratic politics undermined the influence of regional and local traditional elites; and the nationalist party-qua-organization was destroyed by intra-elite conflict and by the recalcitrance of power-hungry national leaders.

*Originally published as 'Centralization and Powerlessness: India's Democracy in a Comparative Perspective', in Joel Samuel Migdal, Atul Kohli, and Vivienne Shue (eds), *State Power and Social Forces: Domination and Transformation in the Third World*, New York: Cambridge University Press, 1994, pp. 89–107.

Given India's plural diversity, the erosion of both traditional authority in the social structure and of the nationalist party created a highly fragmented political society. Leaders with populist and personal appeal offer one ready mechanism for forging a modicum of political coherence in such a fragmented political situation. Once in power, however, populist leaders do not readily perceive the need to build political institutions; rules and procedures of such institutions as parties only put limits on the discretionary power of personalistic leaders. Without parties or other political institutions, however, the links between leaders and their supporters remain weak. Elections are won on general, non-programmatic promises, and it becomes very difficult to translate such general mandates into specific policies. Major policy decisions repeatedly evoke considerable opposition, even from former supporters, and, just as repeatedly, governmental initiatives falter. Policy failure in turn paves the way for other populist challengers, thus perpetuating the cycle of centralization and powerlessness.

The argument developed here with reference to India may also be of some general relevance. First, India is one of the few developing countries that has sustained democracy for nearly forty years. Political patterns within it may thus help analyse what is likely to happen in other low-income democracies over time. One insight of possible general relevance is that the spread of democratic politics in pre-industrial societies undermines domination between traditional 'superiors' and 'inferiors'. As this happens, struggles of domination and opposition emerge from localized, social arenas and enter the national political sphere. One should then expect difficulties in forging new and coherent patterns of national authority. Such a political context, in turn, encourages the emergence of leaders who rule by personal and populist appeal. More often than not, however, personalistic rule of this nature is likely to lead to disappointing results. Without parties and programmes, populist leaders promise too much and are capable of delivering little, especially to the bottom half of the population. The problem of forging coherent authority thus continues. Besides Indira and Rajiv Gandhi in India, this analysis may also apply to such other recent cases as Cory Aquino in the Philippines or Garcia in Peru.

The second general point worth noting at the outset concerns how this chapter's approach relates to other prevailing ones. The issues raised here are similar to some of the earlier concerns of Samuel Huntington insofar as the problem of centralization and powerlessness is an integral aspect of the imbalance between institutional development and mobilized demands.[1] The causal analysis, however, is different. Instead of conceptualizing mobilization

---

[1] See Samuel Huntington, *Political Order in Changing Societies*, New Haven: Yale University Press, 1968, especially chapter 1.

primarily as a function of socio-economic change, this chapter conceives of growing political activism as additionally resulting from the spread of democratic politics.[2] This modification enables one to understand considerable political activism, even in fairly low-income, pre-industrial settings. Moreover, because power-hungry national leaders in India have destroyed or inhibited institutional rebuilding, those who control the state are not viewed here as necessarily the agents of political order and the public good.

Finally, this chapter emphasizes the mutual interaction of the state and society. On the one hand, the centralizing and populist antics of India's national leaders are not comprehensible without situating them in the larger socio-political context, especially at the regional and local levels. On the other hand, the changing societal context of growing authority fragmentation cannot be understood without reference to how India's democratic and interventionist state moulds the incentives of local and regional actors.

In the first of three parts, I analyse the recurring tendency in contemporary India towards the emergence of centralized and personalistic rule. The second part discusses the reasons why personal, concentrated power, while enabling leaders to bloc the access of others to the state, does not readily translate into developmental efficacy. The conclusion investigates the consequences of this recurring tendency towards centralization and powerlessness, as well as some of the broader implications of the Indian materials. (I should note at the outset that the empirical materials for this essay build on some of my other research; details of the Indian materials may be found in this larger body of work.)[3]

THE RECURRING TENDENCY TOWARDS CENTRALIZATION

By 'centralization' I mean control over key national decisions in the hands of a very few (or even a single) political elite. Understood as such, India has always been a fairly centralized democracy. Even during the 1950s and the 1960s, control over important decisions was highly concentrated in Jawaharlal Nehru and those close to him. Nevertheless, important contrasts between India of the 1950s and 1960s, and India of the 1970s and 1980s, help define the analytical problem I seek to explain.

---

[2]This idea has a long intellectual lineage, from Tocqueville, through T.H. Marshall, to Reinhard Bendix and Charles Tilly. See, for example, Reinhard Bendix, *Nation Building and Citizenship*, Berkeley: University of California Press, 1977, especially pp. 62–5, 419–34.

[3]See mainly Atul Kohli, *Democracy and Discontent: India's Growing Crisis of Governability*, New York: Cambridge University Press, 1990. Also see by the same author *The State and Poverty in India: Politics of Reform*, New York: Cambridge University Press, 1987; and an edited volume, *India's Democracy: An Analysis of Changing State–Society Relations*, Princeton: Princeton University Press, 1990.

To simplify drastically a rather complex picture, levels of political mobilization in India during the 1950s and the early 1960s were relatively low, and elite politics tended to accommodate intra-elite struggles. While Nehru was definitely 'first among equals', the fact is that cabinet government during this early period was a reality, the parliament functioned as an important deliberating and debating forum, opposition was treated with respect, the Congress party had internal democracy and an identity independent of the government, chief ministers of states often possessed independent political base, and such other state institutions as the constitution, the civil service, and the judiciary enjoyed a degree of non-partisan integrity. There were thus important institutional checks on the personal power of Nehru. It is also important to recognize, however, that political struggles in this early stage involved primarily a relatively small group of elites, especially nationalist and other wealthy urban and rural elites. The large majority of the Indian population, especially those in villages, were not as yet actively mobilized political actors. Members of dominant castes and other influential 'big men' in villages were thus often able to sway the political behaviour of those below them, namely, the middle and lower rural strata. As these rural elite were incorporated into the fold of the Congress party via patronage links, India's democracy took on the appearance of a relatively well-constructed, elitist democracy in which competing elites managed to work with each other, and into which the elites professed a hope of actively incorporating India's masses.

Political changes over the next two decades present an intriguing paradox: the more the power relations in the social structure, especially in the villages, were democratized, the more personalized and centralized became decision making at the top of India's political pyramid. Can these two processes of change be conceived to have been systematically linked? Before such a case is made, the fact of growing centralization needs to be documented briefly.

Specialists on Indian politics should agree with the broad observation that from the late 1960s onward, decision making in India became more and more centralized in the person of Indira Gandhi. The old Congress party was marginalized and the new Congress party of Indira never became a real party. Indira Gandhi instead won considerable popularity by adopting a populist posture and by establishing direct links with the masses. In turn, she used this popular electoral base as a power resource to make key political appointments. More and more individuals, both in the party and in the government, were appointed rather than elected to power. Issues of personal loyalty and favouritism thus became crucial in this top-down political system. Over the 1970s and the 1980s, nearly all members of the cabinet, the parliament as well as the Congress party officers and chief ministers of states lost their political autonomy; these positions came to be filled by those deemed loyal and useful by Indira Gandhi. As challenges to such personalistic use of power grew, the civil service and the police were also politicized. Eventually, even the armed forces and the constitution were not spared from partisan political struggles.

How does one interpret this trend towards growing centralization in the person of Indira Gandhi? One line of analysis views it as a product of an intra-elite conflict that Indira Gandhi won, partly because of her manipulation skills, and partly because of her populist appeal to India's numerical majority, the rural poor. This victory, the argument would continue, was then used to create a top-down political system to preserve and enhance Indira Gandhi's personal power.[4] Such an argument is not wrong but is incomplete. It is not wrong in the sense that a leader with greater vision, and a greater sense of the public good, would have realized that such a ruling strategy would not only weaken democracy but would also, over the long run, prove self-defeating. As discussed later in this section, when Indira Gandhi needed institutional support to implement her programmes, having destroyed the institutional base of the state, she found the state's arms rather limp. Programmatic failures, in turn, contributed to her political decline, and to her tragic assassination.

The emphasis on power-hungry Indira Gandhi is incomplete, however, because other Indian leaders have also ended up creating a very similar personalistic, centralized, and top-down political system. For example, Rajiv Gandhi sought to reverse these trends after coming to power in 1985, but by 1989, gave up any such effort as quixotic and re-established a personalistic, highly centralized regime.[5] As important are other examples from several Indian states. Non-Congress leaders, such as the actors-turned-politicians, M.G. Ramachandran in Tamil Nadu and N.T. Rama Rao in Andhra Pradesh, also failed to institutionalize their power. They concentrated power in their persons, appointed loyal minions to positions of power, and continued to rule as long as their personal popularity could be maintained.

The wider prevalence within India of a tendency towards centralization and personalization of power suggests the following: certain broader political forces in contemporary India encourage the rise of leaders who rule by virtue of personal popularity and who, in turn, following the logic of personal rule, tend to concentrate power and create top-down systems staffed by dependent appointees. These forces came into play sometime in the 1960s, and over time their significance has grown. Stated baldly, the lower-middle and the lower strata of rural India emerged during the 1960s as independent

---

[4]See, for example, Paul R. Brass, *The Politics of India since Independence*, New York: Cambridge University Press, 1990.

[5]See Kohli, *Democracy and Discontent*, chapters 11 and 12.

and significant political forces. The less these groups were swayed by leaders of the so-called dominant castes, the less electoral utility was served by the old Congress system of a chain of influential 'big men'. As a clever politician, Indira Gandhi sensed this political change rather early and, facing power competition from rival elites, quickly shifted her energies into reaggregating the newly released political forces. The populist slogan of 'alleviate poverty' was aimed precisely at winning electoral majorities in an increasingly fragmented political society, where those traditionally influential were losing their influence. Indira Gandhi's repeated electoral successes further confirmed this hypothesis. The large majorities she won in turn freed Indira Gandhi from coalitional responsibilities and enabled her to create a top-down state system.

Numerous local examples from India's political hinterland buttress the claim that, from the 1960s onward, India's political society became more and more fragmented. I will cite only three empirical cases, and those only very briefly, from three different parts of India.[6] The first example is from Kheda district in the western state of Gujarat. Well into the 1960s, the politics and society of this area were controlled by the landowning dominant castes of the Patidars (the Patels). Even though the Patidars were a numerical minority (some 20 per cent of the local population), their power rested both on control over land and on a relatively high position in the caste hierarchy. Over time, a heterogeneous middle group, the Kshatriyas—who constituted nearly 40 per cent of the local population—slowly awoke to the possibility that their numbers could be translated into political power. The more these 'backward castes' were mobilized as an electoral bloc, the more their leaders wanted to control the local state—for both symbolic and direct material rewards (patronage) that control of a local state provides in rural India. Unfortunately for the Kshatriya elite, the old, undivided, district-level Congress, as well as local government offices, were dominated by the Patidars—well into the 1960s. The resulting political conflict thus posed a fairly classic question of democratic politics: how were Congress's national leaders, like Indira Gandhi, going to incorporate the support of numerically significant groups, like the Kshatriyas, while local party and governmental structures were controlled by hitherto dominant groups like the Patidars?

A second example is from Guntur district in the south Indian state of Andhra Pradesh. The dominant community in the 1950s and the 1960s in this area were the Reddys, who often competed for power and influence with another landowning, relatively high caste community, the Kammas. As long as power conflict was limited to these two elite castes, the old Congress often succeeded in incorporating rival elites. Over time, however,

[6]For details, see ibid., chapters 3–7.

here as elsewhere in India, the capacity of Reddy and Kamma leaders to sway the political behaviour of the backward castes and Scheduled Castes declined. This became clear in the 1960s as many of the old Congress leaders (like a significant national politician, Sanjiva Reddy, who had opposed Indira Gandhi within the Congress) started losing their electoral support. The challenge to the power of the dominant castes was not as dramatic in Guntur as it was in Kheda. Nevertheless, it was becoming clear throughout the 1960s that 'backward castes' would need to be incorporated on a new basis by any leadership seeking their support. Segments of the rural poor in this area had, in any case, been successfully mobilized by the Communist Party of India (CPI). How was the new Congress going to respond to these growing power challenges?

The third and most dramatic example of growing power challenges is provided by India's eastern state, West Bengal. Always more susceptible than other parts of India to radical appeals, parts of the state in the 1960s experienced quite a few radical movements. The well-known Naxalbari movement in the north of the state successfully organized tribal peasants for confiscation of land, till it was brutally repressed. Less dramatic, but probably more threatening, was the fact that the political significance of the old *bhadralok* elite (the Bengali intelligentsia, with a base in land wealth) declined both in cities and in the countryside. Simultaneously, Congress's capacity to win elections declined. As various communist parties gained in significance, the same political question emerged at the forefront: how was a new national leadership of the Congress going to reaggregate electoral majorities in a political context of growing power challenges?

Similar examples could be multiplied. The general point, however, is fairly simple: introduction of democratic politics and competitive mobilization was slowly chipping away at the corporate cohesiveness of India's traditional social structure. As this happened, the old Congress system of patronage-chains-of-big-men was losing its ability to mobilize an increasingly fragmented political society. The sharp downturn in Congress's electoral fortunes in the 1967 national elections must have confirmed this hypothesis for the more astute Indian political leaders, including Indira Gandhi. A new ruling strategy was clearly needed. Many political changes in contemporary India, in turn, are comprehensible if one thinks of them as by-products of the new ruling strategy, namely, populism aimed at building and sustaining majority coalitions in the context of a highly fragmented political society.

We know in retrospect that Indira Gandhi in the early 1970s adopted a political posture that emphasized the alleviation of poverty as a key theme. This populist strategy paid handsome political dividends, generating huge electoral majorities for her. Before investigating the implications of this strategy further, however, we should note that pro-poor populism was by no means an inevitable by-product of a changed political context. It was, rather, a choice from among a handful of other available strategic options. For example, as it became clear during the 1970s that poverty was not going to be readily alleviated, and that empty promises to that effect could not continue to bring electoral rewards, the Congress in the 1980s sought to create winning majorities by flirting with ethnic themes—for instance, Hindus against other Indian minorities. This electoral strategy has, of course, been pursued with a vengeance by other Indian political parties in the 1990s; that, however, is another story.

One question remains a puzzle. Given a number of available ruling strategies, why did Indira Gandhi not attempt to systematically rebuild institutions—such as a reformist party—that could enable her to deliver on her reformist promises, and that at the same time could help solidify her electoral base? A definite answer will never be known, but three possible contributing factors can be proposed. First, it would have required a more visionary leader with a greater sense of the public good than Indira Gandhi possessed. Second, building of parties and institutions takes both time and sustained political attention; Indira Gandhi instead devoted most of her energies to blocking real or imagined power threats. Third, and most important, parties cannot be readily decreed from above. More often than not, parties develop as vehicles for capturing power. Those who are already in power, and especially if their power rests on personal popularity, tend to find rules, procedures, and a robust second tier of leaders unnecessarily constraining; they often view institutions more as obstacles and less as facilitators of effective rule.

To return to the main theme, growing political fragmentation in the 1960s encouraged the rise of personalistic populism. The forces that have propelled political fragmentation, as well as the consequences of personalistic, populist rule now need to be discussed, if only briefly.

Both socio-economic and political forces have propelled growing mobilization, although, on balance, peculiarities of India's democracy have played a very significant role. Students of development often anticipate growing social mobilization in the context of 'modernization'. The spread of commerce, new modes of economic activity, literacy and urbanization, are generally associated with what Karl Deutsch had labelled 'social mobilization'.[7] Social mobilization, in turn, is supposed to erode traditional domination, release social actors for new political commitments, and lead to greater levels of political activism, owing either to anomie or to formation of new interest groups. Marxist analysis of the transition from 'feudalism

[7]See his 'Social Mobilization and Political Development', *American Political Science Review*, 55, September 1961.

to capitalism' is also consistent with this 'modernization' analysis; it, too, emphasizes the corroding role of economic change, especially of capitalism, that supposedly renders class inequalities naked, and thus contributes to class conflict and to new levels of activism.[8] There is enough evidence in contemporary India to sustain an analysis that would emphasize socio-economic changes as the basic motor of growing political mobilization. For example, the roots of radical activism of poor peasants in parts of West Bengal, Andhra Pradesh, and Bihar, and of growing political efficacy of the newly wealthy green revolution farmers of north-western India are located primarily in socio-economic changes.

What is less well understood in the general literature, and to which the Indian experience can contribute, is how peculiarities of democracy in a low-income setting themselves propel higher levels of political mobilization. For example, the state in India seeks to promote development and is thus highly interventionist. This means that a fair amount of a poor society's free-floating economic resources is accessible primarily through the state, which thus becomes an object of intense political attention. Moreover, since this state is accessible via democratic means, the stakes of winning or losing the electoral game become very high. Rival elites thus use all available means, fair or foul, peaceful or violent, to mobilize support from their respective communities so as to secure access to the society's main milking cow, the state. The diversity of India's plural social structure easily lends itself to competitive mobilization. Because political parties are weak in any case, and also do not organize and thus systematize participation, intra-elite political competition is readily transformed into what the Rudolphs have rightly identified as India's growing number of 'demand groups'.[9] The dynamics underlying this process of overpoliticization is both political and economic. Spread of egalitarian values, and of competitive politics within the context of India's low-income democracy and an interventionist state, have politicized social conflict in a manner that has greatly contributed to fragmentation of India's political society.

Some of the evidence for these claims is embedded in the local examples already cited. To recall, the mobilization of Kshatriyas in parts of Gujarat was both political and economic; it was aimed at winning elections and capturing state power, it was led by partisan political elite, and its main demands were economic rewards from the state (for example, more 'reserved' employment for the 'backward castes' or state subsidies). The

[8]See, for example, Antonio Gramsci, *Selections from the Prison Notebooks*, New York: International Publishers, 1971, especially p. 276.

[9]See Lloyd Rudolph and Sussane Rudolph, *In Pursuit of Lakshmi*, Chicago: University of Chicago Press, 1987, especially Part 4.

backward caste movements for 'reservations' across India have followed a more or less similar pattern. Mobilization of various ethnic groups also has not been all that different. Whether at issue are smaller movements, like those of the Gurkhas in West Bengal or Marathi speakers in Belgaum, Karnataka, or movements of much greater significance, like those of the Sikhs of Punjab, or even the Hindu–Muslim conflict in various parts of India, the political dynamics are identifiable: leaders mobilize communities so as to strengthen their own political demands. If demands are met, movements often die down. Just as often, however, demands are not met and movements are intensified, or worse, in spite of concessions—as in the case of the Sikhs—leaders of movements loose control over mobilized followers and fragmented movements develop in volatile and often unpredictable ways.

The most compelling evidence to support the claim that the dynamics of growing political activism are not 'social mobilization' à la Deutsch, but are politico-economic, emerges from regional patterns within India. For example, states as diverse as prosperous Gujarat and poor Bihar have experienced considerable political activism over the last decade. If economic development was the primary driving force, how would one explain the very high levels of activism and political violence in an economically stagnant state like Bihar? A better explanation is, rather, that changing political consciousness and competitive democratic mobilization in a stagnant economy have bequeathed to political demands a zero-sum quality, thus intensifying the sense of threat that political demands pose and periodically lead to political violence. Similarly, the fact that the highly mobilized state of West Bengal has been relatively free of violence and agitations since 1977 must be attributed to a rule by a relatively well organized reformist party. Political and organizational variables are thus crucial for understanding patterns of political activism in India.

To connect the argument back to the main point, introduction of democracy into a highly rigid and inegalitarian social structure has slowly but surely unleashed diverse patterns of mobilization. These activities started intensifying sometime in the 1960s and have continued over the last two decades. A major consequence has been the difficulty in forging moderately consensual authority; the more fragmented the political society, the more difficult it has become to form a democratically constituted, coherent centre of power. This political context, in turn, has encouraged personalistic populism. Leaders who promise a little something to everyone, even if vaguely, and those who possess personal appeal—or, as it were, charisma—often emerge powerful in settings of political fragmentation.

Personalistic and populist rule, in turn, tends to be inherently centralizing and de-institutionalizing and does not offer a long-term solution to the problem of building democratic authority. Because power lines link diffuse masses to a single leader, the person at the top is not as constrained by coalitional pressures as are other democratically elected leaders. Of course, such leaders must respect the socially powerful, but they also possess a considerable degree of freedom, not in social restructuring, but in creating a top-down political system. The more the second- and third-tier officers of the polity come to be appointed from above, the less independent power exists within the polity and the more centralized becomes the top of the political pyramid. Thus emerges the first important paradox of contemporary India: democratization of traditional authority, especially in the rural social structure, has paved the way for centralization of power at the top. The paradox, however, does not stop there. The related, and second, paradox to which I now turn my attention is, why this centralization and control at the top is difficult to transform into real power to solve problems.

THE RECURRING TENDENCY TOWARDS POWERLESSNESS

The use of 'powerlessness' refers to the repeated incapacity of rulers to fulfil their stated objectives. Leaders who manage to centralize control over decision making often appear to be very powerful. This, however, can be and often is misleading, especially in low-income democracies. Therefore, one needs to make an analytical distinction between centralizing power and developmental power. Centralizing power, as already noted, involves growing control over decisions in the hands of a few leaders and, by the same token, exclusion of the second and lower level of political elite from decision making. Developmental power, by contrast, refers to a capacity not only to make decisions but also to carry them through. Developmental power thus is the ability of political leaders to alter successfully the behaviour of social actors and groups.

Some authoritarian regimes within the Third World are able to transform centralized control into developmental efficacy, mainly by utilizing coercion to alter the behaviour of social groups. But this is rare, even under authoritarian conditions. When the polity is organized as a democracy, coercion definitely cannot be the main currency that leaders utilize to influence socio-economic change. Instead, positive and negative incentives, persuasion, and selective use of laws backed by the threat of coercion—legitimate domination—take on an increased significance. Within a democracy, therefore, the capacity to initiate major developmental changes from above comes to rest on a prior capacity of leaders to institutionalize 'blocs of consensus', or to build majority coalitions to support a specific path of change. For majority coalitions not only to elect specific leaders, but also to provide sustained support for the implementation of leaders' programmes, in turn requires that the link between rulers and supporters, or between the political centre and social periphery, be durable. This durability is likely to exist if the relationship of leaders and supporters is institutionalized through such mechanisms as political parties. Democratic leaders, whose power rests on well-organized parties, are thus in a better position to implement developmental programmes than are leaders with a diffuse and populist support base.

These generalizations can be supported with some empirical materials from India. However, one general caveat needs to be made. Leaders in democracies often need the support of multiple constituencies and thus often pursue multiple goals. This simple observation has two important implications for the discussion that follows. First, under the best of circumstances, democratic governments seldom act decisively but, rather, tend to muddle through. This should raise one's tolerance for what is a 'normal' level of developmental performance in a democracy; the 'decisive and flexible' South Korean state under Park Chung Hee, for example, and the 'flabby and muddling through' Indian state reflect, in part, the differences in regime type. Weakness of parties and other institutions that could systematically link the state and society in India is an additional variable that further contributes to the powerlessness of that country's centralizing and personalistic leaders. Second, the capacity to fulfil goals often varies from goal to goal. Whether parties are weak or strong, varying with the nature of the coalitional support, some goals are easier to pursue than others, and the pursuit of some goals makes it difficult to achieve other goals.

Given these caveats, a few examples from contemporary India can now be provided to explain how and why growing centralization did not lead to increased power to achieve developmental goals. Two different types of examples are discussed: the incapacity of Indira Gandhi to follow through on her major commitment to alleviate poverty; and the political difficulties that Rajiv Gandhi ran into when he attempted to redirect India's import-substitution development model in a more 'liberal' direction.

Indira Gandhi and Poverty Alleviation

Garibi hatao or 'alleviate poverty' was Indira Gandhi's main political slogan throughout the 1970s. Yet we know in retrospect that Indira Gandhi did not have much success in alleviating India's rural poverty, certainly not through the mechanism of redistributive state intervention. Because such gaps between rhetoric and outcome are fairly common in the Third World, the gap itself is not very surprising. Why it nevertheless poses an interesting analytical puzzle is because of the following: Indira Gandhi won sizable electoral 'majorities on the basis of her populist slogan; she came to have tremendous personal control over India's crucial political decisions; and for a short while (1975–7), she even possessed near authoritarian powers. Why did it prove so difficult to transform these power resources into a capacity to implement some redistributive programmes, such as land reforms?

The reason is in part that it is very difficult for any state to reach out into the nooks and crannies of a society and hope to restructure social relations in a manner that would benefit the weak at the expense of the socially powerful. Next to making war, redistributive reform is probably the most difficult task a state can undertake. If leaders use standard operating procedures, such as pass laws, and hope the bureaucracy implements them, land reforms do not get implemented. Given that those who own land are often powerful, the lower reaches of the state's bureaucratic arm are seldom efficacious enough to fight the powerful on the behalf of the weak, especially in a society's periphery, where bureaucratic supervision tends to be slack. What is more likely is that lower-level state officials and the socially powerful rural elites establish cozy working relationships and redistributive laws are not implemented. If such reforms are to be implemented, what is needed instead is much more of a political intervention, one that can simultaneously strengthen the weak by organizing them, and utilize politicized implementing agents, usually party cadres, that more readily respond to the decisions of rulers than bureaucrats.

I have argued elsewhere in a book-length study that redistributive intervention in India's low-income democracy has been best facilitated by well-organized, left-of-centre ruling parties.[10] The absence of such an instrument made it almost impossible for Indira Gandhi to follow through on her political platform of garibi hatao. The argument in this other study was developed by a comparative analysis of regional Indian materials. It was documented that redistributive reforms were much more successfully implemented in a state like West Bengal than in several other Indian states, including those run by Indira Gandhi's party. I traced this success to the role of the ruling party in West Bengal, a party that calls itself communist—the Communist Party of India (Marxist) or CPI(M)—but is essentially social democratic in ideology, though sharing a tight organization with other Leninist parties. The party rests its power on a coalition of middle and lower rural classes. This social base, combined with a good party organization, enabled CPI(M) to successfully implement mildly redistributive tenancy reforms in one part of India.

More recent regional evidence from India further supports the significance of well-organized parties as agents of redistribution, although it is also important to reaffirm the issue of the regime's social base. West Bengal continues to be one of the few states in which tenancy reforms have been successfully implemented over the last ten to fifteen years. Nevertheless, having implemented these reforms, the CPI(M) regime has stopped short of implementing any further land redistribution that could benefit the really poor, the landless agricultural labourers. The CPI(M) also has not made any

---

[10]See Kohli, *The State and Poverty in India*.

real effort to organize these labourers so as to improve their wages. The main reason for this is the difficulty the CPI(M) faces in holding together a coalition of middle peasants and landless labourers. Because the middle peasants often employ these labourers and some of their lands may be affected by radical land reform, the CPI(M) has decided, to go slow. The analytical point is clear. Party organization is only one significant variable in successful redistribution. The social base of the ruling party is another important factor that conditions a regime's policy proclivities.

Lest the correspondence between social base of power and a state's policy behaviour be overdrawn, the case of Gujarat in the 1980s provides a ready check. The winning coalition that the Congress party under Madhav Singh Solanki put together in Gujarat was nearly identical to CPI(M)'s power base in West Bengal. As in Bengal, Solanki succeeded in excluding the elite, landholding groups—the Patidars—and rested his power instead on Kshatriyas and Adivasis, the middle and the lower strata. Once in power, however, in contrast to West Bengal, Solanki did not even attempt land reforms. When he tried to implement something as mild as the 'reservation' policy—a policy that would have done little more than ensure a few thousand future jobs in the public sector to the middle and lower strata—Gujarat became embroiled in major riots. These riots were initiated by the Patidars and they severely checked Solanki's power to attempt even token redistribution. Solanki, in turn, could neither hold together the coalition of his own supporters nor fight the opposition with any success. The root of this weakness was the absence of a well-organized party. Without a party, the government's supporters were not deeply attached to a programme, the ruling elite remained factionalized, and a coherent force could not be generated to confront the socially powerful. Clearly, identical social coalitions do not provide a ready explanation of regime's redistributive performance. The ideology and the organization of the ruling party remain crucial variables for understanding success or failure at redistribution in contemporary India.

The absence of a well-organized, left-of-centre party was what made it difficult for Indira Gandhi to translate her left-of-centre political goals into reformist outcomes. In other words, without an instrument to systematically link the state and society, personalistic power enabled centralization but did not generate power to achieve goals. It is important only to add—although the point is relatively obvious—that the presence of a specific type of instrument does not mean that the capacity of leaders to accomplish all types of goals will be enhanced. A well-organized left-of-centre party, for example, may enhance the leadership's redistributive capacity but may have no bearing on the capacity to deal with ethnic conflicts, or may well have a negative impact on economic growth. The issue of when states have capacities to achieve their goals thus remains a highly complex one, varying not only across countries but also across issues within a country.

Rajiv Gandhi and Economic Liberalization

Having recognized that India's industrial growth was relatively sluggish, especially in comparison with such other developing countries as South Korea, Rajiv Gandhi attempted to alter India's development strategy. This was in the aftermath of Indira Gandhi's assassination, and after Rajiv Gandhi had ridden a 'sympathy wave' to power with a massive electoral majority in early 1985. We know in retrospect that Rajiv had some success in implementing 'liberalization', but also that he faced numerous obstacles. Eventually, he had to backtrack in a more populist direction. Moreover, whatever success he may have had probably cost him his electoral support in the 1989 elections.[11] A brief discussion of this example, therefore, highlights a somewhat different analytical point than the one already discussed with reference to the issue of redistribution. The general point continues to be the same, namely, the inability to translate personalistic power into developmental results, but the more specific point here is that the attempt to translate non-specific electoral mandates into specific policy goals quickly run into obstacles.

The first issue that needs to be understood is why recent elections in India have all been won on fairly non-specific mandates. For those who do not follow Indian politics, it is important to know that ever since 1967, most national elections in India have been conducted in the shadow of some extraordinary event. The 1971 election, for example, took place when the nationalist euphoria over the dismemberment of Pakistan (and the birth of Bangladesh) was high, and when Indira Gandhi's sharp shift towards populism had also raised the hopes of many. National emergency was imposed in 1975 as a result of growing and violent political opposition. Indira Gandhi lost the 1977 elections, mainly owing to the Emergency, but the dramatic failure of the opposition to hold the coalition together catapulted her back to power in 1980. There was a widespread feeling in India in the early-1980s that, had Indira Gandhi not been assassinated in 1984, she would have done poorly in the National Elections of 1985. Her assassination, which created a widespread fear of impending turmoil, as well as sympathy for her son, brought Rajiv to power with a large electoral majority in early 1985. The 1989 elections were one of the few 'normal' elections in India since 1967,

[11]The liberalization attempts which began in mid-1991 have been somewhat more successful. The analytical lessons of that experiment, however, will be materials for another essay (see Chapters 6 and 7, this volume).

and it is not surprising that, as in 1967, the Congress party again lost its dominant position. The elections in 1991 that brought Congress back to power again reflected the inability of Congress's opposition to work together, as well as the dramatic assassination of Rajiv Gandhi.

The general point is that the Congress party lost its nationalist hegemony over India sometimes in the 1960s, and ever since then it has been difficult for Congress leaders to put together a winning coalition. This task has become especially difficult because the memory of unfulfilled populist promises is fresh, and populism has probably lost its electoral efficacy. Without parties, programmes, and stable coalitions, therefore, electoral victories have had to be 'manufactured' by creating, or taking advantage of, extraordinary events that generate electorally consequential national moods like euphoria or crises. Electoral majorities based on non-specific and nearly sensational mandates are thus not only fortuitous, they have become an integral part of how to create a coherent centre of power in contemporary India. The analytical issue for us now is, how leaders who win power through such means fare while in power.

Rajiv Gandhi was elected on a very general, non-specific mandate and did rather poorly while in power. His attempts to 'liberalize' India's economy afford important glimpses into the underlying dynamics. Liberalization in India mainly has meant providing incentives—or at least removing disincentives—for the profitability of private production, with the hope that this will improve both the levels and the quality of investment, and lead to higher levels of economic growth. Although eminently 'rational' from the standpoint of improving production output from private sources, attempts to implement such policy measures created major political problems for Rajiv Gandhi.

Rajiv Gandhi did not win by putting together a pro-growth coalition that sought to liberalize India's economy. As a matter of fact, his electoral victory had no or little economic component. As soon as he attempted to translate his broad mandate into a specific economic direction, the first major source of resistance was his own party. Even though the Congress is not much of a party anymore, many of those who had been in appointed positions from the time of Indira Gandhi balked at Rajiv's attempted redirection. The motives behind this resistance were mixed. Some feared that the abandonment of 'socialist' economic policies in favour of a more 'liberal' approach would cost the party electoral support among India's majority, the rural poor, others worried that 'liberalization' would eventually lead to the opening of the economy to external economic influences, thus threatening sovereignty; and yet others saw the new policy regime as signalling that new officers would come to run the party and thus sought to block any major change as a way of preserving personal power. Whatever the motives, and they were mixed, the general point is that because a major policy initiative was not part of the party platform that had facilitated electoral victory, there was no cohesive support for the initiative, even within the ruling party.

Because Rajiv Gandhi stood at the apex of what was by now a top-down political system, the resistance of the party may have slowed his initiatives but was by no means decisive. Rajiv replaced those who really resisted with those who were more loyal, and, at least during 1985–6, continued with his liberalization measures.

Very soon, however, opposition to his new policies grew. For example, Rajiv's attempts to reduce India's public expenditures on poverty programmes evoked considerable opposition, including, once again, that from Congress's own senior political officers. Rajiv backtracked. When plans to remove subsidies on prices of essential goods, like kerosene, were announced, numerous opposition parties threatened a general strike across urban India. Once again, Rajiv Gandhi backtracked. And when plans to invite Japanese auto manufacturers to produce automobiles in India were leaked, India's import-substitution-coddled businesspeople brought pressure on the government and attempts to alter India's foreign investment policies were put aside. Clearly, different components of the 'liberalization' package evoked opposition from all social groups likely to be affected.

Finally, the opposition that really hurt Rajiv Gandhi was that of rural groups, who started viewing the new policy measures as pro-city and pro-rich. While such an interpretation was not necessary, especially because measures like devaluation can shift the terms of trade in favour of the peasantry, the problem was one of political management. Without a party, Rajiv Gandhi simply did not have the political resources needed to persuade and incorporate sections of the rural population behind his programme. What happened instead was that other political actors, at lower levels of the polity, succeeded in counter-mobilizing. Rajiv's new economic policies had led to an increase in industrial production, especially in durable consumer goods. Worried that these goods might not clear the market, the government had also provided numerous incentives for urban consumers to consume more. The resulting development strategy was, and could thus be easily characterized as, benefiting the urban rich. Peasant leaders took advantage of the new opportunity and successfully mobilized rural groups against the Congress party. When Congress lost elections in 1987 in the crucial Hindi-heartland state of Haryana, only then did Rajiv Gandhi realize how politically expensive the new economic rationality had become.

After 1987 one heard less and less about economic liberalization in India, at least until 1991, when another new government started pushing this agenda; that again, however, is a different story. There was no major policy reversal during 1987 and 1991, but there was also no major policy movement.

Instead, Rajiv Gandhi readopted some of the more populist economic programmes. It should be noted in passing that, the more torn he became by the conflicting pulls of economic and political rationality, the less he used economic policies as tools of electoral mobilization. It can be argued that Congress's renewed interest in mobilization around religious sentiments was rooted in this contradiction. Indira Gandhi's populism had won majorities, but poverty alleviation policies were never implemented. As Rajiv Gandhi attempted to reorder economic policies in a pro-growth direction—which might eventually benefit India's poor—the short-term problem became one of securing electoral majorities. If the majority–minority pie is not to be cut along the poor-rich angle, the other obvious angle in India is Hindus versus minorities, especially Muslims. Congress's growing flirtation with a pro-Hindu orientation, and the electoral success of other political parties with similar commitments, is thus partly rooted in these contemporary political tensions.

Rajiv Gandhi did implement some liberalization measures but was also forced to curtail many of his other planned actions. Where he did succeed in implementation, the moves may have cost him important political support. It thus becomes clear that in spite of a massive electoral majority, Rajiv Gandhi could not translate this general support into a force to help him pursue his own policy priorities—mainly because the support he had enjoyed in early 1985 was very diffuse and without a strong mandate to do anything specific. If economic liberalization is what Rajiv Gandhi stood for, it should have been tested in the marketplace of electoral politics. If he could have thus put together a pro-liberalization, pro-growth majority coalition, and given this coalition some durability by incorporating its representatives into a party organization, the problem of implementation would have been qualitatively different. As already argued, however, without parties, programmes, and stable coalitions, non-specific electoral mandates have become a near necessity in contemporary India. Attempts to translate these victories into specific new policies have, in turn, become very difficult. The greater the gap, therefore, between how power is won and how power is used, the more India's political system continues to muddle through at a relatively low level of efficacy.

CONCLUSION

This chapter has sought to identify and explain a recurring tendency in Indian politics towards centralization and powerlessness. Its purpose has been both to analyse an important political problem and to demonstrate the utility of the state–society approach that this volume seeks to advance. It is now important to conclude by drawing together some arguments concerning the substantial analytical puzzle and the approach embedded in the analysis.

The puzzle I have sought to analyse here plagues many developing countries: control over national decisions comes to centralize in the person of a single leader or a few leaders, but the leadership finds it difficult to transform this control into developmental efficacy. The argument I have developed regarding India may or may not apply to other developing countries. My hunch is that it is likely to have some relevance to other low-income democracies but that the dynamics within authoritarian systems are different.

The main condition that helps explain the tendency towards centralization and powerlessness in India is the weakness of systematic authority links between the political centre and the social periphery. The spread of democracy has eroded patterns of traditional domination in the social structure. Numerous groups have thus been mobilized into the political arena, but such mobilization has not been accompanied by a systematic reorganization of the newly mobilized forces. Political parties could have been one major institutional means of such reincorporation. Parties, however, take time to emerge. In India, moreover, power-hungry leaders contributed to the destruction of old, established parties. Weakness of parties and fragmentation of power in the social structure have made the task of forging effective government—a government able to resolve conflicts without violence and follow through on its policy promises—very difficult.

One of the few alternatives for creating a coherent political centre in a fragmented polity is leaders with personal appeal. Following the logic that leaders like power, such leaders characteristically create top-down political systems of loyal minions. Since rules and procedures constrain personal discretion, personalistic leaders also do not always view—especially, if they are shortsighted—the need to create institutions as desirable. Fragmentation of power in India has thus provided the context that encourages personalistic and centralizing leaders to emerge.

We have also noted that personalistic control in India has proven hard to translate into power to achieve policy goals. This was true of both redistributive and growth goals. In both cases, our analysis has suggested, leaders needed a political instrument to translate their goals into outcomes, but such an instrument was missing. Instruments such as parties could have helped bring together leaders and supporters into a durable 'power bloc'. This institutionalized power, in turn, could have been used to pursue specific goals.

The question that remains is supposing Rajiv Gandhi's power had rested on a well-organized growth coalition, what would have been the implication of such a power configuration for redistributive goals? The answer in the abstract is that the implication may well have been negative. The reverse is probably also true: a well-organized redistributive coalition in power can hurt economic growth. How, then, can states simultaneously pursue goals that may be in tension? There is no easy answer. One possible way of thinking about the problem, however, is as follows.

Because interests of social actors vary, one needs in societies parties that emphasize alternative goals. It is no accident that many well-established democracies are served well by alternating rule between growth and redistributive coalitions. Within developing country democracies, where political communities are not well established, and where the state must perform important economic functions, the need for well-organized parties of competing orientations becomes that much greater. Well-organized parties are one of the few available political instruments that can both represent interests and concentrate them at the top, enabling party leaders, if they win majority support, to pursue development democratically. Crafting well-organized parties thus remains an important long-term goal of political engineering in the Third World.

A last set of concluding comments concerns the state–society approach embedded in the analysis here. First, if the argument developed in this chapter is persuasive, it should strengthen the general claim of the volume, namely, that state and society condition each other continuously, and that patterns of political change must be analysed by focusing on state–society interaction. Second, this chapter's analysis suggests that what the national leaders do, or do not do, cannot be discovered without travelling down the political and social hierarchies, where at the 'periphery' the social and political forces provide the context that condition the nature of central rule. And last, this analysis also leads to the argument that our understanding of state and society ought to be deeply political. Instead of a bureaucratic vision of the state, and a tendency to view social structures as given, it is important to recognize that both political and social actors wish to shape the use of authority in social change, and in the process, both the state and society are formed and re-formed. The struggles for domination and opposition are struggles over life chances and thus tend to generate political struggles. How the resulting political struggles are co-opted, repressed, or utilized is essential to an understanding of how political change in developing countries proceeds.

2

Can Democracies Accommodate Ethnic Nationalism?
Rise and Decline of Self-Determination Movements in India*

Numerous ethnic movements have over the years confronted the central state within India's multicultural democracy. India thus provides laboratory-like conditions for the study of these movements. In this paper I analyse three such ethnic movements—those of Tamils in Tamil Nadu during the 1950s and the 1960s, of Sikhs in the Punjab during the 1980s, and of Muslims in Kashmir during the 1990s—with the aim of explaining both their rise and decline. The focus will be less on details of these movements and more on deriving some general conclusions.

I argue below that periodic demands for more control and power by a variety of ethnic groups—that is, self-determination movements—ought to be expected in multicultural democracies, especially developing-country democracies. The fate of these movements—that is, the degree of cohesiveness these groups forge; whether they are accommodated or whether their demands readily escalate into secessionist movements; and their relative longevity—largely reflect the nature of the political context, though group characteristics around which movements emerge and the resources these groups control are also consequential.

*Originally published as 'Can Democracies Accommodate Ethnic Nationalism? Rise and Decline of Self-Determination Movements in India', *The Journal of Asian Studies*, 56(2), May 1997, pp. 325–44.

I would like to thank the following for their helpful comments on earlier drafts: Amrita Basu, Ayesha Jalal, Pratap Mehta, Claus Offe, Susanne Rudolph, Pravesh Sharma, John Waterbury, and the anonymous reviewers. The suggestions made by Ashutosh Varshney need to be singled out for acknowledgement because they were very useful; I incorporated many of them. The paper further benefited from comments of participants at the conference on Political Violence in India, at Amherst, Mass., 23–24 September 1995, and at a seminar I gave at the Department of Political Science, University of Toronto, 9 February 1996. A much earlier version of this paper was prepared with the financial help of the Liechtenstein Research Programme on Self-determination, Center of International Studies, Princeton University.

More specifically, two dimensions of the political context appear to be especially relevant, namely, how well central authority is institutionalized within the multicultural democracy and the willingness of the ruling groups to share some power and resources with mobilized groups. Given well-established central authority and firm but compromising leaders, self-determination movements typically follow the shape of an inverse 'U' curve: a democratic polity in a developing country encourages group mobilization, heightening group identities and facilitating a sense of increased group efficacy; mobilized groups then confront state authority, followed by a more-or-less prolonged process of power negotiation; and such movements eventually decline as exhaustion sets in, some leaders are repressed, others are co-opted, and a modicum of genuine power sharing and mutual accommodation between the movement and the central state authorities is reached. Understood in this manner, self-determination movements constitute a political process whereby the central state and a variety of ethnic groups discover their relative power balances in developing-country democracies.

This bald argument requires some qualifications and caveats that are best stated at the outset. First, in addition to the domestic political context, the comparative analysis of Indian materials suggests that international factors can also alter the underlying power dynamics on which the predicted rise and decline of these movements rests. Second, the analysis is pitched at a fairly high level of generality. This not only obliterates complex details of individual movements but leads one to downplay such important contrasts across movements: some identities (e.g., religion) may be better suited than others (e.g., language) for defining ethnic boundaries and thus may be more readily mobilizable and sustainable in the cause of self-determination movements. Since no single essay can do everything, I hope that the costs of aggregation are worth the benefits of generalizations that emerge. And, finally, there is a need for a normative caveat. The focus on the state and the larger political context ought not to be read as endorsing the actions of state elites at the expense of the rights of ethnic movements. On the contrary, established states often trample the rights of their minorities, sometimes ruthlessly. Whether a state or a demanding group has justice on its side is both important and controversial; it is best decided on a case-by-case basis.

The paper is organized as follows. I first discuss some general issues, explaining why proliferation of group demands ought to be expected in a developing-country, multicultural democracy like India, and why institutionalization of central authority and the nature of the leadership are especially important aspects of the political context that shape self-determination movements. Specific Indian materials follow this general discussion, notably, a comparison of self-determination movements by Tamils,

Sikhs and Kashmiri Muslims. Towards the end, I not only re-summarize the analysis but elaborate on some general conclusions.

POLITICAL CONTEXT: SOME GENERALIZATIONS

Politicization in Developing Democracies

Introduction of democracy to a developing-country setting nearly always exacerbates political conflicts over the short to medium term. Some observers are surprised by such outcomes because, extrapolating from the Western experience, they expect democracy to be a solution to existing, rather than a source of new, power conflicts. In the West, however, if one may over-generalize, democracy evolved over a long time, and both suffrage and political competition expanded slowly within the framework of centralized authority structures at the apex and growing popular pressures from below. Moreover, the question of which groups constituted a 'nation' that was to be wedded to a specific state was often resolved prior to the introduction of mass suffrage. In this sense, democracy in the West indeed came to be a 'solution' to growing power conflicts in society, especially among economic elite and across class lines. By contrast, democracy to most developing countries comes as an imported idea. As these ideas are translated into democratic institutions and these institutions provide new incentives for political actors to organize and mobilize, the results over the short to medium term are often disquieting. Several state–society traits of developing-country democracies help explain why this should be so.

First, prevailing cultural conditions in developing countries do not readily mesh with the imported model of political democracy. For example: mass suffrage is introduced in a context where identities and attachments often tend to be more local than national; authority in society tends to be dispersed but, within dispersed pockets, quite rigid and hierarchical; and community norms often prevail over narrow individualism. As democracy is introduced and competing elites undertake political mobilization, old identities are rekindled and reforged. Modern technology hastens the process (e.g., teachings of Khomeini on cassettes or rendering of the *Ramayana* on television), and collision of mobilized identities with each other or with the state ought not to be totally surprising. Spread of democratic norms also threatens traditional elites, who are more than willing to join hands with all those who perceive the spread of individualism as disruptive of traditional lifestyles. Again, a variety of 'reactionary' movements ought to be expected.

Second, considerable state intervention is inherent to the overall design of 'late development'.[1] This structural trait in a low-income setting generates

---

[1]See 'Conclusion' in Atul Kohli, *Democracy and Discontent: India's Growing Crisis of Governability*, New York: Cambridge University Press, 1991.

special problems when democracy is introduced. For example, ruling elites in developing-country democracies cannot readily claim that distributive problems are social (private) and not political (public) problems; in other words, it is difficult in contemporary developing countries to establish the same separation between public and private realms that many Western democracies developed at early stages. Accumulating distributive claims on these states thus partly reflect the politicization engendered by the state's attempts to penetrate and reorganize socio-economic life. Relatedly, an interventionist state in a poor setting controls large proportions of a society's economic resources, thus attracting the competitive energies of many of those who seek economic improvement. Intense competition over the state's resources, in turn, politicizes numerous cleavages, adding to problems of developing-country democracies.

Third, since democracy comes to most developing countries as an import, and since the transitions to democracy are over relatively short time periods, democratic institutions in most follower democracies tend to be weak. There is some variation on this dimension, and I will return to the issue of relative institutionalization as a variable below (India being more fortunate on this score). For the most part, however, such institutions as norms of electoral politics, political parties, parliaments and constitutional separation of powers are not well established in developing-country democracies. Competitive mobilization, in turn, that is unmediated by institutions tends to spell trouble for most states. Of the problems generated by this well-known condition, the most significant is that power in these settings often comes to rest in individuals rather than in institutions. Barring exceptional individuals, most leaders centralize personal power with long-term detrimental consequences. Because centralization of power in individuals nearly always weakens fragile institutions—strong institutions do constrain the power of individuals—there is a built-in incentive in developing-country democracies for leaders to undertake periodic deinstitutionalization; weak institutions and personal power thus tend to create a mutually reinforcing, vicious cycle. Typically, therefore, developing-country democracies tend to move towards situations in which a centralizing, personalistic ruling elite confronts a variety of oppositional elites, who mobilize that which is most readily mobilizable, namely, community identities, and help transform them into rigid ethnic and group boundaries.

This brings the discussion to the fourth and last distinctive condition of developing-country democracies. Introduction of competitive elections, mass suffrage, and weak institutions will repeatedly generate expansionary political pressures in these democracies, that is, pressures towards a more equal distribution of power in society. A movement towards genuine devolution of political and economic power could accommodate such tendencies, that is, establish a new 'equilibrium' between demands and governance, and help strengthen new democracies. Any such trend, however, is likely to run up against two pervasive global constraints, both manifest as near intellectual hegemonies. These are, first, a belief in strong, centralized states as a necessity for the welfare of nations and, second, in recent years, a widespread acceptance of orthodox economic models as appropriate models of economic development. Whereas the former privileges nationalists, the latter, in spite of the promised dismantling of the state and related decentralization, pushes centralizing technocrats to the forefront.[2] In either case, power devolution in most developing-country democracies is a fairly low priority. A typical outcome is the evolution of these democracies towards two-track polities, with a democratic track in the sphere of electoral politics and a not-so-democratic track in the state sphere, especially in the areas of economic policy-making. The political society of many developing democracies is thus increasingly characterized by 'too much democracy'—that is, by a variety of conflicts, including ethnic conflicts—on the one hand, and, on the other hand, by 'not enough democracy', as the state increasingly insulates itself from social demands and conflicts.

The cumulative impact of these distinctive state-societal traits is that the introduction of democracy into developing countries rapidly politicizes the body politic. Various conflicts thus typically dot the political landscapes of these democracies. Broad contextual conditions, of course, do not fully explain either the variations across such countries or the trajectories of specific conflicts; in the language of social science, a focus on the context provides necessary but not sufficient conditions of specific conflicts. What can be said at the general level, however, is that the four state-societal traits discussed above help explain why democracy in developing countries tends to be as much a source of, as a solution to power conflicts.

These conflicts may precipitate along cleavages of class, interest groups, regions, or ethnic groups. Again, at a general level, it can be noted that ethnic and regional groups are more likely than classes or economic groups to demand 'self-determination', because they can more readily perceive themselves as 'total societies', that is, as social groups with a sufficiently complex division of labour to sustain ambitions of territorial sovereignty. A possibility of a shared cultural heritage further encourages such 'imagining.' The more such groups exist in a developing-country democracy, the more likely it is that movements for 'self-determination' will emerge. If this much is relatively clear, the next interesting question is: why are some such groups demanding greater power and control readily accommodated, while others are not,

[2]For details, see Atul Kohli, 'Democracy Amid Economic Orthodoxy: Trends in Developing Countries', *Third World Quarterly*, 14(4), pp. 671–89.

moving instead into a militancy-repression cycle, escalating their demands into secessionist movements, and threatening the territorial integrity of established states.

Institutionalization, Leadership, and Self-Determination Movements

Continuing the discussion at a fairly general level, I hypothesize that two 'proximate variables' are especially important for understanding the varying trajectories of self-determination movements. The first of these is the level of institutionalization of the central state, and the second concerns the degree to which the ruling strategy of leaders accommodates demands for self-determination. I use the concept of institutionalization in a fairly conventional sense[3]—it has both a normative and an organizational component—but my focus is more narrowly on central state authority than on a host of other norms and political structures that may be more or less institutionalized; I also do not assume that state authorities are always agents of public order. The degree of institutionalization of the central state then influences the degree to which state authorities can 'impose' their preferred vision of the political order on the societies they govern. The vision, of course, may be more or less accommodating of opposition demands, that is, when pressed, the leadership strategy may be more willing in some instances than in others to devolve power. Degree of institutionalization and leadership strategies are thus two important variables, that is, two aspects of the broad political context discussed above that commonly vary within the developing world and influence the fate of self-determination movements. If one dichotomizes these two variables (an action which is clearly quite artificial), and if the mechanical quality of schematic depictions is excused, the resulting 2×2 matrix shown in Figure 2.1 helps clarify some of the issues succinctly.

The main hypothesis I am proposing is well depicted by the first quadrant. All other things being equal, the more the authority of the central state is institutionalized and the more accommodating the ruling strategy, the more likely it is that self-determination movements will traverse the shape of an inverse 'U' curve: they will first rise, because it is 'natural' for them to do so in the political context of developing-country democracies discussed above, but, second, after a more-or-less prolonged period of power negotiation with the central state, they will inevitably decline in intensity as exhaustion sets in and some genuine compromise is reached. The logic underlying this proposition is that a well-institutionalized state sets firm boundaries within which political movements must operate, on the one hand, and, on the other

---

[3]Samuel Huntington, *Political Order in Changing Societies*, New Haven, Conn.: Yale University Press, 1968.

	Central Authority	
	Well Institutionalized	Weakly Institutionalized
Leadership Strategy — Accommodating	1. The inverse 'U' curve of ethnic politics (e.g., Tamils in India, 1950s and 1960s)	2. Peaceful breakup of the state (e.g., Czechoslovakia, 1990s)
Unaccommodating	3. Demands and repression cycle (e.g., Sikhs in India's Punjab, 1980)	4. Turbulence and/or breakdown (e.g., Nigeria, first and second republics)

FIGURE 2.1: Developing-Country Democracies: Political Context and the Trajectory of Self-Determination Movements

hand, an accommodating leadership provides room—of course, within limits—for the movements to achieve some real gains.

The same logic can be readily extended to describe variations on the theme. Given space limitations, I will not belabour the point; a few examples will suffice. A state's leadership may turn out to be not very accommodating to self-determination movements. This may result from something as 'simple' as a different type of leader in power or it may reflect something more complex, such as a different coalition on which the power of the leader rests. Whatever the underlying reasons, unaccommodating leaders in well-established states (that is, quadrant 3 in Figure 2.1) will often channel self-determination movements into cycles of escalating demands and repression. The reason is that a well-institutionalized democratic state both provides room for self-determination movements to emerge and possesses a fair amount of legitimate coercion to repress these movements. Unaccommodating leaders, who define the state's 'good' in terms of denying concessions to demanding groups, will typically repress such movements, only to push them further into more 'extreme' directions of secession as a goal, and militancy as a tactic. The situation depicted in quadrant 3 is then ripe for prolonged, militant self-determination movements. These situations are 'resolved' either when overwhelming force is used and/or when a more accommodating leader comes to power within the established state.

Self-determination movements are deeply threatening to weakly institutionalized states (quadrants 2 and 4 in Figure 2.1). If leaders of such states are relatively accommodating towards movements—such examples in the developing world are rare, suggesting that institutionalization of authority structures and leadership strategies may not be entirely independent of each other—then the peaceful breakup or re-organization of the state is the most likely outcome. By contrast, unaccommodating leaders, especially those who control significant coercive resources, are likely to drive the situation towards considerable turbulence, at minimum, and, at maximum, towards a civil war and possibly even a violent breakup of the state.

In sum, how well the authority of the central state is institutionalized, and what the leadership strategy is, are two important aspects of the political context that influence the pattern of self-determination movements. To repeat, the nature of the groups that are mobilized (i.e., what resources these groups control and whether the groups are organized around race, religion, or language), as well as how intensely such groups come to view their situation as unjust are issues that are by no means irrelevant to the fate of these movements; some of these issues are by their very nature specific to given situations and will emerge in the empirical discussion of specific cases. At a general level, it is my central hypothesis that the nature of the broader political context is quite important for understanding self-determination movements.

EVIDENCE FROM INDIA

India is a noisy democracy. It has over the years experienced a variety of political conflicts. Conflict around cleavages of class, caste, parties, language, religion, and regions thus dot India's political landscape. I have analysed why this should be so in India in detail elsewhere[4]; some of the theoretical generalizations stemming from that analysis were also sketched out above in a highly condensed form. Within that context, the focus here is mainly on ethnic movements demanding self-determination.[5] Again, India has experienced quite a few of these, especially by groups who define their regional distinctiveness along criteria of language or religion. Three of the most significant of these movements, namely, those spearheaded by Tamils, Sikhs, and Kashmiri Muslims are analysed below.[6] Since I have proposed that institutionalization of state authority and leadership strategies influence the pattern of these movements, prior to their analysis a few comments concerning how these contextual conditions have varied in India over time are in order.

[4]Atul Kohli, *Democracy and Discontent.*

[5]As suggested above, I use the concept of self-determination movements fairly loosely. What I have in mind are mainly movements for greater power and control by groups who share some real or imagined characteristics and who are sufficiently large and complex to conceive of themselves as 'mini nations'. Within the Indian federation, then, demands of such minority groups have varied from minimum (i.e., for more power and resources within the federation and expressed through democratic channels) to maximum (i.e., for secession from the federation and expressed through militant means).

[6]I estimate the 'significance' of these movements by the following criteria: the number of people that were mobilized; the cohesiveness and longevity of the movement; and the degree to which they genuinely became a force that the central state could not ignore. It could be argued that this case selection is a little too convenient; that such other cases as in eastern India would be troubling to the argument of this paper.

India in the 1950s was a relatively well-institutionalized polity, especially in comparison to other developing countries. This was especially manifest in a fairly well-organized central state—especially in a highly professional national civil service and armed forces—but also in a well-functioning national political party, the Congress, that generally controlled the state. In addition, India possessed such effective institutions as a parliament, an independent judiciary, and a free national press. How and why India came to have such effective institutions is clearly a complex issue, well beyond the scope of this paper. Suffice it to say that some state institutions were inherited from a colonial past and other more political ones were a product of a fairly prolonged and cohesive nationalist movement.[7] India's rigid and segmented social structure—especially the elaborate caste hierarchies, organized among numerous, relatively isolated villages—kept levels of political mobilization low and, ironically, may have further helped new institutions to take root in the early, post-independence phase.

Over time some of India's political institutions weakened. In terms of periodization, if the 1950s were a decade of relatively effective institutions, the 1960s are best thought of as a decade of transition during which the nationalist legacy declined, political competition and challenges to the hegemony of the Congress party increased, and a new type of political system—a more populist system—with non-institutional methods of securing electoral majorities was created by Indira Gandhi. During the two following decades, namely, the 1970s and the 1980s, some of India's well-established institutions were battered, especially by leaders in power.

Since levels of institutionalization are relative, it is important to remember that even during the 1970s and the 1980s India's central state authority in comparison to most African and many Latin American countries was relatively well institutionalized. Nevertheless, in comparison to its own past, a fair amount of deinstitutionalization occurred: Congress party as an organization was largely destroyed; civil service, police, and even armed forces became less professional and more politicized; parliament became less effective; and the autonomy of the judiciary was reduced. Once again, how and why these political changes occurred constitute a complex story, far beyond the scope of this paper. The only fact I will note is that growing personalization of power was at the heart of the story; growing political fragmentation in society privileged personalism and, in turn, personalistic leaders damaged the institutions that constrained their discretionary powers.[8]

[7]Myron Weiner, *Party Building in the New Nation*, Chicago: University of Chicago Press, 1967 and *The Indian Paradox*, New Delhi: Sage Publications, 1989.

[8]Paul Brass, *Politics of India since Independence*, New York: Cambridge University Press, 1990; Atul Kohli, *Democracy and Discontent*; and Lloyd Rudolph and Susanne Rudolph, *In Pursuit of Lakshmi: The Political Economy of the Indian State*, Chicago: University of Chicago Press, 1987.

As to the other variable of leadership strategy, India has had four main prime ministers who have ruled for more than two to three years each: Nehru ruled India for nearly 17 years (from 1947 until his death in 1964); his daughter Indira Gandhi dominated India for nearly as long as the father (1966–77 and 1980–4); then her son, Rajiv Gandhi, ruled from 1985–9; and finally, Narasimha Rao, was in power from 1991–6. Characterizing the leadership strategies of these leaders in a brief space is clearly to grossly oversimplify a fairly complex reality. I do so only reluctantly.

The main analytical concern here is how leaders typically respond to oppositional challenges, especially to demands of mobilized groups for greater self-determination. On a dimension of leadership strategy that varies from accommodating to unaccommodating, Nehru was closer to the accommodating end of the spectrum. This was in part a function of his own personality and, for the rest, a reflection of his relatively secure power position; a concession from Nehru here or there enhanced his magnanimity rather than threatened his hold on power. The political situation during his daughter's reign, however, was quite different, as were her political instincts. Congress's hegemony had by then declined and Indira consolidated her power against considerable odds. She was always suspicious of power challenges. She re-created a powerful political centre in India mainly by portraying herself as a champion of the poor. As her personal popularity soared, opposition to her also became strident, culminating in the 'Emergency' in 1977, when democratic rights in India were suspended for some two years. When Indira Gandhi returned to power in 1980, she was less populist but, by the same token, needing to mobilize electoral pluralities, she started flirting with communal themes, occasionally courting India's Hindus (more than 80 per cent of India's population) by rallying against religious minorities, especially Sikhs. This strategy made her increasingly less accommodating towards minorities, lest she be viewed as appeasing them. Overall, therefore, Indira Gandhi, in contrast to Nehru, was closer to the unaccommodating end of the leadership spectrum.

Both the subsequent leaders, Rajiv Gandhi and Narasimha Rao, have been more flexible than Indira Gandhi.[9] Rajiv Gandhi was especially accommodating towards self-determination movements in the first two years of his rule. As his political situation became less secure, however, he, too, like his mother, flirted with communalism, tilting occasionally in a pro-Muslim direction, but mainly courting the Hindu vote, becoming more and more indecisive and unaccommodating in the second half of his rule.

[9]The contrast between these leaders and Indira Gandhi helps bolster the claim that leadership strategies are indeed somewhat independent of the degrees of institutionalization of state authority.

Narashimha Rao in the 1990s portrayed himself as a non-personalistic, flexible leader who, at minimum, is not bent on a further centralization of power in his own hands. After the assassination of two prime ministers (both Indira and Rajiv were assassinated for political reasons), this ruling strategy appeared for the time to calm an agitated polity.

To oversimplify a rather complex reality, then, the Nehru period in India, say, 1950–64, is best understood as a period when India's central state was relatively well institutionalized and leadership strategy, though firm, was also flexible and accommodating to demands for self-determination. Subsequently, especially since the mid-1960s, India's political institutions have weakened, though they remain relatively effective by developing-country standards. The leadership strategy over these last three decades has varied. Whereas Indira Gandhi was quite unaccommodating towards demanding groups, both Rajiv and Rao appeared to be at least less threatening, if not actually more accommodating. With this context in mind, we are now in a position to turn our attention to a few specific self-determination movements within India.

Tamil Nationalism

Tamil Nadu is now one of India's important states, an integral part of the Indian federal system. No one now questions, not even those who live in Tamil Nadu, whether they are fully a part of the Indian union. However, it was not always so. During the 1950s and the 1960s, Tamil leaders argued that Tamils were a distinctive people. They mobilized considerable support for a 'Tamil Nation' and demanded, at minimum, greater power and control over their own affairs vis-à-vis New Delhi or, at maximum, secession from India. A very brief recapitulation of the rise and decline of this movement, therefore, will serve our broader analytical interests.[10]

Tamil is a language, and Tamils as a social group are, therefore, mainly a linguistically defined group. Tamil, along with a few other languages in south India, but unlike most languages spoken in northern India, does not derive its roots from classical Sanskrit with its Indo-Germanic roots. Rather, Tamil is a Dravidian language. Tamil nationalists also used to insist that Tamils are a separate racial and cultural group, with their roots in a Dravidian society that was indigenous to southern India prior to the historic arrival of and domination by 'northern Aryans'. Brahmins in Tamil society could thus be viewed, not as natural 'hegemons' of a caste society, but rather as agents of northern domination. That some of the Tamil Brahmin's were of lighter skin colour than much of the darker-skinned Tamil society only added

---

[10]For details, see Marguerite Ross Barnett, *The Politics of Cultural Nationalism in South India*, Princeton: Princeton University Press, 1976.

to the plausibility of such an interpretation. Two other sets of 'facts-on-the-ground' are important for understanding the dynamics of Tamil nationalism. First, Brahmin's in Tamil society constitute a relatively small caste group: less than 5 per cent of the total (in comparison, say, to parts of northern India, where Brahmin's often constitute nearly 10 per cent of the total population). Second, for a variety of historical reasons, the area that is now Tamil Nadu was more urbanized by mid-century than many other parts of India.

The Congress party in this part of India, as elsewhere, built its pre-independence base on the Brahmins. That the Brahmins were few in number and that the non-Brahmin castes were already active in city life provided the necessary conditions for the early rise of an anti-Brahmin movement. Democratization and related power conflicts, in other words, came relatively early to this region of India. The first institutional manifestation of that movement was the Justice Party, which was led by the elite of the non-Brahmin castes and sided with the British against both Brahmins and Congress in the hope of securing concessions in government jobs and in education. The Justice Party eventually was de-legitimized both because of its elitist nature and because of the rising tide of nationalism. That had significant consequences, especially because Congress became identified as a Brahmin party in a region where Brahmins had not been able to establish cultural and political hegemony. The early development of a cleavage between the Brahmin and anti-Brahmin forces opened up the political space for subsequent anti-Congress developments.

The link between Congress and the Brahmins became the target of Tamil nationalists in the post-independence period. The Congress party in Madras could not easily break out of that mould. The continued Congress–Brahmin alliance enabled the regional nationalists to mobilize against domination by both caste and north Indians simultaneously. Hammering on the theme of the distinctiveness of the Tamil tradition and linking that with an opposition to northern Hindi rule and its allies, the southern Brahmins, the leaders of the Dravidian movement, found a ready audience among the numerous backward castes that were already concentrated in the cities. To simplify a complex picture, Tamil nationalism and a 'petit bourgeois' base among the urban backward castes provided the core support for a regional nationalist movement.

The early demands of this self-determination movement were for greater power and control: over time, the broader movement came to include a separatist movement demanding a 'Dravidistan', or a land for the Dravidian people. A number of Indian states in the early 1950s argued for reorganizing the Indian federation along linguistic lines. Most such demands, of course, were not separatist. Nevertheless, in the aftermath of India's separation with Pakistan, Nehru in the early 1950s was reluctant to implement a linguistic redesign, lest it strengthen secessionist tendencies and lead to a further breakup of India. Tamil nationalists and their mobilized supporters were a case in point, insofar as they pressed their identity politics hard through demonstrations that occasionally turned violent and included public burning of the Indian flag and the constitution. When pressed by several states, Nehru recalculated that the dangers of not devolving power to linguistic groups were greater than of doing so. Fully in control at the national centre and widely considered to be India's legitimate leader, Nehru set firm limits on what powers the newly constituted states would have and what would be controlled by New Delhi (which, by the way, was substantial). Within these limits, then, India's federal system was reorganized along linguistic states in 1956. This reorganization gave Tamil nationalists a Tamil state, taking a fair amount of the separatist steam out of the movement.

Having gained a separate state of their own (first called Madras, subsequently relabelled Tamil Nadu, or the home of Tamils), the struggle of Tamil nationalists shifted to oust Congress from power within the state. For this, the Tamil nationalists utilized a political party, the Dravida Munnetra Kazhagam (DMK), and sought to broaden their power base. They adopted a radical rhetoric of land reform and eradication of the caste system, further threatening the Brahmins. Many of the intermediate- and lower-caste dwellers in villages thus came to be attracted to the DMK. The DMK also successfully mobilized cultural themes. In this they were fortunate insofar as many Tamil nationalists were playwrights, literary figures, and theatre and movie actors. Movies were the new emerging medium, and they were used successfully by the DMK to popularize such themes as injustices of the caste system, the glories of Tamil history, and the social need for Robin-Hood-like heroes, who would deliver the poor, the weak, and the dispossessed from the clutches of the rich and the wicked.

As Tamil nationalism became more populist, it simultaneously became less coherent but more capable of winning elections. Following Nehru's death, for example, India's national leaders for a brief moment re-attempted to impose Hindi as a national language on all states. Many states reacted negatively, but Tamil Nadu reacted the most violently. Well mobilized to confront precisely such national policy shifts, the state erupted in language riots. Several students burned themselves to death, protesting the moves of the national government. For another brief moment the national government used a heavy coercive hand to deal with protests. As matters got worse, the national government back-tracked. In principle it was conceded that regional languages, such as Tamil, were 'coequal' to the other two national languages, namely, Hindi and English. This was a major victory for the DMK. Enjoying considerable popularity, the DMK ousted the Congress from power within Tamil Nadu in the 1967 elections. Since then, the Congress has never returned to power in that state.

The rise and consolidation of power by the DMK had a profound impact on Tamil Nadu's politics. The highest leadership posts in the state slipped out of the hands of Brahmins and went to the well-educated elite of the non-Brahmin castes. The intermediate and local leadership more accurately reflected the real power base of the DMK: the intermediate castes. Many of them gained access to more power and resources. As the DMK settled down to rule, the predictable happened. Over time, the DMK lost much of its self-determination, and its anti-Centre militancy, as well as its commitment to socio-economic reforms. The reasons for such de-radicalization in Tamil Nadu were the same as elsewhere. Once national leaders made important concessions, though within firm limits, and the DMK achieved its major goal of securing increased power, realpolitik concerns took over, and mobilizing ideologies slowly lost their relevance for guiding governmental actions. Ethnic nationalism slowly declined, following the inverse 'U' curve discussed above.

Sikh Nationalism

Punjab is one of India's most prosperous states—the home of the green revolution—and Sikhs constitute about half of that state's population (the other half being Hindus). Sikh nationalism was a powerful political force in the state throughout the 1980s. Demands of Sikh groups varied from greater political and economic control within the Indian federation to secession from India and the creation of a sovereign state, Khalistan. The national government under Indira Gandhi, especially during the 1980s, was not only not accommodating, it sought to divide and rule the Sikhs. The strategy backfired. Some Sikh groups turned sharply militant. The central state, in turn, met the militancy with considerable force. Living as they did next to Pakistan, Punjab's militant Sikhs were able to secure arms and support from across the border. Militant nationalists and a repressive state thus confronted each other in a vicious cycle of growing violence. Violence took its toll throughout the 1980s—nearly 1,000 people died every year—peaking in 1990 when some 4,000 people were killed in political violence. Since then, however, the situation has changed. Brutal state repression 'succeeded' in eliminating many of the militants. A more politically flexible Rao allowed state-level elections in Punjab in the early 1990s. As an elected government settled down to rule, an exhausted state went back to work, and both militancy and state repression fell into the background. During 1993, only 73 people died in politics-related violence; over the last few years further peaceful elections have occurred and capital investments in Punjab have grown dramatically.

The underlying 'story' behind the rise and decline of Sikh nationalism is complex and cannot be retold here.[11] What follows, therefore, is only a bare bones account. The Sikhs are a religious group, concentrated mainly in the Indian state of Punjab. Sikh men are distinctive in that they wear religiously prescribed long hair and turbans. Sikhs and Hindus lived side by side, peacefully, for several centuries. Like the Hindus—Sikhism was initially derived from Hinduism in the late medieval period—Sikhs are internally differentiated along caste-like groups. Most Sikhs are relatively prosperous agriculturalists. A sizable minority are urban traders and entrepreneurs; until recently, intermarriage between these groups and their Hindu counterparts was common in Punjab. Sikhs also have their own version of 'untouchables', equivalent to the lowest Hindu castes that generally tend to own no land and be very poor.

Prior to the political turmoil that arose in the 1980s, caste and community divisions in Punjab had given rise to easily identifiable political divisions. In the past, the Hindus had generally supported the Congress party, though a significant minority had also been loyal to a Hindu nationalist party. The Akali Dal party, by contrast, had consistently counted on the Sikh vote, but had seldom succeeded in mobilizing all the Sikhs as an ethnic political bloc.

Given internal divisions among Sikhs, the Congress party during the 1960s and 1970s was often in a position to form a government in Punjab with the help of Hindus and a significant Sikh minority. The Akalis, by contrast, could only form a coalition government, and that only with a seemingly unlikely partner: the pro-Hindu party. These basic political and community divisions provide the background essential for understanding the intensified political activities of the Sikhs during the 1980s. Akali militancy was aimed at mobilizing as many Sikhs as possible around a platform of 'Sikh nationalism'. The analytical issue is why those fairly normal political ambitions generated so much chaos and turmoil.

The Akali Dal as a political party has always exhibited a mixture of religious fervor and hard-nosed political realism aimed at capturing power. Being mainly a Sikh party, there has always been a close relationship between the party and Sikh religious organizations. The Sikh political elite thus periodically utilize religious organizations to influence the political behaviour of the laity. Over the years, the Akalis have been in and out of power. They first came to power in 1966 when they spearheaded a successful movement

[11]For details, see Paul Brass, 'The Punjab Crisis and the Unity of India', in Atul Kohli (ed.), *India's Democracy: An Analysis of Changing State–Society Relations*, Princeton: Princeton University Press, 1990.

for a separate 'Punjabi Suba' (or the land where Punjabi is spoken), and the current boundaries of the state of Punjab were drawn. Given the electoral arithmetic, however, the power position of the Akalis was never secure. Sikhs constituted a bare majority in the state and Congress party leaders consistently sought to draw away part of the Sikh vote through one machination or another. Unlike Tamil Nadu, therefore, where Tamil nationalists came to power around the same time, consolidated their hold, and settled on a slow but steady road towards de-radicalization, Akalis in Punjab have consistently needed to whip up religious and nationalist issues that would keep Sikhs united politically.

During the 1970s, as Indira Gandhi's popularity grew across India, Congress party leaders in Punjab undertook aggressive efforts to divide Sikhs and to consolidate their own hold over state politics. A threatened Akali Dal had little choice but to raise the ante; they started demanding even greater control over the affairs of Sikhs, coming closer and closer in their formal statements to wanting a sovereign state for the Sikhs that they could control. Indira Gandhi countered by a combination of repression—labelling secessionists as seditious—and by further attempts to divide Sikhs. During the 'Emergency' many Sikh leaders were imprisoned. When Indira Gandhi returned to power in 1980 and another round of elections was held in Punjab, Congress won a clear majority, with the Akalis securing only 27 per cent of the popular vote. Congress leaders considered themselves the legitimate, elected rulers. The Akalis, by contrast, viewed Punjab as 'their' state, which they ought to control. The Akalis, cornered in their own state, decided they had to fight for their political life. Much of what followed—some anticipated but most of it unanticipated—makes sense mainly from this retrospective logic of competitive mobilization.

The battle lines were drawn. Indira Gandhi had the popular support. She decided to use her position of advantage to launch a political offensive and consolidate her position vis-à-vis the Akalis. If she could use Sikh militants to split the ranks of the Akalis still further between the moderates and the extremists, victory would be hers. And this is what she attempted. The Akali Dal possessed another set of political resources, however, whose efficacy Indira Gandhi apparently underestimated. The Akalis still could organize around the issue of Sikh nationalism like no other party in Punjab. The chain of Sikh temples, moreover, provided a ready organizational network with money, personnel and the proven ability to sway opinion. A populist, centralizing and unaccommodating national leader, Indira Gandhi, thus came to be pitted against a regional party, the Akali Dal—which had considerable potential to mobilize the forces of religious nationalism.

Both Indira Gandhi and the Akalis assembled militant forces for political ends. In retrospect, it is clear that over the next several years, militancy led to civil disorder that took on a political life of its own, increasingly out of the control of both the Akalis and the national government. Whether that simply was not foreseen or was brazenly ignored under the short-term pressure to seize political advantage may never be known.

What we do know is that, once mobilized, Sikh militants very quickly gained political advantage over moderate Sikh leaders. If the political aim was indeed to create a separate Sikh state, namely, a Khalistan, then moderate Sikh leaders had little to contribute towards achieving such ends. A move towards secession was mainly a political ploy for most moderate Akalis. Having shifted the political discourse in that direction, however, any and all efforts to work with New Delhi simply undermined the legitimacy of this moderate leadership; normal politics made the moderates look like opportunists not worthy of a leadership mantle. True believers, instead, became heroes of the day and gained public sympathy. Flushed with arms that often came from Afghanistan via Pakistan, Sikh militants then unleashed a holy war aimed at establishing a sovereign Sikh state. Indira Gandhi countered by increasing governmental repression. As a militancy and repression cycle set in, Punjab, one of India's most prosperous states, became engulfed in a long decade of violence.

There were at least two important occasions during the 1980s when Congress and Sikh moderates came close to a compromise. Among the demands of Akalis were a number of concrete 'bread and butter' issues that fell well short of secession: control over river waters, over the capital city of Punjab, and over agricultural subsidies. From 1982 to 1984 Indira Gandhi refused these compromises, lest she be viewed nationally as appeasing minorities. This weakened Sikh moderates and privileged those who wanted to use more militant tactics. A second and more important occasion arose when Rajiv Gandhi came to power in 1985. Flushed with victory and committed to resolving the Punjab conflict, Rajiv offered broad compromises to Akalis. The results were dramatic. Elections were held in the state, Akalis came to power, and political violence came down sharply during 1985. Unfortunately, all this was short lived. Very quickly Rajiv Gandhi found it impossible to implement the compromises he had offered to the Akali leaders. While the details are complex, the major obstacle to implementation was Rajiv's own growing political vulnerability: as his national popularity declined, starting sometimes in 1986, he was increasingly pressed within his own party to not make any 'further' concessions to minorities. Once it became clear, therefore, that concessions from Delhi were more apparent than real, the position of elected Akali leaders was again undermined, and the militancy and repression cycle reappeared.

Had India been a weaker state during this period, it is conceivable that Sikh secessionists would have succeeded in establishing yet another state on the subcontinent. As it was, however, even though India's political institutions weakened considerably over the last few decades, India remained a relatively well-established state. National legitimacy of elected leaders, an effective civil and police bureaucracy, and, most important, a loyal armed force are critical components of this state. They were all utilized, especially brute force, to contain and repress Sikh militants. Militants also became marginalized over time, losing popular support. Repression and political marginalization led to a dwindling number of Sikh militants undertaking violent acts to accomplish secessionist goals.

Narasimha Rao finally called for elections in Punjab in the early 1990s. The Akalis boycotted the election, but a Sikh-led Congress government came to power. Over time, when further elections were called, not wanting to be left out, even the Akalis joined in and have now returned to power. For now, therefore, the militancy and repression of the 1980s has fallen into the background.

To sum up, Sikh nationalism in Punjab also traversed the inverse 'U' curve discussed above, but the top of the curve turned out to be prolonged. Among the important underlying contrasts with the earlier movement of Tamils was the contrasting approach of Nehru and Indira Gandhi: Nehru was accommodating and Indira was not. Of course, there were other factors at work: Tamils dominate Tamil Nadu, whereas the Sikhs constitute only half of Punjab's population; Tamils are a linguistic group, whereas Sikhs are a religious group, and, given the close marriage of politics and religion in Sikhism, Sikh religion probably provides a more encompassing identity than does attachment to a language; the threat posed by rapid socio-economic change in Punjab to Sikhism as a religious community was more serious than that to the linguistically defined community of Tamils; and Tamils did not have as easy an access to arms and across-the-border sanctuaries as did Sikh militants. All of these factors played some role, but none of them on their own varies as neatly with the rise and decline of movements as do the relative degrees of institutionalization of state authority and the contrasting strategies of national leaders. Within a more turbulent polity, Indira Gandhi's commitment to dominate Punjab politics pushed Akalis into aggressive mobilization. Once mobilized, professional politicians lost control and militants took over. Finally, over time, militants were repressed out of existence, and a tired population was relieved to accept some concessions from a more accommodating national leadership and to vote an elected provincial government back to power.

Muslim Nationalism in Kashmir

Since 1989 the state of Jammu and Kashmir, especially the northern valley of Kashmir, has been gripped by a militancy-repression cycle. The main protagonists of the conflict are Islamic groups that do not want Kashmir to be part of India, on the one hand, and a variety of Indian security forces, on the other. The dimensions of the conflict are quite severe: in a relatively sparsely populated state of some 8 million people (approximately 65 per cent Muslim), at least 10,000 people (some estimates go as high as 40,000) have died as a result of political violence over the last several years; security forces deployed in the state by now consist of more than 300 paramilitary companies and several army divisions; and at least 100,000 Hindus have migrated from the Muslim-dominated Kashmir valley, mainly to Jammu, the southern, Hindu-dominated part of the state. At the time of writing this article, India's central government is pursuing a two-pronged strategy: it is coming down quite hard on recalcitrant Islamic militants; and it is openly calling for elections in the 'near future', while strengthening the hands of those leaders who are willing to respect 'constitutional boundaries' and to participate in electoral politics.[12] Whether this will generate a result similar to that in the case of the Sikhs in Punjab, namely, a return to normalcy, is not clear as yet.

Once again, the full 'story' behind this specific Indian case of ethnic politics need not be recalled here.[13] The condensed account below suggests that this case does not fit as neatly into the inverse 'U' curve argument developed above. I explain this partial anomaly as partly a result of the fact that the conflict is more internationalized than the other two cases discussed above and, for the rest, that the conflict is still relatively 'young'; as predicted, the decline of ethnic militancy and of the related fratricide may still set in over the next few years. Whatever the eventual outcome, some elements of how and why ethnic conflict flared up in Kashmir are still broadly consistent with the propositions developed above.

Ever since India and Pakistan emerged as sovereign states in late 1940s, Kashmir has been a focus of dispute. As a Muslim-majority state that was contiguous to Pakistan, it is arguable that Kashmir should have become a part of Pakistan. The Hindu head of the Kashmiri state instead chose to join India. Pakistan contested the 'legality' of this decision and, as often happens in interstate relations, it was not legality but might that determined what was right; India and Pakistan fought two wars over the issue and a large part of Kashmir was incorporated into India. What is important for our analytical purposes is that, in spite of these international problems, for much of this period—say 1950–80—ethnic nationalism in Kashmir remained relatively mild. The memory and stories of ethnic injustices were probably

---

[12]As the essay goes to press in early 1997, an elected government has been in power in Kashmir for several months.

[13]For details, see Ashutosh Varshney, 'India, Pakistan and Kashmir: Antinomies of Nationalism', *Asian Survey*, 31(11), 1991, pp. 997–1019.

kept alive. Nevertheless, Kashmir was accorded a 'special status' within the Indian constitution, giving it considerable autonomy within India's federal system; India's central government also provided a substantial financial subsidy to facilitate 'economic development' of Kashmir. This seemed to have done the 'trick'. While both New Delhi and Kashmiri leaders, especially Muslim leaders, viewed each other with suspicion, a working arrangement of sorts operated well into the early 1980s.

Several new factors came into play in the early 1980s. As discussed above, the Indian polity as a whole was by now relatively more turbulent. Old nationalist institutions like the Congress party were in decline. A whole new post-nationalist generation demanded a greater share of political and economic resources. Indira Gandhi was at the helm nationally. In her post-populist phase, in the early 1980s she increasingly flirted with pro-Hindu themes to recreate a new national electoral coalition. This shift in strategy boded ill for states with considerable non-Hindu populations, such as the Sikhs in Punjab and Muslims in Kashmir. Given her centralizing and unaccommodating instincts, moreover, states like Kashmir came under increasing political pressure.

Within Kashmir, the state's 'founding father' and much revered leader, Sheikh Abdullah, died in 1982. His son Farooq Abdullah moved into the resulting political vacuum, both as the leader of the state's main non-Congress political party, the National Conference, and as the head of the state government. State-level elections of 1983 turned out to be quite important. Farooq successfully campaigned on an anti-Congress, anti-Delhi, and a pro-Kashmiri autonomy platform. The campaign caught the imagination of a large majority, especially Kashmir's Muslim majority. Indira Gandhi herself campaigned in Kashmir on behalf of the state Congress party, often appealing to the fears of Jammu Hindus. Communal polarization, while hardly new to Kashmir, increasingly came to be sponsored by competing elites and grew. Farooq's platform fell well short of secessionist demands. Nevertheless, his emphasis on regional autonomy for Kashmir turned out to be very popular, propelling the National Conference to a handsome electoral victory against the Congress.

Farooq in Kashmir had to tread a thin line between emphasizing Kashmiri autonomy, on the one hand, and not appearing as an anti-national, Muslim Kashmiri secessionist, on the other hand. In order to bolster this precarious position, he joined hands with other non-Congress heads of state governments. Hoping to be one of the many who were part of the 'loyal opposition', Farooq hosted a well-publicized conference in Kashmir of all major opposition leaders. Unfortunately, this was precisely the type of move that truly threatened Indira Gandhi. Hoping to clip Farooq's growing political wings, Indira appointed a close and tough personal aide, Jagmohan, to be Kashmir's governor. Jagmohan, in turn, initiated a series of machinations whereby a number of National Conference legislators defected to the Congress, threatening Farooq's position. Jagmohan eventually dismissed Farooq as Kashmir's Chief Minister in 1984, claiming without proof that Farooq had lost the support of a majority in the legislature.

Farooq's dismissal—very much a part of an all-India pattern of a threatened Indira Gandhi, bent on centralizing and weakening India's federal institutions—turned out to be a critical turning point. While public opinion data is not available, it appears that the dismissal sent a strong message, especially to Kashmiri Muslims, that their democratic and legitimate efforts to create greater political spaces within India may well be thwarted.[14] This growing alienation of Muslims, especially of their urban youth, was not helped by political events that followed. As the 1987 state elections approached (Indira Gandhi was by now dead, replaced nationally by her son Rajiv), Farooq Abdullah, both politically pressed and sufficiently opportunistic, formed an electoral alliance with the Congress party. This seemingly innocuous electoral opportunism had the profound impact of eliminating any major democratic outlet for Kashmiri Muslims who sought greater autonomy from Delhi. A number of Muslim groups hurriedly came together in an umbrella organization, the Muslim United Front. They, in turn, mobilized the urban youth and grew in popularity. Elections and the aftermath turned out to be bitter. Mobilized and angry youth were confronted by security forces. Many were roughed up. Further alienated, some went across the border to Pakistan, where they were trained as militants; they returned armed with Kalishnikovs. The National Front–Congress alliance won the election, followed by widespread charges of rigged elections. Whatever the reality, Kashmir was engulfed by a serious legitimacy crisis.

Meanwhile, the Soviet Union intervened in Afghanistan, the United States again rearmed Pakistan, and Pakistani rulers regained a sense of confidence vis-à-vis India that they had lost during the 1971 war over Bangladesh. There is ample evidence to indicate that Pakistan trained alienated Muslim youths from Kashmir and provided them arms and resources. Even when the Pakistani government was not directly involved, India's hostile neighbour became both a staging ground and a sanctuary for Kashmiri militants. The number of Kashmiris trained in Pakistan is by now estimated to be in the several thousands.[15]

[14]See, for example, the essays by George Fernandez (a well-known Indian political leader who directly participated in Kashmiri affairs) and Riyaz Punjabi (a Kashmiri professor who lived through these events) in Raju Thomas, *Perspectives on Kashmir: The Roots of Conflict in South Asia*, Boulder, Colo.: Westview Press, 1992.

[15]George Fernandez in 1990 estimated this figure to be in the range of 3,000–5,000. Since in his former capacity as India's Minister for Internal Affairs (Janata Government, 1989), he had access to all of Indian and other intelligence services data, and since this estimate was provided in a public lecture at Harvard University, one is inclined to give some credence to these estimates. See Raju Thomas, *Perspectives on Kashmir*, p. 289.

Following the 1987 elections, Kashmiri Muslims, especially those in the valley (Muslims in Jammu tend to be ethnically distinct), confronted governments in Kashmir and in New Delhi simultaneously as hostile parties. Kashmiri militants and security forces increasingly met each other in growing cycles of militancy and repression. Human rights abuses occurred. Stories of such abuses must have further alienated the Muslim population. When elections were called again in 1989, militant groups boycotted them quite successfully. The more the democratic political process lost its meaning, the more a full-scale insurgency came to be unleashed.

Factionalism among Islamic militants has also increasingly come to the fore. The Jammu and Kashmir Liberation Front (JKLF)—a nominally secular group that is nevertheless controlled by Muslim leaders—argues for a sovereign state of Kashmir, including part of the Kashmir controlled by Pakistan. The JKLF remains the most popular group. The Hizbul Mujahideen, on the other hand, are modelled after the Mujahids in Afghanistan and argue for accession of Kashmir to Pakistan. While less popular than the JKLF, the Mujahideen receive more support from Pakistan; its hardened militants are better trained and better armed. The popular JKLF faces the enormous obstacle that neither India nor Pakistan supports the possibility of a sovereign state of Kashmir. By contrast, the militant Mujahideen, while a potent armed force, are politically not so popular. The more the Hindus have migrated out of the Kashmir valley, the more the struggle has become one of Kashmiri Muslims vs. India. Most Kashmiri Muslims, however, want a sovereign state; they do not want to join Pakistan. Aside from the fact that neither India nor Pakistan favours such an outcome, Kashmiri Muslims face another major hurdle: there are nearly 100 million Muslims in India, of which Kashmiri Muslims constitute only about 5 million.

Fearing for their own welfare in India if a Kashmiri Muslim state were established by force (such a move would encourage anti-Muslim sentiments and might propel the pro-Hindu BJP party to the political forefront across India), Indian Muslims have generally refrained from openly supporting the cause of Kashmiri Muslims. The overall situation is thus a near stalemate: most Kashmiri Muslims are by now deeply alienated from India; while divided among themselves, a majority among the Muslims would probably opt for a sovereign state of Kashmir; not only will the powerful Indian state not let go of them, even Pakistan does not support such an outcome; finally, Pakistani-trained militants, with arms left over from the Afghanistan Civil War, remain a powerful force, but one which Indian security forces have successfully fought to a standstill. Whether the state elections of 1996 will help break this stalemate remains hard to predict at the time of writing.

Leaving the details of the tragic 'story' aside, what are its analytical implications? It is clear that the roots of the militancy-repression cycle in

Kashmir can be traced back to a power conflict in which Indira Gandhi in her zeal for centralization dislodged the elected government of Farooq Abdullah, precipitating a long-term legitimacy crisis. Had political institutions like parties within Kashmir or the Indian federal system been stronger, such centralizing antics of one leader would not only have been difficult to pursue but, even if pursued, may have been easier to weather. The combination, however, of weakening institutions and an unaccommodating national leader helped push normal power struggles down the path of a militancy and repression cycle. The early trajectory of the Kashmir conflict thus broadly fit the analytical scheme developed above. The obvious fact, however, that the conflict in Kashmir continues clearly defies the predicted journey—given certain conditions—of ethnic conflicts along an inverse 'U' curve. Since India's democratic institutions, despite weakening to some extent, remain relatively strong, and since the leadership of Narasimha Rao was more flexible than that of Indira Gandhi, what explains the persistence of a high-intensity ethnic conflict in Kashmir?

Three different answers (or three components of one answer) are possible to this question, each with different implications for the analytical argument proposed in this essay. The first answer, and the one least compatible with the thesis of this essay, would focus on the distinct values and discourse of Islam, possibly suggesting that political identity based on Islam is felt both more intensely and more comprehensively, and thus an Islam-based ethnic movement ought not to be expected to follow the same trajectory as that followed by Tamil or Sikh nationalist movements. Such an argument, however, would have the burden of explaining why Muslim nationalism flared up mainly in Kashmir (and not in other parts of India) and why mainly in the 1990s.

A second answer would focus on the role of Pakistan in the Kashmir crisis; unlike in Tamil Nadu and even more than in Punjab, the argument contends that Pakistan's continuing involvement in Kashmir has prolonged the conflict. While I have not emphasized this explanation, such an argument is compatible with the thesis of this essay insofar as the logic of the argument developed here is essentially political: ethnic movements in developing-country democracies constitute a political process whereby the central state and mobilized groups discover their relative power balances. Intervention by an external actor then alters the power-balancing process, at least prolonging, if not altering, the overall trajectory.

Finally, the last and simplest answer that is most readily compatible with this essay's thesis is that it is still too early to predict how the Kashmir crisis will end; if Pakistan's role diminishes and if the United Front government maintains a firm but flexible set of policies—that is, if following the state elections it grants the promises of 'maximum autonomy' within the Indian Federation—the ethnic conflict in Kashmir may well decline over the next few years.

CONCLUSION

The argument of this essay ought not to be taken too literally. It merely suggests that in an established multicultural democracy of the developing world ethnic conflicts will come and go. Well, of course! The real message of the essay is thus not so much its literal interpretation but rather some of the implications that flow from it. In conclusion, therefore, I wish to spell out a few of these implications.

The first set of implications concern analytical issues. Indian materials suggest that ethnic conflicts are best thought of as power conflicts. Ethnic conflicts are thus a subset of the larger set of political conflicts that include conflicts along class, caste, or party lines and that dot the political landscape of developing-country democracies. While one can readily emphasize the distinctiveness of ethnic from other types of political conflicts, what ethnic conflicts share with these other conflicts is that mobilized ethnic groups, like other mobilized groups, seek greater power and control, either as an end in itself or as a means to secure a society's other valued resources. Such a perspective, in turn, also suggests what ethnic conflicts are not: they are not inevitable expressions of deep-rooted differences; they are not anomic responses to the 'disequilibrium' generated by 'modernization'; and, while ethnic identities are indeed contingent, the process of identity formation and ethnic conflict is also not so indeterminate as to defy a causal, generalizing analysis.

If ethnic conflicts are mainly power conflicts, then how power is organized in state and society becomes important for understanding their patterns. I have suggested that, given developing-country democracies, when state authority is well institutionalized and when national leaders act in a firm but accommodating manner, ethnic conflicts typically follow the shape of an inverse 'U' curve. Both national leaders and leaders of ethnic movements may be quite calculating, and thus their strategies and counter-strategies may be amenable to a bargaining type of rationalist analysis. The shifts in values and discourses of the broader membership of an ethnic group that inevitably emerge during ethnic mobilization are, in turn, best understood from a close, anthropological type of research. As micro approaches, however, neither the rational choice nor the anthropological approach readily aggregate into macro generalizations.[16] Generalizations about the conditions that help explain the rise and decline of ethnic movements, therefore, are best derived from a direct, macro focus on state and societal conditions. The emphasis on the degree of institutionalization of state authority in society and a focus on leadership held up fairly well in

[16]For a quick review of theoretical debates in the study of, and for further references to, the literature on the politics of ethnicity, see Crawford Young, *The Rising Tide of Cultural Pluralism: The Nation-State at Bay?*, Madison: University of Wisconsin Press, 1993, pp. 21–5.

the preceding discussion of ethnic movements in India. If persuasive, or at least suggestive, such an approach and hypothesis may be worth examining against ethnic movements in countries other than India.

A second set of implications concern normative and policy issues. To the extent that ethnic conflicts are power conflicts, it is often difficult to choose true heroes and villains in these conflicts. It is difficult on an *a priori* basis to hold whether established states are more right or wrong than demand-making ethnic groups. A lot depends on the situation. As a scholar it is as important to eschew the conservative bias that states necessarily act to preserve the public good, as it is to resist the temptation that all comers seeking self-determination have justice on their side. What is clearer is that leaders—especially national leaders, but also leaders of ethnic movements—who persistently choose to be unaccommodating will channel normal power conflicts down a destructive path, a path where calculating leaders drop off and true believers take over, utilizing militant tactics because the cause becomes worth dying for. The true villains of ethnic conflicts are thus those leaders who refuse to see that the failure of timely compromise can only produce and exacerbate political problems, including their own downfall.

Finally, I turn to the question posed in the title of the paper, namely, can democracies, especially developing-country democracies, accommodate ethnic nationalism. Indian materials suggest that the answer has to be a qualified 'yes'.[17] It is ironical that democracy and democratization in a developing-country setting first encourages the emergence of ethnic demands. A well-institutionalized state can put some limits on how far these demands may go. Of course, if the state itself is not well institutionalized, then democracy and multi-ethnic competition spell great political problems; that constitutes a set of cases not discussed here. Given an institutionalized state, however, if some of these demands are not accommodated, the sense of exclusion and injustice may well turn demanding groups towards militancy. That is why democratic leaders with inclusionary, accommodating ruling strategies fare better at dealing with ethnic conflicts. In sum, democracy in a developing-country setting both encourages ethnic conflict and, under specific circumstances, provides a framework for their accommodation.

[17]An important book that after a great deal of valuable empirical work reaches a conclusion that, though not identical, is broadly consistent with this conclusion is Donald Horowitz, *Ethnic Groups in Conflict*, Berkeley: University of California Press, 1985.

3

Enduring Another Election
India Defies the Odds*

Indians appear to love the practice of democracy so much that they are in danger of overdoing it. In February and March of 1998, the world's largest democracy held its 12th General Election since gaining its independence a half-century ago. The voting was largely fair and peaceful. New, right-of-centre rulers led by the BJP replaced the old, left-of-centre ones. The handover of power went smoothly. There is a hitch, however, for while the first eight general elections were spread over the initial forty years of independence, the four most recent have been held within the past decade. The new government—a coalition of disparate parties that together commands a parliamentary plurality but not a majority—is the seventh since 1989. Clearly, all is not well. India's democracy still endures, but frequent elections are failing to produce stable and effective governments.

Table 3.1 compares the 1998 election results with those from 1996. Simplifying somewhat, one can say that the three main contenders in both elections were, respectively, the BJP and its allies on the Right; the Congress party and its allies in the middle; and the United Front (UF) on the Left.[1] After the 1996 election, the UF—an array of a dozen or so groupings including the Janata Party, the Left Front with its collection of Indian communist and socialist parties, and a number of regional parties—had the

*Originally published as 'Enduring Another Election: India Defies the Odds', *Journal of Democracy*, 9(3), July 1998, pp. 7–20.

[1]This simplification can be misleading in two senses. First, the labels 'Left' and 'Right' do not always make much sense in contemporary India. And second, each of the three main groups has numerous, disparate parties under its umbrella, many of which are ready to switch sides at any time. Nearly 40 political parties currently have seats in the Indian parliament. Of these, 30 have fewer than 10 seats each (10 parties have a single seat apiece). Even specialists in Indian politics cannot keep all these parties straight, and often find it difficult to anticipate the variety of alliances that may evolve.

TABLE 3.1: Parliamentary Results in India, 1996 and 1998

Major Parties	1996		1998[1]	
	Seats Won	Percentage of Votes Secured	Seats Won	Percentage of Votes Secured
BJP	161	20.3	179	25.4
Allies of BJP[2]	26	4.0	72	10.8
Congress	141	28.8	141	25.8
Allies of Congress[3]	–	–	26	–
United Front[4]	174	28.6	98	20.9
Others	41	19.3	24	17.5
Totals	543	100	540	100

Notes:

1. These results are calculated from a variety of sources: magazines, newspapers, and especially the website of the Election Commission of India (www.eci.gov.in). These results should be treated as preliminary, especially the percentage of votes secured. The total does not always add up to 100 due to rounding errors. The results do not include three parliamentary districts, including two in Kashmir, whose election results were not available at the time of writing. Blanks indicate that the data are not readily available.
2. Major allies of the BJP in the 1998 elections who have now also joined the government include the AIADMK party associated with Jayalalitha of Tamil Nadu (18 seats) and the Samta Party associated with George Fernandes of Bihar (9 seats).
3. Congress's major ally in 1998 was the Rashtriya Janata Dal (RJD), associated with Laloo Prasad Yadav of Bihar; the RJD won 17 seats. Where data are not readily available, Congress allies are generally part of the 'Others' category.
4. The United Front (UF) was a loose coalition of some ten parties going into the 1998 election. Two UF parties with more than double-digit parliamentary presence are the CPI(M) (main base in West Bengal) with 33 seats, and the Samajwadi Party (associated with Mulayam Singh Yadav of Uttar Pardesh) with 20 seats. Another significant party, the Telegu Desam Party (TDP) associated with Chandrababu Naidu of Andhra Pardesh, won 12 seats but withdrew from the UF after the election; the TDP now has an independent parliamentary presence and so far has supported the BJP government from 'the outside'.

largest parliamentary presence. With support from the Congress, it formed the government for nearly two years, under the prime ministership, first of Deve Gowda, and then of Inder Kumar Gujral.

The 1998 election became necessary when Congress withdrew its support from the UF government. Congress had few, if any, serious policy differences with the UF; the main reason for the split was the Congress leadership's hope—a false one, as it turned out—of gaining political advantage. The Congress held on to its parliamentary strength in the 1998 election, but the UF suffered significant losses. The BJP, especially with its regional allies, increased both its share of the popular vote and its parliamentary presence. While still short of a majority—far short without its allies—the BJP became the largest party in parliament and earned, under the constitution, the president's invitation to form a government. After intense negotiations with and serious concessions to a collection of disparate allies, this government narrowly passed the test of a parliamentary vote of confidence and took over the reins of office.

FILLING A POLITICAL VACUUM

A brief look back will help make sense of the current situation.[2] At independence and for most of the next five decades, the premier political party was the Indian National Congress—the party of Gandhi, Nehru, and the Gandhis again. The original party, with its nationalist orientation, broad social base, and modicum of organizational cohesion, went into decline in the late 1960s. It was re-created by Indira Gandhi in the 1970s, but on a rather different basis. Congress increasingly became a top-down, leader-dominated force that depended for electoral success on the Gandhi family's charisma and populist appeal. This political formula facilitated majority governments for a while, especially during the 1970s and 1980s, but with diminishing returns over time. Sikh bodyguards assassinated Indira Gandhi in 1984. When her son and successor Rajiv Gandhi met with a similar fate at the hands of a Tamil extremist in 1991, it appeared that the years of 'dynastic rule' were at an end. Political space opened up in which a variety of new forces could flourish, among them the BJP. The entry of Rajiv Gandhi's widow Sonia Gandhi into Indian politics in the 1998 election reopened the possibility that the Congress might continue to operate as a leader-dominated organization depending heavily on the popularity of the Gandhi family.

Congress's slow but steady decline has been accompanied by the rise of a variety of opposition forces, especially in the non-Hindi-speaking regions of India. Most of these movements have rural middle-class and lower-class bases and combine themes of regional nationalism and social justice. Thus emerged the pro-Tamil parties in Tamil Nadu, the communists in West Bengal and Kerala, and the pro-Sikh Akali Dal in the Punjab. Within Hindi-speaking areas, similar opposition to the Congress has emerged since the 1970s, often taking the form of a politics of caste that pits middling agrarian

---

[2]I have provided a somewhat more detailed analysis of past political trends elsewhere. See Atul Kohli, 'Indian Democracy: Stress and Resilience', *Journal of Democracy*, 3, January 1992, pp. 52–64. For much more detailed scholarly treatments of the subject, especially of Congress's decline, see Atul Kohli, *Democracy and Discontent: India's Growing Crisis of Governability*, Cambridge: Cambridge University Press, 1991; Paul Brass, *India since Independence*, 2nd Edn, Cambridge: Cambridge University Press, 1994; and Lloyd I. Rudolph and Susanne Hoeber Rudolph, *In Pursuit of Lakshmi: The Political Economy of the Indian State*, Chicago: University of Chicago Press, 1987.

groups—the so-called other backward castes or OBCs—against Congress-affiliated elite groups. Except for the communists, these opposition parties have seldom developed strong organizations or transcended localism and personalism. None has come near to being a national alternative to Congress. The UF government, like the Janata Party governments that came and went before it, exemplified this tendency.

By the late 1980s, Congress's decline was creating a growing political vacuum. Janata and other conglomerations strove to fill it, but none could bring together enough different regional forces to form a lasting coalition government. The BJP's rapid rise since 1990 must be seen in this light. Politics, like nature, abhors a vacuum, and the BJP has been moving—or trying to move—to fill this one.

Clearly, the BJP's ideology and organization have given it advantages.[3] Unlike most Indian parties, it is tightly disciplined and can count on a significant organizational base. Second, its commitment to India as a 'Hindu nation' has enabled it to redefine Indian nationalism and to provide a substitute of sorts for Congress's declining nationalist legacy. If Congress's secular nationalism was particularly well suited to help stabilize a fragile but forward-looking new state during the 1950s, the BJP's religious and backward-looking nationalism satisfies different psychological needs in the 1990s. It holds special appeal for elite and educated Indians who wonder why their country has failed to become a major, modern power, and who simultaneously believe that a fresh beginning must be made, based this time not on borrowed ideas of secularism and socialism, and even less on integration into an open, liberal economy, but on an imagined past evoking the greatness of Hindu India. Blaming non-Hindus seems to facilitate the unification of Hindus, particularly when those blamed are Muslims-members of a group that ruled India in the past, that is numerous in India today, and that predominates in neighbouring countries. Finally, among the BJP's political advantages must be counted its relatively public-spirited leadership. However one evaluates the BJP's definition of 'the public', there is no denying its leaders' intense commitment. Like their communist counterparts, many in the BJP elite are trained cadres who spend long apprenticeships internalizing a notion of 'public service' that stands in marked contrast to the personalistic and corruption-ridden ways of India's 'regular' political class.

[3]Studies of the BJP include Christophe Jaffrelot, *The Hindu Nationalist Movement in India*, New York: Columbia University Press, 1996; and Walter K. Andersen and Shridhar D. Damle, *The Brotherhood in Saffron: The Rashtriya Swayamsevak Sangh and Hindu Revivalism*, Boulder, Colo.: Westview, 1987. For historical background, see Bruce Graham, *Hindu Nationalism and Indian Politics: The Origins and Development of the Bharatiya Jana Sangh*, Cambridge: Cambridge University Press, 1990.

SOURCES OF THE BJP'S SUCCESS

A close look at the 1998 election figures reveals that the BJP's fortunes did not improve all that remarkably. It went from 161 to 179 seats in the parliament's lower chamber, the 545-member Lok Sabha. While its vote share rose by an impressive 5 per cent, some of this resulted from a decision to focus the party's energies on areas where it already enjoyed wide support.[4] Nevertheless, the BJP's share has risen steadily since the 1990s began, which requires an explanation.

The BJP's 1998 platform stressed 'good governance' rather than Hindu nationalism, and the party made most of its gains at the expense of the UF, which headed a wobbly government. As both a social movement and a political party, the BJP possesses a readily comprehensible dual appeal.[5] Whereas most of its growth in the early 1990s came from the social appeal of its redefined religious nationalism, the recent expansion of its support seemingly flows more from its political potential to form the keystone of a stable national government. The entire 1998 election can be interpreted as India's search for such a government. The UF's losses (it went from 174 to 98 seats) can be viewed as a rejection by citizens of the possibility that regional forces can coalesce into a viable, if decentralized, national alternative. The BJP and the Congress each offered its own version of a centralized alternative: the former via well-organized Hindu nationalism; the latter via the well-worn formula of the Gandhis at the helm. Both did much better than the UF at the polls, although it remains to be seen whether either can actually provide the stability that it promises.

The BJP's regional and social bases bear closer examination. The party's core support—accounting for two-thirds of its total seats—continues to come from the three contiguous 'Hindi heartland' states of Uttar Pradesh (UP), Bihar, and Madhya Pradesh. Together, they define a north-central region that is one of India's poorest and most populous, and where Hindi is the main spoken language. In an important sense, therefore, the BJP remains a party of 'backward Hindi-Hindu India'. Nearly 85 per cent of the BJP's parliamentary presence comes from the seats that it won in these three states plus the three western states of Gujarat, Maharashtra, and Rajasthan.

The location of the BJP's bastion in the Hindi heartland and the west provides further clues to the nature of its appeal. These are places where anti-Muslim, pro-Hindu rhetoric resonates. Before the advent of British dominance in the eighteenth century, these areas were either under the rule of Muslims

---

[4]Having made strategic alliances with a number of regional parties, the BJP in 1998 contested 383 seats, compared to 471 in 1996.

[5]For such an interpretation of the BJP, see Amrita Basu, *The Lotus and the Trishul: The Bhartiya Janata Party and the Growth of Hindu Nationalism* (forthcoming).

(especially the Mogul emperors), or thought to be constantly threatened by Muslim rule. The Muslim legacy, particularly in such contemporary states as UP, includes prominent architectural, culinary, and linguistic influences; a significant number of Muslims in the populace; a landscape dotted with mosques; and many stories—real or fabricated—concerning Muslim unfairness towards Hindus. Political entrepreneurs can mine this volatile cultural past for electoral capital in the troubled present, and none have done so more skilfully than the leaders of the BJP. As Congress's power in these regions declined and numerous local opposition parties faltered, the BJP stepped in to fill the breach.

The result was a heady religious nationalism that implicitly or explicitly blamed others, especially Muslims, for India's ills and promised a strong India in which Hindus could finally take pride. BJP supporters destroyed a mosque in 1992, religious violence victimized Muslims, and BJP leaders mobilized new supporters around Hindu symbols. By the early 1990s, the party had catapulted itself to the forefront of political life.

The BJP tempered its stance during the 1998 election, emphasizing instead 'normal' issues of education, health, secure livelihood, and good governance. Although perhaps a threat to the core of its religious and nationalist appeal, this moderation helped the BJP to broaden its electoral base and attract enough regional parties (each with its own calculus of interests) to cobble together a 251-seat minority-coalition government. In 1996, by contrast, nearly all the major parties had joined forces to keep the BJP out of power.

The oldest layer in the BJP's social base is composed of urban traders. Over time, its anti-Muslim militancy and its attempts to unite all Hindus especially appealed to those at the apex of the Hindu pyramid, namely, the upper castes. BJP-led protests against 'reservations' for certain castes (India's version of affirmative action) drew upper-caste urban youth more deeply into the party's orbit. Important newer developments include growing support for the BJP among India's business and industrial groups and among the numerous middling agrarian groups (the OBCs) who make up nearly half of the total rural population. Business's support is readily understandable; it hinges on the BJP's promise of national-level stability and simultaneous commitment to private enterprise and economic nationalism. With its coffers full of contributions from business, the BJP was able to run an effective campaign.

The growing OBC support—if it turns out to be real and durable—is much more perplexing. During the 1970s and 1980s, these groups tended (as many in their ranks still do) to support a variety of anti-Brahmin, anti-Congress parties. Preliminary survey data now indicate that, in 1998, 42 per cent of them voted for the BJP or one of its allies.[6] If subsequent data reveal that OBCs in BJP core areas are swinging over to the BJP on a more long-term basis, then this shift will require explanation. As yet, however, it cannot be considered confirmed.

CONGRESS AND THE UNITED FRONT

The Congress managed to hold on to 141 seats (representing no net change) even though its popular-vote share declined by three points. That dip was only the latest in what has become a confirmed and lasting downward trend. During their two years in opposition, Congress's leaders did little to improve their decrepit organization, choosing instead to focus on jockeying for short-term advantage by exacerbating factional conflict here, joining forces with other groups there, and so on. Twice in less than two years, Congress leaders sought to undermine the UF national government that they supposedly supported, mainly with the hope of forming the government themselves with the UF in a supporting role. The first episode resulted in a prime-ministerial shake-up. The second brought the government down and triggered the election process in February 1998, as baffled observers wracked their brains trying to decipher Congress's political calculus.

Even if viewed in narrow electoral terms, these actions made no sense. Had Sonia Gandhi not entered the fray, Congress's performance would surely have been worse, and even with Sonia, Congress barely held its own. The party had defeated itself with its own machinations, inadvertently toppling a government that it controlled and paving the way for the rise of a BJP-led government. In seeking reasons for these mistakes, one probably need not look much farther than inept leadership.

While Sonia Gandhi has probably played a quiet but significant role in influencing Congress's affairs since her husband's assassination, elections are not won from behind the scenes. Sonia's open participation in politics—and Congress's ready embrace of her as a potential saviour—is instructive in several ways. First, it shows how dependent the party remains on the Gandhi dynasty for its survival and future. When Indira Gandhi transformed the old Congress party into a top-down, leader-dominated organization, she set

---

[6]See the leading news magazine *India Today*, 16 March 1998, pp. 33–5. One problem is that this data may only be capturing the fact that many of the BJP's allies have their core support among the OBCs in one state or another. Without readily available state-by-state data, it remains hard to tell whether the BJP's own support among the OBCs in the Hindi-heartland states actually went up or not, and if it did, by how much. One piece of evidence that raises doubts about whether the OBC vote in states like UP shifted to the BJP is the good performance of regional parties generally associated with the OBCs. Thus the share of Mulayam Singh Yadav's SP in UP actually went up from 20.7 per cent in 1996 to 28.8 per cent in 1998.

in motion a process of deinstitutionalization that no one has yet found a way to reverse. Moreover, Sonia Gandhi's prowess as a vote getter is not obvious. Towards the end of his short life, even Rajiv Gandhi had begun to lose some of the family 'charisma', experiencing serious political competition. Now the Congress is hoping that his Italian-born widow can do the trick. In this last election, the Congress did better in those constituencies where Sonia gave speeches than where she did not, providing some indirect evidence of her appeal. Congress's overall performance was hardly stellar, however, and its share of the popular vote declined, even with Sonia.

Finally, there is the fascinating issue of Sonia's 'foreignness'. During the campaign, she highlighted her role as a dutiful *bahu* or daughter-in-law (in Hindi, the term implies depths of devotion and belonging that the translation does not convey). Having married into India's first political family, she would, now as a widow, continue to shoulder its political responsibilities. While the poor and illiterate, who already tended to be Congress sympathizers, were probably receptive to such appeals, educated, middle-class Indians appeared to be more ambivalent. Some embraced Sonia as a sign of Indian 'cosmopolitanism'. Others, however, felt shame and hostility. In a country of nearly a billion people, they asked, could the grand old nationalist party not find a 'real' Indian to lead it? Which of these reactions to Sonia's 'foreignness' will eventually prevail is not clear. Given India's current political mood, however, a Congress party led by Sonia Gandhi might well just be playing into the hands of the BJP, especially amid the nationalist feeling that seems to be reaching new heights in the wake of the May 1998 nuclear tests.

As Table 3.1 makes clear, the UF suffered serious losses. Not only did its seat count drop, but its popular-vote share slipped by almost eight percentage points. Decisions by several formerly UF-affiliated parties to go over to Congress or the BJP might explain some of this decline. The most prominent example of such a shift was in the state of Bihar, where Laloo Prasad Yadav's Rashtriya Janata Dal (RJD) quit the UF and teamed up with the Congress. While the RJD's electoral performance was not bad, the outcome mainly benefited the Congress. This and other instances suggest that elite factionalism, rather than major swings in voter allegiance, may have been largely responsible for the UF's poor performance. There was also a real drop in the UF's popularity, mainly because of its inability to put together a working national government. Thus the big loser within the UF was the Janata Dal, not the regional parties, which often ran on regional issues and held their own.[7]

---

[7]One apparent exception to this was the electoral loss suffered by the DMK party in Tamil Nadu; however, this was not so much of an exception if one keeps in mind that the DMK lost to another regional party, the AIADMK associated with Jayalalitha.

Janata Dal, by contrast, suffered losses while trying to offer itself as a national alternative to the BJP and Congress. Janata's seats in the Lok Sabha plunged from 46 to 6, and its share of the popular vote went from 8.1 to 3.2 per cent, almost near the 5 per cent mark by which the BJP's share went up. Having presided over a wobbly government, Janata Dal lost ground to a party promising 'good governance'.

The two parties now at the core of the UF are the CPI(M) and the Samajwadi (Socialist) Party or SP (see Table 3.1, note 4). The CPI(M) is a well-organized party, communist in name but social democratic in practice, with a fairly stable electoral base among the lower-middle and lower classes of rural West Bengal. The SP, by contrast, is mostly leader-dominated and has its base among the OBCs of Uttar Pradesh. Several other former UF members have by now either moved closer to Congress or are flirting with the BJP. As a loose coalition of parties with regional power bases, the UF faces a serious collective-action problem. Each of its existing or potential partners responds mainly to its own regional power calculations, and mostly these point in different directions. Their one common policy implication—support of 'reservations' for OBCs—provides less ground for cohesion than it used to because nearly every major party has now embraced it, diluting its appeal.

Drawing as it does from a number of different regional and social bases of support, the UF could offer India a genuine bottom-up political alternative that stands for decentralization and a moderately left-of-centre economic policy. Yet in its present form, the UF is far from providing such an alternative: most of its member parties are too in thrall to the ambitions of their personalistic leaders; common policy positions seldom go much beyond symbolism; and regional rather than national goals continue to dominate.

EMERGING ISSUES

The paradox of regime-level democratic endurance amid governmental instability and turnover has lately begun to concern many friends of India. The 'system' may work for now, but how long can it escape being damaged by the dysfunctional results that it keeps producing? Naturally, India's governability problems are exceedingly complex; it would be a shock if they were anything but so in a polity of such size, multicultural diversity, and political openness. Among many underlying causes, one important contributing factor is the weakness of political institutions, especially parties.[8] Amid a landscape littered with feeble parties, a well-organized formation such as the BJP can plausibly offer itself to voters as a party of 'good government'.

[8]This was a central theme of my *Democracy and Discontent,* cited in note 2.

But can the recently formed BJP-led coalition govern effectively? I doubt it. It does not command a parliamentary majority, the partners are disparate, and, more fundamentally, the BJP itself is trapped between its Hindu-nationalist core and the moderation that it must assume (whether sincerely or not) to govern peacefully and effectively. The nationalist euphoria sparked by the nuclear tests will obviously help the BJP's popularity for a time. How long that time will last is unclear, but even if the effect is enduring, one may wonder whether enhanced popularity will readily translate into effective governance.

The BJP and its coalition partners have been in power for nearly two months at the time of this writing. Prior to the nuclear explosions, doubts about the BJP's capacity to govern had already begun to emerge. Underlying this quick loss of legitimacy was the squabbling within the ruling coalition. Several of the BJP's partners, despite their limited (usually state-level) power bases, have secured senior cabinet posts in return for their support in parliament. They have used these positions, in turn, to press for more power and resources in their respective states. Preoccupied mainly with political management rather than governance, the BJP government had lost the precious capital that electoral victories provide.

This mood of distraction and ebbing legitimacy obviously changed dramatically after the nuclear explosions. The blasts were highly popular in India, with nearly 90 per cent of the population lauding the BJP's decision to declare India's nuclear-power status. It is too early to tell how these developments will alter the BJP's domestic political position. Over the short run, it is likely that the BJP leaders will catch a reflected glow from the nationalist fire that they have lit. Beyond that, however, it is not at all clear whether the BJP has the capacity to control and harness the energy unleashed and translate it into a force for good government.

In the history of India, even governments with clear parliamentary majorities (witness those of Indira Gandhi and Rajiv Gandhi) have often failed to provide effective government. The BJP is better organized than Congress ever was, but the former's record at the sub-national level is not encouraging. In 1998, for example, the BJP saw its vote drop in Rajasthan, Maharashtra, and Haryana—all states where it ruled. This may suggest that the quality of the governance that the BJP offers is not vastly superior to that offered by other parties.

EXTREMISM AND MODERATION

More important still is a deeper issue: How moderate should we expect the BJP to remain if, say by the expedient of calling an early election, it gains a majority in Parliament and can form a national government on its own? This is a central issue of contemporary Indian politics, mainly because, whatever else an aggressive Hindu-nationalist government in India might be, it will not readily qualify as a 'good government'. Such a government would probably be hostile (perhaps even violently so) to minorities, especially Muslims. There would indeed also be international friction, especially with neighbouring countries. Such virulence may satisfy the psychological needs of some groups in India; its capacity to provide the basis for 'good government' is another matter. What then, we might ask, are the forces that are likely to push the BJP towards or away from a more moderate stance?

There are the tremendous pressures for moderation that the contemporary global economy puts on all radical parties once they come into power. Then too, slow but steady deradicalization is a fate of all sharply ideological parties. The BJP shows no sign of being exempt from these powerful forces. Yet if they were determinative, the world would know no radicalism and all democracies would be immune to extremism, which is clearly not the case. During the process of getting from here to there—that is, from extreme religious nationalism to a durable, inclusive moderation—parties like the BJP can excite a lot of emotion and unleash a fair amount of damage.

Leaving the broader context and the longer-term trends aside, the BJP's extremism or moderation over the short run will most immediately be influenced by two factors: its electoral calculations, and its relationship with such 'non-political' organizations as the Rashtriya Swayamsevak Sangh (RSS or National Volunteer Corps) and the Vishwa Hindu Parishad (VHP or World Hindu Council).

First let us look at electoral calculations. The extremism of the early 1990s—as typified by the 1992 destruction of the Ayodhya mosque and the subsequent spate of anti-Muslim violence—paid handsome political dividends. During this last election, however, a more moderate stance enabled the BJP to shed its pariah status and to forge electoral (and now, governmental) alliances with a number of regional parties. This 'moderation' is especially manifest in the avoidance of confrontations over three controversial issues dear to the BJP's heart: (i) the building of a Hindu temple on the site of the razed mosque in Ayodhya; (ii) the enacting of a 'uniform civil code' that would cover the whole nation and do away with pockets of religious exceptionalism such as the Islamic laws that currently govern certain aspects of Muslim communal life; and (iii) the abrogation of some of the special powers that the Muslim-majority state of Jammu and Kashmir currently enjoys. The need for coalition partners forced the BJP to put these volatile issues on the back burner. This moderation in turn helped the BJP to win new supporters in some regions of India. Yet even then a parliamentary majority proved beyond reach, while the policy of moderation proved a liability with core supporters.

The resulting dilemma almost certainly had a role in the BJP-led government's decision to play the nuclear card. There had been no dramatic change in the regional or international security environment to call for India's decision to become an *openly* nuclear state. Past governments had resisted such a demonstration, reasoning that the open secret of India's possession of 'deliverable' nuclear weapons enhanced national security while continued official denial minimized international costs. Although it had arguably served India well for more than two decades, this posture of studied ambiguity had long been rejected by the BJP. In the spring of 1998, the new BJP found that its long-standing commitment to an open embrace of nuclear weapons was one of the few points that the fractious ruling coalition could rally around, and the only one that was certain to evoke widespread support from the broader Indian populace. The nuclear blasts, to which Pakistan replied at the end of May with six of its own, have given Indians a sense, even if only temporary, that despite their country's problems of poverty, illiteracy, corruption, and the like, they are global players, worthy of respect. The BJP is desperately hoping that this response will endure and shore up its troubled political position.

THE TENSION WITHIN THE BJP

In addition to electoral issues, there are organizational factors that will influence the BJP's political posture in the near future. As a political party, the BJP has close affiliations with the 'non-political' RSS and VHP. The avowed purposes of the RSS, for example, are to teach its members pride in the greatness of Hindu civilization, to build 'character', and to develop an ethos of 'serving people'. The RSS is a nationwide organization with an estimated membership of 2.5 million spread across nearly 40,000 tightly organized cells. Members meet frequently, conducting morning calisthenics while dressed in khaki shorts and white shirts and assembled under a saffron Hindu flag. They also hold periodic study sessions that range widely, but that interpret social reality through the prism of pro-Hindu RSS ideology. Even if the comparison is not fully accurate, it is understandable that skeptical observers find these activities redolent of 1930s-style European fascism. The links between the BJP and the RSS, moreover, are fairly intimate. Nearly all the BJP's current leaders are veterans of the RSS ranks. When political conflicts arise among the BJP's political elite, issues are often referred to the RSS for adjudication. Moreover, the RSS organizational network provides indispensable electoral resources. Though a separate organization, the RSS thus provides central ideological and organizational underpinnings for the BJP, and is probably capable of exercising a veto should the BJP stray too far from *Hindutva,* as the somewhat vague but real ideology of Hindu nationalism is called.

The BJP is now a fairly complex political force. The party's political leadership is itself diverse, with leaders like Atal Bihari Vajpayee (the current prime minister) identified as a 'moderate' and an effective parliamentarian, and others like L.K. Advani and Murli Manohar Joshi as 'hard-liners', closer to the RSS and wielding considerable organizational skills. Those who are in the government and those who run the party are also now separate officers; as a result, the party is more likely to remain committed to Hindutva than the government. The party, moreover, has grown rapidly over the last decade, with organized representation in colleges, universities, labour unions, professional associations, and even organizations of retired army personnel. It is safe to assume that while this new growth may help the BJP's electoral strength, it probably also dilutes its character as a disciplined party of RSS-hardened cadres. At the same time, however, the RSS and a few other similar organizations continue to provide a powerful scaffolding of radical Hindu nationalism, which not only narrows the BJP's room to manoeuver, but also provides its core leadership and ideology. The pulls and pushes of these diverse forces, as well as the demands of governance, will continue to mould the BJP as a political actor.

For now the BJP has adopted a fairly mild domestic political posture, balancing this with a more hawkish international one. Both of these tendencies are manifest in the eight-page 'National Agenda for Governance' that lays out the common programme of the ruling coalition. As noted above, this programme eschews most of the cherished but controversial BJP goals that could readily be interpreted as hostile towards India's non-Hindu minorities, especially Muslims. Second-tier leaders, however, have been quick to point out that such compromises are matters of realpolitik, and do not reflect any real change of heart. While such proclamations may themselves be driven by realpolitik (that is, the need to satisfy RSS hard-liners), the truth is that India's Muslims—who number more than a hundred million—can hardly rest easy.

The 'National Agenda for Governance' is relatively vague on other important issues as well. The new government's emphasis on *swadeshi*—Indian goods for Indians—is a somewhat milder version of the economic nationalism for which the BJP is well known. While the need to supplement domestic investment with foreign investment, and India's participation in the WTO, may limit how far the BJP can push its brand of economic nationalism, it is also the case that the BJP is not a party that is likely to spearhead rapid economic liberalization. India desperately needs foreign investment, and the BJP-led government may use its post-bomb-test nationalist credentials to further soften its stance against foreign investment. Yet significant domestic interests back economic nationalism. These include business groups nervous about economic openness (whether to goods or capital); unions worried by privatization and retrenchment; and educated urbanites repulsed by McDonald's restaurants, MTV, and internationally sponsored beauty pageants. The Indian Left and Right often converge on these issues, as dramatically highlighted by the presence in the cabinet of Defence Minister George Fernandes—an old labour-union man who is not a BJP member and who has a record of staunch opposition to foreign investment.

If the BJP-led government is likely to face strict limits in pursuing its preferred political agenda of Hindutva and its preferred economic agenda of swadeshi, where exactly will the BJP make its mark? The nuclear explosions are one early indication. The BJP leaders understand that the present government is not likely to last a full term. Besides the short-term management of a disparate coalition, therefore, the leaders' attention is focused on how best to use their governmental position to improve the party's positioning for the next election. Policy choices based on such short-term political considerations could be very expensive for India, a country exhausted by the repeated use of gimmicky, symbolic politics and desperately in need of some clear and consistent policy interventions with staying power. Yet needs and problems do not always bring forward solutions.

To conclude, the current BJP-led government in India—like any democratically elected government in the contemporary globalized political economy—faces serious outward constraints. Still other limitations are imposed domestically by the government's lack of a majority and the BJP's own internal heterogeneity. Constraints, of course, are never decisive. Politics is, at least in part, the art of the possible. Talented leaders can find creative ways of getting around constraints; less talented ones may also confront these constraints aggressively, only to be defeated. As a recent arrival on the Indian political scene, both heady from its recent gains and insecure about its future, the BJP is likely to push the limits of the possible, as dramatically highlighted by the nuclear blasts. On the 'morning after', however, when the noise of the explosions dies down, the natural question will be: what next? The leadership will remain focused on how to improve its electoral performance in the next election. With enhanced popularity, the option of continuing to work with disparate coalition partners is likely to appear less appealing. A central concern of the BJP will be how to harness its newly won nationalist support. Since building a durable political base requires organization, the BJP leadership may well return to the fold—that is, to the party, to the RSS, and to other affiliated organizations—as the best source of help in this area. Whether that happens or not, it is unlikely that observers of Indian politics have heard the last of Hindutva or swadeshi, or of the greatness of India's 5,000-year-old Sanskritic civilization.

4

From Majority to Minority Rule
Making Sense of the 'New' Indian Politics*

India held its ninth general election in 1989, and it failed to produce a majority government. Although India's premier political party, the Congress(I), remains the single largest group in parliament, its control of 197 of the 545 seats was insufficient to enable it to form a government. Instead, the second-largest group in parliament, the National Front, formed India's first minority government in four decades. Led by V.P. Singh, a former Congress(I) leader, the new government has fewer than 150 seats and rests on the tacit support of two ideologically distinct groups, the avowedly secular but essentially communal and pro-Hindu BJP, which controlled 86 seats, and the Left Front, a group of allied communist and left-leaning parties that won more than 50 seats.

How does one explain this political shift from majority to minority rule, and what are the future implications for an India run by a minority government? In this chapter I propose that the national election of 1989 confirmed and finally brought to the surface three long-term trends in Indian politics: the declining hold of the Congress party; the growing activism of various political groups and their mobilization of support; and the attempts, albeit halting, to forge a national alternative to the Congress(I). A 1989 development representing change rather than continuity was the emergence of a religious party, the pro-Hindu BJP, as a significant political force.

The near future of Indian politics looks uncertain. Good democratic government requires that activism of the citizenry be channelled through coherent institutions. Demands by India's various socio-economic groups are likely to increase, but it is far from certain that political institutions will

*Originally published as 'From Majority to Minority Rule: Making Sense of the "New" Indian Politics', in Marshall M. Bouton and Philip Oldenburg (eds), *India Briefing, 1990*, New York: Asia Society, 1990, pp. 1–24.

be able to accommodate them. In view of recent trends, it is likely that both government and politics will be more unstable in the near future than in the past.

THE LONG-TERM TRENDS

The election and related political issues will dominate any attempt to make sense of Indian politics in 1989. All other major domestic political developments had to do with socio-political conflicts: continuing terrorism in Punjab and growing tension in Kashmir, Hindu-Muslim conflicts in various parts of India, and demonstrations and agitation by various, often privileged, groups against the government's attempts to 'reserve' jobs and educational opportunities for selected underprivileged groups (India's version of affirmative action). Before analysing the elections and other political events of 1989, however, it is important to explore the political background.

The Changing Position of the Congress Party

Although the Congress party has been India's ruling party for most of the past forty years, electoral victories since 1967 have not come easily. As the major nationalist party, the party that had led a successful struggle against British colonialism, the Congress was India's 'natural' ruling party in the 1950s. During the 1960s, however, opposition to the Congress grew in various parts of India. Like India itself, this opposition was quite diverse: it was led by a regional nationalist party in the southern state of Tamil Nadu; by a religious party, the pro-Sikh Akali Dal, in the Punjab; by various communist parties in West Bengal and Kerala; and by parties resting on the support of rural 'backward' castes in the populous heartland state of Uttar Pradesh. (These castes are predominantly composed of landowning family farmers situated between high castes, such as Brahmins, and the lowest, or Scheduled Castes). The result was that the Congress party nearly lost its majority in the national election of 1967.

Ever since that crucial election, the Congress has had difficulty maintaining a stable majority coalition.[1] Indira Gandhi, who inherited power from her father, Jawaharlal Nehru, won the 1971 election handsomely, but by then the political situation in India had changed quite sharply. The old Congress party had split in two, and the segment led by Indira Gandhi never developed the hallmarks of an organized party: regular membership, internal party elections, or a second and third tier of leaders with support from the grass-

---

[1] For a good overview of the Congress's changing electoral fortunes, see Paul Brass, 'Political Parties and Electoral Politics', in Marshall M. Bouton and Philip Oldenburg (eds), *India Briefing, 1989*, Boulder, CO: Westview Press, 1989, pp. 61–106; see also Myron Weiner, *India at the Polls, 1980*, Washington, D.C.: American Enterprise Institute, 1980.

roots. Instead, Indira Gandhi adopted a populist slogan, *garibi hatao*, and used her considerable leadership skills to establish direct links with the majority of Indians, those living in poverty. Having risen to power in 1971 on a wave of populism and socialism, she fought and won the 1972 state elections in the shadow of a regional war that India had 'won' and that had led to the dismemberment of Pakistan and the emergence of Bangladesh.

The rise of a populist Indira Gandhi had several major political consequences; especially important was the organizational decline of the Congress(I) party.[2] The more Indira Gandhi's power came to be derived from a mass following, the more she bypassed established intermediate leaders and sought to appoint new party officers herself. Over the short run, as long as Indira Gandhi's popularity was unchallenged, this strategy of top-down political appointments helped consolidate her power. The strategy, however, had long-term costs. First, it tended to alienate from the Congress many who had independent power bases. Over time, these individuals have sought to combine their oppositional energies. And second, the system of top-down appointments often put in powerful positions individuals who would not necessarily have been the choice of the Congress's grass-roots membership. This development also weakened the Congress by diminishing the legitimacy of its lower-level leadership.

The electoral euphoria of 1971 and 1972 was short-lived. Opposition to Indira Gandhi, which had been there all along, reorganized, and it resurfaced with a vengeance in the mid-1970s. The political style in India had also become more activist. Indira Gandhi's populism and mobilization of support from the mass of Indians came to be matched by the opposition's militancy. States like Gujarat and Bihar became battlegrounds between Indira Gandhi and the opposition, by this time led by an old follower of Mahatma Gandhi, Jayaprakash Narayan. Labour and peasant militancy added to the turmoil. When Indira Gandhi's power was threatened, she imposed a nationwide emergency, in which democratic rights were curtailed for nearly two years.

Indira Gandhi and her Congress party lost the 1977 election. This defeat reflected both popular anger over her imposition of the Emergency and the fact that the diverse opposition to her party had managed to unite, if only momentarily. Factionalism within the opposition, however, resurfaced, and the opposition Janata Party government could not function. This failure, in

---

[2]More detailed discussion of Congress's organizational decline is to be found in James Manor, 'Parties and Party System', in Atul Kohli (ed.), *India's Democracy: An Analysis of Changing State–Society Relations*, Princeton: Princeton University Press, 1988, pp. 62–98; Lloyd I. Rudolph and Susanne Hoeber Rudolph, *In Pursuit of Lakshmi: The Political Economy of the Indian State*, Chicago: University of Chicago Press, 1987, chapters 4–6; and Atul Kohli, *Democracy and Disorder: India's Growing Crisis of Governability*, New York: Cambridge University Press, forthcoming.

turn, created a sense that there might not be a viable national alternative to the Congress. Indira Gandhi benefited from this shift in national mood and won the election once again in 1980.

There was a growing realization in India in the early 1980s that Indira Gandhi might not come back to power in 1985. Her attempts to alleviate poverty had not been very successful. As a result, she had failed to consolidate her populist support into a stable coalition. She was thus increasingly in search of new strategies for securing electoral majorities. Since Hindus are by far the majority in India, Indira Gandhi sought to mobilize support around the issue of Hindus versus Indian minorities. For the first time since independence and partition in the late 1940s, religious themes resurfaced in Indian politics at the national level. While complicated in origin, the government's failure to deal with the demands of Sikhs in Punjab state for religious and political autonomy, which resulted in political turmoil and terrorism, was in part rooted in Congress's political need to win the support of Hindus. Growing Hindu–Muslim problems, though quite complex and variable in origin, can also be traced to the need to build political majorities around religious appeals.

Indira Gandhi's tragic assassination in 1984 by two Sikh bodyguards turned out to be a great political dividend for the Congress(I) party and for its new leader, Indira's son Rajiv. Rajiv Gandhi won by a large majority—nearly 48 per cent of the popular vote and 77 per cent, or 415, of the parliamentary seats. This was mainly a result of Indira Gandhi's assassination, which created sympathy for her son across India. Moreover, the fear of impending political turmoil was skilfully utilized by the Congress leaders to mobilize political support.

The important point is that, ever since 1967, the Congress has won elections under unusual circumstances, whether the leadership actually created those circumstances or simply took advantage of them. These victories were more the result of popular mood swings than of stable social support for the Congress(I) party. What was significant about the 1989 election, therefore, was that it was probably the first 'usual' election since 1967 in that it was not conducted in the shadow of mood-generating euphorias or crises. What looks like a major decline in the Congress's position is in part explained simply by the return to political normality.

Growing Political Activism

The unquestioned dominance of the Congress party in the 1950s and the early 1960s rested in part on the legitimacy it inherited from its role in India's independence struggle and in part on a patronage network that stretched from New Delhi to India's numerous villages. The patronage system worked because the relations between social 'superiors' and 'inferiors', especially in the villages, were characterized in this period by the latter's relative acquiescence. As a result, rural elites were periodically able to sway the votes of the lower strata towards the Congress in exchange for resources that Congress governments controlled.

The spread of democratic ideas and competitive politics has over time helped transform the acquiescence of lower social groups into political activism in many parts of India. These changes started in the 1960s, and their significance has grown ever since. The more active and demanding various groups have become, the less successful has become the old Congress system of patronage networks. If rural elites cannot readily sway the votes of the lower rural strata, what is the political utility of channelling governmental largesse to them? These changing political patterns in the villages have, in turn, contributed to important changes at the top of the political pyramid.

Indira Gandhi was among the first to sense this important political change. It is clear in retrospect that her populist slogan garibi hatao was aimed at capturing the support of the new groups that were emerging from under the sway of traditional rural elites. Her populism, in turn, further contributed to mobilizing India's lower rural strata.

As noted above, the failure to implement anti-poverty programmes in the 1970s made it difficult for Indira Gandhi to consolidate her position with her new supporters. The dissatisfied rural poor of India thus became susceptible to new forms of political mobilization in the 1980s. Their dissatisfaction has found diverse expressions, often varying from region-to-region. One disconcerting nationwide trend, however, has been the attempt by leaders to create new electoral majorities along religious lines. Whether the poorest of the poor support this appeal is not clear. What is clearer is that a failure of the Congress's populism has created a fluid political situation that can now be manipulated by demagogues for other purposes.

In addition to the poor, the somewhat better-off middle groups of rural India have become politically active over the last two decades. Two movements of national significance are worthy of note. First, there is the 'reservation' movement of the 'backward' castes, which demands that government-controlled jobs and educational opportunities be allocated—that is, reserved—according to such ascriptive criteria as caste. Demands of this sort have generally had a top-down quality in the sense that leaders, rather than social groups, have brought the issues to the fore in the hope of gaining the electoral support of the numerically significant 'backward' castes. The more the champions of these castes have succeeded, the more resistance has been put up by elite castes. Some of the political turmoil of the 1980s in states like Gujarat and Bihar can be traced to this type of conflict.

The other movement among the middle rural groups has demanded higher prices for agricultural products and lower prices for such production inputs as fertilizer, electricity, and credit. Such initiatives have often attracted the support of those peasants who have done rather well for themselves by taking advantage of the government's 'green-revolution' policies. These groups now seek to transform their newly acquired wealth into political clout, especially because they feel that the urban rich have done much better than they. The present government is more representative of both the 'backward' castes and the better-off green-revolution farmers, especially those of north-central India, than was Rajiv Gandhi's Congress(I) government.

India's urban middle-income groups are not politically well organized. Their political significance however, is considerable, much greater than their numbers (about 10 per cent of India's total population) would suggest. This is because men and women of letters generally come from this stratum and tend to be society's opinion makers. Rajiv Gandhi benefited greatly from the positive evaluation of these groups in 1985 and 1986, in part because of the pro-urban consumer policies that he pursued and in part because of his initial image as an incorrupt 'Mr Clean'. Between 1987 and 1989, however, many among India's urban educated groups became increasingly disturbed by revelations of corruption at the highest levels of government. The theme of clean government, which India's new Prime Minister V.P. Singh has also adopted, is aimed primarily at these groups.

In a country as diverse as India, a discussion at the national level can hide more than it reveals. The patterns of growing activism vary considerably from region to region. The following brief examples are provided to give the flavour of India's regional complexities.[3]

Punjab state is mired in a violent and fratricidal ethnic conflict involving Sikh militants in a confrontation with New Delhi as they seek greater political control. (Sikhs are a religious minority constituting nearly half of Punjab's population.) While complex in origin, the 'Sikh crisis' is rooted in such factors as the growing wealth of the area's middle peasants, many of whom are Sikhs, issues of ethnic nationalism, and competitive political mobilization by both the Akali Dal (the party of the Sikhs) and the Congress party.

The pattern of conflict in the state of Gujarat is different. Throughout the 1980s, elite and 'backward' castes of the area fought, often violently, for control of state power and over issues of affirmative action for the 'backward' castes. This caste conflict is quickly being transformed into Hindu-Muslim conflict as parties like the BJP succeed in mobilizing support across caste, but along religious, lines.

---

[3]For one study that explores this diversity in great detail, see my forthcoming book, *Democracy and Disorder*. For details of political changes in various states, see also Francine Frankel and M.S.A. Rao (eds), *Dominance and State Power in Modern India: Decline of a Social Order*, 2 vols, New Delhi: Oxford University Press, 1989, 1990.

The government of yet another state, Bihar, has simply stopped functioning. The levels of mobilization along both caste and class lines are so high that nearly all of the groups are fighting each other, often with their own private armies. By contrast, highly mobilized labour, peasant, and student groups have provided the power base of a reform-oriented ruling communist party in the state of West Bengal. However, the resulting political stalemate between the property-owning groups and the communist rulers there has also generated economic stagnation.

In south India, themes of regional nationalism have declined in the state of Tamil Nadu. As a result, while the conflict between Tamil Nadu and New Delhi has receded, it has also become increasingly difficult to carve out a new majority coalition in the state. The new political situation is thus fluid, with wide swings in electoral behaviour likely. The same is true in the state of Andhra Pradesh. The seven-year personalistic rule of the film-actor-turned-politician N.T. Rama Rao has left behind a highly de-institutionalized political system. Weakness of both political parties and bureaucracy has, in turn, contributed to growing caste and class conflict.

In general, the levels of political activity in India are much higher today than they were in the past. This growing activism reflects, in part, the changing socio-economic conditions that development necessarily produces, but, more important, it indicates the spread of democratic values and competitive politics. Egalitarian ideas have eroded the subservient relationships of social 'inferiors' to 'superiors'. Political elites have, in turn, sought to mobilize the hitherto 'inferiors' for their own political purposes. The Indian government controls a great many resources in a very poor society. As the realization has spread that this government, or parts of it, can be controlled by the mobilization of support among new groups, such efforts have spread. High levels of mobilization among diverse groups have made it difficult for governmental consensus to emerge.

Alternatives to the Congress

The organizational and electoral decline of the Congress party and the growing activism of various political groups have been important political trends. If a well-organized alternative to the Congress had successfully accommodated the newly mobilized groups, India might well have had a more effective democratic government than it has in recent years. Unfortunately, the political record of the opposition to the Congress at the national level—certainly up until 1989—has been fairly poor.

The major problem of the centrist political parties opposing the Congress has been their inability to act in unity. In India's electoral system, the candidate who wins the most votes in a constituency wins a seat in the lower house of the national parliament, the Lok Sabha. If more than one candidate opposes the Congress candidate, the typical outcome is that the opposition candidates split the vote and the Congress candidate wins, usually with well under 50 per cent of the total vote. In spite of this situation, in which it would be highly rational for those opposing the Congress to run a single candidate, it has repeatedly proven difficult for the opposition to unify.

A number of factors have inhibited the ability of the centrist opposition parties to unify, the most important of which is probably the ambitions of leaders competing for senior positions. Leaders have often pursued their short-term interests, at the expense of their larger goal of defeating the Congress. This has been true in nearly all of the elections in India except for two: the 1977 election after the Emergency and the most recent one. The Emergency created an intense, though temporary, horror of an authoritarian regime led by Indira Gandhi, thereby uniting the opposition parties under the umbrella of the Janata Party. This temporary unity, however, lasted for no more than two years before conflicting leadership ambitions led to the dissolution of the fragile coalition government.

What is true for the centrist opposition is not so true for opposition parties on the Left and the Right, whose ideology and superior organization have enabled them to tame leadership factionalism and act in relative unity. Both the BJP and the CPI(M) reflect these tendencies. These parties, however, have until recently enjoyed only a limited power base. The CPI(M) has been confined to certain regions of India, and the BJP, to certain segments of the urban population, especially trading groups, in western and central India. The electoral position of the BJP, however, has changed quite sharply over the last two to three years.

Many of the non-Congress parties, whether centrist or ideological, have had some experience of being in power during the last decade, and some political learning has occurred in the parties over this time period. For example, the CPI(M)'s continuing stint in power in the state of West Bengal definitely transformed it from a revolutionary party in the 1970s into a reformist and a pragmatic party in the 1980s. While the BJP has not had an equivalent prolonged experience in running a state government, some of its prominent leaders, such as Atal Bihari Vajpayee, did serve as senior ministers during the Janata government (1977–9). Some of these leaders are also considered pragmatic, not deeply communal, in their management of everyday politics.

Other non-Congress leaders, for example, Ramakrishna Hegde, Devi Lal, and N.T. Rama Rao, also ran state governments (Karnataka, Haryana, and Andhra Pradesh, respectively) during the 1980s. Among their experiences, a particularly valuable one was the attempt to collectively bargain with New

Delhi for more state resources and greater political control. The non-Congress chief ministers met periodically to chart out their political strategies and this provided them with experience in working together.[4]

Despite this shared political experience, one should not overstate the capacity of India's non-Congress parties and leaders to generate a unified opposition to the Congress(I) party. While many leaders are pragmatic, there remain policy differences among them. More important, there is the ever-present danger of competing leadership ambitions. Leaders like Haryana's Devi Lal are especially troublesome because they come from a tradition of mercurial politics in which 'power first' is the main goal. Moreover, the attempts to carve out a unified electoral force during much of the period leading up to the 1989 election were tortuous. Given the history of Janata rule and of numerous failed attempts to create a non-Congress political force, one cannot be too optimistic about the prospects of a unified non-Congress government in India.

THE 1989 NATIONAL ELECTION

The significant political developments in 1989 were nearly all influenced by the imminence of the national election. The first half of the year was dominated by the on-again, off-again efforts of various opposition parties to forge a united front against the Congress. It would have been difficult to predict, say in February or March, whether the opposition parties would be able to work together. The Janata Dal, an aggregation of several smaller parties and now the main constituent of the National Front and thus of the government, was not formally recognized as a party in the Lok Sabha until April. Under the tacit leadership of V.P. Singh, the opposition then went on the political offensive and remained so until Congress's eventual defeat in November.

The opposition parties chose to focus their political energies on the issue of corruption. V.P. Singh and his cronies thus made much of the Bofors scandal: Bofors, a Swedish armaments company, allegedly made payments to high officials of Rajiv Gandhi's government to secure a contract to supply guns to the Indian armed forces. New revelations in July concerning payoffs led 73 non-Congress(I) members of parliament to quit the Lok Sabha en masse, demanding the resignation of Rajiv Gandhi. The opposition thus captured the moral high ground on the popular issue of 'cleanliness' in government.

Rajiv Gandhi responded to the opposition's challenge by downplaying the issue of corruption and focusing political attention instead on decentralization of power. The Congress(I)-controlled Lok Sabha passed constitutional amendments in August that would have transferred a significant share of

---

[4]I owe this insight to Philip Oldenburg.

governmental resources directly from New Delhi to local governments. (The amendments failed to get the necessary two-thirds majority for passage in the Rajya Sabha, the upper house of parliament.) This political ploy was intended to simultaneously weaken the patronage powers of opposition-controlled state governments and enhance those of the Congress. It also aimed to counteract the image of Rajiv's government as elitist and removed from the people.

Elections to be held in November were not announced until October, giving the opposition little time to formalize electoral agreements. Much to the Congress's chagrin, the National Front, the BJP and the CPI(M) quickly managed to reach an arrangement to put up only one opposition candidate per constituency. Once these electoral agreements were reached, the Congress was in serious political trouble. While the magnitude of the Congress's defeat came as a surprise to many observers, part of the reason for this reaction was simply that the opposition parties had come together such a short time before the elections.

Below the national level, the electoral outcomes provided a mixed picture. One fairly consistent result was that nearly all parties in power before the election lost power. As a result, Congress and Congress-supported parties came to dominate much of south India, whereas opposition parties like the BJP, the Janata Dal, and the CPI(M) won power in much of north India, in both western and eastern states.

The elections proved a major setback to Rajiv Gandhi's Congress(I) party. The decline in the number of seats that the Congress won in 1989 was dramatic—it won 197 seats, in comparison with 415 and 353 seats in the 1984 and 1980 elections respectively. The Congress's share of the popular vote, however, did not decline as dramatically (see Table 4.1); the Congress secured 40 per cent of the vote, a drop of some 8 per cent from the 1984 election. One needs to keep in mind, however, that Rajiv Gandhi's spectacular victory in 1984 was something of an exception; the voter turnout in 1989 was 10 per cent lower than in 1984, suggesting that the extra level of politicization engendered by the sense of crisis in 1984 may have disappeared. The Congress's share of the popular vote in the 1980 elections, when the party also secured a comfortable majority in parliament, provides a different, and possibly more appropriate, point of comparison; its share that year was 43 per cent. The decline in popular support for the Congress(I) party between 1980 and 1989 was thus only 3 per cent.

The juxtaposition of the dramatic decline in the number of Congress's parliamentary seats and the much less dramatic decline in its popular vote indicates that the Congress remains a significant political force in India, although its days of unquestioned dominance are clearly over. Even without dramatic changes in Indian politics, it could come back to power in the near

TABLE 4.1: Results of the Lok Sabha Elections, 1989*

	Number of seats won	(Per cent)	Percentage of popular vote
Congress(I)	197	(37)	40.3
National Front			
Janata Dal	141	(27)	18.3
Telugu Desam	2	(1)	3.4
Congress (S)	1	(–)	–
BJP	86	(16)	11.8
Left Parties			
CPI(M)	32	(6)	6.5
CPI	12	(2)	2.7
Other Left	8	(2)	1.1
Others			
AIADMK	11	(2)	1.6
Akali Dal (Mann)	6	(1)	–
Bahujan Samaj Party	3	(1)	–
Small parties and independents	30	(6)	–

Source: Richard Sisson, 'India in 1989: A Year of Elections in a Culture of Change', *Asian Survey*, vol. 30, February 1990, p. 122.

Note: *No elections were held for 16 of the 545 seats in the Lok Sabha: the 14 seats for Assam state and the 2 seats reserved for Anglo-Indians. The total of 529 seats includes seats filled through by-elections held after November on account of vacancies due to resignations and deaths of candidates or incumbents.

future. The shift in India from a majority Congress national government to a minority non-Congress one is due to a small but significant decline in the Congress's popularity and to the changing nature of India's non-Congress parties, including their increased capacity to work together against the Congress.

Rajiv Gandhi's Loss of Support

One should not look for dramatic failures of Rajiv Gandhi to explain the Congress's defeat in 1989. However, his five years in power were not marked by any great successes.[5] When he established his leadership position in early 1985, he had specified the liberalization of the economy, the settlement of regional disputes, and the rebuilding of the Congress(I) party as his political priorities. In retrospect, his performance in each of these areas was at best incomplete and at worst dismal. Even when his performance was relatively satisfactory, Rajiv Gandhi never became a real leader, that is, someone

[5]Two relatively brief assessments of Rajiv Gandhi's performance are Myron Weiner, 'Rajiv Gandhi: A Mid-Term Assessment', in Marshall M. Bouton (ed.), *India Briefing, 1987*, Boulder, CO: Westview Press, 1987, pp. 1–24; and the Epilogue in the paperback edition of Atul Kohli (ed.), *India's Democracy: An Analysis of Changing State–Society Relations*, rev. edn, Princeton: Princeton University Press, forthcoming.

who could persuade his detractors, as well as his followers, of the correctness of his actions.

Rajiv's attempts to liberalize India's economy had some success. India's macroeconomic performance under his rule was also relatively good: the economy grew by nearly 5 per cent; agricultural growth was satisfactory; industrial growth picked up; and export performance was impressive. To the extent that his liberalization measures were responsible for the improved economic growth, Rajiv deserves credit.

Unfortunately for Rajiv, it proved difficult to translate economic performance into political dividends. First, his attempts at liberalization came to be interpreted as an abandonment of socialism. Rajiv's own party, the Congress(I), fearing that such policy shifts would cost the party electoral support, opposed many of his attempts to raise prices, trim public expenditures and provide incentives to private producers. Other political parties took advantage of the opening that Rajiv's new economic orientation provided; they attempted to mobilize the people against the Congress(I) party government, often successfully, and made the image of Rajiv as a pro-rich leader stick. The second reason for Rajiv's difficulty in getting political mileage from his economic successes was that his economic strategy rested, at least in part, on a boom in durable consumer goods purchased primarily by the better-off urban population. This created a sense, right or wrong, that the government was pro-city and less sympathetic to inhabitants of the countryside. The support of landowning peasant farmers may have been decisive in the electoral success of non-Congress parties, especially in such Hindi heartland states as Haryana and Uttar Pradesh.

In addition, for a series of complex reasons, the gap between the government's revenues and its expenditures grew, fuelling inflation throughout 1988–9. Since India's low-income democracy tends to be sensitive to inflation, there is no reason to doubt that dissatisfaction on this score cost Rajiv Gandhi political support. Thus, although India's economic performance—judged by international macroindicators—was relatively good, there was little in this performance to help mobilize the support of its electoral majorities, the peasant farmers and the poor.

Rajiv's attempts to solve such regional disputes as the Sikh crisis in Punjab state did not make much headway. After some initial successes in 1985–6, he abandoned the attempt to find a political compromise between the demands of the Sikhs and the position of the national government. Part of the problem in this area was that the Sikhs are deeply divided among themselves. Equally important, however, was Rajiv's growing fear that such concessions to the Sikhs as the transfer of the city of Chandigarh—currently the joint capital of Haryana and Punjab—to Punjab would cost him political support, both in states like Haryana and within his own party. The failure to find a political solution, in turn, led to a 'law and order' approach that exacerbated both terrorism and governmental repression.

It is not clear whether Rajiv's failures to solve regional disputes like that in Punjab had direct consequences in the 1989 election. It is hard to imagine a poor peasant in Tamil Nadu or West Bengal choosing to vote against the Congress on the basis of what was happening in Punjab. But what is likely is that such policy failures created a more general doubt about Rajiv's leadership qualities, especially in the eyes of India's urban middle classes. Since the opinions of these groups probably have some trickle-down effect, failures such as that in Punjab may have had an indirect negative electoral impact on Rajiv.

The failure that probably cost Rajiv the most in electoral terms was his inability to rebuild the Congress(I) party. Internal party elections were announced, but, after considerable intra-party struggle, they were abandoned. The structure of the Congress(I) party consists of a chain of officials appointed from the top. Replacement of this top-down hierarchy with a bottom-up structure would have reinvigorated the party, but it could also have posed a real threat to the existing party structure, including Rajiv's leadership. Because the effort to rebuild the party was abandoned, however, Rajiv found himself without a dynamic organization to help him through the elections.

The opposition to Rajiv Gandhi, led by V.P. Singh, mobilized primarily around issues of corruption, rising prices, and, most important, the ineffectiveness of Rajiv as a leader—especially around the charge that he was not a man of the people, that he was too westernized to understand the plight of the ordinary Indian. Without detailed public opinion surveys, it is not easy to assess the electoral significance of such a political posture. However, although he stressed his own populist tinge, V.P. Singh did not emphasize any major policy differences with Rajiv Gandhi.

In addition, there were regional variations within this larger national picture. The fact that the Congress did rather well in several south Indian states requires explanation. Regional variations also suggest that local issues may have been as important as, if not more important than, national issues in influencing electoral outcomes. These phenomena are discussed further below.

THE COMING TOGETHER OF THE NON-CONGRESS PARTIES

The arithmetic of India's elections since 1967 has been such that a unified opposition could have kept the Congress out of office for nearly half of the last twenty-two years. How did India's significant non-Congress parties manage to work together in the 1989 election? The simple and powerful answer is that they realized that the rewards of working together would be much higher than those of working separately. However, the inability of these same parties to work together in the past—and possibly again in the future—

requires a further probing of the conditions that facilitated the working unity. Three factors were important: the nature of the main participants, the significant role of a new leadership, and a changing political situation in which the Congress's declining popularity bolstered the prospect of a non-Congress victory.

The parties that form and support the new minority government in India are diverse. Their separate identities, histories, and respective bases of support are difficult even for specialists in Indian politics to master. Fortunately, not all of the details are necessary for an understanding of the three major constituents: the National Front and its main component, the Janata Dal, which have now formed the government; the Left Front, dominated by the CPI(M), which supports but is not part of the government; and the BJP, which is in a similar position to the Left Front vis-à-vis the government.

The party that is at the heart of the new government is the Janata Dal, which was itself put together from other parties and groups in early 1989. The three main components of the Janata Dal were the Jan Morcha, the Lok Dal, and the Janata Party. The Jan Morcha was not a party; rather, it consisted of a group of senior former Congress(I) leaders like V.P. Singh, Arun Nehru, and Arif Mohammed Khan, who had at one time or another served under Rajiv Gandhi but who had later parted company with him and joined the opposition. The Lok Dal was the old party of the late Charan Singh and was itself by the mid-1980s divided into two factions, one led by Charan Singh's son, Ajit Singh, with a base in western Uttar Pradesh, and the other by Devi Lal, with a base in Haryana. As the party of the green-revolution farmers and 'backward' castes, which had always opposed the Brahmin-dominated Congress, the Lok Dal also enjoyed the support of the middle peasantry in other northern and central states like Bihar. The third group, the Janata Party, was an offshoot of the old Janata that had ruled India from 1977 to 1979. Entering into the 1989 election, this group consisted of the remnants of the old Congress party of Morarji Desai from states like Gujarat and Karnataka—identified with individuals like Ramakrishna Hegde, the former chief minister of Karnataka and the present head of India's Planning Commission—and socialist and other parties from eastern Uttar Pradesh and Bihar, represented by individuals like Chandrashekhar.

These groups and parties came together under the tacit leadership of V.P. Singh to form the Janata Dal. The process of party formation went on throughout 1989 and was not easy. The possibility that the group would come apart was alive all year, and it remains an issue. The problems of unity revolved mainly around personalities and leadership ambitions; there were no major ideological or policy divides within this group. What facilitated the eventual unity was the emergence of V.P. Singh as a seemingly reluctant but tacit leader. The members of this group understood that, in policy terms, they were not all that different from the Congress, certainly not enough so as to create a distinct coalition. It must also have been clear to them that they needed a leader who could appear to be a viable alternative to Rajiv Gandhi. The only way to overcome the difficulties of working together was to be led by another popular national leader.

V.P. Singh was in a good position to occupy this spot. As a former raja (prince) from Uttar Pradesh, who had supposedly renounced his principality and associated lands, V.P. Singh is in the mainstream of Indian politics, much more so than other former challengers to the Congress like Morarji Desai and Charan Singh. A trained lawyer and student of physics at Allahabad University, V.P. Singh rose to prominence under the tutelage of Indira Gandhi. Before being made Rajiv Gandhi's finance minister, he had already had a couple of brief stints in the national cabinet and had served as chief minister of Uttar Pradesh. Under Rajiv, V.P. Singh had initiated the liberalization of the economy and had later led corruption raids on prominent businesspeople.

V.P. Singh's parting of ways with Rajiv Gandhi was widely interpreted in India as a result of pressure from unhappy and possibly corrupt businesspeople. This gave V.P. Singh the aura of an anti-corruption champion from the very beginning of his independent rise to power. Having been closely associated with the Congress all along, V.P. Singh wisely chose not to disassociate himself sharply from the Congress's policy positions. Instead he harped more and more on themes of anti-corruption, respect for norms and values in the conduct of democratic politics, and the need to decentralize power in India. The more his popularity rose, the more it must have become clear to the motley coalition that is now the Janata Dal that it could not do without him as its leader. The less contentious the issue of who was likely to lead the opposition to the Congress became, the more likely it became that a new party could be formed.

The only representation the Janata Dal had in the south was in Karnataka. This lacuna was filled by a working alliance forged under the umbrella of the National Front. The Front brought together such south Indian parties as the ruling party in Tamil Nadu, the DMK, and the former ruling party of Andhra Pradesh, the Telugu Desam. Although both the DMK and the Telugu Desam did poorly in the 1989 election, the fact remains that this alliance gave the Janata Dal a semblance of popular support in the south as well as in the north.

Both the communists and the BJP have their own reasons to support the Janata Dal in power. As parties on the Left and the Right of the political spectrum, they are likely to have important policy differences with the centrist Janata Dal. It is important to note, however, that on crucial basics, policy differences among these coalition constituents are not totally irreconcilable. The CPI(M), for example, is in practice more a social-democratic than a communist party. It is committed to a democratic system, it believes in multiclass alliances, it promotes reform rather than revolution, and it has come around to the view that in a private economy, if economic growth is to be facilitated, then private producers need government protection and support. Similarly, the BJP, while pro-Hindu in its overall orientation, is often willing to soften its religious militancy, especially when it is in a ruling position.

The power base of the CPI(M) is essentially regional. West Bengal remains its stronghold, although it also has considerable bases in both Tripura and Kerala. Besides an antipathy towards the Congress and Rajiv Gandhi, the CPI(M)'s main reason for supporting the Janata Dal government is that it views this as an opportunity to broaden its regional power base. Whether the CPI(M) continues to support the Janata Dal government or not will rest primarily on its assessment of whether or not this goal is being met. The CPI(M)'s main differences, in any case, are not with the Janata Dal but rather with the BJP over the issue of communalism, that is, over the appropriateness of religion as a tool of political mobilization. If the prospects of the BJP joining the government grow, this could lead to the withdrawal of CPI(M) support. That, in turn, could mean the end of the experiment in minority government.

The BJP has in the past actually worked fairly closely with several constituents of the Janata Dal, though not always with happy results. The BJP, which is the old Jan Sangh, was part of the Janata Party that ruled India from 1977 to 1979. Its electoral fortunes have fluctuated over the last few decades. Its present strength is in states like Rajasthan, Himachal Pradesh and Madhya Pradesh. These states were at one time Congress strongholds. As there were no other major opposition parties in these states, the BJP utilized its superior organization to piece together a multicaste coalition that used fundamentalist sentiments to unify Hindus around political issues. For example, the BJP or religious organizations loosely allied with it are often alleged to be behind religious riots, especially anti-Muslim riots, that consolidate Hindu support for the party.

Over the last several years the BJP has expanded its political activities, and it has also benefited from Hindu revivalism. In states like Gujarat, for example, the BJP has slowly chipped away at the Congress alliance of lower-middle castes, lower castes, and Muslims against the dominant castes, by trying to unite Hindus against Muslims. Muslim communal violence, such as that in Ahmedabad, which the BJP may itself have instigated, has contributed to the BJP's growing popularity. In other states, for example, Uttar Pradesh, religious organizations such as the Vishwa Hindu Parishad were active throughout 1989, conducting *puja* (religious ceremonies) in villages and collecting money for the building of a Hindu temple on a controversial site in the holy city of Ayodhya, controversial because it overlaps with the site of a revered mosque. Such activities also enabled these groups to mobilize religious sentiments of Hindus against Muslims. Political parties like the BJP, in turn, were well positioned to take advantage of such shifting sentiments, although, to be fair, it must be added that even Rajiv Gandhi attempted to capitalize on such mood shifts by declaring that his main goal in power was to create a *Ram Rajya,* or a kingdom of peace and prosperity such as that associated in Hindu mythology with the revered Lord Rama.

The BJP, more than the CPI(M), would like to join the Janata Dal government. Having won 86 seats in the national parliament, the BJP considers itself deserving of such a role. The arithmetic of the present situation, however, is such that no non-Congress government can be formed without the help of the Left. The Left, in turn, is deeply suspicious of the BJP. It is not likely that the two can join the same government. Hence a precarious situation has arisen in which the current government has assured support from only 144 seats in a parliament of 529 elected members (and worse, only 22 per cent of the popular vote) and must count on the tacit support of another 138 seats from two ideologically distinct groups.

The Janata Dal, the BJP, and the CPI(M)-led Left Front are united mainly by their antipathy to Rajiv Gandhi and their calculation that a stint in power, or near power, will bolster their future electoral prospects. The unity is thus fragile at best.

Regional Patterns

The diversity of regional patterns underlines the significance of opposition unity and enables a further analysis of the reasons behind the decline in support for the Congress(I) party. While the common impression that the Congress did better in the south than in the north is essentially correct, the related generalization that the 1989 vote was a vote against all those in power requires qualification.

To begin with an example from the Hindi heartland, the Congress(I) party did poorly in Uttar Pradesh. Its share of the popular vote there declined by nearly 20 per cent, from 51 per cent in 1984 to 31 per cent in 1989. Even discounting the 'Rajiv wave' of 1984, this represents a substantial shift. What happened? The Congress's traditional power base in Uttar Pradesh had been an alliance of the upper castes, especially the Brahmins; the lowest, or Scheduled Castes; and religious minorities, such as the Muslims. The support for the opposition parties that now constitute the Janata Dal, by contrast, had been from the middle castes: the productive farmers of western Uttar Pradesh, like the peasant castes, had supported the former Lok Dal; and the 'backward' castes of eastern Uttar Pradesh had been behind the old Janata Party. The BJP, the third important party of the region, generally cuts across caste groups; its core support has always been from urban traders, but it has in recent years successfully mobilized support around religious appeals in specific parts of the state.

What happened in the 1989 election was that the Congress lost some of its established vote banks. One remarkable, though relatively unheralded, change was the emergence of a new party, the Bahujan Samaj Party (BSP), which caters to the underprivileged groups, especially to the Scheduled Castes but also to the Muslims. This party received nearly 13 per cent of the total vote. While the figure is not all that dramatic, the results were, because the entire 13 per cent probably came out of the Congress's base, supporting the hypothesis that the Congress's failure to follow through on promises to alleviate poverty, and the subsequent abandonment under Rajiv Gandhi of an attitude favouring the poor, may have ended up costing it dearly in electoral support.

The Congress also lost some Muslim support in Uttar Pradesh. While evidence of this is sketchy, Rajiv's flirtation with pro-Hindu themes, and especially his tacit support for the building of the controversial temple in Ayodhya, led important Muslim leaders to announce their opposition to the Congress. The Congress(I) party lost elections in several Muslim-dominated constituencies. V.P. Singh's firm secular stand probably attracted some Muslim support, although the Janata Dal's tacit alignment with the BJP suggests that such a stance may prove to be temporary.

In contrast to the Congress, both the Janata Dal and the BJP not only maintained their traditional power bases but were also able to broaden them. The Janata Dal benefited from the vote of the Thakurs, a significant elite caste of Uttar Pradesh to which V.P. Singh himself belongs. The BJP, as one would expect, used pro-Hindu themes to expand its base. Equally or possibly even more important was the simple fact of opposition unity: the BJP and the Janata Dal posed one-on-one contests with the Congress for nearly all of the Lok Sabha seats. Add to this the fact that the Scheduled Caste vote for the Congress declined, and the puzzle of why the Congress lost a state like Uttar Pradesh becomes less of a puzzle.

In states like West Bengal in the northeast and Gujarat in the northwest, the pattern was somewhat different. West Bengal was one of the few states in which the incumbents increased their popularity, with the CPI(M) gaining both votes and seats in the Lok Sabha. This continued hold on power by the CPI(M) in West Bengal is in part due to the fact that the Congress is deeply factionalized in the region, but it also reflects the moderately effective performance of the CPI(M) in power: a well-disciplined party has consolidated an alliance between the middle and lower rural strata by implementing mild reforms, and at the same time it has maintained a fairly pragmatic attitude towards businesspeople. In Gujarat, by contrast, the Congress, which had put together a fairly similar ruling coalition of the middle and lower strata, made a mess of it. The Congress failed to consolidate the ruling coalition, both because the party organization was non-existent and because reforms were not implemented. The resulting power vacuum in Gujarat has increasingly been filled by the BJP, which has successfully transformed caste conflicts into communal issues, mobilized Hindus as a bloc, and chipped away at the Congress's traditional alliance. The result was that the Congress's share of the popular vote in this traditional stronghold declined by nearly 16 per cent between 1984 and 1989. The Congress won only 3 Lok Sabha seats to the BJP's 12 and the Janata Dal's 11 in the 1989 election.

The south does not present an undifferentiated picture either. The Congress, for example, did well in both Andhra Pradesh and Karnataka, but the underlying dynamics in the two states were quite different. The Congress's share of the popular vote in Karnataka declined by some 3 per cent, whereas the number of seats that it controls in the Lok Sabha went from 24 to 27 (out of a total of 28). The main reason for this outcome was that the opposition fought against the Congress as two parties rather than as one. Andhra Pradesh, by contrast, provides a much starker picture of a vote against the incumbents. N.T. Rama Rao and his Telugu Desam Party (TDP) lost nearly 10 per cent of the popular vote between 1984 and 1989. While some of this decline was caused by growing caste conflict within the Telugu Desam coalition, it was mainly a result of N.T. Rama Rao's inept and arbitrary rule. After several years of empty promises, the film-actor-turned-politician lost some of his electoral magic.

THE PROSPECTS FOR THE NEW GOVERNMENT

The transfer of power from Rajiv Gandhi and his Congress(I) party to V.P. Singh's coalition government was relatively smooth, emphasizing once again the strength of India's democracy. No sooner were the election results known than Rajiv Gandhi accepted the defeat gracefully and resigned. Even though the Congress(I) party remained the largest group in parliament, it was clear that it could not muster enough support from other parties to form a government. India's president thus called upon the leader of the next-largest party in parliament, V.P. Singh of the Janata Dal, to form a government and to demonstrate within 30 days that he controlled a majority in parliament. With BJP and CPI(M)-led Left Front support, he did so on 21 December 1989.

How well India will be governed by this minority government is a question that many would like to have answered. While predictions of political trends are at best hazardous, some tendencies are easier to discern than others. The answer can be separated into three components: the deeper political trends; the prospects of stability of the new government; and, assuming some stability, the minority government's likely performance.

As already discussed, the underlying political trends in India have been the steady weakening of well-established institutions and the increased mobilization of diverse political groups. Most political analysts understand that such trends do not augur well for long-term stability. This is not to suggest that threats to India's political stability are imminent. Several factors suggest that the Indian polity has considerable resilience: democracy has been practiced for nearly forty years, and the more it is practiced, the firmer tend to be its roots; there is considerable talent in India's ruling circles, both in the bureaucracy and among the political elite; protest and violence in one part of India do not readily spread to other parts; the macroeconomic performance continues to be satisfactory; and the last line of defense, the armed forces, remains efficient, coherent, and largely apolitical. At the same time, however, it would be foolish to be too sanguine about India's growing political problems: major centrist parties are not really political parties in terms of organization, discipline, and programmes; there is growing politicization of the bureaucracy, the judiciary, and even the armed forces; instances of caste, class, religious and ethnic conflict are growing; and the use of force and violence in politics has become common.

These problematic long-term trends will be difficult to reverse, especially for a minority government. It is hard to visualize either the Congress(I) or the Janata Dal becoming a coherent and well-organized party in the near future. Without parties and programmes, the capacity of leaders to create durable ruling coalitions will remain weak, as will their capacity to translate electoral mandates into specific policy outcomes. It is also difficult to imagine that political groups in India will somehow become less active. Mobilization is only in part fuelled by economics; what really fuels political activism in India is competitive politics aimed at securing access to the state and to state resources. Chances are, therefore, that levels of mobilized political activity will remain high, major political institutions like parties will remain weak, and, as more and more groups make demands, the polity will be characterized by a fair amount of turbulence.

The hardest thing to predict in India's new political situation is how long the minority government will last. Many observers, including some of the Janata Dal's senior advisers, feel that a mid-term poll is likely; they expect that V.P. Singh will call elections sometime in 1992 with the hope of enlarging his power base. Whether this comes to pass or not, such anticipations help put boundaries on the likely range of political fluctuations. The new government does seem to have staying power, for several reasons: V. P. Singh has emerged as the pre-eminent leader within the Janata Dal; the antipathy to the Congress will facilitate unity, at least for a short while; both the CPI(M) and the BJP want to use this opportunity to secure their own political goals;

and all the parties are exhausted from the recent elections and would just as soon wait, regroup, and get ready to fight in the near, rather than the immediate, future.

In its early actions the new government has sought to build on the minimal consensus that can be found among its diverse supporters. An important example of this is the partial freeing of television and radio from direct government control by establishing them as autonomous public corporations. The elections in several states in February 1990 further confirmed the popularity of non-Congress parties, especially the BJP, and thus generally strengthened the government vis-à-vis the Congress. And the budget for 1990–1 definitely reflects the capacity of the government and its supporters to work together on important issues.

Against these positive tendencies, however, must be set a number of destabilizing possibilities. At the time of this writing, in early 1990, very few observers think it likely that the minority government will last the full five-year term. A number of conditions militate against such an outcome: the BJP and the CPI(M) are likely to find it very difficult to publicly agree on such major and pressing policy issues as how to deal with political conflicts involving religious divisions, such as the conflicts in Kashmir and Punjab; it is not in the interest of either the BJP or the CPI(M) to sit calmly by and support the Janata Dal while V.P. Singh uses his stint in power primarily as a vehicle to improve his own and his party's position of power; the BJP's impressive performance in the state elections of February 1990 is likely to lead it to want more from the central government, thus pushing the CPI(M) farther from the ruling coalition; and the arithmetic of the current Lok Sabha is such that the Congress can form an alternative government with the help of the BJP, the CPI(M), or even a rump of the Janata Dal—one led, for example, by Devi Lal and Chandrashekhar.

The minority government in power is not likely to be a very effective performer. If Rajiv Gandhi, with his huge electoral majority in late 1984, was unable to translate popularity into effective policies, how likely is it that a minority government will perform better? The actions that the new government undertakes are likely to be those on which not only the government but also the CPI(M) and the BJP agree. Such policies as depoliticizing television and radio, decentralizing some power to the states, and minimizing political interference in the bureaucracy will find broad support. Beyond these, however, the real problem of the new government is likely to be inaction, born of the underlying absence of agreement on policy preferences.

As one looks ahead, therefore, there is no reason to expect crises and breakdown, but there are a fair number of reasons to be concerned about India's political future. The best possible outcome would be if—with the decline of the Congress's hegemony and the beginning of a period of alignments and realignments—the new arrangement that emerges were more truly democratic than past governments in the sense of being more truly representative of India's political heterogeneity. Before one gets from here to there, however, the prognosis for the near future is not good: the minority government is not very stable; even if it survives, its performance is not likely to be impressive; and the long-term political trends are towards institutional fragmentation and growing levels of mobilization of political activity. The most likely near future, therefore, is that India will remain a lively democracy but that this democracy, in terms both of absorbing conflict and of generating effective policies, will continue to muddle through at a low level of efficacy.

II

Political Economy

The essays in this section should be read in conjunction with the Introduction to the volume, especially the discussion on political economy. The focus in this section is on the political determinants of growth and distributional patterns in India. The essay entitled 'India's Fragmented-Multiclass State and Protected Industrialization' is drawn from my book *State-Directed Development* (2004). It provides an overview of the state's role in promoting and hindering industrial growth in India. Unlike neo-liberal accounts of Indian political economy, I argue that growth patterns in India have been influenced, not so much by more or less state intervention, as by the type and quality of state intervention.

This emphasis on state capacity as a determinant of economic outcomes runs through the other essays in this section as well. In the essay, 'Politics of Economic Liberalization in India' I analyse various political obstacles that stymied Rajiv Gandhi's efforts to liberalize India's economy in the second half of the 1980s. Since similar efforts succeeded in the early 1990s, the changing role of business groups in economic policy making in India is especially worthy of serious study. This theme is analysed in much greater detail in the two part essay on the 'Politics of Economic Growth in India'. The focus in these essays is on how best to understand the growth upsurge in India since about 1980. I argue that this is best understood by focusing on the growing alliance between the state and private capital in India.

The focus in the final essay 'Regime Types and Poverty Reform in India' shifts from growth to redistributive issue. This essay was written earlier than all the essays on politics of economic growth; it provides a summary of my 1987 book, *The State and Poverty in India*. As with the other essays in this volume, it is reproduced here in its original form, without any updating. In this essay I argue that the success or failure of poverty alleviation efforts in

India reflects the organizational cohesion and the class basis of ruling regimes. Better organized regimes with a broader social base are thus more effective at reducing poverty. I demonstrate this argument by comparing political efforts at poverty alleviation in West Bengal, Karnataka, and Uttar Pradesh. I have recently updated this earlier study and the related argument has been summarized in the Introduction to this volume.

5

India's Fragmented-Multiclass State and Protected Industrialization*

Sovereign India's experiment with state-led economic growth has produced mixed results. Between 1950 and 1980 the Indian economy grew at a sluggish per annum rate of 3–3.5 per cent, but accelerated to nearly 6 per cent per annum thereafter (see Table 5.1). Nonetheless, this performance of the sovereign state was a considerable improvement over the nearly stagnant colonial economy, especially the pre-1930 period. At the same time, this growth compares unfavourably, especially with that of South Korea but also Brazil, suggesting the need to scrutinize the role of the state in the Indian economy. As for industrial growth, it fluctuated from over 7 per cent in the first fifteen years, to below 4 per cent during 1965–80 and then back again to nearly 6 per cent per annum between 1980 and 2000. There was also considerable structural transformation over the five decades: while agriculture contributed more than half and industry less than 10 per cent of the national product at independence in 1947, towards the end of the century a diversified industrial sector contributed nearly one-quarter and the service sector nearly one-half of the whole.

This chapter focuses on the political determinants of economic performance in India, especially rates and patterns of industrialization, raising questions about the design and the capacity of India's highly interventionist state. Given the mixed outcome, the puzzles for analysis are both why the Indian economy has done as well as it has and why it has not done better. In keeping with the central themes of the study, the main concern is with the state's role, specifically, how the dynamics of a fragmented-multiclass state influenced economic choices and performance.

*Originally published as 'India's Fragmented-Multiclass State and Protected Industrialization', in Atul Kohli, *State-Directed Development, Political Power and Industrialization in the Global Periphery*, New York: Cambridge University Press, 2004, pp. 257–90.

TABLE 5.1: Some Basic Growth Data, 1950–2000
(all figures in percentage per annum)

	1950–64	1965–79	1980–2000
GDP growth	3.7	2.9	5.8
Industrial growth	7.4	3.8	6.2
Agricultural growth	3.1	2.3[a]	3.0
Gross investment/GDP	13	18	23

Source: Government of India, Economic Survey (various issues). Due to numerous statistical complications, these figures should be viewed as broadly indicative rather than as exact or definitive.
Note: [a]Figures are for 1967–80. Inclusion of the two drought years 1964–5 and 1965–6 would make this average figure even lower.

The scholarly scope of this chapter is broad and sweeping in quality, necessarily leading to neglect of nuances and of controversies relevant for a country specialist. I note at the outset that India's political economy can be interpreted from at least two distinct standpoints, only one of which is emphasized below. A more neo-liberal interpretation would suggest that India's lackluster performance results from the sluggish economic growth that followed from the closed and statist model of development adopted by India's misguided nationalist and socialist leaders. According to this line of thinking, the last two liberalizing decades have led to some improvement— higher rates of economic growth and a lower rate of poverty in India.[1] While there are valuable insights in such a perspective, it is not wholly consistent with the facts and it reflects a worldview that this study does not share.

I argue instead that the Achilles' heel of Indian political economy is not so much its statist model of development as the mismatch between that statist model and the limited capacity of the state to guide social and economic change. There have been statist models in other parts of the world that achieved important gains, but they were generally directed by more efficacious states. The cohesive-capitalist cases of South Korea and Brazil both represent models of the Right; the cohesive-lower-class model of communist China is a case on the Left. Trying to reconcile political preferences of both Left and Right in the context of a fragmented state, the Indians failed both at radical redistribution and at ruthless capitalism-led economic growth. The socialist commitment of Indian leaders, for example, was rather shallow. While socialist rhetoric was used to try to build political capital, policies in favour of the poor were seldom pursued vigorously. Such socialist commitments as were pursued, albeit ineffectively, also alienated private

[1]One recent collection that broadly reflects this standpoint is Isher Judge Ahluwalia and I.M.D. Little (eds), India's Economic Reforms and Development: Essays for Manmohan Singh, New Delhi: Oxford University Press, 1998.

investors. The associated difficulties in state-business relations also hurt economic growth. The change in India over the last two decades is not so much that it became more liberal as that Indian politics shifted towards the Right, allowing for more harmonious state-business relations and a positive impact on growth. But at the same time the politicized political exclusion of the poor made governance more difficult and fed neo-fascist tendencies, including the mobilization of nationalism against minorities.

I have divided the discussion of modern India's political economy into three chronological phases: the Nehru era (approximately 1950–64), the era of Indira Gandhi (approximately 1965 to the early 1980s), and the last two decades of the twentieth century, during which numerous governments have come and gone. This division reflects a trend whereby political changes seem to have influenced rates and patterns of industrialization. Thus, I suggest that the state's considerable legitimacy and relatively clear economic priorities in the Nehru period facilitated some economic gains. By contrast, Indira Gandhi's populism hurt investment and growth. And finally, the political drift towards the Right in the third phase has been accompanied by a growing role of the private sector in the economy and improved economic performance.

THE NEHRU ERA

If the 1940s in India are best thought of as the decade in which India marked the transition from colonialism to a sovereign democratic republic, the Nehru era that followed is usefully viewed as the crucible of modern India. It was during this era that a stable democracy took root and the hegemony of a statist model of economic development was established.

Indians by now take their democracy for granted, as if it were the most obvious way of organizing state power in a poor, multiethnic, continent-sized country. Viewed comparatively, however, as well as against the most popular theories that treat democracy as a function of economic advancement, India's democracy is a puzzle.[2] At a minimum the survival of democracy in India suggests that, under specific conditions, a country's political structures enjoy some autonomy from the underlying society and economy. The roots of Indian democracy and of its fragmented-multiclass state thus need to be understood in terms of institutional continuities, including the British political inheritance and, in particular, a relatively centralized and coherent state,[3] with its well-developed civil bureaucracy, its limited but real experience of

[2]For a fuller discussion of this puzzle, see Atul Kohli (ed.), *The Success of India's Democracy*, Cambridge: Cambridge University Press, 2001, especially the introduction.

[3]Those who do not see a ready connection between centralized authority and democracy may consider Samuel Huntington's important argument that 'order' nearly always precedes 'democracy'. See Samuel Huntington, *Political Order in Changing Societies*, New Haven: Yale University Press, 1968.

elections and of constitutional, parliamentary government, and its traditions of independent media and freedom of such associations as labour unions.

Since inheritance is seldom destiny, India, like many other post-colonial countries, could readily have squandered these valuable political resources. Yet it did not. Besides colonial inheritance, therefore, one must underline the constructive political role of India's nationalist movement/party, the Indian National Congress, and of India's leaders in the evolution of the democratic state. In its quest for freedom from British rule, the Congress not only brought together a variety of Indian elites but also established numerous links between elites and the masses, which defined the framework within which India's democracy advanced. India's leaders adopted mass suffrage, committed themselves to a parliamentary democracy, permitted the emergence of a variety of political voices and organizations, and conducted the internal affairs of their hegemonic party in a democratic and inclusive manner.[4]

This combination of a protodemocratic colonial inheritance and a democratically inclined mass nationalist movement provided the institutional preconditions for the emergence of democracy in India. But the political preconditions also helped to lay the foundation for the emergence of a fragmented-multiclass state. The Indian case thus raises the important question: Does democracy in a developing country necessarily lead to fragmented state power with a multiclass social base? The Indian case indeed suggests a strong association between democracy and a fragmented-multiclass state. But as no single case tells us that much about a general relationship, one must be wary of confusing association with causation. For every India, for example, there is also a Malaysia, with less fragmented state authority. And even if democratization in a developing country tends to encourage fragmented-multiclass states, the reverse is certainly not the case: state power in many authoritarian situations can also be fragmented and rest on a plural class base. Most important for the immediate discussion, certain specific political developments during the Nehru period helped consolidate India's democracy while also reinforcing the state's fragmented-multiclass nature.

The colonial bureaucracy that India's leaders inherited was a fine professional force, especially the elite ICS officers, but it was mainly a law and order bureaucracy, not well suited to implement the leaders' ambitious developmental goals. A major overhaul of the bureaucracy, though contemplated, was never really pursued, mainly because the well-trained elite civil servants were indispensable for governing the new state.[5] The size

---

[4]For a good study of how and why the Indian National Congress—even though a single, hegemonic party—facilitated Indian democracy, see Rajni Kothari, *Politics of India*, Boston: Little, Brown, 1970.

[5]For a good study of continuity in the nature and the structure of the pre- and post-independence higher civil service in India, see David C. Potter, *India's Political Administrators:*

of the civil service, including the officer ranks, also grew substantially during the Nehru years. Though renamed the Indian Administrative Services (IAS), the new service reflected the structure of the ICS and still relied for staffing on a highly competitive exam that mainly tested general rather than specialist knowledge. The small fraction of candidates who passed the exam were then trained in more or less the same way as ICS officers had been—first in an institute and then on the job, apprenticing under more senior officers. To keep up the old esprit de corps, many of the ICS traditions were maintained, including the idea that elite civil servants constituted the steel frame that anchored India's political stability. Internal promotions were made on the basis of merit and seniority, and an independent supervisory body helped to maintain the level of professionalism, essentially until the late 1960s, when the IAS became more politicized. The IAS also adopted the core structure of the old ICS, namely, district officers who were responsible for revenue and law and order; new development functions were merely add-ons.

Upon independence, India's leaders faced a cruel choice: advancing the state either as an effective agent of political order or as a successful facilitator of economic development. They opted for the former, which would become a longer-term trend, prioritizing political needs over economic ones and thus initiating what would eventually become a substantial gap between the state's capacities and its developmental ambitions. A similar mismatch came to characterize the Congress party as it sought to be simultaneously a popular ruling party and an agent of socialist development.[6] The majority of Indians lived in the countryside, and most of them operated within a variety of patron–client relationships. One ready way to build political support in such a social setting was to cultivate the support of the patrons—generally the highest, landowning elite castes—who, in turn, could sway the political behaviour of their dependent clients, generally poor peasants. And this is precisely what the party did, building long chains of patronage that extended from the centre to the periphery. This ensured a popular base—at least for a decade or two—but eventually also led to the capture of the party by society's powerful. In this way, more egalitarian ambitions, such as land redistribution and the capacity to tax the agrarian sector, were diluted.

From ICS to IAS, New Delhi: Oxford University Press, 1996. I draw on this study in the next paragraph, especially chapters 3 and 4.

[6]For a fuller discussion of some such issues, see Francine Frankel, *India's Political Economy, 1947–1977: The Gradual Revolution*, Princeton, N.J.: Princeton University Press, 1978, especially chapters 5 and 6. A much more detailed treatment of how the early Congress party 'succeeded' is Myron Weiner, *Party Building in a New Nation*, Chicago: University of Chicago Press, 1967, especially chapter 22.

Another significant political development concerned the evolution of Indian federalism.[7] Soon after India won its sovereignty, each of its numerous ethnic groups began demanding a greater share of power. These struggles came to a head in the late 1950s, when a reluctant Nehru agreed to a linguistic reorganization of Indian federalism. Although this decision accommodated ethnic demands and created a more stable political unit, it also fragmented state power. To the extent that developmental ambitions of India's leaders found institutional expressions—such as the Planning Commission—these were nearly all at the centre. By contrast, lower-level governments were mainly 'machines' with significant powers and resources. While India's central state continued to be quite powerful in relation to its federal units, a federal reorganization of functions also diluted the state's overall capacity to pursue a coherent developmental agenda.

The ruling ideology of the Congress party provides a final example of the mismatch between capacity and ambitions. Congress committed itself to 'nationalism' and 'socialism'—Nehru's creed, which won substantial popularity and legitimacy for him and the party. At the same time, however, these ideological commitments made it difficult to pursue vigorous economic growth, a goal that Congress and the state elites also espoused. In spite of the socialist rhetoric, India was mainly a private-enterprise economy. Vigorous economic growth would be feasible only if there were a vigorous private sector. But the Indian version of multiclass statism found itself at odds with its espoused goals: Nationalism discouraged foreign enterprise in India, and the socialist inclination created difficult relations with Indian entrepreneurs.

Taken together, these political developments during the Nehru era suggest two conclusions. First, there was significant continuity between the colonial state and the sovereign Indian state, even as there were many obvious discontinuities—that the new state was sovereign, democratic and interventionist. The areas of continuity include, most strikingly, the design of the new civil service but also the organization of the legal system and of the armed forces. The latter was especially consequential for helping to ensure civilian control of the relatively apolitical military, a complex story beyond the scope of this study.[8] A more subtle area of continuity was the pattern of the state's alliances with the property-owning elites. The colonial state had rested its

---

[7]A ready and useful overview is Bipan Chandra, Mridula Mukherjee, and Aditya Mukherjee, *India after Independence, 1974–2000*, New Delhi: Penguin, 2000, chapters 8–10. For Nehru's views on this and a host of other related issues, the indispensable source remains S. Gopal, *Jawaharlal Nehru: A Biography*, vols 2 and 3, New Delhi: Oxford University Press, 1984.

[8]This is a surprisingly under-studied area of scholarship on Indian politics. Perhaps 'dogs that do not bark' attract less attention than the ones that do, but probably not justifiably. One study that does address this issue explicitly is Stephen P. Cohen, *The Indian Army: Its Contribution to the Development of a Nation*, Berkeley: University of California Press, 1971.

power with landowning traditional elites and generally had a good working relationship with Indian business groups. While Nehru clearly had a broader social base, the power alliances of India's new rulers with propertied groups also demonstrated remarkable continuities. While it is true that the mega-traditional elites such as the maharajas and the zamindars were eliminated, the Congress rulers still based their rural power on landowning elites, albeit smaller landowners, a 'lower' gentry of sorts.

Second, Nehru and his colleagues placed a high priority on consolidating Indian democracy. They thus incorporated society's powerful and conceded some power to demanding regional elites, but they also encouraged the hopes of the masses by promising egalitarian development to the poor. Although these strategies helped to institutionalize India's fragile democracy, at the same time, the resulting political developments also institutionalized the fragmented and multiclass political tendencies of the Indian state and undermined its capacity to pursue developmental goals vigorously. Was this outcome inevitable?

This is a difficult question to answer unambiguously. Certainly, the power to undertake some basic changes existed, as there was nothing inevitable in the degree of state fragmentation and in the lack of focus in the state's developmental priorities. At the same time, however, the nationalist movement was already straining and losing its way as it sought to create unity in diversity prior to independence. Nehru's specific decisions aimed at maintaining a stable and legitimate democracy in a heterogeneous society further weakened this potential in the post-independence period. Maintaining a 'law and order' bureaucracy hurt the state's capacity to undertake economic tasks directly; a commitment to nationalism and socialism made it difficult to mobilize private capital; and the Congress party's dependence on regional and rural elites fragmented state power, making it difficult to penetrate the rural society directly.

The economic model adopted during the Nehru era was, of course, the well-known model of state-led, import-substituting industrialization (ISI). Once adopted, it endured, even in the face of significant efforts in recent years towards a different model. At the end of the twentieth century, India still exhibited some of the core characteristics of its statist model of development—thus underlining the political nature of India's early economic choices.[9]

Nehru's political preferences, expressed through the Congress party, became India's dominant ideas and stressed the following: maintaining

[9]Good studies of this topic include A.H. Hanson, *The Process of Planning*, London: Oxford University Press, 1966; Jagdish N. Bhagwati and Padma Desai, *India: Planning for Industrialization*, London: Oxford University Press, 1970; and Baldev Raj Nayar, *India's Mixed Economy*, Bombay: Popular Prakashan, 1989.

national sovereignty, the superiority of the state in steering progressive capitalist development, and the need for India's poor to share in the fruits of development. The nationalist commitments of India's leaders translated into a suspicion of an open economy and a preference for heavy industry. In spite of low domestic savings, foreign investors were by and large discouraged, mainly because they might have threatened hard-won national sovereignty. A variety of interests, including Indian business groups, benefited from these ideological choices over time and helped to sustain them. A suspicion of an open trading regime is more difficult to understand in terms of underlying nationalism. Protectionism was justified mainly in terms of prevailing economic ideas of 'export pessimism' and 'infant industry'.[10] In the Indian case, however, there was also something deeply experiential and political about these choices. We have seen that openness during the colonial era had been interpreted by nationalists, not only as killing nascent industries, but also as inhibiting the emergence of indigenous industrial capitalism. Indian businessmen and industrialists, who stood to benefit from a relatively closed economy in which competition would be limited, expressed these preferences openly. Protectionism, as well as an emphasis on heavy industry, was thus seen as serving the interests of nation building. How else, according to India's leaders, could such an enormous country, with its ancient civilization, re-emerge as a powerhouse that was not easily subject to manipulation by external powers?

Widespread was the belief in the state's ability to guide social and economic change efficaciously at the middle of the twentieth century. We have seen this in the Korean and Brazilian cases. This view had a left-leaning tilt in India, reinforced by an admiration of the Soviet Union's developmental 'successes' and by an affinity to the British Labour Party's type of socialism. These ideological proclivities were also consistent with the concrete interests of the Indian political elite, which could channel some of the fruits of development to themselves and their offspring. The statist model translated into both a direct economic role for the state—as, for example, in the widespread creation of public enterprises—and into a more indirect role in guiding the activities of private capital via the 'license-permit raj [or regime]'.[11] What is surprising in retrospect is not so much India's affinity for statism but how little open discussion took place concerning the type of state that could successfully undertake such ambitious economic tasks. While market imperfections were discussed ad nauseam, there was no parallel discussion

---

[10]A good discussion of the belief systems that supported India's economic choices can be found in Sukhamoy Chakravarty, *Development Planning: The Indian Experience*, New Delhi: Oxford University Press, 1988, chapters 1 and 2.

[11]For a highly critical but excellent description of how this policy 'regime' operated, see Bhagwati and Desai, *India*, especially chapter 13.

of state imperfections from the standpoint of developmental capacity. One wonders whether the discussion was avoided because it would have focused attention on the shortcomings of the rulers.[12]

Finally, a vague commitment to the poor and the downtrodden permeated much of the nationalist political discourse. Gandhi and Nehru in their own ways shared this commitment. It found expression in socialist rhetoric and in policy areas such as land redistribution and the laws governing employment of urban labour. Unlike the commitment to nationalism and statism, however, the commitment to the poor was relatively shallow. India's upper-caste rulers may have meant well, but they were no revolutionaries. Barrington Moore's apt description of Nehru as 'the gentle betrayer of masses'[13] probably applies as well to a fairly broad spectrum of India's political class, though not all of them were always as 'gentle'. How else would one explain the limited political energy devoted to land reform or, for that matter, to promoting widespread access to primary education?[14]

What was the impact of Nehru's economic approach, which was statist in intent and emphasized public investment in heavy industry? The modest economic success of the period brings us back to the twin questions: why, in spite of India's fragmented-multiclass state, was a statist model able to achieve some success and why was the performance not better?

We begin by situating India's initial conditions in a comparative perspective. India's socio-economic conditions at mid-century were probably somewhere between the much more favourable starting point of Korea, or even Brazil, and the considerably worse conditions of, say, Nigeria. On the positive side, India had undergone some industrialization; a small but significant group of indigenous entrepreneurs was in place; banking and other financial institutions existed; and technically trained manpower, though not abundant, was not as scarce as it was in many African and Middle-Eastern countries. The agrarian economy, by contrast, had not grown much over the previous several decades; internal demand was limited; savings were low; experience with managing complex modern production was relatively scarce; and the health and educational conditions of the working population were abysmal. Given these conditions, how well designed was the developmental approach of sovereign India's leaders?

---

[12]To be fair, Nehru did on occasion blame developmental failures on the bureaucracy, though this also conveniently exonerated him and his Congress colleagues for the state's shortcomings. See, for example, Potter, *India's Political Administrators*, p. 2. A number of government reports also analysed administrative weaknesses of the Indian state, though without much impact. See Bhagwati and Desai, *India*, chapter 8.

[13]Barrington Moore, Jr., *Social Origins of Dictatorship and Democracy: Lord and Peasant in the Making of the Modern World*, Boston: Beacon Press, 1966.

[14]See, for example, Myron Weiner, *The Child and the State in India*, Princeton, N.J.: Princeton University Press, 1991, chapter 4.

First, the agricultural sector: Nehru's approach to this sector was mainly 'institutional' in the sense that he and India's economic planners hoped that by tinkering with agrarian relations (via land reforms, for example) and by educating the peasantry (via extension programmes, for example), India's agricultural production would improve.[15] After some significant initial public investments, especially in irrigation, the agricultural sector was therefore more or less ignored at the expense of industry. The results reflected this neglect. Agricultural growth was barely able to stay ahead of population growth. More serious was that much of this growth was extensive and not intensive; that is, it was the result of bringing more land under cultivation, not of improving productivity.

The modest increases in agricultural production thus reflected increasing labour input—growing population—and the use of additional land facilitated in part by new public investments in irrigation. Beyond this, the repeal of a variety of colonial-era taxes on agriculture may have created some incentives for agrarian producers that contributed somewhat to higher rates of production. Conversely, the state's downward penetration was minimal and, hence, so was its capacity to alter agrarian relations.[16] The relative neglect of public investments in better irrigation and higher use of such other agricultural inputs as fertilizers further undermined the prospects of rapid increases in food production. By the mid-1960s, then, India's agricultural sector was on the verge of crisis.

Heavy industry, by contrast, was emphasized by Nehru, who used the tremendous legitimacy he enjoyed to pursue his priorities and translate goals into outcomes. In truth, constructing heavy industry was more readily influenced from the political apex than, say, agriculture or land redistribution. The imposition of substantial tariffs and quotas provided a protected environment in which industry could take root. The bulk of this growth, facilitated by rapidly growing public savings and investment, was in the public sector: further development of electricity, railways, and communication, and in such areas as machineries and steel.

The main source of growing public revenues was indirect taxation, especially of consumer goods. There were, consistent with India's socialist leanings, progressive income tax laws in place, but the government's capacity to collect them was limited—a problem that, over time, would become quite consequential. Indirect taxation sufficed in this early period because the government's non-developmental expenditures were minimal: Nehru's

---

[15]For a good discussion, see Gunnar Myrdal, *Asian Drama*, New York: Pantheon, 1968.

[16]I have analysed this issue of the state's limited downward reach in detail elsewhere. See Atul Kohli, *The State and Poverty in India: The Politics of Reform*, Cambridge: Cambridge University Press, 1987.

government spent little on health and primary education, underlining the superficial quality of India's socialism. Moreover, his considerable legitimacy minimized the need to throw money at one group or another to buy political support. The levels of political mobilization in India were also relatively low at this early stage, with much of the lower-class population deeply enmeshed in traditional patron-client relationships. Hence, public expenditures could stay focused on Nehru's priorities, especially the development of heavy industry, which generated substantial production growth.[17]

Critics of this strategy have documented that this growth was quite expensive, in the sense of being relatively inefficient.[18] Some of the underlying causes are inherent to the nature of public sectors—for example, investment in industries that are not immediately profitable or below-market social pricing of output. But others were specific to India: the role of generalist bureaucrats, ill equipped to manage public sector industries, and/or the growing political interference by lower-level political elites who treated public sector industries as one more resource in their patronage networks. The highly protected environment within which these industries operated also contributed to the accumulating inefficiencies.

The Indian state's attempts to guide the private sector have also been roundly criticized.[19] These criticisms, however, need to be kept in perspective. As the role of private capital in industry at this early stage was not all that significant, the prominent role assigned to the public sector is better understood as providing a substitute for a laggard private sector. After all, India's private sector had hardly flourished in the pre-independence period under nearly free-market conditions. That said, however, the socialistic Nehruvian state—unlike the South Korean state—sought more to tame than to encourage private sector development. State intervention had a decidedly regulatory cast. Instead of asking business what it could do and how the state could help, the state itemized what private business could not do and then raised numerous barriers to what it could do. Implementation, too, was haphazard and inefficient: for example, priority industries were not always the ones that enjoyed maximum protection, and overbearing bureaucrats in charge of licensing often deterred private investors. The growing maze of bureaucratic obstacles to private sector development led over time to corruption and to inefficient allocation of private sector resources.

[17]For a good review, see K.N. Raj, *Indian Economic Growth: Performance and Prospects*, Delhi: Allied Publishers, 1966.

[18]See Bhagwati and Desai, *India*. See also Jagdish N. Bhagwati and T.N. Srinivasan, *India*, New York: National Bureau of Economic Research, distributed by Columbia University Press, 1975.

[19]See Bhagwati and Desai, *India*, esp. pt 6.

The examples of the steel and textile industries help to fill out this broad account of the Nehruvian state's role in promoting public and private sector industries, respectively. The indigenous steel industry was initiated in the first half of the twentieth century by the Tatas.[20] To advance their nation-building goals, Nehru and his political colleagues prioritized the development of steel in the 1950s.[21] But, as in South Korea and Brazil, state elites found the private sector not forthcoming. It is true that in India some private steel industries, such as that of the Tatas, continued to flourish, but given the size, complexity, and risk involved, other private sector start-ups were not on the horizon.[22] Steel, therefore, emerged as the leading candidate for public sector development.

But in India, unlike in South Korea and Brazil, the steel industry grew up relatively inefficient, not very competitive internationally. A blanket condemnation of public sector ownership clearly will not do, as steel in all three cases was developed in the public sector. Rather, the culprit was the differing nature of states and patterns of state intervention. Moreover, the problems in India developed only over time. Under Nehru, substantial public investments were devoted to steel and foreign collaboration was sought to help to establish and manage the steel plants. Competent senior bureaucrats at the Planning Commission were responsible for steel policy, and there were good management practices at the plant level. The overall protected environment generated by the import-substitution policy regime ensured a ready market in an economy in which industrialization had begun in earnest. The result was that steel production in India between 1950–64 grew rapidly at a rate of nearly 11 per cent per annum.

The real problems of the steel industry date to the Indira Gandhi period, when it was starved of new investments and thus of new technology and modernization. It was then that the fragmented-multiclass nature of India's developmental state came to the fore to cause problems for the steel industry. First, locational issues that were politicized by India's federal structure were exacerbated during Indira Gandhi's period. Second, policy making was in

[20]I am indebted to my research assistant, Rina Agarwala, for collecting this information on the steel industry.

[21]A useful recent account of the state's role in India's steel industry is Vibha Pingle, *Rethinking the Developmental State: India's Industry in Comparative Perspective*, New Delhi: Oxford University Press, 1999, chapter 3. Earlier accounts include W.A. Johnson, *The Steel Industry of India*, Cambridge: Harvard University Press, 1966; Padma Desai, *The Bokaro Steel Plant: A Study of Soviet Economic Assistance*, Amsterdam: North-Holland, 1972; and Gilbert Etienne, *Asian Crucible: The Steel Industry in China and India*, New Delhi: Sage, 1992.

[22]Vibha Pingle thus notes that T.T. Krishnamachari, a successful industrialist, Nehru's confidant, and subsequently minister of steel, approached Indian industrialists but in vain. It was only then that he and Nehru were persuaded that the state would have to undertake development of steel in the public sector. See Pingle, *Rethinking the Developmental State*, p. 54.

the hands of generalists, the IAS bureaucrats, whose relations with plant-level management were at best remote and at worst condescending and demoralizing for the technocrats. Third, pricing and distributional policies were politicized, with especially damaging consequences. Steel prices were kept below market price and became a public subsidy to a variety of industries, including private sector industries. Although justified in terms of the needs of rapid industrialization, the policy could be sustained only as long as ample public resources to support such subsidies were available. A critical constraint was the state's limited capacity to undertake direct taxation, especially in the countryside, where formal political penetration was minimal. Controlled prices were also a constraint on steel industry profits, reducing its capacity for self-sustaining investments. As long as steel was a priority sector during the Nehru period, with continuous infusion of new resources, these problems remained manageable, and fairly impressive growth continued.

By contrast, large-scale textile production performed rather poorly in Nehru's India, even though at the time of independence, the textile industry, concentrated in private hands in western India, was not insubstantial. It is possible that with pro-business state intervention and subsidies for exports, India's textile production could have become internationally competitive. This was not to be so, however, and the state's legitimacy-driven policy choices were the root cause.[23] We have seen that Nehru was not especially supportive of private enterprise. And within this framework, textiles faced special obstacles.

Recall that the issue of the destruction of small-scale, household-based textile production at the hands of modern textiles played a central role in India's nationalist imagination. Gandhi successfully exploited *khadi*, or hand-spun cotton, as a tool of political mobilization, as witnessed in the symbolism of the Congress elite donning khadi uniforms and caps. With this political inheritance it would have been very difficult to unleash modern textile manufacturing against small-scale production. Mahatma Gandhi's populist commitment to 'love of the small people' cast a long political shadow on India's textile policy. (While championing khadi, however, Gandhi was simultaneously collecting large dues for the Congress from his close friend, textile manufacturer G.D. Birla.) Add to this Nehru's socialist proclivities,

[23]See, for example, S.R.B. Leadbeater, *The Politics of Textiles: The Indian Cotton Mill Industry and the Legacy of Swadeshi (1900–85)*, New Delhi: Sage Publications, 1993; and Sanjib Misra, 'India's Textile Policy and the Informal Sector', in Stuart Nagel (ed.), *India's Development and Public Polity*, Aldershot Ashgate: Policy Studies Organization, 2000. For analysis of related economic issues, see Howard Pack, *Productivity, Technology and Industrial Development: A Case Study in Textiles*, New York: Oxford University Press, 1987; and Keijiro Otsuka, Gustav Ranis, and Gary Saxonhouse, *Comparative Technology Choice in Development*, Basingstoke, Hampshire: Macmillan, 1988.

which inclined him to argue in favour of producing cheap cloth for mass consumption, and the political factors moulding policy choices start to become comprehensible.

Nehru and his colleagues restricted production of textile mills, taxed them highly, and even priced a part of their output below market prices so as to provide cheap cloth for poor consumers. Contrast this pattern of intervention with the one encountered in Korea and Brazil, where state intervention was often supportive of producers, though the political framework necessary for that support was also much narrower and more repressive. This contrast also underlines a central argument of this study, namely, that variations in patterns of state intervention are what matters most when trying to understand varying roles that states play in late-late-development. Thus, Nehru's textile policies undermined private and large-scale textile manufacturing in India but encouraged small-scale textile manufacturing, first with hand looms and then with power looms. Support, that is, went for anything that was less than a modern textile mill, with commensurate consequences: output of large mills nearly stagnated, while that of smaller producers grew sharply. The latter were suitable for the low-end market consumption but not for competitive exports.

The story of industrialization in Nehru's India is thus mixed, characterized by notable achievements but also stupendous follies. As demonstrated with examples of steel and textiles, both these successes and limitations are explicable in terms of the underlying patterns of state intervention. Thus, India's 7 per cent industrial growth rate per annum in this period was respectable. But Brazil in the same period—one of the fastest growers in the world and also a democracy with a strict import-substitution policy regime—industrialized at a rate of nearly 10 per cent per annum. This somewhat superior performance also reflected underlying political and policy differences. The rate of investment in Brazil and India in this phase was more or less comparable. The real difference thus was in capital-output ratios, or in the relative efficiency with which capital was invested in the two countries. The roots of this difference, in turn, can be traced back to the fact that Brazilian democracy was considerably less nationalist and mass-based than that of India. Brazilian leaders thus worried less than India's leaders about legitimacy issues of nationalism or redistribution. The clearest manifestations of this greater political room for manoeuvre in Brazil were the closer cooperation between the state and business and the heavy dependence on foreign investment to facilitate import-substitution industrialization. While this strategy was not without its own problems, the advanced technology and management that foreign investors brought to Brazil was an important reason for Brazil's more rapid industrial growth in this early phase.

THE INDIRA GANDHI ERA

If democracy and a nationalist-statist model of economic development took root in India during the Nehru era, the political economy of the Indira Gandhi era that followed is best viewed as one in which India's democracy became more populist and deinstitutionalized, economic rhetoric moved further to the Left, and the gap between the state's developmental capacities and economic goals widened even further, to the detriment of industrial development. Nehru's death in 1964 marked the slow but steady departure of the first generation of nationalist leaders from the political scene. As nationalist legitimacy declined, numerous movements and parties opposing Congress's hegemony emerged. The party's old ruling formula—a mantle of inclusive nationalism and long chains of patronage fed by statism—was increasingly incapable of generating electoral majorities. Either Congress had to come up with a new winning formula or it would give way to other parties. It was Indira Gandhi who stepped in and provided the winning strategy that revived Congress's sagging fortunes. But her populism and top-down deinstitutionalization of the polity further accentuated its fragmented and multiclass character, with significant developmental consequences.

Under Nehru, India had undergone steady industrialization and experienced modest economic growth, but the poor had not benefited very much. Indeed, the spread of commerce and democracy had eroded patron-client ties, making the poor ripe for new forms of political mobilization. A savvy Indira Gandhi understood these changes and capitalized on them,[24] turning 'poverty alleviation' into her central political slogan. This shift to the Left in India's political discourse yielded handsome short-term political dividends. Indira Gandhi became a darling of India's downtrodden, but her popularity, unlike her father's, was not institutionalized. Whereas he had presided over a nationalist party, the daughter found herself opposed by the old, entrenched Congress elite. Her solution: label the old elite enemies of the poor, exploit her popularity to undermine their power, and appoint loyal minions to positions of responsibility. As India's political system thus became increasingly personalistic, well-established patterns of authority within the party were undermined, and the broader process of institutional development in India's democracy was derailed.[25]

---

[24]Good biographical studies of Indira Gandhi include Mary Carras, *Indira Gandhi: In the Crucible of Leadership: A Political Biography*, Boston: Beacon, 1979; and Pupul Jayakar, *Indira Gandhi: An Intimate Biography*, New York: Pantheon, 1992.

[25]This theme of deinstitutionalization of the Indian polity under Indira Gandhi is emphasized and developed in Atul Kohli, *Democracy and Discontent: India's Growing Crisis of Governability*, Cambridge: Cambridge University Press, 1991. See also Atul Kohli (ed.), *India's Democracy: An Analysis of Changing State–Society Relations*, Princeton, N.J.: Princeton University

The logic of this process of personalization of power was inexorably deinstitutionalizing. Challenged in an increasingly contentious polity, Indira Gandhi not only eliminated her challengers but also weakened the institutions that enabled such challengers to emerge: she tampered with appointments in the civil service and the courts, dismissed 'troublesome' chief ministers, and demanded absolute loyalty from supporters. As a result, the professionalism of the bureaucracy, the independence of the legal system, the functioning of the national parliament and the autonomy of the regional units within the national federation were all adversely affected.

The changing nature of the bureaucracy is especially noteworthy. Though slow and not dramatic, the changes were nevertheless significant, mainly in the direction of undermining the professionalism of the civil service that India inherited from the British. The size of the IAS continued to grow throughout this period, quadrupling between 1950 and 1983.[26] This reflected the overall growth of the public sector, in which employment grew from some four million in 1953 to ten million in 1983. By the end of this period, the IAS employed some 4,000 officers, about 15 per cent of whom served in New Delhi, 25 per cent in the districts, some 10 per cent in public sector enterprises, and the remaining 50 per cent in various state capitals. The basic structure of the IAS in terms of its size within the overall public service or in terms of its distribution across various types of jobs (with the significant exception of public sector enterprises, of course) did not undergo any dramatic changes from earlier times. What changed instead was the diminishing degree to which the IAS was insulated from the broader society, the erosion of professional criteria for internal promotion, and a greater premium placed on connections and loyalty to politicians for securing desirable positions. To some extent these changes reflected the expected indigenization of a colonial state, but they also reflected the priorities of the political elite, as holding on to power became an end in itself.

So, too, Indira Gandhi focused less on matters economic and more on maintaining power. Nehru's statist model of economic development thus essentially continued without major change. Within the framework of continuity, economic policy changes during this era were mainly of two types: a major shift in agricultural policy that had a benign long-term impact on food production and a variety of left-leaning changes that reflected Indira Gandhi's political calculus but helped neither economic growth nor redistribution.

Press, 1988. For a somewhat different interpretation, see Lloyd Rudolph and Susanne Rudolph, *In Pursuit of Lakshmi*, Chicago: University of Chicago Press, 1987.

    [26]The factual information here is drawn from David Potter, *India's Political Administrators*, chapter 4.

Looked at broadly, this was an era of missed economic opportunities in India at a time when other countries exploited such opportunities. From the mid-1960s on, the global economy became more open to manufactured exports from developing countries,[27] and countries as diverse as South Korea and Brazil sought to take advantage of such global shifts. These countries, of course, came to be ruled by military dictators who prioritized economic growth and sought export promotion as an additional strategy. By contrast, India, after a brief flirtation with devaluation in 1966, moved in nearly the opposite direction, becoming more and more obsessed with 'politics'.[28] Indira Gandhi's personalistic governance led India down a path on which democracy was maintained, though tenuously, but on which economic policies became further politicized. And the gap between the state's economic rhetoric and its capacity to implement grew only wider.

A set of agricultural policies adopted in the mid-1960s eventually produced India's 'green revolution'. Insofar as these policies sought to concentrate production inputs in the hands of landowning classes in some regions of India, they did not readily fit in with Indira Gandhi's populist designs. Why and how were these policies adopted?[29] First, they were adopted in the mid-1960s, just before Indira Gandhi's full embrace of 'poverty alleviation' in the late 1960s. More important, India faced severe food shortages in 1965 and 1966, which made the country more open to seeking ways to boost food production and temporarily more dependent on food aid, especially from the United States. The United States favoured green revolution policies and pressured India to adopt them in exchange for aid. But the adoption of these policies was such a politically sensitive matter, in terms of both external dependence and possible distributional consequences, that policies were essentially adopted by a handful of the political elite as executive decisions rather than through any open political discussion.

Various other social and economic policies adopted by Indira Gandhi in the 1970s were aimed at legitimizing populist politics. While the significance of some of these was more symbolic, others turned out to be quite economically consequential. Among the more symbolic—and thus politically consequential—were the removal of privileges that Indian government

[27]See, for example, W. Arthur Lewis, *The Evolution of the International Economic Order*, Princeton, NJ: Princeton University Press, 1977, chapter 6. See also W. Arthur Lewis, *Dynamic Factors in Economic Growth*, Bombay: Orient Longman for the Dorab Tata Memorial Lecture Series, 1974.

[28]For a discussion of the brief experiment with devaluation, see Bhagwati and Srinivasan, *India*.

[29]For a good account, see John P. Lewis, *India's Political Economy: Governance and Reform*, New Delhi: Oxford University Press, 1995, chapter 4. See also Frankel, *India's Political Economy*, chapter 7.

hitherto provided to Indian princes. More economically consequential, Indira Gandhi intensified the rhetoric but also to some extent the efforts to implement land reforms. Land redistribution was a fairly central component of the new 'poverty alleviation' strategy, though the actual impact was quite limited.[30] Similarly, the nationalization of the banks was supposed to 'democratize' lending and so was popular among Indira Gandhi's constituents.

Among the economically most consequential policy developments, the following had an adverse impact on economic growth. First, Indira Gandhi held her populist coalition together by channelling public resources to numerous interest groups—a case of largess that cut into public investment and hurt economic growth.[31] Second, the radical political rhetoric, some seemingly radical policies, and a new level of labour activism alienated private investors, both domestic and foreign. These policies included restricting the growth of private business and industry, nationalization of banks and threats to nationalize other industries. And third, India's closer political links with the Soviet Union and a parallel distancing from the West made it difficult for the Indian economy to derive benefits that might come from further integration with more dynamic economies.

With Indira Gandhi's addition of populism to the statist model of development, the gap between the state's ambitions and capacities that had already existed in Nehru's India grew even wider, and India's fragmented-multiclass developmental state became even less developmental. For example, Indira Gandhi raised the expectations that her policies would help to alleviate poverty—a demanding task that would have required high rates of economic growth, some effective redistribution, and the capacity to penetrate and reorganize the rural society. This demanding task, in turn, would have required a cohesive political party and bureaucracy. Indira Gandhi, however, achieved the opposite, by further deinstitutionalizing the Congress party, further fragmenting the state's authority structure and undermining the professionalism of the bureaucracy. And instead of enhanced public investment in agriculture, infrastructure, public sector industries, and education and health, the state's resources were increasingly directed at buying political support. With growing politicization, the bureaucracy and public enterprises simply deteriorated. And finally, the state simply did not support the private sector and became increasingly anti-capital, with predictable negative results for investment and growth.

As is evident in the figures in Table 5.1, India's economy did not perform very well between 1965 and 1979. As we have seen, Indira Gandhi's populism

---

[30]For an analysis of related failures, see Kohli, *State and Poverty in India*.

[31]See Pranab Bardhan, *The Political Economy of Development in India*, New Delhi: Oxford University Press, 1998.

especially hurt industrial growth. The intervening links need to be clarified, but first a few comments on the agricultural sector. Indira Gandhi's agricultural strategy, adopted under conditions of crisis and external pressure, concentrated agricultural investment in providing better seeds and fertilizer to regions with assured irrigation, such as the Punjab. Price supports were also provided for food producers, thus shifting the terms of trade somewhat in favour of the countryside.[32] While the distributional consequences were decidedly mixed, the new policies did help to improve agricultural production.

On the face of it, the aggregate figures in Table 5.1 do not support this view: agricultural growth between 1965 and 1979 was lower than in the earlier period. However, much of this new growth was based on higher yields. With the possibility of bringing more land under cultivation more or less exhausted—certainly without major public investments in irrigation—productivity-based food growth was essential to feed the growing population. Dramatic increases in wheat production undergirded this new growth, pulling India back from the brink of famine and mass starvation. The state intervened massively to support those property-owning elites who were most likely to generate economic growth, with benign consequences for production. While state intervention was a result of a crisis and though the intervention was concentrated in the agrarian rather than the industrial sector, this alliance of the state and the propertied class is reminiscent of the East Asian cohesive-capitalist state. Over time even the industrial sector moved in this direction but not before a significant populist interregnum and not without being pressed by yet other economic crises.

Industrial growth in India decelerated sharply during 1965–79, leading some observers to dub this an era of 'stagnation'.[33] The underlying cause was mainly declining investment, but there were also accumulating inefficiencies, and both of these, in turn, can be traced back to growing populism. While the rate of investment for this period (see Table 5.1) was higher than in the earlier period, a more disaggregated picture clarifies the apparent contradiction. The higher aggregate rate mostly reflected savings (and thus assumed investment) in the household sector, where the majority of non-consumed resources were maintained in the form of physical assets and were therefore not readily translated into investments with high rates of return. More

[32]For a useful discussion of the politics of agricultural policy, especially of issues surrounding debates on terms of trade within India, see Ashutosh Varshney, *Democracy, Development, and the Countryside: Urban-Rural Struggles in India*, New York: Cambridge University Press, 1995.

[33]See, for example, Isher Judge Ahluwalia, *Industrial Growth in India: Stagnation since the Mid-Sixties*, New Delhi: Oxford University Press, 1985.

significant was thus the behaviour of public and corporate savings in this period, both of which decelerated.

The decline in public investments reflected both a failure to add to the revenue base (for example, by taxing new agricultural incomes or by generating surpluses in public enterprises) and growing public expenditures in such 'non-developmental' areas as 'subsidies' aimed at securing political support.[34] This pattern was a direct function of Indira Gandhi's growing populism: she essentially threw public resources at numerous social classes she sought to mobilize. As public investments declined, industrial growth was hurt on both the supply and the demand side.[35] Infrastructure development suffered, for example, creating serious supply bottlenecks for industrial production. And in the steel industry, reduced public investment hurt production directly. On the demand side also, given the weight of the public sector in India's industrial economy, reduced investment shrank the demand for a variety of industrial outputs, thereby discouraging production.

Since public investments in India have not grown in recent years but industrial growth has, it is also important to consider the role of corporate investments in industrial deceleration during the Indira Gandhi era. Corporate investments also slowed down in this period, especially in fixed capital formation. The underlying causes are difficult to discern but can be traced back to declining profitability. Decline in demand in the overall economy was probably partly responsible. Also at play, however, were more directly political factors. Populist and multiclass politics led to steeper corporate taxes and to labour activism, industrial unrest, and higher wages, probably cutting into profitability. There is also the more diffuse impact of a seemingly left-ward turn in national politics on investor behaviour. While difficult to document decisively, investors may have been discouraged by the growing talk of nationalizing business (and the reality of nationalizing some banks), by new policies that sought to limit their growth and areas of investment, and by the adoption of a general anti-business rhetoric.

Finally, whatever investment was taking place was not always efficient. Since there is little evidence that productivity growth in this period was worse than during the Nehru period,[36] much of the industrial deceleration under discussion cannot be attributed to issues of efficiency. Rather, the main culprit was reduced investment, both public and private. Nevertheless, continuing inefficiencies were certainly at least a part of the overall economic scene. A poorly managed and inefficient public sector repeatedly failed to

[34]For such an argument, see Bardhan, *Political Economy of Development in India*.

[35]For details, see Ahluwalia, *Industrial Growth in India*.

[36]Ibid., especially p. 146, for data; Ahluwalia notes that 'productivity growth estimates do not show a worsening of the situation after the mid-sixties.'

generate investable surpluses and thus contributed to a slowing down of industrial growth. A policy framework that did not encourage domestic competition led to misallocation of resources, hurting growth. Capital-output ratios, a rough indicator of efficiency, increased during this period, especially in manufacturing, underlining that, besides the slowdown in investment, investment was simply not being utilized efficiently.

The evolution of the steel and textile industries can further clarify the changes under Indira Gandhi. After considerable growth in the earlier period, steel production in the public sector stagnated during her tenure, especially between 1964 and 1971.[37] Levels of efficiency in the steel industry also remained relatively low. Again, the roots of many of these problems grew out of the new populist politics. For example, in addition to suffering from a war with Pakistan and droughts in the mid-1960s, public investment declined as well because of Indira Gandhi's new political priorities. The results included declining investment in established steel plants. In the words of one analyst, the steel industry suffered in this period because of 'the state's lack of investment in technological upgrading and plant maintenance and poor plant management.'[38] The problems of an investment-starved industry were exacerbated by low, government-imposed steel prices—again justified in terms of 'socialism'—that deprived firms of internal savings for investment and modernization. And finally, among the political roots of the problems of steel industry was the power of politicized labour. Well-organized unions affiliated with and empowered by the ruling party essentially squeezed the managers of public sector firms, leading to numerous rigidities and inefficiencies.

The problems in textile production, dominated by the private sector, also continued in this period and were probably exacerbated.[39] Controls on the growth of the organized mill sector persisted and were made even more restrictive in the name of protecting handlooms and small producers. The same logic was extended to power looms, a hitherto growing segment of the industry, that had started filling the production space between mills and handlooms. Large mills, moreover, were obliged to provide a significant portion of their output to poor consumers at controlled prices. When less-efficient producers faltered, Indira Gandhi nationalized them. These mills did not perform better in the public sector, at least in part because they were burdened with producing regulated cloth for the low end of the market. Import of new technology was also restricted in order to deal with balance-

---

[37]See the references in note 21.

[38]See Vibha Pingle, *Rethinking the Developmental State*, p. 61.

[39]See, for example, D.U. Sastry, *The Cotton Mill Industry in India*, New Delhi: Oxford University Press, 1984. See also the references in note 23.

of-payment problems. The political context for private textile manufacturers was thus discouraging and contributed to limited growth in both productivity and production.

Finally, a comment ought to be made about the continuing 'closed' nature of the Indian economy. Irrespective of whether arguments about 'export pessimism' or about the need to protect 'infant industries' were ever technically supportable or not, such attitudes were understandable during the Nehru period, given the prevailing political values and popular economic doctrines of the time. By the 1970s, however, many of these assumptions were being globally challenged. Countries such as South Korea and Brazil were aggressively turning towards export promotion and trying to attract foreign investors. Indira Gandhi's legitimacy-driven politics led her instead to adopt a sharply anti-Western and nationalist political rhetoric, pushing India's economic policies in nearly the opposite direction. As a result, India continued to embrace its import-substitution regime fiercely, as well as to resist foreign investment, again hurting growth in multiple ways. Limited exports, for example, remained a key vulnerability, creating periodic balance-of-payment crises. Moreover, by not pushing exports India was not taking advantage of its key resource, cheap labour; it also limited imports of new technology and discouraged economies of scale. Enhanced foreign investment might also have facilitated growth, not only via additional investments, but also and more importantly by contributing to better technology, management, and export promotion.

Populism may be politically expedient and, on occasion, even a political necessity to balance conflicting interests under conditions of weak political institutions, but its economic impact on growth is seldom benign. The Indian case fits this broader pattern. A more genuine social democratic tilt in India, one that would have reconciled better growth and modest redistribution, would have required a well-organized social democratic party and a durable ruling coalition at the helm of a more effective state. In other words, it would have required a cohesive-multiclass state rather than a fragmented-multiclass state. Short of that unlikely outcome, a charismatic and popular leader, promising radical redistribution within the context of a fragmented-multiclass state and a largely private-enterprise economy, was a recipe for failure. Populism doubly harmed economic growth by hurting public and private investments and by further politicizing the statist and closed economic policy regime.

THE PRO-BUSINESS DRIFT

Following Indira Gandhi's return to power in 1980 and later following her assassination in 1984, Indian democracy entered a new phase, marked by a slow and steady decline of Congress's hegemony and by numerous efforts to find workable alternatives, culminating in the emergence of a right-wing, religious nationalist party at the helm.[40] While the 1980s and the 1990s were characterized by a fair amount of governmental instability and even political instability, especially by ethnic and communal violence, India's economic policies took on a more consistent character, generally tending in a more pro-business direction—a process dubbed by some observers as economic liberalization. During this phase the gap between governmental economic ambitions and capacities narrowed somewhat, not so much due to enhanced state capacities as to the scaling back of ambitions, both in the productive and the redistributive spheres. Over the last two decades of the twentieth century, in other words, India's fragmented-multiclass state became not so much more cohesive as markedly less multiclass.

Indira Gandhi's departure from the political scene left India without a charismatic leader capable of holding together an increasingly mobilized and heterogeneous political society. Her failure to make a dent in India's poverty also clarified to her successors (and even to her in the early 1980s) the limits of class politics in India; without a well-organized social democratic party, appeals to the lower classes in India quickly devolved into irresponsible populism that simultaneously hurt economic growth and failed to achieve effective economic redistribution. Subsequent attempts to discover new formulas for ruling have moved in one of three directions, none totally successful: maintaining the Nehru–Gandhi family rule, forging new caste coalitions, and encouraging ethnic politics, especially mobilizing Hindu nationalism. The Congress party pursued the first strategy, and a variety of opposition parties followed the second and the third. Since none of these strategies readily translated into enduring national electoral victories, India's regions also gained national political significance by joining coalition governments at the centre.

The most significant political development over the last two decades has been the emergence of the Bharatiya Janata Party (BJP), a right-leaning religious nationalist party, as a major alternative to the Congress. The BJP emerged as India's ruling party towards the end of the 1990s and remains in power at the time of writing (2003). The rise of the BJP needs to be understood in terms of its ability to fill a growing political vacuum. The assassination of Indira Gandhi's son, Rajiv Gandhi, an heir apparent of sorts, deprived Congress of the opportunity to continue to capitalize on 'dynastic popularity'. With the aim of finding an alternative to the Congress, a series of opposition

---

[40]I have analysed these changes in more detail elsewhere. See Atul Kohli, 'Indian Democracy: Stress and Resilience', *Journal of Democracy*, 3 January 1992, pp. 58–65; Atul Kohli, 'Can the Periphery Control the Center? Indian Politics at the Crossroads', *Washington Quarterly*, 19(4), Autumn 1996, pp. 115–87; and Atul Kohli, 'India Defies the Odds: Enduring Another Election', *Journal of Democracy*, 9, July 1998, pp. 7–80.

parties sought to mobilize hitherto unincorporated middle-caste groups but failed due to factionalism and leadership rivalries, not to mention the absence of any clear political programme.

As a better-organized party, the BJP stepped into this vacuum and sought to unite India's Hindu religious majority into a nationalist political bloc. In a programme reminiscent of European fascist movements, this party sought politically convenient enemies, both within India—India's religious minorities, especially Muslims—and beyond India's borders. The reformulation of Indian nationalism along religious lines paid off handsomely for the BJP, but not enough to win a national electoral majority. The party's appeal remained concentrated in those central areas of India where memories and symbols of rule by Muslims remain mobilizable. Coalition alignments, as well as experience with democratic governance, softened the more extreme elements of the BJP, enabling it to provide a viable alternative to the old Congress, at least over the short term. How the BJP will evolve in the future, however, remains an open question.

From the standpoint of this discussion, it is important to note that shifting governments and coalitions of the last two decades have not translated into sharp economic policy instability. While there have been fluctuations, economic policies over the last two decades have generally moved in a liberalizing or, more precisely, pro-business direction, both dismantling some of the inherited state controls on private economic activities and distancing the state from the rhetoric of redistribution and populism. How can one explain this shift, as well as its consistency, in the face of governmental instability? A few comments will help to round out the story.[41]

Neither state-led economic growth nor political efforts at redistribution and poverty alleviation have proved to be especially successful in India. State capacity to push either the Korean type of high economic growth or the Chinese type of radical poverty alleviation has simply been missing. The more this understanding of past failures seeped into the gestalt of India's political class, however, the more it embraced pro-business solutions to its development problems. Even Indira Gandhi in her later years quietly de-emphasized poverty alleviation as a slogan and courted the business class she had alienated earlier on. Her son, Rajiv Gandhi, embraced the rhetoric of economic liberalization, though in practice his attempts to dismantle India's statism ran into numerous obstacles.[42] Subsequent national governments have more or less maintained a rhetorical commitment to liberalize the

---

[41]One recent book on politics of India's economic liberalization is Rob Jenkins, *Democratic Politics and Economic Reform in India*, New York: Cambridge University Press, 1999.

[42]For a full discussion, see Atul Kohli, 'Politics of Economic Liberalization in India', *World Development*, 17(3), March 1989, pp. 305–28.

economy, moving in fits and starts to produce an incremental progress that suits a large, complex democracy. When questioned as to why, in spite of its nationalist orientation, the BJP sought to liberalize and open India's economy, India's current prime minister, Atal Bihari Vajpayee, replied: 'Nehru Ji's approach was not all that successful. Indira Ji was never sincere. What else can we do now?'[43]

The growing sense among leaders that past strategies were not enormously successful and that there is no alternative but to liberalize is probably the driving force behind the shift in India's development strategy. A moment of reflection, however, suggests that past failures could have been interpreted differently, with different implications for policy. For example, India's leaders could have embraced more fully the model of East Asian 'developmental states', or, less likely but not totally out of question, they could have embraced a more genuine social democratic model based on what has been tried in such Indian states as West Bengal and Kerala. The fact that they did not, in turn, points to another key factor that has pushed India's new economic choices: the liberalizing trend is consistent with dominant interests and ideas, both within India and abroad.

In spite of its socialist flourish, India's statism provided a framework for the emergence of a largely capitalist economy in India. The more Indian capitalism has matured over the last few decades, the more difficult it has become for India's leaders to maintain anti-capitalist political positions. Even India's communist parties now accept market realities and seek to attract private investors. The shifting nature of the political economy has thus bounded the range of economic choices available to India's leaders. International pressures have further reinforced these boundaries. Just as at mid-century statism appeared to be a 'natural' path to adopt worldwide, towards the end of the century the virtues of markets appeared nearly hegemonic.[44] India's leaders could have resisted these national and international constraints, but that would have required considerable political cohesion around alternative values. Having not done so, however, nearly all of India's political parties have sought to work with powerful interests and ideas, especially anti-statist,

[43]This is a translation of a conversation in Hindi between Mr Vajpayee and Atul Kohli in Oxfordshire, England, 19–21 June 1992. Mr Vajpayee at the time was a leader of the opposition in the Indian parliament, and both he and the author were attending a conference on 'India: The Future', organized by the Ditchley Foundation.

[44]This sweeping gestalt shift, which has an ideological quality, should give thoughtful observers a pause. The earlier embrace of statism led to some successes and numerous failures. The new commitment to markets is also likely to lead to a similar, mixed record that will be evident only in the future. For one useful account of this shifting economic mind-set, see Paul Krugman, 'Cycles of Conventional Wisdom on Economic Development', *International Affairs*, 72(1), 1996, pp. 717–32.

pro-business ideas, thus narrowing the range of available options in the economic sphere.

Nonetheless, despite a commitment to economic liberalization, India's political economy still remains quite statist by global standards. Unlike South Korea or Brazil in the 1990s, there was no basic shift in India's development model in the 1990s. Thus, public enterprises remained very significant, tariffs came down but were far from negligible, the role of foreign investment in the economy was minimal, numerous laws governed capital movements in and out of the country, and a variety of labour laws made the economy anything but a model of flexibility. This is neither an endorsement nor a criticism of the state of affairs. The analytical point is that, during the last two decades of the twentieth century, India's leaders sought to liberalize the statist economy they had inherited. This liberalization, while real, was also limited—a mixed result consistent with powerful political forces in India, since a variety of interest groups, especially business, objected to some aspect or another of a radical policy shift. Weak governments, in any case, were reluctant to undertake major policy restructuring. The policy shift in India is thus better understood as a pro-business drift rather than as economic liberalization, but a policy drift that has nonetheless facilitated improved rates of economic growth.

India's rate of economic growth improved between 1980 and 2000 and averaged nearly 6 per cent per annum (Table 5.1). This higher rate was in part a statistical artifact insofar as it reflected the growing share in the national economy of the fast-growing industrial and service sectors. Nevertheless, agricultural growth over the last two decades must be judged satisfactory as both industry and services grew at some 6 to 7 per cent per annum, propelling India into a group of relatively fast growers in the world. How does one explain this improved performance, especially in light of our focus on the role of the state and of state policies? The discussion distinguishes between the higher growth rates in the 1980s and those in the 1990s: growth in the 1980s was debt-led, especially by a growing public debt, and growth in the 1990s was driven by higher rates of investment in the private corporate sector.

Other underlying factors that may have also contributed to this outcome ought to be noted. During the Nehru period India invested in heavy industry and in higher technological education to feed this industry. Returns on these investments typically take time, and India may now be benefiting from these earlier decisions. Consequently, entrepreneurial and managerial skills have been slowly but steadily accumulating in India and probably contributed to better economic performance. There is also some evidence that the structure of industry is steadily shifting towards consumer industries where capital-output ratios are generally lower. India may also have just been lucky over the last two decades, with a spate of good weather, growing remittances from overseas Indians, and better international terms of borrowing

TABLE 5.2: Patterns of Capital Formation, 1980–98
(percentage of GDP)

Period	Total Gross Capital Formation	Private Corporate Sector	Public Sector
1980–5	21.9	4.3	10.2
1985–90	23.7	4.5	10.5
1990–5	23.7	6.0	9.1
1995–8	24.0	8.3	7.0

Source: Adapted from Rakesh Mohan, 'Fiscal Correction for Economic Growth', *Economic and Political Weekly*, 10 June 2000, p. 2028, table 4.

and trade. And finally, as in true for such other cases as Brazil as well, prior industrialization creates its own efficiencies for future industrialization by providing a trained workforce, dense supplier networks, demand for goods, and a supportive tax base.

In spite of the potential relevance of such non-policy variables, there is still something significant to explain. As is clear in Table 5.2, higher growth rates, over the last two decades were accompanied by higher rates of investment, increases that originated in the public sector in the 1980s and in the private corporate sector in the 1990s. What explains these higher rates of investment? Also, what role, if any, have attempts to liberalize the economy played in this improved economic performance? The Indira Gandhi who returned to power in 1980 was considerably less populist than the one in the 1970s. She thus initiated an era—especially marked by a more pro-business Industrial Policy Resolution in 1982—that increasingly came to be characterized by growing silence on issues of deliberate poverty alleviation and by greater public attention directed towards the promotion of economic growth. The appropriate strategy for promoting growth has been evolving. There was a lot of talk of liberalizing the economy in the second half of the 1980s, when Rajiv Gandhi was in power. While some pro-business policy measures—such as a reduction in corporate taxes—were indeed passed, overall liberalization was fairly limited; for example, the average rate of tariffs in India in 1990 was still over 100 per cent.

Following a balance-of-payment crisis in 1991, there was some significant liberalization, especially of the internal economy from state controls, but the pace of change, especially of 'opening' the economy to the world, slowed in the second half of the decade.[45] Tariff rates in India at the end of the century still averaged close to 40 per cent and foreign investment was minuscule compared to, say, China. What continued steadily throughout

[45]For a discussion of policy changes in the 1990s, see Shankar Acharya, 'Macroeconomic Management in the Nineties', *Economic and Political Weekly*, 20 April 2002, pp. 1515–38.

the two decades, however, was a move away from populism and towards a focus on economic growth, and relatedly towards a warmer embrace between the state and national business. The argument I am proposing is that this shift in state priorities and alliances is an important ingredient in improved economic performance.

As discussed above, there was substantial evidence in India in the 1970s of a link between declining public investments and deceleration of industrial growth. With changed priorities, subsequent governments decided that one way to improve growth was to boost public sector investments. This is precisely what happened during the 1980s.[46] The government channelled new investments into promoting infrastructure and industries that provided key inputs for intermediate and final goods, which promoted higher rates of growth. While the direct contribution of an increase of some 2–3 percentage points in public investment to overall growth may be fairly small, given the significance of such bottlenecks as infrastructure, the indirect contribution of this new investment for growth was in all likelihood much more significant.

How was this new public investment financed? Recall that the economic capacities of the Indian state during the Indira Gandhi years had deteriorated, as politicization of the bureaucracy made it difficult to collect more taxes or to improve the performance of public sector enterprises. Some new public resources were found in further taxing international trade (hardly a route to improving economic performance!), but for the most part the role of new resources was limited. The government also did not cut back on the variety of its non-developmental expenditures, such as subsidies. Given weak political parties—essentially, personalistic groupings—it was increasingly difficult to hold together ruling coalitions. Public monies continued to play a key role in buying and maintaining political support. The government thus pursued the only option it thought it had, namely, borrowing—mainly internally but also externally. Given that this borrowed money was being invested in areas with low financial returns and often through inefficient public firms, the results included accumulating debt that created the twin crises of internal and external debt in 1991.

Meanwhile, the economy grew at a handsome rate of nearly 6 per cent throughout the 1980s. Increasing public sector investment was one component of this growth. Private investments also grew, though not by much. There is, however, evidence of improvements in the productivity of investments,

---

[46]See, for example, Rakesh Mohan, 'Fiscal Correction for Economic Growth: Data Analysis and Suggestions', *Economic and Political Weekly*, 10 June 2000. He concludes that 'what becomes clear from examination of the data is that the 1980s were characterized by a significant increase in public sector investment as well as other government expenditure' (p. 2028).

especially in private manufacturing.[47] The underlying causes are not readily evident. Joshi and Little conclude that 'the high level of demand in the 1980s' may be an important part of the explanation.[48] As noted, the roots of this were also the debt-led increase in public expenditure.

The Indian economy continued to grow at nearly 6 per cent per annum during the 1990s as well. It will be a while before all the relevant data for the most recent period is analysed and the underlying determinants of the continuing high growth become clear.[49] Some trends are already evident, however. The crisis of 1991 and the related agreements that the Indian government reached with the IMF led to pressure on government deficits. It is difficult for India's fragmented-multiclass state to collect new taxes, to improve the performance of public enterprises, or to cut back on the various supports and services it provides. The main strategy for debt management is thus evident in Table 5.2, namely, in declining public sector investments. This trend may hurt growth and development in the future, especially because of the woeful state of India's infrastructure but also because of the pressing need to invest more in basic education and health.[50]

In spite of a decline in public sector investments, overall economic growth did not suffer, mainly because private sector investments grew and the share of corporate investments in the GDP actually surpassed the share of public sector investments (see Table 5.2). Private sector industrial investment in India was generally quite productive, though new investment was only partly in new industries. And the industrial sector, especially manufacturing, did not perform all that handsomely in the 1990s. The real locus of growth shifted instead to the less-regulated service sector, especially to exports of information technology, as India's accumulating manpower resources in this area found a niche in the global market.

The success of India's computer industry, including software exports, presents a good example of these broader, changing patterns of state-business relations.[51] The roots of this success are generally traced to policy changes

---

[47]See, for example, Vijay Joshi and I.M.O. Little, *India: Macroeconomics and Political Economy.* Washington, D.C.: World Bank, 1994, chapter 13. Joshi and Little argue that increased investments were too small to explain higher growth rates, which is surprising in light of their own evidence (see p. 327) that public sector investments averaged 7.7 per cent of the GDP between 1960–1 and 1975–6 and 9.9 per cent between 1976–7 and 1989–90. For a discussion of the 'multiplier effect' of public investments in India, see Ahluwalia, *Industrial Growth.*

[48]Joshi and Little, *India,* p. 328.

[49]One such preliminary attempt is Acharya, 'Macroeconomic Management in the Nineties'.

[50]See, for example, Mohan, 'Fiscal Correction'.

[51]See, for example, Peter Evans, *Embedded Autonomy: States and Industrial Transformation,* Princeton, N.J.: Princeton University Press, 1995; and Pingle, *Rethinking the Developmental State,* chapter 5.

in the late 1970s and then especially in 1984 under Rajiv Gandhi, who prioritized this sector for growth. Reminiscent of state-business cooperation in Korea, the Indian government during the 1980s and the 1990s reduced regulations and licensing requirements for this industry, reduced import duties and promoted exports with aggressive marketing in overseas markets. At home, the state helped to create industrial parks and software technology parks with a communications infrastructure, provided core computer facilities and engaged in a type of intervention generally more supportive than regulatory. This strategic state-business alliance was an essential component of the remarkable performance of the software industry, which grew at a rate of more than 50 per cent per annum during the 1990s.

Beyond the information-technology industry, the factors that help to explain growing private sector investments and pockets of dynamism more broadly are the state's increasingly pro-business policies. Over the last decade or so, India's various governments have cut corporate taxes, provided a variety of supports to business, especially for exports, sought to tame labour—evident in the substantial decline of man-days lost due to strikes[52]— and relaxed public controls on entry, exit, and expansion. Tax reforms have included across-the-board reductions in rates and simplification of procedures for paying direct and indirect taxes, lowering of import tariffs by almost one-third between 1990 and 1996, dispensing with industrial licensing agreements for most industries, allowing new entrants—private, semi-private, and foreign—into the banking system and capital markets, and opening up sectors such as power and telecommunications that had previously been limited to the public sector. While champions of liberalization may see all these measures as evidence of a growing free market in India, it remains the case that India's state is still heavily interventionist and that the Indian economy is still relatively closed to external goods, finance, and investors. The policy trend is thus better interpreted as a right-ward drift in which the embrace of state and business continues to grow warmer, leaving many others out in the cold.

CONCLUSION

India's quest for industrialization over the last half-century has produced mixed results. On the one hand, starting from very little, India now has a substantial and diversified industrial base, considerably more sophisticated than, say, that found in much of Africa, the Middle East, or even parts of Latin America. On the other hand, when compared with a South Korea or

---

[52]If the yearly man-days lost due to strikes averaged some 37 million in the 1980s, this average in the 1990s was down to nearly 20 million. See *Yearbook of Labour Statistics*, Geneva: International Labour Office, various years.

a Brazil, the progress of industrialization in India has not been all that rapid and levels of efficiency have generally been low. Industrial performance has also varied over time, moderately satisfactory in both the beginning and the ending periods and punctuated by a fairly lackluster interregnum during Indira Gandhi's rule. This chapter has sought to analyse the political underpinnings of this economic record. Economic outcomes in India, as elsewhere, are of course a product of numerous non-political factors. Nevertheless, the impact of the state's nature and role on the pattern of late-late industrialization is significant and varies systematically across cases and over time within a case.

The analysis has emphasized the impact of India's fragmented-multiclass state on rates and patterns of industrialization. The Indian state effectively controls the territory it governs, provides moderate political stability, is run at its apex by publicly oriented leaders and bureaucrats, and has always included among its multiple priorities promotion of industry and economic growth. Moreover, the state has intervened heavily in the economy to undertake production directly and to protect its indigenous entrepreneurs from global competition. The state took the lead during the Nehru period and increasingly supported the private sector in the last two decades of the twentieth century.

Conversely, however, the Indian state often lacked the political capacity to translate its enormous economic ambitions into outcomes. Central to this incapacity is its fragmented authority, characterized by both intra-elite and elite–mass schisms and ruling coalitions that are generally multiclass. Leaders in such a state worry perennially about their legitimacy, inclining them to adopt economic policies based on whether they can help to consolidate their political position rather than on whether they will necessarily produce rapid industrialization and growth. The impact of these legitimacy concerns was most obvious during the rule of Indira Gandhi.

In conclusion, the impact of India's fragmented-multiclass state on its middling industrial performance may be usefully compared with some other cases around the world. When juxtaposed against Nigeria, what stands out is the economic importance of a moderately effective state that provides order, protects private property, operates according to the rule of law and procedures, is run by an elite with a modicum of public commitment and competence, and thus focuses some of the state's energies and resources on promoting industry. Absent from such minimal capacities, the state in Nigeria has made a mockery of planned economic development, with dismal results. Indeed, Indian specialists have only to imagine all of India being governed in the manner of Bihar—the Africa within India—to understand the positive contribution of the central Indian state to India's industrialization.

Compared with Brazil or South Korea, however, India's economic performance has clearly been inferior, though India's starting point at the mid-century was not as advanced as that of Korea and Brazil—the share of industry in the Indian economy at independence was closer to 10 per cent whereas it was nearly 20 per cent in both Korea and Brazil following the Second World War. This difference was consequential in two ways. First, to the extent that prior industrialization helps subsequent industrialization, India was disadvantaged. And second, India would have had to industrialize even more rapidly than Korea or Brazil to achieve the levels of prosperity that these countries now enjoy. As it was, however, the pace of India's industrialization was slower. The question, then, is what role the Indian state has played in the process.

Although I have studied the subject extensively, I confess that a firm, parsimonious, and confident answer eludes me. Rather, only fragments of long chains of causation suggest themselves. Taken together, these may constitute a complex answer. A comparison with Brazil is especially instructive. Both India and Brazil pursued import substitution in the 1950s within democratic regimes and yet Brazil's industry grew faster and more efficiently. Clearly, blaming import-substitution policies per se is not an adequate explanation. Instead, the role of different types of states in the two countries stands out as significant. The Brazilian state in this period was considerably less nationalist and mass-based than that of India, allowing Brazilian leaders to focus more on industrialization, to invite foreigners to lead the way, to cooperate closely with business groups, and to repress labour. All of these political differences were economically consequential, producing more rapid and more efficient import-substitution industrialization in Brazil.

After the mid-1960s Brazil and India of course took very different political paths, with striking economic consequences. Indira Gandhi sharply politicized economic policies in India, with a negative impact on industrialization. By contrast, the right-wing military regime in Brazil, much more cohesive-capitalist in its make-up and orientation, emphasized economic growth, repressed labour even further, worked closely with private investors, both domestic and foreign, and borrowed heavily, hoping to boost exports so as to pay off its growing debts. Brazil's strategy ultimately backfired, but not before first achieving 'miracle' growth rates in industry.[53] Industry in Indira Gandhi's India, by contrast, nearly stagnated. This economic situation in India changed somewhat in the 1980s and 1990s, but only when national politics also turned more pro-capitalist, with a greater emphasis on economic growth, closer cooperation with business, and further taming of labour.

[53]It may be worth noting that if Brazil's and India's economic growth are compared over the entire period of, say, 1950–2000, the economic performance of the two countries starts to converge more than diverge.

Finally, the comparison between India and South Korea is dramatic. South Korea's cohesive-capitalist state contrasted fairly sharply with India's fragmented-multiclass state. This was evident in how state authority in the two countries was organized—cohesive versus fragmented—as well as in the state's relations with various social classes—narrow and precapitalist in one, broad and multiclass in the other. The South Korean state under Park Chung Hee thus concentrated power at the apex, defined rapid industrialization as essential for national security, penetrated downward, instituted close relations with business, controlled and mobilized labour, and cooperated closely with Japan without creating debilitating dependencies. While Korean citizens paid a heavy price in terms of repression and lack of freedoms, Korea's cohesive-capitalist state intervened heavily in the economy to promote both import substitution and exports of manufactured goods and, judged at least by growth results, did so rather successfully. India's fragmented-multiclass state, by contrast, pursued several goals simultaneously, cooperated with business only sporadically, faced considerable labour activism, resisted integration into the global economy—either for capital, as the Brazilians did, or for trade, as the Koreans did—and has only lately moved in a more developmental direction, but not without a commensurate rise in communal nationalism as the new legitimacy formula. In broad terms, India's middling industrial performance has also reflected these underlying political patterns.

6

Politics of Economic Growth in India, 1980–2005, Part I
The 1980s*

For the last quarter of a century India's economy has grown at an average rate of nearly 6 per cent per annum. Considering that India's economy hardly grew in the first half of the twentieth century, and then following independence, grew at a sluggish rate of some 3–4 per cent per annum, this recent growth acceleration is quite remarkable. It is the case that India's recent rapid economic growth has been accompanied by growing inequalities; the share of the poor in this new growth is also being vigorously debated.[1] Nevertheless, there is no denying that the Indian economy in recent decades has been one of the world's fastest growing economies. Moreover, unlike in much of high-growth East Asia, the Indian economy has grown within the framework of a democracy. The scholarly questions then abound: how has India done it? What lessons, if any, can others draw from the Indian case?

While the cumulative changes in the nature of the Indian economy since independence, as well as the shifts in the global context of India, must be part of any full explanation of 'how India has done it', a central issue for interpretation also concerns the changing role of the state within India: has India's growth acceleration resulted from the state's embrace of neo-liberal policies, or from some more complex but identifiable pattern of state intervention? This paper attempts to answer this question.

One respectable interpretation of the recent Indian experience, let us call it the pro-market interpretation, emphasizes the process of economic

*Originally published as 'Politics of Economic Growth in India, 1980–2005, Part I: The 1980s', *Economic and Political Weekly*, 1 April 2006, pp. 1251–9.
[1]See, for example, Angus Deaton and Jean Dreze, 'Poverty and Inequality in India: A Re-Examination', *Economic and Political Weekly*, 7 September 2002, pp. 3729–48; Abhijit Sen and Himanshu, 'Poverty and Inequality in India', *Economic and Political Weekly* (in two parts), 18 and 25 September 2004, pp. 4247–63 and pp. 4361–75.

liberalization in India that began earnestly in 1991.[2] India's earlier sluggish growth, according to this well known line of thinking, was largely a product of a highly interventionist state and of a misguided import substitution trading regime. In 1991, the argument might continue, India adopted a pro-market strategy that liberalized its internal regulatory framework, reduced tariffs, adopted appropriate exchange rate policies, and allowed foreign investors to play a significant role in the economy. As a result, to repeat the metaphor used by the *Economist*,[3] the animal urges of Indian entrepreneurs were 'uncaged': capital accumulation in and the efficiency of the economy improved, propelling India into the ranks of the world's fastest growers.

While widely embraced, this pro-market interpretation is unable to explain some important empirical anomalies in the Indian record and is plagued by some logical inconsistencies. First, economic growth in India started accelerating a full decade prior to liberalization of 1991.[4] Why? Second, industrial production in India—a key object of reforms—did not accelerate following the liberalizing reforms; if any change is observable when the post-reform industrial growth is juxtaposed against the 1980s, it is nearly in the opposite direction.[5] Again, why? And third, if a set of policies is supposed to work anywhere and at any time, why have some states within India responded well, while others have not?[6]

India's record also has to be situated in a broader comparative context. By international standards, India's embrace of the global economy has been relatively modest.[7] The economic record of many other developing countries

[2]T.N. Srinivasan and S. Tendulkar, *Reintegrating India with the World Economy*, Washington, D.C.: Institute for International Economics, 2003.

[3]'India Survey', 4 May 1991.

[4]R. Nagaraj, 'Indian Economy since 1980: Virtuous Growth or Polarisation', *Economic and Political Weekly*, 5 August 2000, pp. 2831–9; Bradford De Long, 'India since Independence: An Analytic Growth Narrative', in Dani Rodrik (ed.), *In Search of Prosperity: Analytic Narratives on Economic Growth*, Princeton, N.J.: Princeton University Press, 2003; Dani Rodrik and Arvind Subramanian, 'From "Hindu Growth" to Productivity Surge: The Mystery of the Indian Growth Transition', unpublished manuscript, March 2004; and Arvind Virmani, 'India's Economic Growth: From Socialist Rate of Growth to Bharatiya Rate of Growth', Working Paper No. 122, Indian Council for Research on International Economic Relatons, New Delhi.

[5]Sudip Chaudhuri, 'Economic Reforms and Industrial Structure in India', *Economic and Political Weekly*, 12 January 2002, pp. 155–62; R. Nagaraj, 'Industrial Policy and Performance since 1980: Which Way Now?', *Economic and Political Weekly*, 38(35), 30 August 2003, pp. 3707–15.

[6]Montek S. Ahluwalia, 'Economic Performance of States in Post-reforms Period', *EPW*, 6 May 2000.

[7]Baldev Raj Nayar, 'Opening up and Openness of Indian Economy', *EPW*, 15 September 2001.

that have also liberalized, and often more deeply, is, at best, mixed.[8] India's superior economic performance in this comparative context suggests two further observations. First, any analysis of India's recent economic performance must take into account India's relatively favourable initial conditions around 1980, especially a robust indigenous industrial sector and a low foreign debt economy. And second, as the realization grows that the 'Washington Consensus' has not worked very well in many places,[9] it becomes more and more likely that the pro-market interpretation of India is also mistaken, and that what is needed is an alternate account of the state's role in growth success and failure.

In what follows I provide such an alternate political economy account of India's recent growth acceleration, emphasizing the state's changing role since 1980, especially the abandonment of left-leaning, anti-capitalist rhetoric and policies, prioritizing of economic growth, and a slow but steady embrace of Indian capital as the main ruling ally. Let us call such a strategy of development a pro-business strategy. In providing such an interpretation—let us call it the pro-business interpretation—I adopt the view that rapid industrialization in the developing world, as, for example, in South Korea or in some time periods in Brazil, was promoted, not by minimal states that embraced the market, but by highly interventionist states who prioritized economic growth as a state goal, ruthlessly supported capitalists, repressed labour, mobilized economic nationalism to provide social glue and channelled firm activities to produce both for protected domestic markets and for exports.[10] In light of such an analysis of 'success', one might argue that India's sluggish economic growth from 1950–80 was a product, not mainly of state's market distortions, but of a mismatch between the limited capacities of the Indian state and the highly ambitious statist model of

[8]For Latin American, see Barbara Stallings and Wilson Peres, *Growth, Employment, and Equity: The Impact of Economic Reforms in Latin America and the Caribbean*, Washington, D.C.: Brookings Institute Press, 2000; and for Sub-Saharan Africa, see Nicholas van de Walle, *Politics of Africa's Permanent Economic Crisis*, New York: Cambridge University Press, 2003.

[9]William Easterly, 'The Lost Decades: Developing Countries' Stagnation in spite of Policy Reform 1980–98', *Journal of Economic Growth*, 6, 2001; Joseph Stiglitz, *Globalization and Its Discontents*, New York: WW Norton, 2002; and Branko Milanovic, 'The Two Faces of Globalization: Against Globalization as We Know It', *World Development*, 31(4), 2003.

[10]Atul Kohli, *State-Directed Development: Political Power and Industrialisation in the Global Periphery*, New York: Cambridge University Press, 2004. My statist argument, in turn, builds on a number of earlier important studies, especially Chalmers Johnson, *MITI and the Japanese Miracle: The Growth of Industrial Policy, 1925–1975*, Stanford, Calif.: Stanford University Press, 1982; Alice Amsden, *Asia's Next Giant: South Korea and Late Industrialisation*, New York: Oxford University Press, 1989; Robert Wade, *Governing the Market: Economic Theory and the Role of Government in East Asian Industrialisation*, Princeton, New Jersey: Princeton University Press, 1990; Peter Evans, *Embedded Autonomy: State and Industrial Transformation*, Princeton, New Jersey: Princeton University Press.

development. Following 1980, moreover, one can argue, as I did in a recent work, but only in passing, that economic growth in India accelerated as a result of a 'rightward drift' in Indian politics, via which 'the embrace of state and business continues to grow warmer, leaving many others out in the cold'.[11] The present paper provides an opportunity to elaborate and specify this statist argument about India, focusing especially on the pro-business political and policy changes since 1980 that are responsible for the recent growth acceleration.

The argument that growth acceleration in India is mainly a product of the state's embrace of economic growth as a priority goal and of business groups as the main political ally is built in this paper in three analytical steps. First, I juxtapose the more redistributive pre-1980 political and policy orientation in India against the more pro-growth and pro-business orientation that followed in the 1980s. Noting the strong association between this political shift on the one hand, and the improved growth performance on the other hand, I also suggest some possible causal mechanisms that might link political and economic changes. Second, the more liberal policies adopted in the early 1990s indeed ushered in a new policy regime; this regime is best characterized as part pro-business, especially pro-indigenous business, and part pro-market, especially in the sense of an enhanced global opening. After analysing these policy changes, I document the limited impact of these new policies on growth rates in manufacturing and in industry in India. This evidence helps cast doubt on the widespread belief that pro-market policies are helping propel India's economic growth and, at the same time, helps underline the proposition that the pro-indigenous business policies adopted since 1980 are probably still the main dynamic force behind India's sustained but unaltered industrial growth. And finally, a similar pattern is discernible in intra-national variations within India: Indian states with more pro-growth and pro-business governments have tended to experience higher rates of economic growth. An analysis of these variations then provides a further check on the argument.

Of course, what may be a good approach for promoting growth may not always be a popular or a just ruling strategy. When a democratic state is narrowly committed to growth and business groups, not only is the quality of that democracy likely to suffer, but it is also likely to create distributional and political problems. The three most evident in India are: growing regional and class inequalities, with political ramifications; the utilization of ethnic

---

[11] Kohli, *State-Directed Development*, p. 285. Two economists have recently and independently provided a nearly identical interpretation of the Indian experience (Rodrik and Subramanian, 'From "Hindu Growth" to Productivity Surge'). It is encouraging for a political scientist trespassing into the territory of economists to see at least some economists thinking along parallel lines.

nationalism—instead of the less volatile, interest-oriented appeals—as a tool of political mobilization; and a rapid turnover in ruling governments.

The paper is organized as follows. In the first brief section, I deal with some theoretical considerations, establishing the distinction between pro-market and pro-business patterns of state intervention; this discussion then frames the empirical analysis. In the second and the third sections, I document the political and policy changes that occurred in India in the 1980s and the 1990s, respectively, tracing their impact on economic outcomes. I undertake a similar exercise in the fourth section with reference to a few select Indian states. I finally return to some general comments and to the implications of the argument in the conclusion.

PRO-MARKET VERSUS PRO-BUSINESS STATE INTERVENTION

Rare though the cases are, the experience of rapid and sustained economic growth in a developing country has repeatedly provoked scholarly debates. The underlying questions are familiar: how did a country, A or B (say, South Korea or China), get on the high growth path; and does the experience of A or B provide a model or, at least, lessons for others. The main lines of the debate are also familiar: high growth resulted from the state's embrace of a pro-market strategy, namely, a move towards limited state intervention and an open economy; or, no, the growth success was a product of an interventionist state, especially of a close collaboration between the state and business groups aimed at growth promotion. Of course, in popular discourse on development, there is a tendency to treat all pro-business governments simultaneously as pro-market governments. Even some scholars collapse this distinction, either obfuscating important analytical issues, or worse, providing an ideological cloak for what are clearly class issues. Prior to interpreting the recent growth experience of India, therefore, it may be useful to sharpen the distinction between pro-market and pro-business strategies of state intervention; these development strategies vary in terms of the choice of typical policies, the logic and pattern of expected outcomes, and the underlying politics.

Whereas a pro-market strategy supports new entrants and consumers, a pro-business strategy mainly supports established producers.[12] A pro-market strategy rests on the idea that free play of markets will lead to efficient allocation of resources, as well as promote competitiveness, hence boosting production and growth. This simple but venerable idea inspired the so-called 'Washington Consensus' on development during the 1980s and the 1990s.[13]

---

[12]Dani Rodrik and Arvind Subramanian, 'From "Hindu Growth" to Productivity Surge: The Mystery of the Indian Growth Transition', Unpublished manuscript, March 2004.

[13]John Williamson, 'What Washington Means by Policy Reform', in John Williamson (ed.), *Latin American Adjustment: How Much has Happened?*, Washington, D.C.: Institute for International Economics, 1990.

Shorn of numerous complexities, this development orthodoxy consisted of a few key arguments. First, the proponents of the orthodoxy were quite critical of the earlier state-interventionist, import-substitution model of development that was pursued by many countries in the 1950s and the 1960s. Second, the suggestion was instead that economic growth in the developing world would improve if developing country states shrunk their economic role and opened their economies to the external world. A failure to do so, the argument went, would repeatedly produce fiscal and trade imbalances. Pressing policy issues thus involved bringing governmental expenditures more in line with revenues, on the one hand, and opening the economy with the hope of promoting exports, on the other hand. And finally, numerous more specific policy suggestions that emerged included privatizing public sector enterprises, cutting public subsidies, reducing public role in setting prices, devaluation, reduction of tariffs and opening the economy to foreign investors.

All this is relatively well known. What needs to be reiterated is that, if truly pursued, advocates of a pro-market strategy logically expected a competitive, open and efficient economy to lead to a number of additional benign outcomes: for the same amount of investment, a more efficient economy would lead to higher rates of economic growth; pursuing comparative advantage would create labour-intensive industrialization and thus rapid employment growth; competition would facilitate new entrants; the terms of trade would shift towards the countryside, benefiting the rural poor; and since capital moves to capital-scarce areas in search of higher returns, regional inequalities would reduce over time, mitigating inequalities. The major anticipated problems in the pursuit of such a benign strategy were mainly short run, when the transition away from a statist and a closed economy was likely to create disruption and recession. This also suggested that the pursuit of a pro-market strategy might be politically problematic. Since a pro-market strategy bets mainly on future winners, weak states of the developing world were likely to find few domestic allies over the short run. This is why external support for 'reformist' developing country governments was deemed crucial by the proponents of pro-market strategies.

If the pro-market development strategy derived its inspiration mainly from some strands of neo-classical economics, the ideas behind a pro-business strategy have developed more via real world experience, especially from the rapid growth successes of some East Asian economies. The key idea here is that growth success or failure is not so much a function of the degree but the quality of state intervention. More specifically, identifying variations in how states are organized and in the institutionalized relationship of the state to the private sector is the key to understanding the relative effectiveness of state intervention in the economy. This relationship varies along a continuum stretching from considerable convergence in goals to mutual hostility between the state and the private sector. Other things being equal, the setting that has proved to be most conducive (that is, serves as a necessary but not a sufficient condition) to rapid industrial growth in the developing world is one in which the state's near-exclusive commitment to high growth coincided with the profit-maximizing needs of private entrepreneurs. The narrow ruling coalition in these cases was a marriage of repression and profits, aimed at economic growth in the name of the nation. Developmental states of East Asia have generally created such political economies.[14] Turning their countries into state-guided corporations of sorts, they have tended to be the fastest growers in the developing world (e.g., South Korea and Taiwan).

Growth-oriented developmental states pursued their commitment to high growth by developing trade and industry with well-designed, consistent, and thoroughly implemented state intervention. Specific policy measures varied but were generally aimed at easing supply-and-demand constraints faced by private entrepreneurs. Some of these interventions were direct and others indirect. On the supply side, for example, developmental states helped facilitate the availability of capital, labour, technology, and even entrepreneurship. Thus supply of capital was boosted at times by superior tax collection and public investment, at other times by using publicly controlled banks to direct credit to preferred private firms and sectors and at yet other times by allowing inflation to shift resources from both agriculture and urban labour to private industrialists. Repression was also a key component in enabling private investors to have a ready supply of cheap, 'flexible', and disciplined labour. Examples of less-direct interventions on the supply side included promotion of technology by investing in education and research and development, and/or by bargaining with foreign firms to enable technology transfer.

On the demand side, too, developmental states pursued a variety of policies to promote their growth commitment. These included expansionist monetary and fiscal policies, and tariffs and exchange-rate policies aimed at boosting domestic demand. And when domestic demand was not sufficient, these states just as readily adopted newer policies that shifted incentives in favour of export promotion or, more likely, that helped promote production for both domestic and foreign consumption.

There was thus significant variation in the specific policy measures undertaken by developmental states. Only some policies, such as labour discipline, necessitated a repressive state. But what most policies adopted by

---

[14]For a variety of reasons elaborated elsewhere, I have in my recent work replaced the term 'developmental states' with a different concept, namely, cohesive-capitalist states (Kohli, *State-Directed Development*, pp. 383–6). For the purposes of this paper, however, I am continuing to use the more popular concept of developmental states.

developmental states reflected instead was a single-minded and unyielding political commitment to growth, combined with a political realization that maximizing production requires assuring the profitability of efficient producers but not of inefficient ones. Sometimes this required getting prices right, but just as often it required 'price distortions', such as undervaluing exchange rates, subsidizing exports, and holding wages back behind productivity gains. The central issue concerned the state's goals and capacities, expressed in the institutionalized relationship between the state and the private sector. Developmental states in successful late-late industrializers have thus been pragmatically—and often ruthlessly—pro-business, much more than they have been purely and ideologically pro-market.

The empirical discussion of contemporary India that follows is then framed by these general considerations: has India's recent economic growth resulted more from the embrace of the pro-market or the pro-business development strategy? To anticipate, the argument below is that India from 1950–80 was a fairly classic case of a statist, import-substitution model of development, with a socialist flourish. From 1980 onwards, however, the Indian state has shifted Indian political economy towards East Asian models of development. This emulation is, of course, not always self-conscious, and, even then, quite partial, because India cannot readily replicate the cohesion, effectiveness, or the brutality of a Japanese or a Korean state; the Indian state is also not very good at educating or improving the life-chances of its poor. The emulation is thus mainly in terms of prioritizing economic growth and realigning more closely with Indian capitalists. An attempt is thus underway to shift 'socialist India' into 'India incorporated'; this attempt is, and, mercifully, is likely to remain partial. The growth successes in India, as well as the numerous limits on even higher growth rates, are explicable in terms of this partial shift in India towards a pro-business development strategy.

POLITICS OF ECONOMIC GROWTH IN THE 1980s

A glance at both Table 6.1 and Figure 6.1 clarifies that economic growth in India accelerated noticeably around 1980. It is the case that the rate of growth of industrial production from 1980 onwards (Table 6.1 and Figure 6.2) was not all that impressive, both by international standards, and in comparison to India's own record in the 1950s.[15] Nevertheless, the growth in the 1950s was from a very low starting point and the performance since 1980 has been a significant improvement over the 'decade of stagnation' that went before.[16]

---

[15]Jessica Seddon Wallack, 'Structural Breaks in Indian Macroeconomic Data, *EPW*, 11 October 2003.

[16]Isher Judge Ahluwalia, *Industrial Growth in India: Stagnation since the Mid-Sixties*, New Delhi: Oxford University Press, 1985.

Moreover, Virmani[17] and Rodrik and Subramanian[18] have established via a variety of more formal tests that 1980 (or thereabouts) indeed represents a break from India's 'Hindu growth rate'. So, the first empirical puzzle is: what underlying changes might help us understand this break from the past?[19]

TABLE 6.1: Some Basic Growth Data, 1950–2004
(all figures in percentage per annum)

	1950–64	1965–79	1980–90	1991–2004	1980–2004
GDP growth	3.7	2.9	5.8	5.6	5.7
Industrial growth	7.4	3.8	6.5	5.8	6.1
Agricultural growth	3.1	2.3	3.9	3.0	3.4
Gross investment/GDP	13	18	22.8	22.3	22.5

Source: Author's estimates based on Government of India, *Economic Survey,* various issues (http://indiabudget.nic.in).

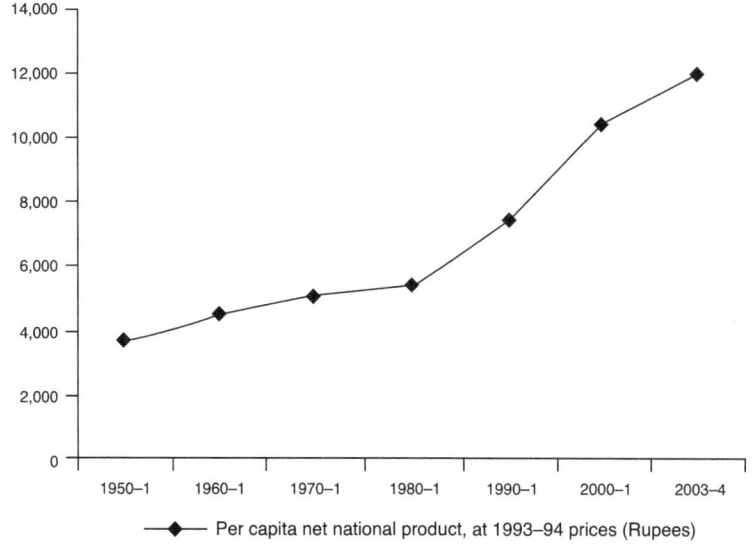

FIGURE 6.1: Growth of Per Capita Net National Product in India, 1950–2004

Source: Based on Government of India, *National Accounts Statistics,* various issues.

[17]Arvind Virmani, 'India's Economic Growth: From Socialist Rate of Growth to Bharatiya Rate of Growth', Working Paper No. 122, New Delhi: Indian Council for Research on International Economic Relations, 2004, and 'Sources of India's Economic Growth: Trends in Total Factor Productivity', Working Paper No. 131, New Delhi: Indian Council for Research on International Economic Relations, 2004.

[18]Rodrik and Subramanian, 'From "Hindu Growth" to Productivity Surge'.

[19]It should be noted that some of those sympathetic to India's liberalizing reforms in 1991 tend not to find the growth pick up of the 1980s all that puzzling, maintaining instead

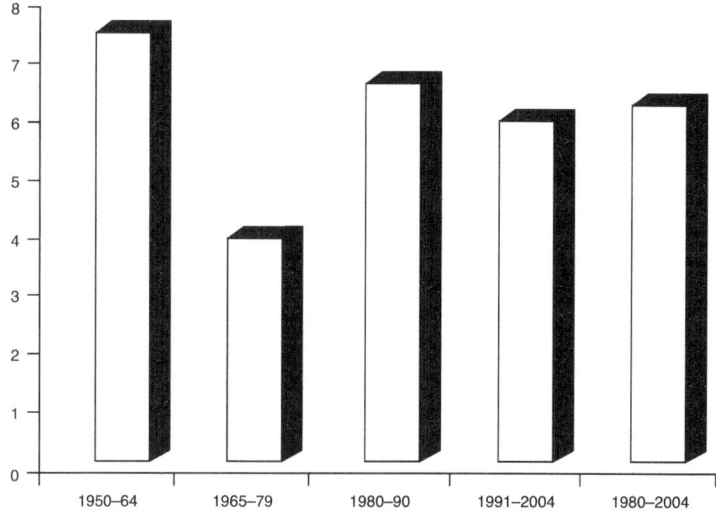

Rate of industrial growth (in percentage per annum)

FIGURE 6.2: Industrial Growth in India, 1950–2004

Source: Author's estimates based on Government of India, *Economic Survey*, various issues.

A brief look at the more proximate economic determinants of rapid increases in production sets the stage for a deeper analysis of the more distant causal variables in the broader political economy. In a rough and ready manner, economic growth accelerated because of improvements in both the rate of

that this growth was not sustainable (e.g., Srinivasan and Tendulkar, *Reintegrating India with the World Economy*; and Arvind Panagariya, 'India in the 1980s: Weak Reforms, Fragile Growth', unpublished manuscript, Department of Economics, University of Maryland). This view is not fully persuasive because the underlying fiscal problems towards the end of the 1980s were not of crisis proportions and the pressure on balance of payments was at least in part generated by unforeseen external circumstances. As to fiscal issues, note that interest payment on government debt constituted about 17 per cent of government expenditures at the end of the 1980s and 31 per cent at the end of the 'liberalizing' 1990s (Rakesh Mohan, 'Fiscal Correction for Economic Growth: Data Analysis and Suggestions', *EPW*, 10 June 2002, Table 5b, p. 2029). The external debt service ratio in 1988 at 29.2 per cent was high but was much lower than the 36.4 per cent average of 'all moderately indebted low income countries'. India's short-term debt was also relatively low (Dilip Mookherjee, 'Indian Economy at the Crossroads', *EPW*, 11–18 April 1992, Table 1). The pressure on maintaining payments on foreign debt was, in turn, exacerbated around 1991 by a sharp drop in remittances by non-resident Indians that at the time constituted nearly a third of India's export earnings (Devesh Kapur, *Democracy, Death and Diamonds: The Domestic Impact of International Migration from India*, forthcoming, Figure 4.2). This drop (and the threat of a drop) was fuelled by such unpredictable external circumstances as the disintegration of India's major trading partner, the Soviet Union, and the first Iraq war and the related increase in oil prices, both creating a sense that devaluation may be imminent. So, while the macroeconomic problems were real, the government also used the occasion to do what it already wanted to do.

investment and productivity. As is evident in Table 6.1, the overall rate of investment in the economy improved from 1980 onwards (the trend actually began in the second-half of the 1970s) and, fluctuations notwithstanding, has remained in the range of 22–23 per cent per annum. The growth in investments was fuelled in the 1980s by both growing public investments and private corporate investments, and in the 1990s, as public investments declined, by a variety of growing private investments (Table 6.2 and Figure 6.3). As to productivity, especially total factor productivity in manufacturing, the literature seems to suggest that there was a surge in the 1980s[20] and then, though still improving, experienced some deceleration in the growth rate in the 1990s.[21] Some support for this overall picture concerning productivity is also evident in Figure 6.4. Leaving aside numerous related measurement and other problems that economists rightly debate, for the purposes of a broad political economy analysis, the first empirical puzzle then translates into this: what political and policy changes during the 1980s help explain improvements in the rates of investment in and the efficiency of the Indian economy?

Before answering that question, however, two caveats. First, it is important to reiterate that higher economic growth from 1980 on, was at least in part a result of the changing composition of the GDP;[22] the outcome one is trying to explain then, namely, improvements in the rate of investment and

TABLE 6.2: Patterns of Capital Formation by Sector, 1970–2002
(percentage of GDP)

Period	Total Gross Capital Formation	Private Corporate Sector	Public Sector	Household Sector
1970–75	18.2	2.8	7.7	7.7
1975–80	22.5	2.3	11.0	10.0
1980–85	21.9	4.5	10.2	7.2
1985–90	23.7	4.5	10.5	8.7
1990–95	23.7	6.0	9.1	8.6
1995–2000	24.8	8.0	7.0	9.8
2000–2	25.3	6.0	6.1	13.2

Source: Author's estimates based on Government of India, Economic Survey, various issues (http://indiabudget.nic.in).

[20]Virmani, 'Sources of India's Economic Growth Impact'; and Rodrik and Subramanian, 'From "Hindu Growth" to Productivity Surge'.

[21]Nagesh Kumar, 'Economic Reforms and Their Macro-Economic Impact', EPW, 4 March 2000; and Sudip Chaudhuri, 'Economic Reforms and Industrial Structure in India', EPW, 12 January 2002, pp. 155–62. It should be noted that assessment of productivity trends raises important measurement issues, especially the measure of real value added that is adopted. P. Balakrishnan and K. Pushpangadan, 'Total Factor-Productivity Growth in Manufacturing Industry: A Fresh Look', EPW, 30 July 1994, thus adjust for changing price of material inputs and challenge the claim that industrial productivity in India improved in the 1980s.

[22]Wallack, 'Structural Breaks in Indian Macroeconomic Data'.

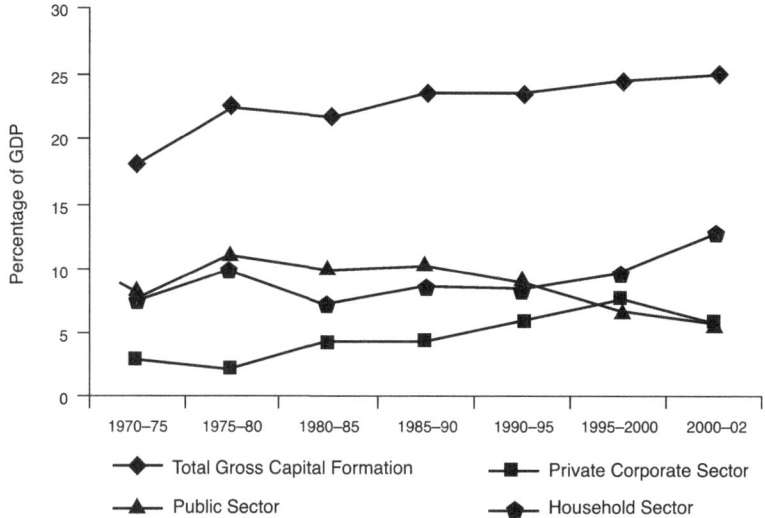

FIGURE 6.3: Patterns of Capital Formation in India by Sector, 1970–2002

Source: Based on data in Table 6.2.

FIGURE 6.4: Economic Performance in India, 1950–2004
(Annual Growth Rates)

Source: Based on data presented in Arvind Virmani, 'Sources of India's Economic Growth: Trends in Total Factor Productivity', Working Paper No. 131, Indian Council for Research on International Economic Relations, May 2004, Table 1.

in the efficiency of the economy, especially of the industrial economy, is mainly of an order that brought to an end the earlier 'era of stagnation'. And second, some non-quantifiable component of the improvement in the growth from 1980 on was clearly a function of building on a good foundation: accumulating technology, entrepreneurship and management; trained workers; a sufficient tax base; dense supplier networks; and adequate demand in the economy.

What eventually triggered the upward shift in the growth rate of the Indian economy around 1980 was a slow but sure adoption of a new model of development.[23] Instead of the statist and the nationalist model of development of the Nehru era, that was then accentuated in a populist direction by Indira Gandhi during the 1970s, Indira Gandhi herself shifted India's political economy around 1980 in the direction of a state and business alliance for economic growth. This change was not heralded loudly and has often been missed by scholars, especially because Indira Gandhi remains deeply associated with the politics of '*garibi hatao*'. Nevertheless, as documented below, evidence shows that the post-Emergency Indira Gandhi was a different Indira Gandhi: she downplayed redistributive concerns and prioritized economic growth; sought an alliance with big business; adopted an anti-labour stance; put brakes on the growth of public sector industries; and demoted the significance of economic planning and of the Planning Commission. As suits a complex democracy, these changes emerged in fits and starts; they were also often camouflaged, helping maintain some of Indira Gandhi's credentials as the leader of the masses. The changes were nevertheless profound; they involved a shift from left-leaning state intervention that flirted with socialism, to right-leaning state intervention in which the ruling elites re-committed themselves to a more sharply capitalist path of development. As important, key economic actors within India, especially big capital, understood these changes pretty clearly, expressing their satisfaction by investing more and helping India's economy grow rapidly.

While Indira Gandhi had already started moving away from 'socialism' during the Emergency, a more consistent shift towards prioritizing economic growth and embracing the private sector began after Indira Gandhi returned to power in 1980. Right after coming to power in January 1980, Indira Gandhi let it be known that improving production was now her top priority. Numerous public statements and policy changes indicated this shift; the shift was also understood well by participants and observers. The *Times of India* thus editorialized within a year: 'A change of considerable significance is taking

---

[23]I have gathered the factual details cited in this paper mainly from three sources: *Times of India*, *Economic Times*, and *Economic and Political Weekly*. Specific citations are provided only when seemingly controversial or debatable observations are made.

place in India...the emphasis has shifted from distributive justice to growth' (22 February 1981). A close advisor noted that, after returning to power in 1980, Indira Gandhi 'was clearly determined to get back to the firm foundations of economic reform'.[24] And the *Economic and Political Weekly* also reported that the prime minister in her various meetings with industrialists had clarified that 'what the government was most concerned about just now was higher production'.[25]

The underlying changes that triggered the policy shift were both of the slow moving type—changes that accumulate slowly but surely, but are not always noticed in daily newspaper reports—and of the more noticeable variety. Among the slow changes was the accumulating evidence that India's economic growth throughout the 1970s had been fairly dismal; accelerating production was thus very much on the policy agenda. The context within which higher rates of growth were to be achieved included the important fact that the significance of capitalism in the Indian economy, both in the countryside and in the cities, had grown steadily.[26] The more this happened, the more anachronistic became the claims of the state controlling the 'commanding heights of the economy', especially in the face of a poorly performing public sector. A growing reliance on the private sector for growth was thus increasingly probable.

Among the short-terms changes, it must have been clear to Indira Gandhi by 1980 that the politics of 'garibi hatao' was running out of steam: anti-poverty policies like land reforms had proven difficult to implement;[27] ineffective socialism had hurt economic growth;[28] and by contrast, putting the weight of the state behind private producers had helped agricultural production, leading to the green revolution in the 1960s. The economic lessons must have been hard to ignore. Politically too, Indira Gandhi and her advisors might have calculated that a realignment with big capital may not be too costly, in part because the poor were already loyal to her, but also because state support of business may lead to higher growth and thus to lower inflation, an outcome that India's largely poor electorate may appreciate.

The three components of the new model of development that Indira Gandhi adopted from 1980 on—and that has pretty well been pursued by subsequent governments—were: prioritization of economic growth as a state goal; supporting big business to achieve this goal; and taming labour as a

[24]Arjun Sengupta, *Reforms, Equity and the IMF*, Delhi: Har Anand Publications, 2001.

[25]'All for Production', Editorial, Review of Management, *EPW*, August 1980.

[26]Baldev Raj Nayar, *India's Mixed Economy: The Role of Ideology and Interest in Its Development*, Bombay: Popular Prakashan, 1989.

[27]Atul Kohli, *The State and Poverty in India: The Politics of Reform*, New York: Cambridge University Press, 1987.

[28]Kohli, *State-Directed Development*, pp. 270–7.

necessary aspect of this strategy. The shape of the new model emerged slowly, but quite, quite surely. First, let us take the issue of prioritizing growth. Within six months of coming to power, Indira Gandhi's government put out a new industrial policy statement that put 'maximizing production' as its top priority.[29] Between then and 1982, a year she dubbed the year of 'productivity', India's development strategy underwent a 'dramatic change': jettisoning redistributive socialism, a move hailed by the Indian press at the time, development was now to be pursued by 'growth first', focusing on improvements in production and productivity.[30]

Indira Gandhi established powerful committees to study how this major transformation was to be implemented: among them were the L.K. Jha Committee to study the overhaul of economic administration; the Abid Hussain Committee to review trade; and the M. Narasimham Committee to consider financial reforms. These three senior bureaucrats were well regarded by the Indian business community.[31] While this long-term process was initiated, with its important signalling effect,[32] numerous policy measures were also adopted right away to give concrete meaning to the 'growth first' policy. These all indicated considerable convergence of views between the government and that of Indian big business (say, as expressed by the Federation of Indian Chambers of Commerce and Industry or FICCI) concerning the factors impeding growth: constraints on and the lack of governmental support for business; labour activism; inefficiency of the public sector; and decline in public investments, especially in infrastructure.[33] Notice also how

[29]H.K. Paranjape, 'New Statement on Industrial Policy', *EPW*, 20 September 1980, pp. 1593.

[30]Nayar, *India's Mixed Economy*, p. 349.

[31]I interviewed these three senior bureaucrats in the 1980s in connection with another study (Atul Kohli, *Democracy and Discontent: India's Growing Crisis of Governability*, New York: Cambridge University Press, 1991).

[32]Note that some scholars (especially Rodrik and Subramanian, 'From "Hindu Growth" to Productivity Surge'; but also, De Long, 'India since Independence') hold that such 'signalling' was somehow sufficient to trigger India's growth acceleration. While sympathetic to their general analyses, I do not agree that mere signalling was sufficient in India to provoke behavioural changes. Businessmen reacted to concrete policy changes that I document below.

[33]See, for example, the lead editorial, 'All for Production' in *EPW*, Review of Management, August 1980. Reporting on Indira Gandhi's 'two well-publicised meetings with selected group of industrialists and businessmen' the editorial noted that 'it was...made quite clear to the industrialists...what the government was most concerned about just now was higher production. Of course, this precisely has been the industrialists position always...(they) have been haranguing the government about the urgent need to remove alleged fetters on larger production...the prime minister herself and her senior cabinet colleagues told the industrialists quite explicitly that the government accepted the position...the government further accepted that industrialists needed to be given incentives to raise production.' Also see B.M., 'FICCI's Blueprint', *EPW*, 26 January 1980, p. 135, where the FICCI's policy preferences at the time are outlined.

the diagnosis within India of factors impeding growth departed from that offered by the emerging 'Washington Consensus' on development of the time. While there was some shared emphasis on deregulation and the inefficiency of the public sector, for the most part, Indian business and government advocated a much more activist state: one that will spend more, control labour more, and support capital more actively. The shared elite policy preferences within India were thus clearly more pro-business than pro-market.

Starting in the early 1980s then, Indira Gandhi's government initiated a series of pro-business policy reforms. First, the government withdrew some important constraints on big business to expand and, going further, encouraged them to enter areas hitherto reserved for the public sector. The Monopolies and Restrictive Trade Practices Act (the MRTP Act), that effectively limited the growth of big business, was thus diluted, removing licensing restrictions, and allowing big business to expand in such core industries as chemicals, drugs, ceramics, and cement. The government also encouraged the private sector to get into such areas as power generation. While small business was not always happy with such changes, big business welcomed them effusively.

Second, if expansion was to be encouraged, there was the question of financing the expansion. The government initially liberalized credit for big borrowers but there was much back and forth on the policy.[34] Additional policies for the provision of finance were instead twofold. The government provided some tax relief to big business to encourage investment. More important, the government altered the legal framework, as well as provided incentives, to encourage the private sector to finance new investments by raising resources directly from the public.[35] As Pranab Mukherjee, the finance minister from 1982 on commented:

An area of strength for the industrial sector today is the highly favourable investment climate, which has prevailed since 1980. This is a result of a series of policy measures implemented with the conscious objective of creating an environment conducive to industrial dynamism. Many of these measures have responded to the felt needs of the corporate sector...the annual budgets for the years 1980–85 have a distinct philosophy. Incentives were provided to encourage savings and channel them into productive investment.... The government has actively encouraged the corporate

[34]A few banks were nationalized during this phase. It would be a mistake to take this as a sign of continuing 'socialism'. The banks were losing money and were nationalized—bailed out really—after mutual agreement. Bank nationalization and credit, however, did become a visible political issue; the government eventually tilted some of the credit towards the countryside, where the majority of the electorate lives.

[35]A useful study of the otherwise neglected subject of politics of private equity markets in India is Echeverri-Gent, *Politics of Markets: Political Economy of Reforming India's Stock Markets*, forthcoming.

sector to mobilize the financial resources it needs for investment and modernization directly from the public. This policy has been highly successful. The total amount of capital issued by the private corporate sector increased from a little over Rs 300 crore in 1980–81 to Rs 529 crore in 1981–82, and further to Rs 809 crore in 1983–84. This is an expansion of 170 per cent in three years.[36]

Third, if private industry was to expand rapidly, both the national government and the business community felt that labour activism had to be tamed. This was difficult for Indira Gandhi in light of the fact that she was widely regarded as a leader on the Left. Nevertheless, she put the 'national situation' ahead of labour's interests and put labour on notice. Strikes, 'gheraoes', 'go-slow' and 'work-to-rule' movements were increasingly characterized by Indira Gandhi as 'anti-social demonstrations of irresponsibility by a few'.[37] Special legislation was passed to discourage strikes and labour and business were increasingly supposed to cooperate. While labour activism continued in the near future—India is after all a democracy—the die for a new government attitude towards labour was cast.

In addition to creating a new pro-business and anti-labour context, that was consistent with its growth-first policy, the Indian government also sought to restructure its own economic role. Of course, it is important to reiterate that what we are discussing here is India, and not some well-constructed, cohesive, and brutal developmental state; this is not a world in which governments pick winners, corporatize interest groups, and balance budgets. Within the limits of India's fragmented state power, the scope of political reordering was nevertheless impressive. Unlike those following the 'Washington Consensus', the Indian state in the 1980s never considered cutbacks in public expenditures that may be recessionary; there was widespread agreement instead in India that public investment in infrastructure 'crowds in' rather than 'crowds out' private investment. Accordingly, Indira Gandhi sought new revenues. Given political limitations, for example, the inability to tax more widely or effectively, and tax concessions to both investors and well-off consumers to keep up demand, the main source of new revenue was indirect, excise and customs duties. With these new revenues, and some borrowing at home and abroad, the government kept up the pace of public spending (Table 6.2), contributing to growth.

With revenues declining from direct taxes on the one hand (resulting from tax concessions for big business), and growing expenditures, including modernizing defence and sustaining investment in infrastructure on the other hand, the fiscal pressure on budgets was significant. In line with its new

---

[36]Pranab Mukherjee, *Beyond Survival: Emerging Dimensions of Indian Economy*, Delhi: Vikas Publishing House, 1984, pp. 58–9.

[37]*Times of India*, 10 July 1980.

priorities—enhancing production mainly via the private sector—the government sought to cut back some of its traditional expenditures. The most significant was limiting new investments into public sector enterprises; the new mantra instead was to improve their efficiency partly by better capacity utilization (read less labour strikes), and partly allowing them to revise upwards the prices they charge for their output. The latter was also consistent with socialism taking a back seat. Other changes of the same genre were cut in subsidies to the public distribution system, and the abandonment of the Food for Work Programme in 1982. While budget deficits and the size of the public debt grew during the Indira Gandhi years, it was downright modest in comparison to what followed in the Rajiv period.

Finally, one should take note of some of the changes in India's economic relations with the outside world.[38] As an oil importer, the second petroleum price hike in 1981 increased India's import costs significantly. A commitment to increasing industrial growth was also going to require imports of machinery and other technology. Anticipating a foreign exchange squeeze, India in 1981 entered a loan agreement with the International Monetary Fund (IMF) for nearly US $5 billion over a few years. India's pro-business policies had already been moving in a direction that the IMF found 'encouraging', though not quite the 'structural adjustment' package more commonly demanded. It is notable that the IMF did not insist that India cut back its public expenditures; apparently Indian policy-makers convinced the IMF of the need to keep up public investments in order to accelerate economic growth via the private sector.[39]

---

[38]Many observers of India, especially those outside of India, often judge the 'progress' of India's 'reforms' or of 'liberalization' mainly by this yardstick. This is understandable, though for different reasons for different actors. First, some serious scholars, often economists, are deeply convinced that global integration of an economy is the key to improving efficiency and growth of an economy. Armed with this 'theory', they often look for evidence of external liberalization—or the lack of it—as key events that will trigger meaningful change. Second, there are those in the international business community, as well as their spokesmen, whose primary interests are opportunities for investment and trade in a potentially large market like India. And finally, there are a variety of other observers—associated with international development agencies or journalists—for whom some combination of ideas and interests leads to rigid (or opportunistic) mindsets that one is tempted to label ideological. While the focus on the opening of the economy to the outside world is thus understandable (or at least, comprehensible), it can also be myopic, especially if one wants to understand some of the key economic dynamics of a giant-sized country.

[39]Sengupta, *Reforms, Equity and the IMF*, Chapter II. It may be worth speculating that this exception was related to the fact that India did not owe any huge sums of money to foreign creditors. In this light, one wonders if the main purpose of subsequent 'structural adjustment' programmes imposed on many Latin American and African countries was mainly to repay loans rather than facilitate growth. In a private conversation (in September 2004), Joseph Stiglitz suggested to me that, to his mind, the main aim of 'structural adjustment' programmes was probably to induce recessions, thus reducing demand for imports, and thus saving foreign exchange to pay back foreign creditors.

What India did do at the time was to open up the economy somewhat to both foreign investors and to foreign goods. Import liberalization in 1981 was especially far from trivial, but also proved to be short-lived. The import bill rose sharply, without a commensurate increase in exports. A variety of Indian businessmen reacted sharply to the threat of cheaper imports and demanded protection.[40] The Indian government obliged; import restrictions were imposed again in the budget of 1983–4, around the same time as India terminated its IMF agreement, even before taking advantage of the full loan.[41] If one ever needed evidence to support the claim that the primary commitment of the Indian state at this time was to established Indian businesses rather than to any general principle of creating free markets and a global opening, here it is. This was also a pattern that would repeat itself during the Rajiv Gandhi years and was not fully abandoned even during the more sharply liberal 1990s.

To sum up the discussion so far, Indira Gandhi during the first half of the 1980s abandoned a commitment to redistribution, and re-committed herself to a 'growth first' model of development. These priorities, in turn, led her to tilt the policy process in favour of big business, against labour, and to restructure the state's own role in the economy towards growth promotion. There were some halting efforts to open up the economy as well. While this model shared some policies recommended by the 'Washington Consensus' on development, it was considerably more statist and more explicitly growth-oriented; it was also more pro-business than pro-market. India's nationalist-capitalist model of development from 1980 on thus started to share some important traits with East Asia, where highly interventionist states commonly ally with business and against labour, and only selectively link their economies to the world, often more via trade than capital. Of course, state power in India is considerably more fragmented and checked by democratic forces than, say, in a South Korea under Park Chung Hee. These differences were also consequential: budget deficits remained an issue as direct taxes were hard to collect and expenditures were hard to limit; mercifully, labour could never be fully tamed; and the state itself remained 'soft', creating numerous problems of inefficiency in the bureaucracy and public management. The shift in development strategy also created significant political problems,

---

[40]By mid-1982, for example, FICCI was arguing against trade liberalization. The demands to restrict imports, however, were not universal. The Birlas were arguing against rayon imports and the Tatas against the dirt cheap Bulgarian soda ash. Select public sector industries were also arguing against cheap imports of computer components. Those benefiting from cheap imports, however, also made some noises but did not prevail; these included some in the textile industry who wanted to import shuttle-less looms and glass manufacturers who wanted cheap soda ash. See, 'Clamours against Liberalization', EPW, 10–17 July 1982, pp. 1135–6.

[41]Kaushik Basu, 'The Budget: A Critique of Its Rationale', EPW, 19 March 1983.

especially how to win the support of a majority, where the majority is poor, or near-poor, and the rhetoric of socialism and of 'garibi hatao' are slowly being put on the back burner. While this is no place to discuss these issues, Indira Gandhi's flirtation with ethnic politics in this period, especially themes of Hindu chauvinism and interfering with Sikh politics, was part and parcel of the new political economy.[42]

The growth-first, pro-business, and anti-labour shift initiated by Indira Gandhi basically continued under her successor, Rajiv Gandhi. Leaving aside a lot of rhetorical flourishes, as well as a fair amount of back and forth on specific policies, Rajiv Gandhi continued the policy changes initiated by Indira Gandhi, moving a little faster in some areas, and little slower in others. By the end of his rule some significant changes in the domestic political economy and a few changes that altered India' s links with the world were put in place. Most significantly, state control of such activities of private Indian firms as entry into production, production decisions and expansion in size were eased even further. Indian business groups were also provided significant concessions on corporate and personal taxes, as well as assurances about future patterns of taxation. On the external front, some import barriers came down, though not dramatically; some import quotas were removed, and there was some devaluation; for the most part, however, the internal changes were more significant than the external ones.

Three important political economy observations concerning the Rajiv period need to be made.[43] First, irrespective of what actual reforms were implemented in this period, Rajiv Gandhi and his advisors decided from the onset to emphasize a break from the past. Whereas Indira Gandhi's growing embrace of big business was increasingly straining her commitment to socialism, Rajiv Gandhi dropped the pretence of socialism altogether and openly committed his government to a new 'liberal' beginning.[44] Among Rajiv's important economic advisors at this point were individuals like L.K. Jha, Manmohan Singh, Montek Singh Ahluwalia and Abid Hussain. These individuals were also critical players under the earlier Indira Gandhi period, and some of them, especially Manmohan Singh and Montek Singh Ahluwalia, played a decisive role in the policy shift in 1991. Two conclusions thus seem warranted: stressing continuity or change was as much a political decision as it had to do with the substance of policy reforms; and more important, the decision to undertake major reforms of the economy was already very

[42]Atul Kohli, *Democracy and Discontent: India's Growing Crisis of Governability*, New York: Cambridge University Press, 1991.

[43]Atul Kohli, 'Politics of Economic Liberalization in India', *World Development*, 17(3), 1989.

[44]During his very first budget, therefore, the word 'socialism' was not even mentioned once. Of course, when faced with declining popularity later during his tenure, Rajiv reembraced 'socialism'. By then, however, the image of a break from the past had stuck.

much on the mind of key policy-makers during the 1980s, who were then waiting for an appropriate political moment, which finally emerged with the 'crisis' of 1991.

Second, it is clear from the policy changes adopted during this phase that the government's commitment was first and foremost to economic growth, and only secondarily to some abstract notions of 'openness' or laissez faire. In spite of growing budget deficits, for example, the government thus kept up the pace of public investments, including in infrastructure. Public spending thus helped growth, not only by boosting demand, but also by easing supply constraints. The government self-consciously lowered taxes to middle classes so as to boost demand, especially for consumer durables. Much of the new private investment flew into these areas, also improving the productivity of the hitherto heavy industry economy. And finally, the state got actively involved in promoting the growth of some such industries as computers and electronics, providing them with supply-side support but also maintaining pressure on them to stay competitive by minimizing protection. While problems of fiscal and of balance-of-payment imbalances were building up, it was also the case that the government was self-consciously promoting growth and succeeding.

Finally, it is important to note that the policy pattern was more pro-business, especially pro-big Indian business, rather than anything else. Much of internal policy reform—such as eliminating many licensing requirements, removing further restrictions on how big businesses can be, and opening up areas reserved for the public sector to the private sector—helped big rather than small or medium private businesses. Moreover, whenever conflicts arose over external opening, especially on issues of foreign investment, but also on trade, the government accommodated the demands of Indian business groups. Spokesmen for FICCI, as well as government representatives, such as L.K. Jha, often reiterated openly that the 'pace of domestic liberalization' would continue but 'external liberalization was not really an objective of the policy'.[45]

Indira and Rajiv Gandhi dominated the Indian political economy during the 1980s. This was also the decade in which India's economy made a breakthrough, moving beyond the 'Hindu growth rate' to a more rapidly growing economy. One central suggestion here is that this shift in economic performance was triggered by the pro-business policy shift engineered by the two Gandhis. Prior to this period, during the 1970s, Indira Gandhi accentuated the democratic socialist content of Nehru's statist model of development. Given the organizational and the class characteristics of the

---

[45]Atul Kohli, 'Politics of Economic Liberalization in India', p. 315.

Indian state,[46] however, Indira Gandhi's efforts at redistribution failed and the democratic socialist tilt evolved into anti-capitalist populism, hurting economic growth. After returning to power in 1980, Indira Gandhi essentially abandoned the redistributive thrust of her rhetoric and policies, prioritized economic growth as the state's main goal, and sought to slowly but surely re-order economic policies to achieve this goal. The story of economic policy changes during the 1980s just recounted is mainly this story of the making of a new pro-business, growth-oriented model of development in India.

The new growth strategy produced both higher rates of investment and improvement in the efficiency of investment,[47] contributing to an improvement in the growth rate, especially in industry. The government's commitment to growth was evident, first in sustaining relatively high levels of public investments in the 1980s (Figure 6.3). This investment helped ease a variety of infrastructural bottlenecks, such as in coal, power and railways; it might also have contributed to higher growth rate via a boost to overall demand.[48] More important than the recovery of public investments was the changing behaviour of the private sector.

Assuming that businessmen react to favourable opportunities for profit making, it is reasonable to suggest that the government's new pro-business policy regime in the 1980s was responsible for the rising share of corporate investments in GDP evident in Table 6.2 and Figure 6.3. Other evidence also supports the claim that private sector companies grew at a relatively rapid pace during the 1980s: whereas the paid-up capital of private companies grew at an average annual rate of 7.3 per cent during the 1970s, the growth rate during the 1980s was nearly double, 14.3 per cent; also, the number of private companies during the 1980s grew at an annual average rate of 13.5 per cent, compared to a growth rate of 3.3 per cent for public sector companies.[49]

[46]Atul Kohli, *The State and Poverty in India*; also see Pranab Bardhan, *The Political Economy of Development in India*, Oxford, UK: Basil Blackwell, 1984.

[47]Virmani, 'Sources of India's Economic Growth'.

[48]Rodrik and Subramanian ('From "Hindu Growth" to Productivity Surge') find that public investments in the 1980s did not impact growth, though they do allow that the relationship holds with some time lag. Most economic analysts of India find instead a strong association between public investments and higher growth rates (see, for example, Nagaraj, 'Indian Economy since 1980'). Even analysts considered 'pro-liberalization', but committed to growth, worry about declining public investments in India (see, for example, Mohan, 'Fiscal Correction for Economic Growth'). Joshi and Little ('New Economic Policies: A Historical Perspective', *EPW*, 4–11 January 1992, p. 43.) also concluded that 'the high level of demand in the 1980s', which was of course in part related to high public expenditures, contributed to improved productivity and growth in the 1980s?

[49]Jorgen Dige Pederson, 'Explaining Economic Liberalization in India: State and Society Perspectives', *World Development*, 28(2), 2000, pp. 268; also see Virmani, 'Sources of India's Growth', p. 35.

We also know that private investment in India tends to be more efficient than public sector investment. It follows that the state's pro-business tilt thus contributed to a higher rate of growth via the enhanced role of the private sector in the Indian economy. While the major beneficiaries were established big business firms, the relative ease of entry and growth enabled new players like the politically well connected Reliance to also emerge as giants, competing with the likes of Tatas and Birlas.

If the partial impact on growth of changing governmental commitment to growth can be traced via changing policies and enhanced investments, both public and private, our understanding of why and how the productivity and the efficiency of the economy also improved remains rather diffuse.[50] Some of the underlying factors were probably not related to short-term policy changes; these might include the building stock of technology and management in the economy, the establishment of a variety of producer networks, sufficient demand in the economy, an adequate tax base, and the presence of a sizable working class. Among policy related changes, firms might have become more productive because many of them by the 1980s were producing more consumer than capital goods, technology imports were easier, and so was the availability of foreign exchange, enabling ready availability of a variety of scarce inputs and thus helping the utilization of industrial capacity at a relatively high level. Internal competition also must have put pressure on some firms to economize, though for others, near monopoly type of growth, and thus achievement of economies of scale, might have helped produce a similar outcome. The precise causal impact of such factors on productivity is hard to establish; what does seem clear is that the shift in the governmental policies and the enhanced role of the private sector helped improve, not only the rates of investment, but also the efficiency of the economy.

While the new pro-business strategy of the two Gandhis was indeed responsible for accelerating India's economic growth rate, it also created numerous other problems. Two sets of problems have been mentioned all along but are worth reiterating. Let us call these sets, political and political economy problems, respectively. The state's narrow ruling alliance with business not only relegated a variety of distributional concerns to second order priorities, but also created the important political problem of how to

---

[50]Writing eloquently, and with an authority that he well deserves, I.G. Patel ('New Economic Policies: A Historical Perspective', *EPW*, 4–11 January 1992, p. 43) thus noted: 'Efficiency, of course, is a dynamic concept and its best promoters, apart from entrepreneurship, skills and capital, are good information, competition with a level-playing field, transparency, relative stability of policies and improvements in technology. Once again, efficiency transcends the domain of microeconomics as narrowly and traditionally conceived, and requires something more than competitive markets.'

mobilize majorities in a poor society. The fact that Congress leaders resorted to mobilizing a variety of ethnic sensibilities in politics—something hardly new to India, but especially evident again after 1980—was deeply related to this narrowing of the ruling alliance; these developments also opened up political room for the subsequent political growth of the Bharatiya Janata Party (BJP). And on the political economy front, given the nature of power in the Indian state, the embrace of a state-capital-alliance-for-rapid-growth model of development could never fully replicate East Asia; India's authority structure was and remains too fragmented, and given democracy, the underlying class basis of state power could never be too exclusively pro-business. The clearest economic manifestation of these political traits was the slow but steady building up of fiscal pressures: the inability to collect more revenues on the one hand, and the inability to limit a variety of public expenditures on the other hand. Even some of the external borrowing mainly fed internal fiscal imbalances. The growing fiscal and balance of payment difficulties, in turn, helped create the 'crisis' of 1991.

7

Politics of Economic Growth in India, 1980–2005, Part II
The 1990s and Beyond*

Having analysed the political economy of the growth experience in the 1980s, the second empirical puzzle for the paper emerges by juxtaposing economic performance—especially performance of the manufacturing sector in specific and of industry in general—during the 1980s against that in the 1990s and beyond. A number of scholars have in recent years demonstrated that, though growth in manufacturing in the 1990s was somewhat lower than in the 1980s, the shift in growth trend since 1991–2 was not statistically significant.[1] The stunning fact then is this: in spite of all the noise about reforms—for and against—the growth rate of India's manufacturing industry was not influenced all that greatly by the reforms (see Figure 6.2, Chapter 6, this volume). The real break in growth occurred around 1980. Since then nothing dramatic has changed in terms of the aggregate outcomes. The growth data is further supported by employment data: employment in manufacturing remained constant at around 12 per cent of the workforce

*Originally published as 'Politics of Economic Growth in India, 1980–2005, Part II: The 1990s and Beyond', *Economic and Political Weekly*, 8 April 2006, pp. 1361–70.

A very early draft of this paper was presented at the 'Crisis States Research Workshop', India International Centre, New Delhi, 16–17 December 2004. I would like to thank Neera Chandhoke and John Harriss for the opportunity, and the workshop participants for their suggestions. A second draft of this paper was presented at the Centre for the Advanced Study of India, University of Pennsylvania, Philadelphia, on 11 November 2005. Many thanks to the centre director, Francine Frankel for the opportunity, and to Sunila Kale and Jeffrey Witsoe, centre staff members, for useful discussions. I would also like to acknowledge the helpful comments of R. Nagaraj, Robert Kaufman, Anil Jacob, and Roy Licklider and the research assistance of Prerna Singh, especially in preparing the tables and graphs.

[1]See R. Nagaraj, 'Industrial Policy and Performance since 1980: Which Way Now?', *EPW*, 30 August 2003; Table 6.3, Chapter 6, this volume.

during the 1980s and the 1990s.[2] The reforms have thus neither helped nor hurt growth and employment by much.[3] Why?

Once again, observing the more proximate economic determinants of these trends helps set up the puzzle for a deeper political economy analysis. It is clear from Table 6.2 (Chapter 6) that the overall rates of capital formation in the Indian economy did not alter significantly between the 1980s and the 1990s. What did alter, however, was the composition of this investment (Figure 6.3, Chapter 6); public investments declined in the 1990s and the balance was filled by a variety of private investors. As already noted, there might have been a slight decline in the growth rate of productivity of the economy, but not by much (Figure 6.4, Chapter 6). So, the second empirical puzzle concerns the impact of reforms on investment—overall stability but changing composition—and on the rate of growth of productivity of labour and capital, where very few gains are evident.

That India in 1991 adopted a fairly significant set of economic policy reforms is well known. A list of reforms undertaken is also readily available elsewhere.[4] The important issues deserving our attention instead are two: why were the reforms undertaken and how have they evolved; and why has the impact of reforms on aggregate economic growth, especially on industrial growth, been negligible. Before tackling these issues, a few interpretive comments on the nature and the scope of the reforms are in order.

The economic reforms undertaken since 1991 have influenced both India's industrial policy and external economic relations. The variety of industrial policy reforms—further de-licensing, removal of MRTP constraints, tax concessions, opening of yet newer areas hitherto reserved for the public sector, and taming labour—are best viewed as continuation of reforms well underway during the 1980s. These reforms also ought to be judged mainly as pro-indigenous business, enabling well-established businesses to grow and allowing some new ones to emerge and flourish. In light of the discussion above, none of these reforms should be all that surprising. Where there was a significant element of discontinuity and thus of surprise, was in the area of India's external economic relations, including, the trade, foreign

[2]Ibid., p. 3708.

[3]There is an interesting parallel here with the situation in Latin America. An important study of Latin American reforms by ECLA thus concluded: 'The reform results were neither as positive as supporters predicted nor as negative as opponents feared. Indeed, the reforms per se seem to have had a surprisingly small impact at the aggregate level (including on growth, investment and inequality)' (Stalling and Peres, *Growth Employment, and Equity*, p. 384).

[4]Rob Jenkins, *Democratic Politics and Economic Reform in India*, Cambridge University Press, 1999, pp. 16–28; Nagesh Kumar, 'Economic Reforms and their Macro-Economic Impact', *EPW*, 4 March 2000; and Francine Frankel, *India's Political Economy, 1947–2004*, New Delhi: Oxford University Press, 2005.

investment and financial relations. As is also well known, starting in 1991, import quotas were removed (fully only in 2001), tariffs came down slowly but surely, currency was devalued, the foreign investment regime was liberalized, and various restrictions on external financial transactions were eased. Some of these reforms helped Indian business; others put enormous competitive pressure on them. In adopting these external economic reforms, the Indian state was responding to a sharply changed world and, in the process, attempting to establish a new social contract with Indian business: we will continue to put our full weight behind you, but you, in turn, must become more competitive.

The scope of India's external economic reforms must be kept in perspective. By India's own past standards, the changes were quite dramatic. In a comparative and global perspective, however, India's opening to the world remains relatively modest. In a useful essay, Baldev Raj Nayar has documented this 'modesty'.[5] On the trade front, for example, tariffs did come down significantly, but the decline began in 1987, during the Rajiv Gandhi years and towards the end of the millennium, still averaged some 30 per cent, among the highest in the world. India's share of foreign trade at some 25 per cent of the GDP was also among the lowest in the world in the early twenty-first century (Table 7.1). The story on foreign investment is not all that different. While the inflows in the 1990s were huge compared to the past—averaging nearly US $4 billion, including both direct and portfolio investments—on a per capita basis India remained one of the least exposed countries to foreign investment in the world. And finally, it is well known that capital movements in India remain relatively restricted.

Now, let us first briefly visit the issue of politics of reforms. Why did the same set of reforms that proved difficult to pursue during the 1980s become more likely in the early 1990s? A superficial answer would point to the economic 'crisis' of 1991. As already indicated above, however, the 'crisis' mainly provided an opportunity for policy reform; the real causes were deeper. A number of political analysts have drawn our attention to these deeper causes.[6] Building on their work, it makes sense to separate the underlying structural variables from the political process, and then to think of the underlying structural changes as both external to India and within India, especially in India's business community. The reforms became more

[5]Baldev Raj Nayar, 'Opening up and Openness of Indian Economy', *EPW*, 15 September 2001.

[6]Jenkins, *Democratic Policies and Economic Reform in India*; Jorgen Dige Pederson, 'Explaining Economic Liberalization in India: State and Society Perspectives', *World Development*, 28(2), 2000; Nayar, 'Opening up and Openness of Indian Economy'; and John Harriss and Stuart Corbridge, *Reinventing India: Liberalisation, Hindu Nationalism and Popular Democracy*, Oxford, UK: Polity Press, 2000.

acceptable during the 1990s then because the world in which India operated changed and because Indian capital split politically, with a significant faction at least willing to experiment with a more open economy. Let us elaborate.

Foremost among the significant external changes was the decline and the disintegration of the Soviet Union. This change was profoundly consequential for India. What I have in mind here is not only the diffuse and the oft cited issue of the decline of a model of development. The resulting pressures were instead more concrete and more serious. First, the Soviet Union was an important trading partner (India-Soviet Union trade was close to US$6 billion towards the end of the 1980s) which provided India, in exchange for a variety of goods, oil, armaments and defence materials. Much of this exchange did not involve use of hard currencies. With a sharp decline in exports to Russia, the issue of maintaining and upgrading defence forces became intimately related to the availability of hard foreign exchange. Improving export earnings and maximizing other sources of foreign exchange thus became issues of national security. While never publicised as such, these issues must have created a new sense of urgency for 'liberalization'. Closely related to this, the disintegration of the Soviet Union also meant the loss of a military and political ally, creating pressures to shore up relations with the US. As most developing country leaders understand, improved political relations with the US, in turn, often involve closer economic relations, especially the opening of an economy to American goods and capital.

A second important global change that developed over the 1980s was the growing availability of investible resources—in foreign exchange, to boot—in the form of portfolio investments. While a Faustian bargain—mainly because of their volatile nature—they might have appeared attractive to foreign exchange starved Indian decision-makers. Even to Indian businessmen, portfolio investment must have appeared less threatening—it is in some ways more akin to selling your shares in public, over which one has some control—than greenfield foreign investment, not to mention acquisitions and mergers.

And, finally, it must have been clear to Indian decision-makers that the World Trade Organization (WTO) was going to happen (it actually came into being in 1994), and that India would be a signatory to the WTO agreement. Given WTO's requirements, it must also have been clear that import quotas would have to go and that tariffs would have to come down within some time-bound period. Mitu Sengupta during her research thus found a number of decision-makers, including Manmohan Singh and Amar Nath Varma, arguing that these external considerations were important in India's road to liberalization in the early 1990s.[7]

---

[7]Sengupta provided this information to me in a personal communication, for which I am much obliged. Also see Sengupta, 'The Politics of Market Reform in India: The Fragile Basis of Paradigm Shift', unpublished PhD thesis, Department of Political Science, University of Toronto.

While India's 'world' thus indeed changed over the 1980s, some very important changes within India must also be taken into account. Most important, the reluctance of Indian business group towards external opening softened, though within limits. During the 1980s, segments of Indian capital became more efficient and business lobbying underwent some significant changes. We have already discussed above the steady gains in productivity of Indian industry throughout the 1980s. One can then suggest that some Indian business groups were probably more ready to deal with foreign competition in the 1990s than in the 1980s. The clearest evidence for this claim is available in the changing patterns of how Indian capital organized itself politically and in the demands it then made on the state during this period.

Stanley Kochanek[8] has ably documented some of these changes in business organization and lobbying. Very briefly, during the 1980s, India's two main national chambers of commerce—the Federation of Indian Chambers of Commerce and Industry (FICCI) and the Associated Chambers of Commerce and Industry (ASSOCHAM)—reorganized. They increasingly became mirror images of each other (with differing regional base), but they also slowly lost ground to the newly constituted Confederation of Indian Industry (CII) in terms of political influence. The CII increasingly came to represent India's more 'modern' industries—especially engineering firms, often located in the south of India—who were more interested in exports. The CII was also run professionally and developed such close ties with Indian bureaucracy that it came to be dubbed as the 'junior partner' of the government; so much so that the 1993–4 budget came to be called the 'Tarun Das' budget, referring to Tarun Das, the director of CII.[9] Over the next decade, these patterns became nearly institutionalized; for example, Montek Singh Ahluwalia in 2004 was openly discussing the need for 'public-private partnership' in industry and inviting the private sector 'to be part of the decision-making'.[10] While not quite 'India Incorporated', there is more than a shade of a move towards 'Korea or Taiwan Incorporated' in these changes.

Though somewhat of an oversimplification, Indian capital basically split during the 1980s in its political and policy preferences. On the one side were the more 'modern', export-oriented businesses, represented by the CII. They favoured a more open, competitive economy. And on the other side were the older business houses that matured during the import substitution regime. They were represented by both FICCI and ASSOCHAM; they were also considerably more wary of external opening. As will become clear

[8]Stanley Kochanek, 'Liberalization and Business Lobbying in India', *Journal of Commonwealth and Comparative Politics*, 34(3), November 1996; 'The Transformation of Interest Politics in India', *Pacific Affairs*, 68(4), 1996.

[9]Kochanek, 'Liberalization and Business Lobbying in India', p. 167.

[10]*Indian Express*, 29 December 2004.

below, the actual political process surrounding economic liberalization was more complex than this characterization might suggest. Nevertheless, with some significant business names and organizations willing to support the opening of the economy, India's pro-liberalization policy makers must have felt emboldened. Changing global conditions and splits within the ranks of Indian capital thus provided the new structural conditions within which India's technocratic elite pushed through some significant policy changes in the early 1990s.

Beyond the structural changes, the political process of economic liberalization was also revealing of the underlying power dynamics. As I analyse this, the basic picture that emerges is one of the political and economic elite attempting to accommodate each other, but within the context of considerable fragmentation of political power; this political dynamics, I will suggest, was economically consequential. To highlight only some of the main events, as the balance of payments situation deteriorated throughout 1990, the issue of India approaching the IMF for a 'structural adjustment' type of a loan was again at the forefront; India accepted such a loan in 1990 with a caretaker government in charge. In early 1991 then, just a couple of months before the 'big bang' announcement of new liberal economic policies, the CII floated a 'theme paper' in April 1991, arguing for radical shifts in India's economic policies towards a more open and competitive economy.[11] When the Congress government, with Manmohan Singh as the finance minister, actually announced the policy shift, the main forces supporting such a shift included the narrow political leadership, the technocratic policy elite, a segment of Indian capital, and external actors, expressing their preferences mainly in the form of policy conditionalities set by the IMF.

In spite of India being a fairly mobilized democracy, it was then the case that major economic policy changes arrived in India with a narrow support base. If further evidence was needed to support this claim, notice, for example, that critical reforms in industrial policy in 1991 were made as executive decisions. Anticipating nationalist opposition to global opening, the government used legal technicalities—they included the policy changes in a 'statement' rather than in a 'resolution'—to avoid any discussion and a vote in the parliament. Similarly, the efforts to reduce fiscal deficits over the next few years encountered opposition. Once gain, as yet another example, the government reduced some fertiliser subsidies and increased petroleum prices (in September 1992) only after Parliament went into recess. Other such examples could be readily multiplied. The simple point, however, is that liberalizing reforms were pushed forward by a narrow coalition, and that an element of 'stealth' clearly characterized the politics

[11]Kochanek, 'The Transformation of Interest Politics in India', p. 538.

of economic liberalization,[12] aimed at circumventing nationalist and popular opposition.

The 'big bang' rhetoric of a dramatic policy shift aside, India's economic policies during the 1990s altered only incrementally, responding to objective changes, the evolving views of key policy makers, and to a variety of political pressures. Early reforms included internal deregulation of industry, attempts to tame the deficit, and slow but steady external opening. The industrial policy reform included further de-licensing of the private sector, removal of MRTP restrictions, tax concessions to business, and some further efforts to tame India's well-entrenched and activist labour. India's private sector rightly interpreted these policy changes as creating 'operational freedom it has never enjoyed before'.[13] The stock market boom that followed was probably not unrelated to what was interpreted as a sharply pro-business policy shift.

In line with the IMF's 'structural adjustment' prescriptions, a second important element of early reforms included efforts to cut the budget deficit. Since it was difficult to increase revenues—especially in light of tax concessions to the corporate sector—the burden of these efforts fell on reducing expenditures. After some early success, say, the first three years, these soon ran into numerous problems. For example, cutbacks in subsidies were resisted by such politically consequential groups as farmers and exporters, further cuts in social expenditures were likely to cost popular electoral support, and decline in public investments was being widely associated with the continuing industrial recession. Even big capital started arguing for greater public investments in such areas as infrastructure. Concerned about economic growth then, the Indian government by 1994 chose not to accept further IMF loans, started arguing that further cuts in budget deficits were neither possible nor desirable, and the decline in current expenditures came to a halt; the reduction in budget deficits that was actually achieved unfortunately came at the expense of social spending and public investment.[14]

The attempt to integrate the Indian economy with the global economy was, of course, the third major component of the reform initiative. As already noted, during the 1990s most import quotas were removed, tariff levels came down, and laws governing the inflow of foreign capital were liberalized. However, the political process of India's global opening turned out to be quite contentious and, in the end, a variety of pressures, especially business lobbying, limited the speed and scope of such an opening. For example, as also discussed above, India's major chamber of commerce, the CII, supported the opening of India's economy in the early 1990s. By contrast, the other

[12]See Jenkins, *Democratic Politics and Economic Reform in India*.
[13]*Economic Times*, 9 November 1991.
[14]Kumar, 'Economic Reforms and their Macro-Economic Impact', pp. 807–8.

two chambers, FICCI and ASSOCHAM, argued throughout the 1980s for internal deregulation but for 'going slow' on the external front. Within two-three years of the 'big bang' opening, as the balance of payment crisis eased, a variety of Indian business houses came together—in a group the Indian press dubbed as the 'Bombay Club'—to oppose India's external opening.[15] They argued that rapid liberalization will destroy India's indigenous industry, especially capital goods industry; according to them, tariffs should be brought down very slowly, and the inflow of foreign investment should be limited. Citing Korea as their model, they asked for more government help and for a more selective integration with the global economy. Along with FICCI and ASSOCHAM members, the prominent spokesmen of the Bombay Club included senior officials of the CII, underlining the point that, as far as external opening is concerned, Indian capital is not as factionalized as the organizational politics of competing chambers might suggest.

The nationalist element in Indian business's protests found a strong echo in the swadeshi politics of India's main opposition party at the time, the BJP. A variety of more diffuse issues—such as intellectual property rights and rapid opening of trade in commodities and services—also fed the nationalist wrath of India's political class. The BJP mobilized these sentiments effectively in the mid-1990s, putting the ruling Congress government on the defensive. The early momentum of reforms thus got bogged down in the nearly normal complexities of India's democratic politics. The results included a steady but relatively slow—paced integration of Indian economy with the global economy, a trend that has pretty well continued into the present period.

Of the major policy reforms initiated in 1991 then, internal deregulation has proceeded the furthest, global opening has been real but slow and modest, and the attempts to trim current public expenditures have not made much headway. Two other reform areas—privatization of public enterprises and labour reforms—were also discussed at the early stages and have been periodically re-discussed. Anticipating serious political opposition, however, various governments have mostly left these policy reform areas alone. A pattern thus emerges. Internal deregulation and the modest global opening were changes that were either demanded by Indian business groups, especially big business, or something a significant faction of Indian business could live with. The unwillingness or the inability to privatize public enterprises and/or to tame India's organized labour in turn underline the 'soft' or fragmented nature of state power in democratic India. The politics of continuing budget deficits is in part a result of similar democratic pressures, but it also highlights the commitment of Indian policy makers to economic growth, and the related willingness to use public expenditures

[15]Kochanek, 'Liberalization and Business Lobbying in India', pp. 168–70.

to facilitate this outcome. In spite of the much pro- and anti-reform rhetoric about India going neo-liberal, therefore, both the political process and the process of policy reform reflect a much more complex pattern of state intervention in the economy: while some liberalization is real, Indian state remains activist, willing to support and to work closely with Indian business, but at the same time state actors remain hemmed in by a variety of democratic political pressures.

Now, leaving aside the issue of politics and policies of reform, the second major vexing issue concerns their limited economic impact. In the words of Montek Ahluwalia, the reforms 'were expected to generate faster industrial growth and greater penetration of world markets in industrial products, but performance in this respect has been disappointing'.[16] With reform advocates themselves expressing disappointment, the real debate in the literature is about explaining the disappointing performance. The 'disappointment' of course has to be kept in perspective: at some 6 per cent annual growth, India is still among the world's fastest growers; exports have grown steadily; and the balance-of-payment situation has improved considerably since the reforms. And yet, it is the case that industrial growth in the 1990s and beyond did not improve over the 1980s (Figure 6.2), growth in total factor productivity in the post-reform period was somewhat lower than in the 1980s (Figure 6.4), the modest export growth continued to be surpassed by growing imports, and public investment declined while the share of public debt in the GDP continued to grow. Contending explanations, as one might expect, tend to suggest either that reforms have not gone far enough,[17] or that they have already gone too far, too quick.[18]

[16]Montek S. Ahluwalia, 'Economic Reforms in India since 1991: Has Graduation Worked?', *Journal of Economic Perspectives*, 16(3), 2002, p. 75.

[17]Ibid.

[18]Prabhat Patnaik, 'The Performance of the Indian Economy in the 1990s', *Social Scientist*, 25(5, 6), May–June 1999; and Chaudhuri, 'Economic Reforms and Industrial Structure'. Advocates and critics alike do not always clarify why they think what they think. Ahluwalia, for example, seems to suggest that further lowering of tariff barriers, further opening of the economy to direct foreign investment, and enhancing labour 'flexibility', are the next steps necessary to improve India's economic performance. Why he believes that these policies will do the trick is never made explicit; it is as if all 'sensible' people must of course agree. An occasional reference is made to East Asia, with a suggestion that this is how East Asia did it. While my analysis too is influenced by East Asian successes, East Asia is a diverse place, and the fastest growing states within that region, such as South Korea or Taiwan, were hardly during their peak performing periods models of open economies with 'flexible' labour regimes (see Amsden, *Asia's Next Giant*; Wade, *Governing the Market*; and Kohli, *State-Directed Development*). Critics of reform, by contrast, seem to hark back to some imagined golden period of Nehru and Mahalanobis. Not only is the desirability of the return to that old import substitution model of development highly debatable, it is also not likely that such a return is a realistic option in the contemporary 'globalized' world.

Focusing mainly on the political economy of growth, what is surprising is that, at least at the aggregate level, India's reforms seemed to have neither helped nor hurt economic growth by much. How does one best understand this outcome? As before, one needs to focus both on issues of rates of investment and of productivity, neither of which improved much in the post-reform period.

Some of the post-reform economic indicators are presented in Table 7.3. Along with the data presented above, they underline the point relatively well known to observers of India, namely, that private investments, including corporate investments, have for the most part remained buoyant in the post-reform period but public investments have declined (see Table 6.2 and Figure 6.3, Chapter 6, and Table 7.1 here). Private corporate investment shot up rapidly after the reforms but peaked in the mid-1990s. Since then the rate of growth of corporate investments has declined but still remained at a level generally higher than in the earlier periods. Capital formation in the household sector by contrast has grown rapidly since the mid-1990s.

One must attribute the continued buoyancy of private sector investments to the variety of pro-business industrial policy changes introduced in the post-1991 period. The fact that the investment boom originated mainly in the 'registered sector', especially in the first-half of the 1990s,[19] further suggests two observations: reform policies initially helped big business more than small business; and that big business felt relatively comfortable with the slow pace of external opening of the economy, at least until later in the 1990s, when continued imports and foreign investor produced goods brought forward protests and discouraged further investments. The relatively high rates of private investment are also one of the main forces propelling steady growth of industry (though not at a very high rate) in the post-reform period. The pro-growth and the pro-business drift of the Indian state—that began in the 1980s and continued into the 1990s and beyond—are thus mainly responsible for the respectable performance of the Indian economy.

Several related observations further support the point that the main dynamics underlying sustained growth is not so much liberalization as it is the state's continuing pro-business orientation. First, contrary to what one might expect from further liberalization, the labour intensity of Indian industry decreased steadily during the 1990s.[20] Second, the unregistered sector of Indian industry—which one presumes to be more export-oriented and less capital intensive—did not attract much new investment in the post-reform period.[21] Relatedly, there is no clear evidence that exports of labour-intensive

---

[19]Nagaraj, 'Industrial Policy and Performance since 1980', p. 3711.

[20]Chaudhuri, 'Economic Reforms and Industrial Structure in India', p. 160.

[21]Nagaraj, 'Industrial Policy and Performance since 1980', p. 3711.

goods grew sharply. Fourth, and this is quite important, the level of concentration in private industry has increased since 1991: for example, market capitalization of the top ten private companies increased from 2.2 per cent of the GDP in 1990 to 12.9 per cent in 2004 and sales of the top ten companies during the same period grew from 2.3 to 9.3 per cent of the GDP.[22] And finally, the share of employment generated by the manufacturing sector has remained largely unaltered over the last decade and a half.

Leaving aside the issue of private industry, public investments in India as a proportion of total economic activity declined noticeably during the 1990s (Table 6.2 and Figure 6.3, Chapter 6, and Table 7.3 here). The underlying dynamics are not hard to understand. Given the fragmented nature of state power in India, public authorities find it hard to raise taxes and revenues. A variety of tax concessions to the rich and middle classes have also cut into the revenue pie, as has the decline of import duties. The service and agricultural sectors remain largely untaxed. The pressure on the expenditure side is merciless, especially paying interest on the growing public debt, and defence expenditures. Faced with severe fiscal pressures in 1991, along with a loan and associated conditions of the IMF, the Indian government sought to trim the deficit. While the successive governments have made some headway, they have been unable to control current expenditures. The budget deficit has thus been reduced mainly by cutting public investments, including in infrastructure. Among the various consequences, notice the sluggish growth of such vital inputs to industrial growth as the supply of electricity (see Table 6.1); the rate of growth of electricity generating capacity in the 1980s was nearly double that of the 1990s.[23] Can anyone doubt that such state shrinkage is hurting India's economic growth? It is no wonder that various analysts, of a variety of persuasions, seem to agree that public investments in India now need to be stepped up.[24]

The continued buoyancy of private investment and the decline of public investment in India constitute key elements of India's economic growth 'story' in the 1990s. An additional issue that deserves further attention is that the rate of growth of productivity of the industrial economy in the 1990s did not improve over the 1980s.[25] While the international opening of the economy

[22]These are my own calculations. Company data was taken from *Businessworld,* 22 August–6 September 1998 and 27 December 2004; the sales data for 2004 were collected from www.valuenotes.com. For one study that documents that further consolidation has been the main corporate response (along with growing use of foreign technology) to economic reforms, see Rakesh Basant, 'Corporate Response to Economic Reforms', EPW, 19 March 2000.

[23]See Nagaraj, 'Industrial Policy and Performance', p. 3713.

[24]Ahluwalia, 'Economic Reforms in India since 1991'; Mohan, 'Fiscal Correction for Economic Growth'; Nagaraj, 'Industrial Policy and Performance since 1980'; Chaudhuri, 'Economic Reforms and Industrial Structure in India'.

[25]Kumar, 'Economic Reforms and their Macro-Economic Impact', pp. 806–7.

TABLE 7.1: Some Post-reform Economic Indicators

Year	GDP Growth (Per Cent)	Industrial Growth (Per Cent)	Capital Formation (Per Cent GDP)		Electricity Generated Growth (Per Cent)	International Trade Per Cent GDP	
			Private Sector	Public Sector		Exports	Imports
1990–1	5.6	7.0	13.9	9.0	9.6	6.2	9.4
1991–2	1.3	–1.0	12.9	9.2	4.0	7.3	8.3
1992–3	5.1	4.3	14.2	8.2	4.8	7.8	10.2
1993–4	5.9	5.6	13.4	8.0	5.0	8.1	9.6
1994–5	7.3	10.3	13.2	8.8	6.1	8.1	10.9
1995–6	7.3	12.3	16.7	7.7	5.8	8.9	12.0
1996–7	7.8	7.7	15.9	6.9	3.5	8.6	12.3
1997–8	4.8	3.8	15.3	6.4	3.4	8.5	12.2
1998–9	6.5	3.8	15.1	6.5	4.6	8.3	11.5
1999–2000	6.1	4.9	15.6	6.2	5.0	8.4	12.4
2000–1	4.0	7.0	15.9	6.0	4.6	9.9	12.7
2001–2	4.4	3.7	16.2	5.9	4.0	9.4	11.8
2002–3	5.8	6.3	16.6	5.6	5.0	10.6	12.7
2003–4	8.5	6.6	16.8	6.0	6.5	10.8	13.3
Average	5.7	5.9	15.1	7.2	5.1	8.6	11.4

Source: Author's estimates based on *Economic Survey,* Government of India, various issues, http://indiabudget.nic

has led to a fair amount of restructuring and consolidation of Indian industry,[26] as well as to increase in technology imports, somehow none of this is adding up to any sharp improvement in efficiency. Why? The answer of reform advocates seems to be that tariffs are still too high and that the labour regime remains rigid. While this may be the case, it is also possible that one should not expect too much from mere international opening, especially in a large economy, with a relatively small role for international trade and investment. Moreover, the claim that trade opening will enhance economic efficiency may also have the causal sequence backwards, at least for late-late industrializers. If East Asian countries like South Korea are to be a model, note that state supported improvements in industrial efficiency came first, and export success only second.[27]

While the Indian state indeed re-committed itself to private sector led growth around 1980, India is no South Korea or Taiwan. The fact is that the Indian state has neither done enough to help improve the efficiency of the private industrial economy, nor has it done much at all to improve the life-chances of its poor. First, India's dismal infrastructure continues to add to

[26]Basant, 'Corporate Response to Economic Reforms'.

[27]Alice Amsden, *Asia's Next Giant: South Korea and Late Industrialization,* New York: Oxford University Press, 1989; and Atul Kohli, *State-Directed Development: Political Power and Industrialization in the Global Periphery,* New York: Cambridge University Press, 2004.

the cost of private industry. Second, while there is much talk of improving the labour situation, not only is the action limited, but even the underlying model of change is mis-specified. Once again, if East Asia is to be the model, labour regimes in such rapid growers as South Korea combined job security, training on the job, continuing skill improvements, and strict discipline, involving repression; the 'model' is thus neither fully desirable nor likely to be replicated in India. Third, the state has done not nearly enough to help improve the technological efficiency of the Indian economy. Imports of foreign technology have helped somewhat. However, with the declining R&D investment in the private sector, and with the continuing cuts in the role of the public sector, the trend is nearly in the opposite direction. Fourth, the efforts to improve India's human capital have been minimal. And lastly, both the incentives and pressures on the private sector to boost exports have remained insufficient. These series of inactions—some as a result of political incapacities and others due to the lack of imagination—may cumulatively help us understand why productivity growth of India's industrial economy has not improved in the post-reform period.

POLITICS OF ECONOMIC GROWTH IN THE STATES

Finally, there is a third puzzle, namely, of considerable variation in growth performance across Indian states in the post-reform period. The basic growth data for Indian states during the 1980s and in the post-reform period (1990–2004) is provided in Table 7.2. The main thing to note is that the rates of economic growth across Indian states started diverging more in the 1990s than in the 1980s; for example, the coefficient of variation in the 1980s was 0.14 and in the 1990s, 0.29.[28] Those who have used alternate measurements, such as gini coefficients, have found a similar pattern of divergence in the 1990s,[29] and even those sympathetic to reforms seem to agree.[30] The analytical issue raised by this trend then is, how to make sense of the diverging growth performance. One strand of market logic would expect capital to move to capital-scarce areas where it might command higher returns, leading to some convergence following liberalization. While a dozen years may be too short a time period to judge, the issue does arise: why are Indian states diverging instead?

Of the sixteen major states listed in Table 6.2, notice that, when compared to the 1980s, economic growth rate in the post-reform period altered significantly

[28]B.B. Bhattacharya and S. Sakthivel, 'Regional Growth and Disparity in India', *EPW*, 6 March 2004, Table 2.

[29]S.L. Shetty, 'Growth of SDP and Structural Changes in State Economies: Interstate Comparisons', *EPW*, 6 December 2003, Table 6, p. 5197.

[30]Montek S. Ahluwalia, 'Economic Performance of States in Post-reforms Period', *EPW*, 6 May 2000.

TABLE 7.2: Economic Growth in Major Indian States, 1980–2004

States	1980–90	1990–2004	1980–2004
Andhra Pradesh	4.81	5.33	5.1
Assam	3.91	3.00	3.4
Bihar	5.20	4.2	4.6
Gujarat	5.71	8.11	7.1
Haryana	6.68	6.63	6.65
Himachal Pradesh	6.10	6.44	6.3
Karnataka	6.10	6.38	6.3
Kerala	4.50	5.69	5.2
Madhya Pradesh	5.18	4.74	4.9
Maharashtra	5.98	5.92	5.95
Orissa	5.85	3.94	4.7
Punjab	5.14	4.14	4.6
Rajasthan	7.17	5.68	6.3
Tamil Nadu	6.35	5.70	5.97
Uttar Pradesh	5.88	3.76	4.64
West Bengal	5.20	7.12	6.32
All-India	5.60	5.90	5.8

Source: Rajya Sabha Unstarred Question No. 1285, dated 14 March 2002 and Lok Sabha Unstarred Question No. 3170, dated 22 March 2002 and Central Statistical Organization (www.indiastat.com). The figures for Bihar, Madhya Pradesh, and Uttar Pradesh are not strictly comparable across years because following 1994–5, they do not include the regions that have come to constitute the states of Jharkhand, Chhattisgarh, and Uttaranchal, respectively.

in only half the states (that is, increased or decreased by one percentage point or more). Economic growth increased notably in Gujarat, Kerala and West Bengal; by contrast, following reforms, economic growth declined by more than a point in Bihar, Orissa, UP, Punjab and Rajasthan. Those working with more specific state-level data on manufacturing in the registered sector have established that the decline in growth in select states was more statistically robust than the growth pickup.[31] Somewhat broader data on growth rates in the secondary sector as a whole, however, are broadly consistent with the overall growth trends in Table 7.2, at least in terms of the eight states in which growth rates increased or decreased by a percentage point or more.[32]

[31]R. Nagaraj, 'Performance of India's Manufacturing Sector in the 1990s: Some Tentative Findings', in Shuji Uchikawa (ed.), *Economic Reforms and Industrial Structure in India*, Delhi: Manohar, 2002, Table 3.

[32]See Bhattacharya and Sakthivel, 'Regional Growth and Disparity in India', Table 6. One exception is Punjab, where the decline in overall growth rate seems to be driven more by decline in the agriculture growth rate rather than by a decline in the rate of growth in the secondary sector, which seems to have remained in the 6 per cent range during both the 1980s and the 1990s. The secondary sector data for the 1990s also indicates considerable growth pick-up in Tamil Nadu and Madhya Pradesh and a considerable decline in Haryana.

		Post-reform Growth Rate (1990–2004)	
		Accelerated	Decelerated
State Per Capita Income	High	Gujarat, West Bengal	Punjab
	Low	Kerala	Rajasthan, Bihar, Orissa, UP

FIGURE 7.1A: Economic Growth in Rich and Poor States

Notes:

1. Growth acceleration and deceleration in all the five figures (7.1A, 7.1B, 7.1C, 7.1D, and 7.1E) is judged by a movement of at least one percentage point over the 1980s.
2. High and low state per capita incomes (or rich and poor) are simply defined as above and below the national income average in 1991.

Given the problems of data quality and availability at the state level, I will focus my comments below on the divergence in the overall economic growth rates across states; moreover, given that only a small number of states are being analysed, where statistical findings are not likely to be robust, the discussion should be treated as rough and ready.

Within these constraints, how does one best explain that economic growth picked up significantly in the post-reform period in Gujarat, Kerala, and West Bengal and declined as significantly in Bihar, UP, Orissa, Punjab and Rajasthan? Figures 7.1 (A, B, C, D, and E) provide some preliminary insights. First, let us set aside some plausible explanations. One might be tempted to hold that liberalization enabled less well-off states to attract capital due to higher marginal productivity of capital and thus to grow more rapidly; this is not true (see Figure 7.1A). One might also be tempted to hold that growth patterns exhibit continuity, that states that grew rapidly in the 1980s also continued to grow rapidly in the post-reform period; again, this is not true (see Figure 7.1D). And finally, though the data on this is not presented here, there is little association between rates of literacy and the rate of growth across Indian states.[33]

What then is the most likely explanation for growth acceleration in some states and deceleration in others? Let us assume as before that growth rates reflect both shifts in levels of investment and in productivity. Unfortunately, unlike the national level, investment and productivity data for individual states are not readily available. On the issue of investment patterns, what we do know instead is that, following reforms, public investments declined across India and that this was also the case for most Indian states.[34] One may propose then that this decline hurt growth prospects of those states

---

[33]Ahluwalia, 'Economic Performance of States in Post-reforms Period', p. 1664.
[34]Ibid., Table 8, p. 1642.

most who are unable to readily attract new private investment. By contrast, the states that have done better are probably those that have attracted new private investment, both domestic and foreign. While direct data to support this claim are not available, the numbers of 'private projects under implementation' collected by the Centre for Monitoring the Indian Economy is broadly supportive, especially at the two extremes. One central component of the larger puzzle of varying growth rates across states is then this: why are some states better able to attract new private investment than others?

Data in Figure 7.1A again provides some clues. The states in which growth decelerated by more than a point—presumably because they failed to attract new private investment—are mostly India's poor states (Figure 7.1A): Bihar, UP, Orissa and Rajasthan. The only exception—Punjab—is really not an exception because growth deceleration in that state was more a function of decline in the agricultural growth rate and quite probably unrelated to the issue of policy reforms; industrial growth in Punjab in both the 1980s and in the post-reform period remained in the 6 per cent range. Whether a direct function of their poverty or not, the poor states then may fail to attract new private investment because of poor infrastructure (Figure 7.1E) or more broadly, an unfavourable investment climate (Figure 7.1B). Moreover, India's two other major and very poor states—Assam and Madhya Pradesh—also fit this pattern, though economic growth in them declined by less than one percentage point (Table 7.2). So, one pattern seems fairly clear: following policy reforms in 1991, India's poor states have not done very well. Growth deceleration in them probably reflects a decline in public investments and a concomitant failure of private investment to fill the gap.

		Post-reform Growth Rate (1990–2004)	
		Accelerated	Decelerated
Investment Climate	Favourable	Gujarat	Punjab
	Not favourable	West Bengal, Kerala	Rajasthan, Bihar, Orissa, UP

FIGURE 7.1B: Economic Growth in States with Varying Investment Climate

Note: The data on investment climate is from *India Today*, 16 August 2004, p. 21. The factors they included were per cent of state GDP spent on administration, capital expenditure, per capita bank credit, industrial disputes, per cent of sick public enterprises, gross capital formation, and industrial workers in the 15–59 population. There are clearly some problems of endogeneity here. The resulting categorization should thus be treated only as rough and ready. A more systematic analysis of investment climate in a subset of these states is broadly consistent with this categorization. See, World Bank, *Improving the Investment Climate in India*, Washington, D.C., 2001, Table 3.1, p. 47.

Instead of seeking a higher rate of return in capital-scarce areas—a trend that may still unfold over the long term—private capital in India for now seems to be shirking India's poor states with poor infrastructure and an unfavourable investment climate. That public action will be needed to reverse this trend ought to be clear.

The issue of why post-reform economic growth accelerated in yet other states is more muddled. As already noted, the three states where growth accelerated by more than one percentage point are Gujarat, West Bengal, and Kerala; economic growth in the secondary sector in these three states also followed this trend.[35] The underlying determinants, however, are not obvious. While Gujarat is clearly one of India's richest states, both West Bengal and Kerala are closer to the national average in terms of per capita income; investment climate in both Kerala and West Bengal is also considered to be not all that favourable (Figure 7.1B). The pattern of post-reform industrial growth in India's other rich states during the 1990s also ought to be noted: it picked up significantly in Tamil Nadu, somewhat in Maharashtra, stayed about the same in Karnataka and Punjab, and declined significantly in Haryana.[36] What conclusions, if any, might one draw about the underlying determinants?

Except for Haryana, one pattern that does seem to stand out is that post-reform industrial growth in India's better-off states either accelerated (Gujarat and Tamil Nadu) or stayed about the same as in the 1980s (Maharashtra, Karnataka, and Punjab). These states are generally blessed with good infrastructure and more desirable investment climates.[37] When juxtaposed against India's poorest states—where economic growth declined across the board in the post-reform period—an important conclusion emerges: private investors in India continue to favour India's better-off states over the poorer

| | | Post-reform Growth Rate (1990–2004) | |
		Accelerated	Decelerated
Labour Unrest	Decreased	West Bengal, Kerala	UP, Orissa, Rajasthan
	Unchanged or Increased	Gujarat	Bihar, Punjab

FIGURE 7.1C: Economic Growth and Labour Unrest in the States

Note: The figures on labour unrest are 'mandays lost' and were taken from various issues of the *Statistical Abstracts of India*. The decrease or increase in labour unrest is estimated by the changing picture in the 1990s when compared to the 1980s.

[35]Bhattacharya and Sakthivel, 'Regional Growth and Disparity in India', Table 6.
[36]Ibid.
[37]*India Today*, 16 August 2004, pp. 20–1.

states. In common sense terms this is not all that surprising. What it does underline, however, is that the pattern of economic reforms in India is not following the free market logic of capital moving to capital-scarce areas. The logic evident instead is more akin to a Mathew effect, namely, to him who hath shall be given.

If 'initial conditions' of Indian states are clearly important for attracting investment and for growing, two important qualifications ought to be added. First, varying initial conditions are themselves a product of past patterns of development, especially the role of varying state governments and of state politics. Thus, such important factors as quality of roads, availability of electricity, levels of education, labour discipline, and law and order conditions—all factors that private investors take into account when deciding in which state to invest—are traceable back to the past developmental activities of state governments. And second, variation in initial conditions does not explain everything; the quality of state governments also matters. For example, why has Gujarat experienced more rapid industrial growth in the post-reform period than other similar better-off states? And why do economic prospects of some such poorer states as Bihar seem a lot worse than of some other poorer states, say, Madhya Pradesh? I will return to some such issues momentarily. For now, why have such middle income states as West Bengal and Kerala experienced rapid growth in the post-reform period? This is especially puzzling in light of the fact that these are India's 'radical' states that are presumably not too attractive to private investors. More detailed state-level research is clearly needed.[38] One tantalizing clue to the economic performance of these radical states is provided in Figure 7.1C. Labour militancy declined in both these states during the 1990s: for example, labour disputes in West Bengal declined from some 9.6 million in 1981 to 3.8 million in 1995, and in Kerala from 2.2 million in 1981 to 1.7 million in 1995. Is it possible that, desiring growth, communist parties in power have demobilized

| | | Post-reform Growth Rate (1990–2004) | |
		Accelerated	Decelerated
Growth Rate in the 1980s	High	Gujarat	Orissa, Rajasthan, UP
	Low	West Bengal, Kerala	Punjab, Bihar

FIGURE 7.1D: Economic Growth in the 1980s and in the Post-reform Period

Note: Growth rates in the 1980s are categorized as high or low simply as above or below the national average.

[38]For one such study, see Sinha, *The Regional Roots of Developmental Politics in India.*

their organized supporters? If so, significant improvement in industrial production might reflect improved productivity via enhanced capacity utilization, as well as by attracting some new investment.

Leaving aside the issue of cross-state variations, let us now briefly contrast the specific states of Bihar and Gujarat to get a sense of how differences in initial conditions are combining with governmental initiatives to create the Mathew effect. Bihar is well known for its poor infrastructure, poor quality workforce, and poor governance.[39] In spite of these obstacles, Bihar's economy during the 1980s grew at a respectable rate of some five per cent per annum. Following the reforms, however, the average growth rate fell by a whole point (Table 7.2). A pronounced deceleration in agricultural growth rate was part of this decline. However, the deceleration of growth in the secondary sector as a whole was also quite significant,[40] and that in registered manufacturing during the 1990s was quite dramatic.[41] While the reasons behind the deceleration are many,[42] the decline in both public and private investments is noticeable. A variety of fiscal pressures, including the need to 'service' a populist polity, led to significant decline in public investment, from an annual average of some 15–20 per cent of total public spending in the 1980s to some 5–10 per cent in the post-reform period.[43]

While data on private investment in Bihar is not available, the data on new state-level private projects collected by the Centre for Monitoring Indian Economy (CMIE) indicates that Bihar in recent years was attracting the fewest projects among all of India's major states. A variety of Bihar's initial conditions, including the investment climate, are clearly part of this 'story.' However, it is also the case that repeated governments in Bihar have simply not been developmental. Consumed by the need to broaden and maintain their electoral power, the priorities of Bihar's political leadership are anything but growth promotion. In the words of the World Bank, yes, the World Bank: 'Bihar has not been proactive in courting private investment or articulating a development strategy and 'vision.' Thus, the government does not have an investment council, conveying a lack of concern about fostering and protecting private investment'.[44] This absence of state activism for development is costing Bihar dearly.

By contrast, 'liberalization' has proved to be a boon to a state like Gujarat. The average annual rate of economic growth in the post-reform period in

---

[39]The World Bank, *Bihar: Towards a Development Strategy*, Washington, D.C., 2005; and Atul Kohli, *Democracy and Discontent*.

[40]Bhattacharya and Sakthivel, 'Regional Growth and Disparity in India', Table 6.

[41]Nagaraj, 'Performance of India's Manufacturing Sector in the 1990s', Table 3.

[42]The World Bank, *Bihar*.

[43]Ibid.

[44]Ibid., p. 32.

| | | Post-reform Growth Rate (1990–2004) | |
		Accelerated	Decelerated
Quantity of Infrastructure	Good	Gujarat, Kerala	Punjab
	Poor	West Bengal	Rajasthan, Bihar, UP, Orissa

FIGURE 7.1E: Economic Growth in States with Varying Infrastructure

Note: The data for the quality of infrastructure is from *India Today*, 16 August 2004, p. 20. The factors they included were standardized measures of availability of electricity, paved roads, bank branches, post offices, and telephones. The top ten 'big states' have been categorized as having 'good' infrastructure and the bottom ten as having 'poor' infrastructure.

Gujarat accelerated by more than 2 per cent over the 1980s (Table 7.2), with the growth in the secondary sector jumping by nearly 3 percentage points, up into the double digits. The underlying dynamics are again not hard to understand. The initial advantages were significant: good infrastructure; productive labour force; and a prolonged record of pro-business government. If Bihar was at the lowest end of attracting new private investment, Gujarat was at the other extreme. As part of an explanation, Aseema Sinha has very nicely documented, how in the 1990s Gujarat became even more of an activist, pro-business state:

The government (of Gujarat) continued to invest in projects and sectors where it expected private investment to need further encouragement. To accelerate development of the electronics industry for instance, the state government announced a special incentive package, which included investment subsidy and sales, tax benefit, and five additional electronics industrial estates were planned. In 1995–2000 many new state agencies were created, such as the Gujarat Infrastructure Development Board and the Gujarat Power Corporation. These signified an enhancement of the state rather than its withdrawal.[45]

This activist industrial policy is a lot more East Asia than neo-liberalism at work.

To sum up, the reforms of 1991 have opened up new opportunities for some Indian states and left others at a disadvantage. While initial economic advantages and disadvantages were important, so has been the contrasting behaviour of state-level governments. Here too, of course, institutional inheritance matters. Nevertheless, the inter-state dynamics of differential growth rates seem to be propelled by similar forces as were evident at the national level: regional states that have effectively created a pro-

---

[45] Aseema Sinha, *The Regional Roots of Developmental Politics in India: A Divided Leviathan*, Bloomington: Indiana University Press, 2005, p. 88.

business alliance for growth seem to be experiencing the most rapid economic growth.

CONCLUSION

In this essay I have argued that the recent acceleration of economic growth in India was more a function of the pro-business tilt of the Indian state and less a result of the post-1991 economic liberalization. In order to support this argument, I have offered three types of evidence: first, growth acceleration around 1980 coincided with the striking but the less noticed shift in the state's economic role initiated by Indira Gandhi; second, the aggregate economic performance since liberalization, especially industrial growth, has not improved over the 1980s; and finally, the inter-state variation in economic growth in the 1990s also seems to follow the same pattern, with pro-business state governments succeeding handsomely in attracting private investment and thus growing rapidly.

With the argument now in place, what remains is mainly to tease out some concluding implications. Readers may wonder what the stakes are in distinguishing pro-business and pro-market policies? The answer is in part scholarly, that is, getting causal connections right, and in part normative, that is, are the ongoing changes fair and just? We are now living in a world in which democracy and capitalism have emerged as the most desirable modes for organizing national political economies. The real debate about national choices is thus increasingly about 'varieties of capitalism'. With advanced industrial economies providing mainly three alternatives—the neo-liberal model of Anglo-America, the social democratic model of Scandinavia, and the statist model of Japan and South Korea—the debate for developing countries increasingly is, which model is best to emulate. My personal preferences are social democratic, but for now that is not too relevant. The neo-liberal model has in the recent years been hegemonic, or near hegemonic. With numerous countries adopting—or apparently adopting—neo-liberal policies, the pressing scholarly issue is: how successful have these policies been?

The discussion about India is part and parcel of this broader global debate. Champions of neo-liberalism generally want to embrace all successful cases—such as recent India—as examples of the virtues of their prescriptions, while distancing themselves from failures, often arguing that their prescriptions were not really implemented, or urging us to imagine how much worse things might be had their prescriptions not been implemented. Against these arguments—which are often put forward and supported by enormously powerful institutions around the world—some lone scholars chip away at this hegemony, arguing instead that growth successes in the developing world resemble more the statist model of Japan or South Korea, where activist states have allied closely with business groups to push national economies on an upward trajectory. Since a narrow alliance of political and economic elite is not easy to institutionalize, East Asian models have also often had unsavoury politics. Against the neo-liberal model that holds that all good things can go together, the East Asian model puts into sharp relief the trade-offs that modern development efforts might involve.

If India's recent economic growth was really a result of pro-market policies, then, in principle, there ought to be very few costs, only widespread benefits: after all, decentralized markets support democracy; competition creates a level-playing field; efficient use of factors of production ought to create labour-intensive industrialization and thus rapid employment growth; terms of trade ought to shift towards the countryside, benefiting the rural poor; and since capital moves to capital-scarce areas in search of high returns, regional inequalities ought to diminish over time, mitigating inequalities. Unfortunately, many of the trends noted above do not fit these expectations. India's growth acceleration is instead being accompanied by growing inequalities, growing capital intensity of the economy, growing concentration of ownership of private industry, and nearly stagnant growth in employment in manufacturing industries. This evidence is more consistent with the view that the development model pursued in India since about 1980 is a pro-business model that rests on a fairly narrow ruling alliance of the political and the economic elite.

Rapid economic growth is essential for poor India. It is also the case that India's development strategy from the Nehru period was much in need of change. However, none of this implies, or ought not to imply, that any new growth strategy that produces these outcomes is beyond critical scrutiny. India's success at growth acceleration is to be admired. However, the current growth experiment has to be kept in proper perspective. India's economic growth has not accelerated dramatically. What aggregate change is noticeable predates the liberalizing reforms by a whole decade and industrial growth in the post-reform period did not pick up. Moreover, the problems posed by India's current pro-business model of development include disquieting implications for the quality of India's democracy. I raise them at the end only as questions. Why should the common people in a democracy accept a narrow ruling alliance at the helm? Is ethnic and nationalistic mobilization a substitute for pro-poor politics? And, is India increasingly stuck with a two-track democracy, in which common people are only needed at the time of elections, and then it is best that they all go home, forget politics, and let the 'rational' elite quietly run a pro-business show?

8

Politics of Economic Liberalization in India*

INTRODUCTION

The capacity of different types of governments for facilitating economic change in the Third World has been a subject of enduring interest in comparative development studies. During the 1950s and the 1960s, this interest was evident in the debates over the developmental capacities of communist versus non-communist political systems. More recently, the impressive economic performance of the newly industrializing countries (NICs), mainly of East Asia, but also of Latin America, has given rise to a challenging new idea: state induced, market-like competitiveness may be the secret for facilitating rapid economic growth. While the economists continue to analyse the economic components of this proposition, political analysts need to investigate the issue of the political prerequisites of economic policy choices. An important question for research is thus, what types of regimes are most likely to choose and to successfully pursue a market-oriented, liberal pattern of economic development?

The existing debates on this issue tend to veer towards one of two positions. A number of analysts have proposed that the observed association between the well-organized, technically competent authoritarian regimes and

*Originally published as 'Politics of Economic Liberalization in India', *World Development*, 17(3), March 1989, pp. 305–28.

This paper is part of a larger research project on 'India's growing problems of governability'. Research for this project has been supported by the Ford Foundation and by Princeton University, especially its Center for International Studies. An earlier version of this paper was presented at the annual meetings of The American Political Science Association, Chicago, 3–6 September 1987. I would like to thank the following for their help: Bashiruddin Ahmed, Jagdish Bhagwati, Donald Crone, Jyotirindra Dasgupta, John Echeverri-Gent, Stephen Haggard, Robert Kaufman, John P. Lewis, GuiUermo O'Donnell, Ashutosh Varshney, John Waterbury, and Myron Weiner.

the pursuit of a market-oriented development strategy is more than a mere association; that authoritarianism of a specific type may well be necessary for adopting a development strategy that strives to promote both domestic and international economic competition.[1] The logic of this proposition often rests in part on the need to contain political pressures generated by those who lose out in a market-oriented model of development, and in part on the need to provide political stability to attract investment. Conversely, other analysts have challenged this emphasis on structural constraints by highlighting various dimensions on which policy choice rests: ideology of the leaders rather than the nature of regime organization, it has been proposed, is a key determinant of economic policy choice; winners and losers of a market-oriented readjustment are difficult to predict and to identify: authoritarianism hardly guarantees political stability; and leaders with will and skill can push an economic programme of their choice quite far.[2]

[1] A wide variety of literature in different contexts tends to argue this position. Only a selected sample of this literature is cited here. First, some scholars have traced the roots of Latin American authoritarianism in the 1960s to the need to 'deepen' industrialization. Implicit in this claim was the argument that moderate regimes find it difficult to adopt a pattern of development that some would consider to be rational and necessary. See, for example, G. O'Donnell, *Modernization and Bureaucratic Authoritarianism: Studies in South American Politics*, Berkeley, CA: University of California Press, 1973. For debates around this hypothesis, see D. Collier (ed.), *The New Authoritarianism in Latin America*, Princeton, N.J.: Princeton University Press, 1979. Second, and related to this, numerous scholars of Brazil have argued that the economic adjustments and the high rates of growth Brazil achieved during 1964–74 would not have been possible without the military regime. For specific empirical materials, see the essays by Thomas Skidmore and Fernando Cardoso in A. Stepan (ed.), *Authoritarianism Brazil*, New Haven, CT: Yale University Press, 1973; and more broadly, see Peter Evans, *Dependent Development: The Alliance of Multinational, State, and Local Capital in Brazil*, Princeton, N.J.: Princeton University Press, 1979. Third, the success of market-oriented industrialization in select East Asian countries like South Korea has been associated with the role of an authoritarian state. See, for example, L.P. Jones and I. Sakong, *Government, Business and Entrepreneurship in Economic Development: The Korean Case*, Cambridge, MA: Harvard University Press, 1980; and the essays in F.C. Deyo (ed.), *The Political Economy of the New Asian Industrialism*, Ithaca: Cornell University Press, 1987. Finally, some development economists, who generally favour a liberal model of development, have also wondered whether it is possible to pursue such a model without an authoritarian regime. See, for example, J. Bhagwati, 'Rethinking Trade Strategy', in John P. Lewis and Valeriana Kallab (eds), *Development Strategies Reconsidered*, New Brunswick, N.J.: Transaction Books, 1986.

[2] In recent years, literature emphasizing the role of leadership and the room for choice has developed around the issue of implementing the IMF's stability programme. See, for example, J. Nelson, 'The Politics of Stabilization', in Richard E. Feinberg and Valeriana Kallab (eds), *Adjustment Crisis in the Third World*, New Brunswick, N.J.: Transaction Books, 1984; H.S. Bienen and M. Gersovitz, 'Economic Stabilization, Conditionality and Political Stability', *International Organization*, 39(4), Autumn 1985; and S. Haggard, 'The Politics of Adjustment: Lessons from the IMF's Extended Fund Facility', *International Organization*, 39(3), Summer 1985.

This essay analyses some empirical material from India that sheds light on the broader question of how much room for economic policy choice a developing country leader has, especially in a democratic setting. India's leaders have over the last decade sought to liberalize the country's relatively controlled, import-substitution model of development. Initial steps in this direction were taken both by the Janata government (1977–80) and by Indira Gandhi during 1980–4. Since coming to power in late 1984, Rajiv Gandhi has made the liberalization of the economy a priority. Significant changes in the domestic political economy and some changes that alter India's links with the world economy have recently been introduced. These include easing of state control on such activities of national firms as entry into production, production decisions and expansion in size; lowering of corporate and personal income taxes; a long-term fiscal policy that substitutes tariffs for import restrictions and assures business groups of future patterns of taxation; some devaluation; and lowering of import barriers on selected items.

These changes do not as yet add up to a dramatic change. A liberal model of development has not replaced the mixed economy model premised on state controls and import substitution. The legal and bureaucratic framework of a highly interventionist state remains intact; so do the numerous public sector activities and governmental restrictions on private economic activity. Nevertheless, policy reforms have been aimed at enhancing competitiveness and at broadening the scope of individual and corporate initiative within the old framework.

The purpose of this essay is not to assess the merits of these policy reforms. Serious debates on the issue of whether liberalization is the right choice for India have been underway for some time;[3] such discussions are also best carried out by policy-oriented economists. The purpose of the present essay

[3] Academic works that would broadly support the liberalization policy prescription include J. Bhagwati and T.N. Srinivasan, *Foreign Trade Regimes and Economic Development: India*, New York: Columbia University Press, 1975; and I.J. Ahluwalia, *Industrial Growth in India: Stagnation Since the Mid-Sixties*, New Delhi: Oxford University Press, 1985. For a brief but succinct statement on the need for liberalization by a policy maker, see P.S. Jha, 'Economic Expansion Ensnared in Red Tape', *India Abroad*, 11 December 1987. For a sampling of the critical views, see B. Datta, 'The Central Budget and the New Economic Policy', *EPW*, 10 April 1985; H.K. Paranjape, 'New Lamps for Old! A Critique of the New Economic Policy', *EPW*, 4 September 1985; P. Patnaik, 'New Turn in Economic Policy: Contexts and Prospects', *EPW*, 7 June 1986; and K.N. Raj, 'New Economic Policy', *Mainstream*, 14 December 1985. Two essays that, like this one, focus on political issues are S.A. Kochanek, 'Regulation and Liberalization Theology in India', *Asian Survey*, 26(12), December 1986; B.R. Rubin, 'Economic Liberalization and the Indian State', *Third World Quarterly*, 7(4), October 1985. Two other essays that came to my attention only after this essay was written are P.N. Dhar, 'The Indian Economy: Past Performance and Current Issues', paper presented at the Conference on the Indian Economy, Boston, 1987; I.G. Patel, 'On Taking India into the Twenty-first Century', *Modern Asian Studies*, 21(2), 1987.

rather is to analyse the political underpinnings of these economic policy changes. What political changes within India have created the pre-conditions for a shift in the development strategy? Are these changes primarily in the ideological realm, or do they also reflect a shifting balance of power among contending political actors? Why has the pace of reform been slow, piecemeal and even hesitant? What forces are constraining a decisive shift in development strategy? Aimed at answering these questions, this essay analyses the recent role of the political elites and of interest groups in India's macro-economic policy making. The analysis has obvious implications for an understanding of the process of India's economic liberalization. It also, however, sheds some light on the broader issue of political conditions under which economic liberalization of a controlled developing economy may or may not be undertaken.

It is argued below that the immediate and the most sustained push for liberalization has come from a group of technocratically inclined leaders that has come to control the levers of India's economic policy making. Business groups have, on balance, supported the government's attempts to liberalize the domestic economy. However, they have opposed any serious attempt at international opening. For reasons to be specified, professional and other groups within India's urban middle class also supported the government's early policy reforms. Conversely, concerted and direct opposition to the reforms has come from three quarters: the rank and file of the ruling party, the Congress; the left intelligentsia; and the organized working class in the public sector. Diffuse but numerically significant opposition has also been expressed by such rural groups as the middle peasants and the landless poor.

The growing opposition to reforms has not forced the government to reverse its economic agenda. On the contrary, both Indira Gandhi and Rajiv Gandhi succeeded in implementing some significant policy reforms. These policy initiatives highlight how and why leaders indeed have some room for policy choice. At the same time, however, the need to build political support has pushed Rajiv Gandhi to slow down his liberalization programme. While liberalization has not come to a grinding halt, a more populist economic programme has been simultaneously readopted. This policy behaviour, in turn, lends weight to those who would maintain that a major shift in development strategy from a state-controlled economy to a more liberal one is not easy within the framework of a democratic regime.

SOME PRELIMINARIES

Prior to presenting a political analysis of India's changing economic policies, it is important to provide three pieces of preliminary information. First, the term economic liberalization is no more than a grab bag for numerous policy measures that governments may undertake selectively. In the Indian case, as will become clear, it does not really refer to an opening of the economy to the outside world in terms of freer movement of capital, goods or money. Privatization of the domestic public sector is also not a policy priority in India. What liberalization, therefore, really refers to is a set of policy measures aimed at loosening governmental controls on the functioning of the private economy. Even within this limited scope, it is important to further recognize that the attempted decontrols influence only the industrial and the service sectors directly and the agricultural sector only indirectly.

A second caveat concerns the fact that the focus of this essay is on the policy process. Therefore, when analysing the forces that have propelled the move within India towards economic liberalization, there is an overemphasis here on the proximate causes—such as the role of the elite—and a tendency to neglect the distant or structural changes in the environment of the elites that are clearly also significant; I will only mention some of these structural changes in both the international and the national context. Careful elaboration of these distant, causal factors would require studies in their own right.

Within India's international context, a number of factors loom large that have inclined its leaders towards liberalizing the controlled economy. The success of the NICs, especially of Asian countries like South Korea, has created a sharp sense of having been left behind. Whereas in the past this sense of being left behind was often blamed on colonialism, a new generation of leaders is now forced to ask if the country's emphasis on socialism and import substitution was mistaken from the beginning. Additionally, the fact that major communist countries like the Soviet Union and China seem to want to embrace the market is of considerable significance. For the present there are few exemplary models left in the world that could help sustain anti-market arguments. Finally, there has been an important change in the nature of external forces that help legitimize Indian technocrats as skilled technocrats. Instead of the left-leaning economists of an earlier generation, who were often trained in England, those deemed as really competent by Indian leaders now generally receive their education in American universities and some of their practical training in such international development institutions as the World Bank. A fair degree of consensus prevails in these legitimizing institutions on the issue of what is an appropriate development strategy. This consensus, in turn, becomes a significant force propelling policy movement towards liberalization.

Within India's national context also there have been significant changes that have proven to be important background variables, which however will not be discussed in any detail here. For example, there is a growing agreement within India that the public sector is grossly inefficient. Along with this, virtually no one would disagree that India's redistributive efforts, such as land reforms, have not been very successful. This sense of the failure of socialism provides a major opening for a new beginning. Of course, as we will see momentarily, there are major disagreements concerning the appropriate future direction—towards more or less socialism. A sense of the past failure of socialism, however, is part of contemporary India's political consciousness. Additionally, over time, the force of anti-colonial and nationalist sentiments has declined. While again there is no consensus on this issue, many of India's new leaders are more willing to open the economy to and learn from the West than the leaders of the post-independence generation. This general decline in a commitment to socialism and nationalism has, in turn, created new political and economic possibilities.

Last in this list of preliminary information, it is important to point out briefly the economic background of the more recent governmental efforts towards economic liberalization. While India's economy continued between 1950 and 1980 to grow at its steady but sluggish pace of 3–4 per cent per annum, India's industrial growth slowed from about 7–8 per cent in the period prior to the mid-1960s, down to about 5 per cent per annum over the last two decades.[4] The overall growth rate has picked up in the 1980s. Much of this growth, however, has been located in the service sector. The slowing of industrial growth has generated an excited debate, especially because India's savings rate over the last several decades has continued to climb, from under 10 per cent of the GNP to over 20 per cent in the early 1980s.[5]

The competing explanations that have been proposed for the deceleration of India's industrial growth can be grouped around three alternative hypotheses: that the root cause of the slow growth are the level of inefficiencies generated by a closed, state-controlled economy,[6] that the sluggishness reflects low aggregate demand;[7] or that the deceleration is associated with

[4]See Ahluwalia, *Industrial Growth in India*.

[5]A good review of this and other debates surrounding India's slow industrial growth is Ashutosh Varshney, 'Political Economy of Slow Economic Growth in India', *EPW*, September 1984.

[6]Two analyses that would broadly support this position are Bhagwati and Srinivasan, *Foreign Trade Regimes and Economic Development;* and Ahluwalia, *Industrial Growth in India*.

[7]For a statement linking limited aggregate demand to slow industrial growth, see S. Chakravarty, 'India's Development Strategy for the 1980s', *EPW*, 26 May 1984. This thesis also crops up in several criticisms of the new economic policy cited in footnote 3. Moreover, a statement by twenty-nine Indian economists, criticizing the government's emphasis on liberalization, suggested that one important component of any new development strategy should be 'expansion of home market'. This statement is further discussed below. It was published in *Mainstream*, 26 October 1985, pp. 24–5, and discussed in many newspapers and magazines, including *EPW*, 26 October 1985, pp. 1813–16.

declining public investments and the related infrastructural bottlenecks.[8] These hypotheses, and especially the policy implications that flow from them, do not have to be exclusive of one another. Nevertheless, each argument is distinct and leads to a different policy emphasis.

As suggested above, the purpose of this paper is not to take sides in this debate and, by implication, to argue for or against the Indian government's attempts to liberalize the economy. The new government is clearly closest to the first of these three arguments. The purpose served by pointing to the existence of these economic debates for the political analysis that follows is somewhat different and is twofold. First, these debates highlight that there is widespread agreement among economists and policy makers that all is not well with India's industrial policy regime. The need for change in the industrial policy regime, therefore, is not itself in question. The second and more important point that the existence of the debates demonstrates, however, is that there is little agreement as to the appropriate direction of change.

This assertion is crucial for the development of the argument below. Policy changes that the Indian government has undertaken over the last several years are not objective responses to an objective situation. That an objective situation exists, namely, an economy whose industrial sector is not doing very well, is clear; the need for change, therefore, may be said to be rooted in the economic situation. There is also broad agreement among economists that many of the governmental controls have outlived their utility in India. The responses to this situation, however, are political choices. Specialists who study the objective economic situation are not in agreement that there is a single, clear way to solve the problem. These disagreements among specialists only add contentiousness to what are already difficult political questions: who has the power to push through their preferred policies and why? Who benefits from these policies and why?

LIBERALIZATION UNDER INDIRA GANDHI

The trend towards the liberalization of the economy was initiated, not by Rajiv Gandhi, but by his mother, Indira Gandhi. This fact has not received as much attention as it deserves. An understanding of why Indira Gandhi initiated such policies after coming back to power in 1980 helps put in perspective what is really new under Rajiv Gandhi. This background is also important for understanding why Rajiv's attempts to liberalize have evoked

[8]This thesis was first put forward by T.N. Srinivasan and N.S.L. Narayana, 'Economic Performance since the Third Plan and Its Implications for Policy', EPW, February 1977. Since then it has been argued by quite a few observers, but especially by P. Bardhan, The Political Economy of Development in India, Oxford: Basil Blackwell, 1984.

considerable reaction, including negative political reaction, whereas Indira Gandhi's went relatively unnoticed.

The Indira Gandhi that returned to power in 1980—after the brief Janata interlude of about three years—was not the firebrand Indira Gandhi of *garibi hatao* (abolish poverty) vintage. While the anti-poverty rhetoric was seldom translated into real policy before or during the Emergency (1975–7), now even the rhetoric was altered. Critical observers have suggested that, after 1980, Indira Gandhi moved 'rightwards',[9] whereas her own former advisors have noted that during this phase, she was more 'pragmatic',[10] or by implication, less ideological. Whether labelled rightward or pragmatic, what is clear is that Indira Gandhi's political and policy orientation during this phase—compared to her pre-Emergency orientation—was distinct.

The changing political orientation was evident in a number of policy areas. Communal themes, for example, especially themes of Hindu hegemony that appeal to India's Hindi heartland, gained currency in Indira's political speeches.[11] Under her son Sanjay's influence, militant thugs were inducted into the ruling party as a source of mobilization for both mass rallies and elections. While the rhetoric of both socialism and nationalism was maintained, anti-poverty programmes were put on the back burner. There was also a change of attitude towards such international institutions as the IMF; negotiations for the largest loan ever granted by the IMF were completed during this phase. Finally, many of the economic policies adopted tended to move in the liberalizing direction.

After completing the loan agreement of SDR 5 billion with the IMF, Indira Gandhi took some important economic policy decisions during 1981–2: steel and cement prices were de-controlled; manufactured imports were liberalized; and controls on both entry and expansion by national firms were relaxed. During 1981, the government sanctioned four times as many applications for expansion and new undertakings as in any of the five preceding years.[12] Over the next two years, as the perspective on the seventh plan developed, it became clear that the new emphasis would be on efficiency of investment and that this would be accompanied by a general move 'away from administrative to financial controls'.[13] Soon thereafter, following the recommendations of the L.K. Jha Commission on Economic and Administrative

[9]See J. Manor, 'Parties and the Party System', in Atul Kohli (ed.), *India's Democracy: An Analysis of Changing State–Society Relations*, Princeton, N.J.: Princeton University Press, 1988.

[10]Interview, Arjun K. Sengupta, Washington, D.C., 28 June 1985.

[11]See Manor, 'Parties and the Party System'.

[12]See P.S. Jha, 'The End of the Tunnel: Return to Sanity in Economic Policy', *Times of India*, 9 April 1987.

[13]For example, see P.S. Jha, 'Seventh Plan Perspectives: A New Direction for Industry', *Times of India*, 13 August 1984.

Reforms, the government placed twenty important industries under 'automatic licensing'.[14] In practice, this meant virtual de-control by the government on expansion and new production in these industries.[15]

Why did Indira Gandhi adopt these policy changes and with what political consequence? As to the reasons for the policy shift, the new economic direction has to be seen as part and parcel of the overall political shift that Indira Gandhi adopted. This involved a move away from India's Left or populist values of secularism and socialism, and towards the package hitherto offered primarily by the right-wing parties, namely, Hindu chauvinism and pro-business. It is important to underline right away that there is no inherent reason why Hindu chauvinism has to go hand in hand with a preference for business or why liberalizing policies, aimed at enhancing market competitiveness, should be pro-business policies. In India's political culture, however, the two packages of secularism and socialism and Hindu chauvinism and pro-business have tended to offer two alternative legitimacy formulae for mobilizing political support. The logic underlying these value packages seems to be something as follows.

Secularism in India has often meant eschewing appeals to caste, religion and community as a tool of political mobilization. While practice often deviated from principles, India's founding fathers understood that national integration in a multinational and multiethnic polity like India could only be facilitated by avoiding the politicization of deep-rooted, 'primordial' loyalties. For the task of political mobilization, therefore, Nehru favoured appeals along economic lines: the need to uplift the poor, the downtrodden, the peasants, etc. Socialism was related to this political logic.

Whatever socialism has meant in practice—in India it has never meant anti-capitalism but rather, state-guided capitalism, involving planning, public sector emphasis, a state-controlled economy and a few anti-poverty programmes like land reform—its electoral significance was always closely associated with a preference for secular over communal appeals.

In contrast, those who wanted to argue for business interests faced a dilemma: in a poor democracy like India, how do you mobilize the support of the majority, who are after all very poor? One solution to this puzzle was to cut the majority–minority pie at a different angle. If the poor were majority by the criterion of wealth, Hindus were the religious majority. Appeals to the majority religious community against minority communities, then,

[14]See *Economic Times*, 1 September 1984.

[15]Most close observers of Indian economic policy agree with this conclusion. See, for example, the editorial in *EPW*, 1 December 1984. Discussions with T.N. Ninan, former Senior Editor (now Executive Editor), *India Today*, New Delhi, 11 December 1985; and with N.S. Jagannathan, Editor, *Financial Express*, New Delhi, 14 December 1985, also confirmed this impression.

can be an alternate strategy for seeking electoral majorities by downplaying class issues at the expense of communal ones. Whereas the Congress traditionally stood for the secularism and socialism package, parties like the Jan Sangh had in the recent past advocated Hindu nationalism and a pro-business attitude.

When Indira Gandhi returned to power in 1980, several things must have been clear to her. In the entire Hindi heartland, Congress had been routed by the Janata Party in the 1977 elections. Even though she had won the 1980 election, primarily due to factionalism and incompetence within the Janata, her support base in the Hindi heartland was, at best, soft. She had to build up this support and fast.[16] The full force that business communities had thrown behind Morarji Desai's government must have also left Mrs Gandhi peculiarly vulnerable, especially for the future of electoral finances. It appears that, after 1980, Mrs Gandhi sought to build her support in the Hindi heartland and with business communities by shifting away from the formula of secularism and socialism and towards one of Hindu chauvinism and pro-business. The new political posture had two ingredients: an emphasis on communalism that has great appeal in the Hindi heartland; and a more pragmatic attitude to build up her support with the industrial and commercial groups.

It must have been further clear to Mrs Gandhi by now that her socialism was not working. Anti-poverty programmes had simply not been very successful.[17] The support she was getting from the poor, therefore, was based not so much on concrete rewards, but primarily due to her ideological and rhetorical appeal. This rhetoric she knew she could maintain, while watering down the overall socialist programme. Further socialist rhetoric would not have brought her much more political capital in any case; the limits of rhetorical socialism had been reached. A movement towards liberalizing the economy, while maintaining some rhetoric of socialism and some of the anti-poverty programmes, she must have calculated, was likely to strengthen her politically.

Besides such overtly political considerations, other factors probably also played some part in pushing India towards economic liberalization. The extent to which the IMF conditionalities influenced policy changes is hard to judge. The World Bank has also periodically kept up the pressure on the Indian government to de-control and open up the economy. In a large and relatively well-established polity like India, however—'well established' in the sense of being staffed by competent bureaucrats—one has to maintain that

---

[16]James Manor emphasizes this as a cause of the more 'communal' Indira Gandhi of the 1980s. See Manor, 'Parties and the Party System'.

[17]See Atul Kohli, *The State and Poverty in India: The Politics of Reform*, Cambridge: Cambridge University Press, 1987.

organizations such as the IMF or the World Bank can never be decisive. Even the decision to enter an agreement with the IMF, and all that involves in terms of policy changes, must be viewed as a prior political decision by the Indian government. Though, once the government chose to enter this arrangement with the IMF, it is clear that this must have created pressures to 'get the prices right' in the economy.

Within the government, report after report put together by bureaucrats and specialists since the 1970s had recommended liberalization of one aspect of the economy or another.[18] The influence of these on real policy changes can easily be overestimated. If one is not cautious, one could easily conclude that policy momentum in India is driven by the expert knowledge that is periodically brought to bear on pressing national problems. Such a conclusion would be misleading. The decision to set up commissions is a political decision. Commission members are appointed by leaders and the policy preferences of these members are generally well known. Most important, whether the government chooses to act on a report is a political decision. For every report that recommends liberalization of the economy, there are literally dozens of others, sitting gathering dust, waiting for some action on their recommendations concerning how to improve the conditions of small farmers or of Scheduled Tribes or how to desilt India's rivers.

Another factor that is worth considering here is the changing economic situation itself. As noted above, industrial growth had been sluggish for quite some time. A particularly bad year was 1979. The Janata government had taken some economic measures around that time that could be interpreted as liberalizing measures.[19] Industrial growth had jumped back to over 8 per cent in 1980. The extent to which this success created momentum for further liberalization is hard to judge; the timing for the adoption of a new political programme seems, however, to have been more than just a mere coincidence.

The issue of a sluggish industrial performance was, in any case, at the forefront. New policies were needed. Various alternative policy measures summarized above were in the air. Whatever their economic merits, some alternatives clearly suited Indira Gandhi's political design better than others. To attack demand constraints would have meant, among other measures, shifting resources towards agriculture—thus alienating urban industrialists

---

[18]Since many of these reports are not public documents, complete citations cannot be provided. The contents of these reports are generally made well known via newspapers. Four of the important relevant documents of the last decade were the reports of the Alexander Commission, Dagli Commission, Arjun Sengupta Commission, and the L.K. Jha Commission.

[19]See Jha, 'The End of the Tunnel'.

and middle classes—as well as attempting what had not worked before, i.e., land reforms and other income generating projects for the poor. Increasing public investments was also not easy. If Bardhan's analysis is right, this would have meant 'rationalizing' the patronage network that holds India's dominant classes in a delicate alliance with one another and is supportive of the state.[20] Given Indira Gandhi's preoccupation with her political vulnerability, she was not about to undertake major surgery on established state–society relations of this scale.

None of this is supposed to lead to the conclusion that the liberalizing alternative is without political pitfalls. On the contrary, as we will see below, of Rajiv Gandhi's many current difficulties, those that have resulted from his attempts to liberalize the economy are not insignificant. Indira Gandhi, however, seems to have made a different political calculation and apparently a correct one. Her credentials with the poor were well established. Since these were based primarily on ideological appeals, she was not about to lose this support over the short run. Given political difficulties elsewhere, she must have decided that communal appeals to the dominant Hindu community and economic measures supporting the business and industrial groups were the way to go.

Now, it was not at all self-evident that the so-called liberalization measures would be welcomed by the business groups. Import liberalization is likely to be and had been seriously resisted by India's well-established indigenous capitalists. So, to put the general political decision of wooing business support into practice, Mrs Gandhi must have asked one or more of her such senior advisors, such as the late L.K. Jha: what is wrong with our industry and what do the businessmen really want these days?

Advisors like L.K. Jha have long worked with both businessmen and the government. Jha had never favoured rapid opening of the economy to external forces. He had, however, argued for removing restrictions on both entry and expansion of firms, and for reduction in direct and indirect taxes.[21] These measures are supported by most business groups: reduction in taxes is supported by all types of businessmen; big business favours removal of constraints on expansion of capacity (in Indian business lingo, removal of MRTP restrictions); while small businesses often fear this, freedom of entry raises even their prospects for competing in some hitherto unexplored areas. As advisors like L.K. Jha were brought into prominent policy roles, and as policies favoured by him and others like him were put into effect, the message

[20]Reference is to the analysis presented in Bardhan, *The Political Economy of Development in India*. An interesting essay that discusses these issues in detail is Rubin, 'Economic Liberalization and the Indian State'.

[21]Interview. L.K. Jha, New Delhi, 16 December 1985.

to the business community must have been clear: socialism was being put on the back burner and a new policy regime that might work to their benefit was being initiated.

The economic policy shift under Indira Gandhi is thus best understood as an integral aspect of her overall political strategy. This, in turn, was aimed at strengthening the soft areas of her support. The question that remains to be answered in this section is why did these policy shifts go relatively unnoticed? Given her socialist commitments, why did a policy trend towards the liberalization of the economy never become a political liability for Indira Gandhi? An important part of the answer is fairly simple: the extent of change was not significant enough to raise too many political eyebrows. Yet, this alone will clearly not do. It, in turn, raises a thorny question of political management: when can changes be made to look marginal and when do they appear significant, deserving political response from all those who may wish to oppose them?

Indira Gandhi was a master political artist. As noted above, she understood well that her popular image was one of a leader on the Left. She had built up these credentials, not by careful implementation of socialist policies, but by undertaking highly visible acts like nationalization of banks, pursuit of anti-monopoly legislation and the adoption of poverty alleviation as the central platform of her party and government. Now, it is a well-established political adage that leaders of the Left can more easily take selected rightist decisions without invoking the wrath of the Left, or vice-versa for that matter. When leaders are judged by their citizens, what leaders seem to stand for turns out to be as important over the short run as the substance of the policies they pursue. Indira Gandhi benefited from this general political trust that groups in the popular sector bestowed on her.

Indira Gandhi further benefited from both the circumstances and the effective stage management she provided for the policy changes. India's political attention was increasingly on such regional issues as Assam and Punjab, rather than on economic policies. Indira herself downplayed the significance of the economy or of economic achievements as tools of legitimacy. When attention did turn to the economy, the picture for popular consumption was more of continuity than of change. The rhetoric of socialism, though toned down, was maintained; so were most of the anti-poverty programmes. Left-of-centre economic advisors like K.N. Raj and Sukhamoy Chakravarty were kept on in visible but largely ceremonial positions in the Economic Advisory Council. The policy changes, however, were being influenced by such advisors in the background as K.C. Alexander, L.K. Jha, and Arjun Sengupta. The changes themselves appeared largely technical: a lowering of a limit here and an expansion of restriction there.

The attempt, it seems, was to depoliticize economic decisions as far as possible. A number of advisors noted this during interviews; the focus they suggested was on 'results', not 'ideology'.[22]

Indira Gandhi's attempts to liberalize the economy did not draw sharp political reaction. This was a result of a number of factors: the scale of change; the conscious attempt to maintain an image of continuity as well as to depoliticize economic decisions; and, of course, other pressing political circumstances that drew attention away from the economy. The tension between the pursuit of economic rationality and the rationality of democracy during Indira Gandhi's last few years was kept within manageable bounds. It is hard to know how far she intended to push liberalization and how far she would have succeeded. Her assassination pushed these questions into the realm of the hypothetical. What we do know is what her son tried; he has pushed liberalization harder than his mother and has also drawn considerably more political opposition.

LIBERALIZATION UNDER RAJIV

In the four years that Rajiv Gandhi has been in power at the time of writing this article, economic policy has gone through three phases. During the first six months of his rule, there was a genuine attempt at a new beginning; an attempt was made to make a decisive shift from the state-controlled and imports substitution model to a liberal model of development. When this attempt ran into political obstacles, the pace of change slowed. The next two years are best characterized as two steps forward towards and one step backward from the defined agenda. With Rajiv's political popularity continuing to decline, the loss of Haryana elections in May 1987 marked the beginning of the third and the present phase. This is the return to India's 'muddle through' model of economic policy making. Within this 'model', the policy makers remain committed to economic liberalization. While the general trend is still in this direction, political considerations have necessitated the renewal of populism. The sense that there was to be a new economic beginning in India has thus been quickly lost.

These three phases of economic policy making—attempt at a new beginning, two steps forward and one step backward, and back to muddling through—are intimately linked to the overall political situation, both as a cause and as a consequence. Since the overall political situation cannot be analysed in detail here, the focus in the next three sections will be primarily on those political factors that impinge most heavily on, and thus help explain, economic policy fluctuations.

[22]Interviews, Arjun Sengupta (see note 10) and L.K. Jha (see footnote 21).

Rajiv's rise to power was largely circumstantial. There is no doubt that prior to Indira Gandhi's assassination, Rajiv had begun to be groomed as the heir apparent. His grooming, however, was no more than two to three years in process when Indira Gandhi's assassination suddenly brought him into power. He was a natural heir in the sense that he had been put into that role by Indira Gandhi and he was more or less accepted as such by Indira's loyal second tier. These political minions in the second tier did not enjoy any independent political support. They must have calculated that their and the Congress' best chance to maintain power was to select Indira's son; he was likely to inherit a fair amount of Indira's popularity and to gain new support in sympathy for her assassination.[23] Rajiv's initial power and legitimacy were thus based on a series of factors, none of which had much to do with Rajiv's preferred economic policies. As Rajiv was thrown in to fill the power vacuum left by Indira's assassination, only a handful of Indians must have known, and the rest probably did not care to know in the post-assassination mood of trauma and crisis, what type of economic policies the new government would pursue.

During the very brief period of his rise and consolidation, Rajiv Gandhi and his advisors must have made a crucial decision: the new regime was going to stress a new beginning rather than continuity with the past. This emphasis on change became clear relatively quickly, in both rhetoric and action, and in both the political and economic arenas. In the political arena, for example, the new emphasis was manifested in a shift away from Indira's apparent recalcitrance (as in dealings with Punjab and Assam) to a more accommodating and compromising set of policies. Similarly, with regard to the issue of primary interest in this essay, the government promised new economic policies. Shortly after winning a massive election, Rajiv summed up his government's economic approach as involving a 'judicious combination of deregulation, import liberalization and easier access to foreign technology.'[24] That this involved a fairly sharp break from Nehru and Indira Gandhi's rhetorical emphasis on 'socialism, planning and self-reliance' should be self evident.

As if to underline the break from the past, Rajiv Gandhi surrounded himself with a new breed of politicians and advisors. Consider some of those who appeared influential, at least in 1985–6. Confidants like Arun Nehru and Arun Singh had backgrounds as executives of multinational corporations. Economic advisors included individuals such as Montek

---

[23]For a detailed discussion of the issue of how leaders in India get into power, see H. Hart, 'Political Leadership in India: Dimensions and Limits', in Atul Kohli (ed.), *India's Democracy: An Analysis of Changing State–Society Relations*, Princeton, N.J.: Princeton University Press, 1988.

[24]Quoted in *Times of India*, 6 January 1986.

Ahluwalia, Abid Hussain, Bimal Jalan, and Manmohan Singh. Individuals like L.K. Jha were considered to have direct access to the prime minister. While clearly a competent group of managers, economists and bureaucrats, they were all marked by a technocratic rather than a political image. Some of them had World Bank backgrounds; most of them were known for their de-control and pro-liberalization proclivities. If one contrasts Rajiv and this group of India's new elite with Nehru and his band of seasoned, left-leaning nationalist leaders and advisors, then the image of a sharp break with the past is unmistakable.

It is important to note here that this issue of change in the nature of economic policy makers is as much or more an issue of image than of substance. For example, if one were to focus primarily on the economic advisors of an earlier generation—Pitambar Pant, I.G. Patel, Bootlingam, Vishnu Sahay, Tarlok Singh, Ashok Mehta, V.T. Krishnamachari—there is probably more continuity than change between this group and the contemporary advisors in terms of both technical skills and preferred policies.[25] What has changed, however, is both the nature of the political leadership and the sense of who—the leaders or the advisors—are really in charge of economic policy making. Since Rajiv and his crucial political aides like Arun Singh and Arun Nehru had a managerial and technocratic image, there was a sense that the political leaders and their technical advisors were cut from the same cloth. Additionally, Rajiv's relative inexperience created a popular image that policy making was increasingly in the hands of bureaucrats and experts. Such considerations added up to an image of a sharp break in the nature of India's economic policy makers.

The image and the real attempt to make a sharp break with the past were probably responsible for Rajiv's early popularity and may well also prove to be his undoing. The issue that presents itself, therefore, is what helps explain the government's emphasis on change over continuity? The question is especially salient because the economic changes that Indira Gandhi had already introduced and those that Rajiv's government has actually pursued since then, could have easily been accommodated within an image of continuity. Why, then, the need to emphasize a sharp break?

An important part of this answer has to be—and this is further discussed below—that Rajiv and his advisors initially intended the changes to go much further than they have actually gone. This, in turn, must have seemed feasible due to Rajiv's unusual rise to power. His massive electoral victory was based on sympathy and fear on the part of the electorate. This victory freed Rajiv Gandhi—if only momentarily and artificially—from coalitional entanglements and interest group pressures. This freedom from politics as usual must have

[25] I am indebted to John P. Lewis for bringing this point to my attention.

heightened the illusion that a sharp new beginning is possible, even in a polity like the Indian one. The politically inexperienced cronies and advisors that surrounded Rajiv, as we will see below, did not help much in dispelling such illusions.

The considerable sense of power, and the hurry in which it had been acquired, must have created a sense among the new rulers that they had hijacked the state. The state suddenly stood quite autonomous, seemingly free of societal constraints, ready to be used as a tool for imposing economic rationality upon the society. Situations of state autonomy like this always encourage the powerful to pursue their ideological whims.[26]

The illusion of autonomy and, with it, the euphoria of a new beginning lasted about six months. The first major product of this new beginning was the 1985–6 budget, presented by the new government in March 1985, less than three months after coming to power. The budget created many ripples. The word socialism was not mentioned even once in the budget speech.[27] Substantial tax concessions were offered to both the corporate and the urban upper-middle classes. Imports were liberalized in certain sectors, especially the sector favoured personally by Rajiv Gandhi, namely, electronics. Most important, licensing regulations for domestic industries were relaxed drastically and the limit on the size of a firm that qualifies it as a monopoly was raised substantially.

The reaction of both business and upper-middle groups was euphoric. India's leading news magazine, *India Today*, ran such cover captions as 'The Economy: Buoyant Mood' and 'We are Gearing for Take-Off'.[28] Other commentators hailed it as 'the most important budget in 30 years'.[29] Since

[26]It is reported that a senior World Bank official flew into India at this time and advised the new government to dismantle the structures of economic control all at once. It is not clear how many of the advisors of the Indian government with World Bank connections were sympathetic to this approach. L.K. Jha in an interview (see note 21) suggested that he reacted 'very negatively to such suggestions'. Given the opposition that even piecemeal liberalization has invoked within India, one wonders about the political sensibilities of both those in power and those who provide 'rational' economic advice around the globe. Do ends justify all means? Does it matter whether the political system can withstand such sharp economic changes? Or is it that, given 'rational economic policies', and thus a 'rationalized economy', all else will work itself out in good time? More sober observers, even economists who favour liberalization of the Indian economy, have openly worried about the capacity of Rajiv Gandhi and his advisors to appreciate the serious political obstacles that such an effort will create. For an extremely well-balanced and sensible essay along these lines, see M. Datta Chaudhury, 'The New Policy', *Seminar*, December 1985. Other economists like Jagdish Bhagwati have also, in a more general context, recognized these obstacles. See Bhagwati, 'Rethinking Trade Strategy'.

[27]For a summary and a discussion of the 1985–6 budget, see *Times of India*, 21 March 1985.

[28]These cover captions are for issues of 15 March and 15 April 1985, respectively.

[29]Nani Palkhiwala in *Times of India*, 2 April 1985.

the parliament was totally dominated by individuals beholden to Rajiv Gandhi for their position, there was no question at this early date of any substantial opposition from this group. The Left and other opposition parties reacted sharply; they characterized the budget as a pro-rich budget and the new government as a pro-rich government. In the middle of 1985, however, these were voices in the wilderness. They were drowned, at least momentarily, in the euphoria of a new beginning.

The opposition that began to simmer at the grass-roots, however, did not take long to crystallize. It was first expressed on a significant scale—much to the surprise of the new leadership—within the ruling party. The occasion was an attempt by Rajiv Gandhi and his cronies to have the Congress party ratify an economic resolution. The politics surrounding this debate is further analysed below. Suffice it to note for the moment that Rajiv ran into considerable and unexpected opposition from the rank and file of his party. The resolution he wanted ratified represented an attempt to get his party formally behind the new economic beginning that he had already begun with the budget. The resolution that was eventually ratified, however, recommitted Rajiv and the Congress party to socialism.[30]

The significance of this dramatic event should not be underestimated. Many in India are so jaded with Congress's socialism that any continued talk of it is deadening to sensibilities; it simply evokes no, or worse, very cynical responses. Even the head of India's leading Chamber of Commerce dismissed this recommitment to socialism on Congress's part as 'mere rhetoric'.[31] Rhetoric it may well be, but its significance was considerable. A recommitment to socialism underlined clearly and starkly that the government's economic policies will maintain continuity with the past, that socialism will define the limits within which new policies will have to fit. Now, it is clear that these limits are very, very flexible; the economic resolution, while reaffirming socialism, also accepted all the policy changes Rajiv's government had introduced so far.[32] Nevertheless, a tolerance for what many observers would consider gross inconsistencies is a very different political picture than one in which the party would wholeheartedly support the liberalization of the economy. Rajiv's first major encounter with his own party thus immediately set limits on how far he could carry economic policy changes. It cannot be doubted that this must have slowed the pace of change Rajiv

[30]These events received considerable attention in the press. For example, see *Times of India*, 7 May 1985; *The Statesman*, 7 May 1985; *Statesman*, 9 May 1985; and *Telegraph*, 14 May 1985.

[31]Interview, D.H. Pi Panandiker, Secretary General, Federation of Indian Chambers of Commerce and Industry, New Delhi, 12 December 1985.

[32]See *Times of India*, 7 May 1985. Also see. All India National Congress(I), *Economic Resolution*, adopted by the All India Congress(I) Committee, New Delhi, 6 May 1985.

and his advisors would have otherwise pursued, had the Congress party supported them fully.

The confrontation with his own party marks the beginning of the second phase in economic policy making. From here on, until very recently, the government continued to push piecemeal liberalizing reforms. Most of these were carried out while reemphasizing the government's commitment to socialism. We will never know what was never attempted because the advisors concluded that it would be hard to justify, even by Congress's standards of socialism. What we do know is that, in spite of these constraints, the government has succeeded in pushing through some important reforms. Others, however, had to be modified or reversed so as to fit the socialist commitment.

The rhetoric on economic policy increasingly became quite confusing. While celebrating Congress's centenary the day after the confrontation with the working committee over the economic resolution, Rajiv reaffirmed that Congress's goal, now as ever, was socialism.[33] Over the next few months, economic policy changes involved several liberalizing measures. These are further discussed below. When presenting the Seventh Plan to the National Development Council in November, however, Rajiv Gandhi once again argued that the 'industrial policy remains unchanged'.[34]

Shortly thereafter, in the same month, Rajiv argued that, when and where 'import substitutes are not cost-effective', India should opt for 'imports, especially of technology'.[35] This was followed by the release of the Abid Hussain Report that emphasized the need for boosting exports and for an outward looking industrialization strategy.[36] Lest the observers nail down the government's real policy, two days later government spokesmen reiterated that, whatever liberalization may take place, the public sector will continue to maintain the 'commanding heights' of the economy.[37] The prime minister himself went on to argue for top priority to the public sector and to reemphasize that there was 'no shift from socialism'.[38] The main thrust of the Seventh Plan, it was further suggested, would be 'eradication of poverty, self-reliance and growth with social justice'.[39] Finally, several months later,

[33]See *Deccan Herald*, 7 May 1985.

[34]See *Statesman*, 19 November 1985.

[35]See *Statesman*, 14 November 1985.

[36]The report was released in mid-November. For an abbreviated discussion, see *Economic Times*, 18 November 1985. The report itself is now a public document. See Government of India, *Report of the Committee on Trade Policies*, New Delhi: Ministry of Commerce, Government of India, 1984.

[37]See *Indian Express*, 20 November 1985.

[38]See *Hindustan Times*, 6 December 1985.

[39]See *Indian Express*, 19 December 1985.

the government let it be known that privatization of the public sector was not on the agenda, that the mixed economy model would stay.[40]

If the rhetoric was confusing, and probably purposefully so, more of a pattern is discernible in the actual policy changes. Shortly after the Congress party had made Rajiv recommit himself to continuity with the past, a new textile policy was quietly passed. Without too much discussion or debate, this policy removed the restrictions on the capacity of the mill sector.[41] While seemingly a minor, technical change, it hit at the heart of some of old Congress's nationalist values. The removal of restrictions, it could be argued, would assure that both the power loom and the hand loom sectors will go into a long-term decline due to the more efficient mill sector.[42] While clearly rational, such a change would have been abhorrent to the first generation nationalists. The dumping of the more efficient textiles by the British had been understood by the nationalists to have caused the destruction of the Indian textile industry in the nineteenth century and thus of nascent Indian capitalism. Now, a generation later, Indian leaders were themselves promulgating similar policies. Old nationalist themes in economic policies are clearly on the decline.

Other important policy changes followed. The role of the Planning Commission was decisively diminished, again without any pronouncements, by the creation of a new Ministry of Programme Implementation. The 'New Fiscal Policy' announced in November 1985 was very significant; it replaced import quotas with tariffs and laid out long-term patterns of taxation, assuring the corporate sector that no negative surprises were looming on the horizon.[43] Despite the worsening balance of payments, the government did not reverse the liberalized import policy, even in the capital goods sector, which had been hurt quite badly. Companies restricted under the monopoly act were, moreover, given further concessions[44] and the budget of 1986–7 brought some further excise and customs relief to national firms.[45]

All these policy changes are clearly part of a pattern. They are aimed at relaxing the scope and the degree of state control over the private economy. What is interesting from the point of view of this essay is the little immediate political response that the changes just documented evoked. A number of

[40]See *Economic Times*, 14 September 1986.

[41]For a critical review of the new textile policy, see L.C. Jain, *Economic Times*, 26 September 1985.

[42]I have chosen not to evaluate the actual consequences of the adopted policies in this essay. It may interest the readers to note in passing that the mill sector of the textile industry has done rather poorly in India throughout 1986 and 1987. The reasons for this, however, are only in part policy related.

[43]See *Hindustan Times*, 12 December 1985.

[44]See *Indian Express*, 23 January 1986.

[45]See the editorial in *EPW*, 1 March 1986.

factors help explain the minimal opposition from the popular sectors. These policies generally tended to affect, as in the case of textile policy, one specific segment of the society more than others. The values violated—in this specific case, themes from the old anti-colonial heritage—are also not felt as deeply as before. Since neither the values nor the interests of the society at large were hurt, political opposition was minimal. Other policy changes that went unopposed, at least over the short run, shared another set of traits: more often than not, they were supportive of powerful business interests; and they were brought about quietly, without much fanfare, as seemingly technical changes in a piecemeal fashion. Very few political groups in India have the resources that it would require to monitor economic policy changes of this minute nature. Opposition groups, therefore, generally concentrate their political energies on policies that are highly visible and that influence widely shared interests and values in the society.

If these policies went more or less unopposed, another set evoked considerable response. The balance has now tilted towards mounting opposition. Policies that actually had to be modified or reversed showed one of two characteristics: they were either opposed by powerful groups like the businessmen; or they created diffuse but real disenchantment among the popular sectors. A number of examples will support these generalizations, as well as highlight the policy fluctuations and reversals that have occurred due to growing opposition.

The Seventh Plan came under opposition from within the ruling party. While the details are not known, it is clear that several groups from within the Congress had approached Rajiv to register their protest, namely, that the plan did not assign enough resources to anti-poverty programmes. The plan was changed to accommodate this political opposition, even though the planners know and argue that resources devoted to such programmes in the past have not been used effectively.[46]

A different type of policy fluctuation characterized the approach the government has adopted towards industries that import goods and thus directly affect the balance of payments. A good example here is the approach towards the automobile industry. During 1985, the government let it be known that it would look kindly on expansion of automobile production, including expansion involving further foreign collaboration—especially with Japanese manufacturers. In early February 1986, after numerous plans to undertake such expansion were underway, the government changed its mind; the implementation of the new automobile policy was postponed indefinitely. Among the reasons cited were the need to conserve petroleum and the

[46]Interview, Raja Chelliah, Member of Planning Commission, New Delhi, 13 December 1985.

worsening balance-of-payments situation.[47] There is also some indication, however, that pressure was brought to bear on the government from those established automobile manufacturers who feared a glut of overproduction and competition from new and probably better products.[48] What adds weight to this interpretation is the fact that the policy was not reconsidered, even when petroleum prices dropped in the world market in July 1986 and India's balance-of-payments situation improved considerably. The government actually used the occasion of a shift in the anticipated automobile policy to make a more general statement that marked an important policy shift: '...pace of domestic liberalization has not been slackened...external liberalization (however) was not really an objective of the (overall) policy.'[49]

More serious opposition, because it was popular opposition, was evoked over the issue of price hikes in February 1986. Within a few days of the announcement of price increases in petroleum and other related products, such as kerosene, every opposition party in the country had announced plans for strikes and the closing down of one city or another. Congress politicians themselves argued against this hike, fearing a popular backlash. Even before the strikes materialized, however, the government reversed its decision.[50]

The above examples demonstrate cases of specific opposition and associated policy reversals. The type of opposition, however, that hurts in India the most politically, and that is the most hard to document, is the more diffuse and growing disillusionment with the national leadership. Rajiv's overall political popularity has gone into a sharp decline since late 1986. He has lost virtually every state election since the assembly elections in March 1985. The loss in Haryana in May 1987 was especially devastating because it is in the area of Congress's power base, the Hindi heartland. Now, it is true that most state elections are influenced by important regional themes. Even when national themes are important, positions on economic policies are only one part of the overall assessment citizens make of leaders. Despite such diffuseness around the issue of loss of electoral popularity, these political changes have two important implications for understanding economic policy fluctuations. First, and this is further documented below, the image of Rajiv and his government as pro-rich has stuck. This is related both to the style of political management and to the substance of the economic policies adopted; it has also contributed to his loss of electoral popularity. Second, irrespective of how damaging these economic policies have been politically, one possible way to recover sagging political fortunes in India is clearly to adopt populist economic policies.

---

[47]See *Economic Times*, 2 February 1986.
[48]Ibid.
[49]*Economic Times,* 24 February 1986.
[50]See the editorial in *Telegraph*, 7 February 1986.

It is this last set of considerations that have come to influence economic policy making in the present and third phase. Throughout the second phase, it is fair to suggest that economic policy changes slowed from what was probably intended to be a major departure from India's mixed-economy model of development. Socialism was re-established as the framework. In spite of this rhetorical reversal, as well as the change of pace and some important setbacks, the overall thrust during this second phase was to continue to push ahead towards lifting governmental controls and restrictions on the Indian economy. With the electoral debacle in Haryana, however, the future of economic policy is now unclear; India has returned to its usual pattern of muddling through.

There was a growing sense in the aftermath of the Haryana elections that a major policy reversal might be in the making. This has not come to pass. It is fair to suggest that Rajiv Gandhi and his key advisors remain committed to liberalizing India's economic policy regime. The opportunities to do so, however, have narrowed. As Rajiv's popularity has declined, the opposition has adopted a relatively left-leaning position that criticizes Rajiv for the neglect of farmers and the poor. This challenge, led by V.P. Singh in the Hindi heartland and by others like Jyoti Basu of the CPI(M) in West Bengal and N.T. Rama Rao in Andhra Pradesh, has exposed Rajiv's electoral vulnerability in the popular sectors. As this challenge has grown, the drive towards economic liberalization has slowed. The angry conclusion of a prominent Indian journalist on this score appears to be only a slight exaggeration:

While no one can doubt that Gandhi was sincere in his desire to liberalize the economy, it is equally beyond doubt that he has failed.[51]

The increased allocation to pro-farmer and anti-poverty programmes in the proposed budget for 1988–9 only highlights the fact that electoral pressures have pushed issues of liberalizing the economy to the sidelines. Some important liberalizing measures are still being pursued. They may also be put back on the agenda if Rajiv reconsolidates his power and popularity after the next elections. For now, pressed politically, Rajiv has slowed down any attempts to change India's economic policies.

In a little more than three years, Rajiv and his bold men have dissipated the enormous political capital that they had acquired almost accidentally. Society has hit back; the state has lost the temporary autonomy it had gained. An enormous sense of power and autonomy during 1985 had encouraged the new leaders to try to impose their own rationality on the society. The loss of this power is now likely to lead to policies that make more sense from the point of view of the logic of winning elections and thus democratic power than of economic rationality. One hopes that it is possible to combine

---

[51]See Jha, 'Economic Expansion Ensnared in Red Tape'.

these two rationalities. Contemporary India, however, continues to search for the appropriate mix.

SUPPORT FOR LIBERALIZATION

So far the focus of analysis has been on the economic policy makers and on the fluctuations that economic policies have undergone. The roles of other actors and groups who influence this policy process have been mentioned, but only in passing. Now it is important to restore the balance. The groups who have supported or opposed the policies are a crucial part of the overall picture of the politics of economic policy making. Some understanding of the role and the views of the more significant actors is thus important. Those who have, on balance, supported governmental initiatives are discussed immediately below and those who have opposed these policies are discussed in the next section.

Business Groups

Business groups have, on balance, been very supportive of Rajiv's government and policies. This support, however, varies along a number of dimensions. At the most diffuse level, business groups have felt in tune with the new government. Rajiv's emphasis on technology and efficiency, rather than on socialism, has appealed to the businessmen's preference for 'results over ideology'. With the early incorporation of former corporate executives like Arun Nehru and Arun Singh into the ranks of the ruling coterie, moreover, business spokesmen have suggested that, for the first time in independent India, they have felt as if they were not cheats or pariahs, that they were part of the national mainstream.[52]

Beyond the most general level, Indian business does not interact with the state elite through any one single organization or with one single voice. A few comments on these issues may help clarify how business and government interact.[53] There are numerous points of formal and informal contact between the state and business. Business groups are formally represented by three national and many regional chambers of commerce. Of three national chambers, only one involving the engineering industries is organized along functional lines. The other two main chambers—the Federation of Indian Chambers of Commerce and Industry (FICCI) and the Associated Chambers of Commerce and Industry of India (ASSOCHAM)—bring together a variety of industries. ASSOCHAM started off as an association

---

[52]Interview, N.D. Saxena, Secretary General, the Associated Chambers of Commerce and Industry of India, New Delhi, 16 December 1985.

[53]For a detailed study, which is somewhat out of date by now, but which still captures important trends in this issue area, see Kochanek, *Business and Politics in India*, Berkeley, CA: University of California Press, 1974.

of British industries in the pre-independence period and has, until recently, maintained its character as a representative of companies with a large component of foreign investment, foreign management or both. FICCI, until recently by far the most significant voice of Indian business, has, on balance, tended to represent indigenous capital. Within the business community, the two chambers are distinguished in a somewhat light-hearted and exaggerated fashion by their cultural composition: ASSOCHAM represents the 'tie-wallahs' and FICCI the 'dhoti-wallahs'.[54]

As long as the overall policy framework was stable, the political task of FICCI and ASSOCHAM was not all that significant. Their role, especially that of FICCI, was to periodically announce policy positions representing interests of their members. FICCI and ASSOCHAM have seldom cooperated on the policy memoranda they present to the government, though they do cooperate on issues of labour management.[55] Clearly, interests combine more easily in some areas than others.

The real points of contact between business and government have generally been quite decentralized. During the 1950s and the 1960s, for example, it is well known that important business houses had certain 'captured' members of parliament. With growing centralization, however, business attention has shifted both to cabinet ministers and other leaders of the Congress party and to the bureaucracy. Members of FICCI are generally understood to have well-established contacts within the Congress hierarchy, where black money is contributed 'under-the-table' to party coffers in exchange for political favours.[56] Most business houses, moreover, maintain liaison offices in New Delhi that wine, dine, and probably bribe bureaucrats and senior politicians to facilitate licensing and access to other resources the government controls. Members of ASSOCHAM claim that their points of contact with the government are not through the party. The Congress culture, they assert, is much closer to the culture of FICCI: 'We would rather deal in a club, over a glass of whiskey, with senior administrators...like L.K. Jha.'[57]

With major policy changes on the horizon, Indian business has tried to come up with a somewhat more unified response than the decentralized mode of operation would have hitherto allowed. However, this has not been easy. Interests of various segments within the business community diverge. One potential divide is between those who favour and those who oppose external liberalization. It would be fair to assume that those in import-substitution industries would oppose liberalizing imports, while those who

[54]The qualification, 'until recently', when discussing FICCI and ASSOCHAM is made because both chambers are currently undergoing major changes in membership.
[55]Interview, N.D. Saxena (see note 52).
[56]Interview, N.S. Jagannathan (see note 15).
[57]Interview, N.D. Saxena (see note 52).

need imported technology and/or produce for external markets may favour a different set of policies.[58] While these are important tendencies, derived from assumed interests, such divisions are not easy to find. Major business houses tend to do all these things; they produce for protected markets; they, on occasion, wish to improve their technology with imports; and many do or want to cater to export markets.[59] A related area of disagreement within the business community crystallizes between the more traditional business houses that fear competition and the more newly established businesses with new technology and imported MBAs who claim to be ready to compete internationally.[60]

Another major divide, about whose political significance much less is known, is that between big business on the one hand and medium and small businesses on the other. It is almost taken for granted by policy makers that the freedom to enter new production lines and to expand existing capacity will primarily benefit those who are already well established, namely, the big business houses.[61] Why should medium, and especially the small businesses, support such policy developments? Are their interests not threatened by the encroaching 'monopoly' houses? Since small businesses are not well organized, their political responses are neither expressed in any aggregated fashion, nor can they be identified easily by observers.

This picture of organizational diffuseness and interest divergence within the business community is not supposed to lead to a conclusion that the Indian business community does not have some clear and coherent policy preferences or that it is politically weak. Those would be absurd claims. What the picture of incoherence helps point to is the mode in and the mechanisms through which business groups have influenced the liberalization agenda. The business community of India has tended to react to rather than lead economic policy. Its power is closer to one of veto than of agenda setting. The policy lead has come from the political actors. The liberalization agenda has thus originated as much in the changing power and interests of the business community, as in the changes within the state, that is, in the coming to power of new leaders with new ideologies.

The nature of the division of power between the state and business is clearly evident in the policy process. FICCI has been making policy demands

---

[58]For an argument along these lines, see Datta 'The Central Budget and the New Economic Policy'.

[59]Interview with a business executive who did not wish to be identified, New Delhi, 14 December 1985.

[60]Several of those interviewed suggested this as the major division among the business community vis-à-vis the new economic policies. For example, both T.N. Ninan (see note 15) and N.S. Jagannathan (see note 15) expressed this view.

[61]Interview, L.K. Jha (see note 21).

for lowering taxes, de-licensing and removing restrictions on monopolies for decades. When these changes finally came in a big way, they came because there was a new government in power. Even business representatives were taken by surprise, for example, when the government chose to raise the limit of the MRTP Act to one billion rupees from 200 million, whereas FICCI had asked for the limit to be only 600 million.[62]

The reaction of business groups to the government's new economic policies has generally been very favourable. The initial package that the Rajiv government offered in the budget of 1985–6, and that has been more or less maintained since, has been received with tremendous enthusiasm by all three chambers of commerce. One major area, however, where business response has been quite hesitant, or even negative, is the extent to which the economy should be opened to external goods and capital. There is a widespread feeling among Indian business groups that both foreign borrowing and direct foreign investment are not desirable.[63] This coincides with the nationalist and cautious sentiments on these issues held by the policy makers.[64] The issue of trade liberalization, however, has proven to be more complex. Many industries welcome liberalized imports of technology, but liberalized imports also hurt domestic producers. Given the import-substitution bias of Indian industry, the overall reluctance of business groups towards import liberalization has emerged fairly clearly in a process that involved some trial and error.

This process of trial and error has proceeded something as follows. The government has liberalized certain imports. It has then monitored the impact of these policy changes on both the balance of payments and on specific groups of industries. Business reactions have similarly developed serially. What has emerged, however, is a fair amount of consensus between the political and economic elite.

Business groups have, on balance, decided that they are not ready to deal with any major international opening of the economy. In the words of the head of FICCI: 'after three decades of highly protective industrialization, liberalization cannot be taken up simultaneously on all fronts—it has to be phased. The first stage has to be to allow domestic competitiveness. Only then (after a while), we should open up to outside forces'.[65] Such views from businessmen pampered by import-substitution are not surprising.

What is interesting and maybe even somewhat surprising is that the government more or less agrees. Those who seem to favour a competitive economy have apparently decided that there is competitiveness and then

---

[62]Interview, D.H. Pi Panandiker (see note 31).

[63]Ibid.

[64]L.K. Jha (see note 21) suggested in an interview that there was no thought to alter the established national approach on these issues.

[65]Interview, D.H. Pi Panandiker (see note 31).

there are the interests of national capital. Senior advisors like L.K. Jha have assured businessmen that domestic industry 'built up with so much effort and sacrifice', will not be allowed 'to be killed by imports'.[66] Even outside experts like Jagdish Bhagwati agree, because of what is politically feasible.[67] Finally, the prime minister himself now feels that import liberalization is not immediately on the agenda: 'Competition within our domestic economy is being fostered. Progressively, we will open our economy to the winds of international competition'.[68]

With the government now having accepted the demand of business groups to limit trade liberalization, one would have to conclude that the present government is more or less in complete agreement with business, especially big business that produces for the protected domestic market. Sporadic efforts to raid business houses under V.P. Singh only underlined the fact that the government badly needed some popular and visible issues—corruption in this case—to distance itself from the image of too close an alliance with business. On substantial issues of policy, however, the alliance of the state and big business has probably never been closer in India than under the first three years of Rajiv Gandhi. Critics of Rajiv Gandhi cannot be blamed, therefore, if they see his economic agenda primarily as pro-business and only secondarily as pro-market and pro-competition.

Middle Classes

Within India's political discourse, the term middle class has come to refer to some 60–80 million urban dwellers who work mainly in the professions and the civil service or are self-employed.[69] The positive support that this motley stratum provided to Rajiv's economic programme in the first two years of his rule can be understood by focusing on two different issues.

First, Rajiv Gandhi's early economic policies provided concrete benefits to the middle classes. Reduction in taxes and abolition of such programmes as the Compulsory Savings Deposit Scheme were received with great enthusiasm. Moreover, the government seems to have decided to hinge its new economic strategy on the buying power of these groups. Controls on production have been released and exports are not going up all that rapidly. Who, under these circumstances, is going to buy all the new products that

[66]L.K. Jha's address to the Indian Merchants Chamber, Bombay, as reported in *Economic Times*, 16 September 1986.

[67]R.K. Roy's interview with Jagdish Bhagwati, as published in *Economic Times*, 16 September 1986.

[68]See *Times of India*, 6 January 1986.

[69]Marketing companies generally arrive at this figure by assuming that 'middle class' is defined by urban incomes of Rs 1000–2500. A good, non-scholarly survey of the Indian middle classes was published in India's news magazine, *Imprint*, March 1986, pp. 14–28.

are now suddenly appearing on the market? Clearly, the government is hoping that the middle income groups will use their increased incomes to soak up the growing supply and thus avoid a demand constraint on growth. Whether this will become the basis of a successful development strategy is not an issue under discussion here; that is for the economists to debate.

From the point of view of the political inclinations of the middle-income groups, the new strategy has meant not only improved incomes over the short run, but also for almost the first time in post-colonial India, an economy that is not beset by shortages of consumer goods. Growing incomes and availability of products have, in turn, helped generate benign views of the government. That such tangible rewards are more important than any set of shared values with the leadership was highlighted when these very middle groups threw their weight against the government's plans to raise petroleum prices during February 1987.[70] Also, with the emergence of corruption scandals within the government during 1987 and 1988, many in this fickle political group have changed their evaluation of Rajiv Gandhi.[71]

A second issue of longer-term significance has not received much attention. Over the last decade, there has been a major change in how Indian industry finances itself. Significant contribution to industrial investment is now made by the sale of public stocks. While exact figures are not known, the phenomenon of middle-income groups, including Indians living outside of India, buying stocks in a big way has been widely noticed over the last decade. This is increasingly creating a structural link between middle-income groups and big business. The political significance of this fact is likely to grow. Middle-income groups now have a growing stake in the economic health of industry and commerce. Policies that facilitate this goal are thus likely to and do receive support.

OPPOSITION TO LIBERALIZATION

If both business and urban middle-income groups have tended to support the government's new economic initiatives, a number of important actors and groups have opposed these efforts. A brief description of the extent and the mode of opposition will set the stage to conclude this essay.

The Congress Rank and File

As noted above, a surprising source of opposition to the new policies has been the rank and file of the ruling party. This is surprising because the party organization of the Congress has been moribund for so long that

---

[70]See the editorial, *Telegraph*, 7 February 1986.
[71]See, for example, the popularity poll published in *India Today*, 31 August 1988.

observers cannot be blamed for having forgotten the party as a source of independent political initiative.

Rajiv's early encounter with his own party provides a reasonably clear picture of his original economic intentions and those of his advisors. A summary of the main events is revealing. Rajiv and a few of his ministers took a prepared economic resolution to the Working Committee of the Congress party, prior to presenting it to the All India Congress Committee (AICC) for ratification. This resolution was reported to have been the handiwork of Rajiv's 'whiz kids' or the 'World Bank *wallahs*'.[72] These references are to the group of technocratic economic advisors of Rajiv discussed above, especially those in the prime minister's secretariat. The resolution was presented to the working committee by the Finance Minister, V.P. Singh. His opening lines, according to the press, included the remark that 'bread, cloth and shelter were not everything of the economy'.[73] The resolution itself did not stress socialism and used language that seemed to suggest that a shift in strategy had already been adopted over the last few months and that this was both necessary and justified: 'The strengthening of the growth impulses of the economy, through absorption of modern technology and through appropriate fiscal and legislative changes, was imperative to sustain the tempo of industrial development. In the process of continued development, the policy instruments relevant to one stage cannot be treated as permanently sacrosanct. Nor are they ends in themselves'.[74]

Many members of the Congress read in this resolution an attempt to move away from the old development strategy of self-reliance and socialism. The details of the internal debates that took place are not known. What is known is that numerous senior party members and elected officials opposed this economic resolution.[75] As discussed above, the resolution that was eventually approved was a radically revised one; it reestablished continuity with the past by emphasizing socialism as Congress's central goal.

What interpretations can one place on these events? First, these events highlight considerable lack of political judgment on the part of Rajiv Gandhi and his economic advisors. The intended plan seems to have been nothing less than a major shift in India's overall development strategy. Even in an

[72]See S. Chakravarty, 'India's Development Strategy for the 1980s', *EPW*, 26 May 1984. Nikhil Chakravarty also brought up these issues, including the fact that he had personally seen the original economic resolution, in a one-on-one discussion in New Delhi, 17 December 1985.

[73]See *Statesman*, 7 May 1985.

[74]Reported in Chakravarty, 'India's Development Strategy for the 1980s'.

[75]See, for example, the reports in *Statesman*, 7 May 1985; and *Times of India*, 7 May 1985.

imperfect democracy like India, this would require a considerable amount of prior discussion and what some euphemistically call 'consensus building'. Forgetting for the moment the various contending interest groups and political forces in the society, the small group of India's technocratic rulers did not even have a clear sense of whether they could carry the ruling party with them, the same party in whose name they rule the country. The explanation for such political behaviour would have to stress some combination of extreme centralization of initiative, isolation of the rulers, and the lack of communication between these elites and the party ranks on the one hand, and on the other hand, the arrogance of power that comes especially from a belief in the righteousness of one's own actions.

Why the Congress opposed the original economic resolution and stressed the need to emphasize socialism is also somewhat of an enigma. Press accounts and discussions suggest that three different sets of motives were at work. The most common interpretation stresses that many members feared the electoral and political ramifications of abandoning socialism. They apparently conveyed to the leadership the following view: 'liberalization of the economy, import of technology and also opening the door to multinationals was not going down very well with the party's ground-level workers, who had to constantly meet people worried by their problems of hunger, shelter and clothing'.[76] Nothing brings home this gap between the leadership and the rank and file more sharply than to sit in a district or state-level Congress office, where the electric fan goes on and off due to an electricity shortage, and ask them what they think of Rajiv's 'march into the twenty-first century with computers'. If they are at all honest, a common answer often is, 'this talk is fine in Delhi, but here it will only make you lose elections'.[77]

A second set of considerations that led some Congress members to oppose the resolution had more to do with ideology than with electoral considerations. The former president of the party, Brahmananda Reddy, apparently made a strong and open speech during the meeting, criticizing the resolution for neglecting what Congress had always stood for, namely, the 'common man'.[78] While cynicism towards such statements from Congressmen is often an appropriate response, it would not be wise to ignore the powerful hold some ideas have on older members. The number of such Congressmen is diminishing, but they have far from totally vanished. Notions of national self-reliance are very dear to this set, as is the idea that, even if you cannot help the poor, the rich should not be pampered. State controls

[76]See *Statesman*, 7 May 1985.

[77]While remarks like this were often made, this specific quote is from an interview with Jinabhai Darjee, a veteran Congress(I) leader in Gujarat, conducted in Ahmedabad on 10 March 1986. The original interview was in Hindi. Translation is my own.

[78]See *Statesman*, 7 May 1985.

on capitalism satisfy this latter ideological urge. Liberalization, by contrast, invokes a knee-jerk reaction because it may involve, first, the abandonment of hard won national sovereignty and second, letting the rich run with all that they can.

Lastly, and probably most importantly, another set of Congress members seem to have opposed the resolution, not because they had any serious concerns over the substance of economic policy. Instead, they were generally disgruntled with Rajiv Gandhi and were in search of an issue over which they could let this be known. This group generally consisted of individuals who were well placed under Indira Gandhi but had lost out in the shuffle. As many as 100 of them, led by Dinesh Singh, apparently met at his house the night before the meeting to chart out an opposing strategy.[79]

Various sets of factors thus mobilized the Congress party to oppose the economic resolution presented by Rajiv and his ministers. The event was significant because it highlighted that the Congress party was not dead, at least not at the top. This same sense emerged when, as discussed above, the party opposed the leadership's decision to hike petroleum prices. What is as significant for the purpose of this essay, however, is a point developed above. This is worth reiterating. The failure to carry his own party put Rajiv on the defensive about his economic programme. This probably put important limits on both the pace and the scope of intended changes.

Moderate Left Opposition

Had Rajiv Gandhi carried his own party, he could have probably ignored the opposition from the Left without significant political costs. The opposition within Congress, however, gelled around what can be considered a 'left' position. This raised the significance of similar opposition generated by non-Congress groups, especially the left intellectuals and parts of the working class. What has made this opposition even more credible is its moderation; the government's new economic policies have been opposed, not from a position demanding massive structural changes, but from one that is claimed to be, though more broad-based, also 'politically feasible'.

An event of some political significance was the joint statement put out by twenty-nine left-leaning economists in October 1985.[80] As discussed above, this statement was sharply critical of the government's new economic policies. The meeting of the economists was sponsored by the CPI(M) and was held in Calcutta. The economists involved, however, were not only Marxists. While the opinions within the group differed, they arrived upon a

---

[79]Discussion with the journalist and political observer Nikhil Chakravarty (see note 72).
[80]See *EPW*, 26 October 1985, pp. 1813–16.

joint position that not only was very critical of the liberalizing thrust of the new policies, but also provided an alternative economic strategy.

The content of both the criticisms and the proposed alternative can be briefly summarized. The group criticized the new strategy because it will undermine cherished national goals of self-reliance and socialism. They argued that the new strategy will not even succeed in its growth objectives because the underlying analysis was wrong; the real constraints on growth are limited demand and declining public sector investment. The way to boost growth, therefore, while preserving national sovereignty and facilitating some redistribution, was to increase public investment, especially in irrigation, improve public sector performance, implement land reforms and facilitate broad-based, agriculture-led economic development.

This event has a number of political implications. First, India's economists are now more divided than in the past on the issue of the economic direction India should adopt for the future. This is not to deny that India has had some vociferous economic debates in the past. From the Second Five Year Plan, onward, however, India adopted a development strategy that has more or less been considered an appropriate strategy for India by most Indian economists. There were always those who thought India should be more export-oriented and competitive, and there were always those who thought that the feudal-capitalist alliance was holding back India's economic dynamism. Towards the middle, however, there were many disagreements, but not over the crucial values that economic development should strengthen. Even today, one should not exaggerate the divisions, especially on the broad issue that controls have outlived their utility. Yet, it is important to note that specialists are now quite divided on the issue of what values economic development should satisfy. The consensus of the specialists, which can be a powerful political glue, has come undone.

Related to this general point is a more specific issue. The divisions among specialists have highlighted the political nature of economic decision making. The new economic policies cannot easily be sold any more as technical solutions to complex technical problems. This has no bearing on which set of specialists is really right. The political point is simply that the technocratic element that could help legitimize economic policies has been weakened. The battle for economic policies will have to be fought more and more openly on political grounds.

This is not to suggest that mere opposition from specialists can form the basis of mass political opposition. That would be a nonsensical claim. The significance of opposition from specialists is that it provides viable, alternative economic plans for political actors to hold on to and mobilize around. It is possible to imagine—though only remotely—that opposition parties like the CPI(M) and the peasant parties like the Lok Dal can come together under the leadership of V.P. Singh around an economic programme that emphasizes broad-based, agriculture-led development. What is a more plausible alternative—and some of this has already begun—is that, as Rajiv Gandhi continues to lose his popularity, he will continue to distance himself from the liberalization alternative and move closer to a more populist programme that emphasizes the needs of the poor and the peasantry.

Another related opposition to the new policies that is worth noting here is the one day national strike organized by the workers in the public sector in January 1986. The strike was organized around mainly political demands: a halt to the policy of privatization; prevention of injecting foreign and national private capital into public sector activities; protecting domestic goods against imports; and the right of trade unions to influence technological changes, especially computerization. The strike was coordinated by an all-India committee and was by all accounts successful.[81]

The strike was mainly around policy issues that public sector workers fear the government may pursue in the future. It is difficult, therefore, to assess the political significance of the strike. Nothing concrete was up for bargaining; there were no identifiable winners or losers. What strikes like this make clear, however, is the type of opposition the government may expect if it ever really gets down seriously to privatize and to modernize the public sector.

Rural Groups

Political attitudes and activities of India's rural groups are the most difficult to ascertain and document. They are important, nevertheless, because it is in the countryside that India's elections are won or lost. What sways the rural voters thus remains both something of a mystery and a subject of considerable importance.

What is known for sure is that, since the new economic policies were initiated, Rajiv Gandhi and his Congress party have lost eight successive state elections. Nearly half of India's states are now ruled by non-Congress parties. All of the South and most of the East are under the control of opposition parties. It would be, of course, stretching the evidence beyond recognition to claim that these electoral losses can be attributed to the government's economic approach. Losses in Punjab and Assam clearly had much more to do with regional than national issues. Losses elsewhere, such as in West Bengal, Kerala and now Haryana, have been products of complex regional and national concerns, including the multi-causal variable of Rajiv's generally declining popularity.

In spite of this crucial caveat, there is reason to believe that the new economic policies have hurt Congress politically among two numerically

---

[81]For example, see 'Public Sector', *EPW*, 24 January 1987.

significant rural groups, namely, the middle peasants and the rural poor of the Scheduled Castes. When trying to understand the political consequences of national economic policies on these rural groups, it is important to bear in mind that political preferences of such largely illiterate citizens are moulded by and expressed in diffuse and general terms; the generality, however, does not necessarily reduce the rationality of these preferences. Nehru, for example, was never preferred by the middle peasants of backward castes because he was seen as a Brahmin who lived among and cared primarily for the city folk. By contrast, Indira Gandhi was much loved by Scheduled Castes because she supposedly stood for the poor, certainly more than the other prominent national politicians. As far as Rajiv Gandhi is concerned, in the words of India's leading news magazine, *India Today*, the 'pro-rich image has stuck'.[82]

The extent to which this image has been created by bad political management, as distinct from the policies pursued, will never be known for sure. The fact is that the image probably was created with Rajiv's first major economic decision, namely, the 1985–6 budget. This budget, one may recall, offered tax concessions to corporations and middle-income groups, as well as other policy concessions that appeared to benefit primarily the urban well-off. The liberalization agenda thus got identified as a pro-rich agenda. In spite of policy changes on the margin since then, Rajiv Gandhi has not been able to shed the pro-city, pro-rich image.

The political reaction of the middle peasants to these images has been quite negative. This is clearest, for example, in a state that is generally dominated by the Congress, namely, Gujarat. Here the backward castes—the Kshatriyas—are also often the middle peasants and are actually aligned with the Congress. In spite of this, over the last two or three years, peasant agitation against the Congress state government has become a regular feature in Gujarat. During March 1987, for example, nearly a million peasants—generally owner-farmers—threatened to *gherao* (coercive encirclement) the state assembly to press for demands for higher output and lower input prices. When government sought to block the action, massive violence resulted: seventy-three government vehicles were set on fire; traffic was blocked; railway lines were damaged; 2000 people were arrested; ten people died; and the former chief minister of the state was beaten up.[83]

Another important example that supports the thesis that middle peasants are feeling more and more alienated from the Congress-dominated centre is, of course, the Haryana elections. Congress has never enjoyed much support with the main peasant caste of this state, the Jats. The popular feeling

[82]See *India Today*, 15 July 1987, p. 22
[83]Reported in *India Today*, 15 April 1987, pp. 22–3.

that Haryana was losing out to Punjab over various regional issues had also raised the odds against a Congress victory. Yet, the massive electoral loss— in a state that Congress formerly controlled, the Congress won only five of eighty-six announced results—points to a further erosion of the peasant base in this largely agrarian state.

The opposition in Haryana apparently emphasized themes that highlighted the vast distance that existed between the needs of humble peasants and the rulers in New Delhi. It is reported that Devi Lal, the new state leader, went from village-to-village in his down-to-earth style, arguing that Delhi rulers were busy with their 'foreign wives, foreign banks and foreign money.'[84] As a newsweekly editorialized:

...in Devi Lal's campaigning there came to be increasing emphasis on the Rajiv Gandhi government's modernization policies. The attacks on these policies were rough and ready, couched sometimes in urban-versus-rural terms of the familiar Sharad Joshi variety and at other times in terms of a western-oriented upper class minority versus the mass of people. Clearly, the raising of these issues and their undoubted impact on the electorate gives the outcome of Haryana election a greater significance than if the election had been more or less exclusively focused on the Haryana-versus-Punjab issue.[85]

The message that the opposition thus attempted to spread and that was apparently accepted was simple but powerful: Delhi rulers do not have peasant interests at heart.

Another related political development that is likely to be of far-reaching consequence is the Congress's loss of rural support. Under Indira Gandhi the Congress had enjoyed the support of the rural poor in general, and specifically of the Scheduled Castes. This was the major political gain that Indira had secured with her emphasis on garibi hatao. If the image of a pro-rich leader is not shed by Rajiv, this support base is bound to erode over time. While hard evidence on this point is not available, there are indications that this trend has already begun. As discussed elsewhere, local-level interviews in India reveal widespread concern among Congress members at the district level and below as to how they are going to maintain the support of the Scheduled Castes, now that Congress talk is all about computers and the twenty-first century.[86] The communist parties, moreover, that now rule West Bengal and Kerala, and other regional populist parties would be difficult to beat without cutting into some of their support base among the landless of the lowest castes.

[84]See India Today, 15 July 1987, pp. 8–10.
[85]See EPW, 20 June 1987, editorial on 'Haryana Elections'.
[86]Many of these interviews have been cited in Atul Kohli, 'India's Crisis of Governability: A Study of Political Change', Mimeo, 1988, chapters 6–8.

None of the above should be read as if there is a groundswell of opposition to Rajiv's Congress in the countryside or that the main cause of this is government's economic policies. Both factually and analytically, such claims would be incorrect. Public opinion polls continue to reflect that Rajiv still remains a competitive leader, though this lead is rapidly declining.[87] Attempts to restore popularity have already pushed Rajiv back in a populist direction. This will probably help Rajiv rebuild his political support among numerically significant groups, but by the same token, the agenda of economic change is for now on the back burner.

CONCLUSION

This paper has sought to present an analysis of the politics of economic liberalization in India. The forces that have pushed and/or opposed governmental initiatives, as well as how this political tug-of-war has influenced the policy process, have been discussed. It is now time to briefly summarize the argument and to draw out some of its implications.

Over the last decade, leaders of India have sought to liberalize that country's relatively controlled and closed economy. There has been no attempt made in this paper to discuss the economic merits of such actions. Whereas such actions are probably necessary for boosting India's relatively slow economic growth, the focus of analysis above has been on the political roots and consequences of economic policy change.

In her last four years, Indira Gandhi quietly initiated some important liberalizing economic initiatives. The interesting issue these developments raise concerns the minimal political opposition that such actions of a socialist leader evoked. There was minimal political opposition because the changes were on the margin and because they were undertaken piecemeal and without political fanfare. Moreover, Indira Gandhi was perceived as a well-established socialist leader. Her attempts to initiate liberalization, unlike her son's, did not evoke a sense that cherished nationalist values of national sovereignty and a concern for the poor were about to be thrown out, only to be replaced by an open embrace of the rich—both Indian and foreign.

Rajiv Gandhi has attempted to push liberalization further and in a shorter time. Major policy initiatives were taken in this direction. The pace of change, however, has now slowed. After some initial successes, there have been important setbacks and the reforms have generated considerable political opposition.

The reforms have been pushed by a technocratic leadership that appears to firmly believe in the economic merits of liberalization. Major support, at least for domestic, as distinct from international liberalization has come from industrial and commercial groups. The motley urban middle classes have

[87]See *India Today*, 31 August 1988.

also appreciated the tax reforms and the availability of consumer goods in the market.

The extent to which the reforms have succeeded is thus best explained with reference to the ideology of the new rulers. These rulers emerged as rulers for reasons that had little to do with their positions on economic policy. Over the short run, these new leaders utilized their considerable autonomous power to push through a few reforms. It is also important to recognize that these reforms were not opposed, but rather were supported, by powerful and vocal urban groups. Those specific reforms—like the attempts to liberalize the automobile manufacturing policy—that met resistance from powerful business groups were postponed. Additionally, the reforms that were successfully implemented tended to exhibit two characteristics: their negative impact was limited to a small and specific group (as, for example, the reforms in the textile industry); and/or they were pushed through as technical changes without political fanfare. A temporary condition of state autonomy, the ideology of the rulers, support of powerful socio-economic groups, and the capacity to de-politicize some of the economic issues thus appear to be the main factors that help explain a partial success in liberalizing India's economy.

Conversely, what looms larger than these partial successes is the rapidity with which the constraints on governmental initiatives came into play. Many political and social groups have come to react negatively to the government's attempts at economic reforms. Their opposition is not based on economic issues alone, nor is it always expressed in a coherent and direct fashion. For some, like the Congress rank and file, the opposition is probably mainly opportunistic but is also in part based on ideology and in part due to the fear of electoral implications of the new policies. The left intelligentsia seems to genuinely believe that the new policies will have disastrous consequences; not only, according to them, is higher growth not assured by the new economic policies, but national sovereignty and a redistributive orientation may also be sacrificed. Labour groups in the public sector fear corrosion of employment security. The political reaction of rural groups is less direct. Even they, however rightly or wrongly, in their own diffuse and haphazard way, seem to be communicating to the government that its pro-rich and pro-urban image is suspect.

Rajiv's declining popularity has clearly not entirely been a product of his economic approach. But just as clearly, it would be foolish to assume that his attempts to liberalize the economy have been politically neutral. Some groups, generally the better-off urban groups, have supported the initiatives. The opposition has come mainly from the groups in the popular sector—peasants, workers, rural poor, left intelligentsia and even the rank and file of the ruling party that has daily contacts with some of these groups. As these groups have reacted negatively, the fear of losing electoral support has forced the Rajiv government to slow the pace of economic change. The society has struck back; the state has lost its temporary autonomy.

It is only with some exaggeration, therefore, that one is led to conclude that attempts within India to implement what leaders consider to be economically rational have come into conflict with the rationality of democracy. All other things remaining equal, either Rajiv Gandhi and his government will not push the liberalization agenda too far, or the pursuit of these policies will continue to cost the ruling groups popular support. Since an internal demand-led, redistributive growth model is even less politically feasible in contemporary India, chances are that the government has few options for stimulating growth but to liberalize the economy. The analysis here suggests that such a policy trajectory will continue to cost the Indian government popular political support.

Finally, these empirical materials from India have a bearing on an enduring debate within comparative development studies with which we began this essay. This debate posits links between specific regime types and development strategies. As mentioned above, some arguments in Latin American studies have suggested that the numerous bureaucratic-authoritarian regimes during the 1960s had their origins in the exhaustion of import-substitution model of development. The implication was clear: moderate regimes may find it difficult to implement policies that, by prevailing economic logic, are deemed to be rational and necessary. This argument has come in for considerable criticism. The issue, however, is too important to vanish. It continues to appear and reappear in different contexts. The success of Southeast Asian NICs has often been attributed to the role of certain type of market policies pursued by authoritarian states. As Latin American countries re-democratize, the issue of their capacities to impose economic rationality has also once again become an open question. The issue of the fit between regime types and development strategies is thus likely to continue to be debated.

Indian materials suggest that it is indeed difficult for a democratic regime to undertake a major shift in development strategy. It has been evident throughout the discussion above that some economic reforms were possible all along. It would thus be absurd to deny that powerful leaders like Indira Gandhi or Rajiv Gandhi can initiate and implement some policy changes that they and their advisors deem necessary. There are, however, fairly sharp limits on how far and how fast a liberalization programme can be implemented in a democracy.

The counter-argument that non-democratic countries have also faced obstacles in liberalizing their economies is simply no argument. All that tells us is that liberalization measures can evoke opposition in numerous settings, and that many non-democratic regimes are also not capable or willing to run roughshod over such opposition. An analysis of a democratic case at least enables one to specify the nature and the mechanics of political opposition. The conclusions are disturbing. In social settings where cultures of efficiency are not well established, calls for efficiency and competitiveness do not buy broad political support. This creates real problems for Third World democratic states that are not products of capitalism, but instead seek to promote efficient capitalist development. The need to build broad coalitions pulls these fragile democratic governments in policy directions other than those that may best promote an efficient and competitive economy. These issues of political rationality ought to complement those of economic rationality when analysing, judging or advising what developing country governments should or should not do.

9

Regime Types and Poverty Reform in India*

Three decades of politically guided economic development have failed to alleviate rural poverty in India. This stark fact raises issues which go beyond the often discussed one of suitable development policies. The more fundamental question concerns the political conditions under which appropriate strategies, aimed at reconciling 'growth with distribution', are likely to be pursued effectively. Given the basic constraints of a democratic polity and a largely capitalist economy in India, what type of regimes can facilitate economic gains by the lower classes? This article suggests an answer to this question by comparatively analysing some recent and varying reform experiences in India.

As a large federal polity, where states are often ruled by political parties other than that controlling the centre, India provides a considerable variety of developmental 'models' within one country. Especially between 1977 and 1980, when India was governed by a highly fragmented Janata Party, the state governments exercised considerable autonomy. Since, by the Indian constitution, the agrarian sector is under the jurisdiction of the states, this autonomy was especially significant in rural policies. Communist-ruled West Bengal, Congress-ruled Karnataka, and Janata-ruled Uttar Pradesh, as three

*Originally published as 'Regime Types and Poverty Reform in India', *Pacific Affairs*, 56(4), Winter, 1983–4, pp. 649–72.

The research reported here is based on two field trips (1978–9 and 1981) to India. While in India, I was affiliated with the Centre for the Study of Developing Societies, Delhi. The funding for the larger research project, of which this article is a part, has been provided by the Social Sciences and Humanities Research Council of Canada; the Institute for the Study of World Politics, New York; the University of California, Berkeley; and Michigan State University. An earlier version of this paper was presented at the 1981 meetings of the American Political Science Association, New York, 3–6 September, 1981. I would like to thank the following for their comments on the earlier draft: Pranab Bardhan, Jyoti Dasgupta, Marc Franda, W.H. Morris-Jones, and an anonymous *Pacific Affairs* reviewer.

of India's more important states, thus provide interesting comparisons of the significance of regime variations for rural reform, allowing us to examine how different patterns of political rule, in similar social structural conditions, affect redistribution policies.

I argue here that, within the general constraints of the democratic-capitalist model of India's development, certain patterns of leadership, ideology, and organization tend to facilitate distribution, while others do not. A well-organized, left-of-centre regime, such as that of the communists in West Bengal, could politically penetrate the rural society without being co-opted by the propertied groups, enabling the leadership to implement a number of redistributive programmes. By contrast, a factionalized government dominated by commercial peasant interests in Uttar Pradesh had little success in its efforts to alleviate rural poverty. The case of Karnataka lies in between: here, a government dominated by a populist leader was able to push through limited reforms. These three cases, then, not only highlight the significance of regime-type in alleviating rural poverty, but also allow the delineation of the specific regime features underlying success or failure in redistributive programmes.

This article summarizes the empirical findings of a larger project;[1] because of limited space, several important issues cannot be considered here. The 'state–society' theoretical framework within which the materials are analysed, and the issue of 'state autonomy' that the empirical materials highlight, have been discussed elsewhere.[2] The central point to note in this regard is that, following the lead set by others, I have avoided approaching empirical materials from those reductionist theoretical perspectives—liberal or Marxist— that treat political structures and processes as derivatives of socio-cultural or economic forces.[3] The empirical materials are instead organized to highlight the 'autonomy of the political'.

Second, I have not provided an overview of India's national developmental framework.[4] Two features of the period of Janata rule, however, ought to

---

[1]See Atul Kohli, *The State and Poverty: Political Economy of Reform in Rural India*, forthcoming.

[2]Ibid., chapters 1 and 6. Also, see Atul Kohli, 'The State and Class in Capitalist Development: Concepts for Comparative Analysis', unpublished paper presented to the 1982 meetings of the Western Political Science Association, San Diego, California, 26–29 March 1982.

[3]This perspective is gaining currency among development theorists. For example, see Alfred Stepan, *The State and Society: Peru in Comparative Perspective*, Princeton, New Jersey: Princeton University Press, 1978, pp. 3–45; Theda Skocpol, *States and Social Revolutions*, Cambridge, Massachusetts: Cambridge University Press, 1979, pp. 3–46, 284–93; Tony Smith, 'The Underdevelopment of Development Literature', *World Politics*, January 1979, pp. 247–88; and Jyoti Dasgupta, *Authority, Priority and Human Development*, New Delhi: Oxford University Press, 1981.

[4]For an overview of the Indian 'political-economy', see Francine Frankel, *India's Political Economy, 1947–77*, Princeton, New Jersey: Princeton University Press, 1979. For a review of

be borne in mind: the Janata leadership did not initiate any major new redistributive programmes; and the weakness of the Janata central government precluded too strict a control over the states. Thus, any turn away from past patterns and towards more or less rural reform was primarily at the behest of the state governments.

Another important caveat concerns the distinction between policy 'outputs' and 'outcomes'.[5] What is analysed here is the impact of regime variation, not directly on such outcomes of redistributive policies as the alleviation of poverty, but on policy outputs, that is, redistributive policies pursued and implemented. Public policies undoubtedly affect living conditions; nevertheless, changes in living conditions result not only from policy shifts, but may also reflect market conditions. Even if it were possible to isolate the consequences of public policies, there would remain the additional problem of time-lag. The consequences of reform policies for standards of living—for example, for income, security, mortality, life expectancy, and literacy—are unlikely to become manifest for some while. Documentation of these changes, based presumably on surveys, usually involves an even longer time-gap.

With these qualifications, the following sections analyse and compare the rural reform experiences of the communists in West Bengal (1977 to the present [1982]), the Congress regime in Karnataka (1974–80), and the Janata rule in Uttar Pradesh (1977–80). The concluding section will summarize the argument, specifying the regime features underlying redistributive success and pointing out some of the broader implications of this study.

THE CPI(M) REGIME IN WEST BENGAL

The Communist Party of India (Marxist) or CPI(M), returned to power in West Bengal in 1977. Unlike the previous United Front ministries, the CPI(M) this time had a clear majority,[6] having won 177 of the 293 assembly seats. With its other partners in the Left Front, the CPI(M) now controlled a solid majority of 230 seats. (The 1982 state elections further confirmed the CPI(M)'s power base in West Bengal.) Since 1977, these 'parliamentary communists' have sought to use their power to introduce elements of redistribution into the process of development. Central to their political-

---

the Janata period, see Jyotindra Dasgupta, 'The Janata Phase in Indian Politics', *Asian Survey*, XIX(4), April 1979, pp. 390–403.

[5]For one use of this distinction, see J. Ronald Pennock, 'Political Development, Political Systems, and Political Goods', *World Politics*, April 1966, pp. 415–34.

[6]For an analysis of the earlier experiences of the CPI(M) and the United Front ministries, see Marcus Franda, *Radical Politics in West Bengal*, Cambridge, Massachusetts: MIT Press, 1971; and Bhabani Sen Gupta, *Communism in Indian Politics*, New York: Columbia University Press, 1972.

economic strategy has been a concerted attack on the rural poverty of West Bengal. Restructuring local government, establishing programmes for the sharecroppers, facilitating credit for smallholders, and mobilizing the landless for higher wages, are all part of the strategy to secure political position by transferring some of the fruits of development to the lower classes. While many other leaders in India have discussed these redistributive goals, only the CPI(M) has made a systematic and impressive effort to implement them. This reformist thrust reflects the pattern of leadership, ideology, and organization of the CPI(M) regime.

The leadership is neither concentrated in the hands of an individual nor, as might be expected in a communist regime, in the party alone. While the party wields great influence, leadership is shared by the three 'wings' of the CPI(M)—the party organization proper, the Kisan Sabha (the peasant wing), and the parliamentary wing. Since the CPI(M) has to compete for votes in an electoral system, the organizational wing of the party cannot simply dictate party policies. The party line has had to take account of both the Kisan Sabha, which provides the crucial link to rural voters, and the parliamentary leaders, who run the government.[7] This sharing of power has not led to the intense conflicts so characteristic of other Indian states. Two important factors have kept such conflict under control. First and foremost has been party discipline. The party is organized along democratic centralist lines: once a party position is adopted, it is binding on all party members. Since members of the government generally belong to the party, party discipline imposes consensus within the government. In other words, while factionalism exists—and at times threatens the process of government—it has not precluded the pursuit of coherent policy. Second, there is a shared perception of the common enemy—namely, the central government of India in alliance with business interests and the landlords. The process of securing and maintaining power is thus seen as an ongoing struggle requiring political unity.[8]

The CPI(M)'s ideology over the years has shifted from a revolutionary to a reformist orientation. Instead of emphasizing 'class confrontation' as a means of establishing the 'dictatorship of the proletariat', the CPI(M) now seeks to preserve democratic institutions, while using state power to facilitate 'development with redistribution'. This 'democratic-socialist' tilt is spelled out in the party programme, which recommends mobilization of 'the broadest possible support' against 'authoritarianism', including 'elements

[7]Interview with Abdullah Rasool, Member of Central Committee, Bengal and All-India Kisan Sabha, Calcutta, 14 March 1979.

[8]Ashok Mitra, Minister of Finance, Government of West Bengal, thus argued: 'What we have to constantly experiment about is how far we can push without invoking central intervention—or what is the feasibility frontier—we have the experience of Kerala in 1959 very much in our mind'. Interview with Ashok Mitra, Calcutta, 16 March 1979.

who do not support the economic programme of the party'.[9] Moreover, the party's 'agrarian program' now seeks the support of 'the rich and the poor' peasants: besides the 'land question', it addresses the problems of 'irrigation, seeds, and fair prices for produce'.[10] No longer does the CPI(M) define its friends and enemies strictly in terms of class: even 'exploiting' classes are not the 'enemy' as long as they are productive and willing to extend political support.[11] This adjustment is quite like that undertaken by the Italian communists.[12] Indeed, a communist party can only justify its ruling position in a capitalist economy by asserting that there are not many enemies—even under capitalism.

Underlying this ideological shift are several factors. First, as the CPI(M) has sought electoral success, there has been greater need for broad-based political support. Recognizing that the rich and the middle peasants are not only numerically significant but, if alienated, can mobilize considerable opposition, the CPI(M) has sought to soften its ideological stance. Second, the CPI(M) has learned from experience: having seen earlier United Front ministries in West Bengal and Kerala collapse because they have not been able to control the class hostilities they unleashed—and also because of pressure by the central government—the CPI(M) has now decided to 'go slow', while assuring the propertied by specifying the limits of the party's 'socialist intent'. And lastly, there is the problem of economic growth. Regime positions perceived as radical will discourage privately controlled economic activity. Regime legitimacy depends on the demonstrated ability of the leadership to manage the economy. The CPI(M) has therefore tried to accommodate those in a position to influence economic performance— landowners and urban capitalists. To gain power and to survive within the framework of democratic-capitalism, the CPI(M) has learned that it cannot be a revolutionary party.

At the core of the CPI(M) as an organizational force is a tightly knit and relatively small party. Party membership is now about one million in a state with a population of 45 million. In the recent past, the membership was considerably smaller, with the bulk coming from urban professional groups. The peasantry was only 'discovered' in the late 1960s. With the spread of

[9]See Communist Party of India (Marxist), *Political Resolution*, Xth Congress, 2–8 April 1978, Jullundur, p. 18.

[10]From a speech by Pramode Dasgupta, Secretary, CPI(M), West Bengal, reported in *Ganashakti*, 10 February 1979.

[11]CPI(M)'s 'class analysis' was explained to the author in an interview with Maujam Hussain, member of Legislative Assembly, West Bengal, and Secretary, Local Committee, Debra Block, Midnapore, West Bengal.

[12]See Sidney Tarrow, 'Communism in Italy and France: Adaptation and Change', in Donald Blackmer and Sidney Tarrow (eds), *Communism in Italy and France*, Princeton, New Jersey: Princeton University Press, 1975.

commerce in the countryside, landlords have lost some of their control over the dependent peasantry. In seeking the support of this newly released political resource, the CPI(M) found itself competing with such 'Maoist' groups as the Naxalites. As the CPI(M) has made inroads into the villages, however, its rural base has continued to develop with the help of groups other than the poorest of the poor. The key linkage groups have been students with rural roots, who come to the cities for education, get politicized, and go back to rural areas to teach and to serve as party organizers and propagandists. As these students often come from at least middle-income families, the social base of the CPI(M) in both the city and the countryside rests on the middle strata.

While the core membership may come from the middle strata, party support is nevertheless widespread among lower-income groups. A series of 'interest group' organizations are affiliated with, support, and are supported by the party. These include the student movement in universities, the teachers' movement in secondary and primary schools, the women's movement, the trade union movement, and the peasant and the landless labourers' movements organized under the Kisan Sabha. These groups provide important links between the party and the society at large. Electoral and other types of political support are mobilized through the various movements; those representing the movements expect rewards from the party, once it comes to power.

The CPI(M) was swept into power in 1977. Underlying its success was not only its own deepening political base but the failure of other parties. Once in power, however, the CPI(M) sought to extend and consolidate its base further, especially in the rural areas. To incorporate the lower rural classes more effectively, the CPI(M) restructured local governments. It was the first time in India that political parties were allowed to compete for local government positions. Well aware of its new popularity, the CPI(M) hoped that its own candidates would be successful. The strategy paid off— 87 per cent of the seats at the district level, 74 per cent at the block level (the block is an administrative unit between the district and the village), and 67 per cent at the village level were captured by those running on the CPI(M) ticket. These 'red panchayats' (panchayat being the Indian term for local government) are now important in the CPI(M)'s overall political and development strategy.

The majority of new office-holders are party sympathizers rather than party members; a large majority are teachers and small landholders, and are therefore from rural lower-middle income groups.[13] This is an extremely significant shift from past patterns. Never have local governments

[13]This is derived from a survey of panchayat members, the results of which have been reported elsewhere. See Atul Kohli, 'Parliamentary Communism and Agrarian Reform: The Evidence from India's Bengal', *Asian Survey*, July 1983, pp. 783–809.

in West Bengal—or, for that matter, in much of India—been so free of the domination of landlords and rich peasants. The CPI(M) has done what no other Indian political force has been able to do—thoroughly penetrate the countryside without depending on large landowners. The CPI(M) regime, along with the newly recreated local governments, thus represents two interlinked patterns of political change: an organizational penetration by the 'centre' into the 'periphery', and a simultaneous shift in the class basis of institutional power.

The CPI(M) has utilized its newly consolidated position to initiate rural reforms. The bulk of the rural poor in West Bengal are sharecroppers and landless labourers; and the programmes have been aimed primarily at these groups, especially the sharecroppers *(bargardars,* in Bengali). Tenancy in the past has been based largely on informal arrangements. As a consequence, laws designed to cut back the amount of the crop that the sharecropper must hand over to the landowner, and laws to increase the security of tenure, have been ineffective. To correct this situation, the CPI(M) regime has undertaken a concerted effort legally to register the sharecroppers,[14] in the hope that this will improve their incomes and provide them greater security.

One of the early acts of the CPI(M) government was to amend the land-reform laws so as to transfer the burden of proof of land-sharing arrangements from the sharecropper to the landowner. With this law on the books, the government undertook a special drive called 'Operation Barga' to facilitate rapid registration of the sharecroppers. Teams of bureaucrats and/or party members, activists, and Kisan Sabha members were sent out to the countryside to announce the laws and to register the sharecroppers on the spot. The operation has had considerable success. While over the previous three decades fewer than 60,000 sharecroppers were registered in the areas where the CPI(M) is now operating, in its first three years the CPI(M) succeeded in registering over one million.[15] Compared to the past performances of Congress and other regimes in the area, therefore, the CPI(M)'s current success is spectacular. Given the size of the problem—there may be nearly 2 million families of sharecroppers in West Bengal[16]—much, of course, remains to be done. Nevertheless, the CPI(M) has taken an impressive first step towards improving the living conditions of the sharecroppers.

---

[14]The 'registration' list is a legal record kept by the local bureaucracy of all bona fide sharecroppers in the area. Once registered, sharecroppers can claim the protection of laws designed to prevent their eviction and reduce the crop share owed to the landlords.

[15]See Government of West Bengal, *Land Reforms in West Bengal: A Statistical Report,* V, Land and Land Revenue Department, 1981. For further detailed analysis of 'Operation Barga' and its results, see Kohli, 'Parliamentary Communism'.

[16]From an interview with Binoy Chowdhry, Minister of Land and Land Revenue, West Bengal, Calcutta, 2 November 1981.

What explains the CPI(M)'s success in registering so large a number of sharecroppers? The very legal act of registration challenges class relations in the countryside, for it is aimed at reducing the landowner's control of his property and the income from it. The act, therefore, is bound to provoke considerable opposition. The sharecroppers are generally afraid to participate in the process without the support of forces outside of the village community. And it is this crucial role of 'outside support' that the CPI(M) regime has played. The power of both the party and the government is being utilized to improve the condition of the sharecroppers. The role of the party has been especially significant. 'Operation Barga' has thus had the greatest success in those parts of Bengal where the party is the strongest. The crucial variable, very likely, has been party-initiated politicization. As a consequence of sustained party activity, the sharecroppers have come to understand the laws, trust the party, and take the final and important step of registration. This act of defiance against the traditional patron perhaps does more to help implement the sharecropping laws than the refinement of the laws themselves.

Modest increases in income and greater security for the sharecroppers have been the short-run consequences of registration.[17] New problems have emerged, however. As the relationship between landowners and sharecroppers has altered, the landowners have grown reluctant to supply the sharecroppers with credit and seed. The CPI(M) regime has thus strived to make it easier for registered sharecroppers to get credit elsewhere. The government has negotiated with the commercial banks and secured an agreement, 'in principle', that banks will lend money not only against land but also against the share of the crop. Furthermore, the government has promised to 'subsidize' the labour-intensive aspects of the banking costs. The party-controlled local governments will prepare the lists of registered sharecroppers and identify their legal share of the crop. This information will be provided to the banks and will save them considerable labour costs. The banks will then offer loans—part in cash and part in vouchers—for agricultural inputs. The government will also subsidize the interest the sharecroppers must pay. The programme is a novel one, and it is too early to judge whether it will succeed or fail. In 1979 and 1980, about 60,000 and 70,000, respectively, registered sharecroppers received institutional credit.[18] If the offering of credit can be sustained and expanded, it will demonstrate how a well-organized, left-of-centre government can imaginatively and

---

[17]The 'land reform' literature is full of arguments and evidence suggesting that secure tenures lead to improved productivity and incomes. For example, see Peter Dorner, *Land Reform and Economic Development*, Baltimore, Maryland: Penguin Books, 1972.

[18]Government of West Bengal, *Land Reforms in West Bengal*.

systematically intervene in a private-enterprise economy so as to strengthen the position of the lower classes.

In addition to programmes for the sharecroppers, the CPI(M)'s efforts have been aimed at providing extra employment and better wages for the landless agricultural labourers. The Food for Work Programme (FWP)—a public-works oriented, employment-generating scheme, in part supported by the wheat/rice grants from the centrally controlled surplus—has been implemented with considerable effectiveness in West Bengal. In 1979–80, the programme generated about one month of extra employment for one-third of all the landless households.[19] Considering that most of the landless usually get no more than four months of employment per year, this increment is by no means insignificant. The implementation of the programme has been facilitated by the party-controlled local governments. Much of the money is channelled through these 'red panchayats'. In consultation with the local party cadres, the panchayats decide which projects will be undertaken, choose who will be employed, and administer the funds. As the political fortunes of the CPI(M) are closely tied to the success of such distributive schemes, sustained pressure through the party has minimized the typical problems of corruption and maladministration of funds.

Party-initiated wage struggles have been the other 'non-governmental' mode of increasing the incomes of landless labourers. As a party in power, seeking to maintain broad-based political support, however, the CPI(M) has not devoted a great deal of effort to organized, union-supported agitation in the countryside. Moreover, socio-economic conditions are harsh. With a massive labour supply, only during the peak employment season do labourers enjoy a favourable bargaining position. Nevertheless, in some parts of West Bengal, where the party organization is strong, unionization has led to a modest increase in wages. My own interviews revealed that wage levels in the unionized blocs tended to be somewhat higher than in the non-unionized ones.[20]

None of the above is meant to imply that rural poverty in West Bengal is on the verge of being eradicated. The problem is massive. The CPI(M) has made a small but impressive beginning towards a solution. They have clearly demonstrated a capacity to implement incremental reform policies. The ultimate effects of these policies will take some time to be felt. Within the Indian situation, however, where poverty stubbornly persists, any small success at redistribution deserves attention.

---

[19]For details, see Kohli, 'Parliamentary Communism'.

[20]For those interested in details, see ibid. Also, 'hard' data supporting this general conclusion have been presented in Pranab Bardhan and Ashok Rudra, 'Labour, Employment and Wages in Agriculture', *Economic and Political Weekly*, 8–15 November, 1980, especially p. 1948.

The CPI(M)'s reform approach has four major characteristics. First, the rule is coherent. The relatively unified leadership has made for clear policy thinking, and for sustained political attention to issues of poverty and development. Second, the ideological goals and the organizational arrangements of the CPI(M) deny the upper classes direct access to the political arena. While the upper classes remain powerful, and significant concessions are made to them, they do not directly control the political process. As a consequence, there is a degree of separation between social and political power. This reduces the possibility that reform programmes will be co-opted by the socially powerful. Third, the CPI(M)'s organization is both centralized and decentralized. While the decision-making power is concentrated, at the same time—through newly structured local government—local initiative and knowledge can be combined within the framework of central directives. Fourth, the CPI(M)'s ideology is flexible enough to accommodate the continued domination of propertied classes in the social and economic sphere. This makes the prospect of reformism tolerable for the upper classes.

Central to understanding the CPI(M)'s reforms and approach are the characteristics of the CPM as a party. A well-organized, left-of-centre party can allow a reformist orientation to be institutionalized within the ruling regime. Political power can thus be used to push through some systematic reforms of the agrarian social order.

THE URS REGIME IN KARNATAKA

Devraj Urs ruled Karnataka for most of the 1970s. His rise to power, while a complex process, was a by-product of the earlier Congress split and the later rout of the old Congress by the Indira-dominated Congress.[21] As the 'Indra man' in Karnataka, Urs sought to create a new power base. Aiming to displace the old ruling alliance of an earlier generation of Congress elites with the propertied members of the 'dominant castes',[22] Urs pursued a two-fold strategy: he brought the hitherto excluded elites into an enlarged

[21]For an analysis of the earlier periods of politics in Karnataka (or Mysore), see James Manor, *Political Change in an Indian State, Mysore 1915–55*, Australian National University Monographs on South Asia, No. 2, Columbia, Missouri: South Asia Books, 1978; James Manor, 'Structural Changes in Karnataka Politics', *Economics and Political Weekly*, 29 October 1977, pp. 1866–9; and B.B. Patil-Okaly, 'Karnataka: Politics of One Party Dominance', in Iqbal Narain (ed.), *State Politics in India*, Meerut, India: Meenakshi Prakashan, 1976, pp. 129–45.

[22]For an elaboration of the concept of 'dominant caste', see M.N. Srinivas, 'The Social System of a Mysore Village', in McKim Marriott (ed.), *Village India, Studies in the Little Community*, Chicago, Illinois: University of Chicago Press, 1955, p. 18. While caste loyalties have in the past provided a basis for mobilizing electoral support, of late the class elements have become more pronounced. For the latter argument, see R.K. Hebsur, 'Karnataka', *Seminar*, No. 278, August 1978, pp. 21–6; also see James Manor, 'Structural Changes', p. 1868.

patronage network; and he sought to implement some highly visible redistributive programmes. Reforms in Karnataka were, however, less successful than in West Bengal: only tenancy reforms were pursued; other programmes were promised but not delivered. Urs' power was not based on a well-organized party, nor was he in any position to prevent the landed elites from penetrating many of the governing organizations. There were no attempts to institutionalize lower-class power within the regime. The resulting reforms, therefore, tended to be piece-meal and unsystematic.

Devraj Urs was a heavy-handed ruler. His leadership style was that of a power manipulator and a 'machine operator'. Party nominations for the legislative assembly, seats on various local governmental boards and cooperative societies, and party funds doled out to loyal supporters, all were part of the patronage network through which Urs built and diversified his power base. Proclaiming himself a 'man of the poor', Urs clothed his regime in a populist ideology. These new patterns of patronage and ideology reflected Urs' political need for a diversified base as a protection against the old guard and the dominant castes. Where political debates of the past had revolved around which caste groupings would obtain the spoils of power, a new element was now added to the rhetoric: the rights of the lower classes.[23] Arguing that planning and development in the past had not served the 'weaker sections', that so far the rewards had been monopolized by the privileged, and that there was a need to 'break the rural power-structure', Urs promised 'social justice'.[24]

The organizational base of Urs' power was minimal. A 'machine' politician, Urs put little or no effort into strengthening the Congress(I) within Karnataka. The party's rudimentary structure was activated primarily for electoral purposes and, occasionally, to influence intra-party factional disputes. The major functions of the party were to collect funds and to nominate candidates for elections. Those who controlled party funds and/or the right of others to run on a Congress ticket were powerful individuals. The party tended to attract opportunists—those seeking electoral office, a job, a permit, or the favourable settlement of a dispute. Leaders and followers alike hailed from varying social backgrounds. Members of an ideologically amorphous, structurally loose organization, they were often bound together by no more than a sense of mutual self-interest.

The presence of a strong leader gave Urs' regime a semblance of coherence. In ideology and organization, however, the contrasts with the CPI(M) are instructive. The ideological positions of the two regimes are alike in having a commitment to the lower classes—but there the likeness

---

[23]Interviews with Devraj Urs, Bangalore, 25 April 1979 and 8 November 1981.

[24]Devraj Urs, *Socio-economic Programme for the Poor: Some Policy Imperatives*, Office of the Chief Minister, Government of Karnataka, April 1978.

stops. The key difference is that the Urs-regime's committment to the poor was not paralleled by a move against the propertied classes. There was little effort made in Karnataka to isolate the propertied from the political sphere. The institutions charged with implementing reforms were not designed to favour the poor. As a consequence, the government had a rather narrow range of reformist options.

The organizational patterns of the Urs regime also contrast sharply with those of the CPI(M) in West Bengal. The CPI(M), ideologically 'tilted' towards the lower classes, largely excludes the propertied classes from its membership, and retains a relatively tight internal control structure. This organizational pattern allows the CPI(M) to act as a cohesive nucleus, both part of and yet distinct from the society around it, capable of generating politically directed social reform. In the case of the Congress in Karnataka, however, social forces penetrated the dominant political organization, reproducing societal hierarchies within it. The Congress's ideological commitments were diffuse, its membership open, and its internal control structure weak. In such a loose and amorphous organization, political behaviour was influenced more by social roles and interests than by organizational imperatives. As class and caste structures were mirrored within the Congress party, the latter tended to become primarily a vehicle for the pursuit of individual or sectional social interests. This relative lack of political autonomy from the social structure generally, and from the dominant social classes in particular, further limited the Congress's prospects of pursuing politically directed social reform.

Between 1975 and 1980, the Urs regime implemented a widely publicized tenancy-reform programme. In early 1975, new amendments, closing old loopholes in the land-reform laws, were passed. And to facilitate implementation, special land-tribunals were created. Each comprising a senior civil servant as the chairperson and four political appointees, 175 tribunals were established throughout the state. Tribunals were to receive applications from tenants, investigate claims and counter-claims, and make final decisions about the tenant's occupancy rights. The land tribunals were thus powerful political bodies with few responsibilities other than tenancy reform, and with authority over decisions affecting the legal status of tenanted land.

How successful were Karnataka's tenancy reforms? Between 1975 and 1980 (the year that Urs lost power), about a third of the tenanted land or about 5 per cent of the total cultivated land in Karnataka was legally transferred from the landowners to the tenants.[25] Did this represent a significant achievement? The answer depends on one's frame of reference. The reform was more successful than those undertaken by other Congress(I)

[25]Figures from 'Land Reform Progress in the State up to the End of November 1980', memorandum from Revenue Department, Government of Karnataka.

governments of the past, but it fell short of both the CPI(M)'s accomplishment in West Bengal, and Urs' rhetorical claims that 'social justice has been achieved'.[26] These limitations become even clearer when two important qualifications are noted: (1) those losing land were not always the rich farmers, and those gaining were not always the poor; and (2) tenancy reforms were the only significant rural reform pursued in Karnataka. Both of these points require elaboration.

In the early 1970s, the tenancy situation in Karnataka did not fit the common pattern whereby big landowners leased out land to the landless or smallholders. Over half the leased land was leased not by the landless and smallholders (owners of 1–2.5 acres), but rather by family farmers (owners of 2.5–10 acres) and the richer landowners (owners of more than 10 acres). Similarly, over half the land leased out was leased out by smallholders and family farmers.[27] This suggests that many farmers leasing land were already well off, and many of those leasing out were relatively poor. There is no reason to believe that land affected by reforms necessarily shifted from the larger landowners to the rural poor. Given the power inequities of the rural social structure, in fact, the opposite was just as likely to occur—with a number of smallholders losing out in the process of land reform, and a number of the larger landowners gaining.

Several features of the Urs regime help clarify, firstly, why the reforms were successful at all and, second, why they were only partially successful. The central point here is that the ruling regime itself provided both the push behind the reforms as well as the means by which the opposition could evade those reforms. To give substance to his 'populist' leadership, Urs needed some visible reformist successes. He himself was thus a major force behind the reforms: it was at his behest that the new legislation was passed, the tribunals created, and the pressure from above sustained. By contrast, the reasons why the tenancy reforms were not more successful are best understood by looking at the design of the implementing institutions, especially the composition of the tribunals. On every tribunal sat a prominent Congress representative, whose ideological outlook was most unlikely to be radical. Additionally, of the thirty-two political appointees I interviewed, over 50 per cent were from the landed classes—and some were extremely rich and locally powerful.[28] It is hardly surprising that these people did not mobilize

[26]Devraj Urs, Socio-economic Programme for the Poor, p. 12.

[27]Based on data from Government of India, National Sample Survey, 26th Round, Report No. 215 (Karnataka), V. II, 1971, Tables 3 and 4. For detailed statistics and analysis, see Atul Kohli, 'Karnataka's Land Reforms: A Model for India?', Journal of Commonwealth and Comparative Politics, November 1982, pp. 309–28.

[28]For details, see Kohli, 'Karnataka's Land Reforms'.

the peasantry to implement land reforms. Moreover, their inclusion in the tribunals provided access to the more powerful opponents of reform.

Regime conditions in Karnataka, then, made for a factional pattern of reform implementation. Larger landowners close to Devraj Urs, to the Congress(I) in general, or to the appointed tribunal members, tended not to lose their land. Those who did were generally not in a position politically to protect their interests. Among these, in addition to some of the smaller landholders leasing out land, were people associated with factions other than the ruling one, and absentee landlords not in a strong position to defend themselves. Without doubt, tenancy reforms resulted in some redistribution of land from the more wealthy landowners to the poor. Still, the reforms were much less of an assault on the entrenched class structure than Urs' rhetoric would indicate.

The limitations of reform in Karnataka are clear, too, in the policy areas other than those affecting tenancy. For example, in contrast to West Bengal, there were no attempts in Karnataka to channel credit to the beneficiaries of the tenancy reforms or to the smallholders in general. The Urs regime neither bargained with the commercial banks to establish new patterns of rural credit, nor attempted to restructure the existing patterns of credit flow. As a consequence, former tenants who became provisional owners of their land were often without any assured source of credit. The traditional sources—landowners and money-lenders—tended to dry up, and nothing new replaced them. Such neglect contrasts with the policies of the CPI(M) in West Bengal, who believes its political fortunes are best advanced by a long-term political incorporation of the intended beneficiaries—the rural poor.

Policies which might improve the livelihood of Karnataka's landless labourers have also not been very effective. First, regarding the employment-generating schemes: unlike the situation in Bengal, where restructured local governments and party supervision have facilitated the clean and effective administration of such programmes, in Karnataka local governments remain a vehicle for the distributing of spoils, and remain dominated by the members of landed classes. In the absence of the party, the local bureaucracy, entrenched in the patronage / corruption network, cannot be used to implement reforms either. Moreover, as the local-level Congress(I) remains dominated by privileged elites, it is unlikely that it will ever tolerate the unionization of landless labourers. Deliberate political intervention here has thus failed to affect the employment and wage conditions of the latter.

In summary, poverty reforms in Karnataka, while more successful than in other states dominated by Congress(I), have had limited success at best. There have been notable achievements in the area of tenancy, but little else has been accomplished. If improved living conditions among the rural poor are a function of redistributive policies, the evidence suggests that the impact of deliberate political intervention here will be marginal. While a strong populist leadership was the most important factor in the implementation of several redistributive programmes, the very nature of political organization and the class basis of the Urs regime made it impossible to initiate a more thorough-going reform. The dominant party and the government were little more than a collection of elites from varying backgrounds, bound together in a large patronage network. Party organization was weak; along with such other institutional arrangements as the land tribunals, it had been penetrated by members of the landowning classes. Thus, there was no organized force capable of implementing reformist leadership goals in the villages. By its very design, the Urs regime was incapable of undertaking systematic poverty reform.

Both the CPI(M) and Urs regimes have operated under similar social structural constraints of democratic-capitalism. But their reformist performances have varied. In its four years, the Urs regime could claim only limited success. These different capacities for reform would seem to reflect varying regime-types. The Urs regime and the CPI(M) regime, of course, shared some characteristics—in particular, a coherent leadership and some ideological commitment to the rural poor. While these allowed the Urs regime to push through limited reforms, they were not enough to enable it to penetrate the countryside without being co-opted by the landed interests, or to mobilize the lower classes to help implement the reforms from above. The reformist capacities of a patronage-based, populist regime were therefore not as developed as that of a well-organized, parliamentary-communist regime.

THE JANATA REGIME IN UTTAR PRADESH

In early 1977, the Janata Party won an overwhelming 383-seat majority in the 425-seat legislative assembly of Uttar Pradesh (UP)—the largest legislative assembly in India. Its victory was short-lived, however. Both at the national level and within UP, the party was marred by internal factionalism.[29] During its term of office, the Janata regime in UP attempted very little in the way of poverty reform; it achieved even less. Land reform was excluded from its political agenda, and, in spite of the much-discussed 'rural tilt', programmes for marginal and small farmers were not very effective. 'Antyodaya' and other publicized programmes for the landless poor also achieved little. Janata

---

[29]For past patterns, with a special focus on factions and fragmentation of politics in UP, see Paul Brass, *Factional Politics in an Indian State: The Congress Party in Uttar Pradesh*, Berkeley and Los Angeles: University of California Press, 1965; Paul Brass, 'Uttar Pradesh', in Myron Weiner (ed.), *State Politics in India*, Princeton, New Jersey: Princeton University Press, 1968; and Saraswati Srivastava, 'Uttar Pradesh: Politics of Neglected Development', in Iqbal Narain (ed.), *State Politics in India*, pp. 323–69. A more detailed treatment of the materials presented below is in Kohli, *The State and Poverty*, chapter IV.

leaders, moreover, often ignored the 'caste wars'—a euphemism for the landlord-sponsored repression of the lower peasantry—occurring in different parts of the state. Instead of initiating poverty reforms, in fact, the Janata regime may, on balance, have actually worsened the living conditions of UP's rural poor.

The Janata Party in UP, as elsewhere, was an alliance of disparate parties united in opposition to Indira Gandhi's Congress. The main components of the UP Janata were the former Bharatiya Lok Dal (BLD), with 164 assembly seats, and the Jan Sangh, with 103 seats. Political conflict in the state revolved around the attempt to accommodate the Jan Sangh faction to BLD leadership, both in the party and the government—an attempt which ultimately failed, for both personal and political reasons.

BLD is Charan Singh's middle-peasant party. An offshoot of the old Congress, BLD has over the years come to be thought of as the party of the Jat castes, that is, the party of those commercial peasants (pejoratively referred to as 'kulaks') who have provided the momentum behind the 'green revolution' in Haryana and western UP. The party's ideology argues for a 'rural tilt' in public investments.[30] Its formal organization is minimal,[31] with most of its core support coming through the kinship network of the Jat community. The Jan Sangh, by contrast, is a tightly organized, disciplined party.[32] The main planks of Jan Sangh's platform have been Hindu nationalism and a belief in free enterprise. Core members of the Sangh acquire party status only after several years of party work. Support groups such as the Rashtriya Swayamsevak Sangh (RSS) provide long periods of socialization in party values and discipline. Once a member, an individual is subject to strict party control.

The UP Janta Party faced the difficult task of unifying the BLD and the Sangh into a cohesive political force. The task proved impossible. The individuals whom competing factions found acceptable to head the UP government were weak leaders. The only qualification of Ram Naresh Yadav to be Janata's first chief minister in UP, besides being a 'BLD man', was the minimal threat he posed to the competing factions. In contrast to the strong and coherent leadership of both West Bengal and Karnataka, therefore, the leadership in UP was weak and fragmented.

The ideology of the UP Janata was likewise a confused amalgam. Goals were vague and perhaps inconsistent: decentralization; a 'rural tilt' in public

[30]For Charan Singh's critique of Nehru's industrialization emphasis and some of his ideas on rural oriented development, see Charan Singh, *The Poverty of India and Its Solution*, New York: Asia Publishing House, 1964.

[31]For example, during a field-trip to Meerut District in July 1979, it was difficult for me to find party committees, party offices, or dues-paying party members below the district level.

[32]This account of the Jan Sangh is based on interviews with two prominent party members in Lucknow who wished to remain anonymous.

investments; and a concern for the 'small man'. Moreover, with its promise of a 'return to Gandhi', the party's ideology was broad enough to allow various factions to pursue their competing mandates irrespective of party positions. But, because the BLD was the most prominent among the competing groups, the 'rural tilt' was emphasized. While the question of which social classes would gain from party policies was never discussed publicly, it was clear that the primary beneficiaries would be the commercial peasants. Janata's seemingly confused ideological outlook, therefore, was not free of class bias: the interests of middle-peasants were favoured.

The attempt to create a well-synchronized organization strategy for the Janata as a whole did not succeed either. The relations between social groups supporting the Jan Sangh and the BLD have often been antagonistic. Reflecting the conflict between urban trading and rural commercial interests, for example, the Jains and Jats of Western UP periodically have been involved in open hostilities.[33] That the BLD and the Jan Sangh found it difficult to cooperate locally is thus not surprising. Uneven organizational development, moreover, and the varying electoral strengths of the UP Jan Sangh and the BLD, also made it difficult for the two parties to cooperate. Jan Sangh had a strong organizational base, while the BLD had the largest number of seats in the legislature. Jan Sangh favoured a membership drive for the new party and organizational elections. The BLD leadership, by contrast, wanted to consolidate its popularity first, and attend to organizational matters later. When it became clear that the Sangh-dominated central organs were going to undertake a membership drive, the already thin veneer of cooperation between the Sangh and BLD began to wear thinner.[34]

Organizational issues and conflicting class interests of the respective supporters of the Sangh and of the BLD thus combined with the ongoing factional conflicts among Janata leaders at the centre. All this made it impossible for the UP Janata to act as a cohesive political force. The Janata Party in UP had little organizational structure of its own. Even the attempts to appoint a state committee got bogged down in factional conflicts.[35] A centrally sponsored election panel for the state was boycotted by the BLD. Few districts had development committees; and in the districts of Basti,

[33]See Arun Sinha, 'Peasant-Merchant Conflict', *Economic and Political Weekly*, 25 November 1978, p. 1929.

[34]As one of the important party advisers explained, the origins of conflict went back to the establishment of the Central Election Panel in late August 1978. Charan Singh was not able to place as many of 'his' candidates on the panel as he would have liked. When the state election panels were thus formed in October/November of 1978, the BLD in UP wanted to boycott them. That Yadav fired Jan Sangh ministers in January 1979 does not then seem unrelated. (Based on an interview with Surendra Mohan, Janata Party adviser, Lucknow, 11 June 1979.)

[35]Interview with Surendra Mohan (see footnote 34).

Jhansi, and Meerut, which I visited, these committees hardly ever met. There was, moreover, no party organization below the district level. Since rural development programmes can generally be effective only when undertaken at levels below the district, there was little that Janata could achieve through direct political intervention. To the extent that ideological and organizational features of the Janata regime were discernible at all, the interests of commercial farmers were dominant. The UP Janata thus had neither a commitment to the rural poor nor an organizational structure to implement reform policies.

Janata's dismal performance was thus no surprise. In the mid-1970s, Indira Gandhi had prodded the UP government to pass some new land-reform legislation.[36] While much of this was not implemented, nevertheless it was the first time since the zamindari abolition laws that potentially significant reform legislation had been put on the books in UP. The Janata regime put a stop to even these mild attempts: land reforms were now virtually eliminated from the policy agenda. In a three-volume, 1500-page Janata Five-Year Development Plan (1978–83) for UP, land reforms occupied two-and-a-half pages. The problem of surplus lands received three paragraphs, which concluded that 'much of the work...has been completed'.[37] The issue of tenancy reforms was not even discussed. Government bureaucrats explained this neglect by arguing that tenancy was illegal in UP; presumably, therefore, tenancy was not a policy problem for the UP government—this, in spite of the fact that about 14 per cent of the total land and 20 per cent of the rural population in the state were tied up in tenancy arrangements.[38] Over the years, moreover, these proportions had increased.[39] Turning a blind eye to the problems of land tenure and rural poverty, the Janata regime downgraded land reforms to the point of total neglect.

This neglect of land reforms was probably a conscious policy decision. While, in part, this decision was simply a recognition of the past ineffectiveness of land reforms, it also reflected the emergence of landowning commercial farmers as a dominant political force within the state. In the past, political leaders had proclaimed their commitment to land reforms but were not in a position to force them upon the socially powerful. This earlier separation

[36]For example, land ceilings were lowered, many of the exemption clauses removed, *sajhedari* (a form of fixed tenancy) made illegal, and the landless of the Scheduled Castes/Tribes assigned priority on the list of who gets surplus lands. See Government of Uttar Pradesh, Revenue Department, *Land Reforms in Uttar Pradesh*, 1975.

[37]See Government of Uttar Pradesh, *Draft Five-Year Plan*, 1978–83, V.II, p. 59.

[38]Government of India, *National Sample Survey*, 26th Round, Report No. 215 (Uttar Pradesh), 1971, Table 4.

[39]See Pranab Bardhan, 'Variations in Extent and Forms of Agricultural Tenancy', *Economic and Political Weekly*, 11 and 18 September 1976, pp. 1505–11, 1541–6.

between political and social power has of late vanished. Landowners have increased their wealth through commercial farming and, thereby, have become more powerful politically. And they are consolidating their political strength through such parties as the BLD and under such leaders as Charan Singh. Landowners' interests are now, therefore, more consciously expressed through the political process.[40] It is not surprising that land reforms are no longer on the political agenda.

The meagre resources allocated to programmes for the small and marginal farmers were further indicative of governmental priorities. Payments of about 2 rupees per year per family of five were unlikely to have much impact on the poverty of 4 million landholding rural poor families.[41] Even when the expenditures were concentrated selectively, organizational problems made implementation ineffective. For example, these programmes were aimed primarily at providing assistance in animal husbandry and granting credit to smallholders. Giving bullocks or other animals to small or marginal farmers was thought to be of possible utility in raising their incomes. But, because the local bureaucracy and the elite-dominated local governments carried out the programme, the beneficiaries were not the rural poor—at least, not in the majority of cases I observed. Whenever poor marginal farmers received animals, they confronted a number of problems: they could not afford the fodder and feed, nor the veterinary expenses; and there was a great temptation to sell the animal to make some quick money. If the goal of the animal husbandry programme was to raise the incomes of even a select number of marginal farmers, it was not succeeding. Without a local-level planning organization which takes into account lower-class interests—an unlikely prospect where a left-of-centre party is not in power—such schemes are not likely to be successful, regardless of how much money is allocated.

Moreover, in contrast to West Bengal, the UP government did little to channel credit towards smallholders. Cooperatives remained entrenched in the patronage network linking political leaders to local notables. Lower classes got nothing out of them. Commercial banks followed their straightforward policy of accepting land as collateral for loans, and were generally accessible only to larger landowners; sharecroppers, by definition, did not qualify, as they owned no land. By the government's own admission, therefore, 'marginal farmers and landless labourers have generally not benefited from [small-farmer schemes] mainly because of the rigid procedures and norms

[40]As Raj Krishna noted with reference to his discussions with members of the Janata central cabinet, 'Charan Singh has No Interest in Land Reforms'. (Interview with Raj Krishna, New Delhi, 22 May 1979.)

[41]See Government of Uttar Pradesh, *Draft Five-Year Plan*, 1978–83, V.II, pp. 158–61 for details of financial outlays. These outlays were later reduced even further.

of institutional finance'[42]—and, it ought to be added, because of governmental failure to make the 'rigid procedures and norms' less rigid.

The Janata Party made no attempts to organize the landless labourers. On the contrary, it often came close to siding with the already powerful landowners in their conflicts with labour. In western UP, for example, recent years have witnessed the unionization of landless labourers under various left-of-centre leaderships. Conflict between labour and landlord has become more common. In one of the villages of Meerut district, Harijan (untouchable) labourers were allotted house sites under Indira Gandhi's 20-point programme. Once the Janata Party came to power, however, local Jats felt strengthened, and they sought to evict the landless labourers from the plots allotted to them. The labourers resisted collectively and sought protection from the police and the bureaucracy. The latter failed to provide support, and the Harijans lost their pieces of land. A senior police officer confided to me that 'interference brings a lot of trouble from the Members of Legislative Assembly (MLAs). We stay out of these things'.[43] The MLAs are, of course, members of the BLD and other parties in the UP legislature.

The problem of Harijan oppression in UP was widespread, and led the government to compensate those Harijan families whose household head had been murdered.[44] While this reflected a degree of humaneness on the part of the regime, it also underlined the incapacity of the leadership to protect the landless. The party had no village presence independent of the landowners; the bureaucracy and police had been captured by landlords, local notables, and their powerful political representatives; and landowners mobilized or hired local toughs to cope with any attempted collective resistance.

To conclude, the Janata 'phase' in UP was characterized by shifting alliances and political instability. Fragmented leadership and the dominant role of a party committed to commercial farmers had a devastating impact on UP's rural poor. Land reforms were eliminated from the policy agenda, and small and marginal farmers were ignored. Landless Harijans may well have been the worst affected: the government not only failed to act on their behalf, but political power was on occasion turned against them to reinforce the already powerful landowning groups. Many in India and elsewhere were impressed by Janata's early commitments to 'a new beginning', 'decentralization', 'a rural tilt', and 'a concern for the small man'.[45] In fact, however, the regime in UP utterly failed to attack rural poverty.

[42]Ibid., p. 160.

[43]The police officer, a Deputy Inspector General, wished to remain anonymous.

[44]See Arun Sinha, 'Uttar Pradesh: Mockery of Reform', *Economic and Political Weekly*, 23–30 December 1978, p. 2065.

[45]For example, see Marcus Franda, *Small is Politics: Organizational Alternatives in India's Rural Development*, New Delhi, India: Wiley Eastern Limited, 1979.

This failure of reform in UP was a systematic consequence of the political and class characteristics of the Janata regime, which contrasted sharply with the CPI(M) regime in West Bengal. The CPI(M) leadership was relatively coherent, while Janata's was fragmented. In West Bengal there was a clear ideological commitment to alleviating rural poverty; in UP there was a commitment to commercial farmers and a neglect of the lower peasantry. The CPI(M) and the Janata regimes differed both in structure and in membership. As a tightly organized 'Leninist' party, the CPI(M) systematically penetrated the countryside without being taken over by the landowning groups. This allowed the CPI(M) both to reach the lower classes directly and occasionally to mobilize them on behalf of reformist goals. Janata had no such organizational framework: the party had hardly any rural presence at all; in so far as it did, it rested on the landowners themselves. Given these contrasting patterns of leadership, ideology, and organization, it is no surprise that the two regimes differed so much in their approaches to reform.

A brief comparison of UP Janata and the Urs regime in Karnataka is also instructive. In organization, the two regimes were similar: both were loosely structured and based on landowning groups—factors which constrained the reform efforts of both regimes. However, there was an important difference in their ideological orientations. Urs, by political necessity, was explicitly committed to the rural poor; the Janata was not. Even more important was the difference in leadership. Urs provided coherent and strong leadership to Karnataka for nearly a decade, which allowed him to take a long-range view of the political situation. Calculating that it would be to his political advantage to provide certain rewards to the lower classes, he undertook a number of reforms. By contrast, the factional infighting among leaders of UP meant that no one could take an 'overview' and push for politically expedient reforms. Moreover, the prominent role of the BLD allowed the interests of commercial farmers to be pursued at the expense of the rural poor. Compared both to the parliamentary-communist regime in West Bengal and to the populist regime in Karnataka, the UP regime held out less prospect of implementing redistributive policies.

CONCLUSION

This article has sought to isolate the political conditions necessary for successful rural reform in India. Three 'models' within the larger democratic-capitalist framework of India's development have been examined, and can be restated as follows. A well-organized, parliamentary communist regime in West Bengal—more social democratic than communist—has initiated systematic social reforms. The fragmented, commercial-peasant oriented regime in UP, by contrast, failed in its reformist initiatives. The case of Karnataka lies in between: a strong leader presiding over a populist political arrangement had limited success in channelling resources to some select groups among the lower rural classes. The analytical question is, then, what conditions explain these variations in redistributive policy outputs?

To restate in a summarized form, the case of West Bengal helps delineate the regime features apparently essential for reforming a social order from above. First, the CPI(M) rule in West Bengal has a relatively coherent and stable leadership. This allows for clarification of goals, arrangement of priorities, and systematic pursuit of the adopted policies. Second, CPI(M) has a clear pro-lower-class ideology. Once democratically elected, this ideological position gave the CPI(M) leaders—even though they did not belong to the lower classes themselves—a degree of legitimate authority to pursue goals beneficial to the rural poor. The long-term political interests of the CPI(M) remain tied to their capacity to bring the lower rural classes into their fold. Third, in spite of being a communist party, the CPI(M) has clearly defined the limits of its redistributive goals. All democratically elected parties in a private enterprise economy, even if communist in name, must set these limits. Predictability is essential for the functioning of the economy. Last, and most important, the organizational arrangement of the CPI(M) regime has enabled it to penetrate the countryside without being captured by the propertied groups. In part resulting from the democratic-centralist nature of the party organization, in part a consequence of the carefully reorganized local government, the CPI(M) can now reach the lower peasantry without direct landlord mediation. This allows the regime to channel some developmental resources to the rural poor, as well as occasionally to mobilize them for fulfilling reformist goals.

Both ideologically and organizationally, the CPI(M) has sought to exclude the propertied from political governance, while allowing them to maintain their social power. The CPI(M) experiment is in its early stages; the extent of its success will depend on its capacity to survive and to sustain its current momentum. Irrespective of its long-term prospects, however, the analytical point is clear. Reformism requires institutionalization of pro-lower-class goals within the governing structures. The case of West Bengal highlights the political features that potentially allow such institutionalization to take place.

The contrasting cases of UP and Karnataka buttress the above argument. The Janata regime in UP was characterized by features quite opposite those in Bengal: a fragmented leadership, confused ideology, and little or no organizational base. As a 'coalition' type of regime, the dominant interests represented within it were, moreover, those of commercial farmers. Little was thus achieved in the interests of the rural poor. On the other hand, the Urs regime in Karnataka had some reformist success, facilitated by a coherent leadership and populist ideology. But, because its organization base was weak, and the propertied classes penetrated the ruling organs, its accomplishments were limited.

The three provincial governments examined operate within similar social structural constraints. They all have to be elected democratically, and the economy in all of these areas is mostly capitalist—wage labour, money as a basis of exchange, and commodity production—with some significant pockets of pre-capitalist formations. The rural social structures are also broadly similar. Although they have operated under similar constraints, however, the three regimes have had varying success in implementing redistributive programmes. This general conclusion has some important implications that need to be stated explicitly.

The first implication concerns the future of politically initiated rural reforms in India. The cases examined above suggest that, barring the ascension of a well-organized, left-of-centre regime in India, the prospects of alleviating rural poverty by deliberate political intervention will remain slight. More specifically, as long as the political alternatives in India are offered by such parties as the Congress(I) and Janata—or its constituents, the BLD and the Jan Sangh—there will be little or no meaningful rural reform undertaken. This is not to suggest that poverty cannot be alleviated by the more indirect mode of 'trickle down' from rapid growth. That issue has not been discussed here. Our concern, rather, is with politically directed social reform; and our comparative analysis suggests that only the CPI(M), or others capable of organizing a similar regime, will have the capacity to push through some effective redistributive reforms. While it seems unlikely that such a regime will come to power in India in the near future—and, therefore, the prospects of politically directed alleviation of poverty appear bleak—a systematic case for the types of regime likely to emerge in India requires a study quite different from the one undertaken here.

The second implication of the above study is for those more broadly concerned about the lot of the 'poorest of the poor' in the Third World. Over the years, some development scholars and international development agencies have proposed varying policies aimed at reconciling 'growth with distribution' in the developing countries.[46] The cases analysed above suggest that developmental outcomes depend not only on which policies are undertaken, but also on what kinds of regimes are in power. Policies are integrally linked to underlying social and political forces. If redistributive goals are to be pursued seriously within the framework of capitalist development models, they must be undertaken by coherent regimes committed to the

---

[46]For example, see Holis Chenery, *Redistribution with Growth*, New York: Oxford University Press, 1974; and The World Bank, *The Assault on World Poverty*, Baltimore, Maryland: The Johns Hopkins University Press, 1975.

interests of the lower classes—regimes which can both translate their commitment into an organizational arrangement capable of penetrating the society without being co-opted by the propertied interests, and, at the same time, provide the propertied classes sufficient opportunity to pursue production based on the principle of profit. Well-organized, left-of-centre parties in power are the most likely candidates for institutionalizing such lower-class goals within democratic-capitalist political economies.

Regimes committed to social reform in the Third World face the danger of alienating both the lower and the upper classes—the upper classes because their interests are endangered, and the lower ones because the reformist promises may not be fulfilled. Such problems are especially serious in the short run, where the upper classes fear the unpredictability resulting from left-of-centre regimes' coming to power, and the lower classes' hope for immediate help. The resulting situation is, therefore, often unstable, having damaging consequences for the legitimacy of reformist regimes. A democratic regime controlled by a well-organized, left-of-centre party, however, may be best placed to assuage the propertied, to bring the lower classes into its fold, and to pursue incremental reform. While the balance is precarious, and thus successful experiments rare, rule by parliamentary-communist or other versions of well-organized, social-democratic parties in the Third World offers the best hope—perhaps the only hope—for facilitating redistribution within the framework of democratic-capitalism.

The last implication of this study concerns some recent theoretical debates in the field of comparative political sociology. I have analysed three cases here that highlight the existence of varying regime types and varying regime capacities for reform within similar social structural conditions. Separating political and social power is thus analytically possible. This suggests that studies which focus too much on the cultural and/or economic roots of political structures and processes can be misleading. Regime capacities to control and to alter the social structure vary according to the patterns of regime leadership, ideology, and organization. This 'autonomous' role of the 'political' has often been ignored in comparative development studies. The present article supports the findings of a number of recent studies that governing structures or the 'state' itself ought to be conceptualized as 'society-shaping institutions'.[47]

---

[47]See the references in fn. 3. The quotation here is taken from a memo (dated 14 July 1982) circulated by Peter Evans, Dietrich Rueschemeyer, and Theda Skocpol about the 'States and Social Structure Project', which was supported by the Social Science Research Council, New York.

III

Politics and Development in Select States

The essays in this section should be read in conjunction with the Introduction to this volume, especially the discussion on 'politics and development in select states'. The essays in this section shed light on the diverging developmental trajectories of the Indian states. As noted in the Introduction to the volume, it makes sense to create a simple typology of Indian states: neopatrimonial states, social democratic states, and developmental states. While most Indian states tend to be mixture of 'types', Bihar best demonstrates neo-patrimonial tendencies; West Bengal is India's social-democratic state; and Gujarat is more and more embodying characteristics of a developmental state. Why and how these states have come to acquire the characteristics that they have and with what developmental consequences are areas worthy of serious scholarly research.

In the essay on Bihar I trace the origins of an ineffective patrimonial state to both the underlying caste politics and the nature of leadership and bureaucracy. The state in Gujarat, by contrast, has increasingly sought to be developmental, especially working closely with the economic elite of the region. This, however, creates a recurring problem of how to mobilize electoral majorities. The soft underbelly of Gujarat has thus repeatedly been the use of violence against one group or another to create 'cohesion' among a majority. While I do not analyse the most recent violence against Muslims, the pattern of fomenting deliberate riots so as to generate electoral majorities has earlier origins and is analysed in the essay on Gujarat.

The two essays on West Bengal analyse the emergence of a left party in that region and the redistributive impact of such a party in power, respectively. The essay on origins focuses both on how a left-leaning elite came to the fore and why it was able to mobilize popular support. The essay on the CPM in power in turn focuses on such policies as tenancy reforms and organizing labour in the countryside.

The final two essays on the south Indian states of Karnataka and Andhra Pradesh can be read as 'stories' of the policy limits of leader-dominated polities. In Karnataka of the 1970s, Devraj Urs sought to implement land reforms and mostly failed. I trace this failure to the lack of cohesive political support. In the essay on Andhra Pradesh I analyse the emergence of N.T. Rama Rao, emphasizing caste fragmentation in the state as the political context. The fact that these political tendencies continued well beyond NTR—notice, for example, the subsequent pattern of rule under his son-in-law, Naidu—underlines their durability and contemporary significance.

10

Breakdown in a 'Backward' State
Bihar*

Bihar is India's poorest state and one of its most violent. Political killings have become so common in Bihar over the past decade that, according to *India Today*, they no longer make news.[1] India's leading newspaper, the *Times of India*, estimated that between 1980 and 1986 there had been more politically motivated murders in Bihar than in Punjab.[2]

Some of that violence has been directed at influencing electoral outcomes. Such violence occurs in bursts and is concentrated in the urban areas. An ongoing, more widespread form of violence is seen in the villages. The primary victims are members of the poor Scheduled Castes and Tribes who may have dared to challenge the age-old patterns of domination. The killers often are members of the landowning castes or their hired thugs, or the police, or some combination of these groups.

As the killings have continued, private caste armies have proliferated. The rise of 'warlordism' has generated new types of violence that do not follow the established patterns. Examples of the 'forward' castes killing the 'backward' or middle castes, of the backward castes killing the forward castes, and of politicized Scheduled Castes and Tribes occasionally killing members of both the forward and the backward castes can all be found. In addition, ordinary criminals, the dacoits, have entered the fray, further confusing the picture of who is killing whom and why.

To the extent that patterns are discernible and systematic analysis is possible, the increase in political violence reflects two trends: the decreasing

*Originally published as 'Breakdown in a "Backward" State: Bihar', in Atul Kohli, *Democracy and Discontent: India's Growing Crisis of Governability*, New York: Cambridge University Press, 1991, pp. 205–37.

I would like to acknowledge the helpful comments of Harry Blair on an earlier draft of this chapter.

[1]15 June 1985, p. 28.

[2]Patna edition, 30 May 1986.

effectiveness of government and the erosion of established patterns of domination in Bihar's predominantly agrarian society. Power conflicts have multiplied, and the state simply does not have the capacity to deal with them. Periodic violence has become a pattern. Several issues are raised by this disintegration of order in one of India's important states: Why did the state become so ineffective? Why did local structures of domination erode so rapidly? How is the disintegration of the state and social order related to the specific patterns of violence?

It is argued in this chapter that the turmoil in Bihar is best seen as a product of two related but independent struggles: a political struggle for control of the state pitting the forward castes against the backward castes, and a socio-economic struggle of the landless lower castes against the landowning forward and backward castes.

The political struggle has been fought with unusual intensity because the forward castes of Bihar, and the Congress party that represented them, had long enjoyed unchallenged supremacy, but the minimal commercial impulse that existed in the state's agriculture had been generated by the backward castes. The backward castes were eventually mobilized politically; they combined their numerical and growing economic strength under the umbrella of the Janata Party. This enabled them to challenge the political hold of both the forward groups and the Congress party. The resulting hostility between Congress and Janata has contributed directly to political violence. It has also had an important indirect impact. Intense political struggle has undermined the state's cohesiveness.

The political elite of Bihar were always factionalized, even within the Congress party, even though they all belonged to forward castes. Growing power conflicts along both caste and party lines added to the political fragmentation. Many elements in the state's bureaucracy, including the police, were dragged into these growing intra-elite power conflicts. Politicization of the bureaucrats, in turn, undermined their professionalism. The civil and police bureaucracies in Bihar are now among India's least effective. In sum, the more the state's cohesiveness, legitimacy, and effectiveness have disintegrated, the less the political leaders have been in a position to deal with political and socio-economic conflicts.

Bihar's growing socio-economic conflicts are best understood as products of Bihar's relative underdevelopment. Although most segments of Bihar's economy have failed to grow, the numbers of its people have not. The people's levels of consciousness and political organization likewise have not remained stagnant. Political mobilization under conditions of terrible economic scarcity has had perverse effects. Attempts by new power groups to challenge any aspect of the status quo have been perceived as zero-sum games and thus as major challenges to the old order. They have been met by force. The landowning castes, especially the middle castes, have sought to maintain their exactions by attempting to impose something like a 'second serfdom', infuriating the lower castes. The state's incapacity to mediate such conflict has further encouraged the formation of private armies. The result has been periodic violence and the vicious cycle of retaliation.

SOCIAL AND POLITICAL BACKGROUND

Bihar is India's poorest state and one of its most densely populated.[3] Nearly 90 per cent of the state's people continue to live in villages, making Bihar one of India's predominantly rural states. Agricultural production between 1969 and 1984 grew at an annual compound rate of around 0.5 per cent. Because the population continued to grow at nearly 2 per cent, overall rural incomes declined.[4] That context of severe poverty, population congestion, and rural economic decline must be kept in mind as we attempt to understand the growing political violence in the state.

Bihar is known throughout India for its rigid caste structure. Caste identities are deeply embedded and influence much of Bihar's social, economic, and political life. Table 10.1 gives a rough estimate of the distribution of various castes within Bihar. The sizable minority of 'twice-born' castes is noteworthy, in contrast with the situations in many other non-Hindi states in the south, east (for example, West Bengal), and west (for example, Gujarat), where the upper castes tend to account for smaller proportions of the whole. The political significance of that fact will be discussed shortly. Although for some purposes the twice-born castes may act cohesively, the cleavages among them are also significant. The Brahmins of Bihar are further subdivided into the Maithali Brahmins, concentrated in the north of the state, and the Kanyakubji Brahmins, concentrated south of the Ganges River. The Bihari Brahmins tend not to marry across these sub-castes, let alone across caste boundaries. Although they own considerable amounts of land, given their priestly traditions, they are seldom agriculturalists; in local parlance, 'they do not pick up the plough'.

The Kayasthas are a very small minority within Bihar and, in strict caste terms, really are not twice-borns. Over a prolonged period, however, they have become the educated elite of the state and have acquired the status of

[3]Bihar's per capita income, for example, was under 1,000 rupees in the early 1980s. That contrasts with more than 3,000 rupees for Punjab and nearly 1,800 rupees for India as a whole. According to the 1981 census, only Kerala and West Bengal were more densely populated than Bihar. Bihar's figure of 402 people per square kilometre contrasts with the all-India average of 216. See Government of India, Ministry of Planning, *Statistical Pocket Book, India, 1983*, Delhi: Government of India Press, 1983.

[4]For a discussion, see Pradhan H. Prasad, 'Agrarian Violence in Bihar', *Economic and Political Weekly*, 30 May 1987, especially p. 851.

TABLE 10.1: Estimated Distribution of Castes in Bihar

Caste		Percentage
Twice-born castes:		
Brahmins and Kayasthas	8.5 ⎫	15
Bhumihars and Rajputs	6.5 ⎭	
Backward castes:		
Yadavs	7 ⎫	48
Koiris	7 ⎪	
Kurmis	4 ⎬	
Other backwards	30 ⎭	
Schedules Castes		14
Scheduled Tribes		8
Muslims		15

Source: The figures for Scheduled Castes, Tribes, and Muslims are 1981 census figures and are taken from Government of Bihar, Directorate of Statistics and Evaluation, *Bihar through Figures, 1981*, Patna: Secretariat Press, 1985, table 18. The aggregate figures for twice-born castes are local estimates derived from interviews, and the aggregate figures for the backward castes are the residuals. Assuming these aggregate estimates to be valid, the further breakdown of both the twice-born castes and the backward castes into specific *jatis* is calculated from a sample of 2,531 households (including 564 twice-born households and 955 backward-caste households) conducted for different purposes. The results of that survey are presented in an unpublished report: P.H. Prasad and C.B. Rodgers, 'Class, Caste and Landholding in the Analysis of the Rural Economy', Population and Labour Policies Programme, Working Paper No. 140, World Employment Programme Research (Working Papers), International Labor Office, Geneva, 1983, table 1, p. 12.

an elite caste. The Bhumihars claim to be Brahmins, of sorts, but are not always recognized as such by other Brahmins. As their name indicates (*bhumi* means 'land'), they are closer to land and agriculture. They tend to own fair amounts of land and are definitely an elite caste. Unlike the pure Brahmins, however, Bhumihars cultivate the lands they own and, as a local observer put it, 'even make their own cow dung'.

The Rajputs are distinguished from other elite castes by virtue of their martial history. Both the Rajputs and the Bhumihars are considered in local cultural stereotypes to be 'tougher' than the 'gentle' Brahmins, and thus quicker to resort to force and aggression. The Rajputs also own a lot of land, but they do not 'pick up the plough' as often as do, say, the Bhumihars.

The backward castes, taken together, compose the largest group within Bihar. It is, however, an extremely heterogeneous group. The Yadavs, Koiris, and Kurmis are the most significant of the backward castes. Their significance derives in part from their numbers, in part from their control over small and medium landholdings, and in part from their relative standing in the caste hierarchy. Though distinctly below the twice-born castes, the

Yadavs, Koiris, and Kurmis are generally the elite among the backward castes. The Yadavs are herdsmen and agriculturalists by tradition. They are followers of Krishna, and on that basis they have often tried, without much success, to raise their status in the hierarchy by organized activity.[5] Among the backwards, the Yadavs are politically the most significant. Kurmis have a reputation of being hardworking agriculturalists. Many of them own sizable pieces of land. The Koiris, by contrast, tend to be poorer than either the Yadavs or the Kurmis.

The twice-born castes of Bihar were in the past also the area's main wealthy landowners. Given their numerical significance and their control over land in an agrarian society, they were politically dominant. Francine Frankel has suggested that in the past in Bihar there was a strong correlation among the factors of high status, landownership and political power.[6] Over the years, that monopoly of privilege has come under considerable challenge. Although the perceived legitimacy of that monopoly probably has been permanently damaged, the twice-born castes continue to control considerable land and power in contemporary Bihar.

Tables 10.2 and 10.3 provide data that help chart the interaction between caste and landownership in contemporary agrarian Bihar. The pattern of ownership according to caste (Table 10.3) is not surprising, especially at the top and bottom ends of the social hierarchy. Most big landowners are members of twice-born castes, and most of the Scheduled Castes are poor, landless labourers. However, a number of historical trends have made the picture in the middle a lot less neat.

There is evidence to suggest that the zamindari abolition (the abolition of large landholdings) of the 1950s may have led to some land transfers from the twice-born castes to their tenants, many of whom were from the backward castes.[7] Two other historical facts increased that tendency. The flight of Muslim zamindars from central Bihar to Pakistan at the time of the partition resulted in some backward-caste tenants becoming de facto landowners.[8] After independence, 'ceiling legislation' was passed and led to

[5]See, for example, M.S.A. Rao, *Social Movements and Social Transformation: A Study of Two Backward Class Movements*, Delhi: Macmillan, 1978, chapter 4.

[6]See Francine Frankel, 'Middle Classes and Castes in Indian Politics: Prospects for Political Accommodation', in Kohli (ed.), *India's Democracy*, Princeton University Press, 1988, especially pp. 236–43. The argument in that essay is a summary of a major piece of research that I have heard Frankel present orally, but to which I unfortunately did not have access when this chapter was being written. That work has now been published. See F. Frankel, 'Caste, Land and Dominance in Bihar', in F. Frankel and M.S.A. Rao (eds), *Dominance and State Power in Modern India: Decline of a Social Order*, 2 vols, Oxford University Press, 1989–90.

[7]See, for example, Thomasson F. Januzzi, *Agrarian Crisis in India: The Case of Bihar*, Austin: University of Texas Press, 1973; and Arvind N. Das, *Agrarian Unrest and Socio-economic Change in Bihar, 1900–1980*, New Delhi: Manohar, 1983, especially chapter 8.

[8]Das, *Agrarian Unrest in Bihar*, chapter 8.

TABLE 10.2: Patterns of Landownership in Bihar

Size of Holding (acres)	Number of Holdings (%)	Area (%)
0–2.5	72.6	23.2
2.5–10	21.4	36.9
10–25	5.2	26.6
25 and above	0.8	13.2

Source: The data are, more accurately, for holdings operated or cultivated, rather than legally owned, by a family unit and are based on the agricultural census of Bihar (1976–7), as calculated from Government of Bihar, Directorate of Statistics and Evaluation, *Bihar through Figures, 1981*, Patna: Secretariat Press, 1985, p. 70.

TABLE 10.3: Landownership by Caste in Bihar

	Big Landowners (over 10 acres)	Midsize Landowners (2.5–10 acres)	Small Landowners (0–2.5 acres)	Landless Labourers
Twice-born castes	80	231	217	32
Backward castes	18	89	457	392
Scheduled Castes	0	7	203	477

Source: Based on a survey of 2,531 households in Bihar conducted in the early 1980s under the auspices of the World Employment Programme of the ILO (see the source note to Table 10.1 for details).

pressure on traditional landowners to sell their excess lands to new groups who could afford to buy, many of whom, especially in central Bihar, belonged to backward castes.[9] One seasoned observer of Bihar estimated that as much as 10 per cent of the state's agricultural land may have been transferred from the twice-born zamindars to backward castes.[10]

Although some members of the backward castes have gained access to land, many more have not. Growth in population and division of holdings through inheritance have created a trend whereby a large proportion of the backward castes are not middle peasants, but rather small landowners and landless labourers (Table 10.3). Similar pressures have made many among the twice-born castes middle and small landowners rather than big landowners. The common tendency to think of the twice-born castes as big landowners, the backward castes as middle peasants, and the Scheduled Castes as poor labourers is an oversimplification.

The pace of economic change in Bihar has been very slow. Leaving to the economists the question why that is so, the fact of Bihar's considerable degree of economic stagnation provides important topics for political analysis.

---

[9]Pradhan H. Prasad, 'Caste and Class in Bihar', *Economic and Political Weekly*, February 1979, Annual Number, p. 483.

[10]Ibid.

Pradhan Prasad probably has done more than anyone else to document the nature of Bihar's agrarian structure within that context of stagnation.[11] His detailed surveys have highlighted the continuing prevalence of share-cropping, usury, and bonded labour in Bihar's agriculture. In conjunction with the data examined earlier, that points to a central line of cleavage in Bihar's villages: many of the landless poor from the Scheduled Castes and other lower castes remain tied to landowning members of the higher castes in a complex web of pre-commercial relationships. Those relationships probably have their harshest impact on members of the Scheduled Castes, who suffer from both economic and social deprivation. As will be discussed later, attempts during the 1980s to alter that severe pattern of subjugation repeatedly led to violence that came to be called caste wars.

The dominant position of the twice-born castes in Bihar's politics went largely unchallenged until the mid-1960s. The educated Kayasthas provided Bihar's earliest leaders in India's nationalist movement. Rajendra Prasad, India's first president, typified that group. Kayasthas were soon joined by other members of the twice-born castes. For example, the two Congress leaders who dominated Bihar politics from 1950 to the early 1960s, S.K. Sinha and A.N. Sinha, were a Bhumihar and a Rajput, respectively. The old established upper stratum, even though fairly narrow, was deeply factionalized.[12] In the words of one observer, that intra-elite conflict occurred mainly in the form of demands for 'circulation of elites'.[13]

The effectiveness of caste domination in Bihar is illustrated by the repeated failure of all manner of reform. For example, in spite of the considerable activism of the 'middle peasantry' and the Kisan Sabha, the pre-independence Congress in Bihar managed to evade carrying out its own 'no-rent campaign'.[14] After independence, the failure of zamindari abolition similarly highlighted the dominant role of the twice-born castes.[15] Finally, even reservation policies did not reach Bihar's political agenda until the 1970s.[16] It is that pattern of fairly effective domination by the twice-born castes over both the Congress

[11]Among his extensive writings on the subject, see his 'Agrarian Violence in Bihar' and the numerous references to his earlier work therein.

[12]See, for example, Ramashray Roy, 'Politics of Fragmentation: The Case of the Congress Party in Bihar', in Iqbal Narain (ed.), *State Politics in India*, Meerut: Meenakshi Prakashan, 1968, pp. 415–30.

[13]See Harry Blair, 'Structural Change, the Agricultural Sector, and Politics in Bihar', in John Wood (ed.), *State Politics in Contemporary India: Continuity or Crisis?*, Boulder, Colo.: Westview Press, 1984, p. 63.

[14]See, for example, Arvind N. Das, 'Peasants and Peasant Organizations: The Kisan Sabha in Bihar', in Arvind Das (ed.), *Agrarian Movements in India*, London: Frank Cass, 1982, especially pp. 71–2.

[15]See Januzzi, *Agrarian Crisis in India*.

[16]See Frankel, 'Middle Classes and Castes in Indian Politics', especially pp. 256–8.

party and Bihar politics that provides an essential background to political changes over the past two decades.

Several important political forces have been eroding that system of domination. When suffrage was introduced at the time of independence, the elite castes were forced to accommodate select members of the numerically significant backward castes.[17] Continuing factionalism among the twice-born elite had a similar consequence. Competing elites sought to incorporate members of the backward castes so as to strengthen their power positions. Thus, in 1957 and 1962 in the Bihar Legislative Assembly, more than 22 per cent of the legislators belonged to the backward castes.[18] Although those legislators clearly were co-opted members of the elite, the perceived need to incorporate them at that time foreshadowed their later emergence as an autonomous political force.

INCREASING GOVERNMENTAL INEFFECTIVENESS, 1967–87

The first-generation nationalist leaders like S.K. Sinha and A.N. Sinha passed from the political scene in the early 1960s. That marked the beginning of a new phase in Bihar politics. Whereas factionalism had been rampant within the Bihar Congress even before 1960, some of its more debilitating consequences had been kept within limits by 'tall' leaders. The deaths of those leaders left behind a highly factionalized and squabbling Congress elite. The growing presence of backward castes among the state's leaders added another element to the factional struggles, and the issue of forward castes versus backward castes began to heat up.

The 1967 elections reduced Congress's majority in many parts of India, and Bihar was no exception. As Table 10.4 shows, Congress emerged as a minority party. Several opposition parties that claimed to represent the backward castes gained in significance. None of those parties was in a position to form a government by itself; only a coalition government was possible. Bihar thus entered a period of governmental instability. Presidential rule was imposed three times. There were thirteen changes in governments in Bihar between 1967 and 1972. The longest that any government lasted was around 300 days, and the shortest was four days.[19]

The simple explanation of that governmental instability lies in the inability of the leaders to form a stable coalition. Closer examination reveals two factors that were at work: the disarray within the Congress party, and the growing power conflict between the forward and backward castes.

---

[17] Ibid., pp. 249–50.

[18] See Chetkar Jha, 'Caste in Bihar Congress Politics', in Narain (ed.), *State Politics in India*, p. 583.

[19] See R.C. Prasad, 'Bihar: Social Polarization and Political Instability', in Narain (ed.), *State Politics in India*, especially pp. 62–3.

The organization of the Congress party in Bihar was particularly weak, and the passing of the first-generation leaders exacerbated the problem. The organizational vacuum, combined with the fact that the forward-caste elite came from divergent backgrounds and did not readily cooperate, contributed to political fragmentation. The rising significance of the intermediate castes was clearly manifest in the fact that seven of the nine chief ministers during 1967–72 did not belong to the twice-born castes. The emergence of those new elites made it even more difficult to achieve any degree of governmental cohesiveness.

Fierce competitiveness among minority parties added to the political turmoil. Figure 10.1 shows that political activism and riots in Bihar reached a peak in 1967, a year of crucial elections in which Congress declined and opposition parties gained. As coalition governments faltered, mid-term elections were called in 1969, and the conduct of politics took on a new ugliness. Most observers of Bihar politics agree that the trend towards the 'criminalization of politics', that is, the use of thugs to intimidate and sway political support, can be traced to the 1967–9 period. One analyst close to the situation commented as follows:

The distinctiveness of the mid-term poll of 1969 [was that] ballot and bullet would now go together; to win the election the ballot must be backed by the bullet. [Fraudulent voting] became a common device to win the poll, acquiesced in by the gun-shy polling officers, and openly resorted to by the local group having superiority in fire arms...it came to be called the device of booth-control: it consists in frightening, through the display and, when necessary, through the actual use of fire-arms, all unfavourable voters and thus succeed in preventing them from coming to the polling station at all for casting their vote. Under the umbrella of superior arms the favourable voters are then encouraged to cast as many votes as they desire.[20]

Unfettered and undisciplined political competition brought criminals into the political system. Not only has that trend continued over time, but many party leaders since the 1970s have received their political education in that milieu of 'democracy' by gun.

In 1969, the national split in the Congress party produced some confusing caste and party alignments within Bihar. Indira's Congress was supported by Brahmins and Harijans. Many of the Yadavs, however, sensing new openings within the Congress party, also supported Congress, if only temporarily. The Rajputs, Bhumihars, and Kayasthas, by contrast, moved closer to Congress(O) and later to the Janata coalition.[21] There is a tendency among some analysts to view the early 1970s as a period when the backward castes were rising

[20]Ibid., p. 57.
[21]Ibid., especially p. 63.

TABLE 10.4: Results of Legislative Assembly Elections in Bihar, 1952–85

Party	1952		1957		1962		1967		1969		1972		1977		1980		1985	
	S[a]	V	S	V	S	V	S	V	S	V	S	V	S	V	S	V	S	V
Congress	240	41.4	210	42.1	185	41.4	128	33.1	118	30.5	168	33.1	57	23.6	169	34.2	196	39.3
Congress(O)[b]	–	–	–	–	–	–	–	–	–	–	30	14.8	–	–	–	–	–	–
Socialists[c]	23	18.1	31	16.0	36	19.3	86	24.6	70	19.3	33	16.4	21	7.0	1	1.6	–	–
CPI	0	1.1	7	5.2	12	6.2	24	6.9	25	10.1	35	6.9	–	–	23	9.1	12	8.9
Jan Sangh[d]	0	1.2	0	1.2	3	2.8	26	10.4	34	15.6	25	11.7	–	–	21	8.4	16	7.5
Swatantra	–	–	–	–	50	17.3	3	2.3	3	0.9	1	0.7	–	–	–	–	–	–
Janata[e]	–	–	–	–	–	–	–	–	–	–	–	–	214	42.7	13	7.4	13	7.2
Lok Dal[f]	–	–	–	–	–	–	–	–	–	–	–	–	–	–	42	15.5	46	14.7
Independents	13	19.6	17	20.8	12	8.4	33	17.9	24	8.3	16	10.8	24	23.7	23	12.0	30	17.9
Others	54	18.6	53	14.7	20	4.6	18	4.7	44	15.3	10	5.6	8	3.0	32	11.8	11	4.6

Source: Computed from the reports of the Election Commission.

Notes:

[a] S, seats won; V, percentage of the total vote.

[b] Formed in 1969 and merged into the Janata Party in 1977.

[c] Includes both the Samukyta Socialist Party (SSP) and the Praja Socialist Party (PSP).

[d] Renamed Bharatiya Janata Party (BJP) in 1980.

[e] Formed in 1977 by a merger of Jan Sangh, Congress(O), Swatantra, and others; broke apart into a number of parties after 1980.

[f] Formed in 1980 as the Janata Party (Socialist), and became the Lok Dal party in 1985.

slowly to challenge the power of the forward castes, culminating in the 1977 victory of the backward castes under the leadership of Karpoori Thakur. Such an analysis is somewhat misleading because it attempts to reduce what was primarily a political conflict to a socio-economic conflict. The caste underpinnings of the rival political forces were quite confusing throughout the 1970s. By contrast, it was easy to identify those who supported Indira Gandhi and those who were against her.

The anti-Indira rebellion reached a crescendo in 1974 under the leadership of Jaiprakash Narain. Figure 10.1 shows the new peak of rioting reached in Bihar in 1974, just before the Emergency. Given the political nature of the anti-Indira rebellion and of the Emergency, a fair amount of Bihar's activism during that period must be understood more as political conflict than as socio-economic struggle. That the rioting declined sharply during the brief Emergency was not surprising. Because opposition leaders were imprisoned, and open political activity was banned, a decline in activism was to be expected, at least for the moment.

The Emergency brought Jagannath Mishra to power in Bihar. Mishra was a 'Sanjay man'. Most observers of Bihar would not disagree with the

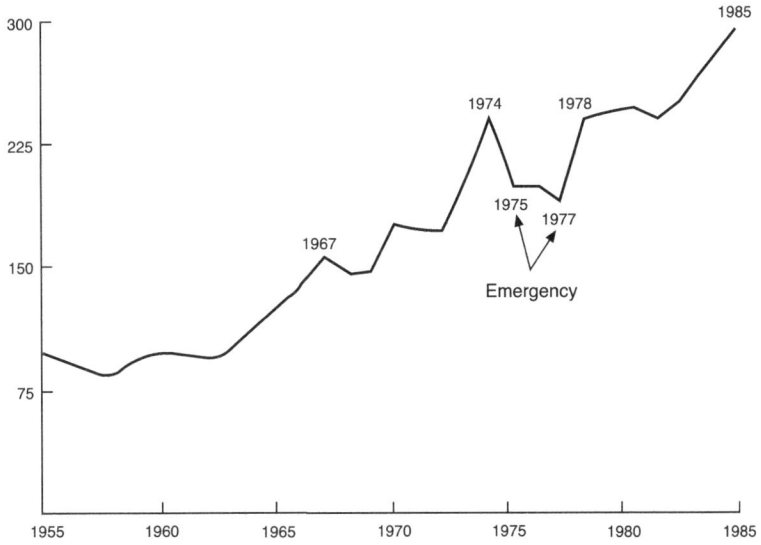

FIGURE 10.1: Riots in Bihar, 1955–85 (number of riots per million population)

Source: Data for 1955–82 are from an annual publication: Government of India, Ministry of Home Affairs, *Crime in India*, New Delhi: Government Press. No data for 1983 and 1984 are available. The 1985 figures are rough estimates provided by state officials. For a discussion of what all the government data on 'riots' include and why they can be used as indicators of public protest and political violence, see Baldev Raj Nayar, *Violence and Crime in India: A Quantitative Study*, Delhi: Macmillan, 1975, especially p. 17.

claim that the Mishra period, especially during the Emergency years, turned out to be 'a dark period in state administration [when] corruption, favouritism and nepotism reached [their] zenith'.[22] Prior to the Emergency, rampant factionalism, governmental instability, politically motivated rioting, and escalating criminalization of politics were the major characteristics of political decay. The trend towards criminalization intensified under Mishra. Moreover, two new developments contributed to the government's growing ineffectiveness: the continuing decline of the police and civil bureaucracies as professional institutions, and the arming of private groups to cope with the increasing agrarian violence.

It is important to remember that by the time Jagannath Mishra came to power in Bihar, the Indian political system had undergone important changes. The most significant for our purposes was that power within states like Bihar had become increasingly a function of loyalty to Indira Gandhi. Indira Gandhi's popularity had soared nationally in 1971; after that, she, or her lieutenant, Sanjay, could pick and choose the chief ministers of states. Over the short run that had the positive impact of reducing the governmental instability that had resulted from coalition governments in Bihar. Indira's popularity enabled Congress to win a clear majority. That victory, however, did not belong to Bihari Congressites. As more and more officeholders were appointed from New Delhi, politics within the state took on a qualitatively new top-down characteristic.

The authority of appointed chief ministers like Mishra within Bihar was, at least initially, fairly shallow. Below Mishra was a highly fragmented political elite and a bureaucracy that did not readily respond to an appointed leader. One of the strategies adopted by Mishra and by nearly all subsequent state leaders was to consolidate control by appointing ministers, civil servants, and police officers who were loyal. Thus, the competence of the ruling elite declined further. Although that was not a new trend, the depth and scope of such political interference, especially in the bureaucracy, increased sharply in the mid-1970s. The long-term consequences of that in Bihar were growing de-professionalization and ineffectiveness in the state's bureaucratic arm.

I interviewed a number of police officers in Bihar in 1986 in an effort to understand why the force was so ineffective in the face of growing urban and rural political violence. How that occurred and with what consequences are best brought out by some excerpts from those off-the-record interviews:[23]

[22]See the analysis in *Hindustan Times*, 15 August 1986, p. 12.

[23]The excerpts quoted here are from interviews with police officers of the rank of superintendent of police or higher. These interviews were conducted in Patna in August 1986.

There is no question that the police are corrupt and demoralized and that they often side with the vested interests. But one has to understand the reasons for this. The professionalism of the police has been totally snuffed out by political interference. At each step, politicians interfere—postings, transfers, execution of duties, arrests and releases....Moreover, most of us have lost respect for politicians. Come election, they will often ask for police support for booth capturing or for this and that. We thus know that many of them are not genuinely elected. This undermines the legitimacy of power. The arrangement between the police and the politicians thus becomes one of mutual convenience. Professionalism is snuffed out. Personalism pervades.

The issue of caste had also become central to police appointments. In the words of one officer:

For example, take the area of Jehanabad [a troubled agrarian area]. Every appointment in that area has to be cleared with politicians. Those appointed have to be more or less the men accepted by the Bhumihars [the local dominant caste]. Officers have to be 'their men'. That is the only way things are workable in that area.

As to when that type of political interference really became the norm:

This probably happened in the 1970s—around the Emergency. Mrs Gandhi had initially found that people would stand up to her. But since then loyalty has been at premium. Jagannath Mishra introduced this culture to Bihar. You had to be loyal to him. This was the basic criteria. Those who did not fall in line were made to or lost out.

The information in such interviews suggests that appointed chief ministers like Jagannath Mishra and his successors had repeatedly interfered in the police service to consolidate their personal control. That undermined the professionalism of the force. What started out as a strategy to enhance political control had unanticipated and unfortunate consequences: when leaders now need to call on the police arm of the state, that arm is relatively limp.

A similar process undermined the efficacy of the state civil service. As one senior IAS officer explained:

Turnover of personnel is everywhere. This is especially true in the districts and in the politically sensitive ministries. Sensitive ministries are those that either control a lot of resources or employment [e.g., departments of personnel, home, finance, agriculture, irrigation, power, and construction]. I used to be transferred every six to eight months.... In the last ten years even the IAS in Bihar is not beyond suspicion for corruption. This is because integrity and competence does not count. What matters is who you are close to. If you are close to powerful ministers [you can get choice positions]. The threat of transfers is very serious....The politico-administrative culture is such that honest and competent people find it hard to survive.

As to how that de-professionalization had affected the functioning of the government and the pursuit of policies:

Well, is there any policy? I still do not understand what the 20 point programme is. Now they have again changed it. It does not make any difference. What goes on is, get into power, amass wealth, keep talking about welfare of the poor, and figure out how to win the next election. No one thinks of policy.[24]

Such cynicism at the highest levels of the government only confirms what casual observers of Bihar politics already understand. Politics in Bihar means mainly a concern with winning elections and office as a source of personal aggrandizement. The concept of politics as a constructive programmatic use of power is simply missing.

The criminalization of politics intensified during Mishra's reign. As one local politician commented, 'the quality of elections has deteriorated terribly since 1977.... There is never an election anymore without murders. [Before 1977] criminal elements used to help politicians. Sooner or later they realized, why not run ourselves'.[25] Individuals like Mishra, coming from a background in the infamous Dhanbad 'mafia', and with links to Sanjay's 'militant' Youth Congress, typified that new genre of politicians. No precise information is available on how many criminals-turned-politicians actually entered the political arena. There is little doubt, however, that their numbers are by now considerable. The *Times of India* reported that 'many MLAs strike terror in the hearts of their constituencies'. That story went on to report what 'most responsible politicians admit in private', namely, 'that the thought that criminal politicians may actually come to control a majority in the assembly can no longer be dismissed'.[26]

Finally, it is important to note that the arming of private groups began at some time in the mid-1970s, probably with government approval. The issues of why and how peasant rebellions have intensified over the past decade will be discussed in the next section. Suffice it to note here that as such rebellions grew, the government found its ability to enforce law and order quite limited. That limitation was a function of two factors. First, as has been noted, the police were becoming increasingly ineffective. In addition, one of the results of the state's low level of economic development was underdevelopment of transportation and communication networks. Police seldom could reach the scenes of disturbances quickly, even when they occurred close to the state capital.

[24]Interview with Arun Prasad, member of the Bihar Board of Revenue, Patna, 23 August 1986.

[25]Interview with Ram Avtar Shastry, member of the Bihar Legislative Assembly (member of the CPI and a former member of Parliament), Patna, 24 August 1986.

[26]Patna edition, 14 July 1986.

In order to cope with peasant rebellions, therefore, the government apparently encouraged the arming of private groups. The evidence on that point is sketchy, but persuasive. For example, the following announcement made by a senior police officer in 1975 was reported in a local paper:

The Bihar government has decided to arm all able-bodied persons in Bhojpur and Patna districts for self-defense to face the extremist menace, who have recently launched an armed struggle.... District magistrates of both the districts have been asked to visit the affected villages and issue licences for firearms on the spot to those who were able to possess them.... The decision was taken following a spurt in the armed attacks on landowners by the extremists in these villages. The trouble was mostly of agrarian nature.[27]

A civil-rights group conducting an investigation of agrarian violence independently reported the following:

One of the most striking aspects of central Bihar is the brazenness with which the police and the administration give support to illegal and violent activities of the *senas* [private armies]. In fact this is a continuation of the policy adopted during the seventies in the counter-insurgency operations against the Naxalites in Bhojpur and other areas, when a large number of firearms were issued to landlords and even centers for training them were set up.[28]

Unable to deal effectively with peasant insurgency, in the mid-1970s the Bihar government abandoned a quintessential task of any state: to maintain a monopoly over the use of coercion. Instead, the Bihar government definitely looked the other way as private armed groups were formed, and it may even have encouraged that practice.

The end of the national Emergency brought the Janata Party to power in Bihar. Karpoori Thakur, an associate of Charan Singh, and popularly identified as a leader of the backward castes in Bihar, emerged as the state's chief minister. Both politically and socially, Karpoori Thakur symbolized a new phase in Bihar's politics: the simultaneous consolidation of an alternative to Congress and the political rise of the backward castes. The Janata reign in Bihar in the 1970s proved to be short-lived; Congress and the representatives of the forward castes came back to power in 1980. The next question is how we should interpret the brief Janata interregnum in Bihar.

[27]Reported in the *Indian Nation*, 28 May 1975, and cited in Kalyan Mukerjee and R.S. Yadav, 'For Reasons of State: Oppression and Resistance, a Study of Bhojpur Peasantry', in Das (ed.), *Agrarian Movements in India*, p. 128.

[28]People's Union for Democratic Rights, *Behind the Killings in Bihar*, New Delhi: PUDR, 1986, p. 29.

The basic facts of that period are well known and require only brief reiteration.[29] Karpoori Thakur headed a coalition of forces that first sought to capture power in the late 1960s. That same coalition then backed Jaiprakash Narain's 'total revolution' against Indira Gandhi in 1974. That group finally came together politically under an umbrella party that was hurriedly formed after the Emergency: the Janata Party. Once in power, Karpoori Thakur sought to consolidate his power base among the backward castes by promising them reservations (quotas) in both government jobs and educational institutions. Attempts to implement that policy shift in 1978 led to a considerable outburst of opposition from the forward castes. Bihar during that period again experienced prolonged agitations and riots against the government. Figure 10.1 shows that rioting in 1978 climbed back to the same high level as in 1974, the year before the Emergency was proclaimed. As a result, Karpoori Thakur's government was forced to resign under pressure. A Janata government under a new leader continued to rule until 1980, but it did not pursue the policy of reservations for backward castes. Eventually, shifts in the national political situation led to an electoral defeat of the Janata Party and to the re-emergence of Congress in 1980.

It is tempting to see in that series of events the makings of a major socio-economic struggle. Analysts with Marxist sympathies have indeed tended to describe a growing struggle between the 'new capitalist kulaks' of the backward castes and the old 'feudal order', dominated by the twice-borns.[30] Prominent non-Marxist scholars like Francine Frankel also have seen the 'backward classes movement' led by Karpoori Thakur as 'the organization of the poor in a double assault on the caste system and the class structure'.[31] That approach overemphasizes socio-economic variables at the expense of political factors.

A number of pieces of evidence indeed support a socially generated explanation of the late-1970s political conflict in Bihar. First, there can be little doubt that patterns of social ascendancy and political dominance have tended to coincide in modern Bihar. Second, the minimal economic dynamism that exists in Bihar's agriculture has been generated primarily by middle peasants concentrated in central Bihar.[32] Many in the old ruling classes, the landowning forward castes, are thus being left behind. The proposition that these middle peasants, the so-called kulaks, have sought a political role commensurate with their improved economic standing is not

[29]For details, see Harry Blair, 'Rising Kulaks and Backward Classes in Bihar: Social Change in the late 1970's', *Economic and Political Weekly*, 12 January 1980, pp. 64–74.

[30]See, for example, Prasad, 'Caste and Class in Bihar'.

[31]See Frankel, 'Middle Classes and Castes in Indian Politics', p. 257.

[32]See Prasad, 'Caste and Class in Bihar'.

unreasonable. Finally, because of conditions of relative economic stagnation, the forward castes consider it imperative that they continue to have access to the state's patronage resources. State-controlled jobs and educational opportunities provide limited but crucial economic outlets for the progeny of an economically lethargic ruling class. As access to such opportunities was threatened by the proposed reservation policies, the new ruling groups came to be perceived as direct economic threats, and that led to the rage and violence that toppled the Thakur government.

Several other pieces of evidence, however, tend to contradict the interpretation of the political discord of the late 1970s as a conflict between the forward and backward castes. First, Table 10.3 shows that as many as 80 per cent of the forward castes were not big landowners, but rather middle and small landowners. There is little evidence to indicate that the 'objective' economic interests of those forward-caste members were sharply distinguishable from the interests of the backward-caste peasants in the middle and small ranks. Second, caste and party alignments during the late 1970s were not clear-cut. Frankel noted that some of the twice-born castes, the Bhumihars and the Rajputs, tended to support not Congress but rather the Janata Party in the post-1977 period.[33] A Yadav leader I interviewed insisted that a significant minority of Yadavs had always supported Congress, even after the Emergency.[34] Thus, the caste, class, and party cleavages were far from being neat and easily identifiable during the political conflict of the late 1970s.

The way in which the political process unfolded during those years also raises doubt that the Janata interregnum should be seen as an example of emerging caste-class conflict. The rise to power of Karpoori Thakur had little to do with his mobilization of people around a pro-backward caste political agenda. On the contrary, in the words of another astute student of Bihar politics:

It is important to note that Thakur did not win the 1977 poll solely or even mostly on the basis of his Backward leadership; rather it was the same anti-Congress sentiment that swept the Indira Gandhi government out of New Delhi. But the fact of getting elected largely on the basis of one issue did not prevent him from interpreting his victory as a mandate to pursue an entirely unrelated policy initiative.[35]

That initiative involved a subsequent attempt to consolidate his power base among the backward castes. The fact that Karpoori Thakur loaded his ministry with members of the backward castes and sought to implement a

---

[33]Frankel, 'Middle Classes and Castes in Indian Politics', p. 256.

[34]Interview with Ram Lakhan Singh Yadav, Patna, 26 August 1986.

[35]See Harry Blair, 'Structural Change, the Agricultural Sector, and Politics in Bihar', note 51, p. 77.

new reservation policy must be viewed as a political ploy to create a power bloc where none had existed. Power came to Thakur first, and the attempt to mobilize and unify the backward castes followed. Although it might be argued that that is somewhat of an exaggeration, the situation definitely was not the other way around.

The opposition that emerged also had a highly political quality. As Thakur himself explained, 'the agitations were definitely politically organized. Newspapers helped them [the agitation leaders] with publicity. There was a whispering campaign...including lies. The crowds were mainly students. Political trouble was mainly all urban.... Rural masses were not involved.'[36] It was that urban concentration of the opposition that gave away the fact that the cleavages in the conflict were created mainly by leaders and parties, rather than by mobilized socio-economic groups. With 90 per cent of the state's population living in villages, a set of civil disorders limited to the cities could hardly be seen as a major struggle between the contending caste groups in the state.

Finally, the 1980 elections, the elections that followed the turmoil over reservation policies in the 1970s, confirmed that the political support of the backward castes was quite fragmented. Despite the fact that the backward castes constituted nearly 50 per cent of Bihar's population, Karpoori Thakur's Lok Dal party received no more than 16 per cent of the popular vote (Table 10.4). The rise and decline of the electoral fortunes of Congress's opposition in Bihar were largely functions of party alignments and realignments and had little to do with a supposed polarization between the forward and backward castes.

Faced with such evidence, one might be tempted to fall back on a modified position, namely, that the conflict of the late 1970s in Bihar was symptomatic of a challenge not to all the forward castes but specifically to the hegemony of the Brahmin ideology and the social order created and sustained by the Brahmin elite. Even that, however, will not do. We shall see in the next chapter that in Gujarat, as in Bihar, a major struggle over reservation policies broke out in the 1980s. The conflict, however, did not involve the Brahmins; the struggle pitted a somewhat lower but prosperous caste, the Patidars, against the backward Kshatriyas.

The late-1970s civil disorder in Bihar was a quintessential political conflict. Although it had certain important socio-economic underpinnings, the evidence suggests that the lines of cleavage involved contending political groups with fairly diverse social support. The rhetoric of the conflict, backwards versus forwards, was aimed at creating caste-based political blocs

---

[36]Interview with Karpoori Thakur, Patna, 23 August 1986. The original interview was in Hindi. The translation is my own.

out of a heterogeneous social base. Even the main political ploy, the reservation policies, would not have hurt or benefited more than a few thousand individuals in a state of some 80 million people. That was hardly the stuff of which major social struggles are made.

The contending political forces throughout the period were pro- or anti-Congress. That was the main line of cleavage in the pre-Emergency mobilization. It continued to be so in the post-1977 battle between the Janata Party and Congress, and it probably was so in the late-1989 elections to the Lok Sabha. In a candid moment, Karpoori Thakur admitted that although he differed with Charan Singh on many issues, 'we both believe in wanting to defeat the Congress'.[37] The main enemy was not the forward castes but the Congress party.

Both Congress and the Janata Party in Bihar were deeply fragmented political parties. Going into the 1977 elections, one analyst described the Bihar Congress as being in organizational 'shambles', and the Janata Party as incapable of working 'as one cohesive unit'.[38] Short-run political gains defined the horizons of both those parties. By late 1977, moreover, rioting as a way of accomplishing political ends was already becoming the norm in Bihar. Congress leaders like Jagannath Mishra had had considerable experience in unleashing semi-organized militancy against their political opponents. The prospect that Karpoori Thakur could utilize his power position to create a political bloc of the backward castes must have seemed quite threatening to the Bihari Congress elite. Students from upper-caste backgrounds were likely to be the main losers in the new policy shift. Thus, the threatened Congress elite allied themselves with the city-based forward castes, especially students, to mount an opposition movement that simultaneously put an end to reservation policies and toppled Thakur from power.

The return of Indira Gandhi to power in 1980 brought Jagannath Mishra back to power in Bihar. One senior civil servant commented during an interview that 'every new government in Bihar makes its predecessor look like angels'.[39] That was mainly because governmental ineffectiveness and agrarian violence were continuing to grow in Bihar. There was no major policy initiative undertaken by Mishra during his three-year rule, or undertaken by Bindeshwari Dubey between 1985 and 1988, that could have reversed the growing trend towards governmental ineffectiveness. As Figure 10.1 shows, political violence in the 1980s continued to escalate. Some examples of recent political developments will further document the continuing decay of political and governmental institutions in Bihar.

[37]Ibid.
[38]See Ramashray Roy, *Battle Before Ballot*, Delhi: Ritu Publishers, 1983, pp. 22, 25.
[39]Interview with R. Srinivasan, Patna, 28 August 1986.

Both the Lok Sabha elections in 1984 and the Legislative Assembly elections in early 1985 were considerably more violent than those in 1977. For example, violent incidents (including assaults, bomb explosions, booth capturing, civilian shootings, and police shootings) increased from some 260 in 1977 to 617 in 1984. Moreover, nearly 100 people were killed in the 1985 election, compared with 34 in 1977, including four candidates running for office.[40] The root cause of that violence was the increasing involvement of criminals and thugs in the political process. As a senior civil servant noted, 'elections have become very violent. Musclemen are central [to this process]. They are not marginal anymore'.[41] The issue of the linkage between crime and politics has already been discussed. It is both a cause and an effect of the growing deinstitutionalization of political parties.

Many other indicators could be cited to illustrate the growing crisis of governability. Factional strife within the ruling party continued to make headlines.[42] Between 1988–9, Bihar had four new chief ministers, with Jagannath Mishra reemerging in late 1989 when Congress(I) finally suffered a humiliating defeat in the Lok Sabha elections. Throughout the 1980s, the Congress government was unable to act with even a modest degree of cohesiveness. Much of the leadership's attention was focused on political intrigue. Solving the state's pressing economic and political problems was far from anyone's mind. Within the first fifteen months of his rule, Dubey transferred nearly 300 IAS officers within the state. That level of turnover of personnel was unprecedented even for Bihar.[43] The traditional mechanisms for expressing and accommodating political discontent had ceased to function. For example, the government's poor handling of the Arawal massacre in 1986 led to considerable controversy and civil-rights groups organized a large protest demonstration. Scared of even a peaceful demonstration, the government unleashed a police assault on the demonstrators and ended up arresting 30,000 people in one day.[44]

Finally, the most troublesome political development throughout the 1980s was the proliferation of private armies. As the government's effectiveness had declined, various socio-economic groups had taken law and order into their own hands. Four to six private armies have been operating in Bihar's countryside at various times over a period of several years. Those armies,

[40]See *Times of India*, Patna, 14 July 1986.

[41]Interview with Arun Prasad (see footnote 24).

[42]See, for example, the discussion of the takeover of the L.N. Mishra Institute in *Times of India* (Patna), 24 April 1986, and the discussion of the continuing caste-based factionalism within Congress in *India Today*, 15 July 1987.

[43]See *Times of India*, Patna, 23 August 1986.

[44]See *Times of India*, Patna, 22 August 1986, for a report, and 23 August 1986, for a biting editorial on 'police terror'.

or *senas,* generally are identified with specific castes. The Lorik Sena belongs to the Yadavs, the Bhoomi Sena to the Kurmis, the Brahmrishi Sena to the Bhumihars, the Kunwar Sena to the Rajputs, and the Lal Sena (or Red Army) to the landless labourers.[45]

Details concerning the operation of the senas are not easily available. Senior police officers in Patna repeatedly warned that the districts of central Bihar, where these armies mainly operate, are not safe. The government's writ simply does not extend to those areas. Any one nosing around, I was warned, could easily get hurt. From the information that I could gather during interviews, these senas are not all alike. The Lal Sena is reputed to be the most disciplined. A government report in 1982 suggested that nearly 200 villages in central Bihar, about 10 per cent of the state's administrative blocs, were under the influence of one 'Naxalite' group or another and that in those areas, various armed leftist political groups were running a 'parallel government'.[46]

The armies of the landowning castes that have been organized to deal with this 'Naxalite menace' vary from ad hoc gangs of hired thugs to uniformed private armies of 1000–1500 men. As one knowledgeable local observer explained, 'these [*senas*] roam around openly in armed gangs in the villages. They are mainly informal organizations. Money is provided by the rich [landowning groups]. Arms are bought. Toughs are hired, more or less permanently. In some places they even have uniforms'.[47] In other places, the private armies have become closely linked with ordinary criminals, the local dacoits. The toughs who are hired for these armies often are mercenaries who double as part-time criminals.[48]

The dynamics of these private armies are best understood within the context of the escalating agrarian conflict in Bihar. For this analysis, the existence of these armies dramatically highlights a government that does not work. If Bihar were an independent country, such conditions of breakdown would by now have precipitated a military coup or external intervention, or some combination of the two.

There is widespread evidence that both the political elite and the police quietly condone the operation of these private armies.[49] Why, one may ask,

[45]For a discussion of these armies, see *Sunday,* 15–21 December 1985, especially p. 14; *Times of India,* Patna, 9 May1986; and People's Union for Democratic Rights, *Killings in Bihar,* pp. 45–6.

[46]Government of Bihar, 'Notes on Extremist Activities—Affected Areas', mimeograph, May 1982.

[47]Interview with Ram Avtar Shastry (see footnote 25).

[48]See People's Union for Democratic Rights, *Killings in Bihar,* pp. 21–31.

[49]See, for example, *Times of India,* Patna, 24 August 1986. Also see the discussion in Prasad, 'Agrarian Violence in Bihar', especially p. 852; Praveen K. Chaudhry, 'Agrarian Unrest in Bihar: A Case Study of Patna District, 1960–84', *Economic and Political Weekly,* 2 January 1988, p. 54; and People's Union for Democratic Rights, *Killings in Bihar,* pp. 45–6.

has the state turned a blind eye to such a development? The need of the haves to protect their threatened socio-economic interests is a fairly obvious point. What is also important to note here is that leaders are worried about their electoral prospects. They are hesitant to unleash systematic state repression against the vast majority, the rural poor. As challenges by the poor have mounted in the countryside, many in the state apparatus have chosen simply to let a decentralized pattern of private responses deal with the problem. It is doubtful that a great deal of thought went into that response. It is more likely that it emerged by trial and error as the easiest way out.

In sum, the growing ineffectiveness of political institutions in Bihar has contributed both directly and indirectly to the increase in political violence. The direct contribution is dramatically highlighted by the fact that the years of peak political violence, 1967, 1974, and 1978 (Figure 10.1), all were years of virulent political conflict between Congress and a motley opposition. The intensity of that conflict in Bihar was unusual for a number of reasons: (i) long traditions of elite factionalism, (ii) unusually weak political parties, (iii) agitations and mass mobilization as established modes of conducting the business of politics, (iv) extreme economic backwardness that made continued access to the state's resources a highly valued good, and (v) the long, unchallenged pattern of caste domination that made the possibility of mobilizing around caste appeals both attractive and dangerous.

Governmental ineffectiveness has also contributed indirectly to the growing violence. Policy ineffectiveness, for example, is at the root of agrarian stagnation. Prolonged political interference with the police forces and tacit political support for the growth of private armies have made the government marginal in regard to agrarian conflicts. These conditions of economic stagnation and disintegration of the government's coercive arm, in turn, provide the broad context within which new patterns of class and caste conflict are emerging.

AGRARIAN STRUGGLES

Agrarian struggles have a long history in Bihar. The conflicts in the first-half of this century were qualitatively different from the more recent ones. Those earlier movements often involved 'tenants', with access to considerable land, against the zamindari system.[50] For nearly a quarter of a century after independence, however, there was a lull. The new movements that have emerged since the mid-1970s often have featured the landless Scheduled Castes against various landowning castes. At stake in these conflicts are mainly economic issues of land and wages. Such non-economic issues as violation of lower-caste women by the higher castes have also been significant.

[50]See Das, *Agrarian Unrest in Bihar*.

The dimensions of the agrarian conflict are difficult to judge precisely. Most local observers tend to agree on the following: these struggles represent a major new trend in the countryside. They are not marginal phenomena, and, most important, they are likely to escalate. The *New York Times,* for example, estimated that some 3,300 people were killed in 1986 in these and related conflicts in Bihar and that this number was 'certainly an understimate'.[51] A well-known agricultural economist in Bihar reported another incredible figure: nearly a quarter of the available land in Bihar was not cultivated in 1985–6 because of agrarian conflicts.[52] It is no wonder, therefore, that even casual observers of Indian politics have come to associate Bihar with periodic murders of members of the Scheduled Castes.

An analysis of these caste wars, as they are called, is best developed inductively. A study of some of the better-known incidents that have been reported and investigated has revealed four basic patterns of conflict.[53] The first and most important pattern involves direct fighting between the landowning castes and the landless Scheduled Castes over socio-economic issues. This frequently results in the deaths of members of the lower castes, and occasionally a member of the higher caste will be killed. Let us label these as incidents of *caste–class conflict.* A second, related pattern is characterized by murders of members of the lower castes by the police. These are often called incidents of *police brutality.* A third and less frequent pattern involves almost random violence and killings between two or more castes. These are cases of *anarchic conflict.* Finally, there is a fourth pattern of increasing conflict that does not concern us directly in this study: looting and plundering by dacoits, the plain *criminal violence* that always increases when law and order disintegrate. Specific examples of the first three types of conflict will help set the stage for development of an adequate explanation of these new agrarian trends in Bihar.

Examples of Caste–Class Conflict

Incidents Following the End of the Emergency in 1977

In Buxara village in Kargahar block of Rohtas district, where the labourers had organised an indefinite strike to secure the revised minimum wages, the landlords ransacked the harijan ghetto on 27 March, shot three labourers and burnt them

---

[51]*New York Times*, 27 April 1987, p. A6.

[52]See Prasad, 'Agrarian Violence in Bihar', p. 852.

[53]In addition to local interviews and news reports, especially from the *Economic and Political Weekly*, I consulted the following sources: People's Union for Democratic Rights, *Killings in Bihar;* a survey of 'caste violence' in Bihar in *India Today*, 31 December 1986, pp. 40–3; another survey in *Sunday*, 15–21 December 1985, pp. 10–15; and a report by Arun Sinha, 'Class War, Not "Atrocities against Harijans"', in Das (ed.), *Agrarian Movements in India*, pp. 148–52.

alive in a haystack. In Gopalpur, where also strikes had been called by the labourers, the landlords on 11 June attacked the harijan ghetto with 50 armed men and wounded some half a dozen workers, humiliated their women, and looted a shop. On 19 June in Pathadda in Bhagalpur district, 36 men and women from the labourers' houses were taken by the landlords and incarcerated in the village school building and brutally assaulted. The cause of feudal anger was the resistance of the labourers to working on old wages and their refusal to pay debts that had been redeemed under the 20-point programme. In Dharampura, four share-croppers were massacred by the landlords for demanding occupancy rights on 20 October.

All these outrages...were committed by big landlords, who hold near-absolute economic, social and political power in their respective areas. In Belchhi it was Mahavir Mahato, in Gopalpur it was Birendra Singh; the landlords of Dharampura and Chhaundadano were led by mahanths who were the biggest landlords of their respective areas. In each case the big landlord concerned is virtually the 'raja' of his area. He possesses one-fourth or more of the total land of his village. He lives like an aristocrat in a large brick house. He employs the largest number of both slave and free labourers for domestic and farm work. He maintains a small private army equipped with guns, spears, lathis and other weapons and himself owns a licensed gun. Often his slave labourers serve as his soldiers but he may also keep, as he does in Chhaundadano, Belchhi, and Dharampura, a permanent contingent of regulars, giving them land for livelihood and cash for liquor.... The big landlord-raja in all the instances belonged to the caste of the dominant section of landlords in the village. To the social, economic, and military power of the raja, 'democracy' had added political power. He has captured the instruments of local government. He now commands the panchayat and thus the various executive bodies at the block level. He has the services of an obsequious police force in the local thana. Mahavir Mahato of Belchhi had nothing to fear from the police. The mahanth of Chhaundadano had the police at his beck and call. When the labourers agitated for minimum wages, the police daroga would report to his bosses that 'Naxalites' had sneaked into the village.[54]

Recent Incidents

[Bihar] has notched up one deadly milestone after another with sickening regularity. Among the major [recent] massacres have been Parasbigha [February 2, 1980; 11 killed], Pipra [February 25,1980; 14 killed], Gaini [June 26,1982; 6 killed], Kaithibigha [May 1, 1985; 10 killed], Arwal [April 19, 1986; 23 killed], Kansara [July 8, 1986; 11 killed], and Darmia [October 10, 1986; 11 killed]. Roughly one caste-cum-class carnage has

[54]From Sinha, 'Class War, Not "Atrocities against Harijans"', pp. 150–1.

been perpetrated here every four months over the last nine years. [Much] of the tension in the area can be directly traced to the juxtaposition of...caste-based senas [and the various left organizations]. [Much horror] has accompanied every killing. In Belchi, the Kurmi raiders prepared a funeral pyre, lined up the Harijans, shot them and tossed the bodies in, one by one. In Pipra, raiders surrounded the Harijan hamlet, set fire to their houses and when men, women and children fled outside, it was only to be tossed right back into the inferno. Parasbigha was virtually a repeat.... In Jaitipur village [Nalanda district], men of the Lorik Sena had captured three extremists, brutally hacked their bodies into pieces and thrown them into a nearby river.... Mere killings have never been enough in Bihar...power [of the killers] must be demonstrated.... The root cause of almost all rural conflicts of course is land.[55]

Conflict over Violations of Individual and Community Rights

1. The 'Naxalite' movement took root in the Sahar block of the old Shahabad district (divided into Bhojpur and Rohtas districts in 1973–4) in the early 1970s. Among the numerous causes of local anger was the local practice that 'poor Harijan women who slept with Bhumihar scions got an extra bundle of grain to carry home. One of the reasons for growing unrest was the fact that the Bhumihar landlords of Chauri [a village in which considerable violence followed] were coercing the lower-caste female labourers to do harvesting work at nights for obvious sexual benefits'.[56]

2. In May 1981, the wife of Ram Pravesh Thakur (a barber) was raped by Tuntun Singh and co-villagers of Raj Kishori Singh of Masaurhi block (Patna district). The landlords managed to hush up the matter, and police also refused to record the case. In retaliation, the landless peasants (mostly of Scheduled-Caste backgrounds) decided not to work at the farm plot of Tuntun Singh, which remained barren throughout the year.[57]

3. It was a common local practice in Bihar that if one owed money to a landlord, the landlord in exchange would ask for one's 'clean daughter' at nights. That sort of thing is now 'being resisted'. Thus, the issues of agrarian conflict are 'status, dignity and economic'.[58]

Examples of Police Brutality

Early in the morning of 21 November, 1985, the police, tipped off by a landlord from Kacharia village, Sravan Pandit, attacked the *beldars* [Harijans working as manual labourers] of Ganga Bigha, killing three. About 35 armed policemen looted and destroyed almost everything in their way, beat the men and children with sticks

[55]Excerpts from a report in *India Today*, 31 December 1986, pp. 40–1.

[56]Reported in Mukerjee and Yadav, 'For Reasons of State', pp. 121–3.

[57]Reported in Chaudhry, 'Agrarian Unrest in Bihar', p. 52.

[58]Excerpts from a discussion with P.K. Krupakaran, special correspondent, *Indian Express*, Patna, 21 August 1986.

and *khantias* [iron rods sharpened at one end] and raped the women. The villagers' crimes: one of them had the courage to quarrel with Pandit over his agricultural wage; the landlord had earlier lodged a police complaint against some of the villagers for allegedly threatening him; and a number of *beldars* had wanted to cut the crop on a 3.75 bigha government plot across the road near their village, which another landlord of the area was claiming as his own. The police, of course, settled the matter in its own way: 40 persons were rounded up and, as the villagers have alleged, made to pose with rifles and booked under several sections of the Arms Act and the IPC [Indian Police Code].[59]

In another case, 23 people were killed on 19 April 1986, when police fired on a group of some 500 people in the small town of Arwal, Jehanabad subdivision, Gaya district. The group had gathered for a political meeting organized by the Mazdoor Kisan Sangram Samiti (MKSS), an organization of poor and landless peasants in the area. The meeting was a product of a prolonged conflict over a small piece of land—about a quarter of an acre. Over the years, the conflict over that land had pitted some nine poor, backward-caste families against an engineer in the Irrigation Department who was himself a Harijan, but was quite well-off and owned this piece of land. This simmering conflict eventually led to the arrest of members of two of the nine families who decided to lay claim to the land. At that point, the MKSS got involved. Meetings were held demanding lawful transfer of the land to the nine families and the release of those arrested. The meeting of 19 April was a product of that prolonged conflict. A civil-rights group that investigated the police firings on that meeting concluded that 'the massacre at Arwal was a barbarous and unprovoked firing at a peaceful meeting'. To understand why the Arwal incident happened, the report went on to note that 'we have to understand why people here are organizing themselves on questions of economic justice and human dignity and the response to this by the local elites and the state'. The civil-rights group also gathered evidence to suggest that the attack may have been a 'preplanned mass murder' as a way of thwarting the organizational efforts of local left groups.[60]

Example of Anarchic Conflict

Caste rivalry between Yadavs and Rajputs led to the brutal murder of forty-two Rajputs in May 1987 in Aurangabad district (Baghaura and Dalelchak villages). Seven families, including women and children, were killed. The brutality of the murders

---

[59]Reported in *Sunday*, 15–21 December 1985, p. 10.

[60]See People's Union for Democratic Rights, *Killings in Bihar*, pp. 32–49. The Arwal incident was reported and discussed widely elsewhere. See, for example, *Times of India*, Patna, 20–7 April 1986, and the editorial on 12 July 1986; *Deccan Herald*, 25 April 1986; *India Today*, 31 May 1986; *Economic and Political Weekly*, 31 May 1986.

was evident from on-the-scene reports: 'frightened womenfolk [were forced] to place their necks on the improvised chopping block and beheaded with country-made axes'.[61] The causes of the killings remain unclear, except for the fact that they were part of an ongoing feud between the two caste communities. Issues of land and members of the left parties may have been involved, but none of that was decisive. Both parties to the conflict were mainly middle or small peasants.[62] A telling piece of evidence, however, was the ineffectiveness of the local police. The growing tensions between the two communities had been evident for more than a month and some outbreak of violence was expected. The state police proved to be totally ineffective, even though the violence was perpetrated openly by a mob of some 700 people. A company of the Central Reserve Police Force (CRPF) that had been posted in the area to prevent violence had to be withdrawn two months before the killings for 'more urgent duties in Punjab'.[63]

Many more examples of the increasing conflict and violence of this nature in Bihar could be cited. The purpose of these specific examples is to illustrate the variety of agrarian conflicts that plague contemporary Bihar. The next problem is how to explain such egregious atrocities. Why has such savagery flourished in Bihar and not in, say, the neighbouring states of Uttar Pradesh and Orissa? And why have these conflicts intensified sharply over the past decade? Leaving the unique features of specific conflicts aside, even a general explanation for these struggles must be multicausal. This is best developed with reference to three factors: (i) Bihar's relative underdevelopment, (ii) the delegitimization of established patterns of domination in the countryside, and (iii) the slow but steady disintegration of the state.

The fact of Bihar's relative underdevelopment within India is well established. A number of important indicators of this have already been cited. The most important of these is worth reiterating: the steady decline in per capita rural income since the late 1960s. Economic failure in the agricultural sector has had a number of perverse consequences.

As noted earlier, Bihar's countryside continues to be dominated by such pre-capitalist economic relationships as usury, sharecropping, and bonded labour. Faced with the prospect of declining incomes in such a context, those who own land and dominate the social structure have sought to improve their incomes primarily by squeezing those below them. The natural instinct to want to maintain or improve one's standard of living has led not to increased investment and to growth in productivity but rather to a labour-repressive strategy:

[61]See *India Today*, 30 June 1987, p. 46.
[62]See *Economic and Political Weekly*, 13 June 1987, pp. 912–13.
[63]See *India Today*, 30 June 1987, p. 51.

In order to maintain their earlier level of prosperity the rural oligarchy resorted to intensification of exploitation. One feature frequently noted in this context was the forceful ejection of sub-tenants and settling the land with others for salami [a modified form of sharecropping]. In quite a few cases landlords attempted to reduce the area of land which was on customary lease to the agricultural labourers for their services.[64]

An increasing use of force to maintain the subservience of labour has been evident throughout this discussion. It indicates a surplus-appropriating strategy that in other historical circumstances has been labelled the 'second serfdom'.

The growing activism of Bihar's rural poor must be understood, in part, as an attempt to resist the imposition of even harsher patterns of domination. Absolute poverty may be politically debilitating, but even absolute poverty has limits. The steady pressure generated by nearly stagnant rural incomes and the simultaneous increase in agrarian militancy appear to be logically connected. Pradhan Prasad's argument on this point is quite persuasive. Those who hold that agrarian capitalism, or the 'green revolution', is the primary motive force behind the agrarian conflicts in rural India should study Bihar carefully. Probably the best thing that could happen to Bihar's poverty-stricken countryside would be the emergence of more owner-producer farms and an increase in irrigation, leading up to a little more of the green revolution and agrarian capitalism of the kind seen in western Uttar Pradesh.

The absence of economic dynamism provides the broad context for the increasing agrarian hostilities. However, it is not a sufficient explanation. It may explain the caste–class conflicts noted earlier, but it certainly will not do as an explanation for the growing police brutality. Even in regard to the former, an important fact must be noted: the agrarian struggles have been concentrated in the area that is 'backward' Bihar's least stagnant region, namely, the districts of the Patna division in central Bihar. If declining income were the sole causal variable, one would expect agrarian unrest to be concentrated in the most stagnant parts of Bihar, the north and the south. Clearly, other factors are at work. Barrington Moore, Jr., one may recall, had forcefully argued that levels of objective exploitation seldom can fully explain peasant proclivities to rebel. What also must be understood is the nature of the linkages, the subjective relationships between the dominant and the subjugated castes.[65]

The worst of the caste carnage over the past decade has been concentrated in the following seven districts: rural Patna, Nalanda, Gaya, Aurangabad,

---

[64]Prasad, 'Agrarian Violence in Bihar', p. 851.
[65]Barrington Moore, Jr., *Social Origins of Dictatorship and Democracy: Lord and Peasant in the Making of the Modern World*, Boston: Beacon Press, 1966, chapter 9.

Nawadah, Bhojpur, and Rohtas. These districts are all located within a 150-mile radius of the state capital of Patna. For administrative purposes, Bihar often is divided into six divisions (Table 10.5). The seven violence-prone districts compose one of these six divisions, namely, the Patna division. This is not to suggest that agrarian conflict does not occur elsewhere in Bihar. Tribal movements for regional autonomy, for example, are fairly strong in the Chotanagpur division. Elsewhere in Bihar, agrarian conflicts are far from unknown. It is important to remember that after Punjab, Bihar probably is India's most violent state today. Within this violent milieu, the worst of the caste killings have been in the Patna division. That naturally raises a question: Is there something distinctive about this part of Bihar?

Table 10.5 lists three agrarian indicators for the six divisions of Bihar. The Patna division stands out on two of the three measures. It has the highest proportion of the Scheduled-Caste population in Bihar, and it has the highest concentration of tube wells within Bihar. Patna, however, scores somewhere in the middle on the measure of concentration of landless labourers. A discussion of these and related indicators may provide some clues as to why Patna has such a high degree of agrarian activism.

The greater use of tube wells for irrigation in Patna confirms that agrarian commercialization and efforts to improve agricultural productivity within Bihar have proceeded furthest in the Patna division. (Perspective is important here. The tube-well concentration in Bihar, standardized for population, is about one-tenth of that in Punjab and nearly half of that in Uttar Pradesh. Even the most advanced division in Bihar, therefore, is not all that well developed agriculturally by all-India standards.) It is this distinctive quality of the central districts that has sometimes led some Marxist scholars to see the emergence of kulaks within Bihar and to relate agrarian

TABLE 10.5: Some Agrarian Indicators in Bihar according to Divisions

Division	Population of Scheduled Castes (as percentage of total population)	Tube-Well Concentration Index*	Agricultural Labourers (as percentage of rural population)
Patna	19.6	2.4	12.4
Tirhut	13.7	1.7	11.5
Darbhanga	14.8	1.4	13.3
Bhagalpur	11.6	.05	11.3
Kosi	13.1	.08	18.4
Chotanagpur	10.8	.01	7.6

Source: All the figures are computed from data in Government of Bihar, Directorate of Statistics and Evaluation, Bihar through Figures, 1981, Patna: Secretariat Press, 1985.
Note: *This index measures the area irrigated by tube wells and is standardized per 100,000 population.

conflicts to agrarian capitalism. The absurdity of that proposition should be emphasized. If this minimum level of agrarian commercialization were at the root of the escalating caste carnage, then much of western Uttar Pradesh and Haryana should by now be in the throes of a full-blown agrarian revolution. Because such is not the case, we need to look for other types of specific links between conditions of modest agricultural dynamism and agrarian conflict.

Some of the peculiarities of the pattern of agrarian commercialization in this part of Bihar should be noted. Even though the efforts to improve productivity have proceeded furthest here, there is no markedly greater concentration of landless labourers in this area (Table 10.5). It is a peculiar kind of 'agrarian capitalism' indeed in which 'proletarianization' does not keep pace. Two detailed studies of the area have further suggested that much of the labour really is not 'free labour'. One of those studies of the Patna district noted that 'payment of wages to agrarian labourers [is] in kind [and] very low wages, forced labour, [and] usury are all common.'[66] A more general survey reported the following: 'Though the old forms of bondage and servitude have practically disappeared, new forms have emerged in response to protective legislations in favour of the poor. Hence, though formally 'free', the majority are virtually dependent on the landowners for subsistence, and given the caste-hierarchy, also victims of caste oppression'.[67]

Thus, the agrarian picture is quite complex. Old patterns of domination have been eroding. Given the relatively low levels of agrarian dynamism, however, there have been renewed attempts to impose new patterns of bondage. It is in the resulting economic and social deprivation that one finds an important clue to the higher levels of agrarian unrest.

The modicum of agrarian dynamism that exists in the Patna division is primarily a product of the actions of backward-caste landowners. Because of a number of processes mentioned earlier—zamindari abolition, abandonment of lands by some Muslim landowners at the time of partition, and the sale of agricultural land necessitated by ceiling legislation—the patterns of landownership by castes in these areas are more mixed than are those in the north of Bihar, for example. The following description of the Patna district probably applies to many of the neighbouring districts as well:

In the western part of the Patna district...the landlords and nonpeasants belonging to upper castes dominate, while in the eastern part...the backward castes, especially Kurmi landlords and rich peasants, dominate.... Brahmins, Bhumihars, Rajputs and Kayasthas form the upper caste. They command strong influence in various political organizations.... A section of the backward castes are rich peasants who were ryots

---

[66]Chaudhry, 'Agrarian Unrest in Bihar', p. 52.
[67]See People's Union for Democratic Rights, *Killings in Bihar*, p. 2.

cultivators before 1952. After the Zamindari Abolition Act, they became owners of big holdings. Through cultivation, employment and other sources their incomes have gone up. They purchased land from ex-landlords at very cheap rates and through various means, they continued to enlarge their holdings. With their developing economic and social position, their political ambition too has grown. These new-style landowners are fiercely aggressive and despotic. They ruthlessly exploit the landless poor and middle peasants in numerous ways.[68]

It is this ruthlessness of a new agrarian class that is behind both the modest agrarian dynamism and the increasing agrarian conflict.

The backward castes as the new overlords enjoy less legitimacy in the social structure than do the traditional upper castes. The old relationships between the twice-born castes and the Scheduled Castes were relatively fixed and legitimized by well-established traditions, and they also had some built-in elements of reciprocity. Although much of the old system has been fundamentally damaged, some of it survives. It is no accident, therefore, that the only major caste in the area that does not have its own private army is the Brahmin. That is probably because the Brahmin landlords still are accorded some degree of deference by others and manage to accumulate their agricultural surpluses through established and accepted mechanisms.

By contrast, the newly emergent classes of backward-caste origin have a difficult time legitimizing their access to surpluses and their new positions of domination. Had the 'mode of surplus appropriation' shifted sharply to a market-oriented mode, as it did in the green-revolution states, the problem of creating a new perception of legitimacy would have been qualitatively different. Thus, it would appear that when new actors on the scene who did not enjoy traditional high status attempted to enforce the traditional patterns of domination—bonded labour, very low wages, usury and master-servant relationships—that effort provoked hostility among the landless lower castes.

It is important at this point to remember the other distinguishing characteristic of the Patna division mentioned earlier—the very high concentration of Scheduled Castes, the majority of whom are landless labourers. They not only are the poorest of the poor but also are socially ostracized, deemed to be the most inferior in matters of social standing. That double economic and social degradation has traditionally made these groups extremely subservient.

It is mainly on these Scheduled Castes that the newly emergent backward-caste landowners have sought to impose their domination. Although the Scheduled Castes may have been habitually subservient in the old elaborate system of traditional caste domination, they fail to see any legitimacy in

[68]Chaudhry, 'Agrarian Unrest in Bihar', p. 53.

this new domination. A growing population and slow economic growth have, in any case, made the problems of eking out a satisfactory livelihood quite difficult. Under these conditions of severe economic vulnerability and decreasing legitimacy of domination, the spread of new political values and organizations has finally taken root. I shall return to this issue of political mobilization later. For now, suffice it to note that challenges from the Scheduled Castes have increased and are being met with sharp hostility. The private caste armies are products of that hostility.

Challenges from the Scheduled Castes are seen by the landowning castes as threats to both their economic security and their social status. There has been a characteristic response from the landowning castes: 'how dare they challenge our authority?' Much of the agrarian conflict is about teaching the Scheduled Castes and their organizers a lesson in subservience, about keeping them 'in their place'. In sum, a social structure that is characterized by minimum economic dynamism, but within which established patterns of domination have lost their legitimacy, provides the context for growing agrarian conflicts in Bihar.

One final set of issues remains to be discussed: the political context. An intriguing aspect of the pattern of agrarian conflict in Bihar is that it is concentrated around the seat of power, the state capital of Patna. This has to be somewhat of a novel trend for students of agrarian radicalism. Peasant rebellions more often than not occur in the political periphery, where the reach of the state is weak, and where political spaces exist to mobilize the peasantry.[69] The explanation for this anomaly in Bihar, however, is not complex: The state has become so ineffective that even in its own backyard its grip is relatively weak.

Once the vitality of the established parties and the effectiveness of the police were seen to be declining, the urban-based counter-elite sensed the opening of new political spaces. As Bihar's infamous but recurring chief minister, Jagannath Mishra, admitted in an interview:

The poor are being neglected by all parties. My own party, Congress, is losing support among the Scheduled Castes and the Scheduled Tribes. The old left has also lost the initiative. Politics, however, does not like a vacuum. Someone will move in. That is why the new left parties are being successful. This is all quite new.[70]

Because these new oppositional elite are concentrated in and around the state capital, the existing agrarian tensions in the adjacent areas have provided

---

[69]See, for example, Eric Wolf, *Peasant Wars of the Twentieth Century*, New York: Harper & Row, 1969, especially the conclusion.

[70]Interview with Jagannath Mishra, former chief minister of Bihar, Patna, 22 August 1986. Most of the interview was in Hindi. The translation is my own.

them fertile ground for their organizing efforts. Every successful mobilization of these groups, however, is labelled 'Naxalite activity'. The activities of the private caste armies grow in proportion to the mobilization of the Scheduled Castes and landless labourers. Some of this conflict is beginning to look like full-fledged class warfare. A fair amount of the conflict, however, is quite anarchic—an uncontrolled police force venting its frustration on one group or another, armed private groups fighting personal vendettas, and, of course, ordinary criminals gathering their booty wherever they can.

Finally, a broader point should also be noted. A clear demonstration of the governmental ineffectiveness in Bihar has been the recurring failure of its policies. Here one does not think primarily of the failure of redistributive policies. Clearly, some degree of land reform would ease agrarian tensions, but failure on that front is common to much of India, and certainly not unique to Bihar. The policy ineffectiveness in Bihar is part and parcel of the overall absence of a developmental state. To be fair, it is difficult to disentangle cause and consequence in this syndrome of underdevelopment. However, government policy remains a crucial variable that could, if properly directed, begin to correct Bihar's underdevelopment. The recurring failure on that front has contributed to numerous problems in Bihar: a failing infrastructure, a low-calibre workforce turned out by ineffective educational institutions, and failure to distribute agricultural inputs in a manner that would stimulate agricultural productivity. The causes of all of these failures are, without doubt, complex. Behind each of them, however, we discover squabbling politicians, massive leakages of public funds through corruption, and, generally, a government that does not work. To the extent that Bihar's underdevelopment sets the context for its increasing agrarian conflicts, Bihar's ineffective government is very much a part of the overall causal framework.

CONCLUSION

I have attempted to document and explain the process of breakdown of political and social order in Bihar. There has been no implicit assumption here that the old order was desirable and the growing turmoil is not. The old caste order in the countryside was inequitable and oppressive. The seemingly stable political rule in the 1950s and 1960s was also rule by the few, a narrow elitist political order. Challenges to the power of the few have grown in both the civil society and the state, resulting in considerable turmoil. Unless one believes that broadening the power base necessarily entails violence, or that good things come out of turmoil, the breakdown of order in contemporary Bihar is a matter of great concern.

This analysis of breakdown has focused on two simultaneous but independent processes: the declining effectiveness of the state, and the increase in agrarian conflict in the civil society. Each of these processes has been caused by a number of forces. In my discussion of governmental ineffectiveness, I have stressed the undisciplined power struggles among the competing political elite as an important causal force. The absence of economic development and the growing delegitimization of traditional caste domination, due to the spread of democratic politics, have similarly been proposed as significant forces generating agrarian conflict. In addition, it is clear that governmental ineffectiveness and agrarian conflict exacerbate one another. Agrarian conflict has given rise to private armies that have further undermined the government's capacity to rule. Governmental ineffectiveness has opened up political spaces within which agrarian struggles are growing.

As one moves from Bihar to other states and towards a comparative analysis, two broad conclusions should be kept in mind: First, the absence of economic development, when combined with a growing population and with political mobilization, can have as corrosive an impact on the social and political order as can high rates of economic development. Those who continue to believe that political disorder in India is a function of economic development should look carefully at Bihar. Second, the disintegration of the state and the growing socio-economic conflict are partially independent processes that have combined to produce a crisis of governability in Bihar. How the parallel but independent forces in the state and civil society mould the overall pattern of political and economic change will be the theme in the cases discussed in subsequent chapters.

11

Growing Turmoil in an 'Advanced' State
Gujarat*

Gujarat is one of India's more prosperous states. Both governmental and political processes in Gujarat used to be relatively stable, but that stability became tenuous in the early 1970s. Violence as a tool to effect political change was rare in the 1970s, but that changed in the 1980s. In 1981, and again in 1985, politics in Gujarat came to be characterized by riots, arson, and other kinds of planned violence, and there was a growing sense that the state's capacity to govern had declined sharply. Whereas the dominant image of Gujarat politics in the 1960s was one of gentility, growing conflict and turmoil characterized the 1980s.

What happened? An answer is developed in this chapter by focusing on the political events of the 1980s. The answer has several components. The main issue that was widely recognized in the literature of the 1980s, had to do with the growing caste conflict between the two major communities in Gujarat: the Patidars and the Kshatriyas. As the socio-economic elite in the area, the Patidars traditionally have commanded both political power and relatively high status in the caste hierarchy. By contrast, most of the Kshatriyas are lower in the socio-economic hierarchy, but they are a significant numerical force. Over time, Kshatriya leaders forged an alliance with other disadvantaged groups, won elections, and gradually pushed the Patidars out of government. As the new leaders sought to use state power to alter the old patterns of socio-economic privilege, the Patidars countered with strong resistance, unleashing violence in the state. That planned violence was successful in the sense that the Patidars achieved their main goals. First, they were able to change the government leadership in 1986. More important, they were

*Originally published as 'Growing Turmoil in an "Advanced" State: Gujarat', in Atul Kohli, *Democracy and Discontent: India's Growing Crisis and Governability*, New York: Cambridge University Press, 1991, pp. 238–66.

able to define the boundaries within which future governments would have to work if they did not wish to invite further violence.

An analysis of political conflict in Gujarat as a conflict involving a privileged minority and an underprivileged majority, though essentially correct, would underemphasize two important issues. First, an important reason why the privileged minority was able to bring down a majority government in 1986 was the organizational weakness of the ruling party. It will be argued that the inability of the Congress government to mobilize political support for its own programme and stave off the Patidar opposition reflected the virtual absence of Congress as an organized political force in Gujarat. This argument will be more convincing when the findings for Gujarat are juxtaposed against the case of West Bengal in the next two chapters. The privileged minorities were excluded from governmental power in West Bengal, but with very different political results: a well-organized party was able to consolidate relatively coherent majority rule in that state.

Another important issue for this chapter is why much of the violence in both 1981 and 1985 was unleashed not against the 'backward' Kshatriyas but rather against the Scheduled Castes, and eventually against the Muslims. The exploration of that issue in this chapter will highlight the way in which violence was targeted against vulnerable groups, both to vent frustration and, more strategically, to undermine governmental legitimacy and destroy the electoral alliance on which Congress's power rested.

The findings reported here regarding the significance of party organization and the need to create and maintain winning electoral coalitions suggest that political variables are as important for understanding the growing turmoil in Gujarat as is the conflict between privileged and underprivileged groups. The crisis of governability in Gujarat clearly is not as serious as that in Bihar. The sporadic periods of intense turmoil, however, are indicative of changing political conditions. Both political factors and variables having to do with the social structure were found to be important in our analysis of the crisis in Bihar, albeit in a setting of nearly stagnant development. The presence of similar causal variables in the context of a growing economy in Gujarat strengthens the case for the 'autonomy of the political'.

An important caveat must be noted: this chapter depends heavily on secondary materials. I conducted many interviews in Gujarat in 1986[1] and

---

[1]I interviewed the following at some length in March and April of 1986: Babubhai Jasbhai Patel (former chief minister of Gujarat), Gandhinagar; Jinabhai Darjee (veteran Congress[I] leader in Gujarat), Ahmedabad (the original interview was in Hindi; the translation is my own); Amarsinhji Vaghela (minister of cooperation, government of Gujarat), Gandhinagar; Govindbhai J. Patel (MLA from the Kheda district), Gandhinagar; Madhevsinh Solanki (former chief minister of Gujarat), Gandhinagar; Hasmukh Patel (minister of education, government of Gujarat, and secretary, Gujarat Paradesh Committee, Congress[I]), Ahmedabad; Shivubhai

have reviewed some other primary materials, but the published studies of Gujarat are quite good. Although the interpretation developed here varies in subtle but important ways from the interpretation in previously published accounts, I have depended on those sources for basic information.[2]

SOME RELEVANT BACKGROUND

Along with Punjab and Maharashtra, Gujarat is one of India's more prosperous states, third in per capita income and second in per capita energy consumption. That prosperity is based in part on relatively high levels of industrialization. Until recently, textiles constituted the mainstay of Gujarati industry. During the 1980s, the industrial base was diversified, especially into oil-related industries. However, the state's prosperity also has a significant agricultural component. The proportions of land and manpower involved in cash-crop production are relatively high. The main cash crops of the area, tobacco, cotton, and oilseed, have fetched relatively high prices in the recent past, adding to the region's relatively high incomes. Gujarat's overall

---

Dave (correspondent for *Indian Express* [Ahmedabad]), Nadiad; Satyam Patel (secretary, Gujarat Pradesh Committee, Congress[R]), Ahmedabad. In addition, I held discussions with correspondents and editors of both the *Times of India* and *Indian Express* in Ahmedabad and with the following academics and observers of Gujarati politics: Sujata Patel, Praveen Sheth, Anil Bhatt, and Achyut Yagnik.

[2] Works by four scholars have been especially relevant: John R. Wood, Ghanshyam Shah, Sujata Patel, and Asghar Ali Engineer. See, for example, John Wood, 'Extra-Parliamentary Opposition in India', *Pacific Affairs*, 48(3), Fall, pp. 313–34; John Wood, 'Congress Restored? The KHAM Strategy and Congress (I) Recruitment in Gujarat', in John Wood (ed.), *State Politics in Contemporary India: Crisis or Continuity?*, Boulder, Colo.: Westview Press, 1984, pp. 197–227; John Wood, 'Gujarat's Anti-Reservation Riots, 1985', mimeograph, 1986, presented at the annual meeting of the Canadian Asian Studies Association, Winnipeg, 5 June 1986; Ghanshyam Shah, *Caste Association and Political Process in Gujarat: A Study of the Kshatriya Sabha*, Bombay: Popular Prakashan, 1975; Ghanshyam Shah, 'Caste Sentiments, Class Formation and Dominance in Gujarat', mimeograph, 1983, revised version to appear in Francine Frankel and M.S.A. Rao (eds), *Dominance and State Power in Modern India: Decline of a Social Order*, 2 vols, Oxford University Press, 1989–90; Sujata Patel, 'Debacle of Populist Politics', *Economic and Political Weekly* (hereafter referred to as *EPW*), 20 April 1985, pp. 681–2; Sujata Patel, 'Collapse of Government', *EPW*, 27 April 1987, pp. 749–50; Sujata Patel, 'The Ahmedabad Riots, 1985: An Analysis', unpublished, undated manuscript; Asghar Ali Engineer, 'From Caste to Communal Violence', *EPW*, 13 April 1985, pp. 628–30; and Asghar Ali Engineer, 'Communal Fires Engulf Ahmedabad Once Again', *EPW*, 6 July 1985, pp. 1116–20. The following sources were also helpful: Praveen Sheth, 'Caste, Class and Political Development', in D.T. Lakdwala (ed.), *Development in Gujarat: Problems and Prospects*, New Delhi: Allied Publishers, 1982, pp. 193–207; Subrata Mitra, 'The Perils of Promoting Equality: The Latent Significance of the Anti-reservation Movement in India', *Journal of Commonwealth and Comparative Politics*, November 1987, pp. 292–317; Howard Spodek, 'From Gandhi to Violence: Ahmedabad's 1985 Riots in Historical Perspective', mimeograph, Department of History, Temple University, 1987.

prosperity should not be allowed to mask the inequalities and poverty that also exist within the state. Scheduled Castes and Scheduled Tribes constitute more than 20 per cent of the state's population (Table 11.1). Living conditions for the many tribal groups, concentrated in the eastern belt of the state, are especially miserable. However, the Scheduled Castes in Gujarat probably are more advanced (certainly so in terms of their level of awareness concerning their rights, but also educationally and to some extent economically) than their counterparts in other states. The roots of such advancement go back to the relatively progressive educational policies of the former Maharaja of Baroda, as well as to the influence of Mohandas Gandhi, who was a native of Gujarat. It will be argued later that the relative upward mobility of select segments of the Scheduled Castes has provoked considerable hostility from the upper castes.

Tables 11.1 and 11.2 show data on caste and land distributions within the state. Brahmins and Banias are among the important upper castes and tend to be concentrated in the cities. Many of the first-generation nationalist leaders in the region and the state's earlier chief ministers, such as Morarji Desai (Brahmin), Jivraj Mehta (Bania), Balwantrai Mehta (Bania), and Hitendra Desai (Brahmin), belonged to these groups.[3] Until recently, the Banias were the dominant group in urban commerce and industry. When one talks about the 'gentler' age of Gujarati politics, therefore, it is important to remember the narrow political base on which the earlier arrangement rested. It was dominated by a few wealthy upper-caste men in Gujarat.

The Patidars are the dominant rural community.[4] Their numbers across the state are substantial, and as Table 11.2 shows, 75 per cent of them own and cultivate landholdings of 5 acres or more. Although a significant amount of the state's land is in very large holdings, this distribution can be somewhat misleading, because many of the very large holdings are concentrated in the arid north, where the quality of land is poor. The popular image of Gujarati agriculture as dominated by medium (5–15 acres) and large (16–50 acres) landholdings, owned mainly by the Patidars, is essentially correct. That is especially true of the central parts of mainland Gujarat. But even in peninsular Gujarat, which historically was dominated by the Rajputs, the Kunbis

[3]For a discussion of politics in Gujarat in the 1960s, see Devarat N. Pathak, 'State Politics in Gujarat: Some Determinants', in Iqbal Narain (ed.), *State Politics in India*, Meerut: Meenakshi Prakashan, 1968, pp. 122–33; and Praveen Sheth, 'Gujarat: The Case of Small Majority Politics', in Narain (ed.), *State Politics in India*, 2nd edn, Meerut: Meenakshi Prakashan, 1974, pp. 68–87.

[4]For studies of the Patidars of Gujarat, see David F. Pocock, *Kanbi and Patidar: A Study of the Patidar Community of Gujarat*, Oxford: Clarendon Press, 1972; and Anil Bhatt, 'Caste and Political Mobilization in a Gujarat District', in Rajni Kothari (ed.), *Caste in Indian Politics*, New Delhi: Orient Longman, 1973, pp. 299–339.

TABLE 11.1: Caste Distribution in Gujarat

High castes	
Brahmin	4.1
Bania	3.0
Rajput	4.9
Other highs	1.1
	13.1
Middle castes	
Patidar	12.2
Kunbi	0.1
	12.3
Lower castes	
'Lower Kshatriya'	24.2
Artisan castes	6.1
Other backwards	13.4
	43.7
Scheduled Castes	7.2 (7)*
Scheduled Tribes	14.2 (14)*
	21.4
Non-Hindus	
Muslims	8.5 (8)*
Other non-Hindus	1.0
	9.5
Total	100.0

Source: Figures adapted from 1931 census, as cited in the following: Ghanshyam Shah, *Caste Association and Political Process in Gujarat: A Study of the Kshatriya Sabha*, Bombay: Popular Prakashan, 1978, p. 9; John Wood, 'Congress Restored?: The KHAM Strategy and Congress(I) Recruitment in Gujarat', in J. Wood (ed.), *State Politics in Contemporary India: Crisis or Continuity?*, Boulder, Colo.: Westview Press, 1984, p. 203.

Note: *The figures in parentheses are from the 1971 census, when the Scheduled Castes, Scheduled Tribes, and Muslims were counted, but not the Hindu castes.

(historically a low-caste group, but now a *jati* or subcaste of the Patidars) emerged as a landowning group after the post-independence tenancy reforms.[5]

The Patidars of Gujarat were mobilized into the nationalist movement in the early part of this century. Their main leader, Sardar Vallabhbhai Patel, rose to be one of independent India's two most important Congressites, second only to Nehru. That gave the Gujarati Patels a powerful role within the Gujarat Congress. Although the top positions within the state were

[5]For a discussion of the land reform and its consequences, see Ghanshyam Shah, 'Caste Sentiments, Class Formation and Dominance in Gujarat'.

TABLE 11.2: Occupations and Landholding by Caste in Rural Gujarat

Caste	Occupation (%)			Landholding (%)		
	Cultivators	Labourers	Others	1–5 acres	5–15 acres	16 acres or more
Brahmin	52	4	44	41	32	27
Bania	30	5	65	55	24	21
Rajput	72	15	13	42	35	23
Patidar	81	7	12	25	42	33
Koli ('lower Kshatriya')	62	24	14	66	23	11
Artisan castes	48	36	16	42	33	25
Other lower castes	45	33	22	43	41	10
Scheduled Castes	43	39	18	69	26	5
Scheduled Tribes	67	21	12	77	21	2
Muslims	44	35	21	36	45	19

Source: Adapted from a survey of 15,680 households conducted by the Centre for Social Studies, Surat, Gujarat, and presented in Ghanshyam Shah, 'Caste, Class and Reservation', *Economic and Political Weekly*, 19 January 1985, p. 133.

occupied by Brahmin or Bania leaders, many districts were controlled by the Patidars. After independence, as the significance of electoral politics increased, the Patidars came to play an even more important role.[6] It probably is only a small exaggeration to say that the Patidars, in alliance with Brahmins and Banias, dominated the regional Congress party and thus Gujarati politics well into the 1970s.

The main challenge to the power of the Patidars in recent years has come from the Kshatriyas. The designation 'Kshatriyas' was essentially political in origin, but has now taken on caste connotations.[7] As seen in Table 11.1, Rajputs are another important high caste in the area. Many Rajputs in pre-independence India belonged to princely families, and most of them cherished their cultural traditions that glorified martial pursuits. Many of the Rajputs formerly owned large tracts of land, parts of which were lost in the post-independence land reforms. The Rajputs never became an integral part of the nationalist movement; as local princes, they were often allied with the British, and some of Congress's programmes, such as land reforms, conflicted with their interests.

Outside of the Congress mainstream, the Rajputs sought to mobilize their own political force. As independence approached, it was clear that voter numbers were going to be crucial for winning elections and thus for state power and patronage. In one of the earliest examples of a 'caste federation',

[6]See Myron Weiner, *Party Building in a New Nation: The Indian National Congress*, University of Chicago Press, 1967.

[7]For a discussion of the rise of the Kshatriya movement, see Ghanshyam Shah, *Caste Association and Political Process in Gujarat*.

the Rajput leaders mobilized several lower-caste groups, especially Kolis and Bariyas, as a 'vote bank' of fellow Kshatriyas. Tables 11.1 and 11.2 show that these lower castes were numerically significant and that they were mainly small farmers. Many of them were actually sharecroppers on Patidar lands. The mobilization of Kshatriyas brought together groups with widely disparate socio-economic positions, but shared cultural traditions and a common antipathy to the Patidars and their organization, the Congress party. As will be discussed later, that Kshatriya unity fell apart for about a decade (1965–75), but was reestablished, though with important differences, in the 1980s.

The current state of Gujarat was part of the larger state of Bombay until 1960, when Bombay was divided into two states: Gujarat for Gujarati speakers and Maharashtra for Marathi speakers.[8] Until well into the 1960s, the narrow alliance that ruled Gujarat—Brahmins and Banias, mainly in the major cities, and Patidars, mainly in the districts—had been cemented by a well-organized Congress party. Because the levels of mobilization among the lower strata were relatively low, and intra-elite harmony was high, the area's politics had an aura of gentility.[9] As Figure 11.1 shows, there clearly was more than an aura; there was a degree of political stability, with depth. Gujarat experienced very low levels of political violence throughout the 1950s and 1960s, not only in comparison with Gujarat in the 1980s but also compared with many other Indian states during that earlier time period.

The gentlemen elite of Gujarat ruled relatively peacefully because they tended to agree with each other on significant issues and because they enjoyed unquestioned dominance in the social structure. Democracy, however, especially when significant socio-economic spoils are available from the state, has a way of quickly bringing excluded groups into the political arena. That is precisely what happened in Gujarat.

The changing caste composition of the Gujarat Legislative Assembly between 1960 and 1980 provides a good indicator of the changing power positions of various Gujarati communities.[10] Three trends are especially noteworthy. First, the higher castes of Brahmins and Banias slowly began to lose political influence. Second, although the middle landowning castes

---

[8]For a historical discussion of the creation of Gujarat, see John R. Wood, 'The Political Integration of British and Princely Gujarat', unpublished PhD thesis, Columbia University, 1972.

[9]Writing in the early 1970s, Praveen Sheth observed that 'modest and moderate, Gujarat politics has on the whole been gentle and peaceful in tradition and commercial in style and technique. Its predominant feature is moderation, and its keynote, its secular character. It has been devoid of anti-Brahminism or rabid caste and communal rivalries'. See Sheth, 'Gujarat: The Case of Small Majority Politics', p. 68.

[10]These figures are derived from Sheth, 'Caste, Class and Political Development', Table 1, p. 198.

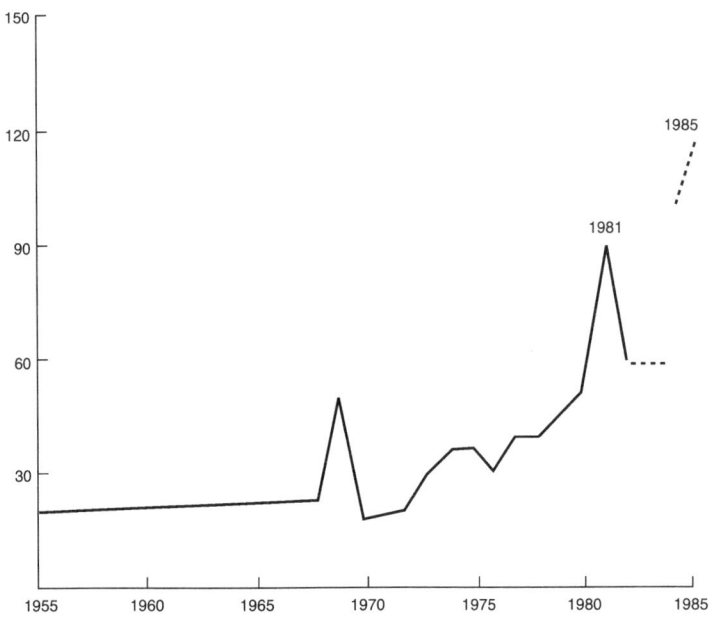

FIGURE 11.1. Political Violence in Gujarat, 1955–85
(number of riots per million population)

Note: The pre-1968 figures are based on average figures for the preceding decade. The figure for 1985 is provisional. No official data are available beyond 1982.
Source: Ministry of Home Affairs, Government of India, *Crime in India*, various years, New Delhi: Government Press.

of Patidars managed to maintain their dominance well into the 1970s, their legislative seats declined from 24 to 18 between 1975 and 1980. By contrast, Kshatriyas and other backward castes steadily improved their access to positions of power.

For the Kshatriyas, 1967 was the big year. Between 1962 and 1967, their legislative seats nearly doubled, from 9 to 17. As discussed earlier, the national position of Congress deteriorated throughout the mid-1960s, leading up to the watershed elections of 1967, when Congress lost control of several Indian states. Gujarat was not one of those states; Congress retained its control over the Gujarat Legislative Assembly. As Table 11.3 shows, however, the strength of the Congress party declined between 1962 and 1967, and a right-of-centre party, the Swatantra, improved its position significantly. Politically mobilized Kshatriyas, unable to penetrate the Patidar-dominated Congress, threw in their lot with some dissenting Patidars and the Swatantra party. Although issues of ideology were not of great significance in determining which groups became aligned with which parties, the fact that Kshatriyas joined a right-leaning party reflected that the Kshatriya leadership, though increasingly challenged by lower-caste representatives, still was in the hands of former princely Rajputs.

Whereas the 1967 elections in Gujarat clarified the growing power of previously excluded groups like the Kshatriyas and of non-Congress parties, the 1969 split in the national Congress party had a decisive impact on Gujarati politics. The power struggle at the national level pitted Indira Gandhi against the Congress old guard, including Morarji Desai. Gujarat was part of Morarji's regional power base. When the national Congress party split, therefore, most of the Congress legislators elected in 1967, as well as senior party leaders, joined Desai in shunning Indira's new Congress and chose to ally themselves with Congress(O).[11] The politics of the state entered a confusing stage of shifting coalitions and alignments that would not be clarified for nearly a decade, until the 1980 elections.

The details of that decade of confusion are not important for our purposes.[12] What is important is to remember that it was a decade of major power realignments within Gujarat. Whereas prior to 1969 Gujarat had been ruled by the old undivided Congress and the upper castes, such as the Brahmins, Banias, and Patidars, Indira Gandhi's new Congress emerged after 1980 at the helm of the state, aligned with many of the state's previously disadvantaged groups, especially the lower-caste Kshatriyas. Something else was also replaced during that period: a relatively well-organized Congress party. Its place was taken by a force more akin to an unorganized populist movement. Those two changes with regard to who ruled and how power was organized, in turn, set the stage for the eruption of the major conflicts and violence of the 1980s.

After the Congress party split in 1969, the major contenders for power within Gujarat became Congress(O), Swatantra, and Indira's Congress, Congress(R). In order to further destabilize the weakened Congress(O) government, Swatantra, with its significant minority within the legislature, intensified its attempts to lure defectors from Congress(O). Congress(R), in control in New Delhi, but fairly weak in the Gujarat legislature, attempted its own defection game, trying to draw people away from both Congress(O) and Swatantra. The ruling Congress(O), in turn, took the political battle to the streets and tried to mobilize public opinion against the 'defection game'. As rival parties competed for the support of legislators and for public opinion, the political situation became turbulent. For a complex set of reasons that have been analysed elsewhere,[13] hostilities broke out between Hindus and

[11]Interview with Babubhai Jasbhai Patel (former chief minister of Gujarat), Gandhinagar, 8 March 1986.

[12]See, for example, Praveen Sheth, *Patterns of Political Behaviour in Gujarat*, Ahmedabad: Sahitya Mudranalaya, 1976.

[13]See Ghanshyam Shah, 'Communal Riots in Gujarat', *EPW*, Annual Number, 1970.

TABLE 11.3: Electoral Performances of Major Parties in Gujarat Legislative Assembly Elections, 1962–85

Party	1962		1967		1972		1975[a]		1980		1985	
	Seats	Vote (%)	Seats	Vote (%)	Seats	Vote (%)	Seats	Vote (%)	Seats	Vote (%)	Seats	Vote (%)
Congress	113	51	93	46	140	51	75	41	141	50	149	55.5
Congress(O)[b]	–	–	–	–	16	24	56	24	21	22	14	19.3
Swatantra	26	24	64	38	0	–	2	2	0	–	–	–
Jan Sangh[c]	0	1	1	2	3	9	18	9	9	13	11	15.0
Independents	7	10	4	10	8	12	15	12	10	10	8	9.3
Others	8	14	5	4	1	4	15	12	0	5	0	0.9
Total	154	100	168	100	168	100	181	100	181	100	182	100

Source: Compiled from various sources, including the report of the Electoral Commission.
Note: [a]Formed in 1969 after the split in the Indian national Congress. Congress(O) was part of the Janata Morcha in 1973 and the Janata Party in 1980 and 1985. The figures reported for Congress(O) in 1980 and 1985 are more accurately figures for the Janata Party.
[b]The opposition to Congress in 1975 fought as a coalition called the Janata Morcha. The main partners in that coalition were Congress(O), Jan Sangh, and several independent legislators.
[c]The Jan Sangh merged into the Janata Party in 1977, broke away in 1980, and was returned as the Bharatiya Janata Party in 1984.

Muslims, leading to the deaths of some 1500 people. As Figure 11.1 shows, that was the first significant increase in the level of rioting and violence in Gujarat politics. That the first outbreak of violence coincided with growing intra-elite political conflict suggests that the civil disorder was more a product of political conditions than of growing socio-economic conflict.

As Indira Gandhi consolidated her power nationally, both Congress(O) and Swatantra legislators in Gujarat began looking at Congress(R) as a potential winner. The first significant change came in 1970, when a group of Swatantra legislators, many of lower Kshatriya background, defected to the new Congress(R). The legislators involved in that defection were too few to create any major political upset. The significance of the transition lay elsewhere: That defection revealed the growing political fragmentation among the Kshatriyas and marked the beginning of a move by lower Kshatriyas towards Indira Gandhi's Congress.[14] Some people within Congress(O), especially those who had been excluded from the perks of power, also began flirting with Congress(R). Indira's Congress began taking on the look of a party made up of previously excluded groups. As Congress(O), Swatantra,

[14]For a good discussion of how the old Kshatriya Sabha fragmented, essentially between the more privileged Rajputs and the less privileged Bariyas, and how a direct patronage-based identification with Indira's Congress reemerged, see A.H. Somjee, 'Social Cohesion and Political Clientelism among the Kshatriyas of Gujarat', *Asian Survey*, 21(9), September 1981, pp. 1000–10.

and Jan Sangh moved closer together politically at the national level, Indira Gandhi and her supporters, both nationally and in Gujarat, gave the political conflict a sharper ideological twist, suggesting that it was a battle of the Right versus the Left. Indira's adoption of the slogan *garibi hatao* for the 1971 national elections finally confirmed that the new Congress had taken a stand decisively to the left of the old Congress.

The widespread electoral appeal of Indira Gandhi's left-leaning populism is well known. Her national victory transformed the trickle of defections to her party in Gujarat into a flood. It was around that time that up-and-coming Gujarati leaders like Madhav Singh Solanki joined Indira Gandhi's Congress.[15] Congress(O) put up a last-minute fight to keep Gujarat under its control, but to no avail. After several short governments and a brief period of presidential rule, Indira's Congress came to power with a huge majority–140 seats in a house of 168 (Table 11.3).

It is important to note that the coalition between the old Congress and Jan Sangh was defeated, but by no means obliterated. As is clear from Table 11.3, the combined popular vote of those two parties still was over 30 per cent of the total. More important, many of the most significant socio-economic groups in Gujarat, such as the Patidars, Banias, and Brahmins, though quite fragmented among themselves, were, on balance, closer in spirit to those old, well-established parties. The political support of the Kshatriyas was similarly divided, though lower Kshatriyas were increasingly attracted to Indira's Congress, both because of the opportunities available within it and because of Indira's anti-Morarji, anti-establishment populism. Although the community's battle lines were still quite fuzzy, an outline was beginning to emerge: the disadvantaged majority aligned themselves with Indira Gandhi, and the privileged minority remained with the Congress(O)–Swatantra–Jan Sangh combine.

The pattern of the political battle was much more clearly drawn. Indira's Congress stood in opposition to the old forces loyal to Morarji. Although the old guard lost a battle, it was not ready to concede the war. It took the opposition only a short time to realize that the rise of Indira Gandhi had changed the rules of electoral politics. The old game of manipulating 'vote banks' was gone; the name of the new game was competitive populism. The capacity of the old established elite to command the support of the lower strata had been diminishing throughout the 1960s. Indira Gandhi was a product of that change, but she also hastened the trend. The Banias, Brahmins, and Patidars of Gujarat could no longer readily mobilize electoral majorities, certainly not through the old methods and especially not when

---

[15]Interview with Madhav Singh Solanki (former chief minister of Gujarat), Gandhinagar, 11 March 1986.

confronted with Indira Gandhi's widespread appeal to the disadvantaged majority. As the old guard contemplated a political comeback, two things must have been clear to them: They would have to do it quickly, before Indira's new coalition took root, and they would have to do it with their own form of populism.

It is against that background that we must interpret the two months of civil disorder in 1974, the Navnirman ('reconstruction' or 'social regeneration') movement that succeeded in dislodging the majority Congress(R) government in 1974. The details of that movement and the civil disorder are available elsewhere.[16] What is important for us to note is that it was a quintessential political conflict, aimed at simultaneously influencing public opinion and toppling the Congress(R) government; it was led mainly by students and other youths, but it was encouraged and supported by the parties out of power, Congress(O) and Jan Sangh, and by those Congress(R) factions that had lost out in the division of spoils. John R. Wood captured the purposive, political quality of those disorders:

Seventy-three days of agitation had left 103 people dead, mostly by police firing, 310 injured, and 8,237 under arrest in Gujarat. And yet, within a week, colleges reopened, students became busy with examinations, and normality returned. The Gujarat agitation, having achieved the two goals of removing the Patel ministry and dissolving the Gujarat assembly, ended as quickly as it had began.[17]

It was as if the tap of violence could be turned on and off for achieving specific political goals. Those who hold the view that the growing political conflict in India reflects irrational, anomic behaviour, or more fundamental socio-economic conflicts, should ponder such examples. The violence was purposeful, and its goal was explicitly political, namely, to remove a government from power.

Indira's Congress lost considerable support in the state election that followed in 1975. Although the new Congress won more seats than any other party (Table 11.3), it was the Janata Morcha, a loose coalition among Congress(O), Jan Sangh, and others, that was able to form a government. Not only had the democratically elected government of 1972 been pushed out of power by street violence, but in the process the opposition had gained enough public support to win the next election. That mode of political change helps illustrate two important points.

[16]See, for example, D.E. and R.W. Jones, 'Urban Upheaval in India: The 1974 Navnirman Riots in Gujarat', *Asian Survey,* November 1976, pp. 1012–33; Ghanshyam Shah, *Protest Movements in Two Indian States,* Delhi: Ajanta Publications, 1977; and Wood, 'Extra-Parliamentary Opposition in India'.

[17]Wood, 'Extra-Parliamentary Opposition in India', p. 319.

First, the success of the Navnirman movement revealed the political weakness of the populist coalition Indira Gandhi had hurriedly put together. The new Congress party in Gujarat had no organization. Praveen Sheth has argued that Congress(R) during that period had 'no party apparatus, no cadre of active members [and] no party offices in sight in districts'.[18] The new Congress(R) could win elections because of Indira Gandhi's personal, populist appeal, but could do little in the way of systematic mobilization to confront a militant opposition. That capacity would change over time, especially after the Emergency, when Sanjay's goons were incorporated within Congress, but in the early 1970s Indira's Congress found itself quite vulnerable to a powerful, mobilized minority.

A second point had long-range significance. An anti-democratic method of turning governments out of power was in the making. That pattern would be repeated in the future. A powerful minority within Gujarat had never acknowledged the legitimacy of Indira's new Congress. Instead of serving as a loyal opposition and accepting electoral verdicts, the opposition took to the streets. Some of that opposition was spontaneous. However, it could not have begun and ended with such precision if it had not been supported by powerful groups, namely, opposition parties with backing from resourceful upper-caste men in Gujarat. Although Indira Gandhi is often held responsible for weakening India's democracy, a non-partisan observer must note the similar proclivities of those in opposition to Indira. Instead of assigning the primary blame to one party or another, it seems fairer to argue that in addition to the increasing power conflicts, anti-democratic tendencies had begun to spread in the polity as a whole.

It is well known that the defeat of Congress(R) in the Gujarat elections in 1975 contributed significantly to Indira's decision to proclaim a national Emergency later that same year. That does not concern us for the moment. What does concern us are the political changes that took place within Gujarat politics between 1975 and 1980, that is, during and immediately following the Emergency. Leaving aside the details once again, the process of political realignment that had begun in 1969 quickened during that period, leading up to the crystallization of an alliance between Indira Gandhi and the disadvantaged groups in Gujarat.

Paralleling the political instability at the national level, four different governments were formed in Gujarat between 1975 and 1980. Interesting patterns of alignments between parties and communities were revealed in an

[18]Sheth, *Patterns of Political Behaviour in Gujarat*, p. 135. Congress's internal weakness, caused by intra-elite factionalism, was also revealed in a number of interviews. For example, Jinabhai Darjee told me in an interview in Ahmedabad, 10 March 1986, that though he was a Congressite, he had supported the Navnirman movement.

important body of data collected by John Wood. The two Janata governments formed in that period had fourteen and sixteen ministers from the privileged castes (Banias, Brahmins, and Patidars) and five and seven ministers from the less privileged groups (Kshatriyas, other backward castes, Muslims, and Scheduled Castes and Tribes). The numbers in the two Congress ministries between 1975 and 1980 were nearly the reverse: fifteen and eleven from the less privileged groups, and seven each from the upper castes.[19]

Although 'polarization' would be too strong a term, it is clear that a two-party system of sorts had emerged, one party aligned with the more privileged socio-economic groups, and the other with the less privileged. The Janata coalition came to be associated with the old established groups, whose influence was steadily declining; Indira's Congress, on the ascent, was increasingly identified as a party of the underprivileged.

THE RIOTS OF 1981

In the summer of 1980, the Legislative Assembly elections marked another important transition in Gujarat politics. As is shown in Table 11.3, Indira's Congress re-emerged as the state's dominant party. The only thing the new Congress in Gujarat shared with the pre-1967 Congress was the name. The new Congress party had virtually no organization, and its social base was sharply different from that of the Brahmin–Bania–Patel-dominated pre-1967 Congress.

The issue of the decline of Congress's organization has been documented in several chapters. As far as the issue of the changing social base of Congress is concerned, only a few more facts need to be added.[20] Whereas the upper castes provided nearly 60 per cent of the Congress legislators in 1967, by 1980 the number was under 30 per cent. The flip side of that change was just as dramatic. The lower castes, tribes, and Muslims held nearly 40 per cent of the seats in the 1967 Legislative Assembly, but by 1980 they held more than two-thirds of the seats. There were parallel shifts in the allocations of the powerful ministerships, as noted earlier. The fact that the number of Kshatriya legislators tripled between 1967 and 1980, and that the new chief minister, Madhav Singh Solanki, was a lower-caste Kshatriya, could not have escaped anyone's attention. Finally, those changing patterns reached into the lower ranks of the government; most of the local government positions at the level of the district had also been appropriated by the Kshatriyas.

It would be only a small exaggeration to suggest that the Kshatriyas had finally begun to push the Patels out of the sprawling state apparatus of Gujarat. The Patels, however, continued to control much of Gujarat's agriculture,

---

[19]Calculated from Wood, 'Congress Restored?', table 8.3, p. 209.
[20]Derived from Wood, 'Congress Restored?', table 8.6, p. 215.

numerous cooperatives, such as dairies, educational institutions, some trade and commerce, and the press. The lines of conflict were drawn. Those who controlled most of Gujarat's socio-economic resources had lost control over the government to the less privileged but numerically significant groups.

Both the 1981 and 1985 riots must be understood within this broad context. It is important to stress that the focus on the Congress–Kshatriya combine against the Patels provides no more than a framework for the political violence that followed. Not surprisingly, the specific patterns of violence, in terms of who attacked whom and with what motive, were extremely varied. Once the government's legitimacy and capacity to maintain order declined, violence broke out in many areas.

In spite of the fact that the Solanki government came to power in mid-1980 with a sizable popular majority (control over 141 seats in a house of 181), within a few months, riots and violence had spread through parts of central Gujarat. The bulk of that rioting took place in the winter of 1981, from January–March, and it shows up as a dramatic blip in Figure 11.1. Nearly 50 people, mostly of Scheduled-Caste origins, were killed. The number of people injured was in the thousands, and property damage was on the order of hundreds of thousands of rupees.[21] What happened? Why did a democratically elected government, with a significant majority, come under attack? More important, why was it unable to control such an outbreak of violence?

The rioting took place mainly in cities, especially Ahmedabad, but also in neighbouring rural areas, particularly the districts of Ahmedabad, Mehsana, Kheda and Bharuch.[22] The most obvious cause of the urban riots was dissatisfaction among medical students in Ahmedabad over the government's reservation policies. Those policies reserved a certain number of admissions for disadvantaged groups, mainly the Scheduled Castes and Tribes, but also some of the backward castes. Medical students, mostly from the upper castes, and especially Patels, had filed a lawsuit in 1979 to test the legality of such quotas. The court issued its verdict in 1980, and the students lost. Once the new government was in power, students, again mostly of Patel background, regrouped and made specific demands on the state government to reverse its reservation policies.[23] The government, hoping to appease the students,

---

[21]Based on press reports, especially those in the *Times of India,* during February and March 1981.

[22]In addition to interviews and press accounts, the following discussion of the 1981 riots depends heavily on an excellent field survey conducted by a Bombay-based human-rights group: Committee for the Protection of Democratic Rights, *The Gujarat Agitations and Reservations,* Bombay: Super Book House, 1981 (hereafter referred to as CPDR report).

[23]For a more specific discussion, see I. P. Desai, 'Anti-reservation Agitation and Structure of Gujarat Society', *EPW,* 2 May 1981; and Mitra, 'The Perils of Promoting Equality', especially pp. 300–2.

quickly offered some concessions. Instead of accepting the compromise, however, the students took that offer to be a sign of weakness and increased both their demands and the intensity of their agitations.

The students wanted to abolish all reservations. They took their fight to the streets. The medical college was closed. Fighting between Patel and Scheduled-Caste medical students broke out and set off a caste conflict in the neighbourhood. After Harijan workers in textile mills were attacked by Patel students, the workers went on strike. The students pressed on with their demand for withdrawal of all reservations. The urban middle classes, many of whom were Patels, and the press, partly controlled by Patels, joined the fray; they were generally hostile to the Solanki government and sympathetic to the students. A number of professional unions, such as the Gujarat association of university teachers, a union of police inspectors, and a secondary-school teachers' union controlled by the Bharatiya Janata Party (formerly Jan Sangh), came out in support of the students' demand. Within a period of two months, the riots had spread farther and police were liberally firing tear-gas shells.

The rapid escalation of the conflict revealed that forces other than a few dissatisfied medical students were involved. The broader nature of the conflict was further evident in parallel developments in the rural areas. A report by the Committee for the Protection of Democratic Rights (CPDR), for example, documented many other incidents of upper-caste violence against the Scheduled Castes around that time.[24] Most such incidents involved Patel landowners burning and destroying Harijan communities and, on occasion, even killing and raping.

How does one account for such rioting and violence? Why was the violence aimed at the Scheduled Castes? The reason the situation is especially puzzling is that the broad political conflict in the state was mainly between the Patels and the Kshatriyas. Perhaps an answer can best be arrived at by first focusing narrowly on the perpetrators and the victims of violence, and then moving outward to link those findings with the broader social and political context.

The Patels in Gujarat are subdivided into numerous jatis. One major division, that between the Leuva and the Kadwa Patels, is especially relevant for our purposes. The Leuva Patels are the highest sub-group within the Patidars, whereas the Kadwa Patels occupy a somewhat lower position, in terms of both income and caste status. Both Leuva and Kadwa Patels had lost out in the long process of political change in Gujarat over the preceding several decades. During the recent conflicts, however, it was the Kadwa Patels, especially the youth of that sub-caste, who were the most aggressive.

[24]CPDR report.

That becomes understandable if one focuses on the differences between the two sub-castes.

Many of the Leuva Patels had long been used to being at the top of the social ladder. They occupied important positions in commerce, trading, education, publishing, producer cooperatives and even agriculture. The loss of political power was a significant blow to them, but not as significant as for the Kadwa Patels. The latter were well entrenched in cash-crop production and depended on government subsidies and price supports. Their children depended on education to lead to upward mobility and public-sector employment. Access to education and employment was heavily dependent on which party was in power. For the highest elite, loss of control over the government was primarily a loss of power as a valued end in itself. By contrast, the same loss of power for Kadwa Patels had more direct material consequences—loss of access to the education and employment opportunities controlled by the state. Thus, the reaction of Kadwa Patels to loss of power was more intense.

In addition to these state-related material considerations, the respective cultural orientations of the two sub-castes also differ. Having long been at the top of the social heap, many of the Leuva Patels cultivated a noblesse oblige that would discourage the youth of 'good families' from participating in the anti-reservation violence. By contrast, the Kadwa Patels are cut from a somewhat rougher social cloth. Many of them do not shy away from aggression and violence as means to achieve their political goals.

Many of the agriculturalists of Kadwa Patel background come into regular contact with members of the Scheduled Castes, who serve as labourers in the fields of the Patels. It is important to differentiate the various sub-groups within the Gujarati Harijans. Bhangis and Chamars are generally lower in the hierarchy than the Vankars. The latter—weavers who lost their traditional occupations with the arrival of textile mills—were the main victims of caste violence, both in villages and in cities. The Vankars often work as farm hands in the countryside and as textile workers in Ahmedabad. As mentioned earlier, the Vankar sub-group had experienced upward mobility because of better access to education and because of Gandhian reforms.

The main line of conflict in the caste riots was not between the highest and lowest groups, that is, not between the Leuva Patels and the Bhangis or Chamars; those groups basically stayed out of active conflict. The direct conflict was between the Kadwa Patels, who felt threatened, and the somewhat upwardly mobile Vankars. The Kadwa Patels often attacked Vankar colonies in the villages. Similarly, it was the young, educated, aggressive Patels who were willing to challenge the educated Harijan youth in the cities.

The main causes of the riots now begin to emerge. The violence was perpetrated by groups who ranked below the highest socio-economic groups, but still were distinctly elite in terms of landownership, education, and caste status. Their increasing loss of power in the state threatened such groups the most. They were the ones whose life-chances were profoundly dependent on government patronage. That access had been decisively blocked by a coalition of lower social groups. The result was a broadly felt dissatisfaction with the new ruling coalition. Despite having been democratically elected, the new government's legitimacy in the eyes of those displaced groups was in question. They were eager for any opportunity to vent their dissatisfaction. The specific incidents did not really matter; the issue of reservations only provided an excuse. The broader, underlying issue was a grave sense of frustration at losing control over the society's main milk cow: the state.

Still unresolved is the question why the caste violence was directed against a segment of the Scheduled Castes and not against the Kshatriyas. The issue is best understood by keeping in mind that the perpetrators of violence were social groups that increasingly felt pressured from many directions. Not only had lower castes and groups wrenched the state out of the hands of the Kadwa Patels, but even the lowest castes had been moving upward. They had begun to demand respect, dignity, and even a greater share of material rewards. Segments of the Patel population thus felt increasingly bitter and threatened. They lashed out at groups that were both upwardly mobile (and thus threatening) and relatively vulnerable.

Groups like the Bhangis and Chamars were not victimized; they were extremely vulnerable, but they were not threatening. Groups like the Kshatriyas were threatening, but they were not especially vulnerable. Their numbers were large, many of their representatives were in direct control of the state, and they could defend themselves well.

To move now to the broader political context of civil disorder, the rioting and violence had a considerable indirect impact on the government in power. It revealed the government's weakness and probably contributed to its delegitimization in the eyes of some segments of the Gujarati population. More important, the sustained rioting revealed the latent potential of an excluded but powerful minority. The Patels of Gujarat had made a statement: Even though the Patels were out of power, any government would be well advised to take their interests into account. Political violence was used by the socially powerful to attempt to define the boundaries of formal state power.

That leads to a final question: Why was a government with a huge majority unable to cope with insurrection from a minority group? One factor was the power the Patels derived from their socio-economic resources, but another factor in the equation was the organizational weakness of the Solanki government.[25] As already noted, the Congress party in Gujarat by

---

[25]One of the few analysts of Gujarat who has also noted this point, but with reference to the 1985 riots, is Sujata Patel. See Patel, 'The Ahmedabad Riots, 1985', especially pp. 21–2.

that time had no organization. That had several consequences. First, the leadership of the Congress party was highly factionalized. Most leaders in Gujarat well understood that the main reason that Solanki was head of the government was because he was favoured by Indira Gandhi. Congress's huge majority in Gujarat elections was not solely Solanki's doing; it also reflected Indira Gandhi's popularity. That knowledge weakened Solanki's legitimacy vis-à-vis other Congress leaders waiting in the wings for Solanki's destruction. Instead of being able to fight a militant minority opposition with a unified political force, Solanki had to worry about his own divided political house. Second, Solanki had no system at his command and had little capacity to organize grass-roots support. He was heading a party without cadres or even committed, active members. Congress could secure votes because of a combination of Indira's mass appeal, caste sentiments, and promises of patronage. However, that basis of support was quite tenuous compared with the power resource that would have derived from committed members in a well-organized party. Without the latter, Solanki could not mobilize his supporters to confront the opposition politically. His support was relatively shallow and unorganized. His opposition understood that vulnerability and took advantage of it.

Finally, a consideration of a somewhat different sort must be noted. If Solanki could not confront a militant opposition politically, why could he not deal with the rioting as a law-and-order problem? Eventually, of course, the rioting died down. But that was only after Solanki had made significant concessions and police had been brought in from outside of Gujarat to control the riots. That highlights another important variable at work: the relative ineffectiveness of Gujarati police in dealing with the riots.

The CPDR report on the 1981 riots documented many instances in which the police either stood by as the powerful Patels wreaked havoc on the Scheduled Castes or, worse, assisted the Patels in the violence. Instances of police violence were especially common in Ahmedabad. The lack of discipline demonstrated by the police reflected both an ongoing de-professionalization of the service and the caste sympathies of the policeman. For example, a union of police inspectors in Ahmedabad voted to support the anti-reservation demands of Patel students. Could such a force act as a neutral agent of law and order?

The political arm of the government was organizationally weak, and the law-and-order arm was less than reliable. When confronted with militant opposition, the Solanki government had little choice but to yield to demands. A similar but more widespread drama would be repeated in 1985. The basic dimensions of the conflict, however, were already clear in 1981: A powerful minority had refused to accept its loss of power in a democracy, and a majority government was institutionally too weak to confront its minority opposition.

THE RIOTS OF 1985

Solanki completed his 1980–5 term as chief minister. That was an achievement, in view of the fact that no other chief minister had completed a term in nearly two decades. Solanki ruled with a comfortable majority. The opposition could create trouble for him in the streets, but could not legally throw Congress(I) out of power. Solanki could, of course, have lost out to other rivals within Congress(I), as he eventually did, but over 1980–5 he managed to avoid that mainly because of his personal rapport with Indira Gandhi. Given the top-down political system then, so long as she had not lost confidence in him, his position was secure. Solanki suggested in an interview that in spite of the pro-lower strata image of his government, he had gone out of his way to avoid radical policies and had done nothing special in the way of socio-economic reforms.[26] As far as real policies were concerned, the message of the Patel-led demonstrations in 1981 had hit home. Solanki would not again provoke the wrath of any of the state's powerful groups.

Solanki's compromises with the powerful and his reluctance to do anything special for his own supporters would appear to have been growing electoral liabilities as the 1985 elections approached. Indira Gandhi was assassinated in late 1984. Rajiv won the 'sympathy elections' that followed, including a comfortable majority from Gujarat, and that must have strengthened Solanki's hand within Gujarat. As a shrewd politician, however, Solanki must have realized that such sympathy waves were likely to be short-lived and that he would need new state-level issues to reinvigorate his campaign. With state assembly elections scheduled for March 1985, Solanki initiated an electoral ploy in January, announcing that reservations for 'backward classes' in government jobs and in educational institutions were being increased from 10 to 28 per cent.

There is little doubt among observers of Gujarati politics that those new reservations were aimed at securing the electoral support of the various intermediate and lower castes, especially the numerically significant Kshatriyas. The timing of the decision is the most important piece of evidence in support of the argument. If there is any remaining doubt, one need only recall that a report recommending increases in reservations, the Rane Commission report, was ready as early as 1983. It recommended the use of economic criteria rather than caste criteria for determining 'backwardness'. Solanki had chosen not to make the report public until just before the elections. More important, he ignored the recommendation to adopt economic criteria for reservations and instead stuck to caste-based definitions. That is readily understandable if one keeps his electoral considerations in mind. The idiom of regional politics was mainly caste-oriented, not class-

---

[26]Interview with Solanki (see note 15).

oriented. Also, Solanki was no socialist. He simply wanted to win elections, and that could best be done by casting electoral appeals in a familiar idiom.

Within a month of the announcement of Solanki's new reservation policies, upper-caste students again initiated an anti-reservation agitation in Ahmedabad. The rioting that followed, though significant, was nothing like what was to follow a few months later. The riots did not get out of hand at that early stage for two main reasons: first, Solanki quickly reacted to the threat of agitations and closed down all the schools until after the elections on 5 March. The second reason was more important: because of the upcoming elections, all the major opposition parties were hesitant to support the agitation. The reservations, including those for Scheduled Castes, Scheduled Tribes, and backward classes, were scheduled to affect nearly half of Gujarat's population. Thus, an anti-reservation stance would be likely to cost a political party support. The opposition parties stayed out of the fray, and the pre-election agitation remained limited.

Congress(I) won a spectacular victory in the relatively peaceful elections held in March 1985 (Table 11.3). Solanki was returned to power with an increased majority, going from 141 to 149 seats in a house of 182. Considering that Congress's share of the vote had declined in other states between the January Lok Sabha elections and the March Legislative Assembly elections, an increase in support in Gujarat demonstrated the rationality of Solanki's electoral ploy to consolidate his position among the various disadvantaged KHAM communities (the Kshatriyas, Harijans, Adivasis, and Muslims), which produced 125 of the 149 Congress(I) legislators. Within the KHAM communities, the Kshatriyas clearly were the dominant group. That was obvious when the new cabinet was announced on 18 March: Fourteen of the twenty ministers, including all the important ones, were from Kshatriya backgrounds.

The rioting that commenced the next day, 19 March, would last for six months. Prior to an analysis of the riots, however, an important question must be asked: Why did Solanki concentrate so much governmental power in the hands of men from his own caste? Given the background of the 1981 riots, and given that everyone in the state was aware of the socio-economic power of the Patels, why did he choose to exclude them from the government? Was that a deliberate challenge, or a stupid miscalculation? Or was there a ruling strategy that made some sense initially but eventually failed?

Solanki was a shrewd politician. One must assume, therefore, that he had some strategy. However, the strategy simply did not work. What was that strategy? Solanki had made it clear all along that in terms of real policies, he was not radical. He had put the government's resources behind production and growth, pursuing policies that would benefit the Patels, Banias, and Brahmins disproportionately. He must have hoped that that policy would appease the most powerful vested interests within the state. In order to win elections, however, he had to create a winning coalition, and one way to do that was to pull together the middle and lower strata. He offered the leaders of those groups direct access to the state's patronage: control over ministries and seats in the assembly, government-controlled jobs, admissions to colleges, and positions in local governments and cooperatives. Thereby he also offered to the unkempt masses the symbolic satisfaction of group political achievements. In addition, Solanki must have known that opposition parties and Patel youth in the cities were likely to create some trouble. By 1985, however, Congress was a different type of party, quite capable of dealing with street violence; it had incorporated many of Sanjay's goons, even in Gujarat.[27] Thus, implementing economic policies favouring the highest groups, holding control over the state and politics in the name of the disadvantaged groups, and using goons to control the opposition's street violence must have been Solanki's ruling strategy. That strategy did not work. The opposition turned out to be stronger than Solanki must have anticipated, and instead of neutralizing each other, the clashing goons created anarchy. As the state lost control and order disintegrated, hostilities broke out along a number of social cleavages. In general, those who could muster force did, and the vulnerable groups suffered the consequences. During the rioting, which lasted six months, approximately 275 people died,[28] thousands were injured, and scores of thousands were left homeless. According to an estimate by the Gujarat Chamber of Commerce, the cost of property damage was 22 billion rupees.[29]

The details of the six months of turmoil are readily available.[30] Most of the facts concerning what happened are well known. However, it is far from clear why events happened as they did and where the responsibility for the anarchy really lay. Therefore, I shall focus on the question: why the riots occurred and, more important, what the specific incidents tell us about the larger issue of concern here, namely, the conditions that lead to crises of governability in India.

[27]Solanki suggested in an interview that 'we can tackle street violence; we have done it before' (see note 15).

[28]See *India Today*, 15 August 1985, p. 32.

[29]See Patel 'The Ahmedabad Riots, 1985', p. 9.

[30]The blow-by-blow details of the riots are available in most Gujarati newspapers between March and August 1985. I consulted the clippings from the *Times of India* (Ahmedabad edition). For a more predigested coverage, see *India Today* for the same period, but especially the following issues of 1985: 15 April, pp. 34–9; 30 April, pp. 20–2; 15 May, pp. 24–34; 31 May, pp. 38–9; 15 July, pp. 18–21; 31 July, pp. 30–5; 31 August, p. 11. For more interpretive accounts by firsthand observers, see the articles by Sujata Patel and Asghar Ali Engineer in *EPW* (see note 2). Finally, for scholarly interpretations, see Spodek, 'From Gandhi to Violence'; Patel, 'The Ahmedabad Riots, 1985'; and Mitra, 'The Perils of Promoting Equality'.

The Gujarat riots of 1985 were concentrated mainly in the cities, particularly Ahmedabad. The rioting went through four identifiable phases. After some pre-election rioting subsided in February, the students resumed their anti-reservation agitation the day after the new government was formed in mid-March. Fairly quickly, the caste riots turned into a Hindu–Muslim riot in which Muslims in Ahmedabad city became the main victims. While both anti-reservation and anti-Muslim rioting continued, the police went on a rampage. Even the army had a difficult time controlling the marauding groups, which included some anti-reservation rioters, politically supported religious zealots, and the police. Finally, as social order totally disintegrated, criminals joined in, ranging from common thugs to well-organized groups of smugglers and bootleggers. All had a heyday looting and settling old scores.

The rioting finally subsided in mid-August, when a political solution was found. Solanki resigned, and a new chief minister agreed to meet all the demands of the anti-reservation students. Some Patels were incorporated into the cabinet. The law-and-order machinery was revamped by creating a totally new chain of command.

The anti-reservation agitations that recommenced in mid-March had a fair amount of continuity from the similar earlier agitations. The stated goal of the new agitation, in 1985 as in 1981, was to force the government to withdraw its recently announced reservation policy. As in 1981, the main participants were upper-caste students in the professional schools of Ahmedabad. Moreover, many of the leaders of the new agitation were the same people who had participated actively or even led the 1981 agitation.[31] The political parties that entered the conflict were also the same. The BJP was actively involved, and the Janata Party lent quiet support, mainly via 'Associations of Guardians', who were directly supporting the agitation. Thus, the main socio-political cleavage was similar to that in the Navnirman movement in 1974 and nearly identical with that in the 1981 riots. The powerful minorities of Gujarat simply were not willing to accept their seemingly permanent exclusion from the state apparatus.

Although the elements of continuity were critical, some differences also were striking. By 1985, both sides were better prepared to pursue street violence. Although the ruling party was not better organized than before, Solanki had employed his own cadre of street toughs. That was the major new development in the Gujarat Congress in the early 1980s. The opposition was also battle-toughened. Therefore, when the agitations began, both in February and in March, instead of attacking vulnerable groups like the Harijans, the students went straight for government property, particularly by burning public buses.

[31]See *India Today*, 15 April 1985, p. 30.

The anti-reservation students organized large, angry meetings in mid-March. They decided to press their demands by calling a *bandh* (i.e., by closing down the city). The bandh was successful, and the government immediately reacted with the proverbial carrot and stick: it retracted its reservation policy, while simultaneously unleashing the police on those still bent on agitating. It is important to note that had the main motive behind the agitations been the reservation policy, the government's immediate retraction should have led to political calm. But it did not. As in 1981, the students took the government's concessions as a sign of weakness; they regrouped and increased their demands.

Alongside the anti-reservation agitation, a perplexing new trend arose. Inter-community riots involving the Muslim and Hindu communities broke out in the crowded inner city. A significant number of Muslims were killed, and a much larger number suffered injury. That pattern of anti-Muslim violence would be repeated periodically over the next six months of rioting. In spite of numerous investigations, however, it remains unclear who orchestrated the violence and why. Thus, the following comments on that aspect of the riots should be treated as informed speculation.

Two aspects of the anti-Muslim violence are clear. First, whereas Ahmedabad periodically experiences inter-community violence, there was virtual unanimity among firsthand observers that in that instance the violence against the Muslims did not result from prior tensions between the Hindu and Muslim communities.[32] Thus, the violence appears to have been deliberately fomented. Second, the direct perpetrators of violence often were hired goons. As one observer noted: 'In the hospitals, doctors describing stab wounds noted that the attackers were striking the liver and other vital organs with an accuracy suggesting professional, and presumably, hired assassins rather than simple retaliation among local communities'.[33] If so, the next question follows naturally: who was hiring the goons, and why? The two main parties to the conflict blamed each other for unleashing the violence. Babubhai Jasbhai Patel, a leader of the Patel community, suggested in an interview that Solanki had unleashed inter-community violence to distract attention from caste riots.[34] By contrast, Solanki suggested that Patels and the opposition parties were behind the inter-community violence; such insurrections, he reasoned, would be designed to weaken his KHAM alliance and would make him 'look bad in the eyes of Rajivji'.[35] As I weigh the

[32]See the articles covering the riots by both Patel and Engineer (see note 2). Also see *India Today*, 15 May 1985, p. 33.

[33]See Spodek, 'From Gandhi to Violence', p. 7.

[34]Interview (see note 11).

[35]Interview (see note 15).

evidence, the overall picture turns out to be more complex than either side is willing to admit, but somewhat closer to the one painted by Solanki.

Solanki had won a huge majority. His government's interests would best be served by rapidly bringing the situation of civil disorder under control, rather than by turning the violence in another direction. Thus, the argument that Solanki himself instigated the conflict between the religious communities seems far-fetched. Solanki was perfectly capable of doing that, but that he actually did so seems doubtful. This in no way exonerates Congress(I) as a whole. Factions within Congress(I), especially those who had failed to get cabinet posts, had an interest in weakening the new Solanki government and thus in encouraging turmoil. It is also important to remember that Congress's national victory in January 1985 was in part a function of the Hindu backlash against minorities. Even before that, since 1980, Indira Gandhi had been counting the pro-Hindu vote. In 1985, therefore, Congress was perfectly capable of committing mayhem against one minority or another. That may have contributed to Solanki's ambivalence concerning how to react to a Hindu-versus-Muslim clash and thus may have exacerbated the problem.

The main force behind the violence, however, appears to have come from militant Hindu groups, many of whom were allied with the RSS and thus with the BJP (formerly the Jan Sangh). The areas in which the initial violence broke out were BJP strongholds.[36] The inflammatory religious pamphlets that were circulated had the tone of right-wing Hindu groups.[37] However community-oriented Congress(I) had become, the religious extremism and bigotry evident in those pamphlets was not the handiwork of Congress. Although Congress was not above using religion for its own purposes, those pamphlets appeared to be the work of 'true believers'. Most important, a message stressing Hindu militancy against Muslims clearly would have worked against the electoral interests of the Gujarati Congress; it would have tended to split the KHAM alliance and unite caste Hindus, presumably within a caste hierarchy, with traditional high castes at the top. That was hardly Congress's political game. It was, however, the BJP's game, and it was a strategy that both the BJP and the Janata pursued throughout the second half of the 1980s, leading up to the electoral defeat of Congress(I) in late-1989 Lok Sabha elections.

The most likely explanation for the inter-community violence in 1985 is that a number of Gujarati groups who opposed Solanki had an interest in promoting political turmoil. Once Solanki retracted the reservation policies, the anti-reservation caste-oriented agitations had to be sustained on the basis

[36]See Patel, 'The Ahmedabad Riots, 1985'.
[37]Patel, 'The Ahmedabad Riots, 1985', appendices.

of other issues. Muslims and other vulnerable minorities have increasingly been seen as easy targets for such hostility in India. Whenever turmoil has seemed likely to be politically advantageous for one opposition faction or another, these groups have been attacked. In 1985, all those with an interest in seeing Solanki's government weakened—Patel youth, opposition parties, especially the BJP, and Congress(I) dissidents—had an interest in promoting the insurrections. Given the meagre evidence, the group most likely to have been behind the communalization of the caste riots was the BJP.

Regardless of who was behind the communalization of the caste riots, a larger analytical point is clear: The violence was deliberately generated as part of a strategy for accomplishing political goals. As far as the chronology of the conflict is concerned, once violence against Muslims broke out, Solanki requested help from the national government. The government had no paramilitary reserves available[38]—most of them were already maintaining order in Punjab and in the northeast—suggesting that India's growing crisis of governability involves far more than an isolated incident in a state here or there. Instead, the army intervened, and order was restored, but only temporarily.

As the army withdrew, the students resumed their agitations. Their demand was that all the students imprisoned during earlier riots be released. The details concerning who was doing what to whom in those riots increasingly become less important for our purposes. It is clear by now that the agitation was politically motivated. Those in the opposition basically did not want the Solanki government to survive. Each concession from the government only emboldened the students and opposition parties. As long as the police force was intact, there was a feeling that order could be restored. In late April, however, even that changed. When the police themselves went on a rampage, people feared that political order in Gujarat had fallen apart completely.

The army was called back in, but it was operating in a 'civil situation', with only minimum powers at its disposal. It was not easy to restore order. An orgy of violence followed. As often happens in such situations, those who could muster force did, and often they used it against those who were easily victimized. Muslim and Scheduled-Caste areas were hit the hardest; they were the ones who lost lives and property.

A discussion of what happened over the next few months would yield only variations on the themes already discussed. The main target of the agitation was Solanki himself. Most groups, including Congress (I), were running out of control. The state had come apart. Rioting had spread to other cities beyond Ahmedabad, and even to some rural areas. Criminals had entered the fray, fully exposing the links among politicians, criminals, and the police.

[38]See *India Today*, 5 April 1985, p. 35.

Leaving aside many of the details, the story ended when New Delhi forced Solanki to resign in mid-July. The new chief minister who replaced Solanki basically reaffirmed the concessions Solanki had already made, and political calm was restored. It is clear in retrospect that the main issue at stake in the six months of rioting was the government itself; the state was the object of contention. Solanki's removal was the main victory for the opposition. The new government went a little further, giving the opposition higher visibility by replacing some of the Kshatriya ministers with Patels. Thus, it was another sweet victory for the Patels; it was sweeter because they had some of their community representatives in power, and they no longer saw the state as being totally in 'hostile' hands. The Patels had again won, and in doing so had once again made a mockery of democratic procedures. They also reaffirmed the significance of socio-economic resources and militancy in struggles for power.

CONCLUSION

Mahatma Gandhi's home state, Gujarat, had once been a model of effective Congress rule in India. A well-organized Congress party had been an important ingredient in that effectiveness. Equally important, however, was a fact that is not always stressed by those who tend to glorify the past: the power competition in the past had been limited to the region's socio-economic elite. The dominance of the upper castes in the social structure had been unquestioned. Competing members of the upper castes had been able to influence those below them for their own political purposes. Over time, those conditions changed. The Congress party was still the ruling party in the late 1980s, but it was no longer a well-organized party. Equally important was the fact that upper-caste leaders had lost their capacity to mould the political behaviour of those below them. The intermediate and lower strata had emerged as significant political forces in their own right. When an alliance of the lower-middle strata and the lower strata captured power through a populist party, the displaced elite sought vengeance. The refusal of a powerful minority to accept the democratic verdict of the ballot box, in turn, became an ongoing source of turmoil in Gujarat. That was true during the Navnirman movement in 1974 that contributed to the proclamation of the Emergency. It was true of the 1981 riots. It was again true in 1985 when Solanki was finally ousted from power. Whether or not the deliberate turn to religious conflict in the late 1980s will fundamentally alter the nature of the caste conflict is a question to which satisfactory answers will emerge only in the 1990s.

The failure of the Congress government to confront the privileged minority politically was a more obscure but also important variable in the political breakdown of the 1980s. Since the rise of Indira Gandhi, Congress has repeatedly won majorities by popular appeal. Just below the appointed leaders, therefore, there exists only a fragmented elite. Little connects these competing elite groups to the mildly supportive masses. This mode of organizing power turns out to be effective for winning elections, but for little else. When confronted with any real obstacle, a government established through populism tends to disintegrate like a house of cards. The opposition in Gujarat understands this vulnerability of Congress governments. As a result, they have periodically resorted to organized street violence to secure what they cannot get through the ballot box.

It should be clear from the discussion in this chapter that the nuances of the specific conflicts vary widely and tend to be quite complex. Some of them have been discussed here; many have not. The purpose of the chapter has been to delineate the major causes of increasing political turmoil in one of India's more developed states. The answer seems to be clear: The major target of the insurrections is the state itself. It is important to emphasize that the importance of the state for opposing groups is not primarily the policies the state pursues but rather the symbolism of power and, more important, the economic resources the state controls. As an articulate participant in Gujarati politics put it: 'If you are not with the ruling party today, chances are life will be difficult. The state is everywhere. Life chances are influenced by the state. If you don't have access to the state, life is difficult'.[39] It is the pervasive presence of the state throughout society, and the related capacity of the state to influence the life-chances of individuals and groups, that has made the state the object of such intense competition. As democracy has evolved, representatives of poorly organized but numerically significant underprivileged groups have gained control of governments in some parts of India, and the socio-economically privileged groups have reacted violently.

[39]Interview with Satyam Patel (secretary, Gujarat Pradesh Committee, Congress [R]), Ahmedabad, 17 March 1986.

12

From Elite Activism to Democratic Consolidation
The Rise of Reform Communism in West Bengal*

The distinctive trait of contemporary West Bengal politics is the rule by a communist party. While the ruling communist party is more reformist than revolutionary, political activism has a long history in Bengal. During the nineteenth century, Bengalis provided the lead in India's militant nationalism. As the leadership of the nationalist movement passed into the hands of Gandhi, and non-violence emerged as his unifying theme, many in Bengal took to violent demonstrations and terrorism. And although the Congress party has dominated Indian politics since independence, its hold on West Bengal has always been tentative. In recent years, communists of various hues have steadily increased their popularity within West Bengal. The CPI(M) has enjoyed an electoral majority for three consecutive terms in the state legislative Assembly. In this chapter on West Bengal, therefore, I will focus on West Bengal as somewhat of an exceptional case within Indian politics. What are the historical roots of elite militancy and political activism in Bengal; why has the hold of the Congress party been weak, and what factors help explain the recent rise of a communist party to the position of West Bengal's ruling party?

The roots of Bengali political exceptionalism, I will argue, can be delineated by addressing three important issues. First, one needs to focus on and explain the early rise of a critical intelligentsia within Bengal, the Bengali *bhadralok*. An understanding of this group is important, not because this intelligentsia was especially radical, but because many of the twentieth century Bengali political activists shared this social background with their

*Originally published as 'From Elite Activism to Democratic Consolidation: The Rise of Reform Communism in West Bengal', in Francine Frankel and M.S.A. Rao (eds), *Caste, Class and Dominance: Pattern of Politico-Economic Change in Modern India*, New Delhi: Oxford University Press, 1990, pp. 367–415.

more conservative counterparts. Radical, conservative or reformist, modern Bengali politics has been dominated by an upper caste, well-off, educated minority. The political proclivities and changing preferences of this high-caste minority thus remain central for understanding patterns of domination and opposition in Bengal.

No leadership succeeds politically without some mass support. The second set of issues requiring explanation, then, is the elite–mass link mediated by structures of caste and class. Class hegemony was never well established within West Bengal and caste affiliations have not provided the basis for state-wide political mobilization. These social structural characteristics have hurt the Congress party while helping the communists gain support. What has finally enabled a communist leadership and their followers to displace Congress rule is a well-organized and a disciplined political party. How such a party has emerged within West Bengal will thus be the third area of discussion. I will locate the roots of this development in the political traditions of disciplined organizations, especially terrorist organizations, within Bengal.

A critical intelligentsia, certain peculiarities of the caste and class structures, and political traditions of disciplined organizations will be treated here as the more important factors helping explain some of the distinguishing features of West Bengal politics. These characteristics, as will be made clear, are historically rooted in Bengali society on the one hand, and in the interaction of the Bengali elite with Hindi-speaking India and British colonialism on the other.

If these factors help explain some exceptional tendencies in Bengali politics, it is further important to analyse the forces which have moulded these tendencies into a reformist rather than a revolutionary direction. The constraints on radicalism, I will argue, stem from the following: the need of seemingly radical parties to gain power through an electoral system; once in power, the need of such parties-in-government to establish credibility as prudent managers of a private economy; and, of course, the regional rather than the national nature of West Bengal's communism.

A chapter-length essay is only suited for the development of a few themes. Several issues related to the large topic under discussion, but not dealt with in this essay, ought to be noted. First, when discussing Bengal's history, I will be concerned primarily with the history of Hindu Bengal. This not only excludes Bihar, Orissa and other parts of the former Bengal presidency, but also, for the most part, the developments within Muslim Bengali society. Second, this chapter does not analyse the whole of West Bengal politics; the focus is rather on certain exceptional tendencies within Bengal's politics. If the continued significance of the Congress party and the structures of caste and class dominance within West Bengal are underemphasized here, it is because the focus in this section is on regional diversity. Third, no study of regional communist parties would be complete without taking into account its linkages with the national and international communist movement. As I do not focus on these themes, this study is by no means a comprehensive study of Bengali communism.

What this chapter does attempt is to explain the weakness of Congress and the relative strength of a reform-oriented communist party within West Bengal. This explanation is best developed by a historical analysis of the interaction of caste, class and politics within Bengal. I have chosen to organize the chapter around analytical themes explaining contemporary patterns of politico-economic dominance rather than present an historical chronology. The latter would dilute the analytical thrust, forcing me to include more historical detail than necessary to explain the issue at hand. The chapter is organized as follows. The nature of politico-economic dominance in contemporary West Bengal is delineated in the first section. This describes the phenomena requiring explanation. The core section then traces the historical roots of the exceptional themes in Bengali politics: elite militancy; weakness of Congress; and the growing strength of a parliamentary-communist party. This is followed by an analysis of the more recent period in which the communists have successfully displaced the Congress party from power in the state.

PATTERN OF DOMINANCE IN CONTEMPORARY WEST BENGAL

Dominance in contemporary West Bengal is characterized by a separation of political and economic power. Power in society continues to reside with the propertied elites. Political power, however, has been wrested from them by an ideological party. The new communist leadership, like the old Congress leadership, belongs to an educated, upper caste, elite minority (see Table 12.3). In order to survive politically, moreover, the ruling party makes significant concessions to the socially powerful. The ruling arrangement is thus a lot more reformist than the label 'communist' may suggest. The governing regime, nevertheless, is not controlled by the property-owning social groups. Political power is rather exercised by a disciplined party allied with the middle and the lower classes.

The exclusion of the upper classes from governance has made it difficult for the privileged to rely on the state for protection. This arrangement may therefore well prove to be an unstable one. In the short run, however, the existence of an elected communist government represents the culmination of some of Bengal's exceptional political traditions: a militant non-Congress elite turned reformist after capturing state power.

Prior to an historical analysis of how this power configuration emerged, it is important to delineate the current situation in some detail. What is the nature of the ruling regime: who rules, who benefits and who opposes?

How is social domination organized: who controls property and who commands status and respect? How do the socially weak and the powerful interact with the regime? And what is the impact of regime intervention on established patterns of social domination?

The simple answer to the question of 'who rules' West Bengal is that power in this state is exercised by an ideologically disciplined political party, namely, the CPI(M). The reason to state the obvious is to resist the analytical tendency that reduces the issue of 'who rules' to underlying socio-economic interests—whether these be a plurality of interests or those of select castes and classes. While the issues of the social origins of those occupying governmental positions, of those voting for the CPI(M), and of those benefiting from regime policies are important, and discussed here, the CPI(M) is first and foremost a political party. Like all political parties, the CPI(M) seeks to win, maintain and, if possible, expand its power base. Social alliances underlying the regime are thus perpetually conditioned by these power considerations. In order to understand the nature of the CPI(M) rule in West Bengal, therefore, it is important to analyse both the social base of the regime and the political characteristics—the leadership, ideology and the organization—of the ruling party.[1]

The leadership of the CPI(M) within West Bengal has remained concentrated in the hands of old revolutionaries whose political careers began in the pre-independence terrorist organizations. Many of these old terrorists, such as the late Pramode Das Gupta, accepted parliamentarianism in the post-independence period. Reconciling communist commitments to 'bourgeois democracy' has not always been easy. Many of these leaders have, nevertheless, brought traditions of integrity, discipline and self-sacrifice to the party organization.

The party has been the dominant force within the CPI(M) regime. Given the electoral framework, however, the party has had to share its power with the members of the legislature and various organizations which help mobilize electoral support, such as the Kisan Sabha. Communist parliamentarians within West Bengal are led by Jyoti Basu. A typical member of the Bengali bhadralok, Jyoti Basu hails from a wealthy, upper caste family. He received his legal education in England prior to becoming a full-time politician. Binoy Chowdhury provides the critical link between the CPI(M) government, where

---

[1]The following discussion of the CPI(M) in West Bengal is based on several research trips to West Bengal over the last five years. These trips were taken in connection with another research project, the results of which are now in print (Atul Kohli, 'Parliamentary Communism and Agrarian Reform: The Evidence from India's Bengal', *Asian Survey* 5(27), July 1983; and *The State and Poverty in India: The Politics of Reform*, Cambridge, 1987). For detailed documentation of the argument, which is based on extensive fieldwork, see these earlier publications.

he is a senior minister, and the Kisan Sabha, which provides the decisive rural electoral support and which he also heads. A quiet leader with an intellectual bent, Binoy Chowdhury's career developed as a peasant organizer in Burdwan.

This varied leadership highlights some of the persistent tendencies among the Bengali communist elite: terrorist past, upper-caste background, western education and long dedicated careers in party organization work. Social background of communist leaders is, however, somewhat less important for understanding their political preferences than party ideology. Party loyalty creates conditions whereby party ideology becomes an important determinant of leadership actions.

While the leadership in the past was marked by intense factional conflicts,[2] those at the top have worked in relative harmony in the last decade or so. Party discipline is an obvious factor militating against open factionalism. Having gained state power, moreover, the stakes of factional conflict have risen. The CPI(M) leadership views political survival as an ongoing struggle with 'reactionary forces'. Party discipline and a perception of continuing struggle have thus facilitated a modicum of cohesive rule and coherent policies in contemporary West Bengal.

The CPI(M)'s ideology has over the years become more and more reformist. Gone are the commitments to 'class warfare', 'land grab' and 'elimination of class enemies'. And in practice, even the goal of establishing a 'dictatorship of the proletariat' now seems to be a distant illusion. Instead, the CPI(M) seeks to 'preserve democratic institutions' and to use state power to facilitate 'development with redistribution'. Electoral strategy seeks to 'exclude' only a few of the highest economic elite: even 'exploiting' classes are not 'the enemy', as long as they are productive and willing to extend support. The agrarian programme, moreover, seeks support of both the middle peasants and the rural poor by simultaneously focusing on 'fair' agricultural prices and marginal land reforms.

The Emergency of 1975 was a turning point for the CPI(M). That brief authoritarian interlude clarified to the leadership the significance of democracy for the party's survival and growth. Certainly, the clear commitment to 'democracy' hardened during and after the Emergency. Other reformist trends were, however, surfacing even earlier. The collapse of previous United Front ministries in both West Bengal and Kerala led the leadership to question those militant tactics which provided an excuse for central intervention. More important, the need to secure electoral majorities continuously pushed the CPI(M) towards accommodating the numerically and otherwise significant 'middle' groups in both the cities and the

---

[2]Marcus Franda, *'Radical Politics in West Bengal'*, Cambridge: MIT Press, 1972.

countryside. And lastly, the sobering reality of governing a private enterprise economy snuffed out much of the remaining radicalism. What remained of communism in the CPI(M), therefore, was a well-disciplined party and a moderately 'social democratic' outlook, rather than any commitment to a revolutionary transformation of society.

The CPI(M) in West Bengal boasts a membership of about one million. In the recent past, much of the CPI(M)'s support was concentrated in urban areas, especially among the literati of Calcutta.[3] Once capturing electoral majorities became a serious goal, however, the need to make inroads into the countryside became obvious. The changing rural social structural conditions—the breakdown of old zamindaris and penetration of commerce—had in any case, made the peasantry a more available political resource than in the past. A break from the Moscow-inspired focus on the urban 'proletariat' was also a liberating influence in the search for rural support. And finally, the success of the Naxalites among the peasantry forced the CPI(M) to take peasant support seriously. The result was that over the last two decades the CPI(M) increasingly became a rural party with the bulk of its seats being won in the rural constituencies and its programme being concentrated in the villages.

The more the CPI(M) has become concerned with maintaining electoral support, the more it has taken on the characteristics of other Indian parties. The CPI(M) is as concerned today about the popularity of candidates it fields as the Congress. This leads the CPI(M) to take seriously such ideologically distasteful considerations as the caste and communal leanings of candidates. The CPI(M) also understands and fully utilizes 'machine politics' for sustaining support. Numerous support groups in both the cities and the countryside are closely tied to the CPI(M). These groups support the communists electorally but, in turn, expect the CPI(M) to channel governmental resources to them.

These characteristics, however, do not make the CPI(M) just another version of the Congress party. The party's democratic centralist organization gives it some genuine distinguishing characteristics. First, party discipline facilitates a strong link between the party leadership and the cadres. This enables the leadership to effectively translate organizational goals into grass-root actions—a capacity few other Indian political parties possess. Second, party followers are ideologically disciplined. This tends to create a degree of separation between the dominant political institutions and the society. As a result, prevailing societal values and hierarchies are not as easily reproduced within the CPI(M) as in the Congress and other political parties.

[3]Bhabani Sen Gupta, *Communism in Indian Politics*, New York: Columbia University Press, 1972.

TABLE 12.1 Seats Won by the Major Political Parties in
West Bengal Assembly Elections, 1952–87

Parties[1]	1952	1957	1962	1967	1969	1971	1972	1977[2]	1982	1987[3]
Congress	150	152	157	127	55	105	216	20	49	40
CPI(M)	28	46	50	43	80	113	14	177	174	187
CPI	–	–	–	16	30	13	35	2	7	11
Forward Bloc	14	8	13	13	21	3	0	25	28	26

Source: Computed from the reports of the Election Commission.
Notes: [1]The other significant parties which have come and gone and are not listed here include the Praja Socialist Party and the Revolutionary Socialist Party. The latter continues to be significant; it won 20 and 19 seats in the 1977 and the 1982 Assembly elections, respectively. [2]The newly formed Janata Party won 29 seats in 1977, only to vanish completely again in the 1982 elections.
[3]Computed from India Today, 15 April 1987.

While the CPI(M) has been the dominant political force within West Bengal over the last decade or so (Table 12.1), the Congress clearly remains the major opposition party in terms of the percentage of votes secured (Table 12.2). It would not be surprising; therefore, if in the future the Congress once again emerges as the ruling party of West Bengal.

In the present situation, however, the Congress within West Bengal remains a highly factionalized political force, looking continuously to the centre for both support and important decisions. The crucial distinction between the Congress and the CPI(M) in the recent past was the ideological orientation, not the social background of the respective leadership or the social basis of party support. There have, of course, been some important differences between the two: the Congress leadership drew a little more heavily from landowning and business classes than did the communists;[4] and the communists continuously drew less electoral support from the upper classes and more so from the lower ones.[5] As discussed below, moreover, the intermediate leadership of the communists has come to rest more and more on the 'middle strata' rather than on the landowning, village influentials, who formed the backbone of Congress's patron–client networks. Both parties, however, drew their leadership from high status, upper caste, educated elites.[6] The electoral support for the Congress party, moreover, was in the recent past at least as high among low income groups as that for the communists.[7] No statistical evidence is available concerning how this situation may have changed over the last crucial decade.

[4]Myron Weiner, Political Change in South Asia, Calcutta: Firma K.L. Mukhopadhyaya, 1963, p. 90.
[5]Sen Gupta, Communism in Indian Politics.
[6]Weiner, Political Change in South Asia, chapter 5, tables 3 and 4.
[7]Rajni Kothari, Politics in India, Boston: Little, Brown and Company, 1970.

TABLE 12.2: Percentage of Votes Polled by the Major Parties in
1977 and 1982 West Bengal Assembly Elections

Parties	1977	1982
CPI(M)	35.8	38.5
Other 'Left-Front' Parties	10.5	9.9
Janata	20.5	0.8
Congress(I)	23.4	35.7
CPI	2.7	1.8
Others	7.1	13.3
Total	100	100

Source: Compiled from the reports of the Election Commission.

The hallmark of the Congress in the post-independence period has been the politics of patronage. Having lost control of the state government (for reasons to be analysed here), the West Bengal Congress has over the last decade found it very difficult to put together a cohesive party. There is hardly a Congress party to speak of in West Bengal today. Old loyalties still generate respectable electoral support; there is, however, no real party organization, distinctive policy position or a significant and popular leader. Old leaders such as Siddhartha Shankar Ray have fallen out of favour with the party High Command; others, such as Pranab Mukerjee, became so alienated from Prime Minister Rajiv Gandhi that they formed their own new party; and yet others are either highly factionalized or are products of the 'Sanjay culture' having open and well-established contacts with 'the underground', making them less than credible as state leaders.

Having very briefly delineated the contemporary political characteristics of the two leading parties of West Bengal, it is important to highlight the nature of the social and the cultural milieu within which these parties function.

The first and most well-known point about Bengali society concerns the strong cultural identity maintained by the Bengalis, especially the elite, in relation to the rest of India. Bengalis tend not only to emphasize the distinctiveness, but also the relatively advanced development of their language, literature, art, music, poetry and even their social and religious practices. Political significance of this regional identity lies in the fact that Congress rule in West Bengal has often been viewed suspiciously as an extension of Hindi domination. The CPI(M) as a regional party has thus benefited from sentiments of regional nationalism. The CPI(M) is conceived of not only as a communist party; it is also a Bengali party. While similar regional sentiments have benefited non-communist parties in other Indian states (e.g., Tamil Nadu, Punjab, and recently, Andhra Pradesh), there are no significant non-communist 'Bengali' alternatives to the CPI(M) in West Bengal. For reasons to be made clear in due course, the CPI(M) has thus

TABLE 12.3 Religion and Caste of West Bengal Cabinet Ministers according to
Parties, 1952–82*

	1952–62 Congress-Dominated Cabinets (in per cent)	1977–82 CPI(M)-Dominated Cabinets (in per cent)
Brahmin	23.0	35.7
Kayastha	31.0	31.4
Vaishya	24.1	22.8
Scheduled Castes	2.3	1.5
Scheduled Tribes	6.9	1.5
Muslims	12.7	7.1
Total	100	100

Note: *The data includes members of council of ministers, ministers of state, and deputy ministers. I would like to acknowledge the help of Sujit Deb and Sajal Basu in the collection of this data.

TABLE 12.4 Changing Caste Composition of West Bengal Cabinets, 1952–82*
(percentage figures in brackets)

	1952	1957	1962	1967+	1969	1972	1977	1982
Brahmin	2(14.3)	2(16.7)	4(28.6)	7(38.9)	9(32.1)	1(7.1)	9(39)	8(36.4)
Kayastha	5(35.7)	3(25)	2(14.3)	4(22.2)	8(28.6)	5(35.7)	8(34.8)	10(45.4)
Vaishya	5(35.7)	5(41.6)	7(50)	4(22.2)	5(17.9)	2(14.3)	4(17.4)	3(13.6)
Scheduled Castes and Tribes	0(0)	0(0)	0(0)	2(11.1)	3(10.7)	2(14.3)	0(0)	0(0)
Muslims	2(14.3)	2(16.7)	1(7.1)	1(5.6)	3(10.7)	4(28.6)	2(8.7)	1(4.6)
Total	14	12	14	18	28	14	23	22

Notes: *The data includes only the members of council of ministers. I would like to acknowledge the help of Sujit Deb and Sajal Basu in the collection of this data.
+ Refers to the ministry formed after the General Election and not to the interim ministry formed shortly thereafter.

been the primary beneficiary of Bengali nationalism. The CPI(M)'s repeated harping, for example, not on 'enemies' within West Bengal, but on centre–state relations, only makes sense when interpreted from this standpoint of political support that the party generates from its regional identity.

The second socio-cultural characteristic deserving attention is the minimum role played by caste in Bengali politics. There is, for example, no equivalent in West Bengal to the role of the Lingayats and Vokkaligas in Karnataka, the Reddys in Andhra Pradesh or the Jats in Haryana. This is not to deny the significance of caste or other local loyalties as a basis for district-level political mobilization; note the role of the Aguris in Burdwan, Gurkhas in Darjeeling, and that of the Mahatos in Purulia. Some caste groupings, moreover, have traditionally been aligned with specific political parties: the Mahishyas, for example, have been closer to the Congress party, whereas the Namasudras opposed the Congress even before independence. There are, nevertheless, no state-wide caste groupings of political significance in contemporary West Bengal.

The question of why caste affiliations are not as politically volatile in West Bengal as they are in Bihar or Gujarat is a complex one. It is sufficient to note here that this condition is rooted in part in certain peculiarities of the Bengali caste structure, marked by a degree of 'pluralism' at the top and weakness of caste identity at the bottom, and in part a result of the non-caste political issues which have fired the imagination of the Bengali elite— anti-colonial struggles, nationalism, militant terrorism and communism. In more recent times, the weakness of caste as a politically mobilizable issue helps us understand the failure of Congress and other non-communist parties in forging significant caste alliances. Caste weakness, moreover, forms a part of the larger explanation of why eventually upper-caste Hindus, as leaders of the 'vanguard', have had some success in forging alliances with lower caste 'peasants' and 'proletarians'.

Some peculiarities of West Bengal's class structure also need to be emphasized. Most important is the historical and continuing failure of Bengali society to generate a commercial and entrepreneurial impulse from within. Rooted in both structural and cultural conditions, this failure has had far-reaching consequences. Urban commerce and industry in West Bengal has come to be dominated by non-Bengalis: first the British and then Marwaris and Parsis. For example, none of the six major chambers of commerce in Calcutta are controlled by Bengalis.[8] This non-Bengali capitalist dominance is, in turn, partially responsible for the failure of capitalism to become an integral part of Bengali social structure. The relative neglect of Calcutta by moneyed urban interests, and the tendency of capital to move away from Bengal at the first sign of political trouble, are thus both related to the non-Bengali nature of Bengal's capitalism.

Bengal's capitalists have also failed to put their weight behind a coherent non-communist political force within West Bengal; they have preferred to intervene in Bengal's politics through New Delhi. While this strategy successfully constrains the CPI(M)'s radical thrust, it does little to encourage political alternatives to the CPI(M). On the contrary, such an alliance between non-Bengali industrialists and New Delhi enables communist leaders to couch their radicalism successfully within themes of Bengali nationalism.

Besides controlling the economy, capitalists usually attempt to mould the values and political institutions, affecting their economic activities. While

[8]Nirmal Chaudhry, 'West Bengal: Vortex of Ideological Politics', in Iqbal Narain (ed.), *State Politics in India*, New Delhi: Meenakshi Prakashan, 1976.

this does not ensure success, a failure to even attempt this intervention is bound to leave a power vacuum. This has essentially been the situation in West Bengal. And the main beneficiary of the resulting political vacuum has been the CPI(M).

The failure of entrepreneurial impulse to take root has also had considerable impact on the nature of the agrarian structure. West Bengal is one of the few states in India where sharecropping as a proportion of overall tenancy actually continued to increase in the post-independence period (Table 12.5). Absentee landlordism has moreover been much more significant in West Bengal than in most Indian states. These conditions have not only been responsible for sluggish agricultural growth in West Bengal; they also have been of political consequence. Failure of landowners to actively participate in village life—which, after all, revolves around agricultural activities—reduces their legitimacy as local influentials. This in turn has made it difficult to reproduce the more common Indian pattern—landed influentials mobilizing support for the Congress party—within West Bengal. As hostility of the lower classes to their superiors is only the other side of the failure of social superiors to legitimize their rank and privileges, radical parties have found Bengal's villages a more fertile ground for mobilizing support than those of other Indian states.

No descriptive picture of contemporary West Bengal would be complete without emphasizing the large proportion of the population that lives under conditions of poverty in this state.[9] While the overall Indian average of population living in poverty is close to 40 per cent, the figure for West Bengal has hovered around 60 per cent (see Tables 12.5 and 12.6). The density of population has continued to increase over the years and the availability of land per person has continued to decline (see Table 12.7). This has swelled the ranks of those who do not own any land or only have access to very small pieces of land, often under sharecropping arrangements (see Tables

TABLE 12.5 Changes in Tenancy in West Bengal, 1953–71

Year	Percentage of Cultivated Area under Tenancy	Area under Sharecropping as a Percentage of Area under All Forms of Tenancy*
1953–4	25.43	89.57
1960–1	17.65	92.53
1970–1	18.73	96.44

Source: Adapted from Pranab Bardhan, 'Variations in Extent and Forms of Agricultural Tenancy', Economic and Political Weekly, 11 September 1976, No. 18.
Note: *Includes sharecropping and fixed rent tenancy.

[9]For details of the following abbreviated discussion on poverty programmes, see Kohli, The State and Poverty in India, chapter IV.

TABLE 12.6 Poverty and Inequality in Rural West Bengal

Year	Percentage of Rural Population in Poverty	Gini Co-efficient of Consumption
1957–8	62.3	.27
1959–60	61.4	.27
1960–1	40.4	.26
1961–2	58.3	.28
1963–4	63.3	.27
1964–5	64.0	.24
1965–6	56.6	.27
1966–7	64.3	.26
1967–8	80.3	.25
1968–9	74.9	.23
1970–1	70.1	.27
1973–4	66.0	.30

Source: Based on NSS consumption data and taken from Montek Ahluwalia, 'Rural Poverty and Agriculture Performance in India', *Journal of Development Studies*, April 1978.

TABLE 12.7: Some Basic Demographic Data on West Bengal

	1961	1971	1981
Rate of growth of population (per cent)	32.79	26.87	22.96
	(1951–61)	(1961–71)	(1971–81)
Density of population (per sq. km.)	399	504	614
Percentage of urban population to total population	24.45	24.75	26.49
Per capita cultivable land (in hectares)	0.18	0.13	—
Literacy (per cent)	29.30	33.05	40.88

Source: Government of West Bengal, *Economics Review, 1982–83*, Statistical Appendix, 2.

12.5 and 12.8). The landless and the sharecroppers both constitute about a quarter of the rural population each, and taken together, form the bulk of West Bengal's poor.

Overall, then, West Bengal is a smallholder state with massive poverty. Lower caste groups, who do not own any land, or have access to some through sharecropping, constitute as much as half of the rural population. They form the bottom of the social pyramid. At the top, the economy has significant non-Bengali presence. This economic elite looks more to New Delhi than to the state government for protection. The political and status pyramids are, in turn, dominated by educated Bengali elites of the 'clean' castes—Brahmins, Vaishyas, and Kayasthas (Tables 12.3 and 12.4). This elite is more divided along ideological lines than along caste affiliations. The left-leaning groups within the elite have in recent years successfully consolidated themselves politically. Through the medium of a communist party and a

'Left-Front', utilizing themes of both regional nationalism and class politics, a segment of the Bengali elite has forged successful political alliances with middle and lower classes. The more this 'communist' alliance has consolidated its rule, the further it has moved away from revolutionary commitments and towards a 'social-democratic' orientation.

The last issue which deserves attention in this sub-section concerns the performance of the CPI(M) regime. Given the overall picture of domination, what contribution has a ruling communist party made towards altering the social configurations of privilege? In general, who supports the CPI(M) and who benefits from its policies?

The issue of who supports the CPI(M) can be interpreted from both the electoral perspective and from the standpoint of the social origins of the power holders. I will come back to an analysis of who votes for the CPI(M) later. Concerning the backgrounds of the politically powerful, one needs to distinguish between the top and the intermediate level of political elite. In an ideologically disciplined party, such as the CPI(M), social origins of the top elite—who are generally long time party members—tell us little about their political preferences and, therefore, little about the socio-economic policies the regime is likely to adopt. Old terrorists like Pramode Das Gupta could adhere to the same overall goal as the England-educated, high caste bhadralok such as Jyoti Basu. A focus on the social background of the leadership in West Bengal thus does not provide a satisfactory answer to who supports and who benefits from the regime. This is because the party line and not social background is the primary determinant of elite behaviour at the highest level. The intermediate level elite, however, are not likely to be as close followers, as the former, of the party line. The social background of these elite is more important for understanding the nature of the regime's social support.

Below the level of old cadres in control of party and government are the intermediate level party elite, often elected to local government positions as party-sponsored candidates. The CPI(M) regime allowed political parties for the first time in India to compete for local government positions. Well aware of its new popularity, the CPI(M) hoped that its own candidates would be successful. The strategy paid off. Of the total seats at the district level—87 per cent, 74 per cent at the block level, and 67 per cent at the village level were captured in 1979 by those running on the CPI(M) ticket. The 1983 panchayat elections were a near repeat performance.

Survey results reveal that the majority of these new office-holders are party sympathizers rather than party members; a large majority are small landholders and teachers; and, therefore, from rural lower-middle income groups.[10] This pattern is significant for two reasons. First, never have local

[10]Kohli, 'Parliamentary Communism and Agrarian Reform', pp. 791–5.

governments in West Bengal or, for that matter in much of India, been so free of the domination of landlords and rich peasants. The CPI(M) has therefore done what no other Indian political force has been able to do: penetrate the countryside without depending on large landowners. The CPI(M) regime, along with the newly created local governments, thus represents two interlinked patterns of political change: an organizational penetration by the 'centre' into the 'periphery', and a simultaneous shift in the class basis of institutional power.

A second aspect of the panchayat officials' background, however, also reveals something interesting about the CPI(M): the CPI(M) is dominated by the lower-middle income rural groups and is not really a party of the poor. This assertion of course needs to be understood in the limited sense in which it is meant. As I will argue, the CPI(M) is *electorally* supported by the poor, and in turn, some government policies do benefit the agrarian lower classes. In this sense, the CPI(M) is a party of the poor. Nevertheless, neither the bulk of the party membership, nor party supporters having access to electoral offices, are the rural poor.

Some of the CPI(M) regime's anti-poverty programmes also deserve attention. While I have discussed these in detail elsewhere,[11] a brief recapitulation of the argument is in order. The CPI(M) has utilized its newly consolidated position to initiate rural reforms. As discussed above, the bulk of the rural poor in West Bengal are sharecroppers and landless labourers, and the programmes have been aimed primarily at these groups, especially the sharecroppers *(bargardars* in Bengali). Tenancy in the past has been based largely on informal arrangements. As a consequence, laws designed to reduce the amount of the crop that the sharecropper must hand over to the landowner, and laws to increase security of tenure, have been ineffective. To alter this situation, the CPI(M) regime has undertaken a concerted effort legally to register the sharecroppers, in the hope that this will improve their incomes and provide them greater security.

One of the early acts of the CPI(M) government was to amend the land-reform laws so as to transfer the burden of proof of land-sharing arrangements from the sharecropper to the landowner. With this law on the books, the government undertook a special drive called Operation Barga to facilitate rapid registration of the sharecroppers. Teams of bureaucrats and/or party members, activists and Kisan Sabha members were sent out to the countryside to announce the laws and to register the sharecroppers on the spot. The Operation has had considerable success. While over the previous three decades, mostly under Congress Party rule, fewer than 60,000 sharecroppers were registered in the areas where the CPI(M) is now

---

[11]Kohli, *The State and Poverty in India*, chapter 3; and Chapter 13 (this volume).

TABLE 12.8: Distribution of Land in West Bengal by Size Class of Operational Holdings, 1953–72

Size Class of Household Operational Holding (in acres)	1953–4		1961–2		1971–2	
	Per Cent of Households	Per Cent of Area Operated	Per Cent of Households	Per Cent of Area Operated	Per Cent of Households	Per Cent of Area Operated
'Landless'[1]	0.89 ⎫ 48.55	–	33.9 ⎫ 48.6	2.3	30.94 ⎫ 50.74	–
0.005–1.0	47.66 ⎭	3.90	14.7 ⎭	11.50	19.80 ⎭	4.34
1.0–2.5	16.61	10.49	16.90	27.90	22.42	20.45
2.5–5.0	17.52	23.27	19.70	32.20	15.77	28.94
5.0–10.0	12.15	31.38	12.40	19.10	8.92	31.05
10.0–20.0	4.14	20.78	3.80	6.60	1.87	12.32
20.0 and above	1.03	11.18	0.70		0.25	2.90

Source: Government of India, National Sample Survey, 8th Round for 1953–4, 17th Round for 1961–2 and 26th Round for 1971–2.
Note: [1]The drastic change in the numbers of the 'landless' between 1953–4 and 1961–2 reflects a change in survey procedure.

operating, in its first five years of its rule the CPI(M) succeeded in registering over 1.2 million. Compared to the past performances of Congress and other regimes in the area, therefore, the CPI(M)'s current success is spectacular. Given the size of the problem—there may be close to 2 million families of sharecroppers in West Bengal—much, of course, remains to be done. Nevertheless, the CPI(M) has taken an impressive first step towards improving the living conditions of the sharecroppers. As the survey data in Table 12.9 indicates, a majority of the registered sharecroppers now only pay their legally stipulated shares—25 per cent—to the landowners. This amounts to a significant—as much as 50 per cent—improvement in the access of share-croppers to the crops they cultivate.

What explains the CPI(M)'s success in registering so large a number of sharecroppers? The mere legal act of registration challenges class relations in the countryside, for it is aimed at reducing the landowner's control of his property and the income from it. The act, therefore, is bound to provoke considerable opposition. The sharecroppers are generally afraid to participate in the process without the support of forces outside of the village community. And it is this crucial 'outside support' that the CPI(M) regime has provided. The power of both the party and the government is being utilized to improve the condition of the sharecroppers. The role of the party has been especially significant. Operation Barga has thus the greatest success in those parts of Bengal where the party is strongest. The critical variable has been party-initiated politicization. As a consequence of sustained party activity, the sharecroppers have come to understand the laws, trust the party, and take the final and important step of registration. This act of defiance against the traditional patron perhaps does more to help implement the sharecropping laws than the refinement of the laws themselves.

Modest increases in income and greater security for the sharecroppers have been the short-run consequences of registration. In order to further improve land productivity and incomes of the registered sharecroppers, the CPI(M) regime is striving to channel credit to them. The government has negotiated with the commercial banks and secured an agreement 'in principle', that banks will lend money not only against land but also against the share of the crop. Furthermore, the government has promised to subsidize the labour-intensive aspects of the banking costs. The party-controlled local governments will prepare the lists of registered sharecroppers and identify their legal share of the crop. This information will be provided to the banks and will save them considerable labour costs. The banks will then offer loans—part in cash and part in vouchers—for agricultural inputs. The government will also subsidize the interest the sharecroppers must pay. The programme is a novel one, and it is too early to judge whether it will succeed or fail. If the offering of credit can be sustained and expanded, it

TABLE 12.9: The Impact of Operation Barga: Household Survey of Registered Sharecroppers*

Question	Tabulated Answers		
1. How much share-cropping land did you register?	Below 1 acre 66%	1–2 acres 25%	2–5 acres 9%
	No	Yes	
2. Do you own any land other than the land held under a sharecropping agreement?	Under 1 acre 37%　　49%	More than 1 acre 14%	
3. Where does the landowner live?	In or around the village 19%	Elsewhere 81%	
	Before registration	After registration	
4. Did the landowner provide any inputs?	Yes　　No 14%　　86%	Yes　　No 3%　　97%	
	Before registration[1]	After registration[1]	
5. How is the output shared?	50–50　　60–40 87%　　13%	50–50　　60–40　　75–25 32%　　2%　　66%	
6. Have you taken out a loan?	Yes 36%	No 64%	
7. If yes to No. 6, how did you use the loan?	Family Maintenance 28%	Investments 72%	

Source: Kohli, 1987, chapter III, table 3.9, p. 130.

Notes: *Based on a survey of 300 households in the districts of 24 Parganas, Burdwan, and Midnapore. The surveys were carried out in July–September 1983. I would like to acknowledge the valuable help of Dr Sajal Basu in supervising the surveys in Burdwan and Midnapore. I did the survey in 24 Parganas.

[1] The first share figure refers to the share of the sharecropper. For example, '60–40' refers to 60 per cent of the share belonging to the sharecropper and 40 per cent to the landowner.

will demonstrate how a well-organized left-of-centre government can imaginatively and systematically intervene in a private enterprise economy so as to strengthen the position of the lower classes.

In addition to the programme for the sharecroppers, the CPI(M)'s efforts have been aimed at providing extra employment and better wages for the landless agricultural labourers. The Food for Work Programme (FWP)—a public-works oriented, employment-generating scheme, in part supported by the wheat/rice grants from the centrally controlled surplus—has been implemented with considerable effectiveness in West Bengal. The programme has tended to generate about one month of extra employment for one-third of all landless households. Considering that most of the landless usually get no more than four months of employment per year, the increment is by no means insignificant. The implementation of the programme has been facilitated by the party-controlled local governments. Much of the money is channelled through these 'red panchayats'. In consultation with the local party cadres, the panchayats decide which projects will be undertaken, choose who will be employed and administer the funds. As the political fortunes of the CPI(M) are closely tied to the success of such distributive schemes, sustained pressure through the party has minimized the typical problems of corruption and maladministration of rural employment schemes in other states.

Party-initiated wage struggles have been the other 'non-governmental' mode of increasing the incomes of landless labourers. As a party in power, however, seeking to maintain broad-based political support, the CPI(M) has not devoted a great deal of effort to organizing union-supported agitation in the countryside. Moreover, socio-economic conditions are harsh. With a massive labour supply, labourers enjoy a favourable bargaining position only during the peak employment season. Nevertheless, in some parts of West Bengal, where the party organization is strong, unionization has led to a modest increase in wages. My own interviews revealed that wage levels in the unionized Blocks tended to be somewhat higher than in the non-unionized ones. The overall success on this front, however, has been minimal. The CPI(M) finds it difficult to hold together an alliance between the landless labourers and the middle peasants who often employ these labourers. Increased wages will put pressure on the politically crucial middle peasantry, thus weakening one of the legs on which the CPI(M) stands. For now, therefore, the CPI(M) has mainly concentrated its energies on improving the lot of the sharecroppers and in supporting the middle peasants. The poorest of the poor have not gained much from CPI(M) rule.

To summarize this section, political and social dominance has come to be separated in contemporary West Bengal. While traditional socio-economic privileges are mostly intact, and the Congress party remains a considerable force, the economically powerful have failed to translate their position and resources into political power. Governmental power is rather being exercised by a well-disciplined, reformist political party. The party draws its cadres primarily from middle and lower-middle income groups. Party-sponsored reforms, however, do benefit segments of the rural poor. How has this relatively rare politico-economic situation emerged in West Bengal? How is it that political power has been successfully wrested from the socially powerful by a reform-oriented, ideological party? Some themes which form the larger answer to these questions have already been touched upon: elite radicalism; regional nationalism; significance of party organization; and weakness of caste and class dominance. As one would expect, such cultural and structural traits do not emerge in decades; they rather reflect centuries of distinctive history. It is to a more detailed historical analysis, therefore, of the factors explaining some of the exceptional tendencies in contemporary Bengali politics that I now turn my attention.

HISTORICAL ROOTS OF BENGALI POLITICAL EXCEPTIONALISM: ELITE ACTIVISM

The exceptional and interrelated tendencies of Bengali politics which I have chosen to analyse in this chapter are: weakness of the Congress party, elite militancy, and the slow but steady rise of an electorally based communist party to power. As one takes a long look at the modern socio-political history of Bengal in search of an explanation for these tendencies, three factors stand out: the nature of the Bengali educated elite; certain peculiarities of the social structure; and traditions of terrorist political organization. I analyse here each of these factors in the hope of elucidating the changing patterns of domination and opposition in India's Bengal.

One important caveat should be noted. While seeking the roots of the present in the past, there is a danger that one may recreate the past so as to make the present an inevitable outcome of that past. This would certainly be fallacious. The present was no more certain yesterday than the future is today. The weakness of Congress and the emergence of a moderate communist government, to put it differently, was by no means an inevitable outcome of Bengali social and political conditions. And yet certain forces and tendencies have given rise precisely to such an outcome. The analytical task is to identify these conditions. If this was mainly an historical essay, I would make an attempt to do greater justice to the past by also identifying contradictory conditions that could have influenced processes of change in other directions. If the recreated past appears occasionally to lead inevitably to the present in the discussion that follows, it is only because of the manner in which the problem has been posed here.

By the turn of this century, Bengal had experienced the rise of an intelligentsia—the Bengali bhadralok. As a leading historian of Bengal has convincingly argued, the members of this group formed a status and cultural elite.[12] While initially rooted in high caste and landed backgrounds, the defining characteristics of group membership were generally acquired through British-introduced education. The 'charmed circle', therefore, though initially rather closed to upper class Brahmins, lost some of its class and caste exclusiveness and, over time, came to incorporate educated and cultured members of intermediate social backgrounds, especially members of such land controlling clean castes as the Kayasthas. Many of the Bengali bhadralok went on to make important contributions in the fields of literature,

[12]John Broomfield, *Elite Conflict in a Plural Society*, Berkeley: University of California Press, 1968, pp. 5–6.

music, art, and religion. Our interest in this social group, however, is limited to their political role. As a self-defined and accepted societal elite, Bengali political leadership, including radical leadership, has originated from this background. Changing beliefs and attitudes of the politically inclined bhadralok are thus of considerable significance, especially if one keeps in mind that much of modern Bengali politics has been elite politics.

The political consciousness and behaviour of the Bengali bhadralok were decisively conditioned by colonialism. As a cultured elite within a colonial setting—a product of that setting first, and then confronting it as 'second class citizens'—the bhadralok found their society backward and wanting. Around the turn of the century, two questions tended to dominate the thinking of the Bengali elite: how to reform or get rid of British rule; and how to reorganize Bengali—or for that matter Indian—society so as to make it respectable and competitive by European standards.

The attitudes towards these two issues of anti-colonial nationalism and social reorganization changed over time. Prior to independence, nationalist themes were dominant. The agitation over Bengal's first partition transformed a sizable minority of the questioning and moderate elite into militant nationalists. From here on, even when militancy was on the wane, the bhadralok were more or less permanently divided between the 'moderates' and the 'extremists'. The differences here were primarily of political tactics; socio-economic outlooks of these groups were essentially elitist and conservative. The moderates slowly lost ground, not initially to the extremists, but to Bengali Muslims, who forged alliances with lower caste Hindus by promising progressive legislation. After independence and the creation of Pakistan, the Muslim leadership departed. West Bengal was thus left with a political vacuum. The moderates under Congress leadership tried to regain the initiative, but for reasons to be specified, never really succeeded. The traditional weakness of Congress in Bengal was never really overcome. Instead, the old extremists, many by now turned communists, slowly but surely gained political prominence and support. Ironically—or may be not so ironically—the more powerful these communists became, the more moderate they tended to be in practice.

Those seeking 'recipes for the Indian renaissance' in the first half of the nineteenth century tended to concentrate on issues of religious and social reform.[13] The major figures within Bengal, and these were also major figures of India at the time, were such individuals as Rammohan, Ramakrishna, and Vivekananda. Paralleling the debates within the Russian intelligenstia

[13]N.S. Bose, *The Indian Awakening and Bengal*, Calcutta: Firma K.L. Mukhopadhyay, 1960; and David Kopf, *The Brahmo Samaj and the Shaping of the Modern Indian Mind*, Princeton: Princeton University Press, 1979.

of the same period, the conflicts tended to be rather tame by later standards. The main conflict was between those who wanted to reform and revive Hinduism so as to find virtue in the 'greatness' of India's past, and those who found the 'evils of Hinduism' intolerable enough to want to embrace Western secularism and emerging liberalism. Eradication of social evils was in either case seen as dependent on the spread of education. The British, however, came to be perceived as obstructing this and other reformist developments. What began as the perceived need for social reforms in those days, easily and often got translated into political demands: if Indians only had greater access to the political arena, they could help improve Indian conditions. By the second half of the nineteenth century, therefore, many in Bengal were demanding political representation in some form, as well as government jobs for the educated Bengalis. While self-serving, these demands were also seen as the means of achieving a desired goal: eradication of Indian social ills.

Failure of the British to offer any substantial concessions tended only to intensify the demands for reforms. By the end of the nineteenth century, therefore, the tone of the argument within Bengal was already quite distinct in comparison to the rest of India.[14] Many Bengali revolutionaries have noted the profound impact that the writings of Bankim Chandra's *Anandamath* had in propelling them to action (see 'interviews').[15] Aurobindo was already criticizing Congress as a 'rich man's club' and preaching the formation of secret terrorist societies as a mode of launching attacks on the British.[16] While these were clearly minority voices at this point, the fact that they were there at all, and beginning to be well received among some of the Bengali bhadralok, was an early indicator of what was to come.

What finally transformed the scattered voices—some demanding social reforms, others political representation and greater access to decision making, and yet others militant action to undermine British power—into a widespread and increasingly militant nationalist movement, was the growing agitation over Bengal's partition. For the purposes of this study, numerous historical details of the anti-partition agitation and the accompanying Swadeshi movement are not important. What is crucial rather is an understanding of two issues: why the movement took on an intense militant quality; and what the consequences were of the movement for future political developments.

[14]R.C. Majumdar, *History of Modern Bengal, Part One*, Calcutta: G. Bharadwaj & Co., 1978, p. 482–537.

[15]Gautam Chattopadhyay, *Communism and Bengal's Freedom Movement*, New Delhi: People's Publishing House, 1970.

[16]R.C. Majumdar, *History of Modern Bengal, Part Two*, Calcutta: G. Bharadwaj & Co., 1978, Chapter 1.

Several factors help explain the increasingly militant nationalism within Bengal. First, there is the readily understandable issue of injured Bengali pride. Political division of an area deemed to be culturally unified was aimed at and was perceived as a conscious British ploy to 'divide and rule'.[17] Bengali opposition was natural. Second, the bhadralok had the most to lose from the partition; it was their sphere of influence—greater Bengal—which was about to be carved up into pieces.[18] Bhadralok-led opposition to Bengal's partition, moreover, had its own internal dynamics. The British policy of 'carrot and stick', instead of arriving at a compromise solution, actually backfired. It legitimized the opposition's goal—reunification of Bengal—without in the early stages delivering on that demand. And nothing radicalizes an oppositional movement like widespread acceptance of the goals sought, and a failure to make concessions necessary for the achievement of these goals.

While the above factors were clearly at work, no explanation of early Bengali militancy would be complete without references to the values and the cultural milieu of the Bengali bhadralok. After all, many of the conditions suggested above could be found in other parts of India during the colonial period, but without similar outcomes. There was, in other words, something distinctively Bengali about the anti-partition militancy. A glance at the works of Aurobindo and Bipin Chandra Pal, for example, reveals the Bengali cultural mood of the period: an unmistakable romanticization of violence. The use of religious symbolism to invoke political acts, moreover, made the leaderships' appeals popular and meaningful. We thus find Aurobindo preaching terrorism against the British in the name of Kali: 'Kali, Goddess of destruction, mother of strength, created by Gods to destroy the demons who had usurped their kingdom'.[19] Others also, including Bipin Chandra, glorified revolution as a religious duty. The goal was to revenge the insult to 'Amar Sonar Bangla' (our Golden Bengal); the means required self-sacrifice as expressed through courting danger—including endangering one's life—aimed at a higher good. Even those not directly involved in militant acts were influenced. Political violence was not to be condemned. On the contrary, it highlighted the selflessness of the participants and therefore invited admiration.

This focus on 'culture' and 'mood' should be qualified in two ways. Firstly, it is difficult to estimate in any precise sense how many of the bhadralok really shared these political values or the extent of their political commitments. A sizable minority of the educated Bengalis, after all, remained entrenched in

[17]Sumit Sarkar, *The Swadeshi Movement in Bengal, 1903–1908*, New Delhi: People's Publishing House, 1973, Chapter 2.

[18]Broomfield, *Elite Conflicts in a Plural Society*.

[19]Ibid.

government services and in the professions. They had little to do with politics and political activism. I am, therefore, not suggesting that the bhadralok as a whole turned to militant politics; only that a significant minority did. And second, as an analytical principle, one should not overemphasize the independent significance of cultural conditions—culture always requires material conditions to be sustained. What is significant about cultural conditions, however, is the fact that once values become deeply embedded in a society, they are a social force in their own right. It would therefore be a mistake to underestimate the significance of the Bengali view of political violence as an act of self-sacrifice and therefore worthy of admiration; giving up of one's self for the sake of a principle was held to be a political act of the highest order. Given this belief, it is plausible to propose that such a cultural mood, legitimated and therefore facilitated the spread of militant tactics for the pursuit of nationalist goals.

The anti-partition agitation and the eventual reunification of Bengal had far reaching consequences on Bengali political psychology.[20] First, it created considerable distrust of the British and of constitutional methods of change. This, in turn, helps explain the reluctance of many Bengali elites to participate in British-controlled legislative councils. Second, the success of the movement encouraged a belief in the efficacy of militant tactics. Many who had participated in the movement joined underground terrorist organizations with the aim of continuing militant nationalist agitation. Related to both of these consequences was a third one, namely, a permanent division of Bengali nationalists between 'moderates' and 'extremists'.[21] The moderates continued to hold that the British could be opposed through electoral means, via participation in legislative councils. The majority were, however, attracted to 'extra-parliamentary' methods; these varied from boycotting of British goods to attacks on the British garrison. While none of these nationalist groups were social radicals at this point—on the contrary, social values were often religious and conservative—tactical divisions would eventually thrust the extremists away from the national political mainstream, and towards more radical political ideologies.

British response to nationalist militancy was to forge an alliance with Bengali Muslim elites and the more moderate bhadralok, aimed at isolating the extremists. Many of the moderates were, however, reluctant to participate in legislative councils, lest they be labelled collaborators. Muslim leadership, by contrast, accepted the British invitation and came to dominate Bengal's electoral politics from the 1930s until the formation of Pakistan.

[20]Ibid.; and Majumdar, *History of Modern Bengal, Part Two*, chapter 1.

[21]For a refined exposition of these simplified divisions see Sarkar, *The Swadeshi Movement in Bengal, 1903–1908*.

The discussion so far has focused exclusively on the political strains among the bhadralok, who were primarily a Bengali Hindu elite. Over half of Bengal's population in the first half of this century, however, was Muslim (Table 12.10). If nothing has been said about the Muslims so far, it is mainly due to the focus of this essay on political trends in today's West Bengal, which were areas of Hindu concentration in the past (Table 12.11). Far less is also

TABLE 12.10: Distribution of Castes in Bengal, 1931

Caste Category	Percentage of Total Population	
Twice-Born		3.13
Brahmin	2.83	
Rajput	0.30	
Upper Shudras		14.37
Vaidya	0.21	
Kayastha	3.04	
Mahishya	4.66	
Others	6.46	
Lower Shudras		5.19
Sadgop	1.11	
Saha	0.82	
Adi-Kaibartta	0.68	
Others	2.58	
Scheduled Castes		15.09
Scheduled Tribes		3.00
Muslims		54.00

Source: *Census of India*, 1931, vol. V, Part II 'Tables'.

TABLE 12.11: Proportionate Distribution of the Population by Divisions on a Social and Religious Classification, 1931: Bengal and Sikkim

Area	Primitive Tribes	Hindus			Total Hindu	Muslims
		Brahmin	Depressed Classes	Others		
1	2	3	4	5	6	7
Bengal	3	3	14	25	42	54
Burdwan Division	7	7	27	45	79	14
Presidency Division	1	4	21	26	51	47
Rajshahi Division	6	1	5	25	61	62
Dacca Division	–	2	13	13	28	71
Chittagong Division	3	1	6	15	22	76
Bengal States[1]	20	1	3	60	47	35

Source: *Census of India*, 1931.

Notes: Burdwan and Presidency Divisions became part of India's West Bengal after Partition, and Dacca and Chittagong Divisions became part of Pakistan. The districts of Rajshahi Division were divided up between India and Pakistan.

[1]Includes Cooch Bihar, Tripura, and Sikkim.

known about the political history of Bengali Muslims.[22] No understanding of bhadralok politics and the eventual weakness of the Congress within Bengal, however, can be complete without some reference to the role of the Muslims.

Bengali Muslims were never as enthusiastic about the anti-partition and Swadeshi movements as were the Hindu bhadralok.[23] The Muslims viewed with suspicion the Hindu revivalist tendencies among the Gita-swearing, Hindu bhadralok. The primary concerns of the Muslim elite were greater access to higher education and those of the Muslim tenants in the east, protection against Hindu landowners. It was not difficult, then, for the Muslims to view Hindu elites as blocking the progress of their community. The Muslims had hoped to ally with the British so as to enhance the oportunities available to them. Even if the partition of Bengal was only one such possible route, for both reasons of religion and socio-economic interest, the Muslims were not ready to accept Hindu leadership.

The early alienation of some of the Muslims from bhadralok politics found institutional expression in the 1920s in the Krishak Praja Party of Fazlul Huq.[24] Interestingly, Muslim leadership was able to forge alliances between lower caste Hindus and Muslims on the basis of promises to reform conditions of rural indebtedness and insecure tenancy. The Huq ministry in the late 1930s was thus probably the last opportunity for communal collaboration, which was opposed both by the majority of the Bengali Hindu bhadralok on the one hand, and by the Muslim League of Jinnah on the other. It was during these crucial years also, that the moderate Hindu bhadralok became increasingly isolated from the Bengali political mainstream and that a sizable minority of the extremists embraced communist ideology.

It is important at this point to divert our attention to the interaction of Bengali politics with Indian national politics. Bengal's attitude towards the emergence of Congress from the very beginning was lukewarm. Bengalis considered themselves politically advanced, and as early as the 1890s criticized Congress as 'three day's fun', 'rich man's club', 'sentimental braggarts' and 'a debating forum for the brown sahibs'.[25] Gandhi's leadership also failed to capture the imagination of Bengali bhadralok. Broomfield has suggested that Gandhi was too much of a social radical for the conservative Bengali bhadralok.[26]

---

[22]As exceptions, see Hossainur Rahman, *Hindu–Muslim Relations in Bengal, 1905–1947*, Bombay, Nachiketa Publications, 1974; Sarkar, *The Swadeshi Movement in Bengal, 1903–1908*, Chapter VIII; and John Gallagher, 'Congress in Decline: Bengal, 1930 to 1939', *Modern Asian Studies*, 7(3), July 1973.

[23]Rahman, *Hindu–Muslim Relations in Bengal*, Chapters 2–4.

[24]Gallagher, 'Congress in Decline'.

[25]Majumdar, *History of Modern Bengal, Part One*, pp. 536–7.

[26]Broomfield, *Elite Conflicts in a Plural Society*.

Whether this was so or not, the elitist orientations of the bhadralok have been well documented. The historian John Gallagher (1983), for example, has traced the weakness of Congress in Bengal during the crucial 1930s to the elitist isolation of the bhadralok. The upper caste bhadralok dominated Calcutta but had relatively few links with the districts, especially the eastern districts. Within Calcutta, moreover, the bhadralok were deeply enmeshed with business and landed interests. When the electorate was enlarged, therefore, the Hindu political elite found themselves in a very difficult situation. In order to build support, the bhadralok would have had to leave the comfort of Calcutta lifestyles, forge alliances with the Muslim majority, and adopt social policies antithetical to their zamindari interests. As none of these changes were forthcoming, the Hindu elite became more and more isolated. The Muslims filled the political vacuum and thus came to dominate state politics.

The national Congress was, in any case, working at cross-purposes with the Bengal Congress. Gandhi had a national vision. By supporting the Khilafat movement, Gandhi wanted to incorporate the Muslims within the Congress. Concessions made to the Muslims at the national level, however, often translated into policies weakening the Hindu Congress elite within Bengal.[27] The bhadralok, therefore, continuously remained ambivalent towards the Congress.

In addition to issues of political and economic interest, there was the persistent cultural issue of the distrust of the Bengali elite of domination by Hindi-speaking India. Gandhi was the quintessential representative of Hindi-India from which the Bengali elite wanted to disassociate. Even from the standpoint of political experience, Bengalis felt they had already tried out 'non-cooperation' as a strategy during the anti-partition agitation. Bengalis, in other words, considered themselves politically developed and therefore natural leaders of India's nationalist movement; even when they did not aspire to national leadership, they were not about to follow Gandhi with the same degree of enthusiasm as the rest of India.

The refusal of the Bengali elite to be absorbed by a Hindi leadership was and has remained a central theme in Bengali politics. This, of course, is not to suggest that no important Bengali leaders came under the sway of Gandhi and the Indian National Congress. It is rather to suggest that the Bengali cultural identity and the related distrust of Hindi-India has proven to be a political disadvantage to Bengal's moderate leadership. Moderates identifying with Gandhi often lost support to those willing to ridicule Gandhi's non-violence as 'tactical weakness'. Bengali nationalism was also on the side of the extremists' refusing to accept Gandhian leadership. And

---

[27]Gallagher, 'Congress in Decline'.

finally, given the intense communal sentiments, Gandhi was often viewed as appeasing the Muslims.

For all these reasons, Gandhi and the Indian National Congress never held the centre stage in Bengal's political drama. Even such well-known Bengali Congress leaders as C.R. Das maintained an ambivalent attitude towards Gandhi's leadership, eventually leaving the Congress to form an independent political party. After Das' sudden death in 1925, even the modicum of support the Congress had enjoyed vanished. When the dust settled after the communal violence of the 1925–37 period,[28] it was Fazlul Huq's Krishak Praja Party that went on to form a government. The Congress party, as it turned out, never formed a government in undivided Bengal.

Throughout the two or three decades prior to independence then, Hindu moderates in Bengal—the most likely candidates for spearheading the Gandhian movement—remained divided and weak. Electoral politics came to be controlled by those Muslim leaders who were first part of the Congress, later part of Fazlul Huq's party, and eventually supported Jinnah's Muslim League. It was during this time also that many of the former extremists and terrorists, then in jail, slowly embraced communism.

Why were a small but significant number of the political elite attracted to communism in Bengal, but not in most other parts of India? The answer is complex and is rooted both in Bengal's elite politics and social conditions.

Elite attraction to socialism and communism was first related to prevailing socio-political values. Even though in practice the Bengali elite were quite conservative, populist themes were central to Bengali culture. Social issues, especially those concerning the position of the poor, were important and integral to the lively Bengali intellectual milieu. Addressing the bhadralok, influential intellectuals like Bankim Chandra Chatterjee argued that 'the downtrodden masses have as much right to happiness on earth, as you have'. Even Tagore had socialistic sympathies: 'Socialism seeks to equally distribute wealth among all—I do not know whether that is practicable or not. If it be totally impossible, then I say, mankind is extremely unfortunate'.[29]

While such 'populist' sympathies were far from a coherent communist ideology, they nevertheless highlighted the general intellectual drift. And such a situation is consistent with the following generalization: if a social setting is dominated by the intellectuals, and if a substantial number of the intelligentsia concern themselves with social issues, it is virtually inevitable that some would actually be attracted to communism.[30] Using Gramsci's

[28]John Broomfield, *Mostly about Bengal: Essays in Modern South Asian History*, New Delhi: Manohar Publications, 1982, chapter 9.

[29]Chattopadhyay, *Communism and Bengal's Freedom Movement*, p. 14.

[30]Karl Mannheim, *Ideology and Utopia*, New York: Harcourt, Brace and World, 1936, Chapter III.

terminology of 'traditional' intellectuals—men of learning, not directly connected with the production process—Sumit Sarkar has similarly explained the political leanings of the bhadralok: the English-educated 'traditional' intelligentsia of Bengal responded readily, even if superficially, to world ideological currents of liberalism, nationalism and eventually socialism.[31]

This general socialistic drift of the Bengali intelligentsia was re-enforced by the coming of the Russian revolution. First, some radicals went abroad, came in direct contact with Bolsheviks and their supporters, converted to communism, and returned to Bengal with Moscow's blessings to carry on political work. More important, many nationalists within Bengal, especially those in prisons, greeted the Russian revolution as a great 'anti-imperialist' event. Interviews with those who embraced communism during this period[32] make it clear that the attraction of the Russian revolution was not only or not even primarily communism; the Russian revolution was interpreted as a victory of 'progressive' forces against western imperialism. The Russian revolution fed the political ethos of Bengali extremists directly: militancy, heroism and nationalism. Bengali militant nationalists thus came to be attracted to communism via a route followed by many other Third World communists, namely, the route of radical nationalism.

Neither sympathies towards socialistic values, nor towards the Russian revolution, however, fully explain why any set of political activists embrace communism. After all, Nehru and others in India's nationalist movement also had similar sympathies but were not communists. The additional condition operative in Bengal, therefore, was the position of 'counter-elite' that most Bengali extremists came to occupy in regional politics. Having refused to be absorbed within the Gandhian mainstream, many of the Bengali militant nationalists can be thought of as oppositional elites in search of an ideology. Theirs was a political battle, not only against the British, but also against what they perceived as Hindi-domination. In order to distinguish themselves from the nationalist-reformist stance of the Congress, Bengali extremists as political competitors had only two options: radical Right or radical Left. Both of these options were tried in Bengal. That the communist elite remained urban-oriented and isolated from peasant majorities well into the 1960s, highlights the elitist nature of Bengali communism. That the communists have turned reformists upon acquiring power, while maintaining a strong tone of Bengali nationalism, further supports the contention that communism was viewed primarily as an alternate route to power.

Political preference for communism within Bengal was thus moulded by the prevailing societal values and by the structural position of political

---

[31]Sarkar, *The Swadeshi Movement in Bengal, 1903–1908*, pp. 513–4.
[32]Chattopadhyay, *Communism and Bengal's Freedom Movement*.

'outsiders' that a sizable minority of the Bengali bhadralok came to occupy within India's national politics. It is important to distinguish this line of argumentation from that conceptualizing Bengali communist leaders as 'frustrated bhadralok'.[33] The so-called bhadralok were a rather diverse social group with divergent political preferences.[34] Any conceptualization which treats them as 'frustrated' *en masse* is likely to be inadequate. I have, therefore, first sought to emphasize the political diversity of this group and then attempted to explain why some members of the intelligentsia were attracted to communist ideology. This shifts the analytical focus to the element of choice: a segment of the Bengali political elite chose to disassociate themselves from India's centrist political mainstream. Having made this choice, but still seeking positions of power, these elite were drawn to radical ideologies.

Many who turned to communism in Bengal were militant activists first and communists later. Most ideological conversions occurred in prisons during the 1930s. Not much is known about how many initially joined a communist party; the historical origins of the communist party in India are itself murky.[35] I will further discuss the mechanics of these conversions within the framework of terrorist organizations. What is important to note here is that Bengali political culture and the position of many militants as political 'outsiders'—at least in part by choice—facilitated the move of a significant minority among the more 'extremist' of the politically active *bhadralok* towards communism in the 1930s. After independence, and the exodus of the Muslim leadership to East Pakistan, this communist elite formed the major opposition to a divided and weak Congress party.

BENGALI EXCEPTIONALISM: CASTE AND CLASS STRUCTURE

A militant elite is only one variable in a long and complex chain of historical causation leading up to the fact that the Congress has been a relatively weak political force within West Bengal and that the state is now ruled by a communist party. Elites need followers to transform their ideological inclination into significant political force. Bengali communists have found such mass support: first, only sporadically in labour union militancy and scattered peasant rebellions; and of late, in seemingly more stable electoral majorities. The next question for analysis is, what aspects of Bengal's social structure help explain the political difficulties of the moderate and the conservative political leaders on the one hand, and the successes of the radicals on the other.

[33]Franda, *Radical Politics in West Bengal*.

[34]Leonard Gordon, 'Radical Bengalis: Alliances and Antagonisms', *South Asian Review*, July 1972, p. 342.

[35]Gene D. Overstreet and Marshall Windmiller, *Communism in India*, Berkeley: University of California Press, 1959.

The relative insignificance of caste in contemporary West Bengal politics is rooted deep in Bengal's history. While old historical records are meagre, the best known history of the area suggests that in ancient times Bengal was outside the zone of Aryan culture.[36] Brahminical Hinduism and related caste structures, therefore, did not sink as deep roots in this region as those to the west and north. The more egalitarian Buddhism survived in Bengal considerably longer than in other parts of India, especially at the intermediate and the bottom end of the social scale. Even when Hinduism took over, Bengal's caste system was less rigid. Around the twelfth and thirteenth centuries several distinctive social traits were observable within Bengal: Bengali Brahmins could eat fish and meat; inter-caste marriage and dining were not uncommon; all non-Brahmins (about thirty-six castes) were considered Shudras and were not further subdivided into rigid categories; and the untouchables could eat with members of cleaner castes.

Mass conversion to Islam during the middle ages further highlights the weakness of caste domination in the area. Those who changed religions were often lower caste Hindus seeking better life chances.[37] Members of lower castes perceived their social situation as unjust and when given an alternative, many took it. Historically, this alternative was religious protest; later, a similar process found an outlet in secular protest with considerable political consequences.

Muslim domination and Islamic conversion within Bengal gave rise to numerous Hindu reform movements. What had existed of Brahminical Hindusim in mass society was further attacked by new religious developments. Tantrism, for example, emphasized worldly pursuits and romanticized physical prowess and even violence. The worship of Kali, for example, with bleeding, decapitated heads as her garland, is rooted in Tantrism—but was also egalitarian in that all castes could become Tantrics. Chaitanya's Vaishnavism was explicitly and radically anti-caste and egalitarian. Sahajivas preached sexual equality and freedom. While the influence of these sects would rise and wane, there can be no doubt that their collective impact was to further weaken the ideology legitimizing rigid caste division and domination, namely, Brahminical Hinduism.

What is important to recognize about all of these trends chipping away at the Brahminical ideology, is that their impact was probably more significant on the lower castes than on the higher ones. The higher castes benefited from Brahminism and were not about to let go of a social system

---

[36]R.C. Majumdar, *History of Ancient Bengal*, Calcutta: G. Bharadwaj & Co., 1971, pp. 25–7, 414–535.

[37]R.C. Majumdar, *History of Medieval Bengal*, Calcutta: G. Bharadwaj & Co., 1973, pp. 189–90.

which served them well. It was the lower castes, therefore, who often embraced Islam or experimented with Tantrism and other reform religions. The reaction of the upper castes to ideological erosion fluctuated between pioneering reform and reimposing orthodoxy, often with a vengeance and militancy characteristic of a threatened elite.

Caste Hinduism thus generally came to have less legitimacy for the lower castes within West Bengal. A large percentage of non-Hindu lower social strata—Muslims and tribal groups still constitute more than a quarter of contemporary West Bengal's population—further reduced the significance of Hinduism for legitimizing the inegalitarian social structure. By contrast, however, those towards the top seem to have held on tenaciously to Brahminism. One is tempted to speculate that this tenacity increased in direct proportion to the ideological erosion at the bottom of the scale.

Bengali caste structure has certain other characteristics which are important for understanding the limited role of caste in later Bengali politics. There are, for example, no indigenous Kshatriyas or Vaishyas in Bengal (Table 12.10). The Brahmins, moreover, constitute a small per cent of the population—much smaller, for example, than in Uttar Pradesh. Historically, the Brahmins were considered just another *jati*.[38] Kayasthas and Vaidyas— which rank just below the Brahmins—are considered clean Shudras in so far as Brahmins will take water from them. Other intermediate castes like the Sadgops and the Tilis have historically experienced considerable upward mobility in the ritual hierarchy.[39] The unclean Shudras and the untouchables, who constituted in 1931 about 40 per cent of the Hindu population (Table 12.10), complete the hierarchy of Bengali Hindu society.

The monopoly of Brahmins over socio-economic privileges within Bengal has never been complete. While the Brahmins have clearly been at the pinnacle of the social ladder, control over land has historically been shared by other intermediate castes. Regional diversity at the village level has been especially significant. Ratnalekha Ray, for example, notes in the following reference to pre-British Bengal:

Each village had its own peculiar caste structure; and while it may appear that in the province as a whole the Brahmins, Kayasthas, and Vaidyas were the privileged caste, in each village there might be a dominant agricultural caste rated quite low in the provincial ritual ranking. In areas of high-caste concentration there were, of course, Brahmin and Kayastha villagers who participated in agriculture and controlled the production of their villages. But more typically such controlling groups came from locally dominant agricultural castes. In the villages of Midnapur, they would quite likely be Kaivartas and Sadgops; in Burdwan, Sadgops and Aguris;

[38]Hitesranjan Sanyal, *Social Mobility in Bengal*, Calcutta: Papyrus, 1981.
[39]Ibid.

in Rangpur and Dinajpur, Muslims; in Kuch Bihar, Rajbanshis; in Jessore, Faridpur, and Bakarganj, Muslims and Namasudras; in Bishnupur, Brahmins.[40]

Above the village level, where the rights to a portion of agrarian revenue resided, such rights were often shared mainly by Brahmin and Kayastha zamindars but also by some Vaidya and Muslim ones.[41] The early introduction of education in Bengal by the British opened opportunities for these land-owning castes. While the Brahmin zamindars were the earliest to 'arrive' upon the scene as the bhadralok, by the turn of the century, there were among the Calcutta bhadralok large numbers of Kayasthas and Vaidyas. The 1931 census, for example, reported that while 14.3 per cent of the Brahmins were literate in English, so were 13.2 per cent of the Kayasthas and 28.1 per cent of the Vaidyas.[42]

Since both access to land and educational opportunities have historically been shared by a number of castes, this may be one reason why political movements within modern Bengal have not precipitated along caste lines. The communal conflict between the Hindus and the Muslims, in any case, provided such a major cleavage in the first half of this century that there was probably little energy left for further intra-Hindu caste conflict. The diversity of dominant castes at the village level, moreover, created a situation in which there were no state-wide dominant castes. Besides zamindari abolition in West Bengal, another reason why caste politics did not emerge, has had to have been the absence of any state-wide dominant agricultural castes whose members may have consolidated political and economic privileges.

To summarize this discussion on caste in Bengal, the Bengali caste structure did not follow the Brahminical division into four *varnas*. A small Brahmin minority at the top was followed by numerous gradations of clean and unclean Shudras, with the untouchables as usual at the bottom. The Brahminical ideology came under repeated attacks historically, especially from Islam, but also from other religious offshoots of Hinduism. The impact of these challenges was probably to weaken the legitimacy of Brahminism in the eyes of the lower castes. At the top of the pyramid, by contrast, the social elite held on to Brahminism tenaciously well into the twentieth century. Even at the top, however, landownership was not a monopoly of the Brahmins. Village-level control was exercised by numerous castes, often lower in ritual hierarchy. Members of several upper castes were able to take

---

[40]Ratnalekha Ray, *Change in Bengal Agrarian Society, 1760–1850*, New Delhi: Manohar Publications, 1979, pp. 52–3.

[41]Ibid., chapter 1.

[42]Marcus Franda, 'West Bengal', in Myron Weiner (ed.), *State Politics in India*, Princeton: PUP, 1968, p. 263.

advantage of educational opportunities. This process truncated the top of the caste pyramid. When competitive politics arrived upon the Bengali scene, therefore, unlike in other parts of India, caste issues were not the major issues of politics; an element of 'caste pluralism' and diversity towards the top and weak caste identification at the bottom, may well be the important reasons why caste issues did not arise as the most significant issues for political mobilization in Bengal.

Private property as a legal right was only introduced to Bengal by the British.[43] Even prior to that, however, control over land revenues, though not necessarily land, was clearly identifiable. When the British came to Bengal, much of the land revenue was controlled by Hindu zamindars. The latter had been relative newcomers on the scene, having supplanted a mostly Muslim aristocracy in the early eighteenth century. What is of interest from our perspective is the fact that the Hindu zamindars did not have deep roots in the land; they had acquired lands either as court favourites, or as effective revenue collectors, or as military lords in control while the Mughal empire disintegrated. Revisionist historians like Ratnalekha Ray have suggested that the sphere of zamindaris lay, not in the economy, but in the polity, implying that the pre-British Bengali zamindars were essentially revenue collectors with established authority rather than landed aristocrats in the English pattern.[44]

These zamindars of the eighteenth century were predominantly of Brahmin and Kayastha castes. They often controlled large areas, many of which equalled what today are districts. Ray suggests that 'at the time of the British occupation nearly 60 per cent of the land revenue of Bengal was paid by 15 large zamindaris comprising 615 parganas out of 1,256 in the province'.[45] It was these zamindars who were well positioned to take advantage of the Permanent Settlement made by the British.

The zamindars owed a share of the revenue they collected to the Nawabs, who occupied the pinnacle of the pre-British Bengali political economy. Real control over land, however, resided below the zamindars at the village level. The village 'landlords'—the *jotedars*—were formally tenants of the larger zamindars. In practice, the zamindars were seldom in a position to bypass totally the local and entrenched village level authority of the jotedars. These jotedars controlled substantial lands, acted as money-lenders and grain dealers, and generally dominated village life. One early survey in 1808 found 'that 6 per cent of the cultivating population enjoyed 36.5 per cent of the land leased by raiyats (read jotedars) from the zamindars, whereas 52.1 per

---

[43]B.M. Baden-Powell, *The Land System of British India*, Oxford: Clarendon Press, 1892, Book I, chapter IV.

[44]Ray, *Change in Bengal Agrarian Society*, chapter 1.

[45]Ibid., p. 27.

cent of the agricultural workforce had no land at all and worked for the rich farmers as hired labourers or sharecroppers'.[46] As noted above, the caste origins of these village-level 'czars' in Bengal was quite diverse: it of course included the upper clean castes of Brahmins and Kayasthas, but often rested in the hands of such cultivating lower Shudras as the Sadgops, Namasudras, Aguris, and Kaivartas, as well as some Muslims.

To simplify a complicated historical picture, prior to the arrival of the British in Bengal, just below the Nawabs, existed a layer of mostly Brahmin and Kayastha zamindars who exercised political-administrative authority, especially revenue collecting authority, over a collection of villages. At the village level itself village headmen, belonging to a diverse set of locally dominant castes and communities, exercised the real control over land. And finally, below these jotedars, existed the low caste and Muslim cultivators in the form of small raiyats, share-croppers and landless labourers.

The staying power of this historical pattern has been considerable, especially at the village level. Once again, to simplify a complex history of 'change without change', the British, in time, replaced the Nawabs, buttressed the authority of zamindars by legal and political changes, but did not alter the pattern of village level domination in any substantial manner. The Congress government in independent India eventually eliminated the zamindars, but even they could not supplant the power of the village level jotedars. On the contrary, Congress governments reinforced the power of the jotedars by incorporating them as the key intermediary figures in patron–client networks of electoral mobilization exchanged for governmental benefits. Finally, the Communists have sought to isolate the village-level jotedars. While jotedars still control sizable village lands, the Communists have sought to build political alliances directly with groups below the jotedar. Efforts to incorporate the smallholders have so far been much more successful than the attempts to channel benefits to those who, throughout history, have been at the bottom of the heap—the landless labourers.

To return to the historical narrative, when the British introduced the Permanent Settlement the consequence was anything but anticipated. Hindu zamindars turned neither into a British style country gentry, nor into productive yeoman farmers. The results were rather twofold: first, a rapid turnover in landownership as those with 'settled' lands often failed to pay their dues to the colonial powers; and second, as ownership stabilized, a tendency to lease and sub-lease land resulting in numerous layers of tenancy and 'interests' on 'settled' lands.

The conventional view of Bengal's history (as in the *Cambridge Economic History of India*, for example) has suggested that rapid turnover in zamindaris

[46]Ibid., p. 64.

brought a spate of Calcutta businessmen on the agrarian scene, thus slowly but surely supplanting a traditional aristocracy by a more money-minded agrarian class, with far-reaching detrimental consequences to the agrarian life of Bengal. Revisionist historians[47] have carefully documented that this was not the case; some of the distressed zamindaris were bought by the better-established, existing zamindars, and other were only made to look as if they had changed hands. What was changing hands, in any case, was not land but title. Given that the real control over land was entrenched at the village level, change in zamindari titles led primarily to a change in those who had access to land revenue rather than to an actual circulation of land. The elites who lived off the land circulated and their numbers actually grew, but the structure of village level control over land did not alter significantly.

The real consequences of the Permanent Settlement were thus to further entrench and enlarge the type of dominant groups—the upper-caste zamindars—which had already existed at the top of the social pyramid in pre-British India. The British buttressed the powers of the zamindars with the coercive machinery of the modern state, in the form of collectorates and the accompanying law and order forces. This enabled the zamindars to squeeze larger surpluses from the land but only at the expense of losing traditional legitimacy. The enlarged surpluses, in turn, supported not only British rule, but also the growth of a high-caste literati with landed connections, manifest as layers of absentee 'tenants', living in Calcutta and the district towns.

Historical evidence also suggests that the burden of increased land revenue was born primarily by the tillers of the soil rather than by the village level jotedars. The jotedars, nevertheless, continuously experienced pressures from the zamindars for enhanced revenues. In this conflictual relationship created by the Permanent Settlement lies an important explanation of the political trends in British-governed Bengal. The Bengali bhadralok, whose connections to the zamindars by both caste and land wealth were considerable, came to spearhead the nationalist struggle. The jotedar class of the Namasudras and the Muslims, the Sadgops and the Aguris, and also some Brahmins and Kayasthas, were rather reluctant to join these bhadralok-led struggles. The economic interests of those in Calcutta and district towns were often at odds with those who dominated villages; they often also did not share caste identities. That the bhadralok-led Congress never formed a government in undivided Bengal, whereas the Muslim and the Namasudra alliance of rich tenants succeeded under Fazlul Huq, thus becomes a little more comprehensible.

The Permanent Settlement was also of far-reaching economic and sociological consequence. From an economic standpoint, layers of tenancy

---

[47]Ibid.

created a situation in which no one had any interest in improving lands. Returns on investment were shared so many ways that agricultural investment suffered, and so did agricultural growth over prolonged periods. As a consequence, Bengal, one of the most fertile parts of India, and with relatively high yields in the nineteenth century, was by the middle of the twentieth century producing considerably less from a unit of land than many other Indian regions. Widespread tenancy has also probably continued to depress agricultural performance in post-independence Bengal.

From a sociological standpoint, those connected with land, but not agriculture—members of high castes with access to land revenue—became Bengal's leisured and cultured classes. Eschewing manual work, these classes indulged themselves in matters of mind and spirit. Land revenues thus provided the material base for the growth of a value system deriding work and the entrepreneurial ethos, but holding artistic and cultural achievements in high esteem. So powerful was the hold of these values that even when the land connection was weakened, the Bengali elite continued to view active pursuit of profit, technical skills or manual labour with disdain. The best Bengali minds thus devoted themselves to music, poetry, literature, art, philosophical concerns, social criticism and even radical politics.

The culture of the Bengali elite also kept them from exploiting new economic opportunities. Calcutta, as the capital city, offered plenty of chances for the enterprising. As indicated, however, most of these opportunities were availed of by non-Bengalis: British, Marwaris, and Parsis. These non-Bengalis were either not interested, or found it difficult to make themselves an integral part of Bengali society. Within British-ruled Bengal, then, urban industry came to be dominated by non-Bengalis, agriculture was ignored as a productive sector and exploited by all for sustenance, and Bengali bhadralok pursued the arts, culture, and of course, politics.

Aspects of Bengali social structure provide one set of insights into why the Congress did not develop a stronghold in British Bengal and why other political forces found a more ready hearing. The Hindu educated elite of Bengal, the bhadralok, spearheaded Bengal's nationalist movement. They were the natural Congressmen of Bengal. For reasons analysed earlier, these bhadralok, often due to their own political values and leanings, tended to be attracted to militant tactics. They remained ambivalent towards Gandhi's Congress. Within Bengal, moreover, both the caste and class positions of the bhadralok made it difficult for them to forge alliances below the district level.

Village level politics was dominated by diverse land-controlling castes. These rich 'tenants', the Bengali jotedars, maintained sometimes cooperative and sometimes conflictual relations with the high-caste bhadralok of Calcutta; they, in any case, did not form long lasting political alliances with the Congress leadership. On the contrary, jotedars of certain districts actually threw their weight behind other political parties, which were anti-zamindar, and which promised 'tenancy reforms'. The jotedars were, however, too diverse a social group to throw up their own party. The Congress thus remained weak, but alternate 'centrist' parties also did not find it easy to forge lasting alliances.

The jotedars were often of intermediate caste status. Their domination was not easily legitimated by Brahminical ideology. Repeated reform movements, including Islamic conversions, had also weakened the impact of Brahminical Hinduism. When the jotedars felt pressured to squeeze the village level peasantry further, therefore, sometimes lower class rebellions resulted, and at other times, the jotedars themselves opposed such demands. It was not easy to forge cohesive and consensus-based political movements in such settings.

Patterns of caste and class domination thus often differed in Bengal from those in other parts of India. The social structure was generally more conflict-ridden at all levels. The issue of elite militancy has already been mentioned and is further discussed below. Instances of conflict around socio-economic interests were also numerous.

While examples of lower class rebellion can be mustered from the nineteenth century—such as the 1857 revolt of the indigo planters and the 1860 Howrah railway workers strike—the significant revolts belong to the twentieth century. The most important of these are the instances where nationalist rebellion quickly turned into class rebellion within Bengal. What started in 1920 as a series of strikes against British-owned factories and plantations—strikes against trade and rule as the two pillars of imperialism— grew into a general strike by 1921.[48] Led by left-leaning Bengali Congressmen, the strike invoked the serious wrath of Marwari businessmen. Not only did Marwaris request Gandhiji, who obliged, to intervene on behalf of 'ahimsa', but they also withdrew money from 'Swaraj funds', and provided armed assistance to the police in dealing with the 'violent strikers'. Bengal's left-leaning leaders had a heyday publicizing the 'Marwari-Khadi-British' link as the link of 'exploiting profiteers' against 'Bengal's working class'. It is also not surprising that communist-led trade union organizations continued to grow in the aftermath, especially in the 1930s and the 1940s.

Gandhi, partly in order to direct attention away from the urban strikes, launched a rural movement against some tax policies. Bengali villagers took over the movement enthusiastically and soon, as in the Midnapur district in 1922, refused to pay all taxes. Gandhi again had to withdraw the movement lest it became too radical. Movements also broke out against the

[48]Majumdar, *History of Modern Bengal, Part Two*; and Chattopadhyay, *Communism and Bengal's Freedom Movement*.

zamindars. These were often led by relatively well-off occupancy tenants. Examples of these include the already mentioned militancy of the Namasudras, who often controlled village-level lands in eastern districts, but who resented their low status as Chandals in the ritual hierarchy. Similar struggles between land-controlling Muslim raiyats and the Hindu zamindars also fed communal movements, first encouraging the Krishak Praja Party and later the Muslim League.

Below these levels, we may also recall the famous Tebhaga Movement.[49] This was a movement of sharecroppers against jotedars for altering the share of crop from 50–50 to 66–33. Led by urban communists, the movement originated among the middle peasants against 'oppression' of jotedars, referring generally to some illegal exactions. The success of the radicals in winning concessions later encouraged sharecroppers in Dinajpur and neighbouring districts to join the leadership of Bhowani Sen in demanding alteration in the share of the crop. Sharecroppers of several districts, mainly of tribal and Muslim origins, rapidly joined the movement in 1946, right after the great Bengal famine. Soon, however, the Muslim League government of Bengal unleashed state repression. Many of the middle peasants also withdrew support, mainly because they often leased out lands to sharecroppers and stood to loose. And as the demands for Pakistan gained momentum, the Hindu communist leaders and their Muslim followers suffered split loyalties, further weakening the class movement. The Tebhaga Movement collapsed in 1947, but left a legacy highlighting traditions of peasant radicalism in parts of Bengal.

All of this suggests that there was considerable lower and lower-middle class rebelliousness in Bengal during the first half of the twentieth century. The primary cause of this was rooted in the historically conditioned caste and class structure of Bengal. Radical elites could not only transform structural conditions into lower class rebellions, but lower class rebelliousness was itself an encouragement to the radical elites. Nothing boosts elite radicalism like responsive lower classes. Peculiarities of the Bengali caste and class structure, and of the militant elite thus mutually reinforced each other helping to explain both the weakness of Congress and a small but growing leftist force within pre-independence Bengal.

BENGALI EXCEPTIONALISM: ORGANIZATIONAL TRADITIONS

An important factor in the contemporary success of left forces within West Bengal has been a relatively effective, centralized political party. What historical factors are responsible for the emergence of such a political force?

---

[49]Hamza Alavi, 'Peasants and Revolution', *Socialist Register*, 1965.

In a part of the world where personalities, factions, and fragmented parties dominate the political scene, what helps explain the existence of a relatively cohesive political organization? In addition to the obvious role of radical political leaders in organizing Leninist or democratic-centralist parties, it is also important to take account of the Bengali terrorist past.

By the turn of the century, many of the militant nationalists, utilizing terrorism as a mode of political activity, organized themselves into highly secretive and disciplined groups. The earliest and the best known of these was the Anusilan Samiti. The Samiti had both a secretive and an open existence. The relatively open activities revolved around periodic political discussions. The issues of concern were the plight of colonial countries, especially India and Bengal under the British, the lives of such important militant leaders as Mazzini and Garibaldi, the revolt of the American colonies against the British, and the struggles of various European peoples against oppression and for independence.[50]

Those convinced of the fact that the British were responsible for India's sufferings and that the British were not likely to leave voluntarily—that they would have to be pushed out by militant tactics—joined these secret organizations. The process of acquiring organizational membership was, however, elaborate. Members had to pass through various stages, proving their skills and trustworthiness. At each stage, members had to take a different vow. Majumdar[51] has traced three such vows and they are worth quoting in full:

First vow   I shall never disassociate myself from the Samiti; I shall always conform to the rules of the Samiti, shall obey without question the orders of the authorities, shall always speak the truth to the leaders and shall never suppress anything.

Intermediate   I shall never communicate the internal matters of the Samiti to anybody; I shall never quit my place of work without informing the leader, shall immediately intimate to him any information about a conspiracy against the Samiti and shall try to meet the situation as directed by him.

Final vow   I shall not leave the organization till the objective is achieved. Love of parents, brothers and sisters and attraction for home shall not make me neglect my duties or falter in the execution of the directions of my leader; if I violate this vow, may I be destroyed by the curse of Brahmins, of my parents and of the patriots of all countries.

[50]Majumdar, *History of Modern Bengal, Part Two*, Chapter V.
[51]Ibid.: Chapter V.

Conformity to these principles was imposed by more than just the 'curse of the Brahmins'. In many instances, Samiti members committed political murders to punish what was conceived to be a breach of membership principles. And all this before Lenin's ideas of democratic centralism had reached this part of the world.

Such secretive and disciplined organizations reflected in part the security needs of carrying on terrorist activities against the British, and in part a Bengali tradition of secretive organization of social dissent. The activities of the Tantrics in the past, for example, when fearing religious persecution at the hands of mainstream Hindus, had for a long time been shrouded in mystery and secretiveness. Militant nationalists developed the art of such organizational principles further. As a result, those attracted to terrorism and militancy within Bengal adopted an organizational ethos stressing discipline, secretiveness, respect for hierarchy and self-sacrifice as the political act of highest virtue.

It is also important to stress that cohesion was not always easy to maintain. Factionalism has been a powerful ingredient of all Indian political sub-cultures. It was difficult to contend with even inside highly disciplined organizations. The Anusilan Samiti split into two over issues of leadership personalities and differences on the role of terrorism. The splinter group, Jugantar party, attracted those favouring greater militancy. From our perspective, however, what is important to note is that both groups were organized along the principles noted above.

The programmes of the terrorist organizations were primarily nationalist—anti-British. Their social philosophies tended to be highly variable. In the early years, prior to the 1920s, anti-Muslim and conservative sentiments were pronounced. During these early years, religious appeals were used for political purposes.[52] Slowly, many of the terrorists were attracted to socialism and communism. The role of the foreign-returned, Bengali communists was quite significant in this process. M.N. Roy had received Moscow's blessing and was sending his emissaries to Bengal. Individuals such as Nalini Gupta and Abani Mukherjee (an anti-Roy emissary with German connections) came from abroad and were often protected from arrest by terrorist organizations. For example, Nalini Gupta lived at various terrorist headquarters upon his return from the Soviet Union.[53]

Leaders of terrorist parties were not necessarily attracted to communist ideology. Their interest in the foreign emissaries was primarily the prospect of securing arms and money from the Bolsheviks. These contacts, however,

[52]Sarkar, *The Swadeshi Movement in Bengal, 1903–1908*, chapter 9.
[53]Chattopadhyay, *Communism and Bengal's Freedom Movement*.

put the returning communists in close touch with intermediate leaders and even the rank and file of the terrorist organizations. Foreign-returned communists had all the necessary ingredients to facilitate ideological conversions: intellectual sophistication; anti-imperialism; blessings of the greatest revolutionary leaders, the Bolsheviks; and most of all, individuals risking their lives, and courting danger for some higher social good.

Foreign-returned communists, as well as the ideas inspired by the Russian revolution, had the impact of converting many members of the Anusilan and Jugantar Samitis to communism. When jailed in the 1930s, often in the Andaman and Nicobar Islands, the committed communists further converted other jailed terrorists to communism. Such were the beginnings of the original conversions to communism in Bengal. Some of these early converts later became leaders of India's communist party. For example, Pramode Das Gupta, Hare Krishna Konar, and Binoy Chowdhury, all hailed from old terrorist revolutionary backgrounds, who converted to communism, and then devoted their lives to building the communist movement in Bengal.

The point of this discussion has been to delineate the organizational characteristics of the terrorist groups, and to stress the link between these groups and the later communist party. A significant minority of Bengali political activists already understood the importance of disciplined organizations when they were introduced to communism. Having embraced the new ideology, the organizational principles of democratic-centralism came relatively easily to this group. Discipline, hierarchy, and party before all else, were values integral to the terrorist political sub-culture. In all probability, these political cultural traditions facilitated the growth of relatively cohesive parties within contemporary West Bengal. Of course, this is not to ignore the legendary factionalism and sectarianism on the Indian Left. Nevertheless, the CPI(M) in West Bengal stands out today as one of the more cohesive political forces in all of India. Long traditions of disciplined organizations are, at least in part, responsible for this political characteristic.

FROM CONGRESS TO COMMUNIST RULE

Having examined the historical record, it is clear that by the time of independence, Congress was not a very strong force in West Bengal and that radical politics had already established strong roots in the area. A significant number of the political elite had embraced communism, and the lower classes—workers and peasants—had indicated ample susceptibility to radical appeals. The two did not always come together as the communist leadership either remained urban-oriented under Moscow's influence, or eschewed mobilizational work due to its own elitist orientations. The political traditions of the area had, however, enabled the radical elite to organize a small but disciplined party, which would in time grow into the ruling party. As I have already examined the more recent behaviour of the Bengali Communists since coming to power, what remains to be analysed so as to complete the picture, is how Bengal's Communists actually displaced Congress rule in West Bengal.

The emergence of the Communists as a ruling force in West Bengal is a function of two related but separate conditions: weakness of Congress and the growing electoral popularity of the CPI(M). Both of these require explanation.

After independence, Congress emerged in West Bengal—like everywhere else in India—as the ruling party. Having been established as the party of national freedom, there was no question of any other party challenging Congress's supremacy at that time. Nevertheless, Congress rule in West Bengal was rather weak and had certain distinct characteristics. As already discussed, prior to independence, Muslims had dominated Bengal's electoral politics. Muslims had also secured the support of Hindu lower castes and classes by promising them agrarian reforms in the 1930s. As Muslim leaders left for Pakistan, the West Bengal Congress found itself weak, fragmented and with little established grass-roots support. Individuals like Atulya Ghosh and B.C. Roy could still muster electoral majorities through their association with Nehru and Congress, but they had little or no autonomous power base within the state.[54] In order to understand this continued weakness of Congress, one must first understand the social structural changes that occurred in West Bengal immediately after independence.

The social structure of West Bengal since independence has undergone important changes. The most visible of these was the abolition of the zamindari system. The zamindars, who in one form or another had mediated the relations of provincial governments to villages for centuries, were finally eliminated by India's sovereign Congress government. As is well known, zamindari abolition was implemented imperfectly. Except for the largest and the most visible zamindars, most of them held on to significant pieces of land. To the extent that zamindaris were broken up, the real beneficiaries were the former 'occupancy tenants', the jotedars.

Many of the former zamindars took government compensations and sought to branch out into various non-agricultural commercial activities; as usual, some succeeded, while others joined the ranks of failed entrepreneurs. Those who held on to sizable pieces of land often became jotedars of sorts, in the sense that their influence came to be limited over one or a few villages where they owned land. The most important consequence of

[54]Chaudhry, 'West Bengal'.

zamindari abolition, therefore, was to transform a three-tier structure of domination involving the provincial government, zamindars, and village-level jotedars into essentially a two-tiered structure of government and jotedars.

As noted, Hamilton-Buchanan had in 1808 found 6 per cent of the cultivating population, the jotedars, enjoying about 36 per cent of the land as tenants of the zamindars. If one thinks of modern-day jotedars as those possessing more than 10 acres of land, it is striking that, in the aftermath of zamindari abolition in the 1950s, about 5 per cent of the largest landowners still controlled around 30 per cent of West Bengal's land (Table 12.8). The continuity in the patterns of land concentration over one and a half centuries is rather remarkable. The share of land revenues that the jotedars keep has obviously changed dramatically over this time, just as have the fortunes of many who either acquired more lands or fell upon hard times. The increasing incomes of the jotedars have probably been eaten up by demographic changes, so that abolition of zamindaris did not result in much wealthier individual jotedars. The share of land controlled by the village-level landowners, nevertheless, has been strikingly consistent.

The declining share of the land of the largest landowners since independence becomes significant in light of this historical continuity. Demographic changes are without doubt the most important factor at work. Land reform legislation, however, also contributed. While little or no land has been redistributed, land reform legislations may well have discouraged further concentration of landownership. This process, coupled with division of property upon inheritance, probably explains the fact that, by the 1970s, landowners owning more than 10 acres controlled around 15 per cent of land—half of what they had controlled in the 1950s.

Below the larger landowners also, the general trend in West Bengal has been towards smaller and smaller landholdings from one generation to another. The ranks of those at the bottom of the social pyramid have swollen. About one-third of the rural households do not own any land. If one combines those who own no land with those who own less than 1 acre, these are the rural poor, constituting over half of all the rural households of West Bengal—a dismal picture of bleak and massive poverty. It is estimated that about half of these rural poor are at any one time involved in some type of tenant farming, creating somewhere between 1.5–2 million families of sharecroppers or bargardars in West Bengal.

What have been the political consequences of these changing patterns in the Bengali social structure? At the top of the social pyramid, the elimination of zamindaris removed the material base upon which the Bengali literati and political elite, the bhadralok, had flourished. The connection of the bhadralok with land in any case, had been weakening for quite some time. As the cultured and educated elite, their political preferences thus came to be influenced by many factors, including, of course, their own material well-being. The partition of Bengal at independence was one of these factors. Many of Bengal's Hindu elite implicitly or explicitly held Gandhi and the Congress responsible for Bengal's final partition. Even those who did not hold this position could not easily bring themselves to be enthusiastic about Gandhi and Nehru; 'golden Bengal' had been reduced to one-third of its size as a result of the great national victory of the Congress party.

A sizable portion of the Bengali literary and political elite thus remained either lukewarm or downright hostile towards the Congress. A significant minority, by contrast, joined hands with the Congress and sought to build a new provincial political base. Those with long-run vision knew that the political future lay where the majorities lived, namely, in the villages.

The Bengali jotedar class were the major beneficiaries of the Congress-sponsored zamindari abolition. These were also the groups upon which post-independence Congress sought to build its power base. While this strategy worked rather well for Congress in many Indian states, the results in West Bengal were not as good. As discussed above, many Bengali jotedars had opposed the Congress and its upper-caste leadership prior to independence. New alliances were made, but they did not always endure.

Bengali jotedars are a highly diverse group, often belonging to various unclean Shudra castes. In contemporary Bengal, the Aguris are significant in Burdwan, the Mahishyas in Midnapur, the Brahmins and the Kayasthas in Bankura and Hugh, the Mahatos in Purulia and the Gurkhas in Darjeeling. In such a diverse social setting, caste identity could not become a basis for long-lasting political alliances.

The Congress sought to rest its power on these diverse groups of local influentials to muster electoral majorities. Myron Weiner in his elite survey in West Bengal in 1958 found many Congressmen to be 'pillars' of local communities.[55] In rural areas, these were generally landowning elites of high and intermediate castes. The capacity for leadership of many of the village headmen of unclean Shudra castes, it is fair to presume, could not have been as great as those higher up in the ritual hierarchy. Caste rigidities and caste identification at the lower end of the social scale, moreover, have been weaker in Bengal traditionally. If one adds to these circumstances the more than sporadic tradition of tenant revolts in Bengal, one is led to see why Bengali jotedars did not provide a stable base of power for the Congress.

[55]Weiner, *Political Change in South Asia*, p. 189.

As the nationalist party, Congress in the early post-independence years won handsome electoral majorities (Table 12.1). Their support base, however, proved to be not as stable as in many other states of India. There were no state-wide dominant castes around on which to build long-lasting alliances. The hold of the locally diverse dominant castes over tenants and landless labourers, moreover, was weaker in Bengal than in other states. These social-structural peculiarities of Bengal did not help the Congress party.

Furthermore, the Congress continued to be thought of as a party of Hindi-India. The traditional ambivalence of the Bengali bhadralok towards Gandhi manifested itself as a belief that Congress and Delhi did not have Bengal's interest at heart. Not only was lower class support thus not universal for Congress, but many of the elite, touched by regional nationalism, held Congress suspect. As the euphoria of national independence fell into the background, issues of regional nationalism became important electoral concerns further undermining some of Congress's support.

Bengali elites and masses alike were thus not incorporated as easily into Congress as they were in other states of independent India. This was a continuation of a historical trend analysed above. The communists, by contrast, emerged as a small but significant and well-entrenched political force. Within the first few years, the Communist Party of India had established itself as the major opposition party in West Bengal. The political significance of the Communists was greater than their small electoral support would suggest. This is because the support the Communists had was 'hard'— ideologically committed and well organized. Initially, this was among the urban intelligentsia, the unionized working class and small pockets of the radicalized peasantry.

The very factors which undermined Congress support worked in favour of the communists. Cultural proclivity to militant activism and Bengali nationalism ensured that the new generation of political activists, especially in Calcutta, would continue to be attracted not to Congress, but to home-grown left politics. The high-caste educated elite, had lost the material base for controlling state-level politics. Those who controlled land, by contrast, often belonged to intermediate castes and did not possess the social esteem necessary to mould political trends. The absence of indigenous social groups possessing both property and social esteem thus ensured the failure of hegemonic politics to take root. Non-Bengali capitalists tended either to withdraw capital or secure central support for ensuring their interests. Either of the moves inflamed Bengali passions and created a further distrust of capitalism. Lower classes exhibited political independence and quite a few were attracted to left parties. Cumulatively, these trends hurt the Congress and continued to benefit Bengal's Communists.

With a few minor swings, Bengal's Communists have steadily improved their electoral support (Table 12.1). In the early years, the Communists were their own worst enemies. Under Moscow's tutelage, they continued to look towards the proletariat in a land of peasants. The split within the communist movement eventually laid the groundwork for the long-term maturation of the CPI(M). The CPI(M) was able to distinguish itself from the CPI, over the years which had been moving closer and closer to the Congress party under Moscow's directions. The CPI(M) also successfully disassociated itself from the more extreme Naxalites. It learned to take the peasantry seriously from the Naxalites. As a party seeking electoral victories rather than a peasant revolution, however, the CPI(M) wanted a broad-based support in the countryside; it sought to build alliances with all those below the larger jotedars—the middle peasants, sharecroppers and the landless labourers. The CPI(M) thus struck a popular image of a party which was both mildly radical and responsible. At the same time, as it did not have a record of collaboration with Delhi, it could capitalize on regional nationalist themes. Radical, responsible, and West Bengal's alternative to Congress, these were the images with which the CPI(M) eventually secured electoral majorities.

The CPI(M) finally came to power in 1977. This was when the anti-Indira 'wave' was sweeping the nation. The sentiments which worked to Janata's advantage in other parts of India, enhanced the CPI(M)'s electoral position within West Bengal. This suggests that while the CPI(M) has a strong political base within West Bengal, its dominant position also owes something to the capricious shifts of public opinion. Moreover, the CPI(M) emerged victorious under the first-past-the-post electoral system in which a divided opposition—Congress and Janata—is always punished. The reason, the CPI(M) has been able to consolidate its position since, of course, has to do with the CPI(M)'s effective performance. Nevertheless, electoral caprice and distortions of the electoral system have benefited the CPI(M) in West Bengal, just as they have often benefited the Congress nationally and in other states. As opposition parties can unite and electoral popularity can be affected by numerous factors, the CPI(M) may well be voted out of power in the future. Those are the necessary hazards of democratic politics. That outcome, however, would not in any way alter the exceptional nature of politics in West Bengal: a relatively weak Congress Party and the significant political position which a 'radical but responsible', or a reformist-communist party, has come to occupy within the state.

CONCLUSION

I have in this chapter sought to delineate and explain the changing patterns of dominance in India's Bengal. Sifting through existing historical evidence, one is forced to conclude that, over time, there has been a lot more change in the fortunes of those who have dominated than in the living conditions and the life chances of those who were dominated.

The top of the pyramid has continuously evolved. The Nawabs and the de facto zamindars of the eighteenth century were replaced by the British and the legally entrenched zamindars. The educated and upper-caste Hindu elite challenged this domination but failed to impose their own rule. Eventually, the Congress as a successful national movement eliminated the Bengali zamindars. The Congress within Bengal also sought to impose order mainly by aligning with non-Bengali industrialists and Bengali landowning village influential of diverse caste backgrounds. This system, however, never struck deep roots. It has now been successfully challenged by a reform-oriented communist party. The communist leadership is well organized and has sought to build alliances with both the middle and the lower classes of Bengal.

Village life over centuries has been dominated by land-controlling or landowning individuals belonging to locally diverse dominant castes. In addition to controlling land, these jotedars have dominated village economic life through money-lending and control of markets. Below the jotedars, again for centuries, actual cultivation has been carried out by small landowners, sharecroppers or hired landless labourers. These cultivators generally have been members of lower castes, untouchables, tribals, or Muslims. Demographic pressures have obviously swelled the ranks of the rural poor. Changing modes of production have brought about some shifts in the proportion of the poor who are sharecroppers or labourers. Some organized lower castes have also successfully raised their status in the ritual hierarchy. None of these changes, however, have altered the overwhelming historical continuity: the majority of the population belonging to the lower castes, and without access to property or gainful employment, have lived under conditions of abject poverty at the bottom of the socio-economic pyramid.

It is within this broad historical picture of 'change without change' that contemporary West Bengal provides the unusual case of the emergence of an elected communist government to power. Can an elected communist government make a dent in rural poverty within the constraints of a private enterprise economy? How has a communist government come to power in any case? Why did India's premier political party, the Congress party, fail to strike deep roots in Bengal? These have been some of the main questions addressed in this essay.

The weakness of Congress and the emergence of the Communist parties to power has been analysed with reference to three historical conditions:

militant activism of the Bengali educated elite; a social structure within which hegemonic domination was difficult to establish and the mobilization of lower castes and classes was possible; and traditions of disciplined political organization.

To summarize, a militant Bengal Hindu elite spearheaded India's nationalist movement, but it eventually failed to find its rightful place in Gandhi's Congress. Having forsaken the political 'centre', this elite experimented with numerous militant tactics and extremist ideologies before settling upon a fairly mild version of communism.

This discontented elite eventually found support within the Bengali social structure. Historically, certain peculiarities within Bengal made it difficult for the upper castes and classes to establish legitimate domination. During the Mughal and British periods, upper castes had access to landed wealth but seldom controlled land directly. After independence, the clean castes lost some of these rights. Those controlling land, by contrast, were of a diverse caste background, often belonging somewhere in the middle of the ritual hierarchy. Their control of property was not matched by their social esteem. Urban industry and wealth came to be controlled by a significant number of non-Bengalis. This diversity at the top of the socio-economic pyramid made hegemonic domination difficult. The educated elite, in any case, had repeatedly challenged one aspect or another of the overall domination. Lower classes and castes also have repeatedly proven restive in this environment. It was not an easy setting for 'consensual' politics of the Congress type to take root.

The communist elite of Bengal did not become serious contenders for power till they gave up their seemingly heroic militancy. Once the Communists decided to build mass support around reformist and regional nationalist themes, however, they found a ready hearing in Bengali society. A well-disciplined party, helped by similar traditions of terrorist organizations in the past, finally enabled the Communists to move to the centre stage of Bengali politics.

Over the last decade or so, the Communist rulers have made some serious attempts to alter historically inherited patterns of domination. The patterns, however, are deep and the problems are massive. The Communists are also constrained both by the larger national framework and by the tensions within their own alliance between the very poor and the moderately well-to-do.

The Communists, nevertheless, have successfully isolated the propertied elite from the political sphere. While the jotedars continue to own land, they cannot easily mobilize state power to buttress their local power any more. They also have difficulty securing governmental resources as patronage. The Communists have instead channelled these resources to the moderately well-to-do. They have also attempted, with some success, to improve the security and the material conditions of the poor sharecroppers. Unfortunately, however, even the Communists have not as yet been able, or have not attempted, to do much for the poorest of the poor—the landless labourers.

13

Parliamentary Communism and Agrarian Reform
The Evidence from India's Bengal*

The Communist Party of India, Marxist (CPI[M]) has survived as an important political force in India. Whereas the more clearly pro-Soviet Communist Party of India (CPI) as well as the 'Maoist' Communist Party of India, Marxist-Leninist (CPML) have paled into political insignificance, the CPI(M) now rules two of India's nineteen states—West Bengal and Tripura— and remains the major opposition party in Kerala. West Bengal is the heart of CPI(M)'s power, where India's 'parliamentary communists' have steadily increased and consolidated their electoral strength. After various 'United Front' experiences, the CPI(M) gained a clear parliamentary majority in 1977. The 1980 elections for the Lok Sabha and those at the state level in 1982 have further confirmed CPI(M)'s secure electoral base in West Bengal. This article assesses the recent governing experience of West Bengal's 'communist' rulers.

What elements of the communist commitment to 'revolutionary class war' and the establishment of a 'dictatorship of the proletariat' has the CPI(M) 'compromised' in order to succeed electorally and survive politically within the framework of democratic-capitalism? Given the 'compromises', does the CPI(M) remain any more efficacious an agent of redistributive reforms than other Indian parties? And, if so, what political features distinguish the CPI(M), while explaining its redistributive capacities? Aiming to answer these

*Originally published as 'Parliamentary Communism and Agrarian Reform: The Evidence from India's Bengal', *Asian Survey*, 23(7), July 1983, pp. 783–809.

The research reported here is based on two field trips (1978–9 and 1981) to India. While in India in 1978–9, the author was affiliated with the Centre for the Study of Developing Societies, Delhi. The funding for the research project, of which this article is a part, has been provided by various sources: The Social Sciences and the Humanities Research Council, Canada; The Institute for the Study of World Politics, New York; University of California, Berkeley, and Michigan State University. The author would like to thank Michael Bratton, Marcus Franda, Jyoti Dasgupta, Pranab Bardhan, and an anonymous *Asian Survey* reviewer for their helpful comments on an earlier draft.

questions, I analyse below the nature of the CPI(M) as a ruling party and its agrarian reform policies in West Bengal.

Based on evidence gathered through fieldwork, I argue that the CPI(M) has moved in an increasingly 'social democratic' direction, while initiating a multi-pronged effort to alleviate West Bengal's rural poverty. Reformist actions have replaced revolutionary goals in face of both a realistic assessment of constraints on the one hand, and political interests of the power holders on the other. Political efforts aimed at improving the lot of the rural poor are nevertheless significant. The restructuring of local government, tenancy reforms, credit for smallholders, and increased employment and wages for the landless add up to a modest set of democratically guided reforms of the rural social structure. The capacity of the CPI(M) to initiate redistributive reforms stems from its political characteristics. The type of leadership, ideology and organization the CPI(M) brings to bear on the operation of political power enables it to perform two tasks important for implementing reforms from 'above': first, penetration of the countryside without being directly captured by the landed classes; and second, controlled mobilization from 'below' to buttress state power as a tool of agrarian reform. The CPI(M)'s developmental experience thus has some general implications as well. It highlights how a well-organized, left-of-centre party regime creates a degree of separation between political and social power and thus enables the implementation of rural reforms within a democratic-capitalist model of development.

THE CPI(M) REGIME

How regime power is structured in relation to society has considerable bearing on regime capacities to intervene for social change. Specifically, regime leadership, ideology and organization are important variables for understanding any regime's reformist potential. Whether the leadership is cohesive or fragmented, what social interests are reflected in the regime ideology and organization, and the extent to which organizational arrangements permit a political penetration of the society, all influence patterns of planned developmental intervention. An analysis of CPI(M)'s reformist role in West Bengal is thus begun by focusing on its leadership, ideology and organization.[1]

Leadership

The CPI(M)'s leadership power is neither concentrated in the hands of one individual, nor in the party alone. The party, of course, wields great influence.

---

[1] For an analysis of the earlier experiences of the CPI(M) and the United Front ministries, see Marcus Franda, *Radical Politics in West Bengal*, Cambridge, Mass.: M.I.T. Press, 1971; and Bhabani Sen Gupta, *Communism in Indian Politics*, New York: Columbia University Press, 1972.

Power at the top is, however, shared by the three 'wings' of the CPI(M): the party organization; the Kisan Sabha (the peasant wing), which provides the vital link to rural voters; and the parliamentary leadership, which runs the government. Pramode Dasgupta, in charge of the party until his death in early 1983, Binoy Chowdhry, head of the Kisan Sabha, and Jyoti Basu, leader of the CPI(M) in the West Bengal State Assembly, were the three most prominent leaders. The intra-party political balance has been more confused, at least temporarily, since Pramode Dasgupta's death.

Pramode Dasgupta, the state party secretary, was the man most responsible for shaping the West Bengal CPI(M) into a well-organized, disciplined party. Of austere tastes, he was respected as a leader of integrity. He wielded considerable political influence and was considered the most 'radical' of the prominent leaders.[2] Jyoti Basu, by contrast, hails from a wealthy, upper-caste background. Educated in elite Calcutta schools and trained in law at Middle Temple, London, in both style and ideology he evokes a 'social democrat' rather than a 'communist revolutionary'.[3] A competent parliamentarian, he was and remains a natural candidate for heading the democratically elected, left-of-center government. Binoy Chowdhry, the low-key peasant leader,[4] is intellectually disposed and eschews revolutionary rhetoric. Though urban in social origin, Binoy Chowdhry has spent most of his life organizing the peasantry. His power base is in the districts, specifically in Burdwan district. As the head of the West Bengal and the All-India Kisan Sabha, his quiet strength within the CPI(M) government is revealed by the fact that his favoured programmes for the sharecroppers top the policy priority list.

While the varied leadership has given rise to more than an occasional factional conflict within the CPI(M), not to mention those within the 'Left Front' government (i.e., the CPI(M) and several other minor political parties), this has not precluded the pursuit of relatively cohesive rule within West Bengal, especially in comparison to many other Indian states. Two important factors, one integral to the CPI(M) and the other circumstantial, have tended to mitigate fragmenting tendencies. The first is party discipline. Since the party is organized on 'democratic centralist' principles, disagreements and power ambitions in the CPI(M), while played out within the party, have not become impediments to a coherent policy. The second and the circumstantial factor facilitating a modicum of governmental unity is a shared perception of the 'common enemy': the central government of India in conjunction with the 'bourgeois-landlord' forces. Whatever the accuracy of these

[2]For a biographical sketch of Pramode Dasgupta, see Bhabani Sen Gupta, 'Pramode Das Gupta: Party Builder in Eastern India', *Perspective*, Calcutta, April 1978.

[3]Based on an interview with Jyoti Basu, Calcutta, 17 March 1979.

[4]Based on interviews with Binoy Chowdhry, Calcutta, 12 March 1979, and 2 November 1981.

perceptions, the process of securing and maintaining power is conceived of as an ongoing struggle.[5] As open conflicts may deprive the leadership of power, there is a perceived vested interest in unity—political survival.

Ideology

Over the years, CPI(M)'s ideology has shifted from a 'revolutionary' to a 'reformist' orientation. Instead of emphasizing 'class confrontation' as a means to the establishment of the 'dictatorship of the proletariat', the CPI(M) has over the years evolved a more moderate stance. This is best characterized as a developmental and a democratic-socialist ideology. It emphasizes the preservation of democratic institutions on the one hand and the use of state power for facilitating 'development with redistribution' on the other.

In the aftermath of the 'emergency' of 1975–7, the renewed emphasis on democracy was clear at the CPI(M)'s Tenth Congress (2–8 April 1978). The 'immediate' as well as the 'long term objective', according to the resolution, was 'expanding democracy and introducing new clauses in the constitution putting the fundamental rights of the people beyond the mischief of any ruling party or government'. Aimed at this, the programme recommends the mobilization of 'the broadest possible support' including 'elements who do not support the economic programme of the party'.[6] The struggle for preserving and strengthening democratic institutions is, in other words, now given primacy; struggles over class issues need to be carried out within the framework of a non-authoritarian, open polity.

This moderation was evident even earlier in the agrarian programme adopted in 1976. The party line stressed that land redistribution, while a useful 'propaganda slogan', should not be made into a 'slogan of action'. In contrast to past practices, land seizures (which were to be encouraged in a resolution adopted in 1969) were now not to be encouraged as a tool of mobilization and politicization. Instead, 'the Kisan (peasant) movement led by our party—will have to channelize many other agrarian currents, like the question of wages for rural workers, the issue of rent reduction, the abolition or scaling down of peasant indebtedness, fair price for agricultural produce, and the reduction of tax burdens'.[7] Pramode Dasgupta explained this reorientation by arguing that the only way to gain the support of all

[5]For example, Ashok Mitra, Minister of Finance (1977–82), argued: 'What we have to constantly experiment is how far we can push without invoking some intervention—or what is the feasibility frontier—we have the experience of Kerala in 1959 very much in our mind.' Interview, Ashok Mitra, 16 March 1979.

[6]See Communist Party of India (Marxist), *Political Resolution,* adopted at the Tenth Congress, 2–8 April 1978, Jullundur, p. 18.

[7]Communist Party of India (Marxist), Resolution of the Central Committee, *On Certain Agrarian Issues,* March 1976.

the peasantry, 'rich and poor', was to pay attention not only to the 'land question' but also to the issues of 'irrigation, seeds, and fair prices for the produce'.[8] The thrust of the agrarian programme was, in other words, increasingly to shift its focus away, not only from 'class confrontation' to electoral competition, but also from narrow asset redistribution to a more broad-based focus on development with redistribution.

The reformist reorientation of the CPI(M) is even clearer in its political analysis of who is the 'enemy' and who is on 'our side'. In contrast to the Marxist emphasis on social classes, the CPI(M) now mixes class with political and other criteria in deciphering potential allies. In the agrarian sector, for example, the only class to be 'isolated' is the 'big jotedar' class. They are 'enemies' not only because they own more land than anybody else, though that is part of it, but mainly because they do not participate in agricultural activities.[9] The support of all other agrarian groups, including larger landowners who supervise production, is to be sought. The resolution on the 'Tasks on the Kisan Front' makes this explicit: 'the unity of the agricultural labourers, poor, middle and rich peasantry (that is, peasantry which uses agricultural labourers and poor peasants) is sharply emphasized'.[10] Accordingly, even 'exploiting' classes (rich peasants utilizing the labour of others) are not 'enemy' classes as long as they are productive and willing to extend political support. Like the Italian communists,[11] the CPI(M) in India can reconcile the prospect of a 'communist state' in a 'capitalist society' only by arguing that there are but few real enemies even in a capitalist society. Broad-based political unity aimed at reform is the essence; revolutionary confrontation with the propertied classes is not on the agenda.

Underlying this 'democratic-socialist' tilt are several factors: the dynamics of electoral-constitutional politics, the CPI(M)'s past experiences, and the need to maintain a healthy economy. As the CPI(M) has sought electoral success, the need for broad-based political support has been deemed important. Knowing well that the rich and the middle peasants are not only

[8]Pramode Das Gupta's speech to the Silver Jubilee Celebration of the Kisan Sabha, reported in *Ganashakti*, 10 February 1979.

[9]The CPI(M) distinguishes jotedars from rich peasants by virtue of the fact that the former do not work the land themselves. While the usage is flexible, the CPI(M) tends to label absentee landlords—generally owning more than 25 acres—as jotedars. CPM's 'class analysis' was explained to the author in an interview with Maujam Hussain, member of Legislative Assembly, West Bengal, and Secretary, Local Committee, Debra Block, Midnapore, 23 March 1979.

[10]Communist Party of India (Marxist), Resolution of the Central Committee, *Tasks on the Kisan Front*, March 1976.

[11]See Sidney Tarrow, 'Communism in Italy and France: Adaptation and Change', in Donald L. M. Blackmer and Sidney Tarrow (eds), *Communism in Italy and France*, Princeton: Princeton University Press, 1975.

numerically significant but, if alienated, can mobilize considerable opposition on behalf of other parties, the CPI(M) has softened its ideological position. Moreover, having accepted constitutional limits, the leadership clearly realizes that the scope for radical property redistribution is minimal.[12] If these electoral and constitutional constraints were not evident in the early life of the CPI(M), active participation in political life for a few decades has clarified both the conditions for electoral success and for surviving as a governing power. Crucial to this 'organizational learning' have been two interrelated experiences. First, the slogan of 'seizure of benami land' (land registered in false names and categories), adopted in 1969, let loose forces which the CPI(M) itself could not control. This led to other political elements, especially the more revolutionary Naxalites, gaining at the expense of the CPI(M), and also to widespread dissatisfaction with the CPI(M), especially among the landed and the middle classes, culminating in repression initiated by the central government. That a revaluation of the agrarian strategy followed is no surprise.[13] Related to this has been the experience of United Front ministries, both in West Bengal and Kerala. As these state governments collapsed under the stress of internal class problems and central governmental pressures, the CPI(M) has now decided to 'go slow', and to assure the propertied of the party's limited 'socialist' intent.

In addition to these constraints, the need to maintain economic growth has led the CPI(M) to take a reconciliatory stance towards the propertied. In the recent past, the economy of West Bengal has been characterized by moderate to low agricultural growth in comparison with India as a whole, and by a tendency for industrial capital to move out of the area. Both characteristics could be easily worsened by radical policies. Had the CPI(M) decided to limit the public investment supporting agricultural production because it benefits the larger landowners disproportionately, agricultural growth would have suffered; had the leadership encouraged labour union activism, the tendency of capital to stay away from, or leave West Bengal, would have continued.[14] The legitimacy of all regimes, however, remains

---

[12]Thus Jyoti Basu argued that 'we recognize that within the larger constraints we are operating under, we cannot bring about fundamental change'. Interview, 17 March 1979.

[13]As a party cadre active in block level organizational tasks explained to the author, 'the slogan to seize benami land was first raised in 1969. The resulting movement was quite irregular and confused. It was not clear as to whose land was to be seized—whether khas [above ceiling land held onto by landowners] or benami or both. Illegal and irregular seizures occurred. When we went out of power, massive repression followed. Only in 1976 we clarified this whole issue.' Interview, Johar Santra, Secretary, Local Committee, Ghatal Block, District Midnapore, 14 March 1979.

[14]For example, see 'Wooing Business to West Bengal', *Indian Finance,* 10 September 1977. This theme of how to attract investment into West Bengal is a continuing one. For a more recent statement, see 'Wooing Industrialists', *EPW,* 12 June 1982, p. 975.

tied to their demonstrated capacity as economic managers. No democratic leadership can afford to take actions discouraging economic growth. Sluggish growth is likely to be followed by shortages, unemployment, general dissatisfaction, and a decline in electoral popularity.[15] Thus, a democratically elected, left-of-centre regime within the framework of a privately owned economy is constrained by the very nature of the arrangement: measures perceived as radical will discourage privately controlled economic activity. To avoid this outcome, the CPI(M) regime has from the outset sought to assuage those in a position to facilitate economic growth—landowners and urban capitalists alike. The CPI(M) has learned that for the sake of survival, it cannot afford to be 'revolutionary'; the most it can achieve is to facilitate 'development with distribution'.

ORGANIZATION

At the core of the CPI(M) as an organizational force is a tightly knit and a relatively small party. In an area with a population close to 45 million, the CPI(M) boasts no more than 40,000 party members in West Bengal.[16] To understand how the CPI(M) has generated a popular and an efficacious political presence with less than 1 per cent of the population as members, one has to understand the nature of the party as well as the link between the party and various 'support groups', such as the Kisan Sabha.

The core membership of the party is a highly disciplined and select group. Each member actually gains that status after several years of 'party work', typically in the trade union, Kisan Sabha, or student movement. Those sympathetic and dedicated to the party's mission are observed closely by those who are already members. Meeting periodically in small groups for political discussions, party members are able to observe at close quarters a prospective member's 'political development' and 'dedication' to the party. The prospective member in turn internalizes the party line as well as an ethos that discipline and loyalty constitute the highest virtue and thereby enable one to become a member.

The pre-recruitment period ends only when a potential member has proven to existing members that he or she understands the party line well and is willing to be a loyal follower of party directives. Those who become members have therefore already agreed to put party considerations before others. Once membership is achieved, the tendency towards loyalty and discipline is only accentuated by the 'democratic-centralist' principles on which the party is organized. Aside from loyalty and/or imposed discipline,

---

[15] For an elaboration of this argument, see Atul Kohli, 'Democracy, Economic Growth and Inequality in India', *World Politics*, July 1980.

[16] Interview, Abdullah Rasool, former leader, Bengal and All India Kisan Sabha, the party headquarters (State Committee of West Bengal), Calcutta, 14 March 1979.

as the ascent in the party hierarchy is also a function of dedication to the party, some of those seeking success find it opportunistic to go along with the party line. Loyalty, discipline, and opportunism thus combine in a tightly knit organization. While none of this eliminates internal dissensions or variations in viewpoints, it does create a relatively cohesive political force consisting of individuals representing the views and interests of the CPI(M).

In the recent past, the core membership of the CPI(M) hailed primarily from urban professional groups. The peasantry was only 'discovered' in the late 1960s. Various conditions facilitated this 'discovery'.[17] The loosening control of landlords over their dependents was rightly perceived as an opportunity to gain the electoral support of this newly released political resource, the peasantry. The more radical elements within or outside of the party, following Mao's teachings, were already beginning to prove that the peasantry offered potentially mobilizable political material. Peasant leaders such as Konar had also gained prominence within the party. He argued for a worker-peasant alliance along Leninist lines. Even to those leaders for whom the primary goal was electoral success, and these have remained dominant, it was clear that this would require successful penetration of the countryside. Aimed at facilitating this rural tilt, therefore, the CPI(M) undertook the recruitment of those university-level students in district towns and in Calcutta who had active rural roots.[18] It was hoped that these students, often turned primary or secondary school teachers, would go back to their areas as party members or near-members, continuing the task of 'propaganda and organization'.

To summarize, as a party in West Bengal the CPI(M) consists of a relatively small group of disciplined and organized cadres. These cadres generally originate from the 'middle' and the 'lower-middle' strata in both the cities and the countryside. This party structure supports and is supported by various 'interest group'-type auxiliary organizations. These include the CPI(M)-controlled student movement, the women's movement, the trade union movement and the peasant movement organized under the Kisan Sabha. These groups provide important links between the party and the society at large. Electoral and other types of political support are generated through the various 'movements'; once in power, those providing support expect rewards from the party in power.

The CPI(M) swept into power in 1977. The number of assembly seats captured by the Left Front (mainly CPI(M), but also including the Forward Bloc and Revolutionary Socialist Party) has been decisive (230 of 293 in 1977 and 238 of 294 in 1982). The percentage of votes secured—46 per cent in

[17]For a detailed analysis of this, see Bhabani Sen Gupta, *CPI-M: Promises, Prospects, Problems*, New Delhi: Young Asia Publications, chapters 3 and 5.

[18]Interview, Sukumar Sen Gupta, Party Secretary, District Committee, Midnapore, 22 March 1979.

1977 (1982 figures are not known yet), however, was less so. Had Janata and Congress not split the opposition vote, the CPI(M)'s overall majority could have been reduced. This potential future 'alliance' between the 'bourgeois' parties is part of the CPI(M)'s overall calculations regarding the necessity of consolidating its power. In spite of these reservations, however, the victory was a heady one. For the first time, the CPI(M) had won a clear majority enabling it to form a government free of 'united front' entanglements.

The factors underlying the CPI(M)'s 1977 success in part reflect its own deepening political base and in part the failure of other parties. In the aftermath of the 'emergency' (1975–7), the Janata Party cut deeply into Congress's support. These two parties split the votes, and the CPI(M) was the beneficiary. Furthermore, having aligned itself with the Congress during the 'Emergency', the CPI lost its credibility and electoral support. As the opposition lay in tatters, the CPI(M) emerged as the major political force in West Bengal. The CPI(M)'s own political work contributed further to this success. Throughout the early 1970s, the Left in West Bengal suffered political repression.[19] Moreover, as the United Front-ministry was dismissed, the landlords used this opportunity to reverse many of the fragile social gains of the tenants. Mass evictions of *bargardars* (sharecroppers), involving the use of police force, followed.[20] Instead of breaking the CPI(M)'s back, political and social repression seems to have strengthened it. According to a party member, 'while this repression was let loose, many of us continued, in a quiet way, to spread our propaganda and organize the peasantry. The electoral success proves that our efforts have borne fruit'.[21] While he may exaggerate the class basis of CPI(M)'s success, the electoral victory of the party in both 1977 and 1982 is a testimony to the fact that not only has the CPI(M) consolidated its old political base, but has continued to broaden and deepen it.

INSTITUTIONAL INNOVATION: THE POLITICIZED PANCHAYATS

Since coming to power in 1977, the CPI(M) has sought to further consolidate its rural power base. In order to incorporate the lower rural classes, the leadership has undertaken a penetration of the countryside. Central to this task are the new politicized panchayats. The CPI(M)'s decision to allow political party competition for local government elections (held in June 1978) constituted a sharp break from past Indian practices. Given that the CPI(M) was in control of the government and that it enjoyed considerable electoral

---

[19]According to Amnesty International, over 25,000 cadres, mostly of the CPI(M) and the CPML, were in jails in the first half of the 1970s. See Marcus Franda, 'Rural Development, Bengali Marxist Style', *American Universities Field Staff Report*, Asia, 1978/No. 15, p. 4.

[20]Interview, S. Sarkar, Director, Land Revenue and Surveys, West Bengal, Calcutta, 19 March 1979.

[21]Interview, Johar Santra, 14 March 1979.

popularity within West Bengal, the leadership calculated that its own candidates would do well in party-based panchayat elections. The calculations were right. Candidates running on CPI(M) tickets won an impressive majority: 87 per cent of the seats at the district level (zila parishad); 74 per cent at the block level (Panchayat Samitis); and 67 per cent at the village level (Gram Panchayats).[22] These 'red panchayats'[23] are now important in CPI(M)'s overall political and developmental strategy. The Finance Minister, Ashok Mitra, went as far as to argue that 'if panchayats fail, the CPI(M) experiment fails'.[24]

What has led the CPI(M) to focus on transforming the local governmental institutions? To answer this, we need to remind ourselves of the CPI(M)'s overall goals. Like any political party, the CPI(M) seeks to win and consolidate power. In distinction to most other Indian parties, the CPI(M) intends to accomplish this political goal by building its power base primarily on the lower-middle and the lower classes. This necessitates involving these groups in the political process, as well as transferring some fruits of power to them. Old institutional arrangements, however, did not facilitate the pursuit of this 'left-of-centre' type of politics. Local government in the past has been dominated by propertied elites, and the bureaucracy has repeatedly proven ineffective in implementing reforms. If reformism was thus the new goal, new institutional mechanisms were needed.

The CPI(M) had two options: rapid expansion of the party or restructuring of the local government. The communist leaders understood well that rapid expansion would destroy the party as a cohesive and disciplined political force. Instead of loyal and committed cadres, those seeking quick rewards of power would be mainly attracted. The party might then grow, but the leadership would not be able to use it for translating its goals into effective rural reform. The CPI(M) thus decided to restructure local government. The strategy is to crowd the panchayats with CPI(M) sympathizers, while leaving the disciplined party cadres to play the crucial supervisory role over the local governmental institutions.

Who are these sympathizers now manning the panchayats? The results of my interviews with sixty members of gram panchayats are summarized in Table 13.1. As these interviews were always carried out in group situations, which included members of the local community, it was difficult for the respondents to hide the length of their party involvement, as well as their ownership and the mode of land use. Considering, however, that there are

[22]Information from Secretary, Ministry of Panchayat Raj, West Bengal.

[23]The term was coined by Bhabani Sen Gupta (1979), *CPI-M: Promises,* chapter 6. While Sen Gupta's assessment of the panchayats is far too optimistic for the minimal evidence he cites, he nevertheless deserves to be credited for being one of the first to recognize the novelty of CPI(M)'s experiment in West Bengal.

[24]Interview, Ashok Mitra, 16 March 1979.

about 28,000 members that won gram panchayat seats on a CPI(M) ticket, a sample of sixty is by no means representative. The accuracy of the sample is nevertheless somewhat greater than its size would suggest, since a degree of control was built into its selection by choosing areas of CPI(M) strength (Burdwan) and weakness (Midnapore). The emerging profile reveals that the majority elected on a CPI(M) ticket are party sympathizers rather than full members, small landowners rather than landless or sharecroppers, and that they use hired labour to cultivate their lands.

A considerable minority are not agriculturalists at all, but rather teachers and social workers. The significance of this minority is greater than the numbers reveal, since the non-agriculturalists were generally more politicized and in positions of leadership within the panchayats. Thus, in Midnapore, for example, a survey of 515 pradhans (heads of gram panchayats) by the district administration revealed that 217 of them were teachers. Of these, 207 had an educational level of B.A. or over.[25] Being more educated and politicized, rural-based teachers were disproportionately in positions of gram panchayat leadership.

Given the social/political composition of the lower-level panchayats, what deductions can we make about the functioning of these reconstructed local governmental institutions in the context of reformist rural development? To begin with, the new panchayats of Bengal represent a break from the past political patterns in rural India. The panchayats in West Bengal, or in most parts of India, have seldom been free of domination by landlords or rich peasants.[26] As the data in Table 13.1 indicate, this is beginning to change in West Bengal. The CPI(M) is carving out a pattern of political organization rare to India, namely, that involving a penetration of the countryside without depending on the larger landowners. Therefore, it appears that politics in West Bengal is undergoing a structural change. While the class structure remains intact, political institutions are beginning to take deep root in the rural society. More important, institutional power has, at least for now, been transferred from the hands of the dominant propertied groups to a lower-middle stratum.

The role of the party in this transition has been central. Through its core as well as auxiliary members, the CPI(M) combined class with political criteria in selecting its supporters. These supporters, riding the wave of the CPI(M)'s popularity, now man the local governments across the province. The new institutional arrangements thus mark a break from the traditional

[25]Information from District Panchayat Officer, Midnapore, West Bengal.

[26]An important government report, while not fully in agreement, sympathetically noted that panchayats are 'dominated by economically or socially privileged sections of society and have as such facilitated the emergence of oligarchic forces yielding no benefits to weaker sections'. See Government of India, Ministry of Agriculture and Irrigation, *Report of the Committee on Panchayati Raj Institutions*, New Delhi, 1978, p. 6.

TABLE 13.1: Political and Class Profiles of Gram Panchayat Members

Political Profile		Vocation	
Relationship with the CPI(M)	Distribution (%)	Type of work	Distribution (%)
Opportunists[a] (less than 2 years of party involvement)	13.3	Agriculturalists	60.1
		Landless agricultural labourers	8.3
Sympathizers (over 2 years of party involvement)	58.3	Non-agriculturalists (mainly teachers and social workers)	31.6
Part time members (over 5 years of party work)	21.7		
Full time members (card carrying members)	6.7		
Landownership[b]		Mode of Land Use[b]	
Size of Holding (acres)	Distribution (%)	Land Use	Distribution (%)
0–2	8.3	Only family labour	0
2–5	69.0	Use hired labour	83.3
6–10	19.4	Use sharecroppers	16.7
10 & above	2.8		

Notes: The data in this table are based on interviews with 60 members of gram panchayats in Burdwan and Midnapore.
[a]The assumption here is that those who started getting involved with the CPI(M) only after it came to power had opportunistic motivations.
[b]Breakdown is for agriculturists only.

pattern of the political elite aligning with landed notables for the mobilization of electoral support. In sum, the new panchayats represent two interlinked patterns of political change in one region of India: an organizational penetration by a left-of-centre party into the villages and a simultaneous shift in the class basis of institutional power.

Aside from the penetration of the countryside, a related goal of the panchayats is to 'tame' the local bureaucracy. According to a new law, legislated in 1977, the bureaucrats at each level—district, block, and village—are from now on to be the executive arm of the parallel, elected governments. The hitherto powerful District Commissioners (DCs) are, in other words, from now on to take their orders from the elected zila parishad. Similarly, the activities of such 'local czars' as the Block Development Officers and of others as the Junior Land Reform Officers and the Kanungos, are now to be carried out in close 'co-operation' with the panchayat samitis and the gram panchayats.

How effective are these attempts to 'tame' the bureaucracy likely to be? Given that the power of local bureaucracy has long been considerable, and that it has come to be accepted by the respective communities as such, the transition will have to be sustained for quite some time before significant change is manifest. In the short run, certain changes are evident in the political-bureaucratic relationships. At the district level, the web of political control over the district commissioner is growing. While the DCs are in part always beholden to local political leaders, especially the members of the legislative assembly in West Bengal, they also now have to pay attention to the district party leaders and the elected zila parishad officials. A potentially significant consequence of this increased control has been the changing use of police to quell 'civil disturbances'. By influencing the DC's rulings on when the police may or may not be used to settle civil disputes, the CPI(M) has sought to 'neutralize' the police as a tool both of landlord interest—especially in harvesting conflicts—and the interests of opposition political parties. At lower levels of bureaucracy also, established bureaucrats repeatedly complained about 'political interference' in their work. This was an indicator of their powers having been curtailed.

The politicization of panchayats in West Bengal is, in sum, aimed at penetration of the countryside. The purpose is to bring lower and lower-middle rural classes within the influence of the party. While the CPI(M) has had more success in incorporating lower-middle classes than the lower ones, it is hoped that by increasing the role of these classes in the governing institutions, as well as by transferring some fruits of development to them, the party position will be strengthened. The past patterns of rural power have involved the political leaders, bureaucrats, and landowners in a tacit pact of domination. The new ruling alliance seeks to diversify this pattern by isolating the significance of the landed to the social sphere, by taming the bureaucracy, and by recasting local government to enhance the political role of hitherto excluded social groups.

POLICIES TO ALLEVIATE RURAL POVERTY

The CPI(M) regime has used its political organization to initiate redistributive programmes. The anti-poverty programme is a multipronged one. Some policies have been accorded priority; some are also achieving more success than others. While in the short run concrete results are less than spectacular, and critics are quick to point this out, regime authorities claim that foundations for systematic reforms are being laid. My analysis leads me to hold that the scope for action is limited and welfare considerations will remain subordinated to power considerations. However, the recent efforts are promising and, over time, may mitigate the worst of rural poverty and insecurity by deliberate political intervention. The CPI(M)'s attempts to implement three major programmes deserve attention: land reforms, especially tenancy reform;

programmes for small farmers, mainly credit for sharecroppers; and employment and wage schemes for the landless labourers.

Land Reforms

Once in power, the CPI(M) faced the option of focusing its efforts either on redistribution of 'above ceiling' surplus lands or on tenancy reform. The leadership has been reluctant to tackle the former. Much of the surplus land is by now 'benami land'—that is, land registered in false names and categories. In order to acquire and redistribute this land, the government would have had to undertake the following: pass controversial legislation redefining family in strict terms; make many of the past land transactions retroactively illegal; and set up party-dominated local committees to identify surplus land as well as the future beneficiaries. Since such moves were likely to tax the energies of a new regime, and invite the wrath of the centre, the issue has been approached slowly. Only now, with the new panchayats beginning to take root and CPI(M)'s political position within West Bengal firmer, has the communist government passed land redistribution legislation.[27] Land redistribution schemes stemming from this legislation are likely to be one major focus of governmental activity in the next few years.

Meanwhile, during the first term, the leadership chose to concentrate on 'operation barga', a type of tenancy reform aimed at improving the conditions of the bargardars. 'Operation barga' is a concerted effort to register the sharecroppers. A sharecropper with a legal record of his or her status can enjoy the protection of legislation already on the books, including security of tenure and modified 'rents'. These protections have in the past not been very effective because of the informal nature of much tenancy. The burden of proof that a tenant was indeed legal, and thus protected by tenancy laws, has hitherto been on the tenant himself. Sharecropping laws have therefore been inherently biased against the sharecroppers. This legal bias has also been reinforced by socio-economic inequalities. As the sharecroppers often depend on the goodwill of the landowner for their livelihood, it is understandable that the former are reluctant to invoke the wrath of the latter by pursuing legalistic demands. Therefore landlord–sharecropper relationships have in the past been marked by insecurity of tenure and levels of rent which many would consider exploitative.

To alter these conditions, the CPI(M) has tilted the weight of the party and state power closer to the side of the sharecroppers. Once the CPI(M) government was in power, one of its early acts was to amend the land reform laws to transfer the burden of proof regarding the status of a sharecropper

[27]Based on Interview, Binoy Chowdhry, Calcutta, 2 November 1981.

to the landowners. Under this amendment, a tenant who claims to be a sharecropper has legal protections until proven differently by the courts. In the wake of this new law, 'operation barga' has sought to: (1) identify areas with a concentration of sharecroppers; (2) send in teams of bureaucrats and the party/Kisan Sabha members to meet, inform, and politicize the sharecroppers; and (3) eventually, after field verification, to legally register sharecroppers.[28] Once sharecroppers are registered, it is hoped that, over time, security of tenure and incentives for production will be improved.

How well has 'operation barga' been working? All measures of success are relative. The CPI(M)'s accomplishments therefore have to be put in perspective. In the same areas where the CPI(M) has carried out its current programme, fewer than 60,000 sharecroppers were registered over the past three decades. In less than three years, however, the CPI(M) regime succeeded in registering over one million bargardars.[29] Compared to past performance of Congress and other governments in the area, therefore, CPI(M)'s current success is considerable. If sustained, CPI(M)'s programmes promise to make a long-term positive impact on the opportunities available to the sharecroppers. When the record, however, is compared to the size of the problem—there are nearly two million bargardars in West Bengal,[30] and most live under conditions of abject poverty—the outlook has to be less optimistic.

What factors have facilitated or hindered 'operation barga'? The CPI(M) regime has used both the bureaucracy and the party (including the Kisan Sabha) to implement the programme. The bureaucratic side is under the jurisdiction of a senior civil servant with impeccable credentials in implementing land reforms.[31] Continuous momentum for 'operation barga' is thus generated from the top. The next rung of relevant civil servants is the Assistant District Magistrates (ADM) in charge of land reforms and land settlement at the district level. Most of these are young IAS officers, who think of their position as a temporary one. As such, their primary consideration is task completion in order to gain promotion. At this level, there was no evidence of either obstruction or enthusiasm. The primary job of the ADM's was to instruct the lower-level bureaucrats on how to conduct the programme

---

[28]Interview, D. Bandopadhyay, Land Reforms Commissioner, West Bengal, 12 March 1979, and 2 November 1981.

[29]See Government of West Bengal, *Land Reforms in West Bengal,* Statistical Report V, 1981.

[30]These are the estimates of the West Bengal government, provided to the author by Binoy Chowdhry in the interview cited in note 4.

[31]The individual in question is D. Bandopadhyay. He made his reputation as an effective land reformer under Hare Krishna Konar, and then moved to the centre for a while. Once the CPI(M) ministry was formed in West Bengal, Mr Bandopadhyay was especially requested to help implement the new government's programmes.

and then to continue supervising it. From the available evidence, this work seemed to be effectively in progress.[32]

The point here is that the upper echelons of the bureaucracy do not create hurdles in the implementation of 'operation barga'. The same, however, cannot be claimed for the lower-level bureaucrats. The lower-level members of the land bureaucracy (Junior Land Reform Officers [JLRO's], Kanungos, and Amins) generally make up the field staff, which is in charge of camping in selected village areas, clarifying the new laws in public forums, urging the sharecroppers to come forward to register, explaining the benefits, verifying from the local sources the validity of claims and counter claims, and finally registering the sharecroppers of the area. It is during this phase of the 'operation' that there is considerable scope for what the party and the government interpret as 'corruption and class bias'. The local bureaucrats often have strong local connections, including those with the landowners. Many field officers expressed personal dissent with the new laws, arguing that the rights of the landowners should be taken into consideration. Moreover, as a group, these are the same set of officers who have often in the past colluded with landowners to foil attempted land redistribution. It would be naive to believe that they have all turned over a new leaf under the CPI(M) regime, now enthusiastically implementing reformist change. Party cadres thus repeatedly complained about the 'corruption' and the 'class bias' of the administration. Some of these complaints were merely self-serving as they tried to place the shortcomings of the party and the government on the bureaucracy. Moreover, as discussed above, there was little evidence to support such allegations at the upper levels of bureaucracy. Nevertheless, village visits revealed that the party perspective was valid for the lower levels of bureaucracy. This was especially borne out by the evidence of the relative success of the programme in areas of party strength.

In visits to the 'operation barga' sites, it became clear that wherever the party or the Kisan Sabha had carried out propaganda or organization work for a few months, the bargardars were more willing to come forward to register. The prior politicization increased the sense of efficacy and reduced the fear of dependence among the bargardars. Moreover, visible party presence, now perceived as the presence of 'state power', created a sense of sustained external support. In a local struggle involving inherently unequal social actors, sustained external support on the side of the 'underdog' was essential to modify the power balance. Active party involvement further minimized bureaucratic corruption while short-circuiting the bureaucrat–

[32]This conclusion is based on long interviews with the ADMs in Burdwan and Midnapore. This information was further confirmed by the potential 'adversaries' of the ADMs, namely, the members of the respective zila parishads in these two districts.

landlord alliance. In other words, the role of the party was central in overcoming socio-structural and bureaucratic obstacles, enabling government's reformist intervention to achieve a modicum of success.

Just as the party organization and presence is uneven within West Bengal, so was the success of 'operation barga'. Where the party is strong, the programme was doing well; where the party is weak, the success was more limited. For example, the registration drive has been considerably more successful in Burdwan and 24 Parganas, areas with strong party presence, than in a weak party area such as Murshidabad. The proportion of registered bargardars to the agrarian population was 0.133 for Burdwan, 0.115 for 24 Parganas, and only 0.084 for Murshidabad.[33]

Members of the land bureaucracy in West Bengal often attributed the problems of 'operation barga' to the CPI(M)'s 'middle peasant' support.[34] The argument was that members of both the Kisan Sabha and the new panchayats own land and use sharecroppers to have it cultivated. As such, the party's own supporters were not in favour of a programme that would undermine their interests. I did not find evidence to confirm this argument. While many members of Kisan Sabha and the new panchayats own land, they are mostly smallholders (ownership holdings of under five acres—see Table 13.1). In a majority of cases, the mode of land use was not sharecropping but use of hired labour (see Table 13.1). The more prominent members of the panchayats are often not even agriculturalists, but rural teachers and social workers. While this evidence clearly indicates that the CPI(M) is not a party of the poorest of the poor, the social origins of its rural support also do not really impart a class bias against the sharecroppers.

In sum, the members of the party and bureaucracy often blamed each other for the shortcomings and claimed credit for programme successes. The evidence discussed above suggests a more complex pattern at work. The obstacles to government programmes are rooted in the social structure, the lower levels of bureaucracy, and the uneven development of the party. Conversely, the forces pushing towards success are generated by the top government leaders and bureaucrats, as well as the action of the party and the Kisan Sabha. The role of the party itself was central. The party's capacity to penetrate the countryside without being co-opted by the landed classes and to facilitate controlled mobilization of the sharecroppers to buttress

[33]Based on 'operation barga' statistics provided by Government of West Bengal, *Land Reforms in West Bengal*, and agricultural working population figures (cultivators and agricultural labourers) from Government of West Bengal, *Economic Review, 1978–79, Statistical Appendix*, Table 2.4.

[34]This almost appeared to be the 'bureaucratic line' on 'operation barga'. Senior civil servants like D. Bandopadhyay and S. Sarkar, Director of Land Surveys, West Bengal, both stressed it during interviews. It was also repeated at lower levels of bureaucracy.

state power for reform has been an important variable in success. Reformist change, in other words, has resulted primarily from the political capacities generated by a well-organized party regime.

In the short run, registration has had both positive and problematic consequences. On the positive side, improved tenure security is the most likely outcome. Whether this will lead to positive economic changes will not be clear for some time. In the short run, incomes of some registered sharecroppers have undergone a small improvement.[35] The laws, for those who can prove their bargardar status, stipulate the ratios of crop sharing. Since unregistered sharecroppers tend to pay higher than the legal shares, once registered, they are not obliged to continue the old arrangements. What allows the old arrangements to snap is of course not the mere shift in legal status, but rather the process of politicization whereby the sharecroppers come to understand the laws, get closer to the party, and take the final and important jump to come forward and register. An act of defiance against the traditional patron, this act itself does more to help implement the sharecropping laws than the refined qualities of the laws themselves.

Sustained party and governmental actions have further contributed to the implementation of the law governing crop sharing. In case of any dispute between the sharecropper and the landlord, the former can now deposit the landlord's legal share with the local bureaucracy, get a receipt, and be free of their legal obligations. The landlords can then collect their shares from the offices of local bureaucrats. The local police have, moreover, been instructed by the government to, at minimum, not side with the landlords, and at maximum, to provide the bargardars with protection in conflicts over crop sharing and disputes over evictions.[36] Wherever the landlords have hired

[35]The evidence for this is somewhat 'impressionistic' and will have to await confirmation by survey data. However, of the six blocks in Midnapore and Burdwan where I carried out research, in only two areas (Duan and Daspur, both in Midnapore) was there little evidence of registration leading to any concrete improvements. In most other areas, interviewed sharecroppers noted that instead of the old 33–67 per cent division between the sharecropper and the landowner, the post-registration arrangement was 50–50 per cent with landlords providing the inputs, or 60–40 per cent with the bargardar providing the input. Some 'harder' data supporting this general conclusion are also provided by village level studies conducted by the Socio Economic Research Institute, Calcutta. See Government of West Bengal, *An Evaluation of Land Reforms in West Bengal,* 1981.

[36]Thus from a memorandum forwarded by the Office of the Board of Revenue to all land administrators, including the district police officers, clauses 4 and 12 are worth quoting in full. Clause 4: 'Where the dispute is between the landowner and the recorded bargardar, the latter should receive full protection from the administration in harvesting the crop and getting proper share of the produce.' Clause 12: 'Government expects that the functionaries at all levels in the district administration should act impartially. They should always bear in mind that the weaker sections of the community who have so far been deprived of and denied their legitimate rights and privileges are given full benefits and protection that they

their own local toughs to settle conflicts by force, the party has attempted to counter by militant mobilization. In an area of Burdwan, for example, where a landlord shot and injured a sharecropper, within 24 hours the party mobilized 5000 supporters. These supporters 'supervised' and shouted slogans as the crop was cut, the share divided, and each party—the injured sharecropper and the landlord—given their legal portion. The landlord backed off from his insistence on evicting the sharecropper.[37]

The political message that the CPI(M) thus intends to convey is that it will take both its 'legal' and 'distributive' roles seriously. Mobilizational power can be generated, but the mobilization is controlled. As in the incident above, neither mobilization led to vengeance, nor was land grab encouraged. As 'revolutionary excesses' are avoided and only 'laws' implemented, the CPI(M) is attempting to convince the opposition that, even as a communist regime, it will operate under constitutional limits. At the same time, however, it provided some countervailing influence against the old alliance of domination among landlords, police, and local toughs. While distasteful to both the more revolutionary and conservative forces in the area, CPI(M)'s strategy of controlled mobilization is in line with its overall reformist orientation. On the one hand, it has facilitated the implementation of some redistributive programmes. On the other hand, the strategy of controlled mobilization has been effective enough so that the past few years of harvesting have been the most peaceful in a long time. Even some landlords were appreciative of the CPI(M): at least, the communist government has managed to bring harvesting violence under control.

Support Programmes for Sharecroppers and Smallholders

The resource base of sharecroppers and many marginal peasants does not facilitate a ready shift in investment patterns. The smallholders are therefore often not in a position to improve their land-based incomes by adopting new agrarian technologies. Among the constraints operating on the smallholders, shortage of credit is an important one. The credit problem is of special significance for the registered bargardars of West Bengal. In the aftermath of registration, some of the old sources of credit and input (via the landowner) have tended to dry up. Having been responsible for registration to begin with, the state is now attempting to provide new and less 'exploitative' sources.

---

are entitled to under various laws.' See Government of West Bengal, Office of the Board of Revenue, 'Guidelines for the Settlement of Harvesting Disputes—Protection of Bargardars and Assignees of Vested Land'.

[37]The incident occurred in a village in Kalna I Block of Burdwan. The various events were related to me by the local party members in the presence of members of the local community and the injured sharecropper. The story was later confirmed by the landlord himself, with the difference that he labelled party representatives as 'hoodlums'.

Organized credit markets in rural India have in the past been notoriously ineffective from a redistributive standpoint. In face of these past patterns, the CPI(M) in West Bengal has undertaken the task of facilitating low interest loans to smallholders as a whole, but especially to the newly registered sharecroppers. Governmental authorities have entered into a series of negotiations with the commercial banks aimed at channelling subsidized credit for the lower agrarian groups. Since the sharecroppers, however, do not own any land, the problem of collateral is the first obstacle to any credit programme for them. The CPI(M) has argued, and the banks have in principle agreed, that loans ought to be given out against crops as well as against land. In practice, however, the principle of loans against crops creates the messy problem for the bankers of identifying the bona fide sharecroppers and their shares in village communities. The bankers definitely do not want to be involved in such a labour intensive and potentially controversial issue area. The CPI(M) has therefore offered the services of the newly created panchayats in undertaking this labour-intensive groundwork requiring community knowledge.

The local panchayats, according to the agreements reached, now prepare a list of the registered sharecroppers in their areas as well as identify their anticipated share of the yearly crop. This information is passed on to the banks, which use it to decide who is eligible for a loan and how large the loan should be. Only a part of the loan is in cash. As much as 50 per cent of the total is in the form of 'vouchers' for fertilizers and other inputs. The interest rate for the sharecroppers is only 4 per cent, the balance being paid to the banks by the government. Moreover, if the sharecroppers pay back their entire loan by 31 March of the next year, the loans are interest free, the total interest being paid by the state.[38]

This programme of subsidized credit (indirect subsidies to the bank in the form of labour cost, and direct ones to the sharecroppers covering interest rates) is presently in its early stages. In 1979 and 1980, respectively, approximately 60,000 and 70,000 registered sharecroppers received institutional credit. These numbers are of course too small to permit any general expectations regarding the future of the scheme. If the programme is not pushed, many of the gains of the 'operation barga', if not jeopardized, will certainly be minimized. Nevertheless, what the beginnings of this credit programme highlight is how a well-organized, left-of-centre regime can intervene in a private enterprise economy so as to strengthen the position of the lower classes.

---

[38]The discussion is based on interviews conducted with both government and bank officials. Especially useful were the insights of D. Bandopadhyay, Land Reforms Commissioner (see note 28).

Employment and Wage Schemes for the Landless

One of the major programmes for creating additional employment for the landless is the Food for Work Programme (FWP), sponsored in part by the centre. The CPI(M) government has implemented the programme with considerable effectiveness. Research conducted in the seven blocks (three in Burdwan and four in Midnapore) revealed a fairly consistent outcome. On the average, employment for 28 days per year was generated by the FWP projects. Most projects were of a 'public works' nature, involving road construction or drainage and clean-up of irrigation canals. The standard wage was 3 kgs of wheat plus Rs 2 in cash per day, a higher wage than the average in the area. Since the total employment availability from agriculture is three to four months, the FWP projects were contributing about 25 per cent over and above the yearly income derived by the landless from agrarian employment.[39]

The FWP employment was of course not available to all the landless, but about one-third of all landless households have had yearly access to this employment.[40] While neither the yearly increment in incomes nor the extent of its coverage is sufficient to alleviate poverty, a 25 per cent increment in yearly income for one-third of all the landless households is something of a modest achievement. Since the FWP has, in the past at least, been sponsored by the centre, the CPI(M) gets no credit for initiating or funding it. What the CPI(M) can claim, however, is its effective implementation.

The FWP projects are now implemented by the village-level panchayats in West Bengal. In conjunction with local party cadres, the panchayats decide the projects to be undertaken, choose who will be employed, and administer the funds. A major short-term consequence of this has been 'cleaner administration'. Resulting from the party-panchayat linkages, and from the party's need to sustain a 'clean reputation' for political purposes, there was widespread agreement that public funds under the new local leadership were not being appropriated for private benefits. Even over the long run then, if the CPI(M) turns out to be not all that redistributive—not an improbable outcome—its contribution to clean administration at the local level will, in the Indian context, remain a major accomplishment. The choice of local projects, however, also reflected 'shared needs' more than the narrow preferences of the village elite. Compared with past practices of 'developmental'

---

[39]For further evidence supporting the thrust of this argument, see the village-level studies in Government of West Bengal, *An Evaluation of Land Reforms in West Bengal*, 1981.

[40]For example, in 1978, 100 million rupees were spent on the FWP in West Bengal. As the average person employed in 1977–8 received 28 × 5 (2 kg of wheat at approximately 2 Rs a kilo and 1 Rs cash) = 140 Rs/year, approximately 10,000,000 ÷ 140 = 714,000 landless labourers were employed.

projects ending up in the backyards of the local notables, the new projects were often of the following type: roads connecting the untouchable colonies to the main road, the cleaning and fixing of village tanks, and the drainage of canals used by many members of the village community. Both in terms of 'corruption' and 'class bias', therefore, the CPI(M) panchayats are considerably more effective in facilitating equitable rural development than the past institutional arrangements.

Other than the developmental impact, the control of CPI(M) panchayats over local decision making and public resources is beginning to have socio-political consequences that should be noted. First, there is an increasingly clear separation of social and political power in the countryside. The landowners and other notables remain economically and socially powerful. Political power, however, is concentrating in the CPI(M) and its representatives. Whether this situation of 'dual power' will prove to be a stable or a desirable one in West Bengal remains an open question. The workability of this unusual situation will depend on the willingness of both sides to leave each other with their core resources: the majority portion of the land for the landowners and control over political offices and policy for the CPI(M). Second, as public resources come to be controlled by a new local elite, new patterns of patronage are developing. Instead of the old landlord-dominated 'vote banks', the panchayat leaders are becoming politically powerful. Many of the landless, working on the FWP projects, regarded the panchayat pradhan (head) as a benefactor. Over time, the pradhans will be able to convert this new-found influence into a tool for mobilizing electoral support. As long as the CPI(M) remains in power, it will be able to buttress its position further through these patronage networks linking the party, local government leaders, and the poor beneficiaries. If and when the CPI(M) is weakened, however, the loyalty of many of the intermediate 'sympathizers' may prove to be short lived.

In addition to the employment-generating developmental projects, the CPI(M) has made efforts to unionize the landless labourers. The unionization is aimed both at building organized political support (i.e., consciousness raising by propaganda and organization) and at conducting wage struggles. This is a decisively political task, and the role of the party and Kisan Sabha is more important than that of the state and local governments. How successful have these efforts been?

To assess this, I compared union activities and wage rates within Midnapore. Of the four blocks I studied, Ghatal and Debra are highly politicized, while Daspur I and II do not have a strong party presence. Moreover, Ghatal and Debra have strong agricultural labour unions with a history of active wage struggles. Not only the local labour, but incoming 'migrant' labour is also controlled by the CPI(M)-Kisan Sabha in these areas. In Debra, for example, the local leadership sought to implement the minimum wage legislation. To dramatize the issue, a strike was organized on the lands of a prominent landowner who was also an ex-Congress MLA. The CPI(M)'s control was effective enough that the land was kept uncultivated for a season. When the landlord decided to comply with the minimum wage law, labour was released to cultivate the land. While cases of this nature are not common, they highlight to the landlords the potential and the threat of the CPI(M)'s rural unions.

The wage levels in the unionized blocks tended to be somewhat higher than in the non-unionized ones. The peak wage in Debra and Ghatal was about Rs 5.50 per day, while in the Daspur area it hovered between Rs 4.50 and Rs 5 per day. Whether economic conditions were responsible for this small differential was not immediately evident, but it is at least possible that unionization had made some impact on wages.[41]

The safest conclusion is probably that CPI(M)-led unions have made some, but by no means a dramatic, difference in the wages received by the landless labourers. The unionization is, however, quite uneven, generally paralleling the variations in party strength. Moreover, the CPI(M) leadership finds it difficult to balance the needs of the middle peasantry, who often employ landless labourers, with organizing 'struggles' for wage increments. As a party in power, the CPI(M) does not prefer agitational modes of political behaviour. There is concern within the party that as party cadres are used more and more in the process of governing—e.g., in panchayats—the politicization activities of the party may be subordinated to more administrative tasks.[42] Given these obstacles, unionized agitation for higher wages is not likely to have a high priority on CPI(M)'s West Bengal agenda.

The improvements in the living conditions of the landless in West Bengal are thus likely to depend on additional employment opportunities. Since the CPI(M) is committed to increasing budgetary resources to this task[43] and, more important, now has an institutional capacity to implement its programmes, one can view the prospects with moderate optimism. This optimism, however, like all optimism concerning the rural poor in India, must be balanced against the enormity of the problem. The unionization

[41]For further data supporting this conclusion, see Pranab Bardhan and Ashok Rudra, 'Labor, Employment and Wages in Agriculture', *EPW*, 8–15 November 1980, esp. p. 1948.

[42]For a discussion of this concern, see *People's Democracy*, 11 March 1979, pp. 10–11.

[43]The CPI(M) government in West Bengal is one of the few state governments in India which now has a progressive agricultural tax on the books. The central government of India has argued, however, that the West Bengal government is financing its welfare programme not from internal resource mobilization but from deficit financing of sorts charged to the centre. For a review of this ongoing debate, see 'Overdraft Politics', *EPW*, 2–9 January 1982, pp. 13–14.

of rural labour is also likely to make some, albeit small, positive contribution. As unionization facilitates organized political support, the CPI(M) will continue to pursue it. Even if wage agitations are not on the agenda, increasing unionization may allow the landless labourers to keep their income share in a growing economy.

CONCLUSION

This article has sought to delineate three themes concerning the CPI(M) rule in West Bengal: the elements of revolutionary communism the CPI(M) has 'compromised' in order to rule in a democratic-capitalist setting; the capacity of the CPI(M) regime as an agent of redistributive reforms; and the political features of the CPI(M) explaining both the limits and the scope of its redistributive intervention. Having analysed the evidence, it is now important to pull together the argument, and suggest some of the more general implications of this one case.

The CPI(M) has moved away from a revolutionary to a reformist orientation. This shift has been evident in the renewed commitment to the preservation of democratic institutions, in forging broad social alliances, and in pursuing not only asset redistribution but a more broadly defined development with redistribution. This reformist re-orientation has allowed the CPI(M) to rule as a democratically elected communist government within a private enterprise economy. In spite of the 'compromises', however, the CPI(M) remains a relatively effective agent of redistributive policies. While comparisons with other ruling parties in other Indian states have not been presented here,[44] the comparisons with past performances of the Congress party in West Bengal are telling. The CPI(M) has initiated a considerably more successful programme to protect and enhance the opportunities available to the sharecroppers. Moreover, the CPI(M) is providing clean local administration, effectively implementing rural employment generation schemes, and organizing rural labour unions. These programmes by no means add up to a radical alteration in West Bengal's rural poverty. Given the enormous poverty in West Bengal, as in the rest of India, no set of government actions is likely to radically alter the poverty conditions over the short run. Nevertheless, within the Indian context, CPI(M)'s actions represent a fairly significant pattern of redistributive intervention. If sustained, these initiatives promise to make a dent in the serious rural poverty of West Bengal.

[44]For a discussion of the Karnataka case, see Atul Kohli, 'Karnataka's Land Reforms: A Model for India?', *Journal of Commonwealth and Comparative Politics*, November 1982; for a comparison of the cases of West Bengal, Karnataka, and Uttar Pradesh within a state-society theoretical framework, see Atul Kohli, *The State and Poverty: Political Economy of Reform in Rural India* (forthcoming, 1983).

Four political conditions, or four features of the regime in power, help explain the existence of the political capacity to reform the social order from above. First, CPI(M) rule in West Bengal has a coherent and stable leadership. This allows for clarification of goals, arrangement of priorities, and then sustained pressure from above for goal completion. Second, the CPI(M) has a clear pro-lower-class ideology. Once the CPI(M) leaders are democratically elected, this ideological position gives them a degree of legitimate authority to pursue goals beneficial to the rural poor. Third, in spite of being a communist party, the CPI(M) has clarified the limits on the scope of redistribution. All democratically elected parties in a private enterprise economy, even if communist in name, must set these limits. Predictability is essential for the functioning of a private enterprise economy. And last, and most important, the CPI(M)'s organizational arrangements allow it to penetrate the countryside without being captured by the propertied groups. In part because of the democratic-centralist nature of the party organization and in part because of the carefully reorganized local government, the CPI(M) can now reach the lower peasantry without landlord mediation. This feature of the CPI(M) distinguishes it from all other organized political alternatives in India. It allows the regime to channel some developmental resources directly to the rural poor, as well as to mobilize them for occasionally fulfilling reformist goals. Taken together, the four features thus explain the reformist capacities of the CPI(M) regime.

Both ideologically and organizationally, the CPI(M) has sought to exclude the propertied from government, while allowing them to maintain their socio-economic power. This ruling arrangement has facilitated a degree of separation between social and political power. It is this separation that allows the CPI(M) regime to pursue incremental reforms within the constraints of democratic-capitalism.

This political arrangement also highlights an issue of more general interest, namely, one set of conditions under which democratically guided social reform may succeed. In order to redistribute income or wealth within a private enterprise economy, the regime must achieve a degree of autonomy from the propertied classes. This autonomy, in turn, is a function of regime organization. The regime must be able to incorporate the interests of the lower classes, while excluding the upper ones from a role in direct governance. As such regimes can easily be threatened from both the Left (not revolutionary enough) and from the Right (too socialist), organizational abilities are the key to effective rule. Well-organized, left-of-centre parties are in a position to assuage the propertied, control the propertyless, and pursue incremental reforms within the constraints of hierarchical societies. Successful cases along these lines are rare. If sustained, the CPI(M) experiment in India's Bengal promises to be an interesting such case of how redistributive goals can be institutionalized within the state structures of a low-income, private-enterprise economy.

14

The NTR Phenomenon in Andhra Pradesh
Political Change in a South Indian State*

The Congress, India's premier political party, ruled the South Indian state of Andhra Pradesh without interruption for nearly three decades. Even when the Congress was routed from power by the Janata Party in 1977, Andhra had remained one of the few Congress strongholds. In 1983, however, a regional party, the Telugu Desam Party (TDP), displaced the Congress as the ruling party in Andhra. Created and led by the movie actor turned politician, N.T. Rama Rao (NTR), the TDP now appears to have established a relatively strong electoral foothold within the state. Andhra was one of the few Indian states that was not totally swept up by the 'Rajiv wave' in the 1984 national elections, and in the 1985 legislative assembly elections, NTR's TDP again defeated the Congress party. The mid-1987 local government elections further highlighted NTR's continuing capacity to attract the popular vote.

The purpose of this essay is to explain how this political change in Andhra has come about as well as to analyse its significance. The first half is an overview of the political change and an assessment of the quality of government that has been provided by NTR's TDP. The focus in the second half of the article shifts to one district within Andhra Pradesh, Guntur, in the eastern part of the state. This specific focus helps to support the general argument with data that is not easily available for the state as a whole. Because Guntur was studied in the 1950s by Selig Harrison and in the 1960s

*Originally published as 'The NTR Phenomenon in Andhra Pradesh: Political Change in a South Indian State', *Asian Survey*, 8(10), October 1988, pp. 991–1017.

The research on which this article is based was conducted in 1985–6 and was supported by the Ford Foundation. The author wishes to acknowledge the helpful comments of Carolyn M. Elliot, Marie Gottschalk, and Myron Weiner on an earlier version of this essay.

by Myron Weiner,[1] a study of this area in the mid-1980s also provides an unusual opportunity to analyse political change over time.

The decline in Congress's popularity in Andhra is traced to both social-structural and political changes. More specifically, the so-called dominant castes of the region have lost their capacity to influence the political behaviour of those below them in the caste hierarchy, creating a fluid political situation. The old, seemingly 'consensual' pattern of politics that revolved around dominant caste leaders and their dependent followers has gone, probably forever. Indira Gandhi's repeated intervention in Andhra politics and the factionalized nature of her party in the state have also contributed to Congress's de-legitimization and to the emergence of an organizational vacuum within the region. NTR stepped into this vacuum, offering a political alternative that stressed the twin themes of populism and regional nationalism. He also put together a coalition of groups that had not benefited from the earlier Congress rule. The unfortunate aspect of NTR's rule is that it also does not offer much hope of institutional re-development. The TDP remains, like the Congress, a leader-dominated organization. Personalization of power has created simultaneous tendencies towards centralization and powerlessness. As the government's authority runs shallow, the future prospects of this regional alternative to the Congress remain fickle. Moreover, the problem of governability in this part of India—as in many other parts—continues unresolved. (Governability refers here to a government's capacity in three areas: durability of the underlying coalitions, policy effectiveness, and ability to resolve conflicts without violence.)

THE CHANGING CONTEXT OF ANDHRA POLITICS[2]

A glance at the electoral trends within Andhra (see Table 14.1) suggests the following: (1) the Congress lost significant electoral popularity during the 1970s before the emergence of NTR and has never recovered; (2) Congress's decline between 1978 and 1983 was much more dramatic in terms of the number of seats than in overall electoral popularity; (3) significant opposition to the Congress was always there, but in the past it was fragmented and usually involved many independent candidates; and (4) over the years, opposition has not only grown but has also come to be focused around a

---

[1]See Selig Harrison, *India: The Most Dangerous Decades*, Princeton: Princeton University Press, 1960, pp. 204–45; and Myron Weiner, *Party Building in a New Nation: The Indian National Congress*, Chicago: University of Chicago Press, 1967, Part III.

[2]In addition to the interviews cited throughout this chapter, I learned about Andhra politics from a number of individuals in Hyderabad and Guntur who, for one reason or another, are not always quoted directly. These included K.C. Alexander, N. Inniah, P.A.V. Prasad, M.V. Rama Murty, Madhev Rao, Narsingh Rao, Balwanth Reddy, and K.R. Sastry.

TABLE 14.1: An Overview of the Results of Assembly Elections in
Andhra Pradesh, 1967–85

	Congress		Main Opposition Parties[1]		Independents	
	Seats Won	Votes Secured	Seats Won	Votes Secured	Seats Won	Votes Secured
	(in per cent)		(in per cent)		(in per cent)	
1967	165	45.1	51	27.3	64	26.0
1972	202	52.3	10	13.0	57	32.2
1978	175	39.2	74	33.9	15	9.3
1983	60	33.6	211	54.9	21	10.0
1985	49	37.0	255	54.5	2	n.a.

Source: Compiled from a series of reports issued by the Government of Andhra Pradesh
and from reports in the Government Central Press, Hyderbad, and the *Indian Express*,
Hyderabad edition.
Note: The main opposition parties in 1967 and 1972 included the two communist parties,
CPI and CPI(M) and the two 'right' parties, Jana Sangh and Swatantra. The Janata Party
emerged as the significant opposition party in 1978, bagging 60 of the 74 seats won by
Congress's opposition. The Janata Party did not win any seats after 1978. The Telugu
Desam was the main 'opposition party' in 1983 and 1985, winning 203 and 194 seats,
respectively, and forming the state government in both instances.

single party, NTR's Telugu Desam. These trends have two important
implications. First, the Congress remains a significant political force within
Andhra. What one is explaining, therefore, is a significant decline in, but
not an elimination of the Congress as a political force. And second, the rise
of NTR is best understood as a 'negative' political phenomenon—that is, as
a consequence of the earlier decline of the Congress.

The Decline of the Congress

Most observers of Andhra politics suggest a familiar story: Congress's decline
was caused by repeated and increasing intervention from the centre. Between
1978 and 1983, for example, Indira Gandhi installed four different chief
ministers in Andhra. None of these men had any significant, independent
political base. Rather, they were all appointed because they had proven their
'loyalty' to Indira or to Sanjay Gandhi. Two of them had actually lost
legislative assembly elections and were brought into power from the political
wilderness. In the words of a seasoned Andhra politician and former chief
minister, such candidates were chosen because they were 'weak men' who
were not likely to present any danger to Indira Gandhi's future power in
Andhra. He explained:

When you put a weak man in, how long is he going to last? The first impression is,
who is this man? Why should he be above us?... An elected person has a different

feeling about his position than an appointed man. An elected man is liked by his people. An appointed man does not have confidence.[3]

The appointment of weak chief ministers without independent political bases prompted the contenders for power to rebel, for competing elites did not accept the authority of these appointed men and found them vulnerable. Indira Gandhi chose to resolve such power challenges with yet other weak leaders, hoping that these subsequent appointees would muster enough support to govern but still not be powerful enough to dictate terms to New Delhi. Thus, Andhra was engulfed with governmental instability. The leadership—not only the chief ministers but also the other important state officials—changed hands almost every year. Worse, every time a new administration was installed, those left out immediately started conspiring for a change. Andhra's Congress leadership thus came to be viewed as grossly opportunistic. It also became quite clear to the citizenry that most of the state's important political decisions were increasingly being made, not in Hyderabad, but in New Delhi. With Congress's legitimacy undermined in Andhra, a growing 'power/authority vacuum'[4] was created and NTR apparently stepped right from the movie screen into it.

While this emphasis on Indira Gandhi's relentless intervention as the primary cause of Congress's decline in Andhra points in the right direction, it also needs some important qualifications. First, it should be noted that by 1978, when the worst of these interventions began, the Congress had already lost a significant amount of popular support in Andhra (see Table 14.1). The fact that the Janata Party won sixty seats in Andhra in 1978 must be attributed to the same national pattern that had brought it to power elsewhere in the country in 1977. Of course, this does not necessarily invalidate the emphasis on Indira Gandhi's post-1978 imposition of chief ministers as a cause of Congress's decline. It still can be argued that the Congress did not recover in Andhra—as it did in many other parts of the country—because of the severe de-legitimization it had experienced between 1978 and 1983.

A second qualification is more important. While Indira Gandhi imposed weak chief ministers upon Andhra, it is not clear whether another national leader could have behaved much differently. The logic of the overall political situation that had been set up—both nationally and within Andhra—was such that weak and appointed, rather than elected and popular leaders were

[3]Interview with Brahmananda Reddy, former Congress Chief Minister of Andhra Pradesh (1963–71), Hyderabad, 22 March 1986.

[4]While I heard this phrase in numerous interviews, it is important to point out that Congress leaders themselves noted this development. These included interviews in Hyderabad with A. Madan Mohan and V. B. Raju, former presidents of the Andhra Pradesh State Congress(I) Committee, 19 and 20 March 1986, and with Brahmananda Reddy.

the likely outcome. Throughout the 1970s, Congressmen in Andhra, as elsewhere, had not won elections because of their individual popularity, but because they were riding the wave of Indira Gandhi's popularity. If the power of the state-level elites derived from Indira Gandhi, it is difficult to imagine how regional leaders with an independent political base could have emerged within the Andhra Congress. Such leaders simply did not exist. These dependent political elites knew that the way to power in such a system was either to be personally close to national leaders or to prove their nuisance value by organizing agitations so that national leaders were forced to co-opt them. Andhra's leaders tried both strategies, and Indira Gandhi, in turn, characteristically played musical chairs. A national leader with greater political vision might have foreseen that such an arrangement was likely to lead to political suicide, but caught in a pattern she had helped create, it is not clear how Indira Gandhi could have found strong chief ministers with genuine state-level authority.

While many political observers are now quick to suggest that she should have left Andhra alone and regional Congress leaders would have emerged, it is important to recall the rampant factional struggles within the Andhra Congress prior to 1978. The state had experienced major agitations in 1966, in 1968–9, and again in 1973, all of which had involved large scale political violence, riots, and death, and had led to the fall of several existing governments and the imposition of presidential rule. Clearly, this and the other evidence that exists on factionalism in Andhra politics suggest that Andhra politicians did not have their political house in order even prior to Indira's interventions, and that such political instability at the state-level invited central intervention. While this argument would be somewhat of an exaggeration—because Indira Gandhi tended to intervene in both more and less stable states—it does help to put her role in perspective. The soundest conclusion on this score probably is that Indira's repeated intervention and the factionalism within the state tended to reinforce each other.

Lastly, among the reasons behind the Congress decline in Andhra was the changing political sympathies of various socio-economic groups within the state. The Reddis and the Kammas have been the two competing 'dominant castes' of Andhra who over the years have continuously jockeyed for power. As long as the Congress was in power, the Reddis—who constitute about 10–12 per cent of Andhra's population and are spread throughout the state—always had the upper hand.[5] The Kammas, by contrast, are

[5]G. Ram Reddy, 'Andhra Pradesh: The Citadel of Congress', in Iqbal Narain (ed.), *State Politics in India*, Meerut: Meenakshi Prakashan, 1976, p. 4. The author summarizes the main reasons why the Reddis were Andhra's dominant social group well into the 1970s: 'Their higher proportion in terms of their numbers among the peasant proprietor castes in Andhra

concentrated in a few districts, including Guntur, and constitute about 5 per cent of the state's population. While they were never ignored by the Congress, the Kammas had always resented the fact that the Reddis dominated the state's politics. Two factors at work throughout the 1970s changed the nature of these caste rivalries and of their relative power positions. First, the Kammas proved to be more enterprising than the Reddis. They utilized their land wealth and spread into numerous commercial activities such as rice milling, sugar production, hotels, tobacco processing, newspapers and the film industry. This changing economic base strengthened their clout and, while some of this economic power found expression in the increased number of ministerial positions secured by the Kammas, members of the caste resented Indira Gandhi's failure to appoint a Kamma chief minister in Andhra. This would have been very difficult for Indira since the Reddis were well entrenched within the Andhra Congress. Of the nine Andhra chief ministers before NTR, six had been Reddis and none had been a Kamma. The growing disjuncture between economic power and the failure to capture the highest political office—with all the symbolic and the real gains that these involve—alienated the Kammas, and they threw their support behind NTR, himself a Kamma and well connected with other wealthy Kammas in the movie, hotel, and newspaper industries.[6]

In addition to losing the financial and other support of one of the two most important social groups in Andhra, Congress during the 1970s also lost significant electoral support among the backward classes. The numerous castes (as many as twenty) who comprise Andhra's backward classes constitute nearly half of the state's population. The Harijans (ex-Untouchables) are an additional 15 per cent. It is obvious that the electoral game can only be won by securing the support of some of these numerically critical groups. Until the early 1960s, the backward classes and the Scheduled Castes did not emerge as independent political forces. In the past, faction leaders of dominant castes often had succeeded in mobilizing the dependent members of the lower castes for electoral purposes. Analysts of Indian politics have noted that this dominant caste control over the political life of villages started declining somewhere during the 1960s, and Indira Gandhi's populist programme was aimed at recapturing the support of these lower castes for the Congress. During the 1970s, however, while the Scheduled Castes more or less maintained their

---

Pradesh; their traditional power in many *taluks* and villages and glorious antecedent of local rule in many parts of *Andhra Desa;* their political initiatives and involvement in the Congress and the Communist politics during the last four decades; the availability of better caste leadership from the village, *taluk,* district to the state level; and, above all, their firm base in agricultural wealth.'

[6]From interviews with V.B. Raju and A. Madan Mohan.

support for the Congress party, many of Andhra's backward classes became alienated, and a survey showed that there was a significant decline in Congress's electoral support in this group by the early 1980s.[7] Observers and participants in Andhra politics repeatedly suggested in interviews I conducted that an important reason for the alienation of the backward classes from the party was Congress's preferential policies towards the Harijans. Brahmananda Reddy noted that whenever he visited villages, members of the backward classes, pointing to such pro-Harijan policies as the granting of land for house sites, would inquire: 'Why should the Congress be so enamored with Harijans? They are poor, but so are we'.[8]

It is also important to note that Andhra's backward castes are extremely heterogeneous. This is quite unlike the case in Gujarat, for example, where the backwards are mainly of one caste, the Kshatriyas whom Congress has been able to mobilize around symbolic appeals and rewards of visible positions to a select few members of the caste. But given the heterogeneity of Andhra's backwards, this option was not easily available, and the party has thus remained an alliance of the Reddis and the Scheduled Castes. As long as the Congress also had the support of the backwards, it could win elections, but as many backwards moved away from the Congress, its electoral hold on Andhra became precarious. By the early 1980s, Congress had lost considerable support amongst 'younger age groups...educated urban voters, middle income groups and backward classes'.[9] As Congress went into a decline—both organizationally and in terms of popular support—no other organized political force was available in Andhra to fill the growing political void. Since politics abhors a power vacuum, sooner or later some force was bound to occupy this space. As it happened, a well-known movie actor turned politician was in the wings preparing to move onto the centre of the political stage.

The Emergence of NTR

N.T. Rama Rao was very well known in Andhra prior to his entry into politics. He had acted in some 100 Telugu movies, often portraying gods from Hindu mythology who ended up saving the poor, the weak, and the dispossessed from all that is wicked. His pre-political popularity among the illiterate rural folk, especially women, was considerable. He skilfully combined this

---

[7]Reported in F.D. Vakil, 'Congress Party in Andhra Pradesh: A Review', in George Mathew (ed.), *Shift in Indian Politics: 1983 Elections in Andhra Pradesh and Karnataka*, New Delhi: Concept Publishing, 1984, esp. p. 68.

[8]Interview, Brahmananda Reddy.

[9]From a public opinion survey reported in F.D. Vakil, 'Congress Party in Andhra Pradesh', p. 68.

popularity with several other themes that helped him put together a motley winning coalition.

NTR emphasized regional themes of Telugu nationalism. He stressed the Congress's corrupt political culture and argued that repeated intervention from Delhi had destroyed the Telugu people's capacity for, and pride in self-government. These themes probably appealed to many amongst Andhra's urban middle class. NTR also promised special new government programmes to help women and youth secure better educational facilities and jobs. 'Reservations', and thus better job and educational opportunities for the backward classes, was another major plank of the campaign platform. Plans to sell subsidized rice and to provide free lunch for all school children were announced. These were aimed at cutting into Congress's support base amongst the poor, especially the Scheduled Castes.

The political symbols and the idiom that NTR used to transmit his message were as important as the substance of his campaign promises. Clad in his saffron robe—the traditional garb of India's holy men—and riding around in a convertible transformed to look like a chariot, NTR might have been a figure from the *Mahabharata*, reincarnated to protect the dispossessed from worldly evils. NTR succeeded, in part, because all his populist promises were made not as an aspect of socialism a la Congress, but 'through home-grown imageries and idioms available in the backyard of the nation'.[10]

Those who have analysed the social backgrounds of the new Telugu Desam legislators of Andhra have noted the following: although the Telugu Desam is not dominated by the Kammas, the caste has improved its political position compared to what it was under Congress rule; backward classes are well represented within the TDP; and many of the new legislators are well-educated professionals (e.g., doctors), with little political experience. While the electoral significance of this changing composition is considerable, it is equally important to note that these legislators probably have had little impact on the quality of government under NTR. Decision making within the TDP is highly centralized, and the legislators play hardly any significant political role. Attempts to build the TDP into an organized party also have not amounted to much. The TDP remains a one-man show.[11] The 'central

[10]Ratna Naidu, 'Symbolic Imagery Used by the Telugu Desam in Andhra Elections (1983)', in Mathew (ed.), *Shift in Indian Politics*, p. 135. One important point made in this article, as well as in several interviews that I conducted, was that the NTR phenomenon should not be viewed as something similar to the situation in Tamil Nadu, since Tamil and Telugu nationalisms are quite different from each other.

[11]See N. Innaiah, *Saffron Star over Andhra Pradesh*, Hyderabad: Book Links Corporation, 1984, pp. 87, 105.

theme' at the TDP's organizational forums is 'hero worship', the hero, of course, being NTR.[12]

As can easily happen in governments dominated by a single individual, NTR's decisions have often been impulsive and arbitrary. For example, in early 1985 he dismissed all village officials, claiming that they represented 'feudal culture', but observers pointed out that the real reason was the established links these officials had with the Congress party. A later high court decision forced NTR to reinstate many of those he had dismissed. Similarly, free midday meals for children were provided for about a year, until the government learned there is no such thing as a 'free lunch'. NTR abruptly discontinued the practice in 1985. His subsidized rice scheme, which had been well received, has also been started and terminated several times; a ban on all tuition fees was announced but not implemented; and loud proclamations were made that Telugu would be made the official language of Andhra, but very little was done up until the end of 1987 to follow through on this promise. NTR's government has also had more than the usual share of problems with the bureaucracy. Several senior bureaucrats, who did not want to be identified, noted that the morale of the civil service was very low and that much of it had to do with NTR's 'heavy handedness' and 'arbitrariness'.

In spite of running a one-man, partyless, relatively arbitrary government, NTR has maintained his electoral support. It should be noted in this context that, whereas NTR has won several sets of elections since 1983, he failed to capture many of the urban municipalities, including the two largest ones— Hyderabad and Vijayawada—in local government elections held in 1986 and 1987, respectively. Whether this is a sign of things to come is hard to judge. NTR's association with recent corruption scandals may also bode ill for his future electoral popularity. But for now, even amid uncertainty, the TDP remains the most popular party within Andhra. Most observers attribute this to several variables, the relative weights of which are difficult to assess: NTR's continued personal appeal, especially to rural illiterates; the visibility of some populist programmes; the establishment of elaborate patronage networks; and the relative organizational mess in the Congress party. One should note that the reasons for NTR's electoral success are fairly similar to those one would list to explain Congress's successes elsewhere in India under Indira Gandhi. The summary observation of a former Andhra politician thus seems appropriate: 'Rama Rao only sophisticated Indira Gandhi's populism'.[13]

[12]This was noted in what was otherwise a very favourable review of NTR in *Indian Express*, Hyderabad, 16 October 1985.

[13]Interview with V.B. Raju.

Growing Violence under NTR

Like the present Congress party, NTR's Telugu Desam does not appear equipped to rebuild institutional authority systematically in Andhra. The authority vacuum emerged as the Congress party's organization and electoral popularity declined; NTR stepped into it but has filled it only as far as electoral popularity is concerned. Electoral fortunes are likely to remain fickle. The absence of a party structure, a coherent programme, and a second or third layer of significant leadership means that the Telugu Desam without NTR is not likely to survive. Even with NTR, Telugu Desam has hardly offered Andhra good government. Arbitrary decision making, as in the case of NTR, is one clear indicator of poor government. The failure to design and implement policies that address the pressing problems of the day is another. A third and very important manifestation of a government without organizational capacity and thus without deep authority is the failure to find peaceful methods to resolve social conflicts. Thus, growth in political violence highlights not only the nature and intensity of socio-economic conflicts, but also always indicates a government that does not govern well. It is important, therefore, to conclude this discussion of Andhra by noting the pervasiveness of violence that has come to characterize the conduct of political affairs within the state.

Andhra's recent past, of course, can hardly be described as free of political violence. Part of what is now the state—the Telengana region—was the scene of a major communist uprising in the late 1940s and early 1950s. Armed forces were used to crush this insurrection as well as to annex the Muslim princely state of Hyderabad into the Indian republic. The decade of 1956–66 was relatively calm, but between 1966 and 1986 Andhra again witnessed three major agitations. These occurred during the time Indira Gandhi was powerful in New Delhi and the Congress party underwent considerable de-institutionalization; each agitation was led by Congress leaders and ended when the implicit or the explicit goals of the leaders, namely, a share of power in the government, were met. This violence in the past tended to follow one of two patterns: political activity by revolutionary elites (e.g., the 'Naxalites') that was met with state repression; or failure to accommodate Congress faction leaders that led to agitation and violence and that subsided when these leaders were eventually co-opted into the power structure. Contemporary violence similarly represents struggles over socio-economic resources and over access to state power. What has changed, however, is the pervasiveness of violence. In the past the incidents were goal specific, time bound, and appeared as exceptions rather than the rule of the system; today, it would be difficult to make a similar statement about Andhra without numerous qualifications. A police report on 'law and order' in

Andhra in 1984, for example, presented the following picture of one year in the state's political life:[14]

- Elections to the eighth Lok Sabha involved 445 incidents of 'law and order' problems, including riots, assaults, arson, cases of bomb throwing and 10 murders.
- There were 167 political clashes during 1984, including 19 murders. These involved the Congress(I), Telugu Desam, CPI and the CPI(M) as either aggressors or victims.
- 115 communal incidents took place, leading to 63 deaths and 584 injuries.
- Violence involving 'extremists' led to 44 murders and 383 other incidents of snatching of weapons, amputation of limbs and attacks on liquor shops.
- Dismissal of N.T. Rama Rao Ministry by New Delhi led to numerous agitations, in which the police opened fire on 16 occasions, resulting in the death of 26 persons and 31 injuries. 48 policemen were also injured. Eventually the army had to be called in to restore 'law and order'.

What the police report underestimates is a different type of violence that has also been growing, namely, a violence inflicted upon the lower castes and classes and their 'extremist' leaders. For example, over the last few years five districts of Telengana have 'been progressively brought under a virtual state of siege' as a result of growing conflict involving 'the region's landlords and arrack and tendu leaf contractors who have found their age-old exactions challenged by organizations of peasants and agricultural labourers'.[15] In other parts of the state a different pattern has emerged. In the southern coastal district of Chitoor, a group of Harijans had acquired valuable tamarind groves from the government as an incentive for sterilization. Local landlords started to question Harijan 'ownership' of the trees, claiming they were 'public property'. They then organized against the Harijans, hired 'goondas', and beat up a group of the Harijans to set an example. The police failed to provide any protection, and when a civil rights group went to investigate, it found the landlords very angry over the fact that the Harijans had become 'well-to-do' and 'uppity'. The landlords had also secured their hold over the tamarind groves.[16] Killings of radicals who organize peasants, tribals and the landless labourers have also become quite common. In mid-1985 a survey done by the Andhra Pradesh Civil Liberties Committee found that thirty-three activists were killed during the first twenty weeks of

[14]Government of Andhra Pradesh, Statement on Demand No. XIII, made by Vasanta Nageswara Rao, Minister of Home and Legislative Affairs, *Police Administration, 1985–86*, Hyderabad: Government Secretariat Press, 1985, pp. 1–5.

[15]*Economic and Political Weekly*, 2 February 1985, p. 174.

[16]Ibid., 4 May 1985, pp. 784–6.

1985. Each of these killings of 'extremists' or 'Naxalities' was done by the police: seventeen in 'encounters', twelve in police custody, and four in police firings. The report also noted that twenty-four people had similarly been killed in 1984.[17]

Growing political violence in Andhra follows one of two general patterns. The first involves violence inflicted upon the lower castes, or those who seek to organize them, either by the socially powerful or by agents of the state; the second evolves from agitations in contests for political power, leading to riots, destruction of property, and murder. The first pattern of violence reflects the failure of the government to perform important 'output' functions. For example, policymaking that might reduce the conflict over scarce resources is so ineffective that administrators are unable to implement even mildly redistributive programmes. Similarly, the police are so ineffective that the government is unable to protect the poor lower castes against the wrath of the upper castes. The second type of violence, in turn, represents a failure of 'input' institutions—that is, institutions such as political parties and party systems that could channel dissent and provide a less-than-violent outlet for the society's normal power conflicts. Taken together, both patterns indicate that political institutions in this part of the country, as in many other parts of India, are not functioning very well and that the state's authority and capacity to deal with pressing problems do not run very deep.

POLITICS IN AN ANDHRA DISTRICT: GUNTUR

The following discussion of political change in Guntur district of Andhra takes Myron Weiner's earlier study of this area (the early 1960s) as a reference point, and moves on to focus on three issues: the role of the contending social groups within Guntur, the organized activities of the political parties, and the struggle to control local government. One general fact about the district should be noted. Guntur is both an old Congress stronghold and, at present, very important to NTR's overall political calculations. Guntur's significance for Congress is evident in the fact that one of Andhra's most prominent Congressmen, Brahmananda Reddy, comes from this district, and that in recent local government elections, Guntur was one of the few districts in Andhra where the Congress won. The fact that the Kammas dominate the district in social and economic spheres makes it of considerable importance to NTR, for if he is to build enduring support Kammas will have to play a significant role. An analysis of this one district helps delineate and specify some important themes concerning Andhra politics that are hard to ascertain at the state level.

[17]Ibid., 22–29 June 1985, pp. 1073–4.

Contending Social Groups

Kammas constitute the most important socio-economic group in Guntur, with nearly twice the population of the Reddis and owning perhaps as much as three-quarters of the fertile land. This gives the Kammas considerable potential power. The Reddis, however, as the most important caste group in Andhra as a whole, were the most influential group within the Congress party, and thus in Andhra politics, throughout the 1960s and 1970s. As a result, the Reddis of Guntur enjoyed a degree of access to state power that they would not have had if the Kammas had successfully transformed their district-level numerical and economic significance into proportionate political power. This disjuncture set up one important conflict within Guntur that was only recently 'resolved' in favour of the Kammas with the emergence of the Telugu Desam as Andhra's new ruling party.

The conflict between the Kammas and the Reddis in this part of India is old and enduring. Local observers trace it back to the middle ages. In more recent times, some analysts have suggested that the hostility between the two may have motivated the Kammas in the 1950s to lead the local communist parties that were pitched against the Brahmin and the Reddi-dominated Congress.[18] Other analysts, like Myron Weiner and G. Ram Reddy, however, have argued that politics in the delta districts of Andhra should not be viewed primarily as a struggle between the Kammas and the Reddis; that the situation is more complex. Still, the emergence of NTR is widely discussed in contemporary Guntur as a defeat of the Reddis and the emergence of a 'Kamma raj'.

On balance, contemporary politics in Guntur does indeed appear to be broadly divided along caste and party lines, with the Kammas mostly aligned with NTR and the Reddis, though hesitant and divided, continuing to hope for a Congress comeback. This is the conclusion that emerges if one investigates the social backgrounds of the respective party elites as well as who votes for which party and the subjective beliefs about who is in and who is out of power. Moreover, I do not believe that this analysis contradicts Weiner's earlier emphasis on multi-caste factions within the Congress as the dominant characteristic of Guntur politics in the 1960s. When Weiner studied this district, Congress was the only game in town, and both of the dominant castes jockeyed for power within the dominant party. The contemporary situation is more akin to the 1950s when Selig Harrison investigated the area's local politics and when two parties—the Congress and the communists—were viable competitors. As two-party competition now has re-emerged—the Congress and the TDP—so have some aspects of the old and well-established community cleavages.

[18]Selig Harrison, *India*, pp. 204–45.

TABLE 14.2: Caste Backgrounds of the Political Elite of
Guntur District, Andhra Pradesh, 1986

Caste	Members of the Legislative Assembly (elected in 1985) Numbers	Presidents of Panchayat Samithis (elected prior to 1983) Numbers
Kamma	12	8
Reddi (and Kapu)	1	8
Backward castes	4	0
Muslims	1	0
Scheduled Castes and Tribes	1	5
Total	19	21

Source: Compiled from local interviews.

Data in Tables 14.2 and 14.3 help unravel the nature of the caste and party linkages in Guntur. The presidents of Panchayat Samithis (village councils) (see Table 14.2) were all elected prior to 1983 and thus prior to the rise of NTR. By contrast, the Members of the Legislative Assembly (Table 14.2) were all elected in 1985 when NTR's party was re-elected to government. The contrast in the caste compositions of Guntur's elites in the two time periods is revealing.

Under NTR, Kammas are by far the most significance group amongst the district's new political elite, followed by the backward castes. The Reddis just as clearly are not favoured politically by NTR. The local elite under Congress, by contrast, were more representative of both the Kammas and the Reddis. The pre-1983 data seems more or less consistent with the situation described for the Congress by Weiner. However, it is important to note that even under Congress elements of caste and party alignments were present. It is clear, for example, that the backward castes were totally neglected under Congress, whereas the Scheduled Castes did rather well. As to the dominant castes, of the eight Kamma local leaders prior to 1983, only three were with the Congress. The other five Kamma elites were either with the communist parties or later joined the Telugu Desam (see Table 14.3). By contrast, as long as the Congress was dominant, Reddis were clearly the largest single group within the party.

Makineni Peda Ratnaiah (MPR) is one of these Telugu Desam assembly men from Guntur whose specific case helps illustrate some general points. MPR is a Kamma doctor who had never been active in politics before. When asked to describe his constituency and who voted for him, MPR noted facts that are both typical and revealing. His constituency is Kamma dominated, numerically as well as in socio-economic influence. In spite of the fact that another Kamma candidate was his opponent, the majority of the Kammas

TABLE 14.3: Caste-wise Party Affiliations of the Political Elite of Guntur
District, Andhra Pradesh, 1986

	Kamma	Reddy	Backward Castes	Scheduled Castes, Tribes and Muslims
Members of the Legislative Assembly (Elected in 1985)				
Congress party	2	0	1	1
Telugu Desam	8	1	3	1
Communists	2	0	0	0
Presidents of Panchayat Samithis (Elected prior to 1983)[a]				
Congress Party	3	7	0	3
Telugu Desam	3	0	0	1
Communists	2	1	0	1

Source: Compiled from local-level interviews.
Note: [a] As Panchayat Samithi elections were not openly contested along party lines till recently, this table represents informal affiliations of Panchayat Samithi presidents with various political parties. Also, since these individuals were all elected prior to the emergence of Telugu Desam in 1983, the affiliation of some presidents to TDP either represents a subsequent switch from another party or interim elections to replace a specific president for one reason or another.

voted for him because he represented NTR's party. Additionally, the backward castes generally voted for him. By contrast, 'Harijans and Reddis tended to vote Congress'. To the question of 'why did the Kammas vote for you', he suggested that this was mainly due to the 'strong anti-Congress feelings in my constituency'. Furthermore, as to why the Harijans did not vote for him, he suggested that this was because, 'they are exploited by the agriculturalists. Kammas are the agriculturalists here. SCs voted against them. They used to vote Communist earlier. But now they vote Congress'.[19]

Some of the important themes that emerged in this interview were repeated in several others. First, many of the Kamma elite, especially the new middle-class elite, have felt alienated from the Congress in recent years. In part this may be the result of having been excluded from Congress's spoils system, but it probably also reflects some genuine disillusionment with what many now consider to be the 'Congress culture'. Second, the Kamma elites joined the NTR bandwagon because they saw in it an opportunity to win political office and the perks that come with it. In this sense, NTR's Telugu Desam is not very different from the Congress. And

[19]From an interview with Makineni Peda Ratnaiah, Guntur, 27 March 1986.

third, the Kammas and the backward castes have been the backbone of Telugu Desam's electoral support in Guntur. A detailed survey might not support these explanations, but assuming that the candidates understood their constituencies, their views are persuasive; local elites repeatedly suggested in interviews that NTR's main support came from the Kammas and the backwards, and that Congress was supported primarily by the Reddis and the Scheduled Castes.[20]

A number of variables that mould local political perceptions help explain this division of the two dominant castes along party lines. Solidarity with the members of one's own caste is, of course, pre-political and an integral aspect of the rural social structure. When the lore of age-old rivalries is transmitted through the generations, as it still is among the Kammas and the Reddis, it provides some of the values that form the basis of cohesive, group political behaviour. Even among the more educated segments, these sentiments run deep. For example, hostels in Guntur's universities are divided along caste lines, and while there is considerable interaction across caste groups in a setting such as a university, local observers note that the Kamma and the Reddi youth 'live and move together' within their own groups. Caste sentiments are thus formed early and continue into adult life. If the political structure enables these caste divisions to be expressed through different parties that hold out a realistic chance of capturing state power, then it is not surprising that the competing dominant castes have come to ally with the two rival parties.

The issue that had done the most to harden this caste cleavage within Guntur is the fact that, until NTR, Andhra had never had a Kamma chief minister, a major irksome issue to Guntur's Kammas. What further exacerbated their frustrations was the fact that a Guntur Reddi, Brahmananda Reddy, had been Andhra's chief minister from 1963 to 1971 and subsequently remained an important political figure, both within Guntur and the state. This gave local Reddis not only better access to state resources than the Kammas but also the psychological advantage of being in power. The elation that Kammas have felt since NTR's victory thus becomes comprehensible. I heard comments from the Kamma elite throughout Guntur suggesting in one form or another that, 'finally, it is our opportunity'.

Some important qualifications to the description of caste alignments along party lines should also be noted. Both the Reddis and the Kammas

---

[20]I interviewed eight of the forty individuals who could be considered 'local elites' in some detail. Local leaders from both the Congress and the Telugu Desam tended to agree with this broad picture of caste and party affiliations. The two local communist leaders, however, disagreed; they argued that both the Kammas and the Reddis had voted against them because they were communists.

have numerous important factions and divisions within their respective communities. The Reddis in Guntur, for example, divided during the Congress split in the late 1960s, moved slowly back together as it became clear that Janata was not likely to be a significant force within Andhra, and now the 'loyalty' of some Reddi elites towards the Congress is once again under strain. They would like to establish a working relationship with the TDP government and yet not abandon the Congress in case it returns to power in the near future. The divisions within Guntur's Kammas have been of a different type. The Kammas in tobacco and cotton production often need to deal with the government in New Delhi to secure export contracts, and therefore have long-established relationships with the Congress party. These Kammas have found themselves in a difficult situation with the rise of NTR. Their solution: pay money to both the parties.[21] Besides such 'rational' divisions within the community, other significant factions involve personality conflicts. The political significance of such factions, however, is reduced under the conditions of two-party conflict. One analyst noted that 'while cleavages often involve two powerful Kammas, when fighting against outsiders, they act together'.[22]

The two other numerically significant groups in Guntur are the backward classes and the Scheduled Castes, and there have been important changes in how these two groups behave politically. The most important is the fact that members of higher castes within villages cannot easily influence their political behaviour. Indira Gandhi thus sought the electoral support of the Harijans by directly appealing to them—offering Harijan elites electoral positions (see Tables 14.2 and 14.3), as well as specific policy rewards like land for house sites. While these measures established a relationship between the Congress and the Harijans that is still more or less intact, several caveats should be noted. First, the Harijans of this area have long been politically active. Well into the 1960s, the Communist parties received as much as 20 per cent of the popular vote in this area. The contradiction within the Kammas, as both the leaders of the communist movement and as the main landowners of the area, could not sustain a viable left alternative in Guntur. Indira's Congress was the main beneficiary, and her left-leaning populism attracted the Harijans. The repeated failure to implement anti-poverty policies, however, could once again lead the relatively politicized local Harijans away from the Congress. Indira Gandhi's well-established image of a pro-poor leader acted as a powerful antidote to this possibility, but with Rajiv Gandhi in power the future of this relationship is in doubt. As a local

[21]Information from P.A.V. Prasad, a Guntur correspondent of *Eenadu,* the largest Telugu daily of Andhra, which played a key role in NTR's electoral success, 16 March 1986.

[22]This point was explained to me by a fellow academic, K.R. Sastry, at the National Institute of Rural Development, Hyderabad.

Congressman tersely noted: 'Our main support is with the Harijans. With this man (Rajiv) behaving like a chairman of an oil company, what is the future of Congress?'[23]

The backward castes of Guntur are extremely heterogeneous. Some are small farmers; many are toddy tappers, washermen, and weavers; probably just as many are landless labourers; and a handful are even quite wealthy. They are neither organized nor likely to be mobilized around simple themes of caste solidarity. Their numerical significance—as much as half of the district's population—and their heterogeneity is likely to add a large degree of electoral volatility to this area in the future. So far the backward castes have tended to behave politically as a group. But it can be argued that, for a number of reasons, this may not continue. First, the category of 'backward castes' is really a residual one, and not an integral part of the social structure. Those controlling state power have imposed a kind of unity upon the motley group that falls between the dominant castes and the Harijans, which could come undone. Second, the backward castes of Guntur moved away from the Congress when they felt that it was favouring the Harijans; their support for NTR is based in part on a negative sentiment towards the Congress. NTR's failure to 'deliver' can as readily change this again. He has, of course, tried to solidify the relationship by offering new reservation policies to the backwards, but these have run into legal problems. The future political behaviour of the backward castes of Guntur remains a matter of considerable electoral significance but is difficult to anticipate.

What does the preceding discussion about the political behaviour of the main contending social groups within Guntur tell us about the modal form of politicized social conflict in this part of India? Factions and the related patron–client links, cleavages around castes, and class conflict are some of the major possible forms that politicization of social conflict can take. The discussion so far suggests that much of the district's politics revolves around alignments between castes and parties. The relationship between castes and parties is now, as always, mutual: while existing caste cleavages shape the decisions of political parties, the nature of the parties and the party system itself moulds how and in what combination the different castes will behave politically. This primary focus on caste, however, should not detract attention from the somewhat secondary but significant role that both factionalism and issues of class conflict also play in Guntur politics.

While the struggle *between* the parties has become more or less a struggle involving different caste groups, jockeying for power *within* the parties, especially the local Congress, still very much revolves around factions, as is

---

[23]Interview, Anjeneya Sharma, former Assemblyman (1972–83) and trade unionist, Guntur, 24 March 1986.

discussed below. Issues of class conflict, by contrast, are relatively new, and while they may be secondary, they are not inconsequential. The overall framework of politics in this part of India has some elements of class politics that are so obvious they can easily fall into the background. The Kammas and the Reddis are the area's landowners. The Harijans and many of the backwards work on their lands. While the Kammas and the Reddis compete for power with each other, it is clear that those who do not own property are not serious contenders for power. Anyone who doubts the significance of property for power should ponder this overwhelming political reality. In spite of this pattern of domination, class conflict is not one of the main forms that local socio-political conflict takes. The poor are actually divided between the Harijans and the various backward castes because of conflicts over relative status as well as mutual jealousies over access to the state's resources. Nevertheless, the dominant groups are quick to perceive any potential threat that may develop along class lines and are just as quick to thwart it.

When Indira Gandhi turned somewhat left in the early 1970s and when Narasimha Rao, the Congress chief minister of Andhra during that time, attempted a mild land reform, 'the landed gentry of the Circars [a set of coastal districts, including Guntur]...found an excuse to start an agitation for a separate Andhra state'.[24] This experience is now an active part of the state's political memory, and it is not surprising that one of the earliest political positions taken by NTR was that he was against all land reform. Local communist leaders often note that the Kammas and the Reddis unite to defeat viable communist candidates in elections, and finally there is the ruthless repression of anyone attempting radical mobilization of the poor, which shows that there are some issues on which most Kammas and Reddis, as well as the Congress and the TDP, tend to agree.

Political Parties in Guntur

Electoral data from Guntur clearly reveal that the Congress and the TDP have become the two main contenders for power in the district since 1983. The TDP controls the majority of the legislative assembly seats, but the Congress and the TDP of late have been running neck to neck in electoral popularity. During the 1987 local government elections, Guntur was one of the few districts in Andhra where the Congress actually won the position of head of the district level government (chairman of zila parishad).

While both the Congress and the TDP enjoy considerable electoral support within Guntur, as organized parties they both are virtually non-existent. Neither has a stable membership, elected officers, or a working district office.

[24]See V. Hanumantha Rao, *Party Politics in Andhra Pradesh, 1956–1983*, Hyderabad: ABA Publications, 1983, p. 262.

The parties have little independent presence or autonomous significance beyond those who actually win elections on party tickets. Since electoral success has mainly been a result of leadership appeal—national leadership in the case of Congress(I) and regional leadership for TDP—the two dominant parties do not behave as organized political actors within the district.

Congress's organizational decline in Guntur, as elsewhere, is due in part to regional and in part to national causes. Even prior to the rise of NTR, local Congressmen had already lost much of their authority in district affairs, partly because traditional authority in the social structure had been eroding. Merely being a prominent Reddi no longer made a Guntur Congressman respected and trusted in the political affairs of the district. The elimination of the more rational-legal basis of authority also contributed to the growing power vacuum. A Congressman noted that 'natural leadership emerges from struggle and competition...from a struggle within the political marketplace'.[25] Indira Gandhi destroyed this 'marketplace'. As a result, the legitimacy of those who were appointed to local positions of power came to be widely questioned, both by the power contenders and by the citizenry. As soon as any individual is now appointed or is nominated to a ticket, all other power contenders are quick to question the decision, often publicly. As a result, squabbling Congressmen, without any independent political following, have come to acquire a very poor public image in local politics.

As to the prospects of rebuilding the Congress party locally, even local Congressmen are not very optimistic. Most of those interviewed suggested that internal party elections, which Rajiv has announced but postponed several times, will either not be held or will be 'bogus'. The general point is that party elections are not likely because they threaten the power of all those appointed individuals who currently run party offices. Genuine elections to party positions could well uproot the entire appointed structure of the Congress party from the bottom to the top. It is also worth noting that being out of power brings out the worst in the Congress party. When the party is in power Congressmen may squabble, but it is squabbling with a purpose: to share the perks of power. Out of power, local party units seem to lose all sense of purpose and political initiative. The main strategy of Congressmen in the districts thus seems to be to hope that 'electoral waves' continue to be generated by the national leaders, and that these leaders, through their benevolence, will somehow find the right local leaders to re-establish Congress's authority.

Although the local-level authority of Congressmen has declined and the prospects of the party are not bright, the authority of those representing the TDP within Guntur has not yet been established. The political careers

[25]Interview, V.B. Raju.

of the thirteen Telugu Desam MLAs in Guntur fall into two broad categories. Nearly half of them had never had anything to do with politics before they ran for and won elections in the 1980s. The other half had repeatedly, but unsuccessfully, tried to win elections on tickets of different non-Congress(I) parties. Several of these individuals had followed a pattern: they started with the Swatantra Party, moved to the Congress(0), then to the Janata, on to the Lok Dal, and finally ended up with the TDP. These two routes to power have created an impression in Guntur that the Telugu Desam MLAs are either political neophytes or opportunists who would have joined any party to win elections.

These MLAs are generally in power due to their personal association with NTR, and do not have an independent political following. This weakens but does not necessarily preclude the possibility of the Telugu Desam establishing a genuine local base. The MLAs are generally well-educated, and many of them are perceived to be honest. Moreover, as local bosses in control of patronage, they could conceivably build an effective machine in the old Congress mould. But the chances that the TDP will establish an enduring local base are not great. As a study of the TDP legislators tersely concluded, their 'clean records' are really a function of their 'political inexperience'.[26] Furthermore, the TDP's control over local resources for building patronage networks is far from uncontested; Congress remains a significant force in local government. Most important, however, the TDP has failed to become an organized party. This has important consequences that are worth noting. NTR, like Congress leaders, has not allowed elections within his party, with the result that no systematic mechanisms for resolving internal disputes exist within the TDP. The word of NTR or of his hand-chosen lieutenants (who so far have been his family members) is what 'resolves' most disagreements. As long as all power and authority is derived from NTR, a functioning consensus is clearly achievable, but without him it is difficult to imagine the TDP as much of a force. The MLAs depend on NTR for their positions and the party does not have much of an existence independent of the MLAs. Not surprisingly, its office in Guntur has seldom been open.

The decline in electoral popularity of the two Communist parties, which as late as 1967 had together received more than 20 per cent of the popular vote, is attributed to the shrinking of the pool from which they drew their leaders and the disappearance of their mass base. It is important to recall that many of the Communist leaders had come from the better-educated Kamma elite of Guntur who resented first the Brahmin and then the Reddi domination of the Congress party. Their success was partly determined by

[26]G. Srinivas, M. Shatrugna, and G. Narayana, 'Social Backgrounds of Telugu Desam Legislators', in Mathew (ed.), *Shift in Indian Politics*, p. 127.

how much of a following they could mobilize among those who depended on them, including other Kammas. A majority of the Kammas, however, must have realized that, caste resentments or not, land ownership and support of communism do not go well together when a massive number of landless labourers are also on the scene. When, over time, the contradiction of a landowning community supporting Communists finally surfaced, it took several forms. First, it led to a significant decline in radicalism among important segments of the leadership, leaving a radical minority sharply alienated. It is this militant minority that, for the past fifteen to twenty years, has generated considerable 'extremist' activity in parts of Guntur and neighbouring districts. But brutal police repression has slowly but surely chipped away at its ranks, and the new post-independence generation of Kamma leaders has sought outlets other than communism to give their community political expression.

The communists in Guntur have seen their support among the masses slip away, in part because of the elitist nature of the earlier leadership. As traditional caste authority has declined, the need to mobilize electoral support around programmatic promises has increased. While the Kamma Communist leaders were downplaying their radicalism so as to maintain the support of other Kammas, Congress—in its rhetoric at least—moved further to the left. Indira Gandhi thus cut sharply into the support that the local Communists had enjoyed among the rural poor prior to 1967. Finally, the sectarian conflict among the communist parties is another factor that helps explain their decline. First came the split of the CPI(M) from the CPI, then the more militant communists divided into numerous 'extreme' factions. 'In the post-1967 period', a veteran communist leader of Guntur noted, 'ideological questions and struggles took most of our time...mass struggles slowed down'. As the fine points of the correct party line were debated with an intensity that only the committed understand, 'divisions within the movement sapped the energy' of the local Communists in Guntur.[27]

The Struggle over Local Government

When NTR won the 1983 Assembly elections, he must have known that this was a victory based primarily on his personal appeal. He had won the elections, but he had hardly gained control over the political affairs of Andhra. In order to deepen his hold, therefore, NTR adopted several strategies, including an attempt to dislodge Congress's control over the rural panchayats. This attempt unleashed a massive power struggle for control of the local governments, the consequences of which are evident today in Guntur. When Weiner studied this area, the introduction of panchayats had

[27]Interview with Kolla Venkaiah, Padanandipur village, Guntur, 28 March 1986.

added new opportunities for patronage, thus broadening Congress's base of support. Local governments still dispense considerable amounts of 'developmental' resources, and as the power struggle between the parties has increased, so has the competition to control local governments and their patronage resources. In principle, such increased political competition is good for strengthening local level democracy, but the manner in which this struggle has been conducted in Guntur has tended both to impair the functioning of local government and erode democratic norms.

Panchayats in Guntur, as in all of Andhra, were dormant throughout the 1970s. The roots of their decline go back to Brahmananda Reddy's chief ministership of Andhra (1963–71) when, in order to consolidate his hold on feuding and factionalized panchayats, he downgraded the powers of elected panchayat officials in favour of local administrators who could be readily influenced through the bureaucratic hierarchy that the chief minister controlled. This prolonged period of dormancy sapped the vitality of the rural panchayats, and even before the emergence of NTR in 1983, they were hardly models of effective local government.

Panchayat elections were resumed in 1981 by a Congress state government, and not surprisingly they led to Congressmen, mainly of the Reddi caste, gaining control over local governments in Guntur. When NTR won the elections in 1983, he found these and other vestiges of Congress power entrenched at the district level and below, and instead of sharing power with those rightfully elected, he adopted several legally questionable strategies to undermine Congress's local hold. First, as noted above, NTR dismissed all village-level officials. Second, to reduce the powers of the Congress-controlled zila parishad, NTR created a parallel governmental structure, the District Planning Board (DPB) staffed by Guntur's MLAs, who were mainly from the Telugu Desam. Having created this parallel structure, NTR's government then transferred programmes with significant financial outlays from the zila parishad to the DPB.[28] The constitutionality of this action was never tested in the courts.

Lastly, NTR abolished altogether the samithi, or the block level of panchayat, and replaced each of them with about four lower level mandal panchayats, the rationale again couched in terms of the 'need for decentralization'. Most observers agreed, however, that the real reason was to weaken, if not to destroy, the established network of support built up by the Congress. In Guntur, at least, the strategy did not work very well. Recent panchayat elections reconfirmed Congress's continued popularity in local governments, and the zila parishad as well as a majority of the mandals have

[28]This information is based on several interviews in Guntur, but especially one with H. Chengappa, District Collector (Guntur), Guntur, 25 March 1986.

again come under Congress's control. It is also noteworthy that these recent elections in Guntur were accompanied by considerable physical violence.[29]

This intense power conflict between the parties has hurt the daily functioning of local governments. The abolition of local officers has eliminated what was often the government bureaucracy's only link to villages, and district officials have complained that 'village level information was not forthcoming'.[30] Implementation of programmes has also slowed down, in part because it is not clear who the beneficiaries should be. Parallel political organizations, dominated by Congressmen on the one hand and Telugu Desam legislators on the other, compete to insure that their respective party supporters benefit from government programmes. While this is often 'normal', local officials noted that power conflicts have at times been so intense that programmes grind to a halt.[31] The vitriolic inter-party conflict also has damaged the morale of non-elected officials, the local bureaucrats. This problem is especially severe in Guntur because, while Congress dominates the district government, decisions on careers of local bureaucrats are made by the state government controlled by the Telugu Desam. As the Telugu Desam strives to deepen its power in Guntur, the insecurity and uncertainty of local government officials increase.

Once NTR had come to power in Andhra, political conflict involving the new Telugu Desam and the old vestiges of Congress's power were to be expected. However, the strategies adopted by NTR to pursue this struggle at the local level have not done much to strengthen local-level democracy. Naked power struggles have been fought with strategies that often involve a flagrant violation of democratic norms. It is important to note this because instances like Indira Gandhi's dismissal of NTR's government in 1983 can create a misleading impression, namely, that only Congress adopts illegal means to fight its political battles. When it comes to winning and securing power, many in India's opposition do not always care much for democratic and constitutional niceties, as the NTR example demonstrates.

CONCLUSION

This essay has sought to analyse the political drama that has unfolded in one of India's important states when the Congress went into an electoral and organizational decline, and a regional party came to power. During the 1960s, scholars like Myron Weiner noted that factionalism and patronage networks were not only the core characteristics of the local Congress but also that

[29]See 'Andhra Pradesh', *EPW,* 4 April 1987, pp. 582–5.

[30]Interview with K. Raju, Joint District Collector (Guntur), Guntur, 26 March 1986.

[31]Interview, H. Chengappa. This general point was also made by several Samithi presidents with reference either to the housing schemes or the National Rural Employment Programme (NREP).

these factors helped explain Congress's local dominance. Over the last two decades, however, the social and political traits on which this ruling arrangement rested have altered. As a result, politics in this part of the country, as in many other parts, has come to be characterized by a growing authority vacuum. This vacuum has resulted both from changes in the social structure and as a consequence of the strategies adopted by the political elite to secure power. It is clear in Andhra today, and especially in Guntur, that members of the so-called dominant castes cannot readily utilize their superior position in the social structure to influence the political behaviour of those below them. Whether this was ever true or not, it is definitely true now that the Reddi elites of Guntur cannot expect to easily sway the members of the backward classes and the Scheduled Castes in the villages to vote for them simply because of their higher caste status. Backward classes and Scheduled Castes have emerged as significant political forces in their own right. As this has happened, the old pattern of politics that revolved around dominant caste leaders and their dependent followers has vanished. Power relations in society have democratized. At the same time, however, the political behaviour of various social groups is far more free floating now than it was in the 1950s, or even the 1960s. The fact that the backward castes constitute a large proportion of Andhra's population and are divided into more than twenty *jatis* only adds further to the heterogeneity and the unpredictability of the political behaviour of local social groups. It would have been difficult for any party to build stable social alliances and a coherent organization in what was increasingly a less oppressive but also a fairly heterogeneous local political society. Indira Gandhi and her Congress followers in Andhra, however, never even tried, and the Congress party within Andhra was highly factionalized. The resentment of the Andhra people towards repeated intervention from Delhi grew. It was into this growing authority vacuum that NTR stepped.

It is clear that the Telugu Desam is mainly an alliance of the Kammas and the backward castes. What is also clear, however, is that the Telugu Desam of Andhra is not much of a political party. The creation of a significant, second tier of leadership below NTR has not been encouraged, and there is really no coherent party programme. Dominated by a single popular leader, the prospects that the Telugu Desam will lay down strong institutional roots are thus not good. While NTR has for now filled the electoral spaces left open by the decline of the Congress, this by itself hardly guarantees authoritative government. The relative ineffectiveness of NTR's government is becoming manifest in the same set of outcomes that often characterizes governments without deep authority: arbitrary decisions, failure to diagnose problems and implement solutions—even modest ones—to some of the society's pressing problems, and most important, the growing role of force and violence in 'resolving' political conflicts.

15

Karnataka's Land Reforms
A Model for India?*

India's land reforms have for the most part been a failure. Only occasionally does one hear of a modicum of success in some Indian state or another. When one does, however, it renews the enthusiasm of those who hold redistributive goals to be important and achievable within the democratic framework of Indian political economy. Karnataka's land reforms belong to this genre. The 'successes' over the last decade led the programme's chief architect, Devaraj Urs, to proclaim that under his political tenure 'social justice was achieved'; that Karnataka's performance ought to be emulated by other Indian states.[1] Some scholars have tended to buttress these claims. One has characterized Urs as a 'pragmatic progressive' and his reform programmes as 'the most promising non-Communist regional experiment' in India.[2] Important policy makers have moreover viewed Karnataka's land reforms as demonstrating how 'production plus social justice' can be 'achieved within the given Indian situation'.[3]

How justifiable is this enthusiasm regarding Karnataka's land reforms? An assessment of this 'most promising non-communist regional experiment'

*Originally published as 'Karnataka's Land Reforms: A Model for India?', *Journal of Commonwealth and Comparative Politics*, XX(3), November 1982, pp. 309–28. The journal is available at http://www.informaworld.com.

The fieldwork for the project, of which this paper is a part, was supported by the Social Sciences and the Humanities Research Council, Canada; the Institute for the Study of World Politics, New York; the University of California, Berkeley; and Michigan State University. While in India (1978–9 and 1981), I was affiliated to the Centre for the Study of Developing Societies, Delhi. I would like to acknowledge the helpful comments of M.A.S. Rajan and James Manor, some of which have been incorporated into this final draft.

[1]Interviews with Devaraj Urs, Bangalore, 25 April 1979 and 8 November 1981; also see, Devaraj Urs, *Socio-economic Programme for the Poor: Some Policy Imperatives*, Bangalore, 1978, p. 11.

[2]See James Manor, 'Pragmatic Progressives in Regional Politics: The Case of Devaraj Urs', *Economic and Political Weekly*, Annual Number, 1980, p. 201.

[3]Interview, G.V.K. Rao, Member of the Planning Commission, New Delhi, 22 May, 1979.

has a bearing on important theoretical and policy debates in India. If Karnataka's land reforms are viewed as successful, it would buttress the claims of those holding that there is scope for deliberate redistribution within a democratic-capitalist developmental model.[4] By contrast, however, if the land reforms are assessed to be not all that significant, it would be another piece of evidence supporting the more pessimistic interpretation: state intervention aimed at alleviating rural poverty in India is—certainly over the short run—not likely to be very successful.[5]

I argue below that Karnataka's land reforms have not been very successful. The Urs regime in Karnataka indeed attempted well-publicized reforms. Moreover, some success was achieved. I do not intend, nor is there any need, to deny the accomplishments. At the same time, however, evidence indicates that serious qualifications on the reformist performance are in order. First, reform policies in Karnataka were not aimed at securing and redistributing 'surplus lands'. They were aimed only at tenancy problems. Second, given the size of the tenancy problem, the achievements are not all that significant. Third, implementation was along a factional pattern: those who lost their lands were not the well-entrenched landowners in close association with the ruling faction, but those who were either in the political wilderness or weak for other reasons to protect their interests. And, lastly the beneficiaries of reforms were not always, and not even predominantly the rural poor. A considerable amount of land was acquired by medium-sized and larger landowners. While the land reforms may then have provided some credence to Urs' populist claims, their redistributive consequences were, at best, quite limited.

The limitations of Karnataka's land reforms are intricately linked with political conditions in the state. I therefore first analyse the leadership and ideology, and then the organizational patterns of the Urs regime. An analysis of the attempted land reforms follows. I conclude by noting that Karnataka-type land reforms do more to 'rationalize' the already emerging owner-producer pattern of cultivation and less to create a somewhat egalitarian agrarian social order.

THE URS REGIME

While formally ruled by a Congress(I) government, Karnataka during the 1970s was very much dominated by the person of Devaraj Urs. A heavy-

[4]For such an argument with reference to India, see Francine Frankel, *India's Political Economy, 1947–1977,* Princeton: Princeton University Press, 1978, especially the conclusion; W.H. Morris-Jones, 'The West and The Third World: Whose Democracy, Whose Development?', in B.K. Nehru and W.H. Morris-Jones (eds), *Western Democracy and the Third World,* London, 1980; and Raj Krishna, 'Next Phase in Rural Development', 278, *Seminar* 1978.

[5]I have developed such an argument elsewhere. See Atul Kohli, 'Democracy, Economic Growth, and Inequality in India's Development', *World Politics,* 1980; and *The State and Poverty; Political Economy of Reform in Rural India* (forthcoming).

handed ruler, Urs leadership style was that of a power manipulator and a 'machine operator'. He used his control over political spoils generously to 'buy support'. The following that he attracted was, in other words, based neither on his personal 'charismatic' appeals nor on such 'primordial sentiments' as caste identity. Moreover, shared agreement on policy issues was also not a basis of the leader-follower relationship. The support that Urs generated was rather based on his capacity as a 'patron' in control of patronage, especially control over the access others had to powerful positions within the state. The leader-follower relationship was thus one of mutual opportunism. This is evidenced by the fact that as soon as Urs' control over power resources (though not necessarily economic ones) 'dried up' in the aftermath of his split with a resurgent Indira Gandhi (late 1970s, early 1980s), his capacity to attract political support within Karnataka proved to be short-lived.

As a leader favoured by the central leadership through much of the 1970s, Urs controlled the crucial resource of the right of others to run for elections on a Congress(I) ticket. Urs utilized this resource repeatedly to pack the legislative assembly with his supporters. Party tickets were given by Urs, as by other leaders, to 'their own men'. 'Irrespective of their public image, work in the party, commitment to the party principles or the ability of the person concerned', the primary criterion for candidate selection was 'loyalty to the leader'. And 'loyalty invariably meant unconditional submission to the leader'.[6] Aside from party tickets for assembly elections, Urs arranged for his supporters to have seats in district boards, *taluk* (administrative unit between district and village) boards, and cooperative societies. These seats, in addition to being positions of power, are coveted as they offer considerable opportunity to divert public funds for private benefit. Moreover, enough evidence was collected by an independently established enquiry, the Grover Commission, to substantiate that illegal funds had been amassed by the Congress(I) under Urs and used for buying political support on an ongoing basis.[7]

As a leader Devaraj Urs thus presided over a 'machine' which remained loyal to him as long as he had the capacity to 'grease' it generously with public funds. This, however, was only one significant aspect of Urs' political strategy. The other was to cast his regime in a 'populist ideology'. The 'ideology' was not so much a coherent set of ideas explaining the present and providing a vision of an alternate future, as a set of idioms aimed at creating a political mood. And the mood was one of people's power'. Aimed at undermining the legitimacy of the old ruling arrangements and, by the same token, enhancing

[6]See B.B. Patil-Okaly, 'Karnataka: Politics of One Party Dominance', in Iqbal Narain (ed.), *State Politics in India*, Meerut: Meenakshi Prakashan, 1976, p. 145; also see R.K. Hebsur, 'Karnataka', *Seminar*, 278, 1978.

[7]See *Deccan Herald*, 4 January 1979.

his own, Urs sought to contrast the 'mass' nature of his regime with the 'elitist' character of previous ones. More specifically, Urs shifted the nature of political debate from caste issues, which to him obfuscated the 'real issues', to 'more important ones' concerning 'redistributive justice' or class issues.[8]

As a leader of a minority dissident faction within Congress, Urs owed his initial rise to power more to being favoured by Mrs Gandhi than to his personal political base. Once in power, however, Urs sought to undermine any possibility of a revival of the older ruling pattern consisting of the Congress 'old guard' in alliance with the wealthy 'dominant castes', the Okkaligas and the Lingayats.[9] In addition to broadening the social base of his regime, Urs altered the idiom of rulership. If past political conflicts had revolved around which caste groupings would obtain favours (spoils) from the leadership, a new element was now added to the debate: the rights of the lower classes. Taking his cue from Mrs Gandhi, but also going beyond her in terms of substantial redistributive actions, Devaraj Urs presented himself as a 'man of the poor'. This populist idiom marked an important political change from 'above' aimed, at least in part, at undermining the legitimacy of the 'elitist' nature of past leadership.

It is important to emphasize the political origins of this populist ideology. The ideological shift to the 'poor' reflects primarily the needs of political competition and only secondarily changes in the class structure. Devaraj Urs, like Mrs Gandhi, discovered the poor when he needed an alternative power resource in his competition with the Congress 'old guard'. In aiming to oust the older ruling alliance, Urs went directly to the 'people'. Of course, this was possible only because social-structural changes had 'released' the 'people'—especially the middle peasantry—from their traditional loyalties and dependencies. At the same time, however, these social changes were not significant enough to be a driving force behind political change. There was little class conflict to speak of in the Karnataka of this period. Even in the latter part of his rule, Urs was still emphasizing the need to organize the rural poor.[10] In other words, it was not the emergence of the rural as an autonomous political force and the need to incorporate them politically which pushed Urs' ideological posture towards populist. Rather, it was the need to mobilize new political forces as a tool of electoral competition that was primarily behind the shifting ideology.

[8]Interview with Devaraj Urs.

[9]For an analysis of this earlier period, see James Manor, 'Structural Changes in Karnataka Politics', *Economic and Political Weekly*, 9 October 1977; and for the historical background, James Manor, *Political Change in an Indian State, Mysore 1917–1955*, Canberra, New Delhi and Columbia, 1977.

[10]Interview with Devaraj Urs.

That the ideological shifts were rooted in political needs is of considerable consequence. First, in the absence of a politicized poor, the gap between rhetoric and actions can, in the short run at least, continue to be large without damaging consequences. Second, once the lower classes have become an object of political competition, no political party can resist the temptation to champion their cause. Especially because the rhetoric does not have to be matched by actions, all parties have been inclined to move towards populist commitments. By the same token, however, and this is the third point, a likely long-range consequence of such drift is political instability. Continued commitments to the poor broaden the range of legitimate expectations from the regime. If the capacity to satisfy these commitments does not expand proportionately, an increasing gap between promises and performance is a sure invitation to long-term instability.

In addition to its leadership and ideological characteristics, the organizational arrangement of the Urs regime needs to be delineated. The organizational patterns were characterized as much by the absence as by the presence of specific forms. Especially notable here is the absence of a well-organized political party. Congress(I) in Karnataka, like Congress(I) elsewhere, has, of course, a rudimentary organizational structure. This is however activated primarily for electoral purposes and occasionally to influence intra-party factional disputes. The major functions of the party are to collect funds and to dole out tickets for elections. Those who control the use of party funds and/or the right of others to run on a Congress ticket are powerful individuals. Those who are attracted to the party often have their own opportunistic motivations. These can vary from something as major as seeking a party ticket for election to something as minor as securing a job, a permit, or a favourable settlement of a dispute by virtue of association with a party influential. Leaders and followers alike hail from varying social backgrounds. They are in turn held together in an ideologically amorphous and a structurally loose organization, bound often by no more than a sense of mutual opportunism.

The ideological commitments of the Congress party are thus multiple, its membership open and the internal control structure weak. In such a loose and amorphous organization, social roles and interests influence political behaviour more than the organizational imperatives. As a consequence, class and caste structures are 'mirrored' within the Congress party. The party itself tends to become primarily a vehicle for the pursuit of individual or sectional social interests. Organizational arrangements here, in other words, do not facilitate much political autonomy from the social structure as a whole and from the dominant social classes in particular. These characteristics of Congress as a dominant party narrow the option of state authorities pursuing politically directed social reform.

Congress as a party and the Congress government in Karnataka have not always worked in unison. Mrs Gandhi occasionally attempted to check the ever-growing power of Urs by assigning his rivals to the state party leadership position. As Urs, however, was a powerful political resource, Mrs Gandhi could not afford to alienate him beyond certain limits. For the most part therefore, and this was especially true in the aftermath of the 'Emergency' (1977–9), Urs managed to control both the party and the government. The party-government relationship was thus a mutually reinforcing one. Control of the party allowed Urs to pack the legislative assembly with his supporters and to use party funds to 'buy' and sustain support. This facilitated control of the government. Governmental control in turn provided further opportunities to dole out patronage and thus to broaden and consolidate the base of political support.

The recipients of patronage increasingly included members of varying social backgrounds. For example, half the Congress tickets for the 1978 assembly elections were given to members of the Scheduled Castes and 'backward classes'. Lingayats and Okkaligas were however by no means fully excluded. Close to one-third of the total tickets were still given to the members of these 'dominant castes'. Potentially troublesome opposition was thus at least partially co-opted. The remaining tickets were given to prominent individuals belonging to higher castes other than the 'dominant' ones. Following the recommendations of the much debated Havanur Commission Report,[11] Urs also increased the share of 'reserved' civil service jobs for the 'backward classes'. Moreover, many of the lesser but significant positions in the rural cooperatives and the taluk boards were given to those previously excluded from political spoils by Congress regimes.

Urs' political acumen lay in recognizing the need to 'buy off' counter-elites. Once bought, his rivals would have less of a reason to mobilize opposition utilizing caste and other 'primordial' appeals. By diversifying the recipients of spoils, Urs diversified his political base. The gains from this mode of accommodating opposition were however not shared by the majority, especially not the rural poor. The elites of the 'backward classes' gained, not the 'backward classes' themselves. What was being offered to the counter-elites was offices or office-related spoils rather than significant concessions on public policy with potentially broad-based social consequences.

Urs regime was, in sum, characterized by a strong leadership, populist ideology, and a loose and amorphous organizational pattern, revolving

---

[11]Reference is to the *Karnataka Backward Class Commission Report*, submitted to the Government of Karnataka by the Chairman of the Commission, Mr L.G. Havanur, November 1975.

around the widespread use of patronage as a basis of political support. The presence of a strong leader gave the regime a semblance of coherence. At minimum, and unlike many other Congress-run states, Karnataka under Urs was not marred by debilitating factional conflict. Populist ideology, while not threatening to the propertied in any fundamental way, created an aura of 'progressiveness' around the regime. The leadership evoked a sense of hope among those favouring the interests of the lower classes. Organizational behaviour however created a sense of *deja vu*. Widespread use of patronage and charges and counter-charges of corruption reminded one that some important trait of the old Congress party remained intact. The party organization itself remained relatively weak, especially in the sense that there was little or no disciplined ideological following. The issue which I now want to investigate therefore concerns the capacity of this leadership-dominant, patronage-based, populist political arrangement for redistribute reform.

LAND REFORMS

As part of its overall populist thrust, the Urs government in 1974 passed a series of amendments to the existing land reform legislation. The new laws hoped to re-inject enthusiasm into a seemingly hopeless and yet important distributional issue. In 1975, moreover, 183 special land tribunals were created, one or more for every taluk, so as to facilitate the implementation of the invigorated laws. With new laws and new institutional arrangements, land reforms appeared to be on the move all over again. How successful have these renewed efforts been?

It is important at the outset to separate the issue of surplus land from that of tenancy reform. It is tenancy reforms which have been pursued vigorously in Karnataka, not the appropriation and redistribution of above-ceiling lands. That the latter has been ignored is clear from the record. In spite of the high land ownership ceilings in Karnataka (up to 54 acres depending on land quality), according to the government's own conservative estimates, there should be close to half a million acres of surplus land in the state. After the four years of publicized land reforms, however, approximately 45,000 acres, or less than 8 per cent of the legal surplus land, had been redistributed.[12] This redistributed land constitutes less than 0.2 per cent of the total cultivated land in the state. It would therefore be difficult to deny that redistribution of surplus land has been a low priority item on the government's policy agenda.

Underlying the reluctance to tackle the issue of surplus land are not only socio-political constraints but also leadership intentions. Surplus land in Karnataka, as in the rest of India, has over the years vanished as *benami*

[12]Figures from 'Land Reforms Progress in the State up to the End of November, 1980', memorandum from Revenue Department, Government of Karnataka.

land (falsely registered land). It would take enormous political capacities to get at this land. The chances are that no government, short of a revolutionary one, would ever be likely to tackle this issue seriously again. Even the communist government in West Bengal, with all its organizational capacities, has been hesitant.[13] With little or no party organization and landlord-dominated local governments, the Urs' regime was certainly in no position to pursue and appropriate surplus land for redistribution. The land tribunals (discussed below) also did not add significantly to this capacity. If the leadership had therefore even wished to get at the surplus land, the complexity of the problem, class opposition, and the absence of organizational capacity would have made it next to impossible.

The issue is however more fundamental. The leadership in Karnataka, as in most of India, had no intention of appropriating surplus land for redistribution. While this is relatively obvious, it is nevertheless important and deserves stressing: a vigorous pursuit of above-ceiling land implies nothing less than a frontal attack by state authorities on the rural class structure. This is increasingly not on India's political agenda. Urs populist rule had some commitment to redistribution, but only within the framework of the existing class structure. The ideology and the organization of 'Urs' regime reflected this class commitment. In an interview, when pressed as to why surplus lands were not being appropriated more vigorously, Urs defended his government's actions in terms of the 'rights of private property'. In other words, rhetoric for public consumption aside, preservation of the basic class structure is part of the regime's commitment. India is after all a private enterprise economy. I do not mean to suggest that there is anything wrong with this. It is just that the gap between the political rhetoric of socialism and the reality of a privately-owned economy tends to be larger in India than in many other countries.

What has been pursued vigorously in Karnataka since 1975 are tenancy reforms: reforms which 'rationalize' rather than seek to restructure emerging agrarian patterns. The new amendments to land reform laws closed off many loopholes which had allowed landlords to escape tenancy legislation in the past. According to the new law, all those who were tenants on the date the law was passed (1 March 1974) now had occupancy rights to that land. While the former tenants would not have all the rights of a legal 'owner' (e.g., the land could not be sold for the first six years), they nevertheless could not be evicted from it. The state would compensate the landlords for their lands, generally at below market prices. And the new 'owners' would pay the state small periodic installments in exchange for the

[13]For a discussion of the West Bengal case, see Atul Kohli, 'Parliamentary Communism and Agrarian Reform: The Evidence from India's Bengal', *Asian Survey*, forthcoming.

land. The new laws further did not allow for any resumption of lands by the landlord for personal cultivation.

The nature of the law, especially the elimination of the 'personal cultivation' loophole, contrasts with much of the tenancy legislation in India. It indicates a seriousness of political intent. To facilitate implementation, moreover, the Urs regime created special land tribunals. Knowing well that existing institutional arrangements would not allow new laws to be implemented, Urs created new, *ad hoc* arrangements. For each of the 175 taluks into which the state is divided, one or more tribunal was created. Each tribunal had five members. The chairman was a bureaucrat at the level of Assistant Commissioner. The other four members were political appointees, including a member from the 'backward classes'. Each tribunal received applications from tenants, checked them for their validity, listened to conflicting evidence (professional lawyers were not allowed), made field visits for necessary verification, and arrived at final decisions regarding the tenant' occupancy rights. The tribunal's decision could not be appealed against in a lower court, only in the state High Court. For all practical purposes therefore, the land tribunals were powerful bodies with considerable final authority over the occupancy rights on tenanted lands.

With laws proclaimed and the tribunals established, applications for occupancy rights on tenanted land flooded in. Over 17 per cent of the total owned land, or about 3.8 million acres, was under tenancy in the early 1970s.[14] As Table 15.1 indicates, applications covering all this (and even more) land were filed over the five years. The mere fact of the filing of applications covering such a large extent of tenanted land is in itself a tribute to the political tilt accomplished by the Urs regime. The act of filing for landlord's land is clearly an act of defiance against the local power structure. How and why this was accomplished, without a strong party organization and thus without any real 'mobilization from below', has important implications.

What the rush of applications indicates is that laws, when genuinely designed to protect and/or enhance the interests of the lower classes, have important social consequences. They strengthen the social position of the lower classes. Protection from above is therefore far from being meaningless. The repeated failure of land reforms in India has led to a widespread feeling that 'mere' legislation is not useful, that only 'actions from below' can resolve the land issue. While this remains important, it can just as easily become an

---

[14]From National Sample Survey, 26th Round, Report No. 215.8, Table 4, 1971. These figures do not correspond with the estimates of the Government of Karnataka. The government chooses to work with figures from the Agricultural Census. The census data, based on 'patwari records', underestimates the extent of tenancy as a rule. This in turn allows the government to make exaggerated claims of successes regarding its own programmes.

Table 15.1: Progress of Tenancy Reforms in Karnataka under
Devaraj Urs, 1975–80

	Number	Area involved (million acres)
Applications filed by tenants	800,355	42.7
Number of applications dealt with by the end of November 1980	566,595	not known
Applications decided in favour of tenants	342,843	1.3
Occupancy certificates issued to tenants	134, 340	0.5

Source: Government of Karnataka, Revenue Department Memorandum, Land Reforms Progress in the State up to the end of November 1980.

alibi for state authorities. For example, it would be totally misleading to argue that the necessary land legislation is on the books in India and that the problem is one of implementation. There is much land legislation on the books, but most of it is inadequate; by design it is full of loopholes. Legislation, and therefore political leaders, rather than bureaucrats alone, are responsible for failures. As the case of Karnataka indicates, when legislation itself is perfected and loopholes are plugged up, the political intent of leadership is clearer. With indications that state power is on the side of a segment of the poor, these poor are not as helpless as some of the contemporary 'organize the poor' literature would lead us to believe.

By the end of Urs' tenure, in 1980 about 70 per cent of all the applications had been processed (Table 15.1). Over 60 per cent of these decisions had been in favour of the tenants and 34 per cent of tenanted land had been legally transferred to former tenants. While only a small proportion had actually received' ownership certificates', site-visits made it clear that land decided upon in favour of tenants was being cultivated by them. About a third of total tenanted land or about 5 per cent of total cultivated land had thus changed hands.

The new Congress(I) government which succeeded the Urs government in early 1980, found itself in a dilemma with respect to these land reforms. If the new government continued the programmes initiated by Devaraj Urs, the resulting political capital would accrue to the opposition, now headed by Urs. By contrast, if the government discontinued the reforms, it would risk losing support due to its 'anti-poor' disposition. The Congress(I) rulers thus decided to rush through the programmes initiated by Urs, 'complete' them, and move on to new ones. This strategy would allow them to claim even more earnest concern for the poor than the Urs regime and yet minimize their involvement in programmes initiated by Urs.

By November 1981, therefore, about a year after having come to power, the Congress(I) government claimed that tenancy reforms had been completed. The government's claims of 'enormous successes' were met with considerable scepticism.[15] The data released in late 1981 are presented in Table 15.2. It would take another study to assess what lies behind the claimed 'accomplishments' of the Congress(I) government. For the purposes of this study therefore, I will assume that (i) land reforms were indeed completed by the end of 1981; and (ii) the credit for these reforms goes to the Urs regime. To the extent that these assumptions bias the analysis, the bias will be in the direction of giving more credit to the Urs regime than it deserves.

As the data in Table 15.2 indicates, 185 million acres of land was legally transferred to tenants during Karnataka's land reforms. This land constitutes nearly half the land under tenancy in the state in the early 1970s. How does one assess the significance of this tenancy reform? Any assessment must take account of several considerations: who lost the land; who received the land; what happened to the nearly half the land under tenancy not transferred to tenants; and what have been the socio-economic consequences for the recipients of land. As direct and hard data on any of these crucial questions is not available, the answers have to be approximated.

Some important data which helps us approximate who may have lost and received land during the tenancy reforms is presented in Tables 15.3 and 15.4. These tables delineate the distribution of land 'leased in' and 'leased out' according to land ownership categories in the early 1970s. The data provide correctives to the crucial assumption on which tenancy reforms were premised, namely, that big landowners lease out land to the landless or smallholders. The tenancy, situation of Karnataka was far more complicated. Over half the land 'leased in' in early 1970s was leased in, *not* by the landless and the smallholders, but rather by family farmers and landlords (see Table 15.3, total).

TABLE 15.2: Progress of Tenancy Reforms in Karnataka up to the 'Completion' of the Programme, 1975–81

	Number	Area involved (million acres)
Applications filed by tenants	813,263	4.60
Number of applications dealt with by the end of November 1980	776,658	not known
Applications decided in favour of tenants	467,298	1.85
Occupancy certificates issued to tenants	305,708	1.03

Source: Government of Karnataka, Revenue Department, Note on Progress Achieved under Land Reforms, 1 November 1981.

[15]Interviews with senior officials (one recently retired, one currently employed) of the Government of Karnataka who wish to remain anonymous, Bangalore, 10 and 11 November 1981.

Table 15.3: Distribution of Land 'Leased In'

Ownership Category	Coastal Districts*		Eastern Districts		Northern Districts		Southern Districts		Total	
	(100 acres)	% of total leased land	(100 acres)	% of total leased land	(100 acres)	% of total leased land	(100 acres)	% of total leased land	(100 acres)	% of total leased land
Landless	1937	38	85	5	1535	7	1138	19	4695	13
Smallholders										
(.01 to 2.49 acres)	2242	44	600	35	7082	30	2622	43	12546	34
Family farmers										
(2.50 to 9.99 acres)	842	16	545	32	8097	34	1600	26	11084	30
Landlords										
(10 acres and above)	104	2	475	28	6952	29	728	12	8259	23

Source: Computed from Government of India, National Sample Survey, 26th Round, Report No. 215 (Karnataka), VII, 1971, Table No. 4, pp. 94, 120, 146, and 172.

Note: *The districts included in the regions are as follows: Coastal (North and South Kanara); Eastern (Chikmagalur, Coorg, Hassan, and Shimoga); Northern (Belgaum, Bellary, Bidar, Bijapur, Chitradurga, Dharwar, Gulbarga, and Raichur); and Southern (Bangalore, Kolar, Mandya, Mysore, and Tumkur).

TABLE 15.4: Distribution of Land 'Leased Out'

Ownership Category	Coastal Districts		Eastern Districts		Northern Districts		Southern Districts		Total	
	(100 acres)	% of total leased land	(100 acres)	% of total leased land	(100 acres)	% of total leased land	(100 acres)	% of total leased land	(100 acres)	% of total leased land
Smallholders (.01 to 2.49 acres)	115.21	12.7	49.9	4.1	669.2	5.4	318.9	10.5	1153.3	6.6
Family farmers (2.50 to 9.99 acres)	313.6	34.7	610.6	49.8	5725.3	46.6	1906.9	63.0	8556.4	49.1
Landlords (10 acres and above)	475.5	52.6	566.0	46.1	5893.1	48.0	801.5	26.5	7736.1	44.3

Source: Computed from Government of India, National Sample Survey, 26th Round, Report No. 215 (Karnataka), V. II, 1971, Table No. 3, pp. 93, 119, 145, and 171.

Similarly, those who were 'leasing out' land were also not always, and not even predominantly, the bigger landlords: over half the land 'leased out' was leased out by smallholders and family farmers (See Table 15.4, total). While this data does not allow a claim that many of richer farmers actually leased land from the poorer ones, it does suggest that many of those leasing in land were already well off and many of those leasing out land relatively poor.

What are the likely consequences when 'tenancy reforms' are politically imposed on this pattern of tenancy? It is important to remember that only about half of the land under tenancy in the early 1970s changed hands as a consequence of the land reforms. Is there any reason then to believe that half of the tenancy land which changed hands went from the richer landowners to the poorer tenants? Given the power inequities which are rooted in rural social structure, it is probable that the small landholders who lost their land outnumbered those who retained it. And many of the already better off must have gained by the land reforms.

In order to further understand the tenancy reforms, one has to go beyond this 'formal' evidence and analyse the workings of the land tribunals closely. Each tribunal was chaired by a career civil servant of Assistant Commissioner's rank. As individuals enjoying considerable authority in the local milieu, the bureaucrats were the most significant members of each tribunal. In addition to the inherited authority of office, the power of the government officials was enhanced by several factors. These included knowledge of administrative/legal regulations as well as sustained activity due to their role as full time, salaried employees. The number of times tribunals met, the number of cases, heard, etc. was also determined by the civil servants. Most important, however, the Assistant Commissioners were responsible to higher bureaucrats for fulfilling their 'quota' or for task completion. Momentum for the tenancy reforms was generated in the Chief Minister's Office and transmitted through the established, bureaucratic hierarchies. The whole programme therefore had a bureaucratic character greater than the inclusion of four political appointees on each tribunal would indicate.

Of the political appointees, the local legislator was included almost as a rule. A prominent Congressman of Scheduled Caste origin was also included in most tribunals. The two additional members were of varying backgrounds. It was widely recognized that Devaraj Urs had packed the tribunals with his loyal supporters. Depicting himself 'a man of the poor', Urs argued that his supporters would ensure 'popular participation'. The reality was however somewhat different. A majority of these members did not have very 'popular' origins. Of the eight tribunals in South Kanara and Mandya that I visited and of the 32 appointed members that I interviewed, over half were of landed origin (owning more than 25 acres). Some were extremely rich and powerful local individuals. Most of them had university-level education. Few, if any, had any real commitment to land reform. In terms of composition, therefore, most tribunals included and some were dominated by middle and upper-class rural Congressmen loyal to Devaraj Urs.

The tribunals served important political needs for Devaraj Urs. For example, each appointed member received Rs 50 per diem for participation in the tribunals. As arbiters of conflict-ridden social situations, moreover, the appointees could use their position to enhance their local influence. Tribunal membership was thus coveted for both pecuniary and political reasons. Urs offered appointments to supporters as favours. Tribunals therefore became one more element in Karnataka's large network of patronage and spoils supporting the Urs machine.

This organizational arrangement provided a 'steam valve' for potential opposition. If the lands of powerful local individuals were threatened, at least some of them, especially those who had personal relationships with tribunal members, could evade the law. Charges of 'corruption' in the local newspapers buttressed the common belief that this was indeed occurring. Opposition to the programme did not therefore develop along class lines. Some members of the landed classes, as suggested by the tenancy data in Tables 15.3 and 15.4, may well have benefited economically from the reforms; others were involved with implementation; and yet others, due to personal association, could minimize their losses. This is not to suggest that some landowners did not incur significant losses. Many lost their lands to former tenants. Opposition however took a factional rather than a class form. Those close to Urs and Congress(I) often did not lose their lands; the propertied of opposing factions did not fare well. The latter constituted the bulk of the opposition. Labelling them as 'anti-people' and 'reactionaries', however, Urs could simultaneously depict himself as a 'people's man' without alienating some of the crucial support of landed groups. And in this lay Urs' political acumen. That only about half of the tenanted land legally changed hands further bears out the reality of this factional pattern of implementation.

It is important to reiterate the role of the bureaucrats. Whatever success the tenancy reforms have had, the civil servants provided an important thrust. Observing the workings of the land tribunals made this clear. The Assistant Commissioner as the chief of the tribunal took the receipts from tenants, proving their bona fides, examined them, asked questions of both parties, and after minor consultations with the other members made the decision. The political appointees, by contrast, were quite out of place in a legal/bureaucratic decision-making set-up, being more like observers than participants.

Following orders from 'above', career civil servants, then, provided the momentum for tenancy reforms. In spite of the popular view, of bureaucrats as an obstruction to radical reforms, the 'professionalism' of senior Karnataka bureaucrats needs to be noted. Given a task, they pursued it diligently. This is of course not to imply that they did not face obstruction or that the other appointees of the tribunals were powerless. On the contrary, the bureaucrats often complained about 'political interference'. The political appointees sought to influence and obstruct cases important to them. These deals were however made out of the 'court room'. The authority of the bureaucrats in the actual legal proceedings may have been great, but out of the 'court room' they had to take into account the power of political figures. Socialized in the Indian legal-administrative system, these officials understand that laws are meant to apply differentially. So they complied with the wishes of the political appointees. The costs of opposing legislators and others close to Urs were unnecessarily high. Ironically, therefore, the momentum towards reform, as well as the obstructions, originated from the power centre. The momentum travelled from the top down, through the bureaucracy, the obstructions from the bottom up, through political linkages.

In many cases the evidence was not clear as to the bona fides of the tenant applicants. This required a visit by the tribunal members to the villages for further investigation. As the workload of the tribunals was heavy, the distances from small taluk towns to villages considerable, and the availability of transport restricted, these visits often did not materialize. Accuracy of decisions thus suffered. Even when the visits were made, rival parties easily mobilized conflicting evidence at the local level. In the absence of personal knowledge and contacts, such problems reduced the efficacy of tribunals as implementing bodies. A more localized organization might have solved these administrative problems, but only at the expense of creating other new ones. Without a strong local party organization, lower-level bureaucrats and landed interests would have indeed created greater obstacles than at the taluk level. In other words, decentralization without centralized tools of control would have solved administrative problems only at the expense of strengthening the forces of the status quo.

Regional variations within Karnataka also ought to be noted. As Table 15.5 indicates, virtually all the land in the coastal districts was under tenancy in the early 1970s. This contrasts sharply with the eastern and southern districts, where less than 10 per cent of the land owned was out on lease. The tenancy pattern in the coastal districts also resembled the more classical pattern, namely land was 'leased in' by the landless and the smallholders (see Table 15.3, coastal districts). The rate of success of reforms in the coastal districts was moreover quite high (Table 15.5). This suggests that the two coastal districts, North and South Kanara, with an extremely high density of tenancy, indeed experienced redistributive reforms. As the land under tenancy in the coastal districts constitutes less than 15 per cent of the land under tenancy in Karnataka as a whole, these localized redistributive successes do not alter

TABLE 15.5: Regional Variations in Karnataka's Land Reforms

Region	Land under Tenancy[a] (100 acres)	Land acquired by former tenants[b] (100 acres)	'Rate of Success' (% of 2 to 1)*
	1	2	
Coastal	5240 (99.25%)**	3138	60
Eastern	1657 (8.19%)	1157	70
Southern	5417 (9.69%)	755	14
Northern	25772 (18.29%)	7955	31
Karnataka Total	38086 (17.14%)	13005	34

Sources: [a]From Government of India, National Sample Survey, 26th Round, Report No. 215 (Karnataka), V. II, 1971, Table No 4 pp. 94, 120, 146, and 172.
[b]From Government of Karnataka, Revenue Department, *Land Reforms up to the End of October 1980.*
Notes: *For this type of formulation see also N. Pani, *Reforms to Pre-empt Change*, Bangalore, 1981.
**Figures in parentheses indicate leased land as a percentage of the total land owned.

the overall assessment. The reformist performance in these areas nevertheless begs the question: what distinct forces were at work here?

The reformist momentum in the coastal districts was primarily a function of the additional 'pressure from below'. This, in turn, resulted from the greater politicization of the rural population in these areas.[16] As one of the Assistant Commissioners, chairing a tribunal, noted, 'the peasants in this area are very shrewd'. This 'shrewdness' is a consequence of several unique features of these districts. South Kanara, for example, has always been more of a 'Kerala type' district. Tenancy here has been largely of *moolgani* type, i.e. permanent, written contracts and based on fixed cash payments. It is therefore easier to prove one's legal status as a tenant. The coastal populations are generally more exposed to the forces of commerce. Missionary and other non-governmental organizations, including the left parties, have also been active in the area. They have on more than one occasion provided support to the rural poor. All these factors have created a greater sense of awareness and confidence among the coastal lower classes. Therefore, once favourable legislation was passed, the tenants of the area, comprising a considerable numerical force, were quick to file their applications, muster the necessary evidence, and press for favourable settlements.

This experience has important analytical implications. These concern the political conditions for poverty reform. Successful reform involved actions from both above and below. Favourable tenancy laws reflected a pro-lower class tilt in state power—at least in this one issue area. A politicized population acted upon these laws and contributed to their successful implementation.

[16]See also Narender Pani, *Reforms to Pre-empt Change*, Bangalore, 1981, p. 205.

The political conditions for successful reform thus appear to be a reformist thrust originating from the state, coupled with actions by mobilized lower classes. The social and political conditions in much of Karnataka however differed from those in the coastal districts. These differences can be summarized as follows: tenancy was a lot less concentrated; patterns of leasing included many larger landowners 'leasing in' land and many smallholders 'leasing out' land; and the politicization of lower rural groups had not moved as far as on the coast. Tenancy legislation did not therefore have the same redistributive consequences in the bulk of the state as it did in the coastal districts. Taking the state as a unit then, two conclusions concerning the reforms would be hard to deny. First, as only about half the land under tenancy changed hands, many of those working the other half are no longer tenants; they were in all probability evicted by one means or another. Given the inequities of rural power structures, it would not be unfair to extrapolate that the bulk of those evicted must have been the already weak, namely, the smallholders. And, second, of the tenanted land which was transferred to the tenants, only a part went from the 'rich' to the 'poor'. For the rest, given the pattern of tenancy, some of the already well-off members must have gained and some of the not so well-off lost.[17]

On balance then, how does one assess Karnataka's land reforms? In any assessment it is important to re-emphasize that little effort has been made to appropriate and redistribute the 'above ceiling' lands. Over the short run, if redistribution is the intent, only land redistribution from the haves to the have-nots is likely to make a real dent into the poverty of the majority, the landless. This was neither attempted nor achieved. At the core therefore, the reformist thrust has been mostly hollow. The policies have focused on tenancy reform. These reforms touch a small but not insignificant proportion of the rural poor. While mildly redistributive, tenancy reforms mainly tend to rationalize the owner-producer mode of production. Even here however the success has been limited. Only half of all tenanted land changed hands during Urs' tenure. What happened to those working the other half as tenants is not definitely known but not hard to guess. Many of them must have been transformed from tenants to landless labourers. Of the land given to tenants, modest redistribution was achieved in some parts of the state. For most of the state, however, given the pattern of tenancy structure analysed above, tenancy reforms could not have been very redistributive. Their consequence, on balance, even if not intended, may have been the opposite: some of the rich getting richer and some of the poor poorer.

Political conditions have both facilitated the modest success and obstructed a more meaningful land reform. The driving force behind the reforms were

---

[17]Ibid., p. 148.

the political needs of a leadership determined to oust the older ruling alliances by creating an alternate and a broader political base. To legitimize his populist regime, Urs passed new legislation, created the tribunals, and applied pressure from above to implement the reforms. An effective bureaucracy and an active population in areas with concentrated tenancy were the other fortuitous factors facilitating a degree of success. Conversely, however, the patterns of tenancy and the nature of the power structure precluded a concerted attack on society. Given that many richer farmers were leasing in land and many poorer ones were leasing out, no blanket legislation aimed at giving land to tenants could have been redistributive. A much more discriminating approach would in turn have required a degree of political organization simply absent in the state. State organization necessitated a 'top heavy' reform. Without complementary support from below, such reforms from 'above' are destined to be less than successful. As a loose and amorphous organization with multiple class goals, the Congress party of Karnataka does not really attract a disciplined and ideologically committed following. Urs therefore had consistently to 'buy' support. The strategy was to exclude some but co-opt most social influentials, albeit from different backgrounds, into a large network of patronage. In the absence of a disciplined party, political survival was contingent not only on not alienating the local notables too far, but also on including them into such reform institutions as the land tribunals. This precluded the possibility of anything but a modest tenancy reform.

Karnataka's land reforms have to be assessed carefully. Control over roughly half the tenanted land has passed into the hands of former tenants. From the stand point of equity, this would appear to be desirable. It is therefore not surprising that the reforms have led to somewhat exaggerated claims of redistributive success on behalf of Devaraj Urs in Karnataka. This paper has sought to balance the 'successes' against the 'limitations'. Land reforms are aimed at promoting either equity or productivity or some combination of the two. While I have not discussed the issue of productivity, Karnataka's land reforms have certainly been short on their contributions to equity.

Many of the powerful among the landed of Karnataka tended not to lose their lands. As much as half the tenanted land may thus remain under the control of the former leasing landowners. Given stringent tenancy laws, one can be sure that these landowners will find ways to transform their tenancy arrangements into something resembling managerial/supervisory farming. Will former tenants turned landless labourers then contribute to greater equity? No. The results are likely to be the opposite. With regard to half of the tenanted land that actually changed hands, the former tenants were of course net gainers. However, whether taking lands away from many a smallholder or others in the political wilderness really constitutes 'egalitarian justice' can at best remain doubtful.

The major consequence of Karnataka's recent land reforms is thus likely to be a hastening of the already emerging owner-producer mode of production. Whether the former landowners turn into managerial farmers (which does not contribute to greater equity), or former tenants become owner-cultivators (which does contribute to greater equity), the results, will be similar: a 'rationalization' of agrarian organization. Policy measures conceived of as creating 'social justice' and a 'better deal for the lower classes' are thus leading to the unintended consequence of promoting a trend already dominant in agrarian India, namely, the trend towards 'capitalist' farming.

Karnataka's land reforms have received considerable favourable publicity. To many they highlight what is feasible within the conditions of a strong populist leadership. Some national policy makers have in any case, for some time, argued against redistribution of above-ceiling lands and for tenancy reforms in India. Karnataka's experience will strengthen this position. The above analysis ought however to give pause to those favouring the Karnataka type of reform, which must be understood for what they are. One thing they are definitely not is what Devaraj Urs and his supporters have claimed they are: a democratically conceived attack on the landed classes in order to benefit the rural poor. What the land reforms represent instead is a set of expedient policy alternatives aimed at giving credibility to the popular nature of the Urs regime. While this did not necessarily preclude significant redistribution, their actual contribution to either breaking the rural power structure or improving the living conditions of the rural poor have been minimal. The major consequence of the attempted reforms has been a further rationalization of the owner-producer pattern of production.

Index